Games of Magic

A Metaphysical Adventure
and Healing Breakthrough
on the Path to Enlightenment

Dennis Dean Alsop

iPaths Publishing

.
ISBN: 979-8-9994268-2-6 (Hardcover)
ISBN: 979-8-9994268-1-9 (Paperback)
ISBN: 979-8-9994268-0-2 (eBook)

Library of Congress Control Number: 2025924064

Front cover design and book design by Author
Cover art inspired by Farscape

iPaths Publishing
Stockton. CA.

www.ipaths.org
www.pipskywalker.com

Dedicated to Patty

"The purpose of a writer is to keep civilization from destroying itself." – Albert Camus

Table of Contents

Chapter 8: Self-Healing Stories – Part 1: The Body 225

Chapter 9: Self-Healing Stories – Part 2: The Mind 242

Chapter 10: The Chronicles of Medic 255

PART III: Real Magic 267

Chapter 11: Everyday Miracles 269

Chapter 12: My Petty Tyrant 280

Chapter 13: Tales of Power 291

Preface

This book is both a chronicle of my lifelong adventure in self-discovery and inner-healing, and an exposition of what I learned and how I now understand the extraordinary experiences I had along the way. Most importantly, it presents some revolutionary information about trauma, and the healing of mindbody issues. This preface is written to get some incidentals out of the way that might be out of place elsewhere, and to help answer a few questions and avoid any confusions that might occur as a result of the way the book is written.

Writing Style

Besides telling my own personal story I will be giving you some important information, but although I have a lot of explanatory material in this book, and some in depth dissertations on various subjects, this is not a scholarly or technical manual. The general narrative style is, for the most part, informal, especially where I'm telling stories and sharing my personal experiences. Interweaving my story with the more expository discussions was necessary in order to make everything more understandable, but it also serves to keep the atmosphere of this whole composition less academic and more personal and human. Incidently, I use several acronyms in this book, but the only one you need to be familiar with is ID-R, which is short for Identity Resolution, the main process I use in my counseling sessions. Most of the others will usually be accompanied by their full name.

Privacy

All of the names of friends, family members, clients, and people involved in my personal life, including the person I call Patty Preston, have been changed. I have disguised many descriptions of people, places, times, and circumstances as well, to avoid controversy and to maintain some privacy and discretion for myself and others. The descriptions of my various professional affiliations are accurate.

Chronology

Any memoir is a slave to its own chronology, but the repeated use of flashbacks, which I employ throughout the book, can be confusing if not done well. So to clarify this in advance, there are two time lines here: the description of my ongoing self-exploration efforts, which is mostly linear, and my descriptions of past events discovered and recalled during those efforts, which are described in flashbacks. Often during my descriptions of events, I go back and forth from the earlier incident itself, to the ID-R session in which I recalled that incident. To avoid repetition and confusion I have tried to minimize my use of dates and ages while still maintaining clarity, by providing some information here in this Preface, as follows. My ID-R sessions began in 1991, and most of the sessions described in this book, unless otherwise noted, took place from 1991 through 1995, when I was between the ages of forty-three and forty-seven. So while I usually give my ages regarding the memories and incidents I describe, most of the work of recalling and resolving those past experiences can be assumed to be taking place in the "present time" of the sessions, which occurred mostly during those first four years.

Credit

Many of the ideas in this book regarding psycho-spiritual models of human nature and methods of healing and self-improvement have been known and used by others for decades or centuries. Some of these ideas are ancient, some are relatively new, and some I discovered and developed on my own, and everything I've learned has contributed to my work in some way. So if you think I got some idea from someone else, you are probably right. If you have studied the history of any invention, you know that most innovations depend on many earlier discoveries, developments, and ideas, and even on language itself. Similarly everything in this book owes credit to many other people, methods, and ideas stretching back through history.

Many of the concepts in this book were ideas I actually had back in the 1970's, although they have changed as I learned more over the years. Other changes in my thinking grew out of working with ID-R, which further modified my understanding of trauma and consciousness, all of which led to the development of the Identity Model of Consciousness described in Chapter 17. Many of the books I cite in this work, I didn't read until after 1993. In most of those later books I was impressed that so much of what was being said, mainly about trauma, healing, and nature of reality, as well as other people's personal experiences, was identical to what I was saying! And I found they were using many of the same quotes and metaphors as I was, because they are so apropos! All this is so obvious that I felt it might look as if I were just copying what others had said, which is what prompted me to write this section of the Preface. But the great thing about these contemporary writings is how they demonstrate that when many of us explore the same territory with scientific intention and an open mind, we will discover the same things, although they may be described and understood in different ways. My understanding of most of the topics in this book has much in common with the works of Francine Shapiro, Bernardo Kastrup, Dean Radin, Charles Tart, Thomas Campbell, Gabor Maté, Bessel van der Kolk, and many others, and yet because we each have different pieces of the puzzle, we all see things a bit differently. But by studying these topics from a truly scientific and rational perspective we will continue to advance toward a more cohesive and universal understanding.

Accordingly I want to express my acknowledgment and sincere appreciation to all the teachers, authors, clients, friends, and others who have contributed to my understanding of life, and to the great many books, studies, and other sources that have helped and guided me along the way. Some of these contributions are mentioned in the Acknowledgments section, and others throughout the book. Still, each new discovery in the world changes how we look at things, and this book presents a new way to explore and understand your own life.

Although I have some very strong convictions which I may express with some certainty, everyone must determine themselves what is true for them. So if I may borrow these relevant words from the author Wei Wu Wei: "This work is essentially a discussion; if occasionally passages should appear to be didactically expressed, please be so good as to interpret them as emphasis." Also, other than my personal experiences, any statements of fact for which I have not given supportive evidence should be considered as my opinion only, until verified.

References

The following pages present a wide range of challenging topics and phenomena about which many books have been written and about which I could write volumes myself from my own perspective. But since in-depth discussions of most of these subjects are not needed here and can be found elsewhere, I will refer you to those references I have personally found to be the most helpful and informative. I recommend using these references to get a more complete perspective on the various topics being discussed, and a better understanding of where my ideas stand in relation to the views of others.

Also, since much of what is written here is controversial, and this is not a scholastic or scientific treatise, I have not backed up many technical statements with extensive or precise references. However, you may find such references in many of the sources I cite. My intention in these pages is not to prove anything or convince you of anything. I'm only presenting a case for some challenging propositions. It is also important to know that while I have taken the required training and received a certificate as an Advanced Clinical Hypnotherapist from a world renown state licensed school, I am not a doctor or a licenced psychologist and have no licence or degree in any field of health. My authority and qualifications are made clear in the introduction. Please research and investigate any of my technical statements for yourself if you have any doubts or questions. I'm sure there will be differing opinions on almost everything I say.

For video clips pop-culture references I make to movies and TV shows, please use the internet link to my blog website in the footnote.[1]

Exceptional Human Experiences – Rhea A. White

I want to end this preface with a quote from a paper by parapsychology researcher Rhea A. White, about Exceptional Human Experiences, or "EHEs." An EHE is any anomalous or paranormal experience that has a transformative effect on the experiencer. There's a more detailed definition of this on the EHE website referenced below.

---

[1] https://www.pipskywalker.com/games-of-magic/

While in college in the 1950's, Rhea was severely injured in a traffic accident and had a profound NDE (near-death experience) that changed the direction of her life. As described by the Institute of Transpersonal Psychology, in a notice by Dr. Charles T. Tart which is posted on the EHE website, "... she found herself seemingly above the earth, bathed in a sense of unity, peace and aliveness while her body lay unconscious on the hood of her car. She thought she had died--and it was wonderful! Rhea heard a voice tell her that "nothing that ever lived could possibly die." She felt the "everlasting arms" enfold her. Then she awakened on the hood of her car, unable to move, and in great pain."[2]

Rhea then began a lifelong quest to understand her NDE, studying all she could on the subject, becoming a parapsychology researcher and working at J. B. Rhine's pioneering Parapsychology Laboratory at Duke University, and later at the American Society for Psychical Research.

As a reference librarian she spent many years compiling reference works on parapsychology. Her unique "outside the box" perspective led Rhea to become the founder and director of the Exceptional Human Experience Network, a project that grew from a vision she had and which was still being developed when Rhea died in 2007. She has been called "parapsychology's bibliographer" and has made many important contributions to the field. This paper, titled "Exceptional Human Experiences: A Brief Overview," is a perfect expression of what this book is, in part, which is a story of exceptional and transformative human experiences. It also places my story, and every other exceptional story, in what she calls the Experiential Paradigm.[3] Here's the quote:

"In science everyone is looking for a new paradigm (or worldview) to account for everything. Physicists are trying to account for the mind-matter interface. Psychologists and philosophers call it the mind-body relationship. We call EHEs preparadigmatic experiences, because they seem to herald a new

---

[2] https://ehe.org/display/splash.html

[3] Exceptional Human Experience Network, *"Exceptional Human Experiences: A Brief Overview,"* EHE.org, accessed September 18, 2025, (https://ehe.org/display/ehe-page53e5.html?ID=5).

paradigm, or at the least, they fly in the face of the one with which we now live. So each one really offers the experiencer (and to some extent, those who read or hear about a given experience) a window with a new view, and they provide an opportunity to choose between belief and doubt. (This is an opportunity of unparalleled importance.) The experiencer must decide whether to provisionally trust the experience or explain it away or dismiss it. Those who choose to believe find they have opened a door leading to additional experiences that provide entrance to a world where their lives become charged with meaning. They have entered what we call the Experiential Paradigm."

Rhea goes on to brilliantly describe the challenges that this new paradigm faces. I considered including the entire paper at the end of the book, but I feel it's better to visit the EHE.org website and read it there, where you will also find many other great articles and personal stories, as well as guidelines for writing your own story.

Although this book includes much additional material, it is basically my own EHE autobiography.

Introduction

"The very cave you are afraid to enter turns out to be the source of what you are looking for." – Joseph Campbell

There is something powerful in this book that will change your life. I can't know exactly what it will be, but no matter what you want in life, what problems you would like help with, or what you might be looking for in any book on mind-body healing, self-help, or self-understanding, you already have it all within you. The trick is getting through all the internal blocks and programming that are keeping those things from you, preventing you from achieving your true purpose – and from accomplishing your dreams. And that makes this book indispensable. I will show you where those blocks come from and what you can do to unlock your true potential.

At its core, this book presents some new and revolutionary ideas about trauma, and it's resolution, that represent an important advance in the understanding of the mind-body-consciousness paradigm. This includes the introduction of a new system of self-discovery and inner healing called "Identity Resolution," or ID-R, which reveals the profound secret of traumatic shock, and utilizes the concept of stuck identity states in the processing of traumatic memory.

I've been a spiritual counselor for over 34 years, helping people heal their deepest psychic wounds, and ID-R has changed my life and helped hundreds of others overcome unwanted mental, emotional, and physical conditions of many kinds. Looking through the portal of trauma has also enabled me to recall many things locked away and long forgotten, and has given me a greater perspective on humanity, and even reality itself. The story of my own healing journey provides a framework and perspective for everything in the book, and it's a story unlike anything you've ever heard.

In addition to a whole new way of understanding and working with trauma, you will find, within these pages, novel explanations of many things, including multiple personalities, out-of-body experiences, spiritual connections, and the "real magic" of paranormal phenomena and miracles. I've also included many related practical tools we can all use for improving our lives, as well as some important discussions about consciousness, memory, past lives, dreams, and the quest for spiritual enlightenment. There is information here regarding these subjects you won't find anywhere else, and I'm happy to share it all with you.

Catalysts

A catalyst is something that instigates or facilitates change, and that's what this book is meant to be – a catalyst for personal insights that can lead to profound healing and a deeper understanding of oneself and others. While I feel internally compelled to share my story and ideas with the public, without really knowing what the deeper underlying purpose and overall future effect might be, I can definitely say that the feeling behind my compulsion is a mixture of excitement, love, and a genuine desire to help. My overall wish and expectation are that this book will inspire hope and curiosity in others and facilitate beneficial changes in people, and the world. I also believe that every positive transformation in ourselves has the potential to ripple outward into the world in many different ways and in many directions, to benefit all humanity. So to that end, I'll be telling you some amazing stories and discussing some very important and fascinating topics. And so as not to bury the lead, there's a secret hidden in the heart of every traumatic experience, that, when properly understood and utilized, is a key that unlocks many doors and can help change things for the better, for every one of us. It's the secret of the "traumatic shock," a discovery that changed my life and which I will describe in detail in Chapter 6.

Overall, this is a book about self-discovery, inner healing, and the incredible things we might find in the course of looking inward into the depths of our own being. What you are about to read is both a memoir of my lifelong quest for better self-understanding, and my description of how our minds function based on what I've learned while using ID-R with myself and others. If you are interested in any of the topics mentioned above, or if you want to get rid of any unwanted mindbody conditions, change your life for the better, have more control and freedom over your automatic reactions, decode your dreams, help others, or just see more deeply into the mysteries of your own life and the truth of what you really are, you should definitely read this book.

"Games of Magic" refers to life itself, in all its forms, throughout the universe. It's all a game, and "magic" is the creative force of Consciousness itself from which springs everything there is. And it all happens through us – through you and me. I'll be explaining all that later, and much more, including how to experience miracles, reclaim your power, know your life's purpose, and find your own best path to enlightenment.

The metaphysical adventure in the subtitle refers to my whole life, which is both my own "hero's journey" and a magical love story. If this introduction were like a good trailer for a fantasy adventure movie, it would probably start with the scene in Chapter 2 where I'm screaming in pain at the top of my lungs, or the childhood scene where I'm being chased by a bully and levitate to the ceiling to escape, and maybe end with the scene where Patty and I meet face to face for the first time, after dying together in a plane crash in France in a past life – the prologue to the whole book. But those are just teasers that don't convey the real purpose and power of this work. In fact while those scenes might interest many people, they might also turn off many of those for whom this book might be the most valuable, by making this information appear less scientific, or seem more like fantasy than reality. My story does play an important role however – several in fact – which I will explain in Chapter 1. But the central purpose of this book is to be a catalyst for change that might benefit you, and the world, for the better. The world only gets better when WE get better, because we are the world. And WE get better when we resolve our inner wounds, overcome the illusions of our internal conditioning, and begin to realize who we really are. As the truth of our connection to each other and everything around us becomes more clear we will be guided by that deeper understanding, and love and compassion will become our natural expression.

The most important information I want to convey in this book is about the healing breakthrough referred to in the subtitle, because it's new, powerful, and few people know about it. ID-R is a tool for self-exploration, and its underlying principles are essentially an advance in the understanding of trauma and its resolution. My own use of ID-R has led to discoveries that challenged the way I understood reality. To make sense of these discoveries requires a new model of the mind, consciousness, and existence, that is both reasonable and more adequately accounts for everything we

experience as human beings. My attempt at describing this new
paradigm is called the Identity Model of Consciousness. But this
isn't academic – everything here is based on actual human
experience, and the basic information can be verified by anyone
willing and able to look through the portal, which is trauma itself.
The cave we fear to enter is the vast unknown within us, because
there is darkness there – the terrifying darkness of past trauma in all
its forms. But having enough courage to enter that cave leads not
only to healing but to unexpected treasures, and what you will find
there can change your life, and your understanding of yourself and
others, in valuable and fundamental ways. Your life may seem
ordinary until you look deeper, but whatever your personal story
seems to be, I guarantee you there's more. There is no novel, no
movie, no legend, no mythology that can compare to the real story
of who and what you are – the story that lies hidden behind the
powerful veils of illusion and forgetfulness – the story that has been
replaced by one of being an ordinary person living an ordinary life.
This may sound silly, but you will never know until you take a look.

Amnesia

So I'm here to help you remember. Most of us have no idea of
what's hidden away in the depths of our own minds and what those
missing pieces can tell us about ourselves, life, and the universe.
Have you ever thought about what it might be like to have amnesia
– to not know who you are or where you came from, and to lose
most of the knowledge and skills you once had? Well, if those gaps
were to be filled in by illusions, like a carefully edited past history,
or none at all before a specific date, and a newly constructed sense
of identity, you would likely not even consider there was anything
missing. Now play along with me here and imagine coming to
realize that your present life memories and self-description are all
just such an illusion. When your memory returned it could be quite
a surprise! It was for me! Many of the personal stories I'm about to
tell you, I did not recall or even suspect had ever happened – I had
no clue. It was all hidden – locked away inside my head – forgotten,
diminished, and suppressed. I had amnesia.

But my amnesia was not caused by a blow to the head – it was
something else, something common to everyone, and discovering
just a little of what I had lost was like magic! My life improved, I
found my purpose, and I knew my path – and much more. It did

take a lot of work though, and I'm certainly not done, but now my mission is to help others know themselves better, and I have a special way to do that, because I believe this is true for all of us – that we all have amnesia. We all have untold treasures of wisdom and power locked away within us – more than we can ever imagine – and yet most of us know nothing about it. How is that even possible? The simplistic answer is, we forgot – but the truth is a bit more complicated.

In order to reclaim yourself though, you must face yourself – the good, the bad, the ugly . . . and the forgotten. A lot of people think that's not necessary. "Why go dredging up painful things from the past?" they say. "Just let the past go and live in the NOW." There is great wisdom in that, but like everything else, it really depends on the context, and the purpose you are trying to accomplish. In addition, this viewpoint is based on a misunderstanding. And no one is really holding on to the past anyway – it's more like the past is holding on to us without our knowledge. Answering the questions of what, we have forgotten, what we might remember, what it takes, and why this is all so extremely important to know, is the essence of this book. And as you will see, this is not just about remembering things – this is about the deeper implications of what we find as we discover more about ourselves. It's about actually seeing why we feel and act the way we do, breaking free from internal programming, rediscovering our true power, understanding our individual life's purpose, and realizing the true nature of our existence, because the illusions we have about ourselves run deep.

The difficulty is that there are many barriers to remembering and knowing ourselves. Sure, we all have the innate potential to accomplish our best as human beings, within the bounds of our physical and mental condition, and there are many methods, programs, and coaches to help us do that, but I'm talking about something else. Also, great successes and achievements don't tell us who we really are. As valuable as those things might be, they only represent a limited version of what we can do in the world. And even successful, wise, or wonderful identities, like all identities, are just temporary masks we wear while living our lives and acting out our various roles. However, those methods that go further and try to help us remove our deeper unconscious barriers and maximize our spiritual wisdom and power, are on the right track, because they do recognize there is more to us than meets the eye, and I have utilized many of them. But methods like these are often hindered by limited effectiveness and dogmatic adherence to unfounded theories or principles. Yet all these things are part of our ever evolving efforts to understand ourselves that have been going on for thousands of years. And these things aren't just the province of theologians, therapists, cognitive scientists, self-help gurus, mystics, or philosophers – knowing the truth about yourself is your birthright.

So what's locked away inside of YOU? There may be a lot of stuff you don't want to know, but what miracles have you forgotten, and what loves, and what joys? What have you lost, and how much of yourself and your true power have you given up? What doors have you closed, and how much of what's hidden away inside is controlling you right now – what's really running your life without your permission? If you have never considered any of this or hadn't believed it was even possible to really examine your own life in any real depth, since most of us don't, or you've never thought that such a thing would be of any value anyway, then what you're about to read will be a wake-up call. I have so much to tell you that I can only hint at some of it in this introduction, but I'm excited to share it all in the chapters ahead so you can clearly see, if you haven't discovered this in your life already, the incredible rewards of making the effort to truly know yourself, and so you can begin to understand and recover more of your own true power, happiness, and freedom. So after reading this introduction, if you think you're ready, prepare yourself for a magical ride on a journey of self-discovery, healing, and spiritual awakening. Let your curiosity and intuition be your guides, and weigh everything against your own experience.

My expertise in all this includes a lifetime of self-study and experience regarding all the topics in this book, and decades of successfully counseling hundreds of others using all the basic ideas and principles you will find here. But most importantly, my expertise is rooted in many thousands of hours of deep and effective introspection, something relatively few people have ever done, using principles that are not generally known. This is not something you go to school for or earn a degree in – this is personal experience. To paraphrase Morpheus in "The Matrix":

"Unfortunately no one can tell you what you really are; you have to see it for yourself."[4]

Understanding Trauma

The subject of trauma is immense, but understanding trauma is important because trauma impedes our memory and it's one of the fundamental barriers that helps keep us trapped in false views of ourselves and reality, on many levels. Traumatic experiences force us to confront things that are beyond our capacity to tolerate or deal with while in our present state of being, at the time they occur. Because of this, trauma changes us mentally and physically, and it changes the way we interact with the world, other people, and ourselves. It affects every aspect of our lives, from our minds, bodies, and health, to our relationships and societies, and even to the very course of civilization itself. There has been a growing appreciation of this for a long time now, but I think this appreciation is finally reaching a tipping point that has the potential to bring about enormous and important changes in the world.

New approaches to working with, preventing, and healing trauma, have been emerging for several decades but in the past, workable trauma therapies have been strongly resisted, often being seen as pseudoscience, fads, or quackery. It's easy to see why – trauma is painful and scary, and the core of any traumatic experience is hidden deep within the unconscious mind, and the pain it contains can cause a tremendous resistance in anyone trying to confront it. Working with trauma can be difficult for the counselor or facilitator as well, when their own trauma gets triggered, which can easily happen. Additionally, healing trauma can have such a profound effect on the body and mind that the results often seem miraculous and hard to believe. Working with trauma can also bring to light things of a dubious or problematic nature, like spiritual or transpersonal phenomena, that might tend to cast doubt on the whole healing process itself. Uncovering what lies within us can feel very threatening. And there can also be various medical, cultural, political, or religious groups at play that have vested interests in suppressing or downplaying the effects of trauma and the value of inner healing practices.

---

[4] Movie: "The Matrix" – 1999

But now, because of the growing understanding of trauma and its impact on our lives, brought about by the many dedicated and courageous professionals in this field, and with a growing body of research like the ACE Study, and with books like "The Body Keeps the Score" by Bessel van der Kolk, "The Myth of Normal" by Gabor Maté," and "EMDR" by Francine Shapiro, it's becoming increasingly clear that one of the most important and urgent things we can do for ourselves, our families, and the entire world, is for each of us to become more "trauma informed."[5] This book takes working with trauma to a new level. The good news is that working with trauma effectively cannot only bring about real and permanent healing and transformation, but can also teach us more about our minds and bodies, and life itself, than you might ever imagine, and it can even serve as a portal to a greater understanding of consciousness and the universe.

Bessel van der Kolk, author of the brilliant book mentioned above, has dedicated most of his professional life to, in his words, "trying to unravel the mysteries of trauma," and he has done a phenomenal job. I hope to unravel a few more of those mysteries for you here. In 1994 while attending an international convention of psychiatrists and therapists studying dissociation, I took part in a workshop discussing traumatic memory. The emphasis was on trying to explain how trauma gets embedded in our systems as it does, to leave its lasting effects on our minds and bodies. Although I had some of the answers the speaker was looking for way back then, I knew it would be futile to try and get anyone in mainstream academia to take my information seriously. However, that was never really my goal. For a new idea or process that has practical value to become common knowledge and be put into widespread practice, if it ever does, it can often take decades. This is especially true if the new thing is truly innovative or conflicts with current beliefs or

---

[5] To be trauma-informed means that we understand what trauma is and how it affects us all. This understanding, when sufficient, will motivate and guide us to adjust our thinking and behavior accordingly so as not to retraumatize others, or ourselves. It also empowers us to be more understanding and more able to communicate effectively with respect and compassion with our fellow human beings, in every area of life.

practices. My present goal is just to get this information into the hands of everyone who might be interested.

Antonie van Leeuwenhoek was the first person to discover microscopic organisms using his specially crafted microscopes back in the 1600's, and his discoveries changed the world by altering the course of science in many areas. According to the Britannica, "Although Leeuwenhoek's studies lacked the organization of formal scientific research, his powers of careful observation enabled him to make discoveries of fundamental importance." Similarly, all I have to offer are my own observations and discoveries, and while some of these are definitely of fundamental importance, they do currently lack any scientific organization or academic acknowledgment. Therefore, this book will have to serve as an introduction to ID-R, and a platform for discussing the revelations that have emerged from working with this powerful self-discovery technique. Revelations like the secret of traumatic shock and the altered state it produces, which I call the "power-zone." This information alone is invaluable, as it explains how trauma happens, why it becomes a problem, why its roots have been so difficult to resolve, and why the effects of trauma can be so profound and so diverse. Other advances include a better description of the nature of traumatic memory, utilizing the concept of "identities" (stuck identity states), as well as a breakthrough understanding of multiple personalities and dissociation that, for the first time, takes consciousness into account. You will also find here a new explanation of paranormal phenomena, of miracles, and the nature of spiritual reality. All these things serve to reveal the universe and life itself to be what they ultimately are – spectacular games of magic that spring from our very minds through the creative power of consciousness itself.

Who Are You, Really?

In the end though, I believe the highest purpose in life, the purpose that serves us best, is to find out who and what we really are. We are not any of the many identities we embody, the social roles we identify with, the story we tell ourselves about who we are, or even the body we appear to inhabit – each of us is the witness of all these things. But who or what is this witness? Discovering our true nature is a spiritual quest, a quest of consciousness that leads to the ultimate fulfillment, happiness, love, understanding, and freedom known as spiritual awakening or enlightenment. Life, love, pain, suffering, joy and sorrow, struggle and healing – these are all part of a journey that eventually leads us to the path toward self-realization, and this has been my path for perhaps my whole life. Healing is certainly valuable and necessary, and that's where my journey began and what most of this book is about. But healing is only a temporary respite. Life is change – we solve one problem and another one comes along – it's inevitable. But "what we ARE" does not change, and what we ARE does not require healing, improvement, or anything other than recognition. What we ARE is already free, and we'll be exploring these things in depth as well.

The effects of trauma are profound and the results of healing it are equally profound, but even more than that, what working with trauma can show us, if we can set aside our preconceptions and be open to it, is some pretty mind-blowing and paradigm-shifting stuff. My own healing journey served greatly to validate what I already believed – that we are much more than human beings and there are levels of reality beyond what we might imagine. I'm fairly sure this book will challenge you, but it can also inspire you if you let it. It's essentially an investigation of life through the lens of trauma that reveals everything I've just described, and much more. The information here, and in the many resources provided, can certainly be of use to anyone interested in deeper self-understanding and in changing lives for the better. So I invite you to join me on this excursion through Wonderland as we explore, from a new perspective, this magical game we call life.

✻ ✻ ✻ ✻ ✻ ✻ ✻ ✻ ✻ ✻ ✻ ✻ ✻ ✻ ✻ ✻ ✻ ✻ ✻ ✻

Part I

♻

Journeys of Discovery

✻ ✻ ✻ ✻ ✻ ✻ ✻ ✻ ✻ ✻ ✻ ✻ ✻ ✻ ✻ ✻ ✻ ✻ ✻

Prologue

"There was a time when meadow, grove, and stream,
The earth, and every common sight,
To me did seem Apparelled in celestial light,
The glory and the freshness of a dream." – William Wordsworth

I was just standing there by the end of the bench facing the street when I heard a voice, distinctly feminine, like a deep breath of air swirling around me but mostly behind me and to the right. The voice whispered "She's coming around the corner."

I was four years old and it was a bright and breezy spring day in the early nineteen fifties. I was standing at a bus stop downtown with my mother. As I watched the people in their colorful attire, and the cars, the yellow cabs, and the buses going by, the ambiance was further enhanced by the different aromas floating through the air: the scent of popcorn and caramel from J. J. Newberry's five and dime across the street, mixed with cigarette and cigar smoke, bus exhaust, perfumes, bubble gum, and other unidentified fragrances that were a signature of this area on a bustling weekend afternoon. This was all experienced with the wonder, openness, and magnified senses of a child.

When I first heard the voice, the atmosphere became alive, vibrant, almost electrical. I was fascinated, more with the voice and the feeling it produced in me than with what the voice was saying, which I found meaningless. In fact it didn't occur to me that the voice was talking to ME – it was just a phenomenon – but neither did it occur to me that anyone else could hear it. I was used to seeing and hearing things that others paid no attention to. There was a very soft yet powerful quality to the voice. It had a kind of melodic fragrance that made it feel musical, and I felt safe and not at all afraid. The voice then said "She's coming toward you." I didn't move. I had no idea who was coming but I had a magical feeling that something amazing was about to happen. I was spellbound.

The voice continued, but it had now become more of a synesthesia of perceptions, less auditory, and more like a strong knowing, mixed with the same vibrant musical quality and vague flashes of color: "She's ten feet away." Entranced, I just stood there facing the street but not actually noticing it anymore. Then I heard/felt "She's right behind you" and I experienced a wave of energy go right through my body, like a gust of magnetic wind! I turned to my left and saw a lady in a dark dress walking by, with a little girl clutching her right hand. I immediately started following them as if I were being pulled along by some inner force. But when I got a few feet from the bench my mother shouted my name and I stopped. This caused the little girl to turn around, and she saw me looking at her.

She continued to walk for another few seconds but kept staring at me, and I stared back. Then she tugged her hand, breaking free from her mother's grasp, ran a few steps in my direction, and then walked very deliberately right up to me with no hesitation, until we were very close. Her eyes never left mine. "Patty!" Her mother called her name, sounding a bit frustrated, but followed her and let her visit. We just stood there looking at each other. The little girl seemed close to my age with blue eyes and dark brown hair. She was wearing a light-colored print dress, a knit sweater, and was clutching a small bag in her right hand. Her mother said "Is that what you wanted – to see this little boy? He's a cute little boy." As we stood there in silence she asked my mother "Is he yours?" and they chatted for a minute.

Since her daughter showed no inclination to turn away, the lady suggested that she give me something out of her bag. She reached in and pulled out a small gift but her mother reminded her that it was for someone else, and suggested giving me another item, a wrapped piece of candy, which she did. Then they had to go, and I just stood there watching as they walked away. I had no idea what it all meant, but I seemed to be in a trance-like state for several hours after that. It was as if I were trying to remember something important, and there seemed to be a lot of chatter going on in my head. Then the experience faded away.

Chapter 1
Taking the Red Pill

"This is your last chance. After this, there is no turning back. You take the blue pill – the story ends, you wake up in your bed and believe whatever you want to believe. You take the red pill – you stay in Wonderland, and I show you how deep the rabbit-hole goes." –
Morpheus - The Matrix, 1999

When I was a child I had some interesting abilities. One of those was that I could see without using my eyes. I could see behind me and all around me and even through walls. I simply had to "look" in a certain way. In India it's what is called a "siddhi," the Sanskrit word for a psychic or spiritual power. Peeking through the back of my head, I would often wave backwards to people who were behind me when I saw them looking at me, like God often did in the TV series "Joan of Arcadia," but they never waved back. I had this ability up until the age of five when I suddenly lost it. I was in my bedroom with my father that day, and while looking backwards and through the wall into the backyard, it suddenly occurred to me that maybe this ability had something to do with why he often seemed to hate me, and was so mean to me.

So I asked him about it. I said "Daddy, I can see outside my head, is that OK?" He looked at me curiously and said "What?" so I repeated it, "I can see outside my head," and he just laughed. Now kids are amazing and we've all heard them say hilarious things that made us laugh or even things that were profound and made us think, but my father had no idea what I meant. However, when he laughed something happened to me – I had a shock – and a darkness formed around my head. I told him I felt sick and there was something wrong with my eyes. He looked in my eyes, felt my forehead, and told me to lie down on the bed for a while, so I did. He came back in a few minutes to check on me, and I tried to describe what I was experiencing, but he didn't understand, and he told me to take a nap. It was like I was wearing a visor or a baseball cap, because there was this hard darkness just above my eyes. I didn't realize that it was just my forehead blocking my view –

something I had never been aware of before. I had lost my special vision and it never returned – until 1991.

One spring day thirty-eight years later, I was sitting across from an older gentleman who was wearing a white shirt and seated behind a large desk. He was asking me questions while I was connected to a GSR meter, a biofeedback device he used to facilitate our counseling sessions.[6] He was training me in a mental technique for resolving unwanted personal conditions. My eyes were closed, and while following his instructions, the darkness behind my eyelids suddenly became gray clouds moving quickly by me as if I were rocketing through them at a high rate of speed. It reminds me of the movie Avatar (2009) when Jake was connecting with his avatar body, and also of the tunnel phenomenon people sometimes have during an NDE. I verbalized what I was experiencing as it was happening. Suddenly the clouds parted, and although my eyes were still tightly closed, I could see the man in the white shirt in front of me on the other side of the desk, smiling at me, as if I were looking up at him from the level of my chest. In fact I could see that whole side of the room. This was all crystal clear. But I couldn't handle it and said so. "It's too much – I can't handle it," I blurted out. I tried to hold on to the vision, but after about five seconds everything went dark.

I opened my eyes, astonished. We were working on that "visor" incident I just described, which I had become aware of several years earlier. I chose to work on this because it was our final training session and I thought it would be fun. I wasn't sure my childhood ability had actually been real, even though I had many memories of it, and I didn't expect to regain this ability even for a few seconds. In fact I hadn't even considered that possibility at all, but it happened – and it was _real_! Although the temporary return of this spiritual gift was very brief and unstable, the training I was receiving was a major turning point in a journey I began as a child. I had now acquired some of the essential keys I had been looking for to help me uncover the secrets of my life, transform myself, and fulfill a promise that was still locked away somewhere deep in my unconscious mind.

---

[6] A Galvanic Skin Response meter is a device that responds to changes in the electrical conductivity of the body by moving a needle. The conductivity of the body is influenced by both physical and mental activity.

Now while this experience may sound too incredible to believe, it was just the beginning of a new phase of my life and a small preview of some of the stories you will find in the coming chapters. Indeed my entire life has been an adventure of self-discovery, of "know thyself," and everything I discovered following that episode, is the subject of this book.

In school I had pursued courses in science with the intention of becoming a biophysicist because I thought that was the best route to understanding life and the universe. I intuitively felt that I had a purpose in life that involved knowledge and helping people on some fundamental level. As my direction became more defined in college, I changed my major to psychology and began studying the mind and consciousness. I eventually set about trying to resolve my own personal issues and to remember more of my life. I also started doing daily meditation with the goal of realizing my true identity as consciousness itself. I'll say more on that later.

So what began as an academic quest for knowledge, turned inward, winding its way through meditation practices, mental exercises, lucid dreams, and out-of-body experiences, to working with childhood trauma and eventually uncovering some secrets of inner healing that were previously unknown, including things about trauma that researchers have been trying to figure out for decades. The result of all this was the development of a self-discovery process I call "Identity Resolution" or "ID-R," which helps us to resolve the effects of trauma and to recall hidden life experiences that were previously inaccessible. These discoveries also opened new doors in dealing with more controversial conditions like multiple personality, spirit attachment, and past life trauma. They further help us to recall and better understand spiritual relationships, paranormal phenomena, and miracles – the real magic that is happening all around us! After a short discussion and a brief synopsis of what lies ahead, we'll jump to the experience that gave me my first real glimpse into the possibilities of inner healing.

Inner Journeys

"I'm just another guy" says Neo in "The Matrix." But he's not – and he soon discovers he has magical superhuman abilities in the dreamworld of the Matrix – he can stop bullets in midair and fly like Superman – he's "The One." And so are you. But you don't know it. We are not who we think we are. We are all inherently magical beings of limitless power and possibility, playing endless games in an infinite universe, throughout eternity. And we're even more than that, and most spiritual traditions tell us this, in one way or another. But if that's really true, why don't we all know it, and how can we use it? Why does life seem to show us the opposite? Instead we appear to be pitiful mortals who live, love, suffer, and die in the blink of an eye, ruled by forces we have little control of. So what's the deal?

To answer these and many other deep questions, I'm going to share with you a true story that is more amazing and incredible than any I've ever heard. This story happens to be my own, and while my life may appear unremarkable on the surface, on a deeper level there is a lot more going on than I could have ever imagined when I began my inner journey many years ago. In the course of doing some deep inner work, I eventually discovered that what I had previously recalled and believed about my life and myself was mostly an illusion. As the illusion dissolved, what I discovered was not only extraordinary, but also incredibly healing, empowering, and liberating.

Although we may all have amnesia, hidden deep within that mysterious forgetfulness is a treasure trove of memories and abilities waiting to be rediscovered, and a magical story waiting to be revealed. On the human level, much of our personality has been shaped by past experiences that have become invisible forces hidden from our conscious awareness. The reality of what these experiences are and how they are affecting us in the present, rarely reaches the surface of our conscious mind except in dreams, deep meditation, or intensive therapy, even though we can be experiencing their effects every day in countless ways. Although these past experiences and the sources of our present difficulties can be brought into full awareness if we do the work, it can be difficult. Because these are mostly memories of trauma, they are by their very nature overwhelming. To avoid the unbearable pain and emotions these memories contain, we may experience great fear and resistance at the prospect of remembering. But our resistance to confronting our past experiences is an automatic mechanism. Once we are encouraged and empowered enough to let down our own inner barriers and confront the truth, we get stronger, and our resistance begins to vanish.

On the other hand, as long as our unconscious fears work to prevent any deeper exploration, we tend to avoid looking too closely at ourselves. Indeed, some of my friends who were given an advance copy of this book were reluctant to read it. They said they felt intimidated for some reason, or were afraid it might trigger something within them that they would rather not have to confront. And they were right – it can definitely stir things up, but if it didn't, it would not be serving its purpose as a catalyst for empowerment. Many of the things hidden deep within ourselves, things we've suppressed and forgotten, can definitely be painful or even terrifying when first uncovered. A few of those friends did have some strong reactions while reading, but they quickly found these reactions to be thought provoking, insightful, and beneficial.

As a memoir of my own life's journey and an in-depth discussion of related topics, this book will take you into areas you may find questionable. And that's OK – we should question everything. The upside is that there is essential and critical information presented in this work, in some detail, that is little known or scarcely accepted, and if you are open to it, you may begin to see life and people very differently, and in the process discover a lot more about yourself. For most of us, before we venture deeper into self-understanding, something has to come along that forcefully awakens us out of our complacency – perhaps the loss of a loved one, a near death experience, an existential crisis, or an intense curiosity – but something. Nevertheless, if you choose to proceed, the possibilities for personal insight, healing, and transformation, as well as some amazing adventures, are unlimited!

When I was ten years old I developed a great passion for knowledge. But my Hero's Journey actually began four years earlier when a series of events led me to choosing a new life purpose. This is what Joseph Campbell referred to as "the call to adventure," and it led me on an amazing quest which, although very difficult and painful, was ultimately fulfilling. One important purpose of that quest, which I discovered much later, was to lead me to find and develop a new way to address the healing of unwanted physical, mental, and spiritual conditions. This is the process that became

ID-R, and it has changed my life in amazing ways and has helped hundreds of people resolve unwanted conditions and limitations of many kinds over the last thirty-plus years.[7]

Many of the ideas and techniques I use are derived or borrowed from other methods. In addition to a few innovations of my own, my contribution to the ID-R process comes from my unique understanding of how these things work after thousands of hours of intensive personal exploration, and counseling hundreds of people over many years. Moreover, what I discovered in working with this method forced me to question the generally accepted materialist paradigm regarding the nature of reality, even more than I already had. Explaining my own life requires a new model of the universe that takes all my experiences into account and still makes sense. Introducing ID-R, and the model that supports it, is the central purpose of this book.

I have no doubt my personal story will challenge you, perhaps even more than Wonderland might have challenged Alice, and if you continue reading, your present view of the world may be imperiled. So if you take the blue pill and put this book back on the shelf, you can continue to see the world as you always have and be none the wiser for it, and none the richer. But all kidding aside, whether you will actually be wiser or richer for reading the rest of this book depends on how willing you are to give real consideration to the things I'm about to share.

Before We Begin
"No, no! The adventures first, explanations take such a dreadful time." – Alice in Wonderland, Lewis Carroll

Yes, there are indeed some interesting stories ahead and some deep discussions, but before we get to the good stuff I want to prepare you a bit in advance so you can get the most out of it all. This is really several books in one. First it's the story of a quest for

---

[7] Throughout this book, when I use the word "resolve" with regard to unwanted conditions, it means to heal or handle completely, to put an end to, or to clear up, so that the issue is gone or is no longer a problem or a concern, and cannot return.

knowledge and self-understanding spanning a lifetime, and of discoveries and ideas that can help all of us improve our lives. Next it's an intensive look into the areas of healing and personal transformation, exploring the immense role that trauma and adverse past experiences play in our lives, the identities we take on, the games we play, the forces that control us, and what we can do about it. In addition to introducing ID-R and the Identity Model of Consciousness, it's also a metaphysical love story that delves into the spiritual nature of the universe, the connections among all of us, and the deeper hidden meanings of our lives. For added clarity these chapters are also filled with explanations and examples of the subjects at hand, and some in-depth discussions of essential or relevant topics as well. So in order to minimize any confusion, I have arranged the book into five parts. While each part can stand on its own to some degree if read separately, it's best to read them in order because they build on each other and will be easier to understand that way. This book is really a journey in itself, or to borrow a quote from the movie "Jurassic Park," "It's a kind of a ride." So to provide a sense of direction, here is a brief overview of each part.

Part I – Journeys of Discovery

My life story is interwoven into the fabric of this book. It's like a carrier wave that not only provides a context and framework for the more important information, but also affords a gradient of understanding for the major concepts, while bringing these concepts to life and establishing them in real experiences using personal examples. In my studies I have found that most of the models and understandings proposed by others, regarding some topics in this book, are third-party intellectual descriptions made by people who have little or no personal experience with these things – outsiders so to speak. For example, many people who pontificate about things like out-of-body experiences, psi phenomena, or multiple personalities, are considering these things from the outside and have not experienced them for themselves on a personal level, and many people who talk about inner healing or therapy have not worked on their own selves to any great degree. Such people, including consciousness researchers, therapists, scientists, medical professionals, and other people closely involved in working with or researching these things, have widely varied ways of explaining them, some of which I find quite sound and others deeply flawed. On the other hand, people who _have_ experienced these things personally, also have many differing explanations for them. The ID-R process has given me some deep insights into many such areas of human experience that I have not found anywhere else. Therefore the inclusion of my personal experiences throughout this book in an intimate and detailed way, will make it clear how I came to my own conclusions, which I think will be of significant value to anyone interested in healing and transformation. Part I, including this chapter, is about the beginnings of my healing journey, and it allows me to share with you how my process of self-discovery began to unfold when I first got serious about it. It is also an essential connection to the epic story presented in Part V.

Part II – The Healing Paradigm

The things that stand in the way of our truly knowing ourselves are not only our illusions of being something we are not, but all the trauma and programming that get in our way as we try and wake up from those illusions. It is important to understand how these things work so we can deal with them more effectively. Part II is the real core of this book – it's where I break down all the main concepts involved in the basic ID-R process and describe what I have learned about healing in general. Here we look at what healing means medically and practically, and we discuss the three basic levels of healing in addressing any problem. When I use the word "healing" with regard to mind, body, or spirit, I mean it in a general way to describe the resolution or betterment of anything from serious life altering physical or mental conditions, to the improvement of minor bothersome impairments or inconveniences. While I use it basically as a synonym for any kind positive change, healing does imply a wound, and the wound is simply whatever stands in the way of improving our situation, whether it's minor or major. Most often this is something traumatic.

From there we dive deeply into how healing and transformation are understood using the ID-R model. This includes in-depth discussions of trauma, dissociation, and multiple personalities, and includes chapters describing many of my own self-healing stories. All the self-healing stories in Part II and Part III serve as examples of both the deep inner healing of trauma, and of the vast variety of trauma-related conditions.

Part III – Real Magic

Knowing yourself ultimately also means knowing ultimate power. Evidence of that power is everywhere, but for the most part we don't see it – we block it. Opening ourselves to seeing it, accepting it, and using it helps us to understand ourselves and life better, which is the path to freedom. That's why knowing about real magic is so important. When it surfaces on the path of self-discovery it can be a source of fear or doubt and become a roadblock. We have all experienced things in our lives that seem impossible and defy any explanation, or at least any explanations that don't depend on spiritual or supernatural beliefs. Part of the problem we have with such experiences is that we don't generally have a convincing theoretical framework in which to understand them. More importantly we often face powerful social pressures and emotional reactions that inhibit us from accepting these things as real, or even from talking about them. The result is that we either dismiss such things entirely or explain them away somehow. However, phenomena that fall under the labels of paranormal, psychic, psi, spiritual, supernatural, or transpersonal, like seeing the future, out-of-body experiences, conversing with God or spirits, telepathy, instantaneous healing, remembering past lives, synchronicity, and many other things that remain "unexplained," are commonly recalled during the work of inner exploration and healing. Acknowledging and working with such experiences can often be a very important part of the healing process, and this doesn't require that we understand them or even believe they are possible. The question of whether or not such experiences are "real" in some explainable way can always be considered later, but they are certainly real as experiences and must not be ignored. Science is about embracing reality and making sense of it, but that often takes a lot of courage, as history has shown.

Part III chronicles my experiences with paranormal phenomena throughout my life. While working on myself I recalled many

extraordinary miraculous experiences that I had completely
forgotten, and which I have no doubt really happened. Paranormal
phenomena have been experienced by most people throughout
history and have been the subject of scientific study for many
decades. In his 2018 book "Real Magic," scientist Dean Radin
recognizes that what we call the paranormal has always been
attributed to the realm of magic and the supernatural. I have a lot to
say on this subject, including why these things are so hard to prove
in a scientific way, and I believe my experiences and explanations
regarding what I prefer to call "spiritual phenomena" or miracles,
warrant serious consideration. Plus, it's all really cool and amazing,
and I hope you can relate. Since recalling such experiences often
calls our memory into question, I've also included a chapter on
memory and reality in this section.

Part IV – Models of Transformation

Part IV gives you methods you can use in dealing with life based
on the three levels of healing described in Part II. The first chapter
in this section presents the Identity Model of Consciousness as a
way to explain how all my experiences are possible in a universe in
which consciousness is the singular underlying reality. It was many
years ago that I came to the conclusion that consciousness is the
source of everything in existence, but I had no real understanding
of how this universe of consciousness works. Although I was familiar
with many theories about these things and they sounded nice, these
were incomplete models based on evidence that was sketchy and
inconsistent. Once I began remembering some of the more
phenomenal experiences from my past, including higher states of
awareness, I began to see an overall pattern for conscious creation.
Consciousness is indeed the ultimate unified field – in fact
consciousness is all there is.

With reference to the Identity Model, this section goes on to
provide tools you can use on your own to understand, manage, and
change your life in profound ways and includes a chapter that will
give you a taste of using ID-R on your own. The culmination of Part
IV is about what I believe is the ultimate purpose of all healing, and
indeed of life itself – the discovery of who and what we really are. In

Chapter 21we explore the ultimate transformative game and the highest meaning of life, spiritual enlightenment.

Part V – Patty Preston

It's unimaginable how we can have entire dimensions of our lives hidden from us and yet they can still rule us and guide us from a realm beyond our awareness for an entire lifetime. Even when we look inside ourselves with meditation, therapy, hypnosis, or drugs, many of us may not find much. When we have not had any deep personal insights into our own minds, we may think there's nothing more there than what we ordinarily experience in our daily lives, but the whole universe is there – we just haven't opened the right doors. In truth, there are higher forces working all around us and through us all the time.

When I finally had the means to resolve my issues and discover my past, the story of my relationship with Patty Preston began to emerge, and it was incredible and exciting. Although we had extensive interactions in school, I barely even remembered Patty before doing all this inner work. When you experience something wondrous and beautiful it's natural to want to share it with others, and that's part of my motivation in sharing this part of my life with you, and setting this story loose into the world. But more importantly, our story reveals what can lie unseen in the secret inner dimensions of our being. Indeed it is working with my experiences with Patty that helped me to remember and understand higher levels of reality. It turned out that Patty was a part of my life story from the very beginning, motivating and inspiring me every step of the way. Without her, my life would have been very different, and this book and all my discoveries would have never happened.

The Power of Story

Lastly, it's my hope that all the personal stories in this book will serve to make it more human and memorable than it might otherwise be, and that offering my own experiences and perspectives regarding all the subjects being discussed here will be a helpful contribution in the world toward greater human understanding and better health, happiness, peace, and wellbeing

for all. You may find many of my experiences too incredible to take
seriously, especially if you don't recall anything similar in your own
life, but belief is not at all necessary. I only care that you understand
and consider the possibilities that they represent.

On the other hand, my story IS a true story, but only for me, just
as your story, your recollection and internal depiction of your own
life is only true for you, because no one else knows your actual
experience or would understand it the way you do, and only you
can really know yourself. What others feel or think about you is part
of THEIR story. Our stories are fables we tell ourselves, and
whether they are mostly rooted in fact or fantasy, they represent our
past, present, and future, and form the recipe for our current
identity. They are composed of all our memories and beliefs
regarding ourselves, our experiences, our relationships, and the
nature of the world, and because of this, our stories are stabilizing
structures delicately bound to every aspect of our lives. Our lives are
continually unfolding, and although our stories regarding the past
can change, normally we stubbornly resist anything that may
threaten our present version, even if for the better. And those
experiences that don't fit with our story because they violate our
most basic beliefs about the world, other people, or ourselves, are
either held as outliers on the periphery of our mind as unexplained
anomalies, or kept entirely invisible, until we can safely and
rationally integrate them into our worldview. Incorporating such
experiences into our story of how things are may require facing
some very intense inner resistance, which may arise in various
forms, like anger, fear, or pain.

For some, this book may threaten their story regarding how
things are and how the world works, but it's the very nature of
science itself to challenge our old ideas about the world while
expanding our knowledge and illuminating the possibilities of what
can be. Sometimes our mental construct of the world has to be
turned upside down and given a good shake. Remember, I'm not
asking you to believe anything – I'm just encouraging you to take a
look for yourself. In the end, hopefully, you can then relate to some
of my experiences and explanations. Besides being informative and
entertaining, these stories are equally there to stimulate your own
curiosity and hidden memories. And that's when the real adventure
begins. Whenever, during your own recollections or in the course

of doing your own "inner work," you find you can relate to some of my personal experiences, I trust you will find these stories inspiring, validating, helpful, or supportive. So while this book may provide some diversion and ample food for thought, the biggest adventures may or may not happen as you sit and read, because the real excitement commences the minute you begin to look deep within yourself with the nuclear microscope of your own attention, and make your own transformative discoveries. Maybe this has already begun. So for you, the reader, my entire narrative is best seen as an allegory representing the real possibilities hidden within us all, because you too will most assuredly encounter the reality of some of these possibilities yourself, in your own experience, and perhaps that will inspire you to share your own story one day, if you feel called to do so.

So now we'll begin this adventure with my first major breakthrough. It was only the beginning, but this experience convinced me I was on the right track, and it was definitely a surprise.

Chapter 2
Primal Pain

"Somatic symptoms for which no physical basis can be found, are ubiquitous in traumatized children and adults."
— Bessel van de Kolk

"I think everybody's blocked, I haven't met anybody that isn't a complete blockage of pain from childhood, from birth on ..."
— John Lennon

I was screaming as loud as I could. The pain was unbearable. My head was being crushed and felt like it was about to burst but I had to stop fighting it. I didn't really know what to expect, I only knew I had to keep going and allow this experience to run its course. The pain was raw, sharp, and cold, and each time I let go to relax into it, the pain intensified. Finally I just let it take over, and as I did I experienced intense electrical sensations shooting through my temples to the back of my neck and down my spine. There was something curiously pleasurable in the electrical feeling, as if I were somehow breaking through to some deep pool of agony and releasing some kind of trapped energy. I screamed deeply with my whole body, as if I were giving voice to all the pain I had ever experienced. It was primal.

And as I screamed, just letting myself feel the pain, something happened – flashes of light, voices, sounds, new sensations. It was as if I had entered another dimension. My temples were throbbing with pain, my face felt rubbery and new, and so sensitively alive that it was like a universe in itself. My eyes watered, my nasal passages filled, and my body made involuntary movements as if I were stuck in quicksand and struggling to Get free.

I heard the doctor yell "Push." "I can't," my mother replied in a strained voice. "Yes you can – take a deep breath." I could feel the cold biting steel of the forceps against my temples as I was being pulled forward – intensely sharp stabbing pains, like crocodile jaws. The vividness of these sensations was amazing.

And somewhere in the first agonizing minutes of allowing these feelings to emerge I realized I was reliving my own birth experience. I hadn't expected this. Although I had read about other people reexperiencing their birth, (no details, just that they had done it), it wasn't something real to me and certainly not on my mind – and now here it was.

I heard the doctor continue to encourage my mother to push. My shoulders were stuck in the birth canal so I began shrugging them up and down, first one, then the other, wriggling my way out. I heard the doctor's voice addressing one of the nurses "Look at that! Amazing. Have you ever seen that before?"

There was a whole body sensation that felt like a deep wave or shudder, and then I was free. But there was a strange pressure building up which I could feel in my entire body, but most strongly in my face and chest.

Suddenly I felt a jolt, like being hit by a freight train, and pain exploded in my left hip joint and stretched every muscle in my back. As the doctor was lifting me up by my feet, my little body actually slipped out of his hands. I dropped a couple inches but he was able to quickly catch me by the left ankle. I could feel the doctor's embarrassment telepathically. That moment passed quickly but it would later have very deep repercussions throughout my entire life. All my attention was now centered on the all-encompassing sensation of heat and pressure in my head, which felt like it would explode. "Slippery little devil" the doctor said with a nervous chuckle. I guess we should get him breathing." There was a huge hiccup, and the enormous inrush of air was like fire, intense yet pleasurable at the same time. And there was a lot of mucous.

Most remarkable, beyond the fact that I was reexperiencing my birth in present time, or remembering it at all for that matter, was how fresh, new, and alive it all was, and the realization of how totally conscious I was during the actual birth process. But I did not reexperience my birth in a linear way. As I was going through this experience on the floor of the spare bedroom in my house in South Sacramento, bits and pieces would burst through and hold my attention for a while, but I kept going back to the pain in my temples which grew more and more intense, and was unrelenting. My attention seemed to be stuck on the pain from the forceps. I was experiencing it over and over, recycling through those few agonizing moments. I could feel myself fighting it but I somehow knew that to release it I had to not resist it. So I tried to allow myself to feel the pinnacle of that pain, the very worst moment – what I now call the "apex." I surrendered to it and just screamed it out.

There was a brief period of exquisitely sharp pain and very strong electrical tingling sensations throughout my head, face and upper body, and then it subsided – it left – it was gone. My eyes and nose were running, and the memories continued to be present. I saw the nurses dressed in white uniforms with their white hats, and the hum of the old fluorescent lighting was very loud. The light was blinding, something was burning my eyes, and I felt lost, like something was missing – something needed and expected wasn't there. This wasn't a thought; it was a deep need, a starving emptiness waiting to be fulfilled. I was cold, empty, alone, but I don't remember crying. I think I just waited for it and eventually it came – someone held me. I remembered wanting to be surrounded, enclosed, secured, as I had been, before my unceremonious expulsion from the womb.

Primal Therapy

When I was done I sat up, sweaty and exhausted and also a bit dizzy from hyperventilating, but the pain was gone, totally gone. Although some remnants of pressure and sensation were still present, they were slowly evaporating. I got up off the floor laughing. For the last two hours I had been reliving an incident that occurred more than thirty years earlier. When my girlfriend Lynne came in I told her about my experience and she gave me a hug. Earlier in the week she had helped me by walking around the perimeter of the house while I screamed in the spare room to see if she could hear me. I was afraid of disturbing the neighbors. Although Lynne had only a cursory understanding of what I was doing at the time, she humored me and tolerated my weirdness.

At the time of this session I had just turned thirty-years old. I had been doing my own version of Primal Therapy, by myself, and with no training or previous experience. I had begun this session with an intense agonizing headache which I experienced as a deep, throbbing pain in both temples, sometimes dull and sometimes sharp. This was a recurring headache I had suffered from for most of my life. It was this pain that I had been working on, trying to feel it all, to scream it out, and to connect with the Primal Scene, which was, according to Primal Therapy, the early trauma from which it originated. The idea was that completely feeling the pain might possibly heal the condition for good. And it worked! For me this was a major breakthrough.

Now I knew two things beyond any doubt: that the root of at least some of my personal problems, including physical conditions, lay in past experiences that were unresolved in my unconscious mind, and that the resolution of these unwanted conditions could be attained by addressing these past experiences in a conscious way. I realized there was fantastic healing potential in this type of inner work and it was very exciting. I had many issues I wanted to work through, and big dreams of transforming our current understanding of the mind and consciousness.

As I understood it then, the idea behind Primal therapy is that we hold the emotional, spiritual, and physical pain of childhood trauma inside ourselves, and that this unresolved pain is the root cause of many problems. The cure for the resulting present day symptoms lies in connecting consciously with this primal pool of pain and letting it out by feeling it, and feeling it may require us to physically express it through screaming, crying, or contorting our bodies. This expression isn't contrived however, but happens naturally in the process of feeling, although one may be encouraged to "prime" the process by moving, screaming, and so forth in the beginning, as a means of helping the feelings emerge. If you were to lie on the floor and just start screaming for a while, as if you were really hurting, besides disturbing anyone within earshot, you would likely connect at some point with some genuine pain from your past. But I don't recommend this without being prepared for what might come up, and without learning how to protect your vocal cords.

So I began this process by simply giving voice to my pain. I had recently experienced several flashbacks of early childhood trauma, so it wasn't a surprise when visual images, feelings, and somatics (physical pains or sensations from the past), began to arise. I was however very surprised to experience my own birth, and I considered, for long hours, the validity of this experience. I could not dispute the fact that the headache was gone and had no

indication of ever returning. In fact everything inside of me said
that this experience WAS that very pain, and that it was no longer a
problem. Although I could remember the pain of the forceps
against my tiny pliable skull, the pain was no longer present and the
memory of it no longer had any force of its own.

An interesting side note: a few years earlier I was doing some
weight lifting in a gym with my younger brother Alan. He was
spotting me as I did some heavy squats. As I struggled to lift the
weight he yelled "Push!" I immediately shouted "I can't." After I
was done he asked me why I had said that. I had no idea at the
time, but now I see that this was a direct connection to my birth
experience and I was repeating my mother's exact words. Traumatic
experiences continue to exist below conscious awareness, much like
hypnotic commands, and can affect us in countless ways.

What I was doing is not really a good example of Primal
Therapy, since I had only read a few books on the subject and had
no other training or guidance. Also, I was mixing it with other
methods as well. For a better understanding of Primal Therapy as it
is today, you can visit their website. It appears there is a great
emphasis now on the whole perinatal experience and its effect on
one's development, personality, and present life. Rather than make
general statements about how such experiences may affect a person,
I prefer to let people discover this directly in private sessions.
However, every person is different, and I generally don't even
suggest looking at one's birth experience or any other particular
incident in one's life. Unless they specifically want to investigate
this experience, dealing with birth only happens when my client is
led there by their own self-discovery process in working through
some issue. This will become very clear in later discussions.
However, birth and prenatal issues have come up for many clients
during ID-R sessions, sometimes at our first meeting!

Understand that my view of these things, specifically the role of
past trauma in present physical pain, illness, or dysfunction, is NOT
generally believed or supported by mainstream medicine, even
though it has been demonstrated innumerable times by doctors and
practitioners around the world and can be demonstrated to anyone
willing to explore. When I mention my own experience along these
lines to doctors, very few give it thoughtful consideration. Most
dismiss what I have to say and are not even curious. They already

"know" that past experience has nothing to do with anything physically present now. They may just humor me or suggest a psych evaluation, so I gave up this kind of discussion a long time ago. I did test it recently though, and nothing has changed. This relates to what I call the "Closed Mind Fallacy." This is the rejection of the reality a phenomenon because it can't be explained in terms of the person's own understanding of things. Since they can't explain it, it doesn't exist and must be a delusion. They've closed their minds to the possibility that there are things they don't yet know. This is anti-science. Whether it's "long covid," telepathy, CFS, the biological harm of cellphone radiation, climate change, or the health risks of tobacco, for those who are not familiar with the massive amounts of evidence that these things exist, and have not been impacted by them personally, they can't be real.

Flashbacks

I had been studying psychology and self-improvement in my spare time since I was sixteen. Six months prior to this session I had a good job as a restaurant manager but one day I suddenly decided to quit so I could devote my time to something more important. It felt like I was on a mission. For the past several years I had this subliminal dream floating around in my mind of exploring consciousness and discovering things that would help me resolve my own issues, help others, and perhaps even change the world. I had no idea why I was drawn in this direction. I was certainly very motivated to improve myself, but it was more than that – there were problems and mysteries in my life that I needed to solve – secrets whispering just below the surface. I didn't have much money at this time and figured I only had a few months before I had to go back to work, so I studied and worked on myself every day.

About a year earlier I had read "The Primal Scream" by Arthur Janov and had begun to casually investigate my own past through memory work, trying to remember my childhood. Until then I had not considered that my personal issues might have originated sometime in the past. Gradually I became convinced that my early childhood experiences held clues to my social issues, and more recently to my headaches and other somatic conditions as well. So after I quit my job I began reading more books by Janov and everything I could find about memory, trauma, and psychological and spiritual healing. I looked into many things including Gurdjieff's "Work," Dianetics, hypnosis, EST, and anything I thought might help me look more deeply into my mind, and I found useful ideas from many sources. Everything I had read about or tried before this period regarding self-improvement had focused on how we could control our minds through changing our thinking, our attitudes, and changing how we use our attention. This led me to believe that I had simply not learned how to use my mind correctly. I had studied Maxwell Maltz, Rollo May, Eric Bern, Abraham Maslow, and Viktor Frankl, among others. What I learned were things which I now mostly include in the category of Identity Management (see Chapter 18). These are basically methods which, although helpful, do not involve the resolution of underlying causes. So while I found methods that made sense and have enormous value, I was looking for something deeper and more fundamental – something more powerful. I didn't just want to solve my problems or be more successful; I wanted to know where my difficulties came from, why they were there, and how to resolve them at their core level. And, most importantly, I wanted to understand myself. Something was driving me and I had a deep intuitive feeling that there was something about myself I needed to know, and making more money or even being happier wasn't going to help.

In the beginning, my self-discovery efforts began awakening many memories from my childhood, most of which seemed interesting but innocuous. For example I recalled standing with my mother outside my kindergarten classroom on the first day of school when I was five, looking at the apricot tree in our backyard when I was three, and holding a tiny glass figurine of a dragon when I was two. I discovered much later that these moments weren't so innocent after all – they were all immediately followed by trauma.

Every day I also did the same deep relaxation meditation, a practice that had caused me to start having out-of-body experiences (OBEs) about two years earlier. I was hoping to relax some inner barriers that might be inhibiting my memory. Although I was exploring Primal Therapy, I wasn't really sure how to approach my issues. Then I began experiencing some unusual symptoms. Sometimes when I was drifting into sleep, my tongue would burn

very intensely. And there were other unexplained aches and pains
that arose in the course of doing this work. Lynne and I were having
a sword fight with rulers one day and she hit me on the right hand.
The hit was just a tap, but my hand was terribly sore for over a
week, which didn't make any sense. Now I realize that some earlier
injury had been triggered.

Then one day during this time, I lay down to take a nap and had
an amazing experience. It was an altered state unlike any I had
encountered before. No drugs were involved. I was drifting off and
just hovering in a semi-sleep state, when I heard a baby crying. As
the sound became louder I could feel the baby screaming and saw
it lying in a crib. Then it was like I was both experiencing it as an
observer while at the same time *BEING* the child. It was
breathtaking. I could feel the whole thing on two different levels at
the same time, and the depth of emotion and lucidity was
astonishing. But this experience was part of a chain of experiences
which unfolded one right after another, almost as if they were all
part of one energetic multifaceted hologram that was rotating to
reveal its different perspectives. I heard a small voice whimpering
"Daddy, don't' make me cwy"and there were several other visions,
feelings, and sounds that simultaneously flowed through my
consciousness. I experienced all these things with the same dual
awareness. I felt myself slowly spinning right to left and floating
upward. There was a little boy hugging the pole of a street lamp
below me as I floated above a busy downtown sidewalk feeling the
deep sadness of total abandonment. This was all perceived with full
consciousness. When I opened my eyes and got up from the bed I
was stunned, shivering, and didn't know quite what to make of it all.
I felt at the time these were traumatic memories that had erupted
spontaneously, and this was soon verified. As I looked deeper into a
couple of these memories over the next few days, I realized what
the last experience was.

When I was six, our family went on a vacation with some friends
to Monterey Bay. At the beach I had collected a small pail full of
shells. I washed the sand off the shells in the sink at our motel room
and left them there before we went out to dinner. When we
returned, I was surprised to find most of my "shells" crawling all
over the bathroom walls – they were snails! When we went to the
beach the next day I took the snails back and collected more shells

but I left my pail there. The pail was an Easter gift which I had grown very attached to. I threw a terrible fit in the motel room later when my father wouldn't take me back to the beach right away to get the pail. It was so intense it was almost like having a seizure! Finally he said we would get it tomorrow.

The next day my father was going into town and I insisted on coming along. I was sure we would go get my pail. We drove for a long time and I started whining about getting my pail back. This irritated my dad and he told me to be quiet or we would never get it. I persisted anyway, until he grumbled that we weren't going back to the beach. But I continued whining until he stopped on a busy downtown street and ordered me out of the car. He kept yelling at me until I got out, and he immediately sped away. I was lost and had no idea what to do. I walked a short distance and finally wrapped my arms around the metal pole of a street lamp, sat on the cement, and left my body. I heard someone saying "Little boy, little boy? Are you alright?" but I was floating away. Then I heard someone calling my name. I came back and looked around. My father was calling me from the car. He had just driven around the block. He told the bystanders I had just gotten lost. Recalling this incident did not completely resolve the trauma, but at least I understood where the vision came from and why it was so intense, and I knew that I was making progress. After this I began having more spontaneous flashbacks.

Another day I was looking at a naked lady in a Playboy magazine and the picture jumped out at me. I was startled for a moment and then had an immediate series of flashbacks of being sexually assaulted by a female babysitter when I was around two and a half. Before this revelation, being around babies and children made me feel very uncomfortable, unconsciously reminding me of these, and perhaps other, early experiences. After looking into these memories, that discomfort disappeared completely. While the past experiences were not fully cleared up, I now felt an empathetic bond with children because I was no longer suppressing my own childhood, and I was remembering what it was like to be a child.

During this discovery period I was smoking marijuana. I had tried it a year or so earlier and found it had a very hallucinogenic effect on me. It had revealed some memories to me, including some past-life memories, and gave me some helpful insights. So one night while under its effects I had a strange physical reaction where it felt like someone was forcing my head downward and my head would stay thrust down automatically until I snapped myself out of it. The next day while recalling this reaction, I discovered I could go into it without the drug by simply relaxing in a certain way. After this, the marijuana ceased to be very helpful. I realized I didn't need it anymore and eventually dispensed with it altogether as a therapeutic agent. Working with that unexpected reaction led me to discover its origin.

I was not yet two and was sitting in a highchair adamantly protesting and refusing to eat my peas. My father finally got so frustrated that he grabbed my head and shoved my face into the plate. I fought him as he held my head down, and when he let go I started screaming in rage. He responded by slapping me on the back of the head, which briefly knocked me out. At first I was out of my body and could have returned immediately, but I stayed out because I was mad and wanted him to worry. There was definitely some adult level thinking going on while I was in that state. He tried to revive me and finally I came to. He then left the kitchen and my mother came in. I remember asking her "Who was that man?" She said "What man? " and I said "The one that tried to kill me." She said "That was your father – why do you think he tried to kill you?" But I remember being fairly sure that wasn't my father.

Thanks to the marijuana, I now had a way to drop into spontaneous memory-reactions, and began using this technique until I figured out how to do Primal Therapy. On a few occasions what arose from this method were verbal repetitions of sounds which eventually turned out to be word syllables coming from forgotten traumatic incidents. The first of these was a word loop that sounded phonetically like "fah dit sah, fah dit sah" repeated over and over. I wrote it down and worked with changing the syntax. I wasn't even sure it was English at first, but the sentence turned out to be "It's a fight, it's a fight." Finally the memory became clear. My parents and I were in a restaurant. My mother was pregnant and I was about two and a half years old. There was a commotion and I looked across the room and saw my father at the counter in a fist fight with a man wearing a white apron and chef's hat, and another man. My mother said "It's a fight – get under the table." So I crawled under the table and whispered to myself over and over "It's a fight, it's a fight," feeling, for some reason, that saying these words would keep me safe.

Headaches

So these few months of research were very fruitful but soon my money ran out and I had to find a job. My brother hired me to work part-time at his restaurant during the day and the job required me to wear a skimmer that was held on my head by rubber bands that pressed against my temples. Every day I came home with a splitting headache. Looking back later, it became obvious that the pressure on my temples from the hat was a big factor in triggering the headaches. After a few days I began to address this problem, using Primal Therapy, trying to feel my way through the pain as soon as I got home from work. I did this for four days in a row. Bits and pieces of my birth experience started to come up on the second or third day, culminating in the session described at the beginning of this chapter. After that session, wearing the hat ceased to bother me, and the headache, that particular headache, which I had experienced many hundreds of times over many years, never returned. This is important. The source of that temple crushing pain from which I had suffered more or less weekly for most of my life, separately or in conjunction with other headaches, was gone. Its root, like that of a nasty weed, had been pulled out. Prior to this I had remembered a few dozen traumatic experiences that seemed to be causing many of the emotional and physical conditions I was experiencing at the time. This headache was the first one to be completely resolved. I still got other headaches, but never THAT headache.

But did I really remember and relive my birth? I've read many arguments against our ability to remember early childhood or perinatal experiences, even though these kinds of memories commonly come up in many types of therapies and self-discovery processes. Were my memories true or just some kind of creation of my mind? And if they were real, how accurate were they? And what difference does it make if this was an actual recall or not? I had a lot of questions. My mother had told me many years earlier that my head looked like a peanut when I was born and had mentioned the forceps. She had also told me that the doctor had said I was a

slippery little devil and she said it almost looked like I had horns.
Maybe they laughed about it. But for me, the use of forceps was a
barbaric torture, and the traumas I experienced at birth were still
affecting me decades later. So did my mind concoct this whole
remembrance from what I had heard? Well, even if it did, the
process of working through an "apparent" traumatic memory of this
kind worked for me, and has worked time and again for countless
numbers of people using many different forms of therapy, including
Primal Therapy, hypnotherapy. EMDR, and basically any practice
that looks for root causes and will accept the client's experience for
what it appears to be in the moment. When these incidents are
handled correctly, the results speak for themselves.

In the areas of memory, reality, and validation, there are many
questions, problems, and controversies, and some of these will be
discussed later in detail. For now let me say there was no question
in my mind back then, nor is there now, that this memory was
absolutely real. The pain of the headaches I was experiencing WAS
the pain I experienced at birth. Not only was reliving the
experience convincing in itself, but it all made sense, was supported
by many things I was currently reading, continues to be supported
by research to this day, and was further validated by the fact that I
was cured.

I had previously heard about psychosomatic medicine, but from
what I read, most of the theory behind it seemed to be couched in
Freudian psychobabble that often sounded reasonable but was
always unsatisfying. Now I could see first hand that the roots of my
own problems lay in my past experiences in a very direct and almost
mechanical way, which was much more understandable. Yet it is
easier to believe that psychological or mental problems, like
phobias or neuroses, may stem from our past, than it is to accept
that a past experience can materialize in the present so as to cause
real time physical pain and other physical manifestations. But this is
exactly what seems to be happening, and it represents a huge
paradigm shift – one that the establishment was not ready for at any
time in the 20th century. This is one reason why things like Primal
Therapy, Dianetics, hypnotherapy, the Relaxation Response, and
many other workable mind-body processes have been rejected by
the mainstream, and may still remain on the fringe. Not to say that
such methods or the theories behind them are perfect or correct by

any means, but their successes, however inconsistent they might be, do provide real clues to inner healing. Physical psychosomatic phenomena can seem to violate our understanding of natural laws, when instead they are simply challenging us to think outside the box of materialistic dogma.

Moving Forward

After this success I thought that all I had to do was to discover an initiating event for any unwanted condition and thoroughly relive it, and the associated problem, including many that seemed to be purely physical conditions, would vanish! Indeed over the next several months I was able to trace many aches, pains, emotions, and psychological reactions, to their origins. I had compiled a list of dozens of such incidents. However, although I did get some welcome changes from recalling and reexperiencing some of these traumas, and they were all traumas in some form, I was unable to get the big results I wanted. I just couldn't make it work. This was especially true of physical symptoms or somatics, which, after their initial discovery, would often recur spontaneously for no apparent reason, like the burning tongue phenomenon. So while I was discovering traumas, I was not healing them, at least not completely, and in some cases uncovering a trauma actually made things worse because the somatic symptoms would then occur more frequently and with greater intensity.

But I knew this was just the beginning of a personal revolution and I wasn't the least bit discouraged. I was on a path that started many years earlier, a path that had deep roots and whose secrets would remain undiscovered until many years down the road. I did however now realize that I didn't actually remember as much about my childhood as I thought I did. Most of it was forgotten, and this seems to be true for most of us, although we might think otherwise. As I recalled it, before I started on my inner exploration, my life was fairly good and I had a lot of freedom in that I was mostly unsupervised.

Backstory – or Keys to the Kingdom
"Sit in a room and read—and read and read. And read the right
books by the right people. Your mind is brought onto that level, and
you have a nice, mild, slow-burning rapture all the time."
– Joseph Campbell, The Power of Myth

"Of all things I like books the best" – Nicola Tesla

A little personal background might be useful. I grew up in a
household with two younger brothers and parents who both worked
full time. We had many babysitters over the years, who also did
housekeeping, and we adopted many pets. My brothers and I had a
lot of fun together but I tended to bully them a lot to get my way.
The holidays were always fun – especially Christmas. However the
fact that no one knew what I was up to most of the time nearly cost
me my life. But with a few exceptions, I thought my life was
basically normal, although I really had nothing to compare it with. I
didn't really know what my friends' family life was like or what went
on behind closed doors in their homes, but I figured it was similar
to mine. My parents were complicated. They both drank and
smoked and had dissociative conditions. My father was an alcoholic
who was occasionally hostile and abusive. After serving in the Navy
in WWII he held a government job for about fifteen years until he
made some mistakes that got him fired. My mother was a
government budget analyst who worked steadily for more than forty
years, rarely taking any days off except around childbirth. She
quietly supported us and held our home together.

As for me, I did have a few useful traits that served me well in
future years – I was a very good organizer and I would take
everything relevant into consideration when dealing with any
problem or situation. I also loved puzzles and would work nonstop
to figure things out. When I was around the age of six my father
tried to keep me from going into the garage for some reason but I
kept getting in, in spite of his repeated injunctions. To me it was a
game. Since it had no lock, he tried jamming the garage door
raising mechanism, among other things. Finally he rigged the door
very securely and said "There, you'll never get in now!" and went in

the house. I took it as a challenge. Minutes later I ran in the house yelling triumphantly, much to his chagrin, "Daddy, I got in!"

When I turned nine, my father got me a book for my birthday, "Gulliver's Travels." I was always curious why he got me a book; we had story books of course, but I had never been given one of my own before, and it puzzled me. However, I loved the book and carried it around. I still remember the wonderful smell of the pages and the texture of the cover. It was hard to read but I did my best, and it swept me into another world, a magical world. I felt like reading it would reveal some secret. Maybe I was just intrigued by the idea that this book was meant for me personally, unlike a school book. But it seemed to represent something important, something mysterious – it was like a shimmering question mark in my head. It reminds me of the movie "Made in Heaven" where, after dying and while in Heaven, Timothy Hutton's character Mike acquires a shovel as a symbol of something he would find useful when he returns to Earth. On Earth the shovel becomes a trumpet, which helps him survive and ultimately fulfill his mission, and find his true love.

It was almost two years later in fifth grade that I was introduced to the school library. It was a revelation - a gold mine. This is what I was looking for, what Gulliver's Travels represented for me – knowledge! I devoured stacks of books. I loved animal stories I think because the animals were often alone, fending for themselves, and struggling against captivity and humans. I was a loner too, and I sympathized with them. But I mostly read science books – every one I could get my hands on. When I discovered the Bookmobile, which stopped weekly a few blocks from my house, I would bring home as many books as I could physically carry. The driver once commented as I walked off with my arms full, "Well, I guess books build muscles as well as minds!" Then I found a nearby branch of the city library that was close enough to visit on my bicycle. I was reading all the time. I was already nearsighted from reading school books and became more so, but I knew a little bit about everything. By age twelve I had some good theories about aging, time, space, life, death, and immortality. I sensed there was something I needed to discover. I didn't know what it was but I felt knowledge was the key. By the time I was fourteen I knew I wanted to become a biophysicist because that field seemed to include everything, and I wanted to know everything.

I remember sitting at my desk working on a physics problem in my organic chemistry class one day in college, having finished my lab experiment ahead of the other students. I had the realization that we didn't really know what mass and energy actually were, or any of the other items we plugged into our equations for that matter. My chemistry professor was a wise old geezer with thinning hair, a grey mustache, and a wry sense of humor. He would often leave the room when we were doing lab experiments – said he didn't want to get blown up, which caused everyone to stop for a moment and look cautiously around, until they realized it was a joke. Or was it? When he came back in the room to check on us that day from one of his breaks, I mentioned my insight to him.

"So we don't really know what matter, energy, and time are, do we?" He looked at me silently for a moment. Then he gave me his knowing half-smile, shook his head back and forth slowly in silent agreement – and without a word, left the room. This moment was a turning point in my thinking – nothing was really figured out – it was all up to me! A puzzle!

Crossroads

But a year or so later at the university I was having a tough time. Over the course of the last eight years, starting with Junior High School, I had become seriously shy and socially inept. The fact that I had to interact with people caused me considerable stress. Also I was becoming disenchanted with being a biophysics major. It just didn't feel right anymore. Most of my fellow students were engineering majors and most of the classes were geared toward creating more cogs in the corporate machine. I wasn't interested in engineering and there didn't seem to be a category called "knowing everything" – and no one from Hogwart's School of Witchcraft and Wizardry had shown up to recruit me.

In the past I had read some psychology and self-help books which had helped me to overcome some phobias, so I began looking for some help in the college library. While browsing the psychology shelves one day for books on hypnosis I discovered the philosophy section! This was exactly what I was looking for! I hadn't even known such books existed. But because of my upbringing I associated philosophy with weakness, and homosexuality for some strange reason, so I felt embarrassed even standing there. It was like being in the pornography section of a bookstore. I nonchalantly maneuvered a couple books to a table to study them, and eventually found the courage to check them out. It was as if I had found a hidden passage through a jungle leading to the Emerald City. Shortly after that I was given a book on Zen Buddhism and this led me to the library's Eastern Religion and Metaphysical sections. These books were about consciousness, and while traditional science assumes that consciousness is an epiphenomenon of matter, it now seemed clear to me that this material universe is created by Consciousness, and it's not the other way around. I had reached a crossroads. In my desire to understand everything, I had been traveling in the wrong direction. I soon came to believe that the world is a projection of our minds. I now felt I was on the right track and changed my major to psychology.

But a few months later I quit college. I was on the track team and enjoyed running and working out, but my stay was putting a strain on my parents' budget, and the stress and anxiety of college life was getting to me. I had begun missing classes, losing track of time, forgetting where I was, and had bouts with a strange paralysis. In the cafeteria at the dormitory where I was staying, there were times when I couldn't raise my fork to my mouth to eat. It was scary. I had to relax and imagine I was alone. There were also moments when I thought I was going crazy. So I dropped out and spent the next three years at home reading, writing, and meditating. Eventually I bought a car, got a job at a restaurant, and got a promotion. Four years later I moved to Sacramento to manage a similar restaurant, but quit after nine months to do my inner work.

So that brings us back to the beginning of this chapter. I was now 30 and I had resumed working full time. Although the birth session had been a genuine breakthrough and I knew I was onto something, it would be more than 13 years before I would really understand trauma and be able to completely resolve anything else. By that time my list of unwanted conditions and past traumas had grown considerably larger!

However my memory had actually begun to open up some time earlier when I first began having OBEs, which is something I was still experiencing once or twice a week. These nighttime experiences started before moving to Sacramento and they will be discussed in the next chapter because they had a major impact on my memory and how I viewed the world. They also helped me more easily accept the things I would be recalling and experiencing in the future. But even long before that, there was the case of the mysterious artifact. This was something I had always remembered, but only partially, and had never understood.

※ ※ ※ ※ ※ ※ ※ ※ ※ ※ ※ ※ ※ ※ ※ ※ ※ ※ ※

The Mysterious Artifact

I still don't really know what it was. My first recollection of it was seeing it in the back of our dark, one-car garage, leaning against the wall, when I was four years old. My best guess is that the artifact was an ornament of some kind, probably part of a hanging lamp. It was made of thin metal and glass and was not quite two and a half feet tall when set on its side. It didn't have a stand or anything and was made roughly in the shape of a flower with five hollow tube-like petals, each about six inches thick in the middle, made of colored glass, curling and tapering off to a point. The metal holding the petals was a dark brass color, and each petal had an exotic twisted shape that reminds me of something out of "The Arabian Nights."

There was something very spooky and mysterious about this object. Every time I walked by the garage when the door was open, I would look at it for a while, as if it might do something. But I was afraid to go near it or to even go in the garage. Another thing that added to the mystery and is still unexplained, was that many times when I stood in front of the garage by the fence, after looking at the object, I heard two voices in conversation in the air above me, in some strange language I didn't understand. This is what I always remembered, but nothing more. One day a few years ago I was thinking about this mysterious lamp-like artifact and decided to investigate using ID-R. It turns out that the lamp was mine, and there was a reason I was afraid of it.

One day my father and I were visiting his friend Derek, a short, stocky man of Dutch ancestry, who was an auto mechanic. This was not long after the event describe in the Prologue. Derek's house included a huge adjacent dirt lot harboring a number of junked cars, with a large exterior garage in the back where he did his work. He was working on a car when we got there. I remember Derek's hands always being black even when clean, as a consequence of his never wearing gloves. While the two adults talked, I was exploring the garage, which was more like a small warehouse. I recall the thick smell of grease and rubber. There were many interesting piles of junk lying around for me to scrutinize – enough to keep me occupied for a while. After poking around a bit I thought I heard something, so I stopped and listened. It was a girl's voice. It was low and faint, more like a whisper, but someone was trying to get my attention. I looked everywhere for the source, expecting to find another kid, perhaps Derek's daughter Jill, hiding in the shadows. I looked in possible hiding places but no one was there. There was something captivating about this girl's presence and I was drawn to finding her. It felt like a game. Her voice seemed to be very close so I whispered "Where are you, I can't see you?" Silence.

After a few minutes the voice took another tack, and now seemed to be coming from a big brass colored artifact lying on top of a pile of beer bottles, broken household items, and auto parts. I gazed at the strange object, which had an exotic beauty about it, until I was sure the voice was coming from there. Now the voice and the object seemed to be one. The lamp was speaking to me! I fell in love with it and asked my dad if I could have it. I was very insistent, so he paid Derek "two bits" for it and we brought it home.

We put the lamp in the garage and I came out every morning to talk with it, but no one was home. Yet there was something beautiful and amazing about it so I kept trying. One morning a few days later I got a response! I was standing in front of the lamp and I heard the girl's voice but she sounded a bit forlorn, like she wanted something she couldn't have. Then she said she wanted to see me and began to sound more forceful and insistent, almost demanding. The energy shifted and I could sense something powerful was present. It felt like something big was about to happen. It was exciting!

She told me to come closer to the hollow lamp and look into it, as if I might be able to see something through its thin pastel sides. So I did – and instantly I was *INSIDE THE LAMP!*

I found myself in a tubular room with soft pinkish light coming from the walls, and a beautiful fragrance, like flowers, in the air. In

front of me, a young girl appeared. She looked about my age with
dark brown hair and a light-colored dress, yet we both seemed older
now, somehow. She appeared to be about ten feet away, if I was still
my normal size, and she was walking toward me. She was talking to
me, and although she seemed to be speaking a foreign language
and I don't recall her words, I understood her perfectly. I knew that
we knew each other and I got the feeling she wanted me to stay
with her. I happily told her I would come and visit her every day,
but she didn't want me to go. She wanted me to stay there with her
– FOREVER! Suddenly I felt trapped, thinking I couldn't get out. I
got scared and had a shock! My enchantment ended abruptly and I
found myself outside the lamp, right where I had been standing
before. I hightailed it out of there and never approached the lamp
again. I seemed to forget what had happened shortly afterwards, but
the lamp still held a strange fascination for me. So although I was
now afraid to go near it, I would often gaze at it from a distance – a
foreshadowing of things to come.

Chapter 3
Journeys Out of the Body

"Wanna take a ride?" – Contact, 1997

It happened spontaneously and without warning. It was almost two years before my breakthrough with Primal Therapy, and an hour's drive south. I was living in my hometown of Stockton with my parents and working at a nearby pizza parlor. On a sunny day in March sometime in the afternoon, I took a nap on the bean bag in my bedroom. I was awakened by what sounded like air rushing quietly into a vacuum sealed coffee can as it's being opened. Ssshhwooooop. The next thing I noticed was that I was seeing the room from above and behind my body – it was as if my "dream head" had popped out of my physical head somehow, but I wasn't dreaming! And I was aware of complete silence; I mean I was hearing the complete absence of sound. It was amazingly peaceful and hard to describe. Visually I could see as if I had eyes. I had the same visual range but my sight was much clearer even though I was normally nearsighted, and everything was very bright and colorful. I was seeing the room just as it was when I had dozed off, yet I was fully conscious – wide awake!

But as I looked at objects in the room they started to morph into different shapes and colors. The red and white striped shirt on my coat rack became a brightly colored parrot, then a banana. It was as if everything was just paint floating around me and I had been holding it in the particular pattern called "my room." It felt like a balancing act and I was losing my balance. The whole room started to change. I was startled and frightened and didn't know what was happening.

Then suddenly I was back in my body looking through my physical eyes. I was emotionally shaken, so I got up and went for a walk. I sat on a grassy mound in a nearby field and contemplated what had just happened. The experience was so profound that I thought I was going to develop spiritual superpowers. You might think this would have excited me but instead it made me feel very depressed for several hours. I discovered the reason for this depression many years later, which was basically, to borrow a phrase from the movie "Spiderman," that "with great power comes great responsibility." And, I might add, the ability to do great harm.[8] Perhaps I was reminded of that Star Trek classic episode where a crewman developed godlike psychic powers and was corrupted by it.[9]

Kenneth Kelzer, who wrote a book on his experimentation with lucid dreaming, had a similar reaction. In the beginning of his journey, after a series of amazing lucid dreams, he developed a recurring fantasy about himself and others developing amazing psychic powers by exploring consciousness through dreams.[10] He saw this as a kind of megalomania – part of his dark side or "shadow" that he would have to deal with in order to continue with his experiment. He also felt there is a part of us that would naturally be tempted to use a new spiritual power for selfish and destructive purposes. His experiences were profound however, and I believe they connected him with a sense of a greater reality in which the powers he imagined are actually possible.

That night, after the beanbag experience, I did my regular meditation and went to bed. My sleep was interrupted however, by a series of very intense out-of-body experiences. Soon after I dropped into sleep I was slammed by intense vibrations, as if my whole body was hooked up to a giant electric generator. The vibrations felt completely physical and would phase in and out from a smooth high frequency humming that might have even been pleasant under different circumstances, to jagged and jolting sensations like my whole body was strapped to a jack hammer. If I tried to physically move I felt completely paralyzed, so I gave up trying to struggle, but I didn't relax either. In the vibratory state I would sometimes feel myself rise up and hover a few feet above the

---

[8] "Spiderman" – 2002

[9] "Star Trek," season 1 episode-3 – "Where No Man Has Gone Before" – 1966

[10] "The Sun and the Shadow" – 1987, by Kenneth Kelzer

bed and sometimes I would sink through the mattress to the floor below. Other times I would feel myself spinning right to left at varying speeds from very fast to very slow. This seemed to go on for hours. At the time, it felt like these things were happening to my physical body, but there were brief moments when I could actually see my body lying in the bed.

The next night it happened again: the vibrations, the spinning, the rising and falling, bizarre sounds, and a host of other strange phenomena and "special effects." These intense nighttime experiences were both frightening and deeply exhilarating, and continued to happen every night when I went to sleep, for about two weeks. I remember standing by my bed each night looking down at my pillow, feeling both terrified and excited at the inescapable prospect of sleep, like a child standing in line at the county fair waiting to ride the Ferris Wheel for the first time. But sleep was inevitable and I could do nothing but let it overtake me. Dream Weaver was a hit song at the time and I would often listen to it before climbing into bed.

During these episodes, which would seem to last most of the night but which may have just been several episodes lasting seconds or minutes each, I had very bizarre dreams that I could make no sense of. In one I was a robot being shot with energy beams and in another I seemed to be in communication with strange beings. But I also had other dreams during these episodes which felt more familiar. After a few nights of this I began to recognize a few of my dreams – they were memories of previous OBEs from early childhood! Some kind of door was opening.

I was desperate to understand what was going on and hit the library and book stores, which I always did when I needed to know something. I rarely if ever confided in anyone. This was 1976 and of course long before personal computers or the internet. I found a copy of Robert Monroe's 1971 book "Journeys Out of the Body," which helped me through this time in many ways. Monroe had been terrified too, and like me, his OBEs began with the use of relaxation techniques, sleep learning audio tapes in his case, which he used at night before bed. Learning that OBEs are a universal and common experience gave me much relief and welcome validation. As I began to accept the reality of what I was experiencing, the

memories of my childhood out-of-body experiences came pouring
in – scores of them!

One night, about two weeks into this, I had enough presence of
mind to utilize an idea I got from Monroe's book, and when the
vibrations hit me, instead of just riding out the experience or
fighting it, I relaxed into it and did what I did every night in my
meditations: I let go.

Then an amazing thing happened – the vibrations stopped! It
was as if I had risen above a storm. There is a scene in the movie
"Contact" in which Jodie Foster's character Ellie gets out of her
chair in the space capsule during its flight through space.[11] The
capsule is basically a hollow sphere in which a person is supposed
to stand, according to the aliens who sent her the design
instructions, but the human engineers decided they had better put
in a chair to make it safer. However the chair begins to vibrate
intensely during her journey through a wormhole and Ellie
eventually decides to get out of it. Once she's out of the chair it
vibrates even more violently until it is ripped out of its fasteners and
flung against the wall, at which point all the vibrations stopped and
there was total silence – total weightless peace. For me it was like
that, and I felt like I was just floating peacefully in space until my
body woke up. After this experience most of my OBEs would occur
without any vibrational effects, and when there were vibrations I
could stop them instantly by letting go, just as I did that first time. I
didn't really think of leaving my body as an ability at this point, only
as a phenomenon, so I had no thought of trying to go anywhere or
do anything, but that changed later.

Robert Monroe

An out-of-body experience or OBE is a term I first encountered
in Robert Monroe's book. It replaced previous names like Astral
Projection or Soul Travel. I also like to refer to an OBE as "being
exterior" or being "in spirit." It's the experience of being fully awake
but with the distinct feeling and perception that you are not in your
physical body. Indeed you may actually even see your body from

---

[11] "Contact" - 1997

some distance but generally you do not hear, see, or feel anything that is happening to the body while you are disconnected from it, although you may. Some people have even trained themselves to be able to physically speak while in the OBE state, in order to record what is happening. I classify lucid dreams as OBEs also. These are dreams in which you are aware that you are dreaming, with some degree of wakefulness or even full waking consciousness. However, there may be no sensation of being external to your body. This may be because in a lucid dream you are more fully disconnected and have less of a sense that there IS another physical body somewhere, especially if you have a strong awareness of having a "second body" or dream-body in the dream.

Many of my OBEs now begin as lucid dreams where I first realize I'm dreaming, and then become fully conscious. The dreamscape then changes and the locale may become the physical world (seemingly) if I am able to control my focus correctly, or it may be some other realm in the vastness of consciousness, or within my own mind. I call the dream realm or locale within my own mind my "inner matrix." The inner matrix is like one's own personal Holodeck (the holographic projection room from Star Trek) where dreaming and lucid dreaming take place. I also think of it as an Astral domain, which I imagine has some kind of boundary that defines one's personal space in the consciousness of the universe and separates it from the spiritual domains of others and the communal realms called the Astral Planes, as well as from everything else, All of this should make more sense after reading Chapter 21.

OBEs have been universally experienced by people the world over since the dawn of recorded history and I believe everyone has experienced being out of their body but most just don't remember. Studies indicate that at least one in ten people remember having at least one OBE in their lifetime, and many people recall having more. In reality the percentage is probably much higher, but within that 10 percent there is probably a Bell Curve with a small percentage recalling many hundreds of OBEs during their lives. But if you had asked me before that "first" OBE on the bean bag or even right after it, I would have said that I had never had such an experience before. I believe most people fall into the category of having had many OBEs but remembering none, or only one. True

OBEs are fully conscious experiences. However, because OBEs happen in an altered state of consciousness, as do dreams, they are very easy to forget. Some say we all have OBEs every night and simply do not recall them. I don't think this is true, but I don't really know.

Memories

So what was happening to me? Was I really out of my body or was it some kind of dream or hallucination or some brain anomaly? At the time these OBEs began I wasn't sure, but my memories were indicating that I could truly leave my body and explore the physical world. If so, what is it that leaves? All I can say is that "I" leave, but what is I, and how can I perceive anything without my physical senses? These were the questions I was asking myself, and we will explore possible answers later on.

As I became more comfortable with these new and unusual experiences, more memories of past OBEs came rolling in almost daily, and some were quite amazing, especially because they were so vivid and clear. Many of my very early OBEs just involved me floating around and checking out my surroundings or seeing what my mother was doing. Most of these first memories were just fragments but still very clear, a few were related to trauma, and some were just fun. Here are a few examples of OBE memories that emerged during that time and over the following weeks, although in some cases the details weren't entirely clear until I explored them later using ID-R.

One Christmas Morning

This is one of the first OBE memories that popped up. I had recently turned three years old, and early Christmas morning I was awakened from sleep by the strong feeling that there was something going on in the living room. Curious, and exterior, I easily moved through the wall, which was transparent to me while in the OBE state at that time. I went into the living room where we had a nicely decorated Christmas tree magically illuminated with multicolored lights. I was surprised to see many toys and gifts around the tree and an electric train set up on its tracks! Excitedly I leapt out of bed and ran directly to my parents' room. I woke my father and told him all about it, in breathless wonderment I'm sure, but he told me to go back to bed and we would look together in the morning – it was probably around 3:00 A.M. But I crept into the dark, tree lit room, filled with the scent of Douglas Fir, and had a peek at everything first. It was magical! It was my first real Christmas experience.

Searching for Mom

When I was about two and a half my mother took me to a new baby sitter. This was after the discovery that my previous sitter had been molesting me, but when I recalled this I was not yet aware of that earlier experience. We went into the living room which seemed to be that of a rich person; it was uncluttered and everything was clean and new and well placed. When we walked into the room I was drawn immediately to the sounds coming from a radio and phonograph console made of dark mahogany wood. It was slow classical cello and violin music. I ran over and sat on the carpeted floor with my ear next to the speaker in fascination. I had never heard anything like it. I was drawn into the sound, the rich deep vibration, merging with it until that's all there was. It was beautiful. My mother chatted with the new lady for a while and then she left. I was fearful of being left alone with another stranger, so as she walked out the door I closed my eyes and quickly let my body fall asleep. I could feel my senses leaving each part of the body until my attention was completely free of it. Once free, I took off after mom. But about twenty feet outside the door I got scared that I would get lost and went back to the body. The importance of this for me is that it was the first time that I recalled using a technique to actually leave my body willfully, while awake, as opposed to waking up exterior during sleep. I was remembering exactly how I did it, although it is not something I can do now.

The Heavy Coat

One morning when I was sixteen, I was standing outside on the front lawn just before dawn. There was a light fog in the air. I was just standing there looking around and watched a small dog with curly black hair sniffing around – he peed on a tree and walked into the next yard. I could feel the cold air against my skin and smell the wet vegetation around me. I was wearing a thick heavy coat and had my hands in the pockets. I tried to pull my hands out but they wouldn't budge and I started to feel alarmed. I struggled to get the coat off but my arms were paralyzed and my fear grew stronger. Suddenly I found myself awake in my bed! The whole thing was strange and frightening because I had been 100% conscious outside moments before. I didn't understand it, so I buried it – forgot about it immediately. One day during these first weeks of having these new OBEs, the fear of them now being gone, this memory came back to me. Although its traumatic aspect was not yet resolved, I realized I had been exterior back then, and the heavy coat was actually my mind's interpretation of the physical sensations of my sleeping body, which I could not move. I later discovered that I started blocking memories of my OBEs at the age of thirteen. I will explain this in Chapter 14.

Carlos Castaneda and the Relaxation Response

This first unforgotten OBE of mine on the bean bag had some important antecedents. For several weeks prior to this incident I had been practicing deep relaxation meditation every night just before going to sleep. I had done Zen meditation in the past and was aware of other meditative techniques such as TM (Transcendental Meditation). I had also read the book "The Relaxation Response" some time earlier and I had a theory I was working on.[12] I was getting about four headaches a week at the time, which lasted an hour or two, and had been since about the age of thirteen, although I experienced headaches earlier in life, but less frequently. I had recently found that if I relaxed the neck and shoulder tension that occurred just prior to getting a headache, I could often prevent the headache from happening. But the relaxation had to be immediate, deep, and continuous for several minutes. Sometimes I didn't catch it in time but I was still able to cut the frequency of my headaches by maybe one third or more. Sometimes I was even able to cause a headache to go away if I could relax deeply enough and long enough. Also I had noticed a similarity between some of my psychological or emotional problems, and stress related headaches. By the age of eighteen I had

---

[12] "The Relaxation Response" – 1975, by Herbert Benson

cured myself of several phobias using a technique that involved relaxation and calming the mind. Maybe if I could reduce my overall stress level, I thought, it might have some effect on these other conditions as well.

Also I had immersed myself in the work of Carlos Castaneda and had read his first four books several times.[13] Castaneda was, at least as a character in his books, an apprentice to a Yaqui Indian sorcerer, Don Juan. Don Juan taught Carlos how to become a "Man of Knowledge," someone able to see things as they really are. To do this he used various techniques which were geared toward shaking Carlos out of his ordinary perceptual framework and his programmed understanding of reality. These techniques involved putting him in psychologically challenging situations and having him practice various mental and perceptual exercises. They also included the use of various medicinal psychotropic plants. During this time I was actively practicing some of the techniques discussed in his books such as breaking my routines, erasing personal history, "not-doing," and basically living as a kind of spontaneous free spirit, although I was not using any drugs at the time. I was aware of lucid dreaming and the magical "dreaming" described in Castaneda's books, but I had never read anything about out-of-body experiences as far as I can recall. And although at the time I thought that Castaneda's more magical experiences might be possible, I couldn't relate to them personally.

So each night I was doing progressive muscle relaxation as deeply as possible for up to an hour, and also trying to relax unconscious tensions which I imagined might be there. I believe it was a combination of all these things that initiated my OBEs, but

---

[13] I greatly enjoyed Castaneda's books and found his stories to be inspiring allegories and treasure-troves of wisdom. It was fun to play along and imagine his adventures being real, but I never really thought they were, any more than "Harry Potter" or "Star Wars" are real. Of course I don't really know. I read an article once where Castaneda said he "dreamed" his books. Still I always felt that the things he described were possible, especially after having read "Autobiography of a Yogi" by Paramahansa Yogananda in college. Once my OBEs began and I did more research, I had little doubt of this. This was before I recalled the more profound miracles in my own life.

that the deep physical and mental relaxation was the most
important factor.

I continued the nightly meditation after the OBEs started but
eventually began doing it less often. Once I began to have more
control over what I did during my OBE excursions, I started calling
my OBEs "power dreams" although I knew they weren't dreams at
all, because I liked Castaneda's idea of "dreaming." He described
"dreaming" as an act of power in which the sorcerer enters a kind of
alternate reality even to the point of creating a "double" which is a
sort of real and solid projection of their body in the material world
while their physical body is sleeping. This materialized apparition,
or doppelganger, had great power because, to the dreamer, the
world is a lucid dream in which "the most astounding feats are
possible," like Neo's super abilities while inside the Matrix. That
was my take on it, but, after my initial depression, I had no
expectation that I might ever be able to do anything like Neo. I did
however entertain the possibility that, while exterior, I could visit
real world places and see what was going on and possibly even
communicate with people or affect the real world by moving
objects or making sounds. It took some time before I actually
traveled farther than my own house in spirit, but I did have some
experiences where I found myself lucidly in other places that might
be called Astral realms.

Sharing

I talked about my OBEs with a few people at the time they
began, but only one of these mentioned having a similar
experience, and he had his first OBE shortly after I began having
mine. Synchronicity! Art was a teacher but moonlighted as a
musician at the restaurant I worked at. He normally appeared
carefree and cheerful, but one night I noticed him sitting alone
during his breaks, looking utterly depressed. I didn't have a chance
to talk with him at the time, but the next night he seemed better
and I sat with him during my break. I asked him about the previous
night. He told me he had an OBE after practicing TM the night
before his depression. A week earlier I had convinced him, and my
girlfriend Lynne, who was one of his students, to take a TM course
being offered in town. They both really liked the course and were

now doing daily meditation, but Art's unexpected OBE had left him depressed, as mine had left me, but not for the same reason. During his meditation he had a profound vision in which he was out of his body and encountered a powerful Being of light. The Being communicated with him and left him with the certainty that he himself was a spiritual being. But he had emerged from this OBE with the deep feeling that this visitation meant he was about to die. But because he didn't die that night, today his fear was gone and he was reinterpreting his experience. I shared Monroe's book with him and we got together occasionally and had some great talks which, he told me many years later, changed the course of his life.

Two years after my initial talk with Art, Lynne was taking a nap on the couch in our house in Sacramento when she suddenly jumped up and said she just had an OBE. She looked astonished. She had not remembered ever having one before this. While exterior she was outside in the back yard looking at our garden and saw that the two marijuana plants we had been growing there, each about a foot and a half tall, were gone. There were two holes in the ground where they had been pulled up by the roots. We ran outside and found that the plants were still there. We talked about her experience, which had been totally real, and considered that she may have actually been seeing the future. However, since no one could see the plants without looking over our very tall fence, I dismissed the idea and took no extra precautions. The next day when we came home from work, both plants had been stolen – pulled up by the roots.

My out-of-body experiences in 1976 seemed to have opened a channel in my unconscious mind and expanded my understanding of myself as a spiritual being. Whatever I really was, I could leave my body, at least in my perception, and still perceive the physical world. Also some of the memories that surfaced a year later, during my hiatus from work, were past-life memories. I didn't know if they were truly past lives but they felt like very real experiences that had each left a strong impression on me.

The concepts of rebirth and karma in the spiritual books I had been reading were also becoming more real to me.[14] The OBEs continued but the frequency tapered off. Still, over the years, these nighttime excursions have led to many discoveries.

Many years later however, I began to remember OBEs that took place on a whole different level, and most of these occurred not during sleep but during dissociative episodes in response to trauma. But the events leading up to those new revelations were not random occurrences – there were unseen forces at work which eventually led me to a man who held the secrets I was looking for.

---

[14] Karma refers to the spiritual principle of cause and effect where intentions and actions of an individual (cause) influence the future of that individual (effect). Every action has a consequence. Good intent and good deeds contribute to good karma and better experiences in this or future lifetimes, while bad intent and bad deeds contribute to bad karma and more suffering for the person until things equal out.

Chapter 4
Synchronicity

"Where some people see coincidence, I see conspiracy"
– Anthony Horowitz, Point Blanc

Carl Jung coined the term "synchronicity" to describe a hypothetical cause behind meaningful coincidences which seem to have to no causal connection but which do have special meaning and seem to be more than random occurrences. We notice such things all the time. Of course we may experience random coincidences that we find very meaningful, but a synchronicity implies there was something deeper going on – a synchronization of forces we don't understand. If I suddenly start thinking of a friend for no apparent reason and he calls a minute later, there may be a real connection, a psychic perception on my part perhaps, but I may choose to think that my thought was random. Or a synchronicity could be the action of a third party that is unseen. If a friend needs $100 but I know they won't accept my help, suppose I drop a $100 bill in front of their house and park down the street to be sure they find it. My friend calls me later to tell me about this amazing coincidence, but I know better. Synchronicity simply implies an event was not really random and there was more to it than meets the eye. In other words, when the cause of a meaningful coincidence is unknown it is always possible that there was an intentional intervention by an unseen third party, or there were other forces involved that are not understood or considered. We live in a miraculous universe and such interventions are going on all the time. When the intervention is not in our favor however, we don't usually call it synchronicity – we call it bad luck. This chapter relates a critical junction in my journey – an intentional confluence of invisible forces that I could only call synchronicity at the time.

Not long after the events of Chapter 2, I was able to get my old job back and Lynne and I got married later that year. However, although we had been together for more than three years, the marriage only lasted a few months. After we broke up, and while pursuing various occupations, I continued, on and off, to look into my past and to try and resolve the many traumatic events I had uncovered, but I never seemed to have the time I needed. I was frustrated that I was making little progress. I moved back to Stockton several years later and became involved in real estate, which occupied much of my time. Finally in 1990 I got serious again – over twelve years since my initial breakthrough. I decided it was now or never, and pushed myself to find the time to do the work and discover whatever was missing. My premise was that most unwanted mind and body conditions had some past traumatic experience at their core, and when this trauma was brought sufficiently into awareness, the problem would dissolve. I began spending about two hours a day trying to resolve items on my expanded list of personal issues, but to little avail. I had discovered lots of incidents and was able to relive them quite vividly but my conditions didn't change much. If the problem didn't go away, I assumed there must be an earlier incident containing the same problem because our traumatic memories are linked by association just as all memories are, but even more strongly. Surely my symptoms had to be originating from somewhere! Maybe I just hadn't found the true source.

I began following my symptoms into past lives and I usually managed to find a similar incident in a previous lifetime. But while these past experiences were interesting, I always felt that I was forcing myself. By that I mean these incidents weren't pulling me into them as my birth experience had, although they were often very vivid and felt real. After pushing myself through these past-life incidents, the memories quickly faded out and the efforts had no effect on the condition I was working on. So I went back to the more natural methods I had used before, minus the Primal Screaming, and tried to improve on them. After a few months, just as I felt I was on the verge of another breakthrough, a series of fortuitous events fell into place one after another, like a row of dominoes, and led me in another direction that would accelerate my progress.

One day when working on a particular incident, I noticed something I hadn't seen before – a kind of pinpoint of bright light right at the moment where the trauma I was investigating had the most impact. This seemed to have some deep significance but I couldn't quite get it. It intrigued me. Then I looked for it in another incident and there was a similar nebulous area. I knew I had discovered something but it wasn't clear and I didn't know what to do with it. There seemed to be a moment in each trauma where everything changes.

Shortly after I had "gotten serious" again about my self-exploration, my brother Alan connected me with a friend of his who gave me some information about a new method for addressing problems, called Idenics.[15] I began communicating with Mike Goldstein who was providing Idenics services and training at Survival Services in Colorado. I was considering learning Idenics, but after speaking with Mike a few times I was still skeptical. However, during a subsequent conversation when I mentioned my "one moment where everything seems to change," he got excited! This was uncharacteristic of Mike, who was usually very low key. He told me I was on the right track and that they _knew_ what it was and that I _had_ to come to Colorado and take the training. Something clicked – it was like a flash bulb went off in my head. I left for Colorado a week later.

Road Trip

Cruising over the scenic Sierra Nevada mountain range and across the Nevada deserts past endless mud flats in my little manual Ford Escort in the late spring, I remember watching a big mother tumbleweed scurry across the road with three little babies tumbling right behind. I had a lot of time to think. There was a point at which I had a momentary feeling that I was wasting my time and money – I felt foolish, like I was being duped. So I asked myself "What am I doing?" From somewhere inside, without any conscious intent, I heard the answer come through with calm confidence: "Exactly what you're supposed to be doing," and at that moment, somehow, I knew it was true! So I braved some treacherous dark rainy mountain passes in Wyoming where traffic was backed up for a mile and visibility was zero, and finally reached sunny Denver on the third day, making my way to Mike's house in the suburb of Aurora.

---

[15] "Idenics - An Alternative To Therapy" - 2007, by Mike Goldstein

Once there I was provided room and board and Mike was a
gracious host. I stayed in a guest bedroom located in the storm
basement. The basement level was huge, brightly lit, and served as
a classroom and storage area. In addition to the guest room, it also
housed the counseling office.

I settled in and spent the next ten days learning Idenics and
getting sessions from the man who developed it, John Galusha.
John had been doing similar work with people for almost forty years
and was very successful. But he wanted better results, so in the mid-
eighties he began to develop something new. He made some great
discoveries and his new process was called Idenics.

On the first day I was there I watched a video of John talking
about Idenics. I remember having more doubts and thinking "What
am I doing here?" I again found myself feeling a bit disappointed
and duped. But I read most of the training manual that evening and
started trying Idenics on myself, although I didn't understand it all
yet – and something happened! I made some headway on an issue I
had been working on. That night I experienced a strange
phenomenon which is still a mystery. As I was drifting off to sleep I
felt a physical sensation, like a heavy burden had been set down and
something inside me relaxed. Actually it was more like I was a
spaceship that had just jettisoned its second stage, and I could
actually see a dark object floating away from me as I lay there with
my eyes closed. Then a silent voice said: "You have just exteriorized
from a huge mass." I later took that to mean that the forces that had
gotten me to this place had done their job – but the strange
sensation remains unexplained.

The Sessions – or Let's Begin!

I met John the next morning; a tall and lean older man, almost
thirty years my senior, with a calm and pleasant demeanor. After
introductions he went into his office and said we would start my
first session at nine. The training included a daily Idenics session
with John and discussions afterwards in which he would answer any
of my questions and provide more detail, examples, and
clarifications of the material if needed. When I went in and sat
down we talked a bit and when I indicated I was ready he said
"Then let's begin!" He reached over with his left hand and swung

the thick heavy wooden door closed. The door slammed shut with great force – *BOOM* – and the impact must have shaken the entire house. It felt like a ceremonial gesture indicating that something of great importance had begun. I don't know if he did this with all his students, but it felt somehow personal, and appropriate.

The first session was strange because I was confused about what had occurred. We addressed an emotional issue and the incidents we looked at were vague, yet I felt better at the end. I was puzzled but continued to study and work on myself for the rest of the day. After our second meeting I had a good grasp of what we were doing, and was feeling excited.

The next morning however, before my third meeting with John, I was feeling very antsy. I felt like I needed to get out of there. There was a very strong urge to grab my stuff and head for home. As nine o'clock grew closer the anxiety increased. But I realized I wasn't choosing to feel this way, and realized that this was just a reaction. When John came in, I told him about it and said I wanted to address it immediately, and so we did. This session blew my mind! John had me engage the feeling, and almost instantly the whole thing changed – I wasn't fighting it anymore, I had merged with it. The source was a vague past-life incident in which I had great power. Someone I loved had been killed and I retaliated with great anger and violence. I don't know the details but it felt as though, in my rage, I had taken many lives, and in the end I had great remorse. I resolved, in that long forgotten moment, to never have that kind of power again. This experience reminds me of the Star Trek TNG episode where a Dowd, a being of great power, had destroyed an entire alien race in a fit of rage for having killed his wife. In his grief and remorse he had become a pacifist, vowing to never kill again.[16] After this session the urge to bolt was gone. This incident also explained my depression regarding the possibility of developing spiritual powers after my seminal out-of-body-experience in 1976. Unconsciously, I feared the same thing might happen with Idenics.

Working with John was inspiring. He had a terrific down to earth presence and a great sense of humor during the sessions, and

---

[16] Star Trek, The Next Generation - 3x03 - "The Survivors"

he seemed to love his work. Most of the remaining sessions were
instructive but not spectacular, with two exceptions: the "visor"
incident discussed in the introduction, and an incident where a
home made bomb exploded in my face when I was fourteen. While
we worked on the latter incident, which was still giving me
headaches, I seemed to recall that I had actually gone back in time
and changed something in the past in order to prevent my own
death! One of the main principles of Idenics and ID-R, and perhaps
the most important, is that only _you_ can really know how things are
for you – that your reality is yours, and only you can sort it all out.
In the Idenics session the counselor may not be aware of many
details about what the client is remembering or experiencing, so I
wanted to discuss this experience afterward. When I told John the
details of what I had discovered, he just looked at me thoughtfully
and said, with genuine sincerity, "Good work!"

Back Home - or Winning the Lottery

Before I left for home, I did three sessions as an Idenics
practitioner with three volunteers, which went very well. I had
never done anything quite like this before but it felt very natural.
Then it was time to go. I remember saying to Mike, just before I
left, that I felt like I had won the lottery.

Earlier, after shaking John's hand and expressing my
appreciation for his help and training, he stopped at the stairs as he
was leaving, and with what seemed to be an afterthought, he turned
to me and said very purposefully "I wish you well." I said something
in reply but when he saw that I didn't get the meaning he intended,
he repeated it: "No" he said, with great intention, "I Wish You
Well!" I looked him in the eye and said "I got that!" He nodded and
walked away. This gesture and many other cryptic things he said
would stick in my mind and not make sense until many months
later. Like when he was telling me about a brainstorm he had
during the development of Idenics. "I was in a restaurant one day
and the ideas just came pouring out!" he said dramatically one day,
while organizing some papers on his desk. But he didn't elaborate
on this cloudburst of inspiration, leaving me a bit puzzled as to why
he had mentioned it.

From that day on, I worked on myself every chance I got, even in my motel rooms on the way home. I now had what I needed to resolve the effects of past trauma and free myself from my long list of issues. It was very exciting! It felt like I had the keys to a great treasure and was anxious to unlock every door I could find. I worked with others too, mainly friends and relatives for no charge. I drove to other cities in California to facilitate Idenics for those who couldn't make the trip to Colorado and were referred to me by Survival Services. I quit my real estate business and devoted all my time to working with myself and others. I lived on credit cards and whatever I could make from my counseling services.

I read numerous books related to my new work including many concerning how to work with others effectively as a counselor or healer. I revisited many methods that had analogs in Idenics and which I now saw in a new light, like Gestalt Therapy, the effect bridge, Transactional Analysis, and various visualization techniques. I also began reading the book "Sybil," about a case of Multiple Personality Disorder (MPD).

In working with myself and others I discovered many new things and had a lot of exciting ideas. I shared some of these ideas with John through letters and on the phone, and while he was very open to communicating with me, he did not seem very interested in my discoveries and speculations. He liked to keep things simple and it seemed like I was introducing complexities. However the real problem, I believe, was that my ideas were unorganized and I didn't express them very well. I was also still very shy and afraid to discuss some of my more radical discoveries in detail because I didn't want to sound crazy or possibly offend him.

In early 1993 I told Mike I wanted to write a book on Idenics. I was very passionate and excited about it, but he said _they_ would be writing the book themselves. Totally understandable of course, and I was very happy at the idea of them writing a book on the subject, but this pretty much took the wind out of my sails. I felt somewhat disheartened, but I remember saying to myself spontaneously and out loud, right after the call: "I'll write my own book – I gave it to them anyway!" I knew the "it" referred to Idenics but I was baffled at these words and why I had said them. How did I give it to them? Yet I could feel that some part of me was amused by this idea for some reason. And, like some of John's enigmatic remarks, this puzzling comment to myself, also stuck with me.

Shortly after this I decided to part ways with Survival Services. This was mainly because I had begun to incorporate some of my own discoveries into the process from the very beginning, so that there were some significant differences between Idenics and what I was doing. I decided to call my expanded process "Identity Resolution," although this name now represents an array of processes in addition to ID-R, which is the heart of the program. Still, many of the core concepts, methods, and descriptions I use originated in Idenics.[17] In the next chapter we will delve deeply into what ID-R and inner healing are all about.

❊ ❊

The IQ Test

I was in second grade when we were bussed to another school to take an IQ test. There were a lot of kids there in a huge cafeteria – possibly every second grade student in town. While I was sitting at the table I somehow realized that *SHE* was there – someone I knew – someone I felt connected to and inseparable from. Like walking by a bakery and the aroma of fresh chocolate chip cookies draws you in, it was as if the whole space of the room had lit up. I left my body to find her, scanning the room for the feeling of her presence. It was more like my perception left my body in the sense that I still felt myself sitting in the chair. When I came back, I knew where she was.

I looked around and saw her at the end of one of the long tables. I felt happy. For the hour or so that we were there, she was the only thing on my mind. I couldn't focus, and my IQ test probably scored below sea level. I wanted to go up to her and stand by her or maybe talk to her, so afterward, as we were all filing out the door, I was trying to figure out how I could do it. In the end there just wasn't a good opportunity and something inside me urged me to wait until

---

[17] Although I acknowledge many similarities with the 1991 version of Idenics, it is important to understand that ID-R is not Idenics. You can learn more about Idenics as it is today from Survival Services at idenics.com.

tomorrow. We had been told that we would be coming back to take part two of the test the next day. The next day she wasn't there however. I sensed she was sick and didn't come to school. I was saddened by this and wondered if I would ever find her again.

✻ ✻ ✻ ✻ ✻ ✻ ✻ ✻ ✻ ✻ ✻ ✻ ✻ ✻ ✻ ✻ ✻ ✻ ✻ ✻

Part II
♻
The Healing Paradigm

✻ ✻ ✻ ✻ ✻ ✻ ✻ ✻ ✻ ✻ ✻ ✻ ✻ ✻ ✻ ✻ ✻ ✻ ✻ ✻

Chapter 5
Inner Healing

"Monsters, John ... Monsters from the ID"
– Forbidden Planet, 1956

"Until we have met the monsters in ourselves, we keep trying to slay them in the outer world. And we find that we cannot. For all darkness in the world stems from darkness in the heart. And it is there that we must do our work." – Marianne Williamson

Temet Nosce

What will it take for you to improve your life, to have more emotional mastery, physical energy, health, and vitality, passion and motivation, to be able to take effective action and become more successful, to have better relationships and more abundance?[18] What do you need? Do you need to get your chakras balanced, have your aura cleansed, do better self-talk, have better strategies, read more books, visualize success, correct your "erroneous zones," overcome your fears, unblock your Qi, get physically healthy, be hypnotically reprogrammed, get psychoanalyzed, communicate better, take supplements, exercise more, become vegan, meditate, do yoga, scream out your pain, have better self-esteem, commune with Nature, pray, get a better self-image, eliminate limiting beliefs, normalize your brain chemistry, explore your past lives, learn martial arts, or tap your meridians? There are literally thousands of theories, models, and ideas about what goes wrong with us or limits us on every level, and treatments, programs, pills and potions, crystals, chants, and therapies to fix and improve things. Entire books have been written just listing some of them. And most of

---

[18] Know Thyself – a Delphic maxim emphasized by Socrates who said "To know thyself is the beginning of wisdom." He believed that an unexamined life is not worth living.

these seem to work for some things, at least to some degree for some people, or we wouldn't use them at all.

But if we imagine that there are basic underlying principles and a definite system regarding the operation of our mind, body, and consciousness, and the world in general, even while we don't understand it all yet, then any effective technique IS USING that system in a beneficial way, even if the explanation and theory behind that technique or program and how it works are completely wrong. In fact we know from studies of hypnosis and the mind-power effect (placebo effect), both of which are only utilizing the power and unlimited potential of our own minds, things can change simply because we believe they will or we expect them to. Many of the methods mentioned above may therefore be useful whether or not the evidence for the theories behind them is valid. But what's really going on? What's the common denominator?

I spent decades looking into many such models and methods with the goal of finding out how we really operate as human beings, because unless we really understand what's going on, we will be mostly guessing and depending on trial and error, or the fad of the day. We've come a long way in the field of mainstream medicine in our understanding of the physical nature of disease and malfunction, but in the areas of consciousness, psychology, and mind-body interactions, not so much. Yet a better understanding of these things is crucial if we want to improve the status of mental, physical, spiritual, and psychosocial health for ourselves and others in this world! This may seem obvious already, and it will become even more clear as we explore how all these factors are connected and intertwined.

In the classic science fiction movie Forbidden Planet, a distant and ancient alien race called the Krell had constructed enormous and powerful machines on their world that could read minds. From one's thoughts these machines could materially create whatever the person desired. But their own thoughts destroyed the Krell's entire civilization until only the machines remained. This was because these people had not understood their own minds. "Monsters from the id" refers to the primitive and dark unconscious impulses and conflicts inside all of us. When the machines received subliminal impressions of desires based on greed, jealousy, anger, hatred, depression, violence, narcissism, and other wayward impulses, they manifested these too, into reality, leading to the Krell's extinction. Our own unconscious manifestations, in the form of reactive mind-body states, which I call "identities," are similarly responsible for most of the ills of our world. These identities could be called our monsters from the id. They can range from irritating inconveniences and limitations, to the monsters of fear, depression, addiction, anger, hatred, cruelty, violence, and insanity, and we created them ourselves.

After learning Idenics I continued doing multiple solo sessions every day, and began incorporating my new discoveries into ID-R as they emerged. Over the course of the next two years, as I gained more awareness of my forgotten past, my awakening memory revealed things about myself I had never imagined. Many of these things I had deliberately blocked myself from remembering, and others were hidden behind the partition that separates different levels of consciousness. Most of the stories in this book were completely unknown to me until they arose in my sessions, but after arising they seemed perfectly natural, as if I had known about them all along – because of course, on some level, I had.

However, many of the incidents in my life that I will be recounting were never forgotten, although what I remembered of them was not the whole story, like the previous story of the mysterious artifact, the time the bomb exploded in my face when I was fourteen, or going into the hospital for surgery at the age of five. Much of my memory of these traumatic experiences was absent, and I believe this is true for most of us – that much of our life story is missing from conscious recollection, and those missing parts can hold important keys to self-understanding and transformation. Remembering as much of my life as I do now, did take time, and I had to break through many barriers, but the rewards have outweighed the effort a million times over. Even today my sessions continue to provide new revelations and insights.

We may think we know ourselves but we don't – we only know what's on the surface – the tip of the iceberg. Yet there is nothing more important than knowing oneself, because if we don't know ourselves how can we really know anything else? I believe knowing ourselves, being in touch with our own feelings, and recalling our own true history will promote empathy and compassion for others,

and that healing our wounds allows wisdom to prevail over
unconscious responses. For the Krell, self-knowledge would have
made the difference between death and life, and for us it can make
all the difference in the world.

The Healing Journey

In the current mainstream medical model, healing refers to the
physiological or functional return to some degree of normalcy with
regard to a medical or psychological problem. A cure might mean
complete recovery of function, disappearance of symptoms, and
elimination of the cause, if known. But treatments and cures can
have a down side. For example we all know that many drugs have
adverse side effects. I was cured of bacterial meningitis but the
antibiotics that saved my life also damaged my inner ear on one
side leaving me with permanent hearing loss and balance problems.
Because our mind, body, and consciousness are interdependent
aspects of who we are as human beings, and not actually separate at
all, for our purposes "healing" will refer to the resolution of any
kind of problem involving our mind-body-consciousness system.

However, this definition of "healing," being specific and limited,
must not displace the larger concept of what healing represents.
Resolving or curing some ailment or difficulty, as monumental as it
might be sometimes, is never a total healing. I like Gabor Maté's
expanded meaning when he refers to healing as "a natural
movement toward wholeness," and as a "direction, not a
destination." So for me healing is therefore also a lifestyle and an
attitude – it's my own natural movement along a path toward
greater self-understanding and wellness on every level, following the
recognition that, to again quote Maté "... each of us contains as-yet-
unimagined possibilities for wellness, possibilities that reveal
themselves only when we face and debunk the misleading myths
about normality to which we have become passively accustomed."[19]
As we move toward wholeness we will, of course, want to heal those
difficulties and speed-bumps along the path, but we will recognize
that we must not allow the wonderful things that happen along the

---

[19] "The Myth of Normal" 2022 by Gabor Maté, page 6

way to make us complacent. As long as we are vulnerable to trauma, suffering, and death, we had best remain self-observant and maintain an openness to the ever-present possibility for greater self-understanding and wholeness. I want to be always moving forward.

Because our mind, body, and spirit compose a complex interactive system which is still a mystery on many levels, recovering from a physical illness or injury, a mental condition or psychological limitation, or a combination of these, can be a real journey involving a great many factors. Since there are so many things that can affect us in positive and negative ways, the best means of healing needs to be comprehensive, safe, and balanced. One's personal healing journey, whether it involves recovering from some mild acute viral infection, a life threatening disease or injury, or a chronic debilitating condition, is best when it is personalized. It can be very helpful to listen to others who are struggling with these things or have made the journey back to wellbeing. It's also helpful to research a wide variety of approaches and opinions and work with trusted practitioners whenever possible. Developing your own plan, trying different things, and finding what works for you and sticking to it, are all keys to success. I recommend books like "The UltraMind Solution" and "Brave New Medicine," and "The Pain Chronicles" because these are books that highlight the complexities of healing, promote functional medicine and holistic approaches, and provide personal stories of persistence and recovery. And there are many others. But remember, nobody has all the answers to anything, and not everything anyone says will be true or complete, or apply to you. We're all learning. It's up to you to evaluate things for yourself. We must all be our own advocates for our health and happiness, get multiple opinions when there's a problem, and gather as much useful information as we can. So with respect to healing, in this book my main focus is on the healing of trauma and its effects, on understanding the kinds of things that can emerge in the process of intense introspection, and how this information can change our understanding of life.

Three Levels of Healing

When doing ID-R, the goal is to either to discover or understand something about yourself, or to resolve an unwanted personal problem or condition at its core. But before we get into how that works, there are actually three basic levels of healing or transformation I want to share with you, regarding any unwanted condition or situation. These are resolution, management, and transcendence. If you have a pebble in your shoe and no time to remove it, you can manage the problem by walking differently or pushing the pebble around with your toes until it is less painful, or not a problem at all. That's management – the source of the problem is still there but it's being handled effectively to some degree. Resolution would be to simply stop, remove your shoe, and dump the pebble out – problem solved. You could get another pebble in your shoe of course but that one is gone. Transcendence, the highest level, would be to not mind the pebble while it's there, whether you could manage it well or not. You have actually gone beyond the need to heal or fix the problem, at least in terms of suffering. I refer to these levels as Identity Resolution, Identity Management, and Identity Transcendence and they are all covered in detail in Part IV.

In this chapter we explore the level of resolution, which is the curative level of healing that permanently removes the source of the problem, preferably with no downside. This is the goal of ID-R, but ID-R is not a solution for everything. Like a good microscope, ID-R can address virtually anything but this does not mean it will solve every problem. As a healing practice, ID-R mainly works by resolving the effects of traumatic shock. However, as I hope to make clear, traumatic shock can affect any aspect of our minds, bodies, and lives, in countless ways, and it is possible that any problem or condition might have trauma as a cause or a contributing factor. This fact has been shown scientifically in the ACE Study which tracked the mental and physical health effects of adverse childhood experiences on thousands of people over decades. The ACE Study (The Adverse Childhood Experiences Study) is a research study conducted by Kaiser Permanente and the Centers for Disease Control and Prevention beginning in 1995. I consider it to be the most important health study ever done! It clearly shows that traumatic life experiences during childhood and adolescence are common and pervasive throughout our society, and reveals child abuse, in all its forms, to be the single largest health crisis in the

U.S. The trauma we experience in our first ten years of life has an incredible effect on the entire rest of our lives. In this book you will find many examples of how childhood trauma can affect our health and wellbeing on many levels. The psychological effects are usually obvious, and research into the physiological and neurological effects is ongoing.

Medicine which deals with the body only, misses 90% of what ails us. OK, I made that number up, but I believe it's close. In fact, I believe that, on a spiritual level, ALL our problems, regardless of their nature, stem from a common misperception of reality, and we'll look at that in a later chapter. While the body has a tremendous capacity to heal itself from disease or injury, and modern medicine can assist us in this in countless ways, understanding the power of consciousness and the role of our own minds on our health and wellbeing, as well as all aspects of our lives in general, can provide us with tools to heal and enhance our lives in every way. So the first thing we will look at is how our adverse life experiences can have such a powerful and permanent effect on our health and wellbeing. Then we'll see what we can do about it.

Trauma

When I first attempted to deal with my own fears and anxieties back in the 1970's, the only methods I could find were based on changing my emotional responses by either consciously controlling my focus and thinking, or by reprogramming my mind. These types of processes do work to some degree, but they do not address the underlying cause of a condition. So while I found nothing much that was convincing at the time, about underlying causes, I was still able to cure those phobias I had while in high school, and later I learned to reverse negative thinking and think more positively, to be more mindful of my mental states, and to relax more deeply, among other things. I also learned many techniques that reduced the effects of stress in my life, and I found all this extremely valuable. But after healing my birth headaches and stirring up many other issues from the past, I knew there was a deeper, more powerful level of healing available.

Although some effective methods like basic hypnosis and NLP work on a deeper level by reprogramming our unconscious minds

in various ways, they still don't get to the root cause of any problem.
These and similar workable methods are discussed in Chapter 18.
There are many methods however, like regression hypnotherapy,
EMDR, Primal Therapy, and others, that can help us discover the
roots of our adverse conditions, and it is almost always found that
the root causes of persistent internal problems that aren't purely
physiological, lie in trauma. So we'll start our discussion of inner
healing by defining "trauma."[20]

In her book EMDR, Francine Shapiro states the definition of
trauma as "*any event that has a lasting negative effect*."[21] Of course
we're not talking about getting a bad tattoo; we're talking about the
psychophysical effect of a damaging experience on a conscious
being. Shapiro also refers to big Traumas [capital T] like a horrible
accident or losing a loved one, and little traumas [small t], like
being stood up on a date, and implies that not all experiences that
have a lasting negative impact are of the kind that we would
necessarily expect to do so, or that we would even call "traumatic."
In "Getting Past Your Past"[22] she states: "… if someone who was
raped a year ago or molested fifty years ago has PTSD, the past is
present. When they think of the incident, it can feel as though it's
happening all over again, or they can be fearful and anxious when
around certain people or places. But regardless of how long ago
something happened, and regardless of how long symptoms have
been there, it doesn't need to be permanent. The research is clear
on that. Also important, although a major trauma such as robbery or
violence is needed to give a formal diagnosis of PTSD, a number of

---

[20] EMDR stands for "eye movement desensitization and reprocessing." It is
a method of psychotherapy developed by Francine Shapiro in 1987 to
address and resolve trauma related issues. When using EMDR the client is
asked to bring their problematic issues to mind while the therapist guides
them using bilateral stimulation, such as side-to-side eye movements or
hand tapping, during which significant insights, reprocessing, and healing
can occur.

[21] "EMDR" (Updated Edition), 2004, xiii, Id. – note: this is not the last
edition

[22] "Getting Past Your Past", 2013, by Francine Shapiro Chapter 1

recent studies have demonstrated that everyday life experiences, such as relationship problems or unemployment, can produce just as many, and sometimes even more, symptoms of PTSD."

This is absolutely true! This fact is something I wish everyone was aware of, and you don't need any studies to find this out for yourself. I highly recommend these two books. Although ID-R is a more powerful technique based on a better model, the models are very similar. The EMDR approach definitely works and has clearly demonstrated the same basic understanding of how trauma affects our lives in a great many ways. The aftereffects of trauma exist on a continuum from mild to severe. Whether an experience is a devastating catastrophic event or a momentary confusion, it is traumatic when it is preceded by a shock and creates a reactive program in the mind-body system. This is my definition of trauma, because not all traumas will have a negative effect later. I'll discuss what I mean by "shock" in detail in Chapter 6. Some traumatic reactions can become dormant, causing no adverse psychic effects, but will always have the potential to be reactivated and cause problems later. Also, defining trauma as _any_ event that has a lasting negative effect suggests that trauma is the cause of _all_ permanent unconscious programming. However, it is possible for similar unconscious negative effects to originate in ways not connected with trauma, as I've defined it.

The common premise here is that in life we often have experiences that overwhelm us enough that we are traumatized, which means they impact us in a way that leaves a permanent scar on our psyche. Existing now as a sort of unconscious imprint, a trauma can affect us in negative ways long after it occurred. I've heard many people say they've never experienced trauma, but besides all the disturbing experiences we have that we would not normally call traumatic, people can have a major trauma and not even remember it. The fact is that probably all of us have had thousands of past traumatic experiences that have influenced our lives and personalities in countless ways, and continue to do so.

The most effective programs I know of for dealing with PTSD or any unwanted conditions arising from trauma, invite us to consciously examine the related trauma in some way. EMDR, for example, helps us discover the traumatic sources of our difficulties and reprocess the feelings and thoughts that arise from them. Primal Therapy emphasizes reexperiencing the trauma and feeling the pain and emotions that are embedded in it. Other programs might have you look at the traumatic experience in a more detached way, help you work out the conflicts involved, and guide you in noticing any distorted thinking or detrimental past decisions that can now be discarded. Psychedelic drugs like psilocybin, used with the proper support, may also help you see your problems and their sources from a completely new perspective so as to bring about healing and transformation. All these ideas have value and are utilized in ID-R in unique ways. There are many different theories as to why these kinds of methods work, but there is a common theme, which is that unconscious programs and reactions are the source of most of our unwanted mind and body conditions, and the remedy lies in consciously addressing them in a way that brings them out in the open. We can't effectively deal with something we are unaware of, but when we make the effort we will find that everything we need to know is already within ourselves. I won't be discussing other workable theories in much detail but I will provide you with a model that I feel makes sense of them all.

The Consequences of Trauma

So how exactly does trauma affect us? Asking about the consequences of trauma is like asking what problems can be caused by germs. An infection can cause anything from a cold or tooth decay to meningitis and death. The problems these invisible microbes might cause can be short or long term, mild or severe, with almost every kind of physical symptom imaginable. Past trauma is also invisible and its consequences can cause or influence every malady of mind and body there is. Trauma can have a hand in everything, from fears and phobias, acute and chronic pain, addictions, a weakened immune system, anger issues, worry, depression, sleep problems, sexual problems, nightmares, procrastination, attention disorders, dissociative conditions, multiple personalities, eating disorders, weight problems, seizures, and even paranormal and spiritual phenomena, and this brief list is barely a drop in the bucket of possible trauma related conditions I don't mean to be tedious here but I want to give you a panoramic view. Physically trauma can affect every aspect of our biology including our hormones, our brain and nervous system, every other organ system, and even our epigenetic gene expression, and it can do this in amazing and powerful ways. The magnitude of all this will become clearer as we go on. One problem however is that many symptoms of trauma are most often not considered to be related to trauma at all. Another problem is that when a symptom IS connected to stress or trauma, the condition may then be considered to be a mental illness, a designation which has unfortunate consequences. And the detrimental effects of trauma go far beyond the individual to include all of human civilization, as well as future generations. For a much deeper, all encompassing, and quite compelling perspective on all this I highly recommend Gabor Mate's 2022 book "The Myth of Normal," a book I consider to be one of the most important books on human health and wellbeing ever written.

When we are born, our minds are not a blank slate – various aspects of our personality are already in place, as every parent knows – but we are in an extremely vulnerable state and dependent on the people around us for everything. From there we learn, grow, and begin to take control of our bodies, our perceptions, and our surroundings. If we were never permanently affected mentally or psychologically by anything that we experienced from birth onward, then it seems reasonable that we could modify anything that was false or ineffective, in terms of information, feelings, or behavior, and continue to learn and improve throughout our lives. Nothing we experienced could permanently hold us back. We might still fall into various negative states or mindsets and intellectual habits regarding what we believe and how we function, but theoretically there would be nothing to prevent us from mentally changing any such pattern if we wanted, unless the cause was purely physiological. And although our bodies could be damaged or impaired, we would still be able to adapt to that psychologically as well, because our initial negative or maladaptive responses to the onset of such things would only be temporary. We might get angry at someone for something but we would quickly adapt and then forget about it. But this is hard to imagine because the reality is that we ARE permanently affected by many of the things we experience. If this were not so, our world would be a very different place.

The effects of trauma can be devastating at any time during our lives, but are especially profound and harmful to our minds and bodies during the developmental period starting from before birth and extending through infancy and childhood, and the results can be very difficult to undo. When you get a real sense of the extent to which our own internal programming controls or affects every aspect of our lives, it's absolutely mind-boggling! We can hardly imagine the magnitude to which we, and the world, would be different without the negative impact of trauma on the human mind and body.

"Programming" is what I call our automatic mental, emotional, and psychological responses to the things we experience. The key word here is "automatic." I call these automatic responses "reactions," as opposed to a "response" which appears to be freely chosen. By "freely chosen" I mean that the response didn't happen automatically but occurred with awareness and deliberation, even if the response only takes a fraction of a second, whereas a reaction occurs without any free consideration. We can, of course, train ourselves to react automatically in certain situations, which we do when forming a new habit or developing skills like dancing, martial arts, or playing music, and this is also a form of programming, although I prefer to call these kind of automatic responses "learning" or "conditioning." The difference here is that these programs are patterns that were intentionally learned and can be easily changed on the fly. We'll explore these differences in more detail in the section on identities.

So in the aftermath of a traumatic experience, we are stuck with unconscious programming that can affect how we feel, think, and behave, and even how our bodies function, whenever that programming is activated. Also, some reactions can become chronic, meaning they are affecting us all the time, like chronic pain, depression, or anxiety. It is my opinion that virtually every single symptom in the DSM-V, the comprehensive manual psychiatrists use to diagnose mental disorders, could be the result of trauma! In other words, there is really no limit to the variety of negative effects that can be caused by the trauma people experience. I will be giving you many examples of how trauma can impact our lives, but for now I want to give you more insight into the enormity of that impact.

Here is a statement from a 2014 document from the U.S. Department of Health and Human Services titled "A Treatment Improvement Protocol – Trauma-Informed Care in Behavioral Health Services."

"Trauma, including one-time, multiple, or long-lasting repetitive events, affects everyone differently. Some individuals may clearly display criteria associated with posttraumatic stress disorder (PTSD), but many more individuals will exhibit resilient responses or brief subclinical symptoms or consequences that fall outside of diagnostic criteria. The impact of trauma can be subtle, insidious, or outright destructive. How an event affects an individual depends on many factors, including characteristics of the individual, the type and characteristics of the event(s), developmental processes, the meaning of the trauma, and sociocultural factors."

This is all true, but it's only the tip of the iceberg. As implied by the ACE Study of the long-term adverse effects of early trauma mentioned earlier, childhood trauma in particular can affect every aspect of our mental and physical health and wellbeing for our entire lives! Our resilience in the aftermath of trauma is only an outer manifestation – the internal damage and its consequences in our lives may never be readily apparent because those consequences are "subclinical," meaning we may never seek counseling for them, or, even if severe, they may be determined to be caused by other factors not associated with trauma. Your heart attack for example may be blamed on your being overweight when stress is the real cause – stress which causes hormonal changes, adverse epigenetic expression, high blood pressure, and many other physiological responses directly, and which may fuel behaviors and various addictions that contribute to poor diet and lifestyle – stress which is, at its root, the product of trauma. Everything is connected.

PTSD, as a specific diagnosis, is considered a mental disorder that can take many forms. Symptoms can include intrusive and disturbing thoughts, feelings, dreams, mental and physical pain and distress, changes in behaviors, and even hallucinations. You can think of PTSD as one of the more severe effects of past trauma, but maybe it's only the most obvious. Getting upset that someone got your order wrong at a restaurant or cut you off in traffic may seem like a normal response, and it is, but only because so many other people may respond similarly to similar situations. Because we live in a traumatized world, behaviors fueled by anger, fear, hatred, and greed, that would otherwise be considered abnormal, have become the norm. The truth is that ANY automatic response that you are not happy with is most likely a reaction – an internal program with a traumatic experience at its core.

If we are mindful, we can notice our reactions and their automatic nature when they occur. The problem is that most often our reactions just seem like conscious choices we make in the moment – until we take a closer look. But many emotional reactions are easy to spot, especially anger, fears, and phobias. Much of our programming however, takes the form of personality traits, including our personal preferences, mood swings, self-image, limiting beliefs, prejudices and biases, feelings and judgements about others, mental habits and self-talk, our posture, facial expressions, and even physical pain and disease. There is virtually no area of our feelings, thoughts, behaviors, and lives that our programming doesn't touch. There are countless stories of people discovering the roots of their problems in traumatic experiences, using various methods, and finding resolution in consciously processing those experiences. I will be sharing many personal stories as examples of this in the chapters ahead, but here's a brief illustration.

Using ID-R, I recently worked with a lady who was stuck in a job she didn't like. Brenda wanted to make a change but found herself unable to move forward. It didn't take long for her to see why she was afraid to get a better job. Brenda is a caring person from a dysfunctional family, and several of her relatives were addicts and unemployed. They would often ask her for money and she would give what she had, to help them and their children. She described her reaction to their manipulations as "being guilted" by them, and she would always eventually give in. In one instance of doing this she experienced a traumatic shock when she gave all of her money to a relative with four hungry children. The shock came during this transaction when Brenda realized she was betraying the trust of her boyfriend. She had promised him she would not part with this money. This realization was traumatizing and resulted in many negative feelings and self-judgements. In addition, her betrayal of her partner's trust resulted in the end of their relationship. Now the thought of having more money brought up all the feelings of guilt, shame, heartache, and failure that were present during the trauma. She felt if she had money she could not say "no" to her family, and would again lose everything. These feelings and decisions were subliminal, but they effectively paralyzed her from moving forward. Emotionally it was safer to stay where she was, but she wanted to change this. Brenda had two ID-R sessions and after resolving this trauma, and some others, things did change. She can now say no to her family's manipulations, and she got a new job. Exactly how and why Brenda's realization of betrayal was traumatic for her may not be readily apparent at this point, but how our own thoughts can impact us so deeply will be explained in detail in the next chapter where we take a deeper look into the heart of what trauma actually is.

Is it possible Brenda could have been empowered to make the changes she did using hypnosis, NLP, assertiveness training, a Life Coach, or some other method, without addressing any underlying causes? Absolutely. There are many helpful methods available, although, in my experience, to be more than superficially effective and short-lived, this usually takes considerably more time and effort. These and many other helpful management techniques, which do not address the real source of our problems, are discussed in Chapter 18. But even when they work, if the root of a condition is not resolved, the underlying emotions, thought processes, and internal stress, can still cause problems even though one's behavior has changed. This isn't speculation; I'm telling you this from experience. When the roots of these things are gone there is internal peace regarding the issue – the trauma is now only a memory with no force of its own to affect body or mind.

In summary, trauma can be a factor in every problem we might have, every physical illness or dysfunction, every ache and pain, every psychological or mental problem or limitation, and every roadblock we find in any area of our lives. It can affect our health, success, relationships, energy, motivation, emotions, and general wellbeing – everything I mentioned at the beginning of this chapter. I agree with Gabor Maté when, in the 2021 documentary "The Wisdom of Trauma" he says: "... in thirty years or more of medical practice and of addiction medicine, what I found was that the common template for virtually all afflictions, mental illness, physical disease, is in fact trauma." All this has deep social repercussions as well. The unconscious effects of trauma underlie most of the reactions we call "stress." The trauma factor in all of these things can be insignificant or huge, but the point is that trauma is always an important consideration.

Finally, I don't think we can fully understand and appreciate the consequences of traumatic experiences until we are able to see directly how it has affected us personally. Even when we see how it has affected other people we know, if one has not observed this in theirself, it may still be very hard to grasp. And in order to grasp it we have to see the direct connection between the past experience and its effects in the present, as I did when healing my headaches by resolving my birth trauma. Until then, much about our own health and behavior, and that of others, will remain a mystery, or be subject to many disputable explanations. In many of the stories that follow, such connections will be described in detail to illustrate what I'm talking about here. It is also hoped that you will begin to make some connections between the past and the present regarding your own life situations.

Healing Trauma

Most people who seek counseling or therapy are probably not thinking about past trauma – they just want to get rid of their problems or get help with their goals. But when we help someone find the unconscious sources of their issues, we most often find the root cause in some kind of difficult past experience. When it comes to our own personal issues, I believe that we each have, within ourselves, all the answers and solutions we need, if we could only find them, and ID-R is one means to that end. ID-R is not really a therapy or a treatment for anything, but is instead a guided self-discovery technique that can have a transformative and healing effect. It's perhaps like a more advanced version of Gabor Maté's method of "compassionate inquiry." When we see the things we need to see regarding the underlying sources of our unwanted conditions, those conditions tend to evaporate automatically. When that happens, new possibilities and realizations can arise spontaneously. For example, when Brenda, in the previous example, resolved her feeling that she was a bad person, and her fear of making more money, the idea that she could move forward in her life suddenly became a real possibility. When old programs fall away like this, it can be like a fog lifting and the sun coming out. What was unseen suddenly becomes clear and what seemed impossible becomes a possibility. New positive cognitions like this usually arise immediately once the filters and blinders of old programming fall away.

Using ID-R we make no diagnosis. The client's issue is whatever they say it is. If they have a "nervous toe" then that's what they've got. I don't even have to understand what they mean by that, because THEY know, although I may ask for clarification. Whatever the issue is that they want to resolve, once some important preliminaries are taken care of, we start by addressing it directly. This usually involves bringing the issue to the surface, which means having the person focus on it, think about it, or get into the feeling state of it.

I may then ask the client to recall the first time they ever experienced that condition. I consider this a shortcut. In practice, they often do know where the problem began and sometimes they bring it up before I ask. There are also people who do come in wanting to resolve a specific trauma they experienced. If a client is wrong about the source of their condition, we will find out in due course. The point here is that if we already have an idea of the initial experience or the source of the problem, we have saved a lot of time.

When I ask a client about the first time they had a specific symptom, one common reply is that it was too long ago to remember. Even if they do remember something from many years ago they might feel that the memory is too distant or too vague to be of value. But if the client's problem is indeed related to a past experience, then whenever they are experiencing that problem, or any symptoms of it even if only to a tiny degree, they are already "remembering" the initial trauma! The body knows! In other words, whatever the problem is, the symptom IS the source. Whatever its nature, physical, mental, or spiritual, the condition being addressed IS their memory of what happened, playing itself out in the mind and body to some degree, in an automatic way. It's the same as when we purposely remember something – we are bringing the past into our present awareness, and we can do this with any experience. Another important point is that we remember past physical pain with the body, we remember past thoughts in our thought field, and we remember past visual images in our visual field – in other words, whatever the perception is, when we are remembering the actual experience itself, we remember it as it was: as pain in the body, as emotion, as a visual image, as thought, or as behavior, etc. The difference between a so-called traumatic memory and a normal memory is that a traumatic memory has explosive power, like emotion, pain, or the urge to take action, and these can burst into awareness and be nearly as intense as they were in the original experience. In contrast, few of us can summon up a past experience voluntarily with as much intensity and clarity, and even if we can, the recall is under our control and has no power of its own.

It is certainly possible for us to resolve the effects of trauma by working with the symptoms directly and without ever knowing clearly, or in any detail, what the trauma actually was, where and when it took place, or who was involved. This is because these details are not what keeps the trauma embedded in our system. If we can access the essential unconscious factor that does keep the traumatic memory stuck – the lynchpin so to speak – and bring it into awareness, the symptoms will resolve. This can be a decision, a realization, pain, emotion, resistance, an effort, or something else. It could also be more than one thing. Most of the time however, in an ID-R session, the root incident does become known, often in great detail.

The real key to resolving past trauma therefore, lies in bringing into awareness whatever has been keeping the condition unconscious and stuck, and this usually lies within some kind of overwhelming experience, or overwhelm. Whether the overwhelm is physical pain, intense emotion, an unbearable realization, or whatever, this experience has been hidden from complete conscious access, but may still surface as an adverse physical or mental condition.

ID-R

The focus of ID-R is to get the client to look at things connected to the issue at hand, and to do so in a guided way that leads to a resolution. It is similar to EMDR in this respect. There are several things that differentiate ID-R from EMDR and other methods, including all of the following components. The first is a new basic model of how we operate as human beings and of how we get compromised by the things we experience, most importantly by trauma. The Identity Model is a spiritual model in that it takes consciousness into account. For me, spirit simply means consciousness. Also this model is based on experience alone, and does not require or rely on any deep understanding of the brain or neurology, or any particular brand of psychology. Instead, this is an empirical and pragmatic model based primarily on the personal observations made by the person undergoing the process. I will describe this model in detail later. At its core, ID-R utilizes uniquely defined concepts of various phenomena including "identities," traumatic shock, conscious viewpoints, identification, multiple personalities, the "power-zone," and relationships among all these things. It also employs, in a unique way, the concepts of state-dependent memory and recognition triggers. Ultimately ID-R is a way to find and uproot the effects of trauma more quickly and more deeply than most other methods, so as to provide permanent relief. It can also be used in conjunction with other methods when needed. These statements are based on my own observations however, and you should be skeptical until you see this for yourself.

Also of critical importance, is the adherence to some essential guiding principles in the application of every aspect of ID-R. Without complete adherence to these tenets, ID-R will fail. The first of these principles is that only the client or subject can know what is true for them, and they are the sole authority on their own experience. An ID-R practitioner recognizes that everyone is a unique individual with their own reality, and that anything is possible. The practitioner's job is basically to help the client find their own truth, without any judgement or criticism. Invalidation, analysis, critique, or anything less than our full support, is antithetical to the whole purpose of promoting self-understanding and healing. The practitioner must understand that they are only acting as a guide, and as an ally who is there to support the client, to ask questions, and to facilitate the discovery process. We trust that they will find the answers themselves. These principles also apply when we work on ourselves. We must suspend judgement and not invalidate our own experiences when things arise that we can't accept or don't understand – it will all sort itself out in the end. On the few rare occasions when I had a client with whom I felt I could not maintain a nonjudgmental viewpoint, I have referred them elsewhere.

Working with trauma also requires a safe space for both the practitioner and the client, as well as a presence that engenders trust and fearlessly welcomes the client's personal truth. Also, in ID-R there is no diagnosis beyond the client's own description of their issue. However, since a client could be delusional, incompetent, or otherwise compromised, all this is mediated by rational thinking and practical common sense, but we do our best to adhere to these ideals.

There are also several unique ways we can begin working with any mind-body issue using ID-R, but the most basic way is to find and resolve any underlying causative experiences that created the problem in the first place, and this approach is common to many other therapeutic practices as well. In ID-R we work with the aspect of the experience that is still with you, the program itself – the so-called traumatic memory. This unwanted program has power because it's embedded in the unconscious mind, and is resolved when it is sufficiently brought into conscious awareness. For example, suppose I hypnotize someone and have them make a fist. I tell them that when they awaken they will still be making a fist and will find they are unable to open their hand no matter how hard they try. I also tell them that they will not remember that I told them this, and they will not know why they are making a fist. Then I awaken them from the hypnosis and ask them about their hand. They find that they cannot open it and don't know why. So I help them explore this issue. They quickly realize that the cause must be a hypnotic suggestion I gave them, but their hand is still frozen.

Now I ask them to see if I did indeed give them a suggestion, but they can't remember, so I encourage them to try. You see, I have no power over my client, they simply agreed to follow my instructions unconsciously, and just because I said they couldn't remember, that doesn't mean they can't. That suggestion only works as long as they agree with it or want it to work. Their agreement is unconscious however, so it takes a little effort. They soon recall what I said, and suddenly the clenched fist relaxes and the hand is back to normal. All they had to do was see the truth – the power of the unconscious command they were following was actually their own power, which they reclaimed through awareness alone. Here's a simplified illustration of an ID-R session:

Michael

Michael is three years old and is having a great time at the beach building his sand castle. His mother is some distance away talking with a friend. While he stacks up fistfuls of sand, scrunches them together and pokes holes in them, he can hear the sounds of ocean waves and children laughing, and the plaintiff squeals of sea gulls gliding overhead. It's a warm sunny day and he feels very good, breathing in the fresh ocean air and digging his fingers into the warm moist sand. He's enjoying himself, and his sand castle is coming along nicely.

Then out of nowhere an older kid appears standing next to him with a devilish grin on his face. He kicks the whole sand castle down, laughs, and runs off. Michael is not used to this kind of thing and it's a total shock to him. He feels surprise, confusion, and anger and he jumps up and runs after the kid screaming, and throws a handful of sand at him. He is enraged, his face is red, his heart is pounding, and his jaw muscles have tensed up. The kid disappears in a crowd and Michael hears his mother calling him so he turns around. He sees her twenty feet away holding some colorful balloons and an ice cream cone for him. He walks over to her while wiping the tears from his face. He tells her what happened and she makes a sympathetic face and says she will help him build another sand castle, as she hands him the ice cream. He quickly forgets his anger and the sand castle, and doesn't think about it again.

Twenty five years later Michael is sitting at a desk in his office quietly building a house of cards with a poker deck. He has a hangover and is coming down with a cold. He feels miserable and is not having a good day. Outside it's warm and sunny, the window is open and he can hear the sound of birds chirping. His friend and co-worker Dick walks in, and with a mischievous smile, blows down Michael's house of cards, which he had been working on for the last ten minutes, and chuckles. Any other time Michael would have just said "Thanks a lot butt-head – what do you want?" But suddenly his mood shifts – his face turns red and he feels anger from head to toe but tries not to show it. Dick asks if he wants to go to lunch. "Not today," Michael grumbles. "I'm feeling crappy. I'm just going to rest awhile and probably go home early." He really wants to scream at Dick but restrains himself and remains quiet. He realizes that the house of cards was nothing to get upset over so he searches his mind for other reasons why he should be upset with Dick, and several previous incidents come to mind wherein Dick had caused him some difficulty, anger, or irritation. Today his good friend Dick is a jerk, in Michael's mind, and he finds ample justification for his reaction.

Days later however Michael notices that he is more easily provoked to anger than before. Whenever anyone gets in his way or upsets his plans his face reddens, his heart pounds, his jaw muscles tense up and he has to restrain himself from expressing his anger. He even notices that the sound of birds irritates him as does the sound of people laughing. He realizes something is amiss. People and situations seem to keep pushing his anger button. He doesn't like this so he comes to see me for an ID-R session.

After some conversation I ask him about the first time he ever had these same feelings. He has no idea. He can tell me many times he felt angry but not like this and not for no reason or over something silly. However, after a little work with his thoughts and feelings, he mentions that he keeps thinking of the ocean and seeing a sandy beach in his mind. Finally, he recalls being at the beach as a young child. As I direct him to look at various things, with nonsuggestive questioning, he discovers that these same feelings of anger were indeed present in this memory of being at the beach.

Although Michael eventually recalls the entire experience, at first he is sure that this happened too long ago for him to remember any more details but I encourage him to relax and trust himself. We are looking for a "shift," which is a sudden change in his state of being. This can be emotional, physical, or anything else. He notices a "cloudy" part in his memory of playing in the sand. On further inspection he starts to feel some physical sensations and recognizes that there was indeed a shift but is not sure what caused it. The shift took him from feeling great and having fun, to being filled with anger and rage. He even notices that he is experiencing some of those feelings right now as we talk about it in present time! Now we look for what caused the shift, which lies in the center between feeling good and feeling rage. I ask if there is a "moment of shock" right before the shift – a moment when he felt overwhelmed or confused. This is usually just a split second in time. For him it first appeared as a cloudy area but now he is able to see the exact moment that this incident impacted him, which, as you would expect, was when his sand castle was destroyed. When asked what made this moment traumatic for him, he tells me that when he realized what had happened he felt totally disrespected and reduced to nothing. It was as if his reality had been stolen from him. These are his words, not mine. I simply have Michael notice this moment a few times. This whole incident is becoming more clear to him.

Further questioning helps him to see, and actually feel, the emotions of surprise, confusion, anger, and "loss of reality" present in this incident. He can also feel the joy of playing in the sand, the safety and love of mom, and other good feelings. When asked about any decisions he might have made during this traumatic moment, he says that he decided that he had to do something about this transgression, and chose to act on his anger, rather than the other thoughts and feelings he had during the shock.

After inspecting this "shift in state" a bit more I have him turn his focus to the moment of shock itself. The moment of shock has two aspects. First there is the shock moment, which moves him out of his state of play and into a new mental space where he can decide what to make of this situation and what to do about it. Then there is the new mental space itself, which lies in the middle of the shift and can also be called the middle of the shock. There, Michael seems to be in a quiet place where he can think about things. One might characterize this as an altered state of consciousness or perhaps a dissociative state. It's really a special kind of "time out" which I will describe more fully in the next chapter. From this vantage point many things go through his mind. He can see the demolished sand castle and the mean kid running away; he recalls the ride to the beach with his parents, and imagines his sand castle being completed and looking like the plastic toy castle he has at home.

In this "time out" he also imagines various strategies about how to deal with what just happened. He could decide to just not be interested in building things anymore. He could run to mom and cry and she would comfort him. He could do what dad does when he gets angry, which is to puff up, grit his teeth, and have a red face; seems to work for Dad. Or he could scream like mom does when her feelings are hurt, and throw things. Using his parents as models he decides to express his anger and scream at the kid, run after him and throw sand. As Michael looks at the shock, and at his emotions, decisions, thoughts, and physical sensations, he feels a lot of the pressure of the whole experience dissipating. This is called "unburdening."

Before the shift, Michael was just having fun. To work with this "before" state of mind, I have him put himself in that same state now. I want him to actually _be_ that three-year-old at the beach and to look at things from that viewpoint. While he's playing that role, I again ask him some specific questions. It's like asking the three-year-old, twenty-five years ago, what he is feeling and thinking while building the sand castle. This method is related to the concept of "state-dependent memory." It's easier to recall something if you can put yourself in the same mental, emotional, or physiological state you were in when the experience was happening. This is called "being in the right viewpoint." We often do this when retracing our steps to find objects we've misplaced. I have successfully used hypnosis in a similar way to help people find objects they have lost, sometimes after many years.

After working with this "before" viewpoint for a bit I have him assume the viewpoint he adopted AFTER the shift – that of an upset and enraged person chasing after his assailant. Through this process Michael was able to clearly see what had happened and how he had shifted from being happy to being angry, as well as how he had used his parents as a model for this shift in character. He could also see how his decisions had solved his dilemma of what to do about the situation. At one point Michael becomes noticeably more relaxed and at ease, and laughs at the whole thing.

At the end of the session he reports that his "grumpiness" and chronic irritability have gone and he doesn't feel they will return. Something has changed! He reports later that this particular state of anger never came back.

The Healing Factor

The session just described illustrates one part of the basic process of ID-R for resolving unconscious reactions. In Michael's case he had recently been shifting into the same state he had shifted into that day on the beach when he was three. When his partner Dick had blown down his house of cards, that earlier childhood response had been reactivated in present time. Michael is not a real person but his case is based on my many years of experience working with myself and hundreds of other people. A session like this could take anywhere from fifteen minutes to two hours, and averages about ninety minutes, but the time depends on many factors.

I used this fictional case to present a simplified example of how we get programmed because an actual case won't always show all these elements in a clear and orderly way. Michael's problem could have been headaches, a terrible phobia, difficulty studying or taking tests, procrastination, recurring nightmares, or many other things. While Michael's example was very simple and straightforward, traumatic situations, and our reactions to them, can often be much more complicated, powerful, damaging, and difficult to work with. I could have presented a more painful example of Michael being a battered child, a war victim, or worse. Still, the process is the same, although the catharsis of emotion and pain in a more severe case might be much more intense.

The basic ID-R model of trauma is very simple: during a traumatic event we experience a disturbance that overwhelms us

and causes a shock. We respond to that shock with a shift in our
state of being, and the whole experience somehow sticks with us
such that it can emerge in some form to affect us later on. If we can
become aware of the factors within or surrounding the shock that
keep it stuck, the entire reaction or program will lose all power and
cease to be a problem. Varying degrees of emotional release or
catharsis, cognitive reorganizing, and memory integration can
occur during this process, and they are all guided, encouraged,
supported, and reinforced by the facilitator whenever this is needed
in the session. Most of the time all these various aspects of the
healing process happen spontaneously when the client gains
enough insight into the sources of their condition. Awareness itself
is the main healing factor.

Now here I want to make an important point. Although I just
described someone having a reactive condition and eliminating it
for good, as I said earlier, unless you have had an experience like
this, it may be hard to truly understand what Michael was
experiencing during the session, and how becoming aware of the
trauma, or specific aspects of it, could possibly heal it. From the
description it may have seemed that we were just having a
conversation, but I was helping Michael open doors that had been
closed for many years, and to become aware of things that he
normally would not have access to, the discovery of which
precipitated an internal transformation. The secret to all this will be
covered in more detail in the next chapter. So again, think about
any unwanted condition that you have – some reaction or recurring
phenomenon that is causing you a problem. You may be able to
recall a time when you did not have this condition, and you may
possibly be able to imagine having it disappear and never coming
back, even if right now that might seem unlikely. But you will
probably not be able to imagine how looking at things that
happened many years ago could cure a condition like that. The
process is similar to hypnosis in the example I described earlier, but
it's something you have to experience for yourself. Here's another
metaphor to give you an idea of what it's like.

Suppose you live in an area where there are poisonous snakes.
You walk outside one evening at dusk and see a coiled snake close
to your leg, ready to strike. You freeze. Many things go through your

mind as you try to decide what to do. Can you move away fast enough or will that cause the snake to attack? Can you slowly back off? Is there something nearby that you can use as a shield or a weapon? What will you do if it bites you? Your muscles are tense, your heart is pounding, and you're filled with fear. Then you notice the snake isn't moving. You slowly pull out your cell phone and shine a light on it. Then you see it's not a snake at all but a coiled rope. You immediately relax, your heart rate becomes normal, blood pressure drops, and you feel relieved. You look around and verify that you are safe. The "problem" is gone. So how did your physical and emotional state of alarm get resolved? Well, it was caused by something in your mind, and when you saw that there was no foundation for concern, the problem simply vanished.

The resolution of a problem caused by past trauma is similar, though more complex. In both cases, relief comes from seeing something for what it really is, but the mechanism is different. In this example the alarm reaction was triggered, or stimulated, by the thought that you saw a snake, and relieved, or destimulated, by realizing the truth, that there was no snake. In the healing of trauma there is also a realization that brings relief by permanently removing the unwanted state from its seat of power. In the case of trauma, something that was deeply hidden and unconscious has become conscious, and, in a cathartic process, has released any emotion, pain, and effort it contained, as well as its stuck and automatic nature. Still, this is something you have to experience yourself to truly understand. But maybe you already have experienced this kind of relief, either through some kind of therapy or healing process or just in the course of living, where you realized the truth about something and felt better immediately.

I will present real life examples in more detail later on. Although in the end, most sessions will probably fit a basic framework similar to the one above, every person and every session is different. Often different elements emerge that require taking a different direction or using alternate or additional methods. ID-R is a spontaneous process and the way each session unfolds will be unique, and not all will be as simple and straight forward as Michael's.

Identities: the Roles We Play in Life

"A man has as many social selves as there are individuals who recognize him." – William James, The Principles of Psychology

What happens in trauma can best be understood using the concept of "identities." For our purposes the term "identity" is used in a specialized sense to mean any temporary "identity state" that serves a purpose. Whatever you are experiencing right now is part of your present identity state. If you are happy at the moment, rather than saying "I'm experiencing happiness," you would say "I'm happy," because you are identifying with that state. Our various identity-states generally serve a purpose, so an identity is simply an operational state of being. For example when we learn how to drive a car we acquire many different associated skills and habits as well as information, relevant to driving. When we sit in the driver's seat we automatically know what to look for, what to feel for, and what to do, from releasing the parking brake to turning the key, and so forth. Once these associations are learned and become habitual we don't have to put any extra thought or effort into operating the vehicle. You could call this set of associations and habits your "car driver" identity. This identity may even include various attitudes and emotions, most of which are acquired during the course of driving over many years. And this identity comes into play automatically the moment you get behind the wheel. Identities such as this one are changeable and not problematic. Although learned identities may be habitual and more of a reflex, they can easily be modified or expanded to adapt to new situations, like driving in a foreign country which observes different driving rules, or learning to use a manual transmission after driving an automatic.

So normally, identities are ways of being that serve a purpose, and they are composed of whatever has been learned or put in place to suit that purpose. Identities may be functional in this regard or dysfunctional. For example, in learning tennis you may have acquired some bad habits that need to be unlearned if you want to be a better player. So you would have a dysfunctional, or at least a "less than optimal," tennis identity. An identity's usefulness also depends on the innate abilities of the person employing them. If you are not very good at mathematical thinking then, no matter how much you try, your "math identity" might do poorly on a math test. But maybe that's all you've presently got for math. You may be a virtuoso when playing the guitar however and the identity you develop for that may serve you well. If you have a lame leg, your bowling identity will include physical adjustments you have learned in order to compensate for it. So an identity includes whatever you have come up with to do whatever you are doing. John Galusha described an identity as "a way to be in order to accomplish something." As used in the Identity Model, identities are the roles we play in life. An identity is like a suit of clothes or a uniform we put on for a particular purpose or occasion.

In fact, identities are how we operate in general. That is, we operate using _states_ that have mental, emotional, physical, and spiritual components. These states can be very simple or very complex. We can have a different identity for every person we know and one for each role we play in our lives – roles like teacher, student, spouse, parent, dancer, soldier, child, boss, employee, as well as for different aspects of these roles and the different situations we may encounter. In daily life we shift seamlessly in and out of identities all the time. You can observe this in yourself and others. Identities are really just a useful way of looking at our temporary operational states, and are not to be confused with the larger concept of the totality of who we are, or who we believe ourselves to be. In that case the word would constitute our overall identity as a person, which includes our entire personality, our history, and our personal story. We will look at these things in more detail later on. Nor should identities be confused with alter-personalities, which are something else, and will be discussed in Chapter 7.

Identities, as I have described them, are what I call "free identities," as opposed to identities that become "stuck," which I will explain shortly. Although free identities may sound like discrete entities, they generally have no clear boundaries or limitations. An identity is simply a cohesive grouping of associations – a set of traits a person has learned to draw on, consciously and unconsciously, to suit a particular situation. Normally, identities are dynamic and flexible tools we use, and they have no individual autonomy – it is YOUR autonomy that creates them and uses them. They are roles in our acting repertoire, and each of us has thousands of identities at our disposal. When we have a goal, we will shift into the identity state we need to fulfill that goal, modify it if necessary, or create what we need in the moment. The difference between an identity and a "state of being" in general, is that an identity has a purpose – a dedicated function. Whatever its primary goal or intention is, it is that which drives the person while they are in that particular state. For example, when shooting an arrow, the primary goal might be to hit the target. So an identity is a set of learned responses from which one can also improvise. If some aspect of an identity becomes useless or hinders our purpose, it may be dropped, modified, or replaced – it becomes information that is no longer valid.

So the key to understanding identities is to see them as established states – states of being that serve a purpose. They are created by strong associations made in our physiology, our emotions, our thoughts, our intentions, and other things. While the many aspects of any particular identity may involve very different and complex cognitive brain functions, neurological pathways, different types of memory, trained perceptual discrimination, and specialized motor coordination, somehow they are all associated in an organized way to create the end result, like the ability to dance, to make people laugh, or play the piano. You could also say that identities are just packages of specially organized information.

The identity concept has many uses. Tony Robbins developed a method of modeling the identities of people who excelled at certain things like target shooting or other sports or activities, and described this in his book "Unlimited Power."[23] He would study the beliefs, feelings, perceptual filters, meta-programs, physiology, and other pertinent factors of highly skilled people, and effectively install these traits in himself and others. This is a way of quickly becoming proficient at something by creating an identity that emulates or duplicates the necessary qualities of someone already adept. This is a very workable method that goes beyond concept learning and practice, although these are both aspects of the process. It embraces, ideally, the whole working identity of expertise, not just a few parts of it, and helps one get there faster. Tony was highly successful at this. Although he used the word "state" instead of

---

[23] "Unlimited Power" – 1986, by Anthony Robbins

"identity," his suggestion that the way to get good at something is to begin by modeling someone who is already accomplished at it, makes obvious sense. And this works best by embracing the whole desired identity with all its nuances and secrets, instead of focusing on one small part, as Tony has demonstrated.

Great sports coaches and life coaches have the ability to enable people to change their mental and physical states instantly and consistently. Most of what we see in the world of self-improvement and success-coaching falls under the category of what I call Identity Management – the art of disrupting and changing negative states and of creating and maintaining the most effective identity states for one's life and goals. This is covered in Chapter 18.

Stuck Identities

All of you are nothing but a crowd of different people, some better and some worse, and each of these people – each of these 'I's in you – at particular moments takes charge of you and makes you do what it wants and say what it wishes and feel and think as it feels and thinks." – Maurice Nicoll – "Psychological Commentaries on the Teaching of Gurdjieff and Ouspensky"

The concept of identities is of particular importance in ID-R. It has been known for many decades that a traumatic experience somehow gets embedded in our minds in a way that can come back to haunt us later. The example of Michael illustrates this fact, and it also illustrates a key point. Remember how Michael shifted from being in one state before the shock at the beach to another state immediately afterward? The identity Michael was in before the shock, embodied a different set of intentions, emotions, and behaviors than his identity immediately after the shock. Michael shifted from being in the identity of "happy castle builder," to being in another identity, "angry retaliator." Under the right conditions, this shift can happen again and again, and not as a response to anything traumatic. Once _established_ and _activated_, this same shift becomes an automatic reaction that can be triggered by specific external or internal events, which we call, oddly enough, "triggers."

In any traumatic event, the identities present before and after a shift become, in a sense, solidified, like a multidimensional photograph which is now frozen in time. But when I say "frozen" I don't mean "immobile." These frozen or "stuck" states, when active, are something like a 3D video or GIF image on a computer playing in an endless loop – a hologram where all parts are functioning just as they did when they were captured in the shock. They might also be likened to a hypnotic spell. When a shift is triggered later, we find ourselves in a past identity state reenacting the earlier event and experiencing, to some degree, the same emotions, sensations, thought patterns, expressions, and behaviors as we did during the earlier event. Our bodies may even respond in ways we have no conscious control over. We may try to control some aspects of these automatic responses, but since we do not remember the past event in that moment, our reaction seems to be totally about what's happening now, when it's not. So when we work to resolve an unwanted condition like anxiety, understand that the anxiety is not isolated somewhere in the mind all by itself, but is part of a larger cluster of things cemented together in a package we're calling a "stuck identity." Reactive programs like Michael's anger are actually stuck identities. When a stuck identity gets triggered, we don't just experience the anger or anxiety; we get the whole thing – the whole ball of wax.

By the way, while traumas, in their reactive form as stuck identities, programs, reactions, or inner wounds, are often referred to as "traumatic memories" or "reactive memories," and I often use these terms myself, I prefer to think of an inner trauma less as a memory, and more as a "place inside" that needs proper care and attention in order to be brought fully into awareness. A reactive memory feels to me, in a way, like something that is somehow out of alignment. I also want to point out here that a person's response to trauma, when it first occurs, involves their total being, mind, body, and spirit – it's a total transformation that can have a wide range of ramifications which are always individual and specific. Please keep in mind that our identities are not what we really _are_, they are only what we are "_being_" or acting out, in the moment. The many "I"s that Gurdjieff talked about correspond most closely to what I call stuck identities, as do the "games" described in Eric Bern's 1964 book "Games People Play."

By using the "identity bridge," which is similar to the "affect bridge" in psychotherapy, we can usually find the source of a condition, that is, the originating incident, if it cannot be easily recalled.[24] We can also try hypnotic regression, EMDR, or other methods for this if needed. But as I mentioned earlier, we do not necessarily need to find the initiating incident of an unwanted condition in order to resolve it. By working with stuck identity states we can successfully resolve issues even when the source is unclear or cannot be found, by tapping the unconscious root of what keeps those identities stuck. Finding the source is ideal however, and usually does occur in due course. Here is a more personal example of some of these processes.

Quadrophobia

One night when I was fourteen I was watching TV and drinking a glass of Coke when an ice cube got stuck in my throat. I couldn't breathe. I jumped up in a panic but couldn't yell. I ran into the kitchen but my mother was in the bathroom and no one else was home. I instinctively tried to breathe but the ice cube went deeper. I couldn't cough it up, and in a moment of shock I pictured myself lying dead on the kitchen floor. Then the ice cube just popped out. I had coughed it up, seemingly without trying. I caught my breath and felt OK. A second later my mother was there, a bit shaken, and said she could hear me gasping for air. We both calmed down and I returned to watching TV.

The next day was uneventful until supper time. Suddenly I couldn't swallow my food! I balked every time I was ready to swallow. I kept thinking I would choke, so I would panic and hesitate, and chew some more. I had to chew my food until it was liquid, which I had less trouble with. This continued every day.

---

[24] The identity bridge is a process in ID-R utilizing "state-dependent memory." We use specific questions designed to trigger associations by the power of recognition. By putting oneself in the viewpoint of the identity that embodies a particular feeling or condition, one has greater access to all memories associated with that state, including its origin – in fact the state itself is a partial memory. We can even say that the unwanted state actually IS the past incident superimposed on the present moment.

From then on, dinner could take me hours to eat! It was like a similar story depicted in an episode of Young Sheldon, where Sheldon choked on a sausage and couldn't eat solid food for several weeks, except in my case this condition lasted for months.[25] My family could see that something was wrong but no one said anything, and I was too ashamed to volunteer my dilemma. It was dreadful. At every meal I felt like I was walking a tightrope.

A few days after the choking incident I noticed my heart beating and I had the sudden feeling that something terrible was about to happen. This caused me to panic, and I had a very strong urge to run, so I ran out the door and down the street – and then, amazingly, the panic disappeared.

Some months after that panic incident I was climbing a tree, and when I looked down from about ten feet up, I panicked at the thought I might fall. From that time on I had a fear of heights. Mind you, I had never had this fear before. Many times prior to this my friend Jeff and I had scaled giant oak trees by clinging to the thick bark and even hanging upside down twenty feet off the ground with no fear at all, so that we could sit up in the top branches.

One day while out hunting with my dog King down by the river I was attacked by a very nasty hornet. At first I stopped and tried to be very quiet. I knelt down and held my breath, but strangely, it continued to harass me. When I felt the hornet land on my shoulder, I suddenly became terrified. I began running, waving my arms, but it chased after me. I was stung on the left arm as I ran, panic stricken, into the nearby field, thinking I was going to die. I didn't die of course, and when I calmed down I spotted the stinger in my arm and pulled it out. In younger years I used to catch bees and let them walk on my hands. I even got stung a few times but it never bothered me. But now I had another phobia.

All these new phobias were extremely embarrassing, but especially the bee phobia. Wherever I was, if a bee or wasp flew by, I had to run. Even the buzzing of a fly could spook me. I didn't always run, but it was difficult to restrain myself. In Junior High

---

[25] Young Sheldon - 1x04 "A Therapist, a Comic Book, and a Breakfast Sausage"

School I would eat lunch with friends on the benches outside the cafeteria. Bees were usually present, attracted to the discarded soda cups and half-pint ice cream cartons in the trash cans. If one flew near me I would move away as nonchalantly as I could, or pretend I had to go to the restroom, while trying not to run or reveal my discomfort. I managed to hide this phobia from my friends fairly well but it was agony.

My phobias, which, lasted about three years, were stuck identity states with specific triggers. When I was seventeen, I began reading psychology books in the hope of finding some answers. I discovered behavioral conditioning and learned the process of desensitization. I decided to work on my fear of heights by jumping off higher and higher places, after getting relaxed and calm. I started by jumping two feet off a box – then three feet. Next was the five-foot fence. I graduated to jumping off the roof of our house, eventually advancing to the highest point which was about eleven feet to the grass below. My friends didn't know why I was doing this, and thought I was crazy, but it worked. I successfully handled swallowing food in a similar way, although it had become less of a problem on its own since I had to eat every day.

Buoyed by this success I decided to tackle my bee problem. I was now eighteen. When spring came I drew a line about thirty feet from a row of several of blossoming rose bushes in our backyard that were swarming with bees, and stood there with my eyes closed, getting as calm and relaxed as I could. Then I would look at the bees and remain relaxed. Each day I would move the line one foot closer to the bees, and spend several minutes repeating the desensitizing process. After about three weeks I could stand right next to the rosebushes with bees buzzing all around me, feeling no fear at all. In fact I was feeling rather ecstatic. I did this last step for about a week. One day a bee landed on my hand. I watched it calmly until it buzzed off. It worked! I had created a new calm and stable identity regarding bees, and had basically deactivated bees as a trigger.

But still, sometimes, for no apparent reason, I would feel a panic coming on, and would have to run – at least that seemed to provide the most effective relief. The fear of swallowing was an obvious consequence of the ice cube choking incident, which I had always assumed had something to do with the other phobias as well, through some kind of sensitizing or generalization. Twenty-five years later I discovered and resolved a childhood incident that was the real source of _all_ these reactions.

A Race with Death

One afternoon when I was about six years old I was walking with my father, holding his hand. Ahead of us was Pearl, a family friend, and her daughter Jill, who was a few years older than I. We were walking across a parking lot toward the back door of Pearl's house. Jill was telling her mother about using some colored pencils. Earlier that day when we were alone, Jill had colored her lips with her colored pencils, using them like lipstick, and had encouraged me to do the same. Pearl seemed upset when she heard this, and said something to Jill about going to the doctor. Pearl explained to my dad that Jill was allergic to the chemicals in the pencils, and that an allergic reaction could even kill you.

I suddenly became concerned, since I too had used the pencils, although I had no idea what the word "allergic" meant. I tugged on my dad's hand, and told him that he needed to take me to the doctor too. He ignored me. I kept tugging and insisting, and after a few seconds he stopped and turned to me while I explained. He then knelt down, looked me right in the eye and said, quite solemnly, "Son, you're gonna die." Feeling desperate I pleaded, "No, you just have to take me to the doctor!" "No. You're gonna die. I'm sorry, but there's nothing anyone can do," he said with finality, and he stood up and walked away.

I stood there for a moment, frozen – then I panicked. I ran over to the chain-link fence nearby and rapidly tried to find a solution. This was an emergency and, for all I knew, I could die at any moment. I wasn't really sure what death was, but it seemed to be the scariest thing imaginable. I could feel my heart pounding. Maybe I could find a doctor myself or get someone else to take me. But for me, a little kid, it all seemed hopeless. In the middle of the shock of "no hope" I decided that whatever death was, maybe I could outrun it! I imagined death as a shadowy monster that was coming to get me. I decided that if I could just beat death to the gate in front of the house, about thirty yards away, I would be safe.

So I ran with all my might, as fast as I possibly could, racing past everyone else. I could feel Death right behind me, practically breathing down my neck. But when I got to the gate I knew I was safe, and Death turned away and disappeared. I experienced great relief, and I knew I would be OK. I forgot this experience until a couple hours later at Pearl's house when Pearl said she was impressed by how fast I could run. I started crying, and she comforted me as I told her what had happened, and then scolded my father for being so mean.

The trauma then receded into dormancy, but was reactivated when I was choking on the ice cube, eight years later. After that, this panic reaction became linked to four things that represented the possibility of death, including swallowing, falling, being stung by a bee, and just noticing my heart beating. It could have also become linked to many other things, given the right circumstances. This program of fear also included a mysterious solution, running, which always brought relief. When this incident and its stuck identities of "must find a solution" and "must beat Death to the gate" were resolved, the last traces of this reaction evaporated. Of course I also worked through the "ice cube" incident and the "mad hornet" adventure using ID-R, and while these shocks did harbor panic, discomfort, and thoughts of death, most of those feelings had their source in the "race with death" incident from eight years earlier.

This story demonstrates the basic pattern of programmed reactions. First the reaction must be established, which is what happened in the original shock. The whole experience became an unconscious program. Such programs often quickly become dormant and may pose no problem until they are reactivated later. Many traumas are never reactivated, and some never become dormant. A dormant trauma with its stuck identities can be reactivated at any time in the future by an experience that is strong enough to awaken, or connect to, the traumatic memory. The activating experience may be another shock or any event that has a strong physical or mental impact and is associated with some aspect of the earlier trauma. If someone is in a weakened condition due to illness, drugs, or stress, as adult Michael was with his cold and hangover in the earlier example, they may be more prone to such activation.

This story also illustrates how a shock can connect a person to earlier shocks if it bears a close resemblance to them, and this is extremely common. Another factor is that during a traumatic moment we often scour our memory for similar experiences, perhaps in an effort to discover a past solution. In my case, the shock of choking was about death, which connected me to the earlier shock about death. These two shocks were instigated by very similar thoughts and feelings, and a connection was made instantly on a deep unconscious level. This explains why a stressful experience that later seems minor on the surface can have a devastating effect that seems to make no sense, by reactivating something earlier. This is why panic attacks or other problems can sometimes originate for no apparent reason. They seem to come out of the blue, but something, maybe even a single thought under the right circumstances, has activated a trauma long forgotten.

Once my earlier fear-program was activated, it could now be restimulated or triggered by a reminder. A reminder can be anything that is associated with the program; even a thought or a subliminal perception like a sound or an odor. These triggers are sometimes called "buttons" as in"pushing one's buttons."

In a phobia, the main trigger is simply the thing you are afraid of, snakes for example, although other things could become triggers as well once an association is made. A snake phobia can be triggered just by thinking about snakes, anticipating seeing a snake, or seeing something that looks like a snake.

Ghosts in the Machine

The following chapters contain many examples of the kinds of aftereffects that trauma can create, but there is no limit. Your anxieties and fears, your emotional reactions, your aches, pains, and physical dysfunctions, even your attitudes and preferences, can all have their roots in past trauma that you may not even remember at all. These reactions are like gremlins wreaking mischief from the shadows – ghosts in the machine. As I mentioned earlier, I was able to resolve a wide variety of problems and conditions in myself by working with their underlying causes, and many of these will be described throughout the book. Everything in time and space has a cause – something that preceded it and set it in motion. That's simply part of the mechanics of our present world. When we find the experiential causes of our personal unwanted conditions and bring them sufficiently into our awareness, those conditions vanish.

What does this mean for you and me? The fact that trauma affects our minds and bodies in so many profound ways, and that these effects can be reversed, takes us into a whole new realm of understanding about ourselves that has far reaching consequences. Trauma is very much like microbes were before the invention of the microscope. Until then we knew nothing of the existence these tiny invisible entities or their role in causing disease. They plagued us with sickness, disability, and death, while we remained oblivious to the greater truth. But now that we understand how microbes work, we can see their effects everywhere. Similarly, the effects of trauma are invisible to the untrained eye. But once we better understand how our mind-body-consciousness system works, we can see the effects of trauma everywhere also.

For virtually every problematic mental, spiritual, and physical condition we have, we can probably attribute some aspect of it to trauma, and there are many conditions that are entirely the result of trauma. If we have the means to either relieve or resolve the negative effects of past traumatic experiences, we can use these means to address practically every problem and limitation we have.

Taking my cue from Gabor Maté, from here on I will refer to the mind-body-consciousness system as simply the "mindbody." Some unwanted mindbody conditions might be benefitted in a minor way and others completely cured, all by mental processes alone. Once germs were taken into account, the field of medicine took an enormous leap forward. When the real effects of trauma are taken into account and worked with effectively and routinely, I believe we will see another renaissance in the advancement of human health and wellbeing on every level. In fact this renaissance has already begun and is apparently beginning to accelerate. The vast ramifications of this will be astonishing once we truly understand the enormous impact traumatic experiences have on the body and mind, and every aspect of our lives. I hope to provide at least a glimpse of this. Probably all of us have many hundreds if not thousands of traumatic moments in our lives that have shaped us, and yet our present state of being may seem fine and normal. But if you think you have never experienced anything traumatic, just think about how much if your childhood you don't remember, and be sure to read the next chapter. Even while we may have many things about ourselves we would like to change or improve, we have gotten used to our programmed condition, whatever it may be. We accept this as our "normal" state of being. But if the effects of all traumatic experiences in our lifetime were undone, what would be the result? How might we change? We have as yet, no idea!

Overview

When psychology first emerged as its own science in the late nineteenth century, it did so as a respectable extension of medicine, developed by physicians who also studied the human mind and consciousness. But since then psychology has taken a back seat to physiology in the field of medicine, and as a result, it has struggled to be more than a kind of pseudoscience or a minion of advertizing and propaganda agencies. Psychology broke out of this mold somewhat by aligning itself with the physical sciences and becoming, in many ways, more like a branch of neurology and biochemistry, and even statistics, and becoming less a science of the mind. The main reason that progress in understanding human psychology has been so slow compared to progress in medicine and industrial technology is, I believe, largely due to the dogma of materialism. When dealing with the mind, we must consider consciousness – and consciousness defies any materialistic explanation. Studying the mind and consciousness also reveals phenomena that are scientifically problematic and inconvenient. A great book to read if you want to explore this in more detail is "Irreducible Mind."[26] Another is "Real Magic" by Dean Radin. But the main point I want to make here is that understanding our own mind is the key to unlocking the unlimited potential in each of us.

The process of how we get programmed and stuck with the effects of past experience is very simple in theory, and so is the

---

[26] "Irreducible Mind" - 2007, by Edward Kelly et al.

remedy. We have a traumatic shock and the whole experience gets locked into our system. These trapped traumas reemerge as identities, which are mind-body states that we experience as automatic reactions and unwanted conditions. The resolution of these unwanted conditions involves clearly inspecting the original shocks and their resulting identities in a way that ends the unconscious reactive nature of the trauma and frees us from its effects. If the original shock cannot be found, working with the stuck identities (feelings, decisions, beliefs) can still bring about a resolution.

I've already restated this several times in this chapter, but it is critical to understand that our unwanted conditions are _states_, that they are mechanical reactions, and that _we are not our states_. If we are in a "poor-me" identity for example, nothing we are thinking, feeling, or doing, regarding that state, has any basis in reality – it is simply being projected into our awareness and it affects the way we see ourselves and the world. We are _identified_ with this identity _if_ we believe its thoughts, accept its feelings as our own, and let it dominate us. But if we can just pause and take a mental step back any time we "shift" into a reactive state, then in that noticing, we can see the identity for what it is, an automatic reaction, and not allow it to be in control. Then we can see that _it_ is not who we are, and we begin to get free of it. This is not so easy at first, and takes practice! By being more self-aware and practicing Self-Observation, we can make this a habit and thereby experience many immediate and long term benefits. We will cover this more thoroughly in Chapter 18.

There is, of course, a lot going on with us humans, and we've just scratched the surface. The ideas in the next chapter continue our exploration of the basics of our reactive nature and can be powerful doorways to self-understanding. Now let's look into the heart of trauma and explore what makes something traumatic.

Chapter 6
Explosions in the Soul

*"Human freedom involves our capacity to pause between the
stimulus and response and, in that pause, to choose the one response
toward which we wish to throw our weight. The capacity to create
ourselves, based upon this freedom, is inseparable from consciousness
or self-awareness." – Rollo May,* "The Courage to Create"

There are many levels to our existence. Just above our conscious
mind, just out of sight, is another world. We can call it the
unconscious or subconscious mind, the superconscious mind, the
collective unconscious, or the spiritual universe. Or if you like, we
can just call it the brain, but it contains all those aspects of
ourselves of which we are presently unaware, and there is evidence
it includes the complete memories of everything we have ever
experienced. There are things we can become aware of, hidden in
this unknown and mysterious realm, that can transform our lives in
profound ways. We've had a glimpse of how trauma can program
us, on an unconscious level, with various adverse conditions, and in
this chapter we will go deeper into how that works and take a closer
look at the far-reaching effects our unconscious reactions have on
our lives.

The Shock

In every trauma there is a moment of shock, which I described
briefly in the last chapter. The traumatic shock is the critical
element and holds the key to understanding many things, and the
proper application of this information can change the world. A
traumatic shock is like an explosion in the soul. It's like being
silently blasted into another dimension. In general, a shock may
occur when we cannot confront, tolerate, handle, or deal effectively
with what we are experiencing. The experience can be as loud and
violent as a bomb explosion or as silent and invisible as a thought
while lying in bed in the dark of night, but whatever it is, it's too

much; it's an overwhelm. From the beginning of using ID-R, I've often referred to the shock as the"oh shit!" moment. Imagine the feeling of turning a corner in your car and seeing that you're about to go over a cliff. You get the idea. Others have independently used this phrase as well, in describing the onset of trauma.

Common experiences that could cause a shock include a confusion that leaves one vulnerable, a question that can't be answered but must, recognizing an immediate threat to life or limb, a problem that requires an immediate solution when you have none, a broken expectation, something too difficult to believe, physical pain that is beyond one's threshold to tolerate, unbearable emotional pain, the unwanted end of something, the unwanted beginning of something, catastrophic failure, overwhelming loss, overwhelming success, loss of status, and on and on. Whatever the cause, it's a state of emergency! There are countless situations and experiences that can cause a shock, and I will be providing numerous examples of these.

The shock itself is experienced as just that – a shock to our mindbody system. It's an impact to our entire being – a sudden moment where we shift into an altered state of consciousness, at least for a split second. Exactly why this happens I do not yet know, but it's most likely a preconditioned response of some kind. It happens so fast that it seems instinctual, like pulling your hand off a hot stove, but being in this fleeting altered state is what traps the experience in the unconscious mind. It's almost like a portal opens, captures the whole experience, and closes back on it. This is just a metaphor, but the space in the middle of the shock is normally not remembered because it lies beyond ordinary experience, and in fact, it lies outside of physical space and time altogether. Normally this makes the moment of shock itself invisible to our memory unless we focus directly upon it, and one can investigate a trauma a thousand times in therapy and never see it, or see what happens within it. What is experienced in the middle of the shock therefore becomes unavailable for recall, either entirely or to some degree. This can make the entire memory of the traumatic experience difficult to access clearly, even when the experience is not intentionally suppressed and hidden from oneself.

That's about all I can say for now as to _why_ traumatic experiences get trapped in our system as they do. I'm sure there will be more neurological or metaphysical theories advanced about this but the fact is, every shock is <u>an experience</u> which does produce a momentary altered state of consciousness, and things do get trapped there. Anyone can verify the truth of this personally by inspecting their own traumatic moments in depth, with the right technique and precautions.

So ultimately a shock is whatever impacts you in a way that propels you into that momentary state where things get stuck. It's caused by something that you can't handle as you are, in your present state of being, for whatever reason. In that sense, every shock is a failure, at least momentarily. That special state produced by the shock occurs in the middle of the shock moment, which is also the middle of the shift between one identity state and another. I call this special state the "power-zone." During an ID-R session I simply refer to the power-zone as the middle of the shock. Although it is normally out of sight, it is possible to see what happens in the power-zone with the proper focus, and people often recall remnants of it right after a shock. For example you might recall a moment where your whole life flashed before your eyes, or where everything was moving in slow motion, or where time seemed to stop. The power-zone is not however, a state that can be entered into intentionally by will alone, or via drugs or hypnosis, or any other method I know of, nor is it the same state as an out-of-body-experience, although one may feel dissociated or bodyless in that space, and it may induce and out-of-body state that occurs afterward. It's something we do with our attention as conscious beings. It's more like a "beyond-the-body-experience" where we are closer to being our true self, but it's always temporary.

Kodachrome – or
Planes, Trains, and Automobiles

Here's another example of a shock. When I was thirty-one, I lived on the outskirts of town and was driving home from work by myself, late one night, down a long and very dark road. I was rounding a curve going between forty and fifty miles per hour, and there was a slight mist in the air, but I could see the road in front of me clearly. I was listening to Paul Simon singing Kodachrome on the radio. The windows were rolled up and the music was loud.

While I was singing along, I noticed three moving lights ahead of me and to the left, about 300 yards away, although at the time I thought the distance was much greater. The lights were above the horizon, so I thought it must be a low flying airplane, but I really couldn't tell. After a few seconds I noticed that the plane was getting closer, so I kept glancing at it. Perhaps being a bit nearsighted played a part in this, as well as the fact that the road was on a slight upgrade. The lights were now coming right at me, which created some anxiety and puzzlement; something wasn't right! My eyes were now transfixed on the approaching plane that was apparently going to crash into my car! The idea of pulling over to the side of the road flashed only briefly in my mind. Finally I turned my attention back to the road ahead, and that's when I saw the flashing red lights of the railroad crossing gate – which was down! I was about ten feet from the tracks.

There was a split-second of confusion. I had mistaken the lights of a train for an airplane. I immediately floored the gas peddle and blasted through the crossing gate, cracking my windshield. I looked back a few seconds later and saw the train moving well on down the tracks. I also saw the dangling broken half of the gate swinging back and forth, hanging from the electric wire that connected the warning lights. The crossing gate sat very close to the tracks. If I had taken any other action I would have died. I reported the broken gate to the police as soon as I got home.

I was unhappy with myself for not seeing the train, although it was completely hidden by the darkness, with trees and houses behind it so that only its lights were visible at night. I checked all this out the next day. But I was somewhat proud of hitting the accelerator and escaping death. Still, I was always curious as to how I arrived at that decision so instantaneously. There seemed to be something missing – a tiny gap – something I couldn't recall. It was many years later that I took a look at this moment with ID-R and spotted the shock. The shock occurred right after I saw that the crossing gate was down. I didn't know how close the train was but I knew I was in trouble and that there was no time to think about it. It was one of those "Oh shit!" moments. Death was immanent! My mind stopped – I blanked out.

And in that moment some interesting things happened. I was out of my body and there was another spiritual entity helping me.

This being appeared as a naked child with no discernable gender, reminiscent of Casper the friendly ghost. During this "time-out," time in the physical world was frozen – nothing was moving. Yet we were both flying around in the air measuring the speed of the train, its distance from my car, and other factors. We were operating in what I call "sideways-time."[27] We arrived at the conclusion that I should step on the gas without hesitation, which is exactly what I did. From what I remember about the proximity of the train, I would say it missed the back of my car by only few inches. This is what I recalled. As I said earlier, amazing things can happen in moments of trauma

I have now heard many stories of people doing amazing things in critical moments and getting themselves out of dire predicaments without having any idea how they did it; the solution just mysteriously happened. Perhaps they just don't remember because the solution occurred while they were in the altered state of the power-zone, which, as I said, is resistant to ordinary recall. I recently read one such story in Eben Alexander's wonderful book "Proof of Heaven," where he describes miraculously escaping death during a skydiving incident. In his case he eventually came to recognize that something extraordinary had indeed happened in the midst of this perilous experience. Sometimes people make up a story to explain the mystery, but they know there's still something missing. Clients with these kinds of stories are usually able to see what really happened, using ID-R, just as I did in the above example, and I have worked with many people who did just that.

---

[27] Sideways-time occurs when we experience events outside of the normal chronological time of the material world, which I call "real-time" by convention. They are both experientially the same but take place in different spaces so to speak. Everything we experience occurs in time, which is an essential quality of all experience. So sideways-time is like another dimension in which you can operate while time in the real world appears to be stopped. Sideways-time is often experienced in the power-zone, but it is not "timelessness," which is something else altogether.

The Power-Zone

It's important to understand that a trauma is a personal
EXPERIENCE. It's not something that happens to your body or
your brain, though these are of course involved – it's something that
happens to YOU. It's also important to realize that everyone of us is
unique in our psychological makeup, and that what constitutes a
shock for one person may be nothing for someone else. And a shock
can never be seen from the outside – only the person theirself can
know exactly what something means for them and how it affects
them. A trauma is a situation that presents a problem, and how
someone perceives that situation determines the reality of it for that
person. A traumatic situation for one person may not be a problem
for someone else, or it may instead pose a very different problem.

When faced with an overwhelming situation, the middle of the
shock affords us an opportunity to assess our predicament, to make
decisions, and to take action. It's a special pause between an
extreme stimulus and our ultimate response. I call this momentary
time-out the "power-zone" because it's an untouchable space where
we can access inner power and knowledge to help us deal with the
situation. Sometimes this access to our own inner resources is very
limited and sometimes our responses don't help much or may even
make things worse. A child has to rely on very limited conscious
knowledge of life and how things work, so the solutions they come
up within a trauma will usually reflect that. We do the best we can.

However, sometimes our internal access is phenomenal and we
may, even as infants, tap into everything we have ever known,
including past lives or higher wisdom, and utilize this knowledge in
our decisions. We may also awaken and employ the amazing
strength and spiritual power sleeping within us. We have all heard
stories of people doing phenomenal things that were physically
beyond their ability, like incredible feats of strength, in a moment
of emergency. It's not just adrenaline.

By addressing the power-zone, ID-R is, in a very real sense, like a
microscope for the mind, and one that can routinely reveal things
of a spiritual or supernormal nature. Based on the experiences of
many people, here are some of the things that can and do happen
in the power-zone, in a fraction of a second.

★ We may assess our situation in great detail – this may include detailed spiritual perception of our body, inside and out, even on a microscopic level, and an enhanced perception of our environment. ★ We may access pertinent information from our past experience and knowledge, or even from past lives. ★ We may tap into a higher source of wisdom or intelligence, or just suddenly know things we didn't know previously. ★ We may imagine positive or negative possibilities or outcomes. ★ We may practice many scenarios in our minds, like chess moves, in trying to figure out what to do. ★ We may make decisions, choices, promises, rules, or vows, and employ concepts like "never" or "always" in our considerations, like "I'll never trust anyone again." ★ We may create machinery or psychic mechanisms that are set up to work automatically under certain conditions. ★ We may utilize previous programs already in place. ★ We may open ourselves to other spirits attaching themselves to us in some way. ★ We may accept help or guidance from other entities who are watching us or already attached to us. ★We may telepathically communicate with other people we know, or entities which we may regard as guides, angels, or God. ★ We may see the past or the future. ★We may make judgements about ourselves, others, life, God, or situations. ★ We may make requests of a higher power, which may or may not be granted. ★ We may ask for help in the form of a helper personality which is then created from our own consciousness to assist us or trade places with us for a while. ★ We may momentarily acquire great strength, great speed, great skill, or the ability to heal something instantly. ★ We may suppress pain or become numb to what we are experiencing. ★ We may suppress our memory or our senses or alter these in some way. ★ We may make adjustments in our body to compensate for what is happening to it physically. ★ Miracles can happen.

In the end there may be no limit to what can occur, or appear to occur, in the power-zone. In my stories of working with myself and others you will find examples of all of these and many other things occurring in that brief phenomenal state. If some of these things seem impossible, unreal, or conflict with your belief system, please keep in mind that these are people's actual experiences. Their source, meaning, and reality will be discussed later. However, acknowledging and working with any experiences or considerations a person brings up in an ID-R session, regardless of their nature, is of crucial importance. Invalidating a person's experience, or your own, is a critical error in doing this kind of work, and one which may even halt all future progress. Each person must discover for theirself, what is true for them and what is not.

A word of caution here: there were times as a child when I injured myself unintentionally because I did something dangerous and thought I would not be hurt – I thought my magical powers, or some guardian, would protect me. I was wrong – every time! Once, while in a slightly higher level of awareness, I kicked a wall with my foot thinking I would be able to leave my body at the shock of the pain. The only thing that happened, while in the power-zone, was that I had to deal with the pain in my foot. In looking into these moments I learned something that reminds me of the TV series "Limitless." In this series the hero, Brian Finch, accepted a job with the FBI in which he was given a dangerous drug called NZT that unlocked the full potential of his brain, making him super-intelligent for twelve hours. He agreed to work with the government because he was the only person they knew of who was immune to the lethal side effects of NZT, but he was only allowed to take one pill a day while working. When he was off NZT and back to normal, he sometimes had goals or inclinations which, once he was back on the drug, he could clearly see would be disastrous to pursue. The obvious lesson is that what you might want when in one state of mind, might be unthinkable in a higher state of clarity.

The bottom line here is that if you try and give yourself a shock in order to access the power-zone for some specific outcome, _you will always fail_. This is because in the power-zone we only address the immediate shock. If however, the solution to a problem during a shock is to leave my body, that _may_ happen, but what actually does happen is _completely unpredictable_. If you jumped off a building thinking that in the power-zone you would acquire the ability to fly, in the shock of plummeting to your death you would only realize that you can't fly, and have to deal with THAT. Miracles can and do happen, but they come from another realm and cannot be forced or predicted. It would be like tempting God. We can access our higher states through meditation and other means, but not by self-inflicted trauma. Furthermore, what we can and can't do in this world is governed by rules that are enforced by higher powers, as I will explain later, and some things are simply not allowed.[28] Although this means that you can't use a shock to make something happen, you can definitely inspect past shocks and see what _did_ happen. Sometimes we are gifted with great power, but that power can vanish at any moment.

What Gets Stuck

The stuck identity states that result from a trauma contain everything experienced during the trauma, including any physical pain, grief, fear, shame, guilt, numbness, hopelessness, dissociation, dispassion, rage, hatred, tension, confusion, positive emotions, or anything else, including all the decisions, solutions, judgements, and compensations that were put in place. ID-R resolves unwanted conditions by resolving the shock itself, and thus releasing everything that was attached to it. To really see what gets stuck in a traumatic shock you have to work through the trauma and see what gets UNstuck. When a traumatically generated reactive program is effectively resolved, its entire assemblage of identities, emotions, decisions, limiting beliefs, and goals, falls away. The power that drove the reaction is released, and the stuck nature of the traumatic experience disappears. All that remains is the memory – a memory that has no more power than any ordinary memory. Although ID-R has specific ways to address various things like stuck mechanisms and machinery created in the shock moment, these seem to fall away on their own as well, once the incident is handled.

But some things created during a trauma do not get resolved immediately or automatically, including multiple personalities, spirit attachments, and physical manifestations in the body, among others. Such things may be the products of a traumatic experience, but they remain external to it. However, these issues can also be resolved, and they are considered in every session, and addressed whenever suspected or discovered.

After experiencing a trauma, the trauma may remain as an active program, which means that the person will shift into the reactive identity whenever it is triggered. If the trauma becomes dormant, it will have no effect until it is reactivated, which could be many years

---

[28] See page 371.

later, or never. Once reactivated, a trauma usually does not go dormant again until death and can be triggered acutely by association, as when my birth headaches were triggered by stress, or by wearing a hat. A trauma may also remain in a constantly stimulated condition, causing chronic pain, numbness, depression, anxiety, weakened immune system, hormonal dysfunctions, or other problems. While such conditions may have other causes, because of the possibility that they could be the mindbody effects of past trauma, it is always worthwhile to explore that possibility first or in conjunction with medical or physical approaches. Although every aspect of health and ability, whether physical, mental, psychological, or spiritual, can be affected by trauma, and trauma can be the cause of, or a factor in, any unwanted conditions we may have, there is no way to know for sure unless this possibility is explored with an effective method.

Collateral Healing

Often after doing ID-R there are unexpected benefits, usually because the trauma you resolved was affecting you in ways you hadn't realized or considered. And sometimes things get resolved which weren't specifically being addressed. I call this collateral healing! In addressing any issue there are always things happening unconsciously, behind the scenes so to speak, that we may never see or understand. But even though we may not see everything, and while some of what we do see may remain vague or incomplete, during the ID-R process we only need to see enough to resolve the problem. Also, sometimes a problem seems to go away over a period of time after the session, even though the issue was not resolved at that time and there was not much insight into its source. It's as if we poked a microscopic hole in a balloon, which didn't burst it, but caused it to gradually deflate over time.

It is also possible for there to be negative effects after a session. This can be because the issue was not completely resolved or because other reactions were stirred up that were never addressed. ID-R sessions can be highly restimulative and triggering, causing new symptoms to appear afterward. Other phenomena may also occur after an ID-R session. These include having flashbacks of past incidents and changes in the quality or content of dreams. I have had several clients who found themselves in a temporarily uncomfortable state after a session, but in each case the discomfort faded in less than a day and never returned. After this, the positive effects of the session were even more pronounced. Some of the work, it seems, had continued unconsciously.

Somatic Conditions

The word "psychosomatic," which means "pertaining to the mind and body," is often equated with the word "psychogenic," which refers to something created by the mind. While these words usually refer to physical symptoms that are generated unconsciously, they are commonly thought of as meaning "imaginary," as in "it's all in your head," and have been used over the years to disparage people who have conditions with unknown causes. In the medical field however, these terms refer to very real physical conditions thought to have a mental or psychological origin, although exactly how psychogenesis works is unknown. The words "psychosomatic" or "psychogenic" may sometimes just be words to use when all known physical causes are ruled out.

I once commented to a girlfriend that her painful jaw might be psychosomatic. She got very angry. She thought I was invalidating her or telling her she was crazy. I was unable to clear up the confusion so I never used the word again. She was a nurse, and this made me wonder how often the word "psychosomatic" is being misunderstood and misused within the general milieu of the medical profession. In conversation I rarely use the word now, even with those who understand its true meaning, because it still unfortunately can elicit a negative response.

The word "psychosomatic" simply means the mind and body are an interactive system, not that the condition is unreal or imaginary. Understanding how this works is important because it affords each of us tremendous power to transform both our minds and our bodies. The word "psychosomatic" is being replaced more and more by the word "mind-body" or mindbody (unhyphenated) which does not share the same negative connotation. In the field of psychosomatic medicine, mindbody interactions are perceived and acknowledged as real. This field is vast and contains many decades of evidence of the effect of the mind on the body. ID-R reveals and confirms at least one actual mechanism by which the mind can affect the body, which is through the reemergence of past trauma in present time, in the form of pain, dysfunction, and other symptoms, and is confirmed by the resolution of such symptoms using mental processes.

Mind and Body

So what is the mind anyway? For now we can say that the mind is the sum of all the things about us that cannot be identified as part of the body, even if they depend on it. This would include our thoughts, emotions, memories, abilities, knowledge, personality, and conscious perceptions – all those internal conscious and unconscious aspects of ourselves that are not identifiable physical objects. We could liken the mind to the software in a computer system and the brain and body would be the computer hardware and peripherals. A purely mental or psychological complaint would then most likely be a software problem and best handled by working out the bugs in the programming. Using the computer metaphor, a hardware problem is resolved by fixing or replacing the hardware, which would include the body and all its systems. But the key lies in ascertaining whether a problem is caused by the hardware or the software, because in either case, both are involved. Faulty hardware in a computer can cause many problems, including total destruction of the system. Similarly software errors, or "bad code," can do the same.

In traditional medicine, any kind of physical complaint is thought of as entirely physiological and amenable to medical treatment – a hardware problem. A spiritual tradition or shamanistic approach would consider spiritual aspects as well, with the understanding that what happens in our lives, our minds, our bodies, and our communities, can be a manifestation of unconscious and spiritual conflicts, imbalances, and other influences. The mindbody system is complex – what affects the mind affects the body and vice versa. By convention, when I use the word "psychosomatic" I'm referring to that part of any condition that _originates_ in the mind, the software, and affects the body. My birth headaches affected my body but originated in a past trauma which was active in my mind. A broken finger is a physical condition that can affect us emotionally as well, but would not be called psychosomatic. However, if it failed to heal correctly or if there was unexplained pain in that finger later, those effects could very well be psychosomatic.

Gall Stone

Years ago I had some pain in the area of my gall bladder and it kept getting more intense. I figured it might be a gall stone, but I worked on it and here's what I found. One weekend when I was maybe three and a half years old I was visiting with some kids a few houses down from mine who were having some kind of play market using book shelves and cans of food. One of their mothers was helping them. I wanted to play too and they said I had to bring something, like a can of fruit, so I ran home to get one. My father was working on his car and saw me. He yelled at me to stay where he could see me. I went in the house and asked my mother for a can of fruit. She gave me a can of peaches but said I would have to ask my father before going back down the street. Instead, I went out the front door and tried to sneak past my dad. I saw him by the garage and his back was turned so I sped off down the street, legs moving with the blazing speed of a three-year-old. Suddenly I was swept up in the air, experiencing a terrific pain under the front of my right ribs. My dad had run after me and caught me from behind. But he didn't realize how hard he had grabbed me. The pain was quite intense and definitely a shock. I reexperienced that pain during the session, and resolved the trauma. The pain from the gall stone was almost immediately reduced by about 90%. The pain lingered on for a couple days and then was gone, I don't know for sure that it was a gall stone, but I do believe it was something physical. In any event, it's an example of a physical malady triggering a past trauma, whose symptoms then become part of the condition, in this case adding to the pain.

A somatic condition or symptom can come in many forms and be _acute_, like recurring pain, nausea, or dizziness, or _chronic_, like chronic pain, numbness, or infections. Such somatic conditions can be entirely or partially psychosomatic. I use the word "somatic" as a noun to refer to part of the physical pain or sensation emanating from a past experience. A somatic can be triggered by something mental or physical. Psychosomatic headaches, for example, can be triggered by a physical condition such as a tumor, an injury, or a psychosomatic headache from another source. They could also be triggered by a feeling or a thought.

The Aetiology of Hysteria

Sigmund Freud presented his seduction theory of neurosis in 1896 in a paper titled "The Aetiology of Hysteria," before an audience of colleagues and peers.[29] He was a brilliant man. He had apparently discovered that childhood trauma, particularly in the form of sexual violation, could have serious and debilitating effects on people for their entire lives.

In this paper he describes or alludes to most of the basics of ID-R. He discusses primal scenes (early trauma), traumatic force (the shock), chains of associations, trauma dormancy and reactivation, restimulation and much more. He even unknowingly points toward the shock moment and the power-zone when he mentions the "hypnoid state" aspect of trauma proposed by Jean-Martin Charcot and Josef Breuer. According to Jeffrey Masson, former projects director of the Freud Archives, Freud most likely even visited the Paris Morgue to observe the autopsies of young children who had been brutally assaulted physically and sexually.[30] Freud had done his research and could answer most objections. His presentation to a potentially hostile audience took considerable courage as well. He was incorrect about a lot of things, especially in his emphasis on sex, but he was on the right track, and if he had stayed on this path he might have changed the world in a positive and profound way.

Unfortunately Freud soon reversed his theory, replacing sexual trauma with sexual fantasy, so that although his psychology did have a huge influence, it placed the blame for neurotic symptoms on the fantasies of the victims of childhood trauma instead of the real cause. Why? Was this truly the rational result of his scientific and objective research, or did he succumb to fear, peer pressure, or his

---

[29] Reprinted in "The Assault On Truth" - 1984, Jeffrey Masson, Appendix B, & available online.

[30] Masson, 1984

own ego? In Masson's controversial book "The Assault on Truth," fear of being ostracized seems to be the predominant motivation, since his ideas were not well received and threatened to bring incest out in the open, and possibly expose some of his peers. This theory has been disputed. Or was it, as others believe, that Freud was reacting to the possibility that his own father might be a sex offender, as noted in a letter to his colleague and confidant Wilhelm Fleiss?[31] Possibly these were all factors but we will never know for sure. But we do know that before his reversal, Freud was on the right track.

Childhood sexual trauma is common, family members are often involved, and any unwanted conditions such traumas generate can be traced back to these incidents. In addition, as Freud himself discovered, the types of neuroses and hysterical symptoms he was investigating can and do emanate from such experiences, as well as from nonsexual trauma, and they can be resolved by correctly addressing them. Freud had abandoned this truth and instead came up with a complicated fantasy of his own, which became psychoanalysis. Freud's work reminded me of Claudius Ptolemy's geocentric astronomy many years ago, in a way which I later found beautifully expressed by Dr. Colin Ross in his book "Multiple Personality Disorder," in discussing MPD:[32]

"In Ptolemaic astronomy a vast machinery of cycles and epicycles was invented to explain the motion of the stars and planets. The cycles and epicycles were circular mechanical pathways that exerted force on the heavenly bodies and interacted like gear wheels to coordinate their motions. After Keppler the entire machinery was simply dropped. There are no epicycles in nature."

"Although Ptolemy was a genius, his astronomical theory is best described as antiquated. His genius lay both in his ability to observe

---

[31] "The Complete Letters of Sigmund Freud to Wilhelm Fliess 1887-1904" p264 - Masson - 1985

[32] "Multiple Personality Disorder: Diagnosis, Clinical Features, and Treatment" - 1989, Colin A. Ross M.D., p.140 - later revised and renamed "Dissociative Identity Disorder" in 1997.

and in his theory, but the theory was wrong. This is the situation with Freud. His vast and elaborate theoretical machinery is currently in peril and is endangered by Occam's Razor.[33] As an observer of psychopathology Freud will always be one of the greatest psychiatrists."

I mention Freud here to provide a little perspective, validation, and historical support for the concepts I've been discussing. More than a hundred years ago Freud was about to change our view of life in a different way than he did. But he and the world in general, were not ready for it. And for many reasons, the world is still not ready for the deeper understanding that can be provided by a clearer insight into human consciousness. But every step we as individuals take in the right direction brings us closer to the time when these things will be common knowledge.

Trauma and Recovery

Other psychological theories and healing methods based on resolving trauma were present in Freud's time and many others have been developed over the intervening years. However Freud's Psychoanalysis dominated psychiatry up until around the 1960's, while behaviorism dominated academic psychology. In the 1970's biological psychiatry began to dominate the mental health scene as it does today, for many reasons. But the effect of trauma has been effectively downplayed for a long time. One of the best books I've read on the subject of the history of the conventional understanding and treatment of trauma, is "Trauma and Recovery" by Judith Herman.[34] This book brilliantly describes the many social, political, and psychological forces that have conspired through history to keep the impact of trauma hidden from consideration and open discussion, and highlights the courage of those who worked hard to bring it out in the open. These early negative forces still exist, and the courage to overcome them must continue and be supported if

---

[33] Occam's Razor is the problem-solving principle that the simplest solution tends to be the correct one.

[34] "Trauma and Recovery" - 1992, Judith Lewis Herman

we want to see further progress in the understanding and healing of trauma.

Psychiatrist Bessel van der Kolk clearly describes the challenges he and those working with trauma in the medical fields have faced in the last four decades in getting trauma and its effects properly researched, understood, and treated, in his powerful best-selling masterpiece "The Body Keeps the Score."[35]

Many therapeutic methods were developed over the last century that specifically look to trauma as the cause of mental, emotional, and somatic conditions – methods like Primal Therapy, rebirthing, transpersonal psychology, the mindbody approaches of Dr. John Sarno, Peter Levine and others, EMDR, the Trauma Model Therapy of Dr. Colin Ross, psychedelic therapy, and many more. I'm sure there are many reasons why the effective aspects of these various approaches are not widely known or given more credit, although probably many thousands of practitioners worldwide now employ these and related methods to heal trauma and its effects, as opposed to just alleviating or managing symptoms. I mention these methods here because they represent the growing awareness of the effects of trauma and the value of mindbody approaches, and ID-R has much in common with all of them.

I believe that working with trauma does not yet dominate the mental health system and this approach is resisted as a methodology for three main reasons: pain, ignorance, and fear. Firstly, no reasonable person wants to experience pain or see someone else in pain. The issues that come up in processing trauma can be painful and frightening for both the client and the practitioner. This may seem like a questionable argument, but what I'm talking about includes fear of the unknown, which can be a very powerful force. There is nothing more terrifying than what lies hidden within our own minds. What we've experienced, what we've done, the pain and reactions that we may find within us, and the idea of losing control, can all be too difficult to confront. When inner pain starts coming up, it's common to want to stop it, or avoid it and cope in some other way, like drinking, taking drugs, and immersing ourselves in work or some other compulsive distraction or

---

[35] "The Body Keeps the Score" - 2014, Bessel van der Kolk

addiction. For a therapist, the things that come up for a client can be powerful triggers for their own reactions, especially if they are at all empathetic, which any good counselor should be. It's easier to avoid the truth, as Freud did. To quote Dr. van der Kolk, "Nobody wants to remember trauma. In that regard, society is no different from the victims themselves. We all want to live in a world that is safe, manageable, and predictable, and victims remind us that this is not always the case. In order to understand trauma, we have to overcome our natural reluctance to confront that reality and cultivate the courage to listen to the testimonies of survivors." Fortunately, the pain we encounter in counseling can be safely handled if approached with care and compassion.

The second reason for resistance is that most practitioners in the psychological healing arts are simply not aware of the impact of trauma on the human psyche, outside of a diagnosis of PTSD, although this is changing. Nor is there a clear consensus on how the human mind really works. Also, prior to the last three decades, the effectiveness of available methods for dealing with trauma was mostly hit and miss. They might work spectacularly sometimes and fail miserably most other times, and sometimes they make things worse. Without a good model of the psychological effects of intense experiences, this might lead us to think that trauma therapy is of little use, or even dangerous. When I asked several therapists about working with trauma many years ago, some were very much against it and seemed to think that the only things that come up in such work are false memories. It's as if many therapists have become brainwashed by the popular media. This is the result of both inadequate and misleading education on the subject, and the lack of awareness of effective treatment models in traditional education, even though there are many such models around.

The third reason for resisting working with trauma and the unconscious mind is a kind of fear that will take some explaining because it treads on controversial ground and is a central theme of this book. Some of the things that come up in sessions involving memories of trauma can be frightening to some people. They can challenge one's reality and threaten one's belief system, causing them to be judged as false or imaginary. When someone's experiences seem too unlikely or strange to be believed, the methods that brought these things to the surface may be considered

less credible or even abandoned. This is what happened with
hypnosis.

Hypnosis

In the mid-1800s, some medical practitioners in Europe,
especially in England, Germany, and France, were getting
extraordinary results in treating patients suffering from a wide
variety of problems using Mesmerism and other early forms of
hypnosis. Some results seemed miraculous. Hypnosis was used
during major surgeries, including amputations, as a way to
eliminate pain without anesthetics. Patients apparently experienced
little or no pain and superior healing. Because the results of
hypnosis and hypnotherapy rely on a passive belief and trust in the
process, they can easily be adversely influenced if that trust is
negated, by the same mechanisms that make hypnosis effective in
the first place. That is, negative suggestions can render hypnosis
ineffective. And that is precisely what happened after about 1867.
For various reasons, there was extreme opposition from the medical
establishment, which began an intense negative media campaign to
discredit hypnosis, and it worked! Soon hypnosis became less
effective and fell into disrepute.

Eventually hypnosis became more connected with the occult
and with stage hypnotists and entertainment, effectively reducing its
respect and significance as the powerful and authentic healing
method it is, in the eyes of the general populace. Unfortunately,
these attitudes still prevail. Even so, hypnosis was a staple for early
psychiatrists, and there are still many thousands of medical and
professional practitioners, as well as lay people, successfully using
hypnosis and hypnotherapy around the world today.

I earned my certification in advanced clinical hypnotherapy at
the Hypnotherapy Training Institute, a top state-licensed school in
California. One man who later came to see me at my office wasn't
aware I was a Hypnotherapist. When I told him, he quickly averted
his eyes. He was afraid I would put him under my spell like
Svengali. He was OK after I set him straight, and we both laughed
when he said he could now see that I looked "normal." When I
applied for a business license for hypnotherapy in 1995, the only
category it fell under in my city at that time was "Fortune Telling."

Part of what has worked against hypnosis, besides the fact that its often amazing results cannot be explained in purely physiological terms, is that very often spiritual phenomena emerge as a natural part of the process. Past-life memories, communication with spirits of the deceased, and people exhibiting psychic abilities, are just some of the many extraordinary things that often occur in the hypnotic state, and these kinds of experiences are often decried by religious authorities as being of ungodly origin, and are seen as imaginary or scientifically unfounded by the scientific establishment. Because these things are not religiously or scientifically acceptable in general, they are rejected by mainstream society. The history of hypnosis, the general bias against it, and the neglect in the reporting of various paranormal phenomena that regularly arose from its use, is well reported in Michael Murphy's phenomenal book "The Future of the Body."[36]

Considering what happened with hypnosis, I believe every method of human introspection and psychological advancement runs the risk a similar backlash if we are not careful, because we ARE spiritual beings and we HAVE spiritual experiences – experiences that transcend what is presently considered normal and explainable. The best way to approach any memories or experiences that appear while using hypnosis, ID-R, EMDR, meditation, or any other method of addressing the deeper hidden aspects of our minds, is to just be accepting of whatever comes up and to not immediately jump to any conclusions one way or the other. However, I believe many mainstream practitioners who use such methods of exploration usually ignore, avoid, or downplay any spiritual phenomena out of disbelief or for fear of delegitimizing their practice. This failure to accept and work with these experiences only contributes to the ongoing lack of acceptance of such phenomena, and fear of it, by most of society. On the other hand there are also many effective practitioners who do not ignore these things and who recognize, as I do, the importance of acknowledging all human experience. I am particularly impressed by veteran EMDR therapist Laurel Parnell, who has for many years recognized and effectively worked with the transpersonal

---

[36] The Future of the Body – 1992, by Michael Murphy

phenomena that arise in her sessions. I commend her courage to
write and speak about these things and highly recommend her 2007
book "A Therapist's Guide to EMDR" for anyone interested in a
deeper understanding of this process.

I used hypnosis in the mid 1990s to develop successful stop-
smoking and weight-loss programs. Hypnosis, hypnotherapy, and
self-hypnosis are powerful tools for transformation and I believe
everyone should know their basic principles and uses. They provide
very easy and powerful tools to help oneself and others, allowing us
to tap into our own deep well of power and potential. I think it's
critically important for doctors and other medical professionals to
be familiar with the power of suggestion, and most especially for
nurses who are in constant communication with people who need
help. Using the power of communication through facial expression,
words, and touch to change beliefs and expectations, can be a
powerful healing method when used wisely. Conversely, suggestive
communications that convey things like worry, doubt, and negative
outcomes can have very undesirable effects.

We may rarely think about how we are being influenced by
everything around us, but we are stimulated to be mass consumers,
pacified by the entertainment industry, addicted to the unhealthy
food we eat, controlled by every service we depend on, and
conditioned to accept it all as normal. By learning about hypnosis
you will become more aware of how the powers of the media,
advertising, the internet, religion, politics, social media, and
culture, are attempting to influence and control you every day, and
you will be less vulnerable to the propaganda and manipulation
which are so pervasive in our time.

Someone is Here

In 1997 a client named Wanda came in for help to stop
smoking. When I first got Wanda into a very relaxed hypnotic state,
she unexpectedly began speaking, saying that someone was with us.
Being ready for anything, I let her continue. She described an older
white-haired lady who said she was my mother. My mother had
died three years earlier. This lady had a message for me which was
then delivered. I didn't pursue this by asking any questions,
although I could have asked the client's permission during the

hypnosis. But I didn't want to interrupt the flow of communication or take advantage of my client's time for personal benefit. Instead I simply acknowledged the message, after which she said the lady was gone, and we continued with the session.

The message made perfect sense to me and allowed some closure. Among other things my mother thanked me for protecting her. I had taken care of her during her final years when she had cancer, and I had indeed been protective, from her viewpoint, although I had simply felt I was watching over her. After awakening Wanda, I questioned her and found she had no memory of the conversation concerning my mother, so I didn't discuss it with her. She never mentioned it again, and our other sessions were uneventful. I mention this experience as a personal example of the kind of things that occur in hypnosis that are often not reported. I have had many other experiences with clients during hypnotherapy or ID-R sessions, which involved spiritual or paranormal phenomena as well, and although these have been in the minority because we were not usually pursuing such things, they are still quite common. I learned hypnotherapy in 1994 because some of my dissociative ID-R clients were spontaneously going into trance states. I wanted to better understand those states and be more skilled at working directly with the unconscious mind, which is what hypnosis is all about.

Summary

Trauma has been studied for a long time, and in traditional psychology it is mainly acknowledged as the cause of its namesake, PTSD The fact is however that trauma, in all its forms, because of its lasting effects, is the most pervasive and detrimental causative psychological factor in the lives of every human being on Earth! The effects of trauma are especially significant during our developmental years. Developmental Trauma Disorder, or DTD, as a diagnosis proposed by Dr. van der Kolk, is a better way to classify the vast and long term effects of childhood trauma in general, in psychological terms. The devastating neurological and psychological effects that can be caused by trauma during our developmental stages are enormous, and are now well documented.

But what actually happens in a trauma has never been adequately understood for many reasons, and one reason is that trauma induces a profound altered state that is not remembered. The observation that post-traumatic symptoms form cohesive packages of associations, described here as identities, has also apparently been overlooked although alluded to in the Third Edition of the EMDR book.[37]

What ID-R reveals and what the model of how it works explains, once a general consensus of the reality and efficacy of these things is established, allows us to reinterpret most or all of the present workable therapeutic methods of working with trauma and its effects in a better way.

Furthermore, trauma is an EXPERIENCE, and some experiences are traumatic solely because of the conceptual MEANING we give them. So what one experiences in a shock, is subjective – it is not a piece of neurology or chemistry that can be altered in a material way, regardless of what materialists would like to believe. Traumatic impressions may well be stored in the brain, if "stored" is even the appropriate word, but they are primarily contained in consciousness, which is beyond the brain. Remember, there is no scientific explanation at all that accounts for the existence of consciousness itself in the universe, or proof that it is created by the brain. The good news is that what happens to someone in a traumatic shock can be recalled, if approached correctly, although there can be many obstacles to that. ID-R is just a better microscope to see through some of those obstacles, and we still have a long way to go. With care, persistence, and the right tools, trauma can be reversed. What hasn't been emphasized is the incredible potential that the healing of trauma can have in changing our lives, our societies, and the world.

---

[37] Eye Movement Desensitization and Reprocessing (EMDR) Therapy" Third Edition – 2018, Francine Shapiro

Chapter 7A
Multiple Personalities – Part 1
Introduction

"The best thing about being me ... there's so many of me."
– Agent Smith, The Matrix

When I was a child, the bedrooms of the house we lived in had crystal doorknobs. They looked like big diamonds with many facets and would reflect different colors from different angles. From the right perspective I could see my own reflection in several of the inner mirrors. I remember staring into my bedroom doorknob on a particularly gloomy day and fantasizing. I was maybe ten or eleven years old. I imagined that there were dozens of tiny children imprisoned there, trapped within the facets, sad, tortured, and frozen forever. I spoke quietly to them and promised that one day I would rescue them and set them free. My promise was prophetic.

Everywhere and Nowhere

Bats are one of the most prevalent mammals on Earth. There are more bats in this world than people, and they are estimated to number over ten billion. The number of bat species alone comprises more than one fifth of all mammalian species. They're everywhere. There are lots of bats in my area but I've never seen one, have you? Sure I've seen them in pictures and videos and documentaries, but I've never seen one for sure in real life, although I have seen evidence of them. Of course many people have seen bats in real life, especially those who live near huge colonies, but the vast majority of us probably have not. Ever seen a shrew? I haven't; yet shrews are another of the most common mammals in the world. So if these animals are all around, why don't we see them? Well, bats come out at night and fly silently in the dark sky and shrews live underground. Neither are easy to see unless you go looking for them, and to do that you have to know where, when, and how to look.

Multiple personality is a very common condition, as I will establish, yet it is rarely seen by anyone besides therapists who recognize and work with it. Although its foundations are simple, multiple personality is a vast subject, considering all its possibilities and ramifications. In this chapter I just want to give you a little preliminary information about this condition. We will be looking at what it is, how it comes into being, how it can affect one's life, and how it can be resolved, not as a disorder or even as a problem, but as a human condition.

When I was a senior in high school, we moved to a new house. We had been there a few weeks when a lady knocked on our door. My mother answered and the lady said she was our next door neighbor. She seemed quite freaked out and wanted to know if someone in our house had come over and washed all her dishes for her. She was home alone and apparently there were dirty dishes in the kitchen when she went to take a nap. When she walked back in the kitchen later, all the dishes had been cleaned. She swore she didn't do them herself. She feared an intruder. It was quite strange, and we just figured she must be crazy. If it turned out that she had multiple personalities however, it wouldn't be strange at all. She had dissociated, and while she "napped" the dishes were done by another personality, completely unbeknownst to her.

Most people have never seen a person with multiple personalities and don't know much about it except what has been sensationalized in movies or on TV talk shows, although there are now many videos on the subject on the internet. But multiple personality is unseen even when it's in plain sight because the fact is, multiple personalities can't be seen at all from the outside like you can see a bat or a shrew; an observer can only surmise its existence based on evidence. The _external_ evidence for multiple personalities is, as yet, entirely circumstantial. However, consciousness itself cannot be seen from the outside and cannot even be scientifically proven to exist, and yet we all know it's real. The only evidence for consciousness is personal and subjective; anecdotal if you will. Books on the subjects of dissociation and multiple personality, like Marlene Steinberg's excellent "Stranger in the Mirror" from 2001, will give you a better perspective on the likely prevalence of this condition in the population. Colin Ross made a sound argument in 1989 that at least 1percent of the US population has MPD, (multiple personality disorder) which is about the same rate as schizophrenia, a much more debilitating condition. He speculated that the percentage could be much higher. It is.

Multiplicity

MPD and its present DSM-V designation DID (dissociative identity disorder) are diagnostic labels applied to people who have multiple personalities.[38] Calling any condition of the psyche a disorder or a mental illness has traditionally been an aspect of the treatment process of categorizing such conditions as if they were medical disorders, when often they are actually something else.

A person with multiple personalities, who may be referred to as a "multiple," seems to have one or more additional personalities. Such people behave as if their body houses two or more different people, called "alters," any one of whom might take temporary control of the body and be the one in charge at various times. Alter personalities can be different ages and can differ in many ways, including how they look, speak, and act, and they can have very different attitudes, mannerisms, skills, and proclivities, as well as different memories. These different personalities, of which there could be many, may or may not know anything about each other. When an altar personality takes control of the body from the host or another alter, it's called "switching." If you are familiar with any of the literature on this subject, you will know that each of these unique people or personalities came into being to play a specific role in the person's life. They were considered by the person to be necessary in some way for survival or sanity during times of extreme duress or trauma, and were created somehow by the person's mind at those times to help in a particular way. I usually refer to alter personalities as "helpers."

It is believed that people with multiple personalities most often had a very traumatic early childhood that may have included unimaginable pain, betrayal, stressful conflicts, abandonment, cruelty, and sexual violation. This is often borne out in any valid

---

[38] Diagnostic and Statistical Manual of Mental Disorders, 5th Edition (DSM–5) - 2013 American Psychiatric Association

treatment process that explores the client's past either through
memory, corroborative witnesses, or material evidence. Many books
have been written about MPD and there are many ways of looking
at it and thinking about it. There are also many doctors and
therapists who believe it doesn't exist. They believe that all the
symptoms can be explained in other ways that don't require
believing there are separated aspects of the mind that act
independently as if they were other people. The very existence of
multiple personalities is very controversial, as are the various
theories about what they are or what the symptoms of MPD/DID
really represent. However, my observations and pragmatic
explanations in the following chapters render all debates on these
issues moot.

    MPD is considered a dissociative disorder, which means it
involves dissociation as one of its essential characteristics.
Dissociation in this context refers to the feeling or experience of
being detached or disconnected in some way from one's body,
perceptions, or surroundings, compared to what one would
normally be experiencing. Dissociation is often described as a
continuum from mild and normal to extreme and pathological.
Being mentally preoccupied or daydreaming where you are only
vaguely aware of what's going on around you is a mild dissociation
that we all experience. Various trance states or other altered states
induced by hypnosis, drugs, meditation, or even intense
concentration on a task may be experienced with a much greater
detachment, like you are in your own private world. In a dream you
are dissociated from your body perceptions, and usually experience
a diminished sense of reality. In an OBE or a lucid dream you are
dissociated from the body but may experience a normal or
enhanced sense of reality. None of these states of dissociation need
be a problem. Dissociation is labeled pathological when it is seen as
part of troubling conditions like dissociative fugue states, amnesia,
sleepwalking, depersonalization, derealization, and MPD/DID.[39]

---

[39] While depersonalization and derealization are altered perspectives that
may occur in dissociative states where one might feel the world or the self is
unreal, I do not consider them forms of dissociation in themselves. They
may be problematic however, or they may actually be signs of a spiritual

From the outside perspective a counselor can only hear the client's words, observe their behavior, and speculate about what's going on. A multiple might tell their counselor that they have periods of amnesia, during which they seem to have done or said things that they do not recall, or that they have been accused of things they didn't do. They may be cutting themselves or engaging in other maladaptive behavior that they seem to have no control over or don't even remember doing. They seek counseling because their lives have become unmanageable or they are suffering emotionally. They may hear voices or feel like they are going crazy. Or they may just be in counseling seeking relief from depression or anxiety. They usually have no idea that they might have other people within them. Without an understanding of dissociation or multiple personalities the counselor will never really understand what's going on in these cases. It's easy to be skeptical that a person has amnesia for things they obviously did, and if amnesia is confirmed it may be considered a neurological problem instead of a psychological one. If it is considered to be psychological in nature there are many theories to account for this and many treatment approaches which may be explored. Even when the therapist sees other personalities coming and going they may interpret these as mood shifts, acting, or as bizarre manifestations of mental illness, not as multiple personalities.

Multiple personalities cannot be seen or detected in any physiological way, although evidence of their existence has been well established through brain neuroimaging scans. Additionally it has been demonstrated that there is a brief interruption in EEG readings when a personality switch occurs, although brainwave patterns do not change, as far as we can see. This makes sense. Every alter personality is using the same nervous system, but the switch is a momentary disturbance in that system and probably should be detectable. Indeed, when using my GSR meter with clients I often see readings that indicate to me the possible presence of another personality. Also dramatic physiological changes can sometimes be shown when a switch occurs, including changes in physical appearance, voice, hearing, eyesight, health conditions,

---

awakening.

and other things. All these validating signs do not prove however that there is another personality present, no matter how obvious it is. That such changes have anything to do with an actual other personality existing can only be speculative, from an evidence perspective, even if it's true. So in spite of this being a real phenomenon there is no real "proof" so to speak, that this is not simply ONE person who is lying, acting, or just dysfunctional in some other way. Similarly, without the existence of microscopes someone could postulate the theory of microbes causing disease, but the evidence, however powerful, would still be circumstantial.

It's important to realize that most people would never suspect anyone of having multiple personalities. It's not a common perspective. We all tend to see people as single individuals, not a multiplicity of different characters. Even for someone who counsels people with this condition, multiple personality is not always readily apparent, and indeed my experience tells me that most cases of multiple personality are not likely to ever be discovered or even suspected by most conventional therapists. Part of the reason for this is that the media and the psychiatric community have labeled this condition as something extremely rare and bizarre, and whose very existence is still controversial. And there are other reasons we don't see it, one of which is that this condition is a protective measure whose efficacy usually relies on the truth remaining hidden. A chameleon wouldn't want you to know it can change colors; it just wants to hide and be safe.

The reality of multiple personalities is often first discovered in the therapist's office and born out by the therapist in conversations with the alters. Since we all have many different social identities which may present very different sides of our psyche, and which can display many different moods, emotions, and attitudes in different situations, distinguishing an alter personality from that mix can be very difficult, even when you are looking for it. And even if you suspect an alter personality, you will never know for sure until you actually "meet" them.

Prevalence

In his book "The Body Keeps the Score" psychiatrist Bessel van der Kolk describes his first encounter with a patient who had other personalities. Her name was Mary and he had actually been counseling her for about three months. When he was confronted one day by Jane, one of Mary's helper personalities, he was stunned, but maintained his composure and handled the situation well. However it seemed obvious to me that he had already had many patients with this condition and simply did not recognize it. He says "the emergence of distinct identities experienced in DID represent only the extreme end of the spectrum of mental life." I believe this probably reflects the majority consensus among those in the mental health fields who recognize MPD/DID as a valid condition, but it's totally incorrect. Multiple personality appears to be an extreme condition only because it is rarely diagnosed until it has _become an extreme problem_, or just too obvious to ignore.

The truth is that it doesn't require a severely traumatic childhood filled with sexual abuse for us to call a helper personality into being – anyone can have other personalities. All it takes is a specific need at a specific time during a traumatic moment. And other personalities can also come into being under conditions outside of trauma, although they cannot be created simply by hypnosis. Alters have reportedly been created in barbaric mind-control experiments under traumatic conditions, which is also a possibility. We will go deeper into all this later, but the creation of other personalities is a universal ability inherent in our own consciousness.

The incidence of childhood sexual abuse in the U.S. is said to be about 25%, affecting one out of every four people by one estimate. I believe it is much higher. Most childhood sex abuse is unreported. The incidence of childhood trauma of any kind is undoubtedly 100%, and everyone has experienced dissociation in some form. I don't think we all have alter personalities, but as I said, I do believe this condition is very common. Based on what I know about dissociation and multiple personalities, and what I have experienced with my clients, my guess is that _at least_ 30% of the people in the U.S. have other personalities, but I could be way off. In my own practice the percentage is higher, but this is obviously because I routinely check for it. By the way, I never tell a client they have other personalities. If they do, THEY tell ME. All I do is ask questions.

Many people with multiple personalities never switch or rarely do, some do so occasionally, and some do many times a day every day. Just as every person's internal programming and system of identities (operational states) is unique, every multiple's internal system of helpers is different and may be simple or very complex. I often hear people describe family members or friends as "Jekyll and Hyde" types who occasionally behave in uncharacteristic ways or shift into strange moods at the drop of a hat. This is a sign they could possibly have multiple personalities, but is not definitive. Some people with multiple personalities have lives so out of control that their behavior seems crazy to the people around them. Once their multiplicity is recognized however, their behavior becomes easier to understand. These would be people like Sybil (Shirley Mason) who was depicted in the book of the same name by Florence Schreiber, or Truddi Chase who wrote "When Rabbit Howls." I have had several clients like this.[40]

In 1992 at the age of forty-four I discovered that I had other personalities myself. My own case fell somewhere between the first and second types mentioned above, as I would switch occasionally when triggered to do so. Using ID-R I was able to heal the trauma that caused my dissociation and to integrate with every helper personality I found. As it is for most people, my multiplicity was very well hidden – nobody ever knew. Most of the time multiplicity remains hidden very easily since most people are not even aware of its possibility. Even when you have watched documentaries and seen multiples on talk shows, you will not consider it as a possibility in real life until it somehow affects you personally. Even then it may be difficult to believe. Yet when you understand multiplicity and work with it extensively you tend to see possible signs of it

---

[40] There is some controversy as to whether Shirley Mason was faking her condition and whether both her psychiatrist and the author of "Sybil" were complicit. They all may have tried to capitalize on the sensationalism, but given all the information and the deep biases, ignorance, and dubious motives of those who support such theories I find this untenable. In the book, one of her alters claimed Sybil was faking her condition. This was a self-protective reaction and is understandable. I've done the same thing myself.

everywhere. However, since it can't actually be seen, one can only suspect it, until it's too obvious to dismiss.

MPD is a condition that can be completely resolved through trauma resolution and integration. It is also possible for someone to resolve the problems they were having and still retain their other personalities. Most people who have multiple personalities are oblivious to the fact, and are living normal lives. These may include many of the people you know, or even yourself.

I believe there are many very good clinical practitioners around the world who have workable understandings, theories, and treatments of trauma, MPD, and other dissociative conditions. In the arena of those who accept these diagnoses, the most widely accepted treatment protocols do recognize alter personalities as individuals and work with them as such, in the context that they form a part of a more or less complex system – a system which is ultimately one individual human being. The idea is that the person has split their consciousness and fragmented their mind in a way that allowed them to survive and function in intolerable circumstances. I see all this a bit differently.

Working with someone with many personalities who has experienced massive childhood trauma can be difficult, for many reasons, and ordinarily may take several years to complete, depending on the desired outcome. Today the treatment usually involves, to some degree, confronting and healing the traumatic foundations of a client's condition and integrating the various personalities into one unified person. While this approach is basically the same as my own, I believe my experiences, both personal and in working with others, will provide a better and more accurate understanding of the condition of multiple personalities, and a simpler and faster means to its resolution. Discovering my own multiplicity was a major revelation that is hard to describe!

Chapter 7B

Multiple Personalities – Part 2
My Cast of Characters

"Some friends can be quite a pain and still be a true blessing."
– Pipananda

In the summer of 1991 I was reading "Sybil" by Flora Schreiber. Here was the story of a lady who had sixteen separate personalities who each seemed to be a different person altogether. I assumed this was a real phenomena, and the alter personalities were just specialized identities, as defined earlier. I was trying to figure out how Sybil had managed to create all her alter personalities and operate within each of them without any memory of doing so when she was in her primary identity. Actually there were a great many puzzling questions regarding her condition. I imagined that part of the structure of these special identities was that the specific memories and abilities of each one was set up in such a way that while she was operating from one identity viewpoint, other parts of her memory track were somehow blocked. She was in effect "being" these different people. and would "switch," or become a different character, when specific conditions triggered the necessary reaction. This would require immediately accessing all the memories and abilities of the new character while blocking all her own memories and those of all her other characters – quite a phenomenal feat!

If an actor had to perform in five different plays in one day and act as a different character in each one, I imagine it would take a lot of practice. Mel Blanc, who provided the voices of Bugs Bunny and dozens of other cartoon characters, reportedly could switch between characters instantly and effectively at a moment's notice, which he had to do when playing multiple characters in one cartoon. When doing a different voice, his whole expression and posture would change to that of the character, as any good impressionist does when performing. Each character he portrayed was a different identity state. Yet what Sybil seemed to be doing was a thousand times more complicated. I wasn't even considering at the time how these personalities all seem to exist and interact at the same time with all their various differences. The whole system of memory, ability, and personalities had to be unthinkably complex. Also the basic nature of this condition of multiple personalities had to be hidden in the unconscious mind and not under conscious control. Although this is precisely how our programming works, as an unconscious matrix of many interacting parts, and while I intuitively felt that Sybil's condition was probably real, I couldn't really understand it. The current thinking at the time chalked it all up to the creative use of imagination in the face of terrible trauma. But if this was imagination, it had to include some very powerful and unexplained mental abilities, like the ability to completely block pain or turn off fear at will. But then again, our minds can do some amazing things. I felt I would understand all this better in time.

Almost from the beginning of working with the concept of identities I was noticing in some of my own traumatic incidents, identities that seemed to interact. One aspect of dealing with stuck identities during the ID-R process involves looking at the relationships between various identities, particularly the "before" and "after" identities appearing in a shock. This can often clear up hidden inner conflicts. Sometimes there seemed to be more than two identities involved in a traumatic shift, but I attributed this to there probably being more than one shock in that particular incident. This does happen quite often and many traumatic incidents are actually a whole cluster of shocks. However sometimes an identity seemed to have a life of its own, or at least a mind of its own. At the time I just took this as me being in various viewpoints and having feelings of conflict or support for the previous states I was operating in. For example you could be angry at someone, then mad at yourself for verbally expressing it to them, and then sad that you hurt their feelings – three conflicting identity states in a few seconds. It was interesting, but I didn't puzzle over it too much because I assumed I knew what was going on. I didn't.

In October of 1991, I was working on an issue that led me to a past life in which I had multiple personalities. The details are unimportant but what was interesting was that I recalled being three different people, or at least three very different identity systems, in one male body – a man, a woman, and a child. All three were interacting during some inner turmoil surrounding my death in that life. I still thought these personalities were just very discrete identities and I spent a year pondering this whole phenomenon, thinking I had some understanding of it. As a side note, this incident, and some others, suggested to me the possibility that at the time of death there is an automatic and total integration of any and all alter personalities.

Later I discovered a childhood incident where I was being threatened or tormented in some way. The situation was unclear but something was created in the shock which seemed to me to be an imaginary child. I called him Safe Place. He was created to live behind a brick wall and always be safe even if I wasn't. This seemed to give me hope and the ability to go on by preserving a sense of safety for me. I assumed this was all imaginary however, and that he didn't actually exist. I discovered soon after this the existence of an imaginary friend when I was around two years old. No one would interact with me and I was feeling all alone. I had a shock at the idea that my life would always be this way. Suddenly this friend was there. He talked to me and made me laugh so I didn't feel so alone. Once again I assumed this was purely imaginary but operating unconsciously – a mental mechanism or robot friend if you will. Discovering Bill changed everything.

Bill

Sometimes to initiate a session, instead of working on some particular issue, I simply look around "in my space." What this means is, I close my eyes and let myself be open to whatever is around me in my psychic, emotional, or physical space. To understand this, just sit and close your eyes and be quiet – something is there. In fact your whole mind is there, and if you try to remember something, something will show up – and if you ask your unconscious mind to show you something significant, it may appear. Sometimes nothing much shows up and other times I might notice a sensation or a pressure in my body, an emotion, an attitude, or something visual. What shows up could be anything. Sometimes I simply ask my unconscious mind to show me something useful or important to work on. This is a simple autosuggestion that does not require being in hypnosis but which brings something up in my awareness. Usually though, I notice something looming somewhere within or around me right away.

On one occasion of checking my "space" I noticed a hazy red splotch that seemed to have some solidity to it. As I worked with this, it soon became a vision of a red couch and I was feeling very sad and humiliated. Then I was watching a young boy being raped by an adult man on the red couch. I was out of my body floating helplessly above the scene. I worked through this trauma, as ghastly and as difficult to confront as it was, and when I was done I felt a strange sense of relief. But there was still this poor kid on the couch. That was me of course, I thought, but there was still the viewpoint of being in the body while this assault was taking place, which I had not yet experienced in a physical way, but only as an observer from a distance.

The "before identity" in this trauma was "me being cornered" and assaulted. The "after identity" was "me being out of my body watching." But there was this third viewpoint. I had to go in and assume the identity of being in the body – I had to BE the guy this was happening to. So I did. I imagined going into his body and looking through that identity's eyes with the intention of feeling my emotional and physical states at that time.

As I did this there was an odd subtle sensation of entering another reality, and as I looked through the body's eyes, something happened. For a moment I felt very different – I felt like someone else! This feeling passed quickly, but I now found myself in a strange emotional state with lots of images and thoughts buzzing around, beneath the surface. Suddenly, I had the experience of looking down a long corridor that had many doorways and in each was a memory of a past event. It wasn't literally that way but that's the best way I can describe it. I became aware of several powerful and disturbing memories, and I had to work through a few of these as soon as I could. It's like I had broken through a wall into a hidden room in my mind filled with previously unknown past experiences. What had happened?

Without any preconceptions or any intention to do so, I had integrated with an alter personality. His name turned out to be Bill, and I had immediately gained access to his memory track. In the incidents I worked through later that day, I was able to recall each entire event both as myself and as Bill. We were two separate people. He wasn't imaginary, and he wasn't me. And yet now we were one. How can this be? I believe that what happened cannot be understood properly without a better understanding of consciousness itself, and I will discuss this in more detail in the sections on integration.

So I experienced the initial incident on the red couch as myself and as Bill, and had resolved the trauma and gained an amazing sense of freedom. The disturbing nature of the memories that surfaced right after that had little to do with Bill's emotions. Bill was a victim personality who took my place whenever sexual assault was eminent. The sexual assaults didn't bother Bill as much as they did me, as he had accepted his fate and adjusted to it long ago. In fact he saw himself as a protector and found meaning in being the victim. The problem was that I had blocked my memories but Bill hadn't blocked his. Integrating with Bill forced his memories upon me immediately. Fortunately my ability to confront these awful experiences had become greatly enhanced from all the work I had done on myself up to this point, and I was not retraumatized. However, I don't know that the preparation was actually necessary. I now believe that if I were not ready to integrate, it simply would not have happened. I would have protected myself from that until I was ready. I call the method I used for merging with Bill's viewpoint "Directed Confluence" (DC), which is a good descriptive term, but I usually just refer to it as "personality integration" or PRI.

After this session it was necessary to work through the new incidents I now recalled, right away, because, while to Bill these kinds of events were ordinary, to me they were very upsetting. It was like trying to hold on to a hot potato. They were there and I had to do something with them immediately, so I worked through these new memories and felt amazingly transformed. These incidents included a later rape by a scout master when I was in the Boy Scouts, and a few embarrassing moments when something triggered me to switch with Bill. I later discovered many more of Bill's memories including the incident of his origin, but for some reason these few initial emergent memories were right on the surface. After the integration, other phenomena occurred which verified even more, to my own mind, that Bill was a separate person with his own physical posture, facial characteristics, and "projected presence," and that he was nothing like me. He was a victim and a replacement for me when I was faced with a certain type of threat, specifically male sexual predators.

After these sessions my memories of the traumatic assaults felt very impersonal in that I felt no sense of identification with them. There was no sense of anger, grief, shame, or any other negative emotion present in a personal sense, when I thought about them. Those had been experienced and released during the process. Now it was more like I was observing things that happened to someone else, even though I knew they had happened to me, and I felt the natural and appropriate feelings as I might when thinking about these things happening to others. I simply no longer had any personal stake in these events in any emotional or psychological way. This is healing, and this is freedom.

Incidently, when I speak of "projected presence" I mean a specific vibe, energy, or charisma someone projects to others – it's the feeling you get around them and the atmosphere they seem to create. Whether it's love, calmness, authority, confidence, gloom, humor, fun, or fear, we've all experienced people with a strong presence. It's quite amazing how perpetrators can spot people who are easily victimized and how victims often have a sort of internal radar to detect these predators as well. It's about being sensitive to an aspect of the other person's presence. While I see this to be primarily a psychic or spiritual phenomenon, you may also think of it as being sensitive to subliminal perceptual cues. This phenomenon has been described to me by many clients I have worked with and is commonly described in the literature regarding sexual abuse and multiple personality.

Bill's "projected presence" was quite strong, as was his radar. After integration, this presence disappeared and I noticed very significant positive changes in a few people's attitudes toward me. One in particular was quite dramatic, but this was all subliminal – these people were not consciously aware of the change. Some people are more sensitive to these things than others while some seem to have no such sensitivity at all. Of those who are sensitive, some seem to "tune in" to one particular aspect of a person's presence, or that of an alter personality, and sense mainly that.

Bill's Origin and Transformation

After discovering Bill I could have attempted to recall many more of his experiences but decided to just continue to work on the issues that came up each day. However, many more incidents involving Bill did come up over the next four weeks as new memories and emotions bubbled to the surface, allowing me to see how he had transformed and aged over time. Finding his origin showed me how helper personalities are usually created, at least in my own case.

In the incident of Bill's origin I was less than a year old and could not yet talk although I understood my name and many words. I was lying in a crib when a strange man began to rape me. The pain caused Medic to appear and I left my body. Another shock was caused by my confusion about what was happening – I needed to know what to do. The man kept calling me "Baby William" which of course was the wrong name. Because of this, while operating in the power-zone, I decided that he had the wrong person and that this was a big mistake. It instantly occurred to me that someone else was supposed to be there whose name was William, and this solution became a request. Immediately another person appeared and went into the body to be the unfortunate victim. William was basically a duplicate of me except that he appeared to have an enhanced ability to physically tolerate being raped. From then on, he took over immediately whenever similar circumstances or threats occurred. The switches were automatic. Something would trigger me to dissociate and William would be "called," so to speak, to step in. When I was in my twenties William started to grow up and began calling himself Bill.

When I was five years old, after dealing with another sexual assault, Bill protested to me that he didn't want to be the victim anymore. He wanted to play and have fun and do different things like I did. I told him that being the victim was his purpose and that I needed him. I said that without him someone else would have to suffer. He had a big shock of his own at the prospect of being doomed forever to playing this role. His solution was to find meaning in it as a protector and to see this as a sacrifice. However this trauma left him in a strange stunted and depressed state because he had to suppress all prospects of joy and ambition. It left me feeling guilty and very sad as well. After working through this experience, all of these negative feelings vanished.

Bill was created by my own higher consciousness (or unconscious mind or brain if you prefer) in response to a request. This request wasn't verbal but was a felt sense of need for a specific kind of solution. In almost every case in which I have had an insight into the origins of my helper personalities, there was a similar knowing request for a helper, and the helper appeared, possessing whatever attributes and abilities they required to do their job. I never imagined them or dreamed them up consciously in any way that I recall – I only asked for a helper. Some people however, may imagine having a helper or an alternative self, for some time, and find that image brought to life later during a shock, as a real being. There were a few incidents where I needed a helper and one appeared but I couldn't spot any request, although I suspect there was one. In looking at a traumatic shock, the goal is mainly to resolve it, so I don't presume that I've ever seen everything that occurs in any particular shock.

Before I go on, I want to express something that I may not make clear elsewhere. I have made it a point, for the most part, to avoid dramatic, detailed, and emotionally triggering descriptions of the unimaginable pain, terror, rage, grief, and horror, that were a part of many of my traumatic experiences. Trauma is always overwhelming, by definition, but there are degrees of suffering in others that we can't even imagine or relate to until we recall such things in ourselves. When I leave such descriptions out of my narratives, or downplay the soul-crushing impact of some of these experiences, it is mainly to lessen the triggering effect on the reader, and to maintain a lighter narrative atmosphere more conducive to my message of healing and hope. I also don't want to give the impression that working through trauma is easy. Even with ID-R it takes some work, and while this work is totally worth the effort, it can temporarily be very uncomfortable.

Integration

In the Identity Model, every helper personality is a viewpoint in the host's own consciousness that branches out like a tributary stream that flows from a river. In fact the host theirself is a tributary of this river. The main river in this metaphor is what I call the Higher Self. And the Higher Self is a viewpoint which flows from the ocean of consciousness itself which is Infinite Aware Being. In this multidimensional model each of us is a viewpoint of a Higher Self which may have many such viewpoints, some of whom may be helper personalities existing with us, while some may be living parallel lives in other bodies in other places and even other times. This will all be discussed more completely later on. "Directed confluence" refers to the merging of two tributaries of consciousness into one stream, by intention. By directing your attention into the conscious viewpoint of a helper personality to experience what they experienced, your viewpoints will merge and become one. This is integration. Integration can happen in other ways as well but the result is the same. Theoretically integration should allow the host to have access to all of the memories and abilities of the helper, but this does not seem to happen automatically, and may not happen at all. It appears that most of the memories and abilities of helper personalities submerge into the unconscious mind and may become very difficult to retrieve.

For me, over the next two years after discovering this integration technique, I discovered, within myself, a total of seventy-two helper personalities. After that I stopped counting. Most of these helpers were only active once or twice and were otherwise dormant or perhaps became commentators or observers behind the scenes. For example one, called Juke Box, would play songs in my head that fit the situation I was in, usually to cheer me up and with a quite humorous effect. While all of my main characters have been integrated, I could possibly have a few more of these "one time" helpers who still remain dormant and undiscovered. However, since I healed my reactive dissociation long ago, switches are no longer possible.

Since every alter personality is created to help, I prefer to call them "helpers" or PRs, for "personalities," or perhaps jokingly "Public Relations." The original person being helped, Dennis in my case, is usually referred to as the "host" personality. As I progressed in my sessions I integrated with each helper as soon as they were discovered, using directed confluence as I did with Bill. I also once asked another personality to integrate with ME. I had a dream of a silhouette of a person trying to communicate with me.

When I worked on this dream, I realized it was a helper that wanted to integrate. I explained to him how to do it himself and waited to see what happened. It worked! I felt the momentary joy of being out in the physical world as if for the first time and a brief sense of relief, but I don't know anything more about him.

With regard to safely working through trauma and integrating helper personalities, I don't know that everyone can do what I did on their own, but it can be done, and it can certainly be done with the assistance of a good facilitator. There can be difficulties however, when doing this type of work solo, without help. Some of the things we experience can be horrendous and extremely difficult to confront by ourselves. There were a few times when I felt like I was literally going to die or go insane, and times I had to stop due to excessive pain or anxiety. But these difficult states were just reactions connected to the very issues I was dealing with, and my fears were never justified – I always ended up laughing about it later. In working with others I have employed the same methods of trauma resolution and personality integration, and have facilitated the integration of any discovered helpers quickly, with no problems. This is not always possible, but in people who are relatively stable, as I was, this seems to be the best route. In the stories that follow, whenever I mention discovering another personality in a session, that helper was normally integrated right away, although I may not describe it.

A Condition with Consequences

According to the latest official diagnostic manual of mental disorders, multiple personality refers to the experience of having two or more distinct identity or personality states, each with its own relatively enduring pattern of perceiving, relating to, and thinking about the world and the self. However, a diagnosis of MPD or DID also requires that a person dissociates – or forgets – between the different states, and that the experience impacts them negatively. The assumption is that multiple personalities are different states of one person, one consciousness. But this is only how the condition appears from the outside and does not explain what is actually happening.

The term "dissociative identity disorder" was adopted in the U.S.
by the American Psychiatric Association and is used by those who
adhere to its diagnostic guidelines. I prefer to call the condition
Multiple Personality, as do many others. But DID is actually a
better name for MPD, except that multiple personality is not a
disorder. An alter personality IS like a dissociated identity in a way,
but it is SO dissociated that it actually IS another person – a person
with their own experiences, memories, and different identity states.
However, the DID label still implies, at least for me, that these
identities are not real or that their separation is the result of some
kind of splitting or fragmentation. In truth, alter personalities are
created from whole cloth, in one moment, to be what they are.
Helpers are people, even if some helpers may seem to be mere
fragments of a person, and they were created to help, regardless of
how it might seem. Nothing is split, shattered, fractured, splintered
off, or anything of the sort. Although this may have been a
reasonable model in the past, these types of metaphors are
antiquated and based on a fundamental misunderstanding.
Unfortunately they still persist to this day.

All that being said, a person could perceive the creation of a
helper personality as some part of theirself being split off or lost, but
that would just be a story – a way they explain it to themselves to
give it a particular meaning. For example I might recruit a helper
who is cheerful because I have decided, in a shock, that I will never
be cheerful again. I may tell myself that this helper is the cheerful
part of me which has split off so that at least my cheerfulness can
still exist somewhere and not be completely annihilated. In
actuality I have only suppressed my own cheerfulness, but this story
preserves the desired illusion that it's permanently gone while still
allowing the possibility of presenting a cheerful face to the world,
via my helper, when necessary.

Moreover, in a multiple, various functions and situations may be
handled by specific helpers, kind of like an internal government,
giving the illusion of fragmentation. Every person's internal psychic
organization and programming is unique anyway, and if multiple
personalities are involved, things can be quite complicated and
chaotic because, in such a case, we have a mix of automatic
reactions, including dissociation, along with autonomous

individuals acting according to their nature, who themselves have automatic reactions.

Having multiple personalities is considered a disorder because it is thought to be a disruption in the normal functioning of the mind, when in fact it is caused by the utilization of natural human abilities. The result can be "disorder" in the sense of chaos or confusion in one's life, but not in the sense of a medical problem or a mental illness or abnormality. All these terms have negative social connotations as well.

In the movie "127 Hours" (2010), which was based on a true story, a young man is trapped in a desert canyon for five days with his arm pinned under a rock. Alone, and with no way to get help, he eventually amputates his injured arm to free himself. He was facing certain death and had to do this in order to survive. Now he is missing an arm, which is a limitation but not an illness or a disorder. This man made a choice in order to stay alive, and now he has to live with the consequences. Although the choice was radical and had a major impact on the rest of his life, to him, at that time, it was absolutely necessary. He could not see any other options. Creating other personalities to help one survive or maintain sanity or integrity in threatening situations is a similar choice with its own unique set of consequences. But it is not a disorder, a pathology, or a mental illness. It is simply a condition, and one that has been misunderstood, doubted, and feared for far too long.

Most people with multiple personalities would not be diagnosed with MPD because their lives are not so out of control that the condition is their main problem. My main problem in life was not the fact that I might dissociate under certain conditions or that I had helpers – it was my social fears and lack of confidence, which had been set up by all the trauma I had experienced. In fact it's hard to say that there was a "main" problem really – our personal predicaments are the sum of all our experiences. If a person is trapped under a large pile of rocks, some rocks might be heavier than others, but which rock is the main problem?

In my case some of my helpers were major players in my life, guiding me, taking my place under certain conditions, and generally always coming forward automatically when needed if something triggered me to dissociate. Other characters surfaced once, when they were created, or a maybe few other times, and

remained either asleep, or perhaps as silent witnesses the rest of the
time. There were nine helpers whom I would call main characters.
The two of those most important to my life's direction were
Dennis–2, and Lydia. Of the others, Bill, Denise, Hero, Buffer (also
called Gordie), and Medic, were involved in protecting me from
abuse, physical assault, and pain. Meany (also call Harry) and
Cindy also had a good number of appearances. While I have
recalled hundreds of stories involving my team of helpers since my
integration with them, I've tried to select only those that are useful
in telling my story and providing a basic understanding of the
origin, operation, and integration of multiple personalities. I will
introduce some of these characters here and others later on.

Dennis–2

Even before I discovered Bill, I was aware of Dennis–2 but I
thought he was some sort of identity – just me operating at a
different level of consciousness or perhaps just an aspect of my
unconscious mind acting as a guide. I even called him Dennis–2
without knowing why. When it became apparent that he was a
separate entity, I still didn't know what to make of him. Later I
discovered his unique origin but I was not able to integrate with
him and he seemed to disappear. However, he initiated our
integration himself two weeks after I had integrated with Bill, once
he had become sure that he was no longer needed in his role as my
primary guide toward my life's purpose.

Dennis–2 was created when I was around six-and-a-half years
old. He seemed like a duplicate of me but unfettered by the
personal issues I was hindered by. Yet Dennis–2 was a mysterious
and powerful force. On the one hand he was funny, confident,
inventive, fearless, and, since he was rarely in the body, he had
great psychic abilities and possessed knowledge which I did not. He
even seemed to be present in some of my prenatal and early
childhood experiences long before his own origin. This baffled me
at first and I thought I had missed something. Now I believe that he
could actually time travel and went into the past to guide me,
perhaps from the beginning of my life. I'll explain how this might
be possible later on. When a switch with another helper was
triggered, Dennis–2 usually didn't interfere, although he had the

ability to switch with any of us voluntarily. Our switches were never automatic; it was always his choice to come out.

And that was a problem, because there was a dark side to Dennis–2. Sometimes he was a valuable ally and other times he appeared to be a mean and mischievous spirit who delighted in making my life miserable. Although he got me out of some jams and helped and supported me many times, he also interfered in my life in emotionally devastating ways, getting me in trouble, and coercing me with frightening threats into doing things I didn't want to do. However my awareness of him, or any of my helpers, was fleeting and usually occurred only during moments of shock, or during a switch. At these times I either felt gratitude for his help or fear at his threats. I actually experienced him as two different entities – one was my guide and savior and the other was my adversary – I didn't know he was playing both roles. His ability to kick me out of the body was frustrating and often made me feel crazy. But he was untouchable and I could do nothing to stop him. Dennis–2 altered the course of my life.

Buffer and Medic

Buffer and Medic were discovered shortly after Bill, when new somatics from my birth experience started occurring. I was experiencing pain in my lower left hip and groin. As I described earlier, when the doctor was holding me upside down after delivery, he dropped me and caught me by the left ankle before my head could hit the table. Although it was a very short drop, it caused incredible pain to shoot through my hip and groin as my muscles and joints were jolted. Every muscle in my body tightened in response. In that moment my life depended on taking my first breath, and this shock was interfering with that – I needed help. I needed someone to hold that pain for a moment so I could focus all my attention on this immense and desperate burning need that became my first breath.

Buffer came into being to hold the pain for me for just a moment, while I dealt with the pressing problem of breathing. She seemed to emerge from some inter-dimensional or temporal doorway to appear precisely at the moment of shock in order to take it from me, even though I experienced it first. It was as if she stepped backward a moment in time, but this may have all taken place in the power-zone which lies outside of time. Buffer only had the ability to hold the pain briefly without doing anything about it, but her time quickly expired, and I was still not breathing. Now SHE needed help and Medic was born. Medic pictured herself dressed like one of the nurses and wore a white hat. She received the pain from Buffer and handled it herself by deeply suppressing it, as most of us often do with traumatic pain. Meanwhile, I was finally breathing and had been spared the whole ordeal of having to also deal with the pain and injury of being dropped.

The creation of a helper personality usually presents a great liability. It jeopardizes autonomy and can create other problems. I think we instinctively know this on some level, and don't call for such help unless we can see no other viable alternative. However, after one has begun acquiring helpers, at some point there may be less concern, and their creation can become almost routine.

Buffer was supposed to have a very limited role – to provide a time-buffer or queue, so to speak, between the shock of physical pain and my dealing with it. Once I was breathing she would pass the pain back to me, and I would deal with it myself. When this strategy failed, Medic was created because Buffer was not equipped to actually handle the pain. Medic, however, could handle anything. The problem is, that from that moment on, EVERY shock that was CAUSED by pain was immediately captured by Buffer and handed off to Medic, who dealt with it. They worked as a team. As a result, whenever something caused me intense pain, if it was enough to cause a shock, I experienced it so briefly that it was as if I didn't feel it at all. This doesn't mean I never felt pain; I felt lots of pain! But when pain reached the shock threshold, it disappeared. Although I always experienced the initial pain-induced shock myself, my reaction was to dissociate and let the dynamic duo handle it, just as I did at birth. Here's an example:

When I was thirty, I accidentally cut my nose on a nail that was sticking out of a kitchen cabinet. I picked up something from the floor and when I stood up quickly there was a tremendous impact. I dropped to the floor and said to myself "I'm dead" and started laughing. I wasn't sure what had happened. I knew I had hit the cabinet door but I thought it was a blunt impact. Amazingly, there was no pain at all. Then I felt the blood running down my face and went to the hospital with a deep rip in my nose. Although I didn't remember feeling any pain at the impact, Medic's pain, as I discovered later, was intense. I did feel a lot of pain minutes later, but it was tolerable.

Hence, Medic became the repository of all my traumatic physical pain from the day I was born, and this pain was all deeply suppressed. Buffer, on the other hand, never held on to any pain. Since they were partners, Medic wanted Buffer, who had no gender in the beginning, to be a girl. In my mind I saw them as two young girls with long curly ringlets of light brown hair. Buffer was taller and chunkier and they were always smiling. I called her Buffer from the beginning but later discovered that Medic had named her Gordie, after Flash Gordon, who we watched on TV when I was a child, because Buffer always appeared instantly, like a flash of light. Medic named herself. While handling painful situations, Medic would also become concerned whenever the body was in danger of being damaged. She would usually be the one who called upon Hero, when his services were needed.

Hero

Once I knew what to look for, discovering my helpers became easy. Any time I noticed I was exterior during a shock, I would look to see if another personality was present. By "exterior" I mean viewing the scene as if you are outside the body, outside of yourself, or dissociated in some way. You may be viewing events looking down from above or from some other vantage point. You may be close to the body, far away, or partially in the body. You may be in or near the body and able to hear but not be able to see. There are many possibilities. You may even be in the body and seeing everything through your physical eyes yet not be in control of what you are saying or doing. You may be feeling what is happening, or be completely numb to it. Whatever the dissociated viewpoint is, I look from there to see whether the body is active or unconscious. If the body is active, I check to see if there is another personality taking my place. I also look to see if there are any *exterior* helpers present. If I do spot any helpers, I integrate immediately after resolving the trauma. Since the memories may be somewhat vague, and since part of this process is visualization, it may seem at first that this is all imaginary, until the integration happens. It's one of those things you have to experience to really understand.

I first discovered Hero after recalling an incident I had completely blocked from my mind. It was a drunken brawl outside a downtown tavern I worked at for awhile in my early thirties. I was trying to protect a young lady co-worker named Claudia from being raped by two men. It was around 3:00 A.M. and we had just gotten off work. I was going to walk Claudia to her car, but while I spoke to these two guys she lay down on the bench we were standing next to. She was very drunk and passed out. At this time of night the streets were deserted and we were the only one's there. One of the men suggested they rape Claudia, and I told them that wasn't going to happen. But something one of the men said triggered me to switch with a personality called Bodyguard. His only job was to keep Bill from taking over. One of the men got Bodyguard in a headlock and began hitting him. While he was getting pummeled, Medic was doing her part but was in fear that we would sustain some serious physical damage. Medic quickly called for the warrior.

The warrior didn't have a name. He seemed to come from some far away place and usually took several seconds to appear, as he did this night. Once he arrived, he immediately reversed the headlock and told the guy that he would kill him instantly if he didn't stop. When the guy laughed and said "How ya gonna do that?" the warrior explained calmly, with absolute confidence, exactly what he would do and began to demonstrate. The guy got scared and let go. He backed off and both men hurried away. Our protector then revived Claudia and walked her to her car. She knew nothing of what had happened. When I came to, I was in my own car with no recollection of these events. I had never before understood why Claudia began feeling closer to me – in fact she smiled at me one day at work and exclaimed "I feel like you're my best friend!" – but now it makes sense. I resolved this incident and integrated with this new character, who I called Hero. A few days later I had a strange dream.

In the dream I was sitting in a dark room at a small table. It seemed to be in some kind of eating establishment but there were these strange boxlike things that were like dressers without drawers, and they each had a TV sitting on them with something showing on the screen. I was sitting across from a slight, blond lady, and we both had beer mugs in front of us. My feeling was that I had no idea where I was or how I got there, yet I felt in control. There were other people in the room and several were standing in front of the TV structures. Nothing was familiar, yet it felt like a memory. I was doing my sessions early in the morning at the time, and often worked on dreams. I quickly realized what this was. This dream was one of Hero's memories. As soon as I assumed Hero's viewpoint in the dream I recognized the place. It was an upper level of the same tavern where the previous brawl had taken place. In the dream I was seeing it through Hero's eyes. To Hero it was strange and dark, like a cave, and he had no idea that the TV boxes were video arcade games. It was surreal and fascinating to experience it as he had. But why was he there? As I worked on this memory, the following incident unfolded.

It was the early nineteen-eighties and I had just gotten off working the day shift in the kitchen at the tavern. I was tired, hot, and I had a throbbing headache in the back of my head. I went upstairs to play Karate Champ, which was my favorite game at the time. The game was occupied so I was playing an adjacent game when a fight broke out next to me and I turned and saw two men violently wrestling on the floor. This short thin blond lady started screaming for someone to help her boyfriend and she started pulling on my arm pleading for me to do something. I was feeling terrible physically, and was very reluctant to get involved. But when I realized I had to intervene I had a shock. I was already feeling the humiliation I was sure was about to come, but in the power-zone I seemed to be conferring with my helpers and I heard a tall hazy figure off to my right say, matter-of-factly, "I'll do it." The rest of the incident will be described from Hero's viewpoint.

I (Hero) emerged and looked at the two men struggling on the floor. I grabbed the guy on top and threw him off and he quickly jumped up to face me. The other guy was now on his feet and standing behind me. I heard him say "I don't need your help" but I ignored him. The lanky man I was now facing was about five inches taller than me. He said "Who the hell are you? You work here or somethin'?" "I don't know" I replied truthfully. "Well you don't look so tough" he smirked, obviously ready to fight. So I said "Take your best shot."

My attitude was one of total ambivalence. He took a swing at my face. I could see streams of energy flowing through his body, mostly in shades of blue and some red, and there was one at the level of his sternum that seemed very vulnerable. I blocked his punch with my left hand by hitting his right elbow joint, in the middle of the energy stream running through his arm. With my right hand pointing straight out like a spear, I simultaneously stabbed him at exactly the right point on the blue energy stream running vertically through his trunk. It was as if I had hit an "off" switch. His legs buckled and he dropped straight to the floor. I actually saw his spirit standing there for a split second before he went back into his body. He got up and looked at me, confused by what had just happened. When I asked, impassively, "Do you want to try again?" he just grumbled "Fuck you!" and left. The other guy said nothing and went back to his video game.

The blond lady touched my shoulder and seemed amazed. We'll call her Faye.

Faye: How did you DO that!? That was amazing!
Hero: "It was easy"
Faye: Thanks for helping. Do you work here?
Hero: I don't know?
Faye: You don't know if you work here? What's your name?
Hero: I don't know.
Faye: "You don't know your own name!? Are you OK? Do you need some help?" She looked concerned. "You must work here – you're wearing one of their T-shirts" she said, pointing at my chest. (I tilted my head a bit to focus on the voices which were mainly Dennis–1 and Dennis–2)
Hero: "They said I'll be fine"
Faye: Who said?
Hero: "The spirits." I said, quite innocently.
Faye: You're talking to spirits!?
Hero: Yes.
Faye: I think you'd better sit down for minute. Come over here. I'll get you a beer.

We sat at a tiny table for two against the far wall and she went to the bar downstairs and came back with two beers. She was interested in the spirits and had a lot of questions for them. The "spirits" gave me the answers and I relayed them to Faye, who was quite amazed. I was telling her things about her life and about people she knew, which only a real psychic could know. I was apparently also giving her some good advice and possibly information about the future. At one point she called her boyfriend over and said "You have to listen to this guy – this is incredible." He didn't seem interested though, and shortly disappeared. When they were leaving Faye asked if I needed a ride anywhere and I said I'd be OK.

After Faye left, I switched back. A minute later an assistant manager and a bartender came running up the stairs and rushed over to me asking where the fight was. Hero was gone and I remembered nothing of the preceding events. I said I hadn't seen any fight. The two guys ran upstairs to the top bar area and came back down. They told me that a lady had said someone might be in trouble, but I assured them it wasn't me. They left scratching their heads. I didn't even question how I got a beer – I just took it all in stride.

Hero was an expert in martial arts.[41] He was also like the alien in the movie "Star Man" (1984) in some ways. He knew nothing of pop culture and didn't understand common social references. He took everything literally and was very honest and blunt. But he had absolutely no fear and, although he never seriously hurt anyone, he had no qualms about killing if necessary to save someone's life. He saved my life on at least one occasion but he also got me in trouble more than once. One time after skillfully escaping a deadly situation some guy asked him "Who are you, James Bond!?" to which he replied flatly "I just may be." I soon discovered his origin while exploring the source of a feeling of humiliation.

---

[41] It is not uncommon for people with multiple personalities to have helpers who have skills or knowledge that their host doesn't have. Billy Milligan for example (The Minds of Billy Milligan – Daniel Keyes, 1981) had a helper who spoke Serbo-Croation and was a karate expert, abilities he himself did not possess. Chris Costner Sizemore (A Mind of My Own, 1989) had a helper who could play the piano, having had no lessons.

A Warrior from the Past

I was in seventh grade and it was between classes. I was getting some M&M's from a vending machine outside the cafeteria when two ninth-graders came over and started harassing me and took my candy. I wasn't afraid of these guys and I was willing to fight them off, but I switched with Bill when one of them suggested that they "pants" me – an embarrassing bully prank. They pushed Bill into a side corridor and one held him facing the wall while the other tried to pull his pants down. I was exterior watching the whole thing and feeling deeply humiliated. I also got very angry and wanted to do something but felt helpless because I couldn't get back in the body, and this caused a shock.

In the shock I asked for a helper, and Hero appeared. He seemed to come from a long way off and it took a few seconds for him to arrive. Most of my helpers arrived instantly, even at their first appearance, so this was unusual. He emerged from a colorful swirling vortex of energy and jumped right into the body. He turned around and punched one of the boys behind him. The boy fell to the ground, out cold. The other boy stood there for a moment staring at Hero. He looked confused and ran away. I switched back and walked away as the first boy started to come to.

Two years later when I was fifteen my brother Blake gave me a book for Christmas titled "Zen Combat" which described several martial arts. I loved it and began to practice Karate and Aikido. But in discussing this with Blake many years later, it was a mystery to both of us as to why he had gotten me that book. He doesn't remember, and I had never shown any previous interest in the subject as far as I knew. But after discovering Hero I had some visions of being exterior, watching Hero showing Blake and his friends some self-defense moves.

There is evidence that helper personalities can be created who can speak other languages or play musical instruments that the host cannot, or have other skills and aptitudes that were not available before their arrival. The host may have a physical condition, like poor vision or diabetes, while a particular helper doesn't. These and many other documented phenomena of multiple personalities are controversial and unexplained. There have been attempts to disprove the existence of such reported phenomena or to find conventional, material world explanations for them. In order to satisfy a nonspiritual worldview, we can speculate that the human brain and nervous system are capable of a great deal more than we have ever believed, not on the level portrayed in the movie "Lucy" of course, but perhaps enough to account for some of these observations.[42] However this is merely a concession on my part to those who cannot yet see the greater reality. I believe that consciousness, in the form of a higher-level conscious agent which I call the Higher Self, provides helpers when needed, and can give them whatever resources they require to be whatever they need to be, within limits. This is debatable and cannot be proven, but I do know that before Hero appeared I had none of his abilities – nor was I ever as good at math as Cindy.

Cindy

When I was a senior in High School, I was taking an advanced math class from Mrs. Krutz, an older lady who was quite arrogant, and full of herself for having written the textbook we were using. I was not studying much and my performance in school was deteriorating due to the emotional stresses I was under. One day she criticized me for not doing my homework and I said something flippant back to her. She made me stand up at my desk and gave me a royal dressing down. Then she compared me to a baby and asked me if I was a baby. I said no but she said something like "Everyone else seems to be able to do their homework. I think you must be a baby – tell us you're a baby and can't do your homework." She paused. "Say you're a baby." I was silent. She repeated her domineering command and I was on the spot. I didn't know what to do and had a shock. In my shock I felt a lot of anger and hatred toward her for embarrassing me in front of everyone. I hated her from that moment on. I decided that I had to say I was a baby or endure even more humiliation, but vowed to myself, in that moment, that I would never do homework in her class again. And I never did.

---

[42] Lucy (2014) - A powerful new drug allows a woman to access 100% of her brain giving her superhuman intelligence and paranormal abilities.

One of the things causing me stress was that I had registered to enter the Naval Academy, under some pressure from my father, but it was something I really did not want. I was also considering going to the local community college. The next time I had to do homework for Mrs. Krutz I had a dilemma. I didn't want to fail the class because I needed it to graduate. But the idea of giving in to that woman was unacceptable and put me in a quandary. I also had to make my decision about the academy right away. That and other things on my mind made my head swim. Sitting at my desk in my bedroom, I felt trapped and overwhelmed. I needed some time to think and I just wanted to escape. It was all too much.

My inner conflict caused a shock. At that moment I heard a girl's voice. "I'll do it" she said, sounding light and perky. I immediately became aware of Cindy, who was happy and eager to do my homework for me. Cindy was a math genius, born years earlier. She asked if she could take my tests too. I approved but made her agree to not get more than a C grade if she took the tests. I then stayed out of my body while she did the homework. I went to a peaceful place surrounded by white fluffy clouds and did a lot of thinking. I worked out my conflict about the Naval Academy and decided to go to college instead. I felt greatly relieved afterward, and was impressed by the neatly completed homework I found on my desk. Mrs. Krutz probably thought her bullying tactics would spur me into being a better student but it only made me hate her, hate myself for allowing her to humiliate me, and prompted me to find a way out of doing what she expected. I underperformed just to spite her. I think I got a B anyway. Teachers and parents who use fear, derision, and punishment to gain compliance, always do everyone a disservice, even if it appears otherwise. Students may learn in spite of this, but not usually because of it, and they are left with other byproducts like hatred, resentment, and impaired function, that do no one any good.

Denise

Denise was a young girl who, like Bill, helped me by being a victim of sexual assault when I was very young. Her origin was similar also in that the perpetrator was using the wrong name. He knew my name but was purposely calling me Denise instead.

Denise had a high-pitched little girl's voice. Unlike Bill she was not depressed, was always in good spirits, and liked talking with other girls. Her unexpected appearances created some hilarious moments. People always thought I was creating that voice on purpose but I couldn't have duplicated it even if I wanted to. I was also never aware of Denise.

I switched with Denise on the first day of fourth grade as soon as I saw the teacher – something about her white hair spooked me. Denise took my place for all of that year while we were in the classroom. I remember almost nothing of that class. Now that we are integrated, I can remember being her on that first day of school, and wondering why I wasn't wearing a dress like the other girls. If Denise spoke in class during that year, it must have been interesting. I haven't tried to remember, but I do recall that I had to meet with a counselor a few times that year for speech therapy because I wasn't pronouncing certain words properly. However the counselor was confused since I had no problem with those words. But that was because outside the classroom I was back in control. A few times that year, I did switch with Denise while we were in the classroom, but because I had no idea what was going on, I felt lost and confused. I would dissociate pretty quickly and Denise would take over again. I'm sure she did all our homework too.

Pseudo-Personalities

Let's review the definitions I'm using here, and add a few more. Identities are the many mind-body states we have at our disposal. They are the simple or complex groups of associations of feelings, thoughts, skills, and whatever else is needed, to accomplish a particular purpose. Free identities are developed through learning, practice, and experience. They are flexible and can be changed or discarded. Stuck identities are created in traumatic moments and we shift into them automatically as a reaction when they are triggered. These are mostly a hindrance and the source of, or a factor in, most of our problems and limitations. They can be deactivated and still remain intact until resolved and relieved of their reactive status. "Groups" are composed of two or more stuck identities that get triggered by the same or similar stimuli and are active, to some degree, at the same time. In actuality we are often in many identities simultaneously. Unlike identities, personalities are separate viewpoints within our own consciousness, and are created to help us in some way. These helpers are people and have their own personality traits, identities, memories, and abilities, and they can be traumatized just as anyone can. Their consciousness cannot be destroyed (it was never created) but their apparent mental separation and individuality can be resolved through integration, which results in a merging of viewpoints and memory tracks. These alter memory tracks may or may not be easily accessible to the now unified host.

The "spirit-self," or soul, is the host – the "atman" in Hinduism – the person born in the present body. The spirit-self may appear to reincarnate through countless lifetimes, although past-life memories are usually not readily available for most of us without some effort. The Higher Self is a higher level viewpoint of our own consciousness and it is aware of us and everything we experience although we are not aware of its presence. We could call the Higher Self our superconscious mind, but it's really our own self operating at a higher level. I believe we each have our own Higher Self, which has unlimited power. It is our personal creator and may seem like God to us but it is not the ultimate God, in my model, which is consciousness itself. God is the self-aware totality of existence. In India, God (Brahman) is referred to as The Self, meaning the universal Self, as opposed to a self. Jesus called this universal Self "the All." You don't have to buy into any of this metaphysical stuff, but it's important to understand so that later you may see how our experiences can be effectively modeled in this way. This will be discussed further in Chapter 17.

In Latin "persona" means mask or role. In the Identity Model, what I call a "persona" is a character that one plays. Actors take on a persona when they immerse themselves in a role. It's a "pretend" personality. They act and express themselves as the character they wish to portray, assuming whatever mannerisms and physical characteristics are required. They become someone else, but of course they know it's just an act. Sydney Bristow in the TV series "Alias" took on various personas to infiltrate nefarious organizations and she had to play these roles perfectly in order to avoid being caught or killed. So a persona, is a temporary identity state with the purpose of portraying a complete personality.

We identify with most of our identities, believing that the way we are feeling, thinking, and acting is a true expression of ourselves in that moment, even though they are just roles. While many of these roles are an authentic expression of our personality when intentional, when they are unconscious reactions, they are not. Using the examples above, we can say that the real identity behind a persona is the state of "you being an actor" or "you being a spy" and the "persona" is your mask. Impressionists like Rich Little and Jim Carrey, create a persona to represent each celebrity they impersonate. As with any identity, a persona can be momentary and simple, or complex and well established, like a TV actor's role in a series.

What I call a "pseudo-personality" is also a persona, but one that is unconsciously stuck in some way. It is not a helper personality and is not autonomous – it's just you playing a role. As a general description, a pseudo-personality is a role in which someone pretends to be someone else or pretends to be different in some significant way that is unlike their ordinary personality. This person usually knows that their persona is a pretense, although it is possible in some cases that they may think it's who they really are.

We may adopt a pseudo-personality for many different reasons. I had a client, Nancy, who was going to law school but had a job as an "exotic dancer." Her stripper persona was very much like a different person and I suspected it was a different personality, but she was totally aware and in control of everything she did as a dancer. I had worked with another topless dancer who actually did have multiple helper personalities, one of whom did the dancing. She was also aware of what she did as a dancer, and she was comfortably aware of her other "people" as well, but she was not in control. Although this was NOT the case with Nancy, there were several traumatic moments in Nancy's life that led up to a shock in which she decided to BECOME the kind of woman that men appeared to want. She later became a stripper in an environment where no one knew her, although she was not at all secretive about it. This pseudo-personality was a complete character which served several purposes for her, like making money and providing her a sense of being in control of her life. It was very much like having an acting role except that her attachment to it was programmed – stuck. Through ID-R the stuck nature of this persona appeared to have been resolved, and if so, I suspect Nancy abandoned this role when it no longer served its original purpose. Still, for her it was like having two separate lives, and she shifted easily between them. This is how it was for me when I became Pete.

Being Pete

I was working on a dream where I had two friends at school but I didn't recognize them or the school, and it turned out to be an experience I had not thought about for decades. I had gone to summer school in the summer of 1959, but barely remembered anything about it. My fifth grade teacher, Mrs. Goodman, had a talk with me at the end of the school year and told me there was a new experimental class for gifted and creative students that summer, and that it would be a great experience for me. She pushed hard to convince me to go and I reluctantly acquiesced. But I felt coerced, and I wasn't looking forward to going; who wants to go to summer school!? I had disappointed Mrs. Goodman in the past but I sensed her sincerity – she seemed concerned about me and said I had special gifts that should not go to waste, and I was a bit curious.

The Creative Thinking class was held at another grammar school, about a mile or so down the road from mine. The kids in the class were almost all a year ahead of me so I felt alienated from the start. I also don't recall there being any girls there. However the teacher, a tall lively man with light brown hair, was passionate about the class and somehow managed to make me feel important.

On the first day of class, I was tying my shoe by the bike racks at the beginning of a recess period when one of the boys asked me if I wanted to play basketball, as he walked by. As I considering whether I wanted to interact with anyone at all, given the risk of being teased for being a fifth-grader, I had a startling revelation. No one here knew me! I had no past here. A world of possibilities seemed to open up! I realized that, with these people, I could be anyone I wanted – I was free! I could start over! Could I dare take the risk? I had a shock at what I might do. There was no dissociation involved in the shock (outside of the shock itself), but there was an inner transformation as I felt all of my poor self-esteem and shame wash away. I was reborn. It was like going to another world and starting a new life where there were no expectations or preconceptions of who

I was. The old Dennis was gone. So I went and played with the other kids. And I told them my name was Pete.

Pete was me, not an alter personality. I had made a decision to become Pete and created a template for him. Pete had none of my past restrictions. In fact, he was me without a past. A persona is an identity, and purely an act, but when it is created or rooted in a shock, it becomes a pseudo-personality. In my case, being Pete was actually an expression of my natural personality; it's how I would have been without all the trauma in my life. Pete was just me being my confident, uninhibited, and unaffected self. But Pete was born in a shock; not the name, but the idea of being myself as I wanted to be, and in that shock there were some decisions and psychic maneuvers which enabled me to put the idea into action. It was as if all my previous programming and personalty traits were set aside, behind a wall, so my real self could shine through.

In my new guise as Pete I quickly made some friends, two in particular, John and Lantz. When I hung out with John and Lantz during recess and after school on the playground, I was great. I was the leader, even though they were older than me. We had fun and I was able to express my genius and creativity in suggesting and carrying out bold adventures or explorations of the school buildings, most of which were unused during the summer. I was brave, confident, funny, and charismatic. As Pete, I was amazing.

Back then I believed the persona of Pete was not the real me but a "pretend me," an "alternative me," the me that I wanted to be but wasn't, but who I COULD be in this environment. So while the pseudo-personality of Pete was closer to my natural self, I thought he was a lie, a trick, a con, and that I was hiding the truth of the "real" me. I could have continued to use the name "Dennis" instead of "Pete" and THAT "Dennis" would have still been the same upgrade – a pseudo-personality with all of Pete's qualities – but I used Pete instead, to further distance myself from my old personality, which, by the way, was also a pseudo-personality but one I DID identify with and thought was the real me. (That's right, whomever you think you are right now is a false persona and not the real you, but we'll get into that later).

As Pete, I felt, thought, and acted much differently than I would have without the shift that set me free from "being Dennis," and there was a new energy and a great sense of joy in that. It was like

taking a drug, and I always looked forward to becoming Pete. So
every weekday, as I rode my bike or walked the two miles to
summer school, I shed the old me, and became someone else. Just
past the half-way point there was a certain telephone pole that
served as a landmark. I became Pete when I passed it in the
morning and became Dennis when I passed it on the way home,
and I was fully conscious of doing so.

Several times however, Pete's mettle was tested and for the sake
of remaining true to my new persona I had to meet challenges with
novel solutions – solutions which surprised me not only because
they showed wisdom and restraint, but also because they were
unanimously well received by everyone. There are three instances
that stand out.

Dodging Bullets – or You're the Boss!

I was feeling very good about my "new"confident self, almost
arrogant. My charisma was infectious with my small group of
friends, which led me to assume that everyone would welcome my
input in the same way, perhaps hanging on my every word. Not so,
young grasshopper! One day the class was divided into two or three
groups for some project or creative exercise, and there was a heated
discussion going on in my group about how we would approach our
challenge. I attempted to interject some ideas but it was difficult
There were two rather large boys, Bart and Eddie, who had
basically taken charge of the project and were debating ideas with
some intensity. When I found a break where I could speak I said my
piece and was stared down by Bart. Ignoring my idea, Bart
continued his heated discussion with Eddie.

I tried again to express an idea and this time Bart was in my face,
belittling me for being an ignorant fifth-grader who should keep his
stupid ideas to himself. The implied threat of being pounded was
quite obvious. But as Pete, I dared not show any fear. I was in
eminent danger of losing face. The shock occurred because I took
any defeat or embarrassment to mean that my ruse was up. I would
be exposed for who I really was, a pauper pretending to be a prince,
and my days as Pete would be over. A deflated Pete would be no
Pete at all.

In the power-zone I knew what "Pete" would do, so I showed no sign of being intimidated in the slightest. I just smiled and said to Bart, whose face was inches from mine, "You're the boss!" My tone was confident and almost cheerful. He looked at me for a moment and seemed perplexed. I had validated his status, ended the conflict, and left him speechless. So he immediately went back to debating Eddie. I had dodged a bullet. I realized now that my brilliance could not stand up to the brute force of ruthless sixth-graders. I understood that this was an ego thing – a power play – king of the hill. So I remained quiet for the rest of the project. This experience was still affecting me decades later, inhibiting me a bit from speaking up in groups.

I was fleshing out this Pete persona with true wisdom and rationality, and this incident is where that growth really started, when the waters first got rough. So now I realized there was a lot more to this game than just having fun. It wasn't going to be easy. I was vulnerable and I had to be careful. I had an identity to maintain and protect, not just so I could keep enjoying my new secret life away from home, but so I could hide my dark side. Exposure would mean ridicule, and banishment from Camelot.

Down in the Dirt – or The Phoenix Rises

Another day, while playing football on the grass during the exercise hour, my boldness rubbed Bart the wrong way. Bart, who was much bigger than me, verbally assaulted me and then jumped on me and rubbed my face in the dirt. I could have been embarrassed, felt demeaned, cried, or gotten angry, but I was Pete, and Pete handled things differently.

I was the quarterback for our team, which in itself was amazing, and as I walked back to the huddle, John asked me if I was OK. I was. I was surprisingly unruffled, and I continued to play as if nothing had happened. I had decided during the shock of being bullied that I would protect my endangered status as Pete by rising above this affront. I would treat Bart with respect, not be angry or hurt, and keep playing with total aplomb. So I was unoffended, calm, and cool. I even joked about it. I don't recall everything that happened but I do recall the feeling. I had put all the negative reactions out of my mind – I paid them no heed at all – and the effect on my team was that they respected me even more.

As we walked back to the classroom later, John seemed genuinely in awe. He said that my response to having been put down by Bart was the most impressive thing he had ever seen. Pete was alive and well, and wiser and stronger for the experience. And I have recalled later situations in my life where I used the same strategy to great advantage, without knowing where the idea came from, or recalling anything at all about my summer as Pete.

Over My Head

The third incident that stands out involves my helper Cindy. In my session I was working on a feeling that I was in over my head in some situation. I had a flashback to being Pete in the summer classroom while the teacher was demonstrating some kind of mathematical process on a large white blackboard using black chalk. On this occasion he called on me to come up and try to solve the problem on the board. I wasn't understanding his demonstration and felt completely lost. But as Pete I had to be cool. Pete couldn't afford to look stupid in front of his friends, but this was way over my head. I had a shock in realizing I was about to fail and look bad. Dennis–2 could have joked and charmed his way out of this, still looking good, but he wasn't there and I needed help. That's when Cindy was born. She saw the math puzzle clearly, provided the solution, and answered the teacher's questions about how she solved it. Back in my seat I wasn't sure what had happened, but I felt like I had cheated or bluffed my way through this somehow. I was relieved, but a bit anxious that someone might figure out my charade. Cindy was exactly what I needed her to be in that situation – a math genius who could solve whatever problem the teacher presented, while remaining calm and collected.

Pete's Farewell

On the last day of summer school, as I was leaving, I said goodbye to John and Lantz. John said we should keep in touch and do some things together. But even as we were talking, I felt a great sadness. As we said our goodbye's I knew I would never see them again. This was the last day I would ever be Pete. Once I left, they could never find out who I really was. My bike had been broken for a few weeks and it was a long sad walk home. I knew that when I passed that telephone pole for the last time, Pete would become a distant memory.

Some time later, maybe a few weeks, John called me on the phone to suggest the three of us get together. I was surprised because I had intentionally given him the wrong phone number. I explained that I couldn't see him. He didn't understand so I had to be adamant. It was awkward and I felt bad, but it had to be done. I didn't feel like Pete at all. If I had not done the work of looking into this, I would have never remembered anything about being Pete that summer. My previous "edited" memories of summer school were only that I had attended, along with a few dim images of being in the classroom, a white blackboard, and sitting with a bunch of older kids; less than a minute's worth. This wasn't amnesia, it was just too sad to recall, so I had tucked it all away in some back corner of my mind.

Masks

I created two other short term pseudo-personalities later on as a teenager for basically the same reason: to push my old conditioning temporarily aside so that I could act more freely with people. One persona I called Dennis and one was Rod. They were basically masks. They each lasted less than an hour but allowed me to be more free during that time.

When I was in my twenties, I read some of Maxwell Maltz's books on psycho-cybernetics. Maltz was a plastic surgeon who noticed how people's personalities would sometimes change for the better after cosmetic surgery. He ascribed this to their new look giving them a new and better self-image. I suspect that their new self-image was a pseudo-personality state that allowed them to suppress their old personality for an extended period of time, as I did while being Pete. Maltz also noticed that many people had a bad impression of their appearance even when they looked fine and didn't really need the surgery they wanted. And many times the cosmetic changes didn't help his patients with their feelings about themselves at all. So he developed techniques to help people improve their self-image mentally. Being very shy at the time, I

tried his techniques in the early 1970's but was unable to maintain
the new self-images I created, for more than a few minutes.

However one Halloween I had an interesting experience which I
never forgot. I was working at a restaurant and we were allowed to
wear masks while working that night. Behind my goblin mask I felt
very free. All my shyness and awkwardness were gone for those few
hours, and I had a great night because I felt no one was actually
seeing ME. I realized that while in my "behind the mask" persona,
I had the potential to be the person I wanted to be, and I became
confident, funny, and outgoing with everyone around me. I didn't
remember Pete, but perhaps that night was his encore. When the
stuck nature of a persona is resolved through ID-R, it will simply be
abandoned if its original purpose is gone, unless it is still useful, in
which case it will simply be a conscious act.

Voices Within

Mel Blanc, who I mentioned earlier, was a master voice actor in
the last century who created many memorable cartoon character
voices like Bugs Bunny, Daffy Duck, and Foghorn Leghorn. He
would immerse himself very deeply in the characters he created,
becoming those characters with his whole body, and he could shift
from one voice to another instantly and perfectly. Each character
would be a free identity of course, but also a persona because he
was portraying someone else.

In 1961 Mel suffered a head injury in a near fatal car crash that
left him in a coma for two weeks. His prognosis was not good. As an
experiment, in an effort to communicate with his comatose patient
when nothing else had worked, Mel's neurosurgeon addressed him
as Bugs Bunny and asked how he was doing. To the doctor's
astonishment, Bugs replied! "Eh... just fine, Doc. How are you?"
The doctor said it was as if Bugs Bunny was trying to save Mel's life.
Other characters replied as well, when addressed, and this helped
Mel come out of the coma, and he soon recovered. This story has
raised questions about the nature of identity and personality and
who we really are, because we haven't had a clear understanding of
these concepts. It is most likely that being prompted to shift into the
Bugs Bunny character and other well established personas simply
triggered Mel to partially awaken in these states and helped him to

regain full consciousness. It was obviously the right stimulus at the right time.

I do want to mention that it is equally possible for a helper personality to be created in the guise of a cartoon character, an alien, a saint, a devil, a robot, an animal, or anything else, and they will believe themselves to be that, although these are only roles they are playing. Helpers are created for specific purposes to be whatever they are needed to be. However there is no reason for me to believe that any of Mel Blanc's characters were anything other than well-established personas, acting roles, or neural patterns, if you prefer.

Are Helpers People? – or What is a Person?

The ideas about multiple personality that are found in the literature do not, for the most part, address consciousness itself as having any role in this phenomenon, and certainly not in any supramundane way. But, as I mentioned earlier, to understand multiple personalities we must have a better understanding of consciousness itself. I already said that alter personalities are people and that they are not imaginary, but this is counterintuitive, very difficult to understand, and goes against mainstream thought.

Dr. Colin Ross is a foremost expert on MPD/DID and someone whose work I greatly admire and respect. He is one of the most brilliant, knowledgeable, and level-headed psychiatrists in the field. Here are two rational and definitive statements about multiple personalities Ross made in 1989. He may possibly have a very different perspective these many years later, but I'm using these quotes as a segue into further discussion because they are so well stated, and I believe they represent a generally standard view of MPD, and one which I hope to change.

"What is MPD? MPD is a little girl imagining that the abuse is happening to someone else. This is the core of the disorder to which all other features are secondary. The imagining is so intense, subjectively compelling, and adaptive that the abused child experiences dissociated aspects of herself as other people. It is this core characteristic of MPD that makes it a treatable disorder, because the imagining can be unlearned and the past confronted and mastered." ("Multiple Personality Disorder," page 55)

This reminds me of the old "solar system" model of the atom –
useful up to a point, but ultimately incorrect. The main problem
with this definition besides being simplistic, is the word
"imagining." This is purely a theoretical position based on a very
limited paradigm. The features of multiple personalities cannot,
and do not, appear by any ordinary human imagining. The
appearance of helpers *IS* a creative process, and previous
imagination may have some relevance to their creation, as I will
explain later, but alter personalities come into being from beyond
ordinary conscious awareness. This is not willful imagination by the
person; it is something else. It would have been better to say that we
just don't completely understand it yet. Alters appear in a split
second, fully formed. There can be multiple conversations between
them taking place at the same time. They can be aware or unaware
of other helpers. Some can have mental or physical conditions that
the others don't have as well as their own unique abilities. They
have their own memories, beliefs, and other defining
characteristics. The number and degree of amazing phenomena
arising in multiplicity cannot be simply "imagined up" and
maintained day in and day out for a lifetime, by any human being,
much less a child.

Of course, I have seen the truth, at least for myself, and
regardless of where my helpers came from, whether from my brain
or my Higher Self, I didn't imagine them or sustain them in any
way I have knowledge of. To call this mysterious process
"imagining" is just a way to make it sound as if it is understood,
when it is not. There has been a lot of speculation about
"precursor" imaginary people becoming helpers and this can
happen, but such fantasies would only be models from which a
helper personality is fashioned in a traumatic moment, just as other
people in the child's life, a character in a book, or a TV personality
might be. And yes, multiple personalities absolutely can be
resolved, but by the specific processes of trauma reduction and
personality integration, as previously noted, but not by any kind of
"unlearning." I'm sure Ross knows this and was just being
metaphorical. He continues:

"The most important thing to understand is that alter
personalities are not people. That may seem obvious but it is a truth
that one may lose sight of during therapy. Alter personalities are

highly stylized enactments of inner conflicts, drives, memories, and feelings. At the same time they are dissociated packets of behavior developed for transaction with the outside world. They are fragmented parts of one person: There is only one person. The patient's conviction that there is more than one person in her is a dissociative delusion and should not be compounded by a _folie a deux_ on the part of the therapist."[43] Ross continues: "MPD is elaborate pretending. The patient _pretends_ she is more than one person in a very convincing manner. She actually believes it herself. Some MPD patients enter therapy aware that the different parts are all parts of one person, but most don't." ("Multiple Personality Disorder," page 109)

From my current viewpoint these statements are inaccurate in many ways and represent a delusion on the part of the therapist who is trying to maintain a specific worldview. And if alter personalities are "highly stylized enactments of inner conflicts, drives, memories, and feelings," doesn't that describe each one of us as a person? The main problem here is that no one has ever bothered to define "a person" in this context. What IS a person? If a person is defined as a body, then there is only one person regardless of having multiple personalities, by definition – end of story.

Of course that definition is not very useful and does not change the reality, whatever it might be. But then what about Siamese twins? We wouldn't say someone with two heads or two brains is one person. It is generally accepted that our brain is the center of our "self" – our individual consciousness and personality. But what if someone was born with two brains in one head, either of which could take control of the body as helper personalities do? With appropriate medical analysis we might conclude there were indeed two brains, and therefore two people there. But we really don't know what constitutes one's "self" in a neurological way. In other words, we really don't know what it is about the brain that allows us to experience life as one separate individual person, although there is ample speculation.

---

[43] A "folie a deux" is a shared madness, or two people sharing the same delusion.

What if we discovered that one's sense of self and one's entire personality and memory were contained in one distinct module, holographic system, or isolated network, within the brain, and that other similar modules or isolated networks could be formed that were also completely separate individuals? What would we then conclude? Perhaps we would see people as we see computers. Each personality would be like a separate, self-contained computer program, operating system, hard drive, or computer chip, each with its own consciousness. In fact, from a completely neurological view, our personality can already be seen as a vast and complex interaction of many different processes – a cooperation of many different "minds" so to speak.

Alter personalities may also be referred to in some systems by various names like "inner critics," inner children, "child parts," "protective parts," sub-personalities, compartmentalized aspects, "dissociated memory networks," and so on.[44] While such names may have some descriptive merit, none of them convey the whole picture of what helpers are, any more than such a description would define what YOU are as a person. One way or another, the human system CAN house multiple personalities, as multiple people, in one body. There is no real evidence that helpers are NOT exactly what they appear to be. To believe otherwise is merely a philosophical stance. And what real harm does it do if the therapist does engage in a "_folie a deux_" of seeing multiple personalities as separate people? Hopefully in the end they are integrated anyway, regardless of how they are categorized, until only one person remains. The therapist would not be playing along with a delusion but would be engaging with an "apparency" which may or may not be what it seems, without presuming to know better when they do not. Previous views of multiple personality were the natural consequence of some basic and plausible assumptions. But I have seen first hand more deeply into this issue than most others, I

---

[44] Inner children or inner critics can also refer to stuck identities that have these qualities. These are not separate autonomous entities. When we talk to them we are simply talking with ourselves by playing different roles, as we might do in Gestalt Therapy. They have no autonomy apart from our own.

believe, and taking consciousness into consideration here, as we're about to do, constitutes a major paradigm shift.

But what difference does it make anyway and why is this point of recognizing helpers as people so important? One objection to this approach is that calling helpers "people" supports a delusion and makes therapy more difficult. This is false. In actuality, clients can be healed and personalities integrated without any consideration of these issues whatsoever, and this may happen spontaneously in many forms of therapy, like EMDR or IFS, rendering the whole matter moot! But the reason this IS important is twofold. Firstly, recognizing the personhood of helpers validates their existence, respects their suffering and service, and aids in recovery. It also validates the client's own experience. Whether helpers are separate people or the host is just one delusional person who we are playing along with, this respectful approach is essential for healing work and is practiced by all the best counselors already anyway! Helpers are treated as, and respected as, individual people, regardless of what they are called, even if the therapist sees only one person playing different roles, or one person with many "parts".

But now it's time to bring consciousness into the equation. Consciousness is the elephant in the room and nobody talks about it, at least not with any real understanding. I define a "person" as "a unique and dynamic viewpoint in consciousness." Regardless of whether one's helpers are real people or the host is pretending, we are always dealing with a conscious being. So secondly, and of primary importance for me, besides being the truth, is that seeing helpers as people is a better model because it corresponds to one's actual first hand experience, and explains things much better. Every person has their own individual consciousness, which is a sense of their own existence. The mind and personality structure of any person is centered upon that consciousness, without which there is no person at all. If, as I believe, there exists in this universe only one consciousness (the universal field of existence) of which we are all a part, then from that perspective we are all individual aspects, multiple personalities if you will, of that one self-aware Being. So ultimately, we are all one. Our individual personalities, memory networks, experiences, and life stories, are separated by barriers of mind only, and these dissociative barriers are actually illusions. But I'm getting ahead of myself.

Multiplex Thinking

I remember suggesting to some people, to much skepticism, the possibility that the famous athlete turned actor, O. J. Simpson, presented a classic case of multiple personalities where a helper committed murder but O. J., unaware of this, believed himself to be innocent. Of course I don't know if O.J. was guilty or innocent of anything, and this is just some speculation, although there is plenty of supporting evidence, and I'm just using his case for the sake of discussion. For example, Simpson even confessed to a friend of having had dreams in which he committed the murders. There is also much evidence of Simpson's Jekyll and Hyde nature throughout his life, including people's descriptions of him switching. In the words of Denise Brown in her court testimony "It wasn't as if it was O. J. anymore." I recall having thoughts, when I was younger, of doing things that I wouldn't actually do, but that my helpers went ahead and did anyway, often to my mortification – like when my helper Jack ran me head first into a brick wall at school, after I merely considered it briefly one day when I was feeling upset. Jack had been created earlier to punish me once by stabbing me with a pin when I couldn't do it myself. Unfortunately he continued his employment long after his services were no longer needed.

To many people my O. J. theory would sound far fetched and difficult to believe, especially regarding such a well-known figure. People have a hard time believing someone could do something and not remember it. But when an alter personality is in charge, if the host is completely dissociated, then they won't remember anything of what happened because they never experienced it. If they had a small degree of awareness, they might think the experience was a dream or their imagination. If a helper personality was indeed responsible in O. J.'s case, then he didn't do it. That doesn't mean O. J. is not responsible, which is a separate issue, but it would explain his apparent amnesia. We all have periods in our lives that we don't remember at all, like birth, infancy, early childhood, and aspects of various traumas, and yet experiences during these periods can often be remembered with the right effort. We also can intentionally block things from our memory, and memories around traumatic events are often incomplete or altogether missing. As a side note, there is also much evidence that "O. J." may have been a persona for Simpson, similar to what Pete was for me. Many people have commented on the "O.J. character" that he created, as if it were an act, and many people saw through this act, including friends, sportscasters, and other actors.[45]

You may be wondering why YOU haven't seen people switching personalities, acting out of character, or talking in different voices. My answer is that you most probably have, but if you are like most people it's unlikely that you recognized it. Hard to accept? "Change blindness" is the failure to register that something has changed in whatever you are perceiving. We all experience this. A woman may spend all day getting beautified only to be disappointed when her partner doesn't notice anything has changed. This has to do with how we use our attention and how we process information. Daniel Schacter in his excellent book "The Seven Sins of Memory"[46] relates the following psychology experiment measuring "change blindness" in live interactions: "One experimenter would ask someone on a college campus for directions. While they were talking, two men walked between them carrying a door that hid a second experimenter. Behind the door the two experimenters traded places, so that when the men carrying the door moved on, a different person from the one who had been there just a second or two earlier was now asking for directions. Astoundingly, only seven of fifteen participants reported noticing this change." Now this was a unique situation, but if some people are unable to notice that the person they were just talking to has become someone else, and that even their clothing has changed, how many people would notice such a change when the person switching has the same face, the same voice, the same clothing, and was never out of their sight? And there are other contributing factors as well, so that people almost never notice a switch.

Most depictions of multiple personalities in movies or on TV are silly, have little to do with reality, and they have a detrimental impact on the public perception and understanding of multiplicity.

---

[45] "O.J.: Made in America" - 2016

[46] "The Seven Sins of Memory" - 2002, by Daniel Schacter

There are so many times the multiple turns out to be an axe
murderer or otherwise psychotic. But there have been and continue
to be exceptions. I liked the 2023 TV series "The Crowded Room,"
in spite of its flaws, which was inspired by the book "The Minds of
Billy Milligan" My favorite however is "Voices Within, the Lives of
Truddi Chase" from 1990, mainly because of the realistic way
Truddi, portrayed by Shelley Long, was shown to switch many times
in front of people in a matter of minutes, and they didn't notice a
thing. All of us are conditioned to interpret what we see in specific
ways. We each have a vast unconscious system of perceptual and
psychological filters in the form of identities, programs, and meta-
programs, that determine how we experience life. Although these
things can be changed, until we take the time to consciously
reconsider them, they tend to conform to those of the people
around us.

A simple example of the power that focusing our attention has,
as a perceptual filter, is a classic selective attention experiment. In
this experiment a group of people is shown a one-minute video of
six students on a stage, passing a basketball around. Half the
students are wearing white shirts and the others have black shirts.
The viewers were asked to focus on the basketball and count the
number of passes between the white shirted students during the
video, as if it were a test of concentration. After the video they were
asked for their count. Then they were asked if they saw the gorilla.
What gorilla?! During the video someone in a gorilla suit walked
through the middle of the scene, beat their chest, and walked out.
More than half the viewers failed to notice the gorilla because they
were completely focused on their task. You can find this video
online and try it yourself. How we focus our attention, filter our
perceptions, and interpret our experiences determines our reality.
When multiplicity is not part of your understanding of life, you
simply won't see it.

So the basic universal reason we don't see multiple personalities
in people is that we don't know it exists so it's not part of our reality.
We are not expecting to see it and are not looking for it. We see
people as single individuals only, not as a group of more than one.
This is called "uniplex thinking." Uniplex thinking is a perspective
in which we see everyone as a "singleton" – a single individual. You
may see people switch and behave differently, but you will only

understand it in a context you are familiar with, such as your own behavior. Shifting moods, attitudes, and behaviors are mostly identity shifts anyway, not personality switches. "Multiplex thinking" on the other hand considers that any person could have any number of autonomous parts or helpers available to listen or participate at any time. When you start seeing people in this way it is much easier to notice possible switches, or notice the presence of helpers.

Another reason we don't recognize multiplicity even though we've heard about it, is that it's freaky. and it's easier to put the idea out of our minds and find another explanation. The idea that the person you were Just talking to has been replaced by someone else can be quite weird, threatening, and stressful, if you don't understand what's going on, or if you already have scary ideas about it. Spooky experiences of people switching can easily be quickly forgotten when a reaction is triggered. There were several times that my mother said things like "I'm not your mother" and I forgot them all immediately. This is reactive forgetting. We may do the same thing when we experience paranormal phenomena. We can reactively forget what we saw by blocking it or putting it out of our mind right away. A more usual solution however is to find an alternative explanation that provides a more suitable answer – one that we are more comfortable with. If we can fit an experience into a familiar framework, we are not only more at ease with it but we have a better idea about how to respond, and we feel more in control.

There are many good and well-known therapists who choose to look at helpers as "parts" and not as multiple personalities or people. They have reframed this phenomenon in a way that is more comfortable for them, and I respect that, because however it is framed, the condition is real and working with our "parts" is essential, whether those parts are identities, helper personalities, thought patterns, feelings, brain or body processes, or something else. Others may see all "parts" as autonomous people. Internal Family Systems Therapy (IFS) is a wonderful program developed by Richard C. Schwartz, which recognizes and works with all our "parts" in a very effective and nonthreatening way.[47] When he first encountered what seemed to be different autonomous "parts" in his clients, Schwartz admits that the idea that his clients had multiple personalities was scary. I believe this is a common reaction due, unfortunately, to various factors I've already mentioned. Instead, being a Family therapist, Schwartz reframed the situation and worked with these internal parts just as he would with members of a family, and developed a very effective program incorporating "systems theory."[48] Although I employ a different model of our internal psychic dynamics than Schwartz does, I have studied his methods and incorporated some aspects of IFS into my current program because, among many other advantages, it can quickly dissipate any fear and concern about multiplicity in a client. Also this approach provides an easy way to begin working with a person by addressing and handling, right from the start, any inner obstacles to change they might have. This is also something that can be used very effectively with oneself.

Integration Revisited

I would like to make a few more points concerning integration. While helpers live in our bodies with us and can even share our thoughts and feelings, they are in some ways as separate from us as our next door neighbors. But as aspects of our own personal consciousness, that separation is ultimately an illusion, and one that can be rectified easily through integration. But that separation, illusion or not, is the reality we have to deal with, and to deal with it effectively we have to understand it. Every helper has a reason for existing and they are all our friends, even if they seem to be our enemies, because they are "the way they are" in order to help us in some way. If that way is destructive or even depraved from the start, it was our own decision that this be their nature, even if we don't

---

[47] "Internal Family Systems Therapy" 1995, by Richard C. Schwartz; and 2020 with Martha Sweezy.

[48] Psychological systems theory is a holistic approach that emphasizes an understanding of the well-being of the whole person, rather than just changing a set of problem behaviors.

want to admit it. In a sense, they are only obeying their instructions. However they too can learn, evolve, grow and heal, or they can be traumatized and change in a negative way as well, just like anyone else.

In the rest of this book when I refer to my helpers, I will mostly refer to them in the third person to help avoid confusion. But understand that I have integrated with every alter personality I have found, which means that I AM all of them. They are no longer separate individuals, and their memories have merged with mine. When we were separate, I didn't know what they knew, but now I do – not totally, but to some degree.

In the literature on multiple personalities and in various workshops and groups I have attended, different methods for the integration for multiple personalities have been described. Some methods employed the use of suggestion and various metaphors of merging. Sometimes integration would happen spontaneously between helpers, after two helpers had developed a closeness of cooperation and communication. I was skeptical that integration had actually occurred in many of the stories I heard. The evidence usually accepted as conclusive for integration, in addition to the client saying so, was that the helper and its attendant behavior seemed to be gone and didn't return. But that can happen for many reasons and does not necessarily mean integration was successful at all. A switch usually occurs because something triggers the person to dissociate and the appropriate helper then takes over. In my case I was actually able to overcome some triggers that would cause me to dissociate, long before I knew I was dissociating at all. Whenever I learned to confront a certain type of situation where I would normally switch, so that I no longer would dissociate at those times, then the switch would not happen. But there was no integration at those times; I had simply become stronger.

Directed confluence is the easiest and most sure way I know of integrating. After integration I always test my clients by seeing if they can recall BEING the helper. If they say they can, this is a good sign, but I also look for other things. Sometimes there are no signs, even if it worked. Other times the signs are unmistakable, as in the case of Betty, which I will relate in Part C of this chapter. Some of my clients who discovered another personality in a session seemed to integrate on their own as soon as I described the process, as if they intuitively knew what to do, which of course they did on some level. A few others integrated immediately before I even suggested it, and others avoided it by pretending to integrate, until they realized it was safe to do so.

Although, with regard to the mind, the word "integration" has different meanings in different contexts, with regard to multiple personalities it is the same as merging and fusion. These terms may have specialized meanings in different systems in this context, but for me they all mean the same thing – two separate personalities have become one. The host and another personality are now one conscious viewpoint, one person. The memories of both are now theoretically accessible to the integrated host in that there is no longer a disconnection between their minds and memory tracks. This can happen also between helpers, with two helpers becoming one. There are no partial integrations, as far as I know, although there are some interesting phenomena that might suggest otherwise, like my relationship with Lydia, discussed in Chapter 24.

Chapter 7C

Multiple Personalities – Part 3
Adventures in Multiplicity

"What a strange world we live in ...Said Alice to the Queen of hearts" – Alice in Wonderland

In the course of remembering my own various dissociative misadventures, I began recalling incidents in which I witnessed multiplicity in other people. As a young child I saw both my parents switch countless times. When a different personality was present, I often knew it immediately but as I got older I recognized it less, and then not at all. This was because my worldview had changed and I saw people in a more uniplex way, so that when people did switch, either I didn't notice it, or it was so freaky it caused me to block it out or dissociate and switch myself.

Each of my parents had at least one helper personality who was dangerous to me. My father was an alcoholic. Earl was my father's alter who would come out when my father was drinking, and he could be mean, violent, and abusive. Adrienne was my mother's alter who would often hurt me or threaten me, in my younger years. After becoming aware of these things in my sessions, I researched my parents' histories a bit. I had some enlightening conversations with my mother and did a few ID-R sessions with her, which revealed some dissociative problems early in life. I also had a very long talk with my father's oldest sister, after my father passed away. She had taken care of him when he was a child. It was quite evident that both my parents were dissociating as children. But despite their troubling helpers, they could both also be compassionate and caring.

I recall a time in my early twenties when I was in the dining room at home and my mother was sitting at the table. I asked her something, calling her "Mom," and she responded, somewhat hesitantly, "What if I told you I wasn't your mother?" She seemed

sincerely concerned about my response. I remember having a
strong reaction of fear and I said "I don't know," and left the room. I
never remembered this again until I was doing a solo session on a
similar feeling of fear, which I traced to the following incident.

I was alone in the car with my two brothers one night when I
was maybe six or seven. The car was parked on a downtown street
where it was very dark and quiet, and our parents had most likely
gone into a local bar. Our mother returned alone after some time,
and got in the back seat with me and my youngest brother, and lit
up a cigarette. She seemed angry but didn't say a word. I can still
see the glowing end of her cigarette moving around in the darkness.
My brother in the front seat queried: "Mom ... ?" "I'm not your
mother!" she snapped, in a bitter tone. We were all paralyzed! We
sat there in tense silence for a few more minutes, until she got out
and left. I recall many other examples of my parents switching and
even times when their alters were talking with each other about
their hosts. I know this sounds quite bizarre, but for me as a kid it
was ordinary.

How do I know that these were other personalities? When you
absolutely know that multiple personalities exist, and you have seen
people switch, and there is a ton of circumstantial evidence as well,
it's like knowing that a person is speaking a different language
because you have learned that language and you understand it.
Imagine if you knew several foreign languages, including Chinese.
If someone came up to you and spoke Chinese, it would be obvious
to you. But if you translated for someone who didn't know that there
were ANY other languages, and they doubted you, you would know
at least three things they didn't: that other languages exist, that the
language spoken was Chinese, and you would know what the
person speaking Chinese was saying. As I said earlier, you may not
really know what's going on in someone else's consciousness, but
you can learn to recognize clues. It's like recognizing a language or
someone's face. But it's deeper than that – there are signs of
multiplicity that simply cannot be duplicated intentionally. Once
you become accustomed to seeing people in a multiplex way, it's
like learning Chinese – at some point you recognize it and
understand it – it becomes familiar.

Once I had integrated with all my main helpers I felt my
understanding of multiple personalities and the integration process

was an original and phenomenal breakthrough. I had been working with clients for about a year and a half by then, and I recognized that I now had a new and very powerful way to work with people with dissociative conditions. In a short time I was able to find and help integrate alter personalities in several of my clients, but these people were not dissociating and switching every day. Their situation was not quite as volatile as mine had been, and the impact of their integration was not always apparent. Also I wasn't aware of anyone actually switching in the session, but sometimes it's very difficult to tell anyhow, even with experience. I had read many leading books and journal articles regarding MPD and I believed that ID-R and Directed Confluence were superior to the mainstream therapeutic approaches being used in the 1990's. But these are only tools, and working with a person who is having serious problems with switching would take a lot more experience and resources than I had at the time. Although I had no formal training as a counselor or psychologist, I did have a lot to offer.

So to get more experience and help people who possibly couldn't afford seeing a therapist, I put out a notice for a free Multiple Personality Pilot Program to help people with this condition, one on one. After making sure it was all legal, I put the ads out and got calls right away. I ended up working with eight people. Interestingly, and with one exception, none of these clients had been diagnosed with anything other than depression or anxiety but they all thought they might have multiple personalities, and it turned out they all did.

I was a little nervous about how I might react when I saw someone switch, even though I had been switching my whole life, but I figured I would just deal with it and resolve my own reactions as they occurred. I have already described how, as a child, I experienced some very frightening moments when my parents switched, leaving me confused and worried as to what they might do. I had worked through those shocks but I knew there could be many others.

Alice

One of my first clients in the program was a man in his thirties who had been taken to psychiatrists as a child and also had received shock treatments, although he never understood why. As an adult he would sometimes find himself in other cities or even other countries, with no idea how he got there. I had a female client who experienced a lot of dissociation phenomena but did not know about any alter personalities. These clients and others just seemed to be drawn to this program by a feeling or intuition. They did indeed have other personalities but in the end did not choose to do the work required to get their issues resolved. I ended the program when I realized that many of my clients had helpers anyway and that it takes a strong commitment of time and effort on the part of the client to resolve all the trauma needed to become fully integrated, and this is not a goal many would pursue.

As it turned out my very first client in the Pilot program, Alice, HAD been diagnosed with MPD and had been in treatment for six years. Yet she was still skeptical of this diagnosis. She did concede however that what her therapist had told her made sense and accounted for a lot of strange things, like her inability to understand time. Whenever she looked at a clock, the time made no sense. One minute it would be three o'clock for example, and a few seconds later it would be 5:25. She seemed to function OK in life but she had no idea how she was actually managing her time each day.

Alice was a tall, somewhat heavy lady in her early 40's with light brown hair. When I first met her she seemed nice, sensible, and a bit nervous. She wanted to see me because she felt she wasn't really getting anywhere after six years of therapy. A few minutes into the initial interview as I was explaining my process in a general way, I glanced down at my notes and when I looked up there was someone else there, where Alice had been sitting. If I hadn't been somewhat prepared I might have fallen out of my chair or dropped my pencil, but I didn't.

It was obvious that Alice had switched with someone else. Maybe if I hadn't known anything about multiple personalities I wouldn't have noticed the switch at all. I would have noticed something had changed however, but I would have interpreted it in a different way, perhaps thinking it was a drug reaction. As it was, I did have a brief moment of confusion but I quickly recovered. Everything about her was different. Her posture, her face, her expression, and her energy (what I call projected presence) were unmistakenly that of someone else. She was a big lady but she now looked smaller. She appeared to be a young scared child of about seven or eight. So I just smiled and said "Hi."

It turned out I was indeed talking with a young child named Sally who said she was twelve but seemed younger. Sally appeared to know most of the other helpers inside, and after a brief conversation I met Allie, a responsible helper who was able to stay out longer than the others. Allie didn't know all the others but understood their multiplex condition and was trying to learn more about the people inside. I made some agreements with Allie, who, along with Alice and Sarah, became my primary contacts during the limited sessions we had. I was introduced to seventeen additional characters but interacted with them only very briefly. They all had names and I could tell who was "out" (in control) immediately just by their physical appearance. I could also tell when someone came out whom I had not yet met. Other personalities were mentioned but not named, like the "children of the night, " and the "scary ones." Alice's inner matrix (personal inner world) was structured like a tall building with many levels and had elevators between floors. Symbolically, the top levels were closer to the control center where switching could occur and the lower levels were further below the surface. Everyone had their own room and the children of the night were kept way down on the lower levels. They never came out and were managed by a sad caretaker who would sometimes hurt herself. I have interacted with many other people's helpers and there are often unmistakable changes in attitude and expression, but rarely have I seen the extreme physical changes I witnessed in Alice. I have to say that Alice was an unusual case, although I have seen similar changes in videos of other multiples.

With my free program for people with multiple personalities I did expect to be talking with helper personalities but I was hoping this would be minimal. I was very naive. In a session with a more stable person I don't encourage switching because it is simply unnecessary and eats up time. But sometimes working with helpers is the best approach and is often unavoidable anyway, and this takes added skill and experience to do well. In one session I tried to get Alice to communicate with Allie. I discussed it with Alice and she was willing to try it. But she had a habit of disappearing at the drop of a hat, and although this attempt at inner communication started out OK, Alice quickly found it all too spooky and switched with Allie. Allie also told me about strange physical phenomena that sometimes occurred around them, and there were several unexplained bangs on the wall, and the lights blinked on and off once, during our sessions.

Although I learned a lot from working with Alice I wasn't able to help her much in our eight ninety-minute sessions, mainly because she was never there more than a few minutes and Allie and I hadn't gotten to the point where we could actually begin using ID-R. We never even discussed Alice's childhood or anything traumatic that might have caused her problems. Part of this was due to my inexperience at the time and Allie's past experiences with psychologists. Although Alice was not stable enough to remain in session, I really felt I could have made good progress with Allie if the sessions had continued. Still, my resources were limited and she needed more time than I could provide to make it work.

After my first session with Alice I had a very strong urge to cry and felt an unusual need to be nurtured, and I don't know why, but I had no such reaction in our later meetings. While working with Alice I had several dreams about her, and in these dreams every time she switched, her whole body and clothing changed as well; she physically became other people. Perhaps I was seeing her helpers as they saw themselves, but the dreams were quite strange! I wondered if others in her life recognized her switches as such, or just thought she was weird – or maybe her switches were less obvious outside of counseling. Later I talked with two friends of hers: my ex wife Lynne, and Christina, an ex-girlfriend, both of whom had referred Alice to me at different times. They were aware of her condition and each of them had indeed seen what I had seen.

I discontinued the free program for multiples after a few months because the participants were mostly just curious and not willing to make the commitment required to make some significant changes. But I learned a lot, and I was already incorporating my understanding of multiplicity into my regular sessions.

Something's Different About You

My encounter with Alice also made me wonder how people had perceived my own switches so I began looking into that. I saw that in my case, for the most part, people didn't notice at all. Either they just thought my mood had changed or assumed I was just acting differently on purpose for some reason. I do remember a switch that happened in my early thirties when I lived with three college students. As far as I know, none of them had yet seen any of my helpers. One very late night my helper Bill was awakened from sleep by Donny, one of my roommates, who was banging on the front door. He was drunk and had lost his key. I was not present and was probably off on some OBE adventure. When Bill got up and let him in, Donny asked Bill if he was OK. When Bill asked him why, he said "You look depressed." Bill turned away, and then turned back around smiling, like when the T-101 cyborg tried to smile in the movie Terminator-2. He asked "How do I look now?" Donny looked tired and perplexed. He just shook his head and said "This is too weird ... I'm goin' to bed" and went upstairs.

On another occasion when I was ten, my favorite bully Terrence was tormenting me. He was always out to get me and today he was laughing at me and saying he knew I was crazy because he had heard me talking like a little girl. He had obviously seen Denise. This was during fourth grade when Denise was taking my place at school and she was probably "out" a lot at home doing her homework.

I was denying everything Terrence said, since I didn't know what he was talking about, but he seemed very excited about this evidence and went on and on mocking me, laughing at me, describing all my mannerisms, like my high-pitched voice, and repeating what Denise had said. Finally Dennis–2, who was always listening, had enough of this and came to the rescue. Dennis–2 smiled at Terrence and started laughing and teasing him back: "I really had you didn't I! You really believed me! I wanted you to think I was crazy and it worked!" Then he started talking just like

Denise in her high-pitched voice (which I'm sure I could not possibly have duplicated) saying the things she had said. Finally he laid into Terrence about how easily he was fooled, and how the joke was on him. Terrence got fed up and left in an angry huff. I seldom prevailed in my battles with Terrence, but I had my moments, usually with a little help from my friends.

Split Personality

Here's another time that a switch was noticed. When I was a senior in High School, my first class of the day was History at eight in the morning. One day in class I sensed Patty was in trouble and left my body to help. Dennis–2 took over and I was gone for most of the class. I returned near the end of the period and was so upset with what had happened that I ran to the back of the class and threw up. I was sent to the nurses office but I never made it. As I was walking across the campus I left my body again to check on Patty. This time Medic took over, which was very unusual. She didn't know what to do so she just stood by a tree and waited. A teacher walked by and asked her what she was doing there during class time. She just smiled and told him she was just waiting for her brother. Fortunately she sounded like me. The teacher went his way.

In history class we each had a partner for our current assignment, and my partner was a girl named Cathy. The next day in history class, after the above episode, I was sitting at a table across from Cathy. We exchanged some ideas and then went back to reading our textbooks. After a while she asked me "How come you're not like you were yesterday?" "How was I yesterday?" I asked. I didn't recall yesterday at all. "I don't know" she said. "You were just more fun. You were funny, and lively, and you made jokes about everything." "I don't know" I responded. "I don't remember." She thought for a moment and said "Maybe you have a split personality." Something about that statement felt right. I looked at her and replied "I think maybe I do," and we went back to reading.

Cafeteria

This story describes a more dramatic confrontation with my own multiplicity, and it affected me for many years. When I first started working around people, I was in my early twenties. The job was at a local restaurant. As I tried to become more social I was encumbered by a great shyness, and this kept me distant from others. I would avoid eye contact and felt nervous about being too "open." If I did not keep my distance, so to speak, I would have a strong panic sensation and feel as if my whole body were on fire. I called this the "flash" reaction. People just thought I was shy, and so did I.

When I began to investigate this with ID-R, I kept getting a picture of being in line at my college cafeteria. Something happened there! I then recalled seeing this image several times before, when I had worked on my shyness issue. Now I know why.

During my third year of college I stayed in an off-campus coed dormitory and ate meals in the cafeteria, which was on the first floor. One day while standing in line with about ten people ahead of me, two guys behind me began heckling me for some unknown reason. Maybe I had snubbed them somehow or didn't respond to a question. Whatever it was, they kept making jokes and goading me. I just tried to relax and ignore them but at some point, as my irritation increased, I heard someone behind me yell at them to leave me alone. However, their insults only became more intense and abusive, Now they were saying things like "Whoa ... we've got a real psycho here, he must have escaped from the looney bin." At this point I knew something weird had just happened – something I couldn't quite recall. But as I stood there I tried to remember, and I noticed a blank moment from a few seconds earlier. So I looked deeper and saw that I had turned around briefly, looked at the two guys and said forcefully "Leave him the fuck alone – he didn't do anything to you!!" But it wasn't me! I had lost all control, and realizing this was a shock. I panicked, and my whole body experienced an adrenalin rush. My immediate response was to tense up, stay conscious and in control, and to suppress all impulses to interact. There was definitely something wrong with me and I worried maybe I WAS crazy. As the heckling continued, I left the line and went back up to my room. I soon forgot the whole thing, but I had a strange nervous reaction whenever I tried to eat in the cafeteria.

This incident was the source of my "flash" reaction. This reaction wasn't shyness; I was afraid of losing control and doing something crazy. I was trying to protect myself and others. I didn't

know that it was just my helper Meany defending me in the
cafeteria, because I was rarely ever aware of switching or losing
control.

Carlos and the Bad Guy Inside

I have had many encounters with multiplicity in others, but
before my own healing, very few of these were remembered. I
blocked most of them out. There were also situations that I did
always remember because of their strangeness, which I now realize
were episodes of other people dissociating or switching
personalities, but at the time I did not understand them in that way,
so they didn't make much sense to me. My experience with Carlos
is one of the crazier episodes that was completely blocked.

While I was in college I had a job during one summer break,
working at a government warehousing facility. I worked with a small
crew sorting nuts and bolts, moving pylons around, and doing
cleanup work. There were about three dozen warehouses
surrounded by train tracks and situated on an inland island. I was
twenty at the time, and most of the guys in the crew were my age or
younger except for the two supervisors: a tall skinny "forty-
something" African American man named Jim, and Carlos, a
younger, tall, muscular, and good-looking Hispanic man who
occasionally came around to take some of us to do other jobs.
Whenever we could get away with it, we all played penny ante
poker wherever we could find shade, and were out of sight of any
other crews. Jim was easy going and would play poker with us
unless he wanted to be off doing who knows what; I think he
actually started the whole poker playing thing. So, being the
scientist that I was, I did what I always do, I got a book on poker,
studied it, got good at it, and started winning all their money. I still
remember the time Carlos thought I was bluffing and I had four
jacks!

One day Carlos took me off to help him with something and it
was the first time I got a look inside the warehouses, which stored
hundreds of pieces of heavy machinery and vehicles, all covered
with thick grey or black tarps, made of plastic, I believe. It was hard
to tell what the material was because the sheets were heavy with
thick layers of peat dust. Carlos was usually very upbeat and jovial

and had a way of making you feel good. I remember successfully mimicking some of his mannerisms outside of work, to great effect.

Today however, he seemed very different – he seemed greatly agitated and resentful toward his bosses, as best I could discern from his disjointed comments. It was more like he was talking to himself. I didn't know what to say, as his outbursts of angry words escalated, so I just kept quiet and went along with him. The warehouses were unattended so no one heard him but me, but when we did run across someone else, he would suddenly become his familiar genial self, until they were out of earshot. I was definitely seeing a different side of Carlos. I found him very intimidating and couldn't wait to get back to the crew.

Our task was to locate some machinery and take the covers off and get them ready to be moved. But at one point as we were leaving a building, going down the back steps from an office area, Carlos began acting extremely distressed, said he couldn't take the humiliation anymore, and was going to kill himself. At this point he pulled out a gun and started waving it around. That's when I switched, and Dennis–2 took over.

Dennis–2 was very sympathetic with Carlos and tried to help him and calm him down. At first Carlos was argumentative but then after about a minute or so his intention seemed to change; he seemed to forget about his outrage and self-pity and was now trying to bully Dennis–2 and had him pinned against the outside wall of the building. Dennis–2 could sense that Carlos was now being sexually aggressive, so he suggested they meet in a more private place. Carlos pointed at a building about fifty yards away. Dennis–2 agreed to meet him there but Carlos was skeptical, thinking this was a trick, which of course it was. So he told Carlos that he could always shoot him if he didn't follow through. Carlos smiled and agreed to let him go, saying he'd meet him there shortly, and went back inside the building we had just left, in order to finish something. Dennis–2 quickly ran out of sight, hitched a ride on a truck that was passing by, and went back to the crew. We promptly switched and I was back, not realizing I had some missing time. Jovial Carlos came by later also showing no indication that any of the previous events had occurred. And since I didn't remember anything either, it was just another ordinary day.

Then perhaps a week or so later, Carlos took Eric and me out on
another job that involved moving some crates around in an
unoccupied section at the far end of the facility. Carlos was driving
a small tractor which was pulling a small open trailer. Eric and I sat
in the trailer while Carlos drove us around. Eric was about my age,
going to college, and had a dry, cynical sense of humor. I liked Eric
and found we had a similar taste in music. As we chatted in the
trailer, Carlos switched and began a foul mouthed barrage of insults
directed toward individuals unseen. His voice was very gruff and he
didn't sound like himself at all. Eric and I looked at each other, our
expressions conveying the mutual sentiment of, "What the fuck?!,"
half in amusement and half in nervous angst. It was definitely
spooky.

My first thought was that Carlos was just messing with us and
trying to scare us. But his agitation increased and he stopped the
vehicle and told us to get down. He was acting very weird and
ordered Eric and I to perform a sexual act. Eric told him we were
leaving and Carlos pulled out a knife and said that if we didn't do it
he would kill us. I switched several times but Dennis–2 bumped
everyone back in.

Suddenly I found myself up in the clouds and there seemed to
be other invisible spirits all around me. I heard a voice telling me
that Carlos couldn't kill me because I was immortal. But I wasn't
immortal. When I found myself back on the ground and facing
Carlos, I had a shock at the possibility of death, and Immortal was
created. When I first remembered this shock, I thought Immortal
was an alter personality, but upon trying to integrate I realized that
he was just me in a temporary pseudo-personality state, like Pete,
but with a special ability. I, as Immortal, took off my shirt, walked
right up to Carlos, and said with complete confidence "You CAN'T
kill me, I'm immortal."

Eric was standing behind me, appearing immobile. He was
probably terrified, not knowing wether to run away or try and help
me. Carlos stabbed me in the chest, although it was just a tentative
stab to see if I would react. But I, being Immortal, didn't flinch,
although the pain was intense enough to be a shock. I said "See?
You can't even hurt me." The knife had barely penetrated the skin
but Carlos pushed it in a bit deeper and there was no blood. Carlos,
or more correctly his malicious helper, seemed to accept this and

was unfazed! He pulled the knife back and said "Well, HE'S not immortal – I'll just kill HIM," and took off after Eric.

I shifted back to being my normal self but I was still in a higher state where I was aware of everything that had just happened, but was somewhat dazed by it all. I heard a voice say "Get a rock and throw it at him!" This was more like a complete instantaneous thought that only took a fraction of a second. We were a few feet from the train tracks and there were lots of rocks. I quickly grabbed a big rock, which was actually half a brick, and ran after Carlos. This all happened fast but by now he was maybe thirty yards ahead of me. The two warehouses on my right stretched about 150 yards in the direction we were running, and Eric was about 10 yards ahead of Carlos. I spoke mentally to the voice, "I can't hit him from here." I was running very fast but Carlos was so far ahead that I doubted I could throw the rock hard enough to even reach him, much less hit him. But the voice commanded "JUST THROW IT!" So I heaved the brick as hard and as far as I could.

I sensed an unseen force guiding the brick, and when I look at this from Dennis–2's viewpoint I can see that the voice was his and that he was indeed controlling the brick's movement. It struck Carlos in the back, at the top of his right hip, and he went down instantly. Eric disappeared to my right around the far side of the last warehouse and Carlos lay on the ground writhing and moaning, "What happened, what happened?" I still had my shirt in my hand so I put it on and walked up to Carlos, feeling a lot of compassion. In my current state I knew exactly what had happened. I helped him up and said "You tried to kill us." I then helped him over to the tracks and we sat on the rails.

He was rocking back and forth, obviously confused, repeating things over and over: "What's happening, what's happening?" "There's a really bad guy inside of you" I told him. Carlos was now holding his head, rocking and crying, repeating the question "What did he do?" "He pulled a knife and was saying really bad things" I said. "What am I gonna do? Am I crazy?" he moaned. "No," I replied, "I have people inside of me too. You just have to try and be good."

Once he quieted down, I left him there and walked back to Jim's office. I was back to normal by then, and it was time to punch out. I didn't see Eric, and I had already forgotten everything that had just transpired.

The next day Eric didn't show up for work, nor did Carlos. I never saw either of them again. I also don't recall my asking about them or anyone saying anything about their absence. This seemed strange to me at first, but it could be that I just blocked out any mention of them so as not to be reminded of what had happened. However I do clearly remember thinking to myself, when Eric didn't show up, "Good for him" but I didn't know why at the time. I suspect that Eric reported the incident and quit, and that Carlos quit or was fired, but I'm sure someone would have questioned ME about it also – maybe they did, and maybe Dennis–2 told them what happened – I haven't tried to remember. I also don't recall having any wound on my chest and there is no scar. I recalled these incidents while working on a sharp pain in my chest where Carlos had stabbed me. The pain disappeared.

Betty – or Dining by Proxy

After my personal success with personality integration I added some simple questions to the regular ID-R process to help discover helper personalities during sessions. Asking about helpers, and integrating them when found, became routine, and the results were often phenomenal. Other times nothing much happened. Sometimes the results weren't noticed until after the session, as is often the case with ID-R and other techniques.

A middle-aged woman named Betty saw me several times wanting to deal with her depression, which she described as tiredness, sadness, and lack of motivation. She was also overeating but didn't enjoy her food at all, and in fact couldn't even taste it. What struck me the most was her description of an "in and out" sensation that she felt on the way to our first session; something she had last felt more than nine years earlier during a problem period in her life. This sounded like a typical dissociation feeling and I felt this might be a helper who was coming forward and who might want to talk with me. I verbally gave her a questionnaire called the "Dissociative Experiences Scale," which could tell me how much she was dissociating. I mainly used this in our session as a segue into discussing multiple personalities. She scored low on the scale but had mentioned some OBEs earlier, so I hypnotized her and, using ideomotor response signals, I learned that there was indeed another female personality who had some important information to share.[49] She revealed to Betty a childhood incident that had been long forgotten. Once Betty was aware of the incident, I awakened her and we used ID-R to resolve it.

Betty came to the U.S. after World War II, as a European refugee, when she was seven and a half years old. In her home country, she came down with whooping cough around the age of five or six. She was not eating and was losing weight so her parents admitted her to a sanitorium for six weeks where she joined a group of other sick children. At some point during her first few days there, the staff tried to force her to eat. They gave her some kind of ultimatum to which she was forced to respond, and this was traumatic for her. She faced a tremendous conflict because she really did not want to eat. In working through the shock, we discovered a helper who had been created to eat her meals for her, so that she didn't have to. This was her solution to her dilemma at the time.

Before guiding her through the integration process with this newly discovered helper, I told her I was going to ask her unconscious mind a question and asked Betty to tell me whatever answer came to mind. She was not hypnotized. I asked: "Is there someone inside who has been eating Betty's food for her?" She immediately responded verbally with "I do!" Taking this to be Betty's helper I asked "So you're the one who eats Betty's food?" "I still do" she replied. I complimented her on her service, and then addressed Betty so we could complete the integration. I normally do not address helpers or call them out at all unless it becomes necessary, but this was in the early days and I wanted Betty to get a sense of the reality of her inner helper, although I now believe this is not generally a good idea for reasons described earlier, and the client may find it confusing or distressing. Betty's integration went

---

[49] "Ideomotor response" refers to the practice in hypnotherapy whereby the therapist asks a question of the hypnotized client's unconscious mind, and receives answers using prearranged motor signals, like "yes" and "no" finger movements, in order to bypass any conscious intention.

fine and she felt better, but there was no other noticeable change. She then recalled that, during her stay in the sanitorium, people began calling her Elena for some reason, but the name meant nothing to her.

Later that evening however, I was surprised to get a call at home from Betty. She sounded very excited. "I can taste my food!" she sang into the phone, and described how this was the first time in almost her whole life that she could taste and smell what she was eating. She later reported other new sensations. Betty had been unable to taste her food because, while her helper was in control during meals, she was dissociated from her body and the sensations of eating, although she could remember sitting at the table and going through the motions. Finally she could enjoy her meals and perhaps even be more in control of her diet. Evidently, Betty had been automatically dissociating during meals ever since Elena's first appearance.

While on the phone we discussed our session a bit, but when I asked if she had heard her helper's responses to my questions, she said no – her mind was a blank. I suggested that because she and her helper had merged, the taste of food she had eaten in the past, but never tasted before, might now be familiar to her.

Betty's "in and out feeling" however, was not gone and was even stronger, which disturbed her. In the next session we traced this to an experience during birth in which a spirit, perhaps her mother communicating telepathically, told her that she shouldn't be born. The "in and out feeling," which was stuck in this trauma, was due to a conflict with her mother, and was finally resolved in this session. So that feeling of hers, and my earlier intuition about a possible helper wanting to talk, were actually two separate things.

It is very important to understand that, while the facilitator's intuition and transpersonal impressions can be very useful during a session, they are only hunches and should be treated as such, and dropped if they don't lead anywhere. The client will always find the answers they need if you just trust them. In my case, I find that even though I have a lot of experience, my suppositions are often wrong, and even when they are correct, they are rarely complete or exact unless they are true visions. But whether I am right or wrong in my feelings or speculations is immaterial. Usually my intuition is most helpful when it leads me to ask a good question.

The Conference

In 1994 I flew to Canada to attend the annual meeting of the International Society for the Study of Multiple Personality and Dissociation (the ISSMP&D – now the International Society for the Study of Trauma and Dissociation), an organization I had joined earlier. I didn't learn anything of a technical nature that I could use, or meet any self-proclaimed multiples, but I did learn something about the status of research and the current state of understanding of dissociation at that time. What I found most valuable however, were my interactions with some of the other attendees. It helped me to have a better understanding of how other people think of, feel about, and react to multiplex people or other people who have been diagnosed with a mental illness. I was very naive at the time and for some reason felt that these would all be rational, understanding, and nonjudgmental people that I could share with. Right. Well let's just say I was optimistic. I had to learn the hard way how things really are, and got a huge dose of reality.

On the first day I hung out with a group of lively therapists who seemed quite amiable – at first anyway. During lunch, using their terminology, I mentioned that I had discovered a few years back that I had MPD and had integrated with all my alters. I may have shared a relevant story or two and there were a couple of questions. After lunch we walked back to the hotel as a group. We took a couple of detours through some shops along the way and I noticed that no one in the group was talking to me. They seemed to be ignoring me, not looking at me, and behaving in an exclusionary manner. Whenever I would walk close to someone, they would increase their distance from me and I soon realized I had spooked them. I don't want to be unfair here but they were definitely acting differently toward me than they had at first when they assumed I was a licensed professional and one of "them." Was I imagining it? I didn't think I had acted in any way that might be construed as strange, but their body language made me feel like they were seeing me as a mentally deranged individual who might be dangerous and unpredictable. It didn't matter that I had said I was cured or that I presented no signs of being any less normal than they were. Then I realized it was very likely that these people had never actually worked with anyone with multiple personalities and had no real sense of reality about it whatsoever. Perhaps some of this was even a manifestation of an unconscious fear of their own multiplicity – who knows? In any event, thanks to widespread ignorance and the misperceptions generated by the media and psychiatry, I had become a pariah, an untouchable, for the moment.

I had one other similar experience at the end of the conference and it was clearly the subject matter that was problematic and not me. Of course I'm biased in favor of myself, but when I kept quiet about my "history" I had no problem socializing whatsoever, and everyone was quite normal and friendly.

In stark contrast to these few rather awkward encounters, I had dinner the first night of the conference with a delightful young lady who was an office assistant for a well-known psychotherapist, and I mentioned my multiplicity and its resolution to her. She thought it was fascinating and we had breakfast together the next morning. Talking about my past condition with her was like talking about gardening or baseball. At first I was baffled and speculated that she was unaffected because she was young and naive, but I observed her carefully and concluded that she wasn't an air-head at all, but actually comprehended what I was saying. She just didn't have the negative associations and evaluations that many others have. We also talked about her work, aspirations, and her further education. I gave her a few suggestions, which she found helpful, and when she left I felt very light hearted, and generally more hopeful for the human race.

I had lunch the second day with a quiet gentleman whom I had chatted with during a lecture. In discussing my case he was sincerely interested and wondered how he would know if he himself had alter personalities. He seemed to understand easily and had no outward fearfulness, skepticism, or other concerns. He seemed introspective. We hung around together for another two lectures.

I attended several gatherings and spoke with quite a few psychiatrists, doctors, and psychologists. Some were arrogant know-it-alls, some were quite humble and rational, a few were brilliant, and many were asking important questions and sincerely looking for answers. Mostly what I learned from the conference was that more effort was needed in developing a common terminology in discussing trauma and dissociation, and that there was almost no real understanding of the nature of traumatic memory and its resolution – just a lot of theories.

I refrained from mentioning my personal history quite so freely after the first day and had some good conversations. One psychologist does stand out though, because when I did mention to him my past dissociative condition, his identity shifted dramatically. He became deeply sympathetic, as if he were talking with a burn victim or other severely traumatized person who had just arrived for help. He seemed to be a sincerely compassionate person but his sympathetic manner toward me was nauseating. Explaining that I was completely healed and integrated had no effect. He was fully in his "compassionate therapist" identity. He wasn't seeing ME; he was only seeing his own mental projections, so I made an excuse and cut our conversation short. The lesson here, about how people only see their own projections of you, works both ways, which reminds me of another story worth relating that demonstrates this.

Years later my brother and his family were moving and I was helping unload some trucks at the new house. There were many other people helping as well. When I went to leave I decided to back my car down the long narrow driveway. There was an open gate at the end but I failed to notice a short metal post that was slightly away from the gate and too low to the ground to see. I ran into it and there was a loud bang! I got out to investigate. Nothing seemed damaged so I was getting back in the car when Jacob, a young man who had heard the noise, ran up to me from the house and asked if I was all right. He seemed totally sincere but somehow condescending. Everything about him irritated me. He asked a couple times if I was sure I didn't need any help. I said I was sure and left quickly, feeling insulted and quite angry. His tone of voice, facial expression, and body language were such as to make me think that he took me to be mentally incompetent. It was as if he were talking to a small child, but not exactly. I thought about it for a long time. I was taking it personally.

When I came back to help the next day around noon, I was hoping Jacob wouldn't be there. Our brief confrontation was still bothering me, as I hadn't tried to resolve my reaction yet. I went in the house and there were about fifteen people on a lunch break standing around the dining room table in happy conversation. There was plenty of food including tasty sandwiches, cheese, soda, and other snacks. I saw Jacob on the other side of the table, and tried to contain my laughter. Instantly it all made sense.

Standing next to him was a younger man with Down Syndrome and they were both wearing T-shirts connected with a local organization that helps developmentally disabled children. Jacob's job was working with kids with special needs. When he had come out to help me the day before, Jacob had shifted into his caregiver identity because that was his normal state when helping people in distress. He was treating me like one of his charges. It may or may not have been a stuck identity in his case, but, at the time, it wasn't appropriate in addressing me or the situation. The goal of that identity was probably something like "to understand and be understood by someone who has a mental deficiency." I had picked up on this immediately. I do have a strong ability to read people, but I think anyone would have gotten a similar impression. His manner may or may not have been appropriate in addressing someone who has such a deficiency, but it was his way of communicating with them. I was laughing at myself. I had let him put that "incompetent" identity on me, and I had reacted to it. The lesson is that people are always presenting us with an identity that has little or nothing to do with us, and everything to do with what they feel they need to be at the time. And this is usually automatic. As it suggests in the book "The Four Agreements," it's best not to take anything personally.[50]

Overall the conference in Vancouver was a fascinating experience. It connected me with many useful resources and I left a wiser person. However, I didn't see the need to attend any more in the future. I also decided afterward that if I did attend anything like this again, I would most likely not mention anything about my own case to anyone at all. I had gotten that out of my system.

---

[50] "The Four Agreements" - 2001, Don Miguel Ruiz

Chapter 8
Self-Healing Stories – Part 1
The Body

"The source of most disease is in the spirit" – Nikola Tesla

One of the things I like best about Francine Shapiro's books "Getting Past Your Past" and "EMDR," and other books on EMDR as well, including most notably those by Laurell Parnell and David Grand, are the many greatly detailed accounts of sessions the authors did with their clients.[51] These accounts help provide a clearer and deeper understanding of what trauma does, the kinds of issues one can address, and the relief and life-changes one gets when trauma is resolved. The personal accounts of my own sessions throughout the book are included to help expand that understanding.

The summer of 1992 was a period of many breakthroughs for me, including learning about multiplicity, personality integration, and understanding my life purpose. But throughout the first few years of my working with ID-R, beginning at the age of forty-three, and later, while the story of Patty and I was becoming more clear to me, I was also working on many other issues. These next two chapters and Chapter 14, explore my personal experiences with some of the many diverse conditions that I worked on, and will give you a small sampling of the wide range of problems that can result from trauma, and which can be healed when the trauma is resolved.

The majority of the unwanted conditions I tackled in the beginning were somatic in nature like headaches and other body

---

[51] See these two books by David Grand: "Emotional Healing at Warp Speed", 2001 and "Brainspotting", 2015. They provide more examples of the many kinds of problems that can be resolved by healing trauma.

aches and pains. I worked on these mainly because they were a daily occurrence and I was working on whatever came up. As soon as I resolved one thing, something else would present itself. It was fun and exciting and I was discovering unbelievable things about myself. But mainly I felt like I was doing what I'm here to do, and the conditions I worked on were clearing up, one after another. After about two years I ceased having headaches altogether. I also felt stronger and healthier, especially after doing more than seventy personality integrations and clearing up some major emotional trauma. In working with others I found that I could identify with most of my clients in that I had so often experienced the same or similar issues.

The following accounts are more than just stories – they reflect the deeper unconscious decisions and emotions that were uncovered in the sessions. Most people would not remember these details, and it is important to understand that I only recall them because the process enabled me to see into the altered state of traumatic shock where they were embedded. This chapter will focus on conditions that were mostly somatic in nature, while the next chapter includes issues that were mainly mental or psychological. Issues that are more spiritual in nature are described in Chapter 14. The sessions mentioned in these chapters took place between 1991 and 1995.

Epilepsy

When I was thirteen, I began having strange seizures at night during sleep. The first one was preceded by a dream of someone shooting me with some kind of ray gun through my window while I was lying in bed. I immediately felt something like electricity running through every nerve in my body. There were other strange phenomena as well, including a loud buzzing sound composed of many frequencies. My whole body felt paralyzed and there was a strong physical vibration that is hard to describe – but my whole body was humming. Also, the intensity of this whole experience of vibration and sound was cyclical – the vibrations would get very coarse and intense and then speed up and crest at a very smooth and high frequency, then drop down again, morphing into a very rough experience. The whole cycle would then repeat. It was very much like riding a roller coaster. During this time I was completely conscious. Each episode seemed to last less than a minute, after which I would awaken. Each time upon awakening I could still hear the buzzing sound in my head to some degree, and I felt kind of spaced out and dizzy. These aftereffects would pass after a few minutes.

I didn't tell my parents about the seizures, but instead hit the library to figure this thing out. I thought it might have something to do with my recent accident. A week or so before the seizures began I had fallen at school, hit the back of my head on the pavement, and experienced a grand mal seizure. I was a bit jangled afterwards, but got back to normal by resting a bit in the nurse's office.

After some research I figured I had some form of epilepsy. These episodes would recur about three times a week, and less frequently later on, but they only happened at night. I decided that all I could do when the seizures began was to just ride them out. When I was twenty years old, they took the form of what I called "fear dreams." These were brief moments of intense fear during which I would be fully conscious but find myself paralyzed, unable to move, and I would wake up before the "roller coaster" effect could begin. After I started meditating at the age of twenty-one, even the fear dreams stopped.

In 1976 when I began having the out-of-body experiences described in Chapter 3, I recognized the similarity of the vibrations I felt during these episodes, to the epileptic seizures. At that time, I thought that although the seizures originally may have been due to my head injury, the main triggering culprit was inner tension, which is why the meditation and deep relaxation had stopped them. This made sense, especially after I found that by relaxing during an OBE, the vibrations stopped immediately. But there was more to all this, which I discovered later, using ID-R.

In eighth grade my friend Ross and I were at the school bicycle racks. The school day had just ended and we were getting our bikes to go home. While backing my bike out of the rack I ignored the person behind me, as a prank, and experienced instant karma. His front tire hit my back wheel and I fell over my bike, hitting the back of my head on the asphalt. At first I was conscious. I didn't hit my head very hard, and I told Ross I was OK. It seemed like the impact on my head was very minor. But then everything went black and the seizure began.

I experienced intense vibrations throughout my body for a moment and then I felt nothing, and although I could still hear, I could not see. I heard Ross say "Are you fakin' it?", and later I heard Mr. Buckley, the Dean of Boys, saying he was putting a stick in my mouth so I wouldn't bite my tongue. The seizure must have lasted a few minutes. Mr. Buckley then brought me around with smelling salts, but I was unsteady on my feet and unable to speak. I remember that clearly, because when Mr. Buckley reprimanded me, saying that this should teach me a lesson, I had a great sarcastic comeback, but all that came out of my mouth was gibberish. He then escorted me to the nurse's office. That's all I remembered consciously, until my ID-R session thirty years later. Here's what actually happened:

When everything went black, I suddenly found myself twenty feet up in the air with full perception. I saw my body on the ground and the people watching, and while I could hear and see perfectly from this viewpoint, I could also hear through the body's ears and see darkness through the eyes. I had dual awareness. But from my exterior viewpoint I didn't care about any of it because I was delirious with joy – I was free! The genie was out of the bottle! The body seemed like an empty shell and I felt no connection to it. I thought I could now do anything I wanted. But a voice behind me reminded me that I couldn't leave – that I had some kind of contract or promise to fulfill. While in that expanded state, I knew it was true. I also realized it had something to do with Patty. Reluctantly I went back in the body.

The smell of ammonia from the smelling salts was very vivid during this session, as if it was actually present. I remembered that while in the nurse's office I asked the nurse if I could cry. She seemed hesitant to say yes, probably since boys aren't supposed to cry, but she replied, with a sarcastic and disapproving tone, "If you want to." I needed to cry, not because of the accident, but because I could not have that amazing freedom I had experienced earlier. I was back in prison, a hostage of the body. But I soon forgot the whole thing.

As real and visceral as these experiences were, I am quite sure that the nighttime "epilepsy" I experienced after the convulsions at school was a replay of that trauma, and nothing more. This replay was triggered by my having an OBE during sleep. As soon as the OBE would begin, my reaction was to jump back in my body and ride out the seizure. This whole experience was an automatic repetition of what had happened in the incident at school.

As to why this reaction only occurred during sleep and not other times I was exterior to my body, my guess is that these experiences were not similar enough to the incident or that there is something about sleep that is more specifically connected to that experience. It is important to note that in the school incident I was in a higher state of awareness than that of an ordinary OBE. In an ordinary OBE the feeling is that I am temporarily out of my body but intimately tied to it, not entirely free of it. During the school experience I knew that I was not the body and did not have to be tied to it, giving me a sense of freedom I had never experienced before in an ordinary OBE, and this was a big difference. (See page 343 for a discussion of levels of awareness.)

Two days before I worked on this incident, I had discovered an earlier similar incident. When I was still learning to walk as a child, I got out of my crib and attempted to traverse the vast terrain known as "the hallway." Unfortunately I slipped and hit the back of my head on the hardwood floor, causing me to go into convulsions, just as I had at school. If I had not had this accident, would I have experienced convulsions from a minor blow to the head when I was thirteen? I don't know, but there is a connection. As the young child, I also left my body and watched it twitching on the floor until the sitter came and picked me up. But back then, I did not have the same sense of freedom I experienced later, but neither did I have any sense of being trapped within a body.

Circumcision

"Circumcision, the surgical removal of the male foreskin, usually during the first few days after birth, is an emotionally charged subject that most people are reluctant to discuss openly, let alone objectively."
– Dr. Christine Northrup (2004)

Circumcising male children as babies is controversial. I find the reasons for it dubious myself. I have heard many circumcised men say, in interviews, that it has had no effect on their sex lives. This is possible, but my question is, if they consider their own degree of genital sensitivity and feeling to be normal, how would they know? New born babies are exquisitely sensitive to everything, and circumcision with no anesthetic is at least as traumatic as it would be for an adult – really. And just imagine what that would be like! Still, it is possible for any trauma to become dormant and have no negative effects. But in the case of a traumatic injury to one's sex organs which results in reduced sensitivity to feeling, afterward, one may not have any idea that what they feel has been numbed out to some degree. If one's orgasms are normal, they may feel that everything is fine.

When I was a baby, many times I was given milk that was too hot. After working through one of these incidents, I drank some ice water, and for the first time ever, I could actually feel the cold liquid enter my stomach! It was amazing! Until then I didn't know that people could feel hot or cold food entering their stomach, because my reaction in this incident, with the aid of my helper Medic, was to make my stomach numb.

Regardless of the motives behind involuntary circumcision, genital mutilation without any anesthetic is a barbaric act given the fact that babies are completely conscious and can feel and suffer pain just like anyone else, anytime after birth and even before they are born. The argument that we won't remember it anyway is not only untrue, but can be used to justify any kind of inhuman conduct toward children. And even if not remembered consciously, trauma can stay with us forever and affect us in profound ways, until resolved. Until I recovered from my own traumatic circumcision, my penis was basically numb on the surface.

I was circumcised when I was two years old. A doctor came to our house with his black bag, and, with my father present, prepared to do the circumcision with no anesthetic. My father objected to this, so the doctor reluctantly went to the nearest pharmacy, just two blocks away, and came back with sodium pentothal. He said it was the only anesthetic they had, but it should do the job. He gave me a shot, and, after the drug kicked in, proceeded to do the operation. I felt everything at first – all the drug did was paralyze me. But after the initial painful shock, it was Medic who felt everything, and responded by suppressing all feeling in the injured area. My father could tell that I was in severe pain, and he was complaining about it the whole time. The doctor said he was almost done, and he was allowed to finish, but I could feel his stress. When it was done, my father, a onetime boxer, angrily assailed the guy telling him, "I should just bust you one!" He paid him, begrudgingly, and told him "Get out of my house, and hope I don't ever see you again." He then came and apologized to me. I was still spaced out and just looked at him. What could I say? To me, it was just another day of people hurting me.

Since other issues took precedence, it took me a few sessions, done randomly over several years, to actually resolve this issue, but when it did finally get resolved, the difference was like night and day. The numbness was completely gone and the feeling returned so that the sensitivity was comparable to touching any other sensitive part of my body. Still, I have no way to compare how things would feel if that foreskin tissue had never been removed.

Leg Rash – or Feel the Burn

In my twenties I developed a rash on the back side of my left leg. It was a few inches away from the groin area and was not jock itch, but it was caused by the same common fungus. Although drugs and ointments would cause it to go away temporarily, it always returned. One doctor said I would probably have it for life. I had discovered the rash's origin long before I began using ID-R, but had been unable to resolve it until now. After this session the rash cleared up and never returned.

I don't know how old I was, maybe seven months more or less. My mother was changing my diaper on the bedroom floor, while smoking a cigarette. The burning end of the cigarette was very close to my left leg. At some point it grazed my scrotum and I felt it, but it was not a shock to me. It was more of an intense new feeling I didn't understand. Then the cigarette pressed directly into the back of my left leg. The burning sensation grew rapidly stronger but it took some moments before it became a shock. Perhaps the time was only milliseconds but in my state of consciousness as a child my experience of time was more flexible. Finally the pain reached a critical point and became overwhelming. Medic started kicking and screaming while I watched my mother do her best to help me.

When I was back in the body, the pain was suppressed, but still very distressing. My mother told my father that I had turned beet red when it happened. I have no idea what the burn looked like at the time.

A doctor was called to our house, and I recall he and my father leaning over me discussing the injury. The doctor asked if this was my first trauma. He then explained what he meant, and my father said it probably was. He then asked the doctor how long it would take to heal. "It may never heal," was the doctor's response. This guy knew his stuff! He also asked my father if I had experienced other injuries or accidents around my mother. "Do you think she did this on purpose?" my father asked, somewhat surprised. The doctor said he was just trying to get a clear picture of the situation.

Later however, my parents got into an argument about this injury possibly being intentional. I heard my mother say "You think I did this on purpose?!" and then "Fine, I'll never touch him again!" I'm sure this was a big shock for her, and that she made a decision. From that time on, the only physical contact she had with me was to do what was necessary to take care of me. But she never held me, hugged me, nursed me, or had any loving contact with me ever again, whereas before this incident, she occasionally had. But I know she didn't hurt me on purpose. It was her mean helper, Adrienne.

Anesthesia

I recalled the following when I was working on some pain which I traced back to an operation I had as a child. I had to have a relatively minor operation when I was four to correct a hydrocoele which is a fluid leak in the groin area. I speculate that this condition was possibly the result of a weakness caused by the doctor holding me upside down by my feet and dropping me when I was born. In any event, after having the fluid drained I was scheduled for surgery. I can still recall the smell of the ether that was used as an anesthetic. However, I could feel the pain of the surgeon's knife even while I appeared to be unconscious. At one point my left leg began kicking, as it did during my birth trauma, and they had to give me extra drops of ether on the sponge or whatever it was over my face. After the initial pain, I found myself exterior, floating around the room until the surgery was over, watching everything. It was all quite clear. After the operation I had some very colorful psychedelic dreams.

At the age of two I was running through the house with an open can of baby food, fell, and cut myself on the lid. I still have the small scar in the middle of my forehead. I was taken to the hospital a few blocks away and had the wound stitched up. While in the doctor's chair, I was given nitrous oxide. At first I wouldn't inhale it, so my father told me it was laughing gas and pretended to breathe it from the mask, and then started laughing. He promised he would be there with me the whole time. After I inhaled the gas I could still feel the pain of the suturing, and left my body immediately, fully conscious. My father left the room as soon as I was unconscious, and came back before I woke up. I let him know right away I was mad that he had lied to me and left the room, although he denied it. But I had been exterior and watching the whole time.

Because I was in an altered state of consciousness or exterior during my operations, the trauma from the pain was usually momentary. Still, as we have seen, these traumas did cause problems later. This is probably how it is for most people. Most of us seem to remember nothing from being put under anesthesia, and there appears to be no problem afterward, but since trauma can occur even while we are apparently "out," problems may occur at any point later on. And there are some people who, for one reason or another, have found themselves fully conscious during a medical procedure while under general anesthesia, and have awakened with considerable distress, having recalled the whole thing. In such cases the trauma is more like being tortured and the post-traumatic effects can be severe. A very moving case of this kind is related in Chapter 12 of the book "The Body Keeps the Score.".

I have had many clients who reported remembering things that happened while they were under general anesthesia, including pain, while doing ID-R, although they had never remembered these things before. Waldo was a client in his seventies who I worked with on and off for two years, to heal his sciatic pain, among other things. I had taught him how to turn off the pain using hypnosis and it worked very well, but he just wouldn't use it at home. We worked through several injuries that caused his original problem but he still had a lot of pain. Eventually we got to the root of where the pain was now coming from, which was one of the back operations he had many years earlier in an effort to fix his original pain. The fact was that while under general anesthesia Waldo could still feel the pain of the surgery, and it stayed with him. He had assumed the operation had simply failed to correct the problem. After we worked through that surgery the pain didn't diminish right away, so I thought we had missed something. But a few days later something made him angry and he yelled at someone. At that moment all the remaining back pain suddenly came shooting out and disappeared. He came in later and happily told me that his sciatica was gone and declared himself cured.

Because we can still feel pain while under some forms of general anesthesia and be traumatized by that, and yet remember nothing of this at the time, it seems that local anesthesia should also be employed concurrently. But I'm not a doctor and I haven't researched whether this is a common practice or even whether it is medically feasible or safe. If it is feasible, I speculate that it could reduce complications, promote faster recovery from surgery, and prevent problems later on. It would also be best if there was minimal talking, or no talking at all, when general anesthesia is used or during any painful medical procedure or childbirth. Whatever words a person hears while in the drug induced unconscious state, or any state of shock or trauma for that matter, can have the same effect as a post hypnotic command. I have presented several examples of this from my own experiences. If words are spoken beyond what is necessary, they should all be helpful, hopeful, and positive words, or at least neutral. When you understand how the mind works, this is all simply common sense.

One last thing – when we undergo a dental or medical procedure in which a local anesthetic is used, and we are given pain medication to use after the anesthetic wears off, I would recommend using that medication when the pain starts to return so that it can take effect *BEFORE* the pain can become a shock, *IF* the anticipated pain might possibly be that extreme.

The Cruel Shoes

We all have hundreds of moments in our lives that change us – they change our ideas of who we are, our direction in life, our attitudes, predispositions, and propensities – and then we forget them. But everything about us has a cause, a history, and a reason for being. In my thirties I used to come home from work and sit down or lay on the bed and occasionally experience an overwhelming need to remove my shoes. The feeling was quite maddening but vanished instantly, once I kicked the shoes off. I experienced this feeling again many years later, and found the original shock.

I got some new shoes and they were very uncomfortable. I may have been around eight years old. My mother said they had to be broken in. So on the day I got the shoes she wouldn't let me take them off, which added a control issue to the situation. This only caused me to put more of my attention on my discomfort. I found myself mentally resisting the tight feeling of the shoes and continued to whine about them. But my mother was unrelenting. I wanted to scream but she told me to be quiet and that I only had to keep them on for one hour and walk around in them. For me that was an eternity. When I could no longer tolerate the agony, which I was mostly creating myself by my own resistance, I had a shock. This shock was not painful enough for Buffer and Medic to handle, so my solution was to suppress the discomfort by distracting myself. I began pounding my fist on the couch and repeating some words over and over for about ten minutes. I don't yet recall what I was saying but I basically put myself in a trance in which those words became a powerful suggestion that made me not feel the shoes at all. This new state remained in effect until I was able to take the shoes off. The reaction soon went dormant and was reactivated many years later. It was now finally resolved.

Turning a Blind Eye

I was sent to see the school nurse about my vision when I was in fifth grade, and I was told I was nearsighted and needed glasses. I didn't like the idea so I didn't get any. I later learned that reading, and similar close work, when done in childhood while the eyes are still developing, is the primary cause of almost all myopia or nearsightedness. This is something everyone needs to know, and especially parents and teachers.

But there can, of course, be other contributing physical and psychological factors affecting vision as well. When I was between three and four years old, I was with my father at the office of some kind of doctor or teacher. The room was a kind of Romper Room place and I was instructed to do various activities which seemed like games. It was all designed to be fun, but I was more interested in trying to understand what the adults were talking about. At one point I was given an eye test. My father bragged that he had pilot's-eyes and that my vision would be as good as his. I had a lot of anger toward my father and felt the need to do the opposite of whatever he wanted. So when I was asked to describe the symbols on a chart, I had a shock in considering the consequences of performing well, and I rebelled. But I could see the chart fine so my solution was to make my vision blurry so I could not see it clearly. I also lied when necessary. My father was predictably upset but decided I just didn't understand the test.

There were also several other times later on when it was important for me to *NOT* see clearly as a solution to some traumatic situation, and these identities contributed to my problem. I recall my vision not being perfect in second grade, but it was in fifth grade, after I began reading for many hours every day, that my vision rapidly deteriorated. I finally got a pair of glasses when I was fifteen, but because I was already very self-conscious about my appearance, I threw them away. When I was sixteen, I found a book called "See Without Glasses" and found that looking through a pinhole, which I could simulate with my right thumb and two fingers, allowed me to read the blackboards at school. Also I learned some good reading habits, which, along with the relaxation exercises in the book, did improve my vision. However many of the ideas in the book about how the eyes work were incorrect. I found this out in college by researching eye physiology.

In my twenties I found the book "The Myopia Myth" by Donald Rehm, which correctly explains how the eyes work and describes the causes of myopia.[52] When the lenses of the eyes are relaxed, they are focused in the distance. Focusing on something close involves tension, but reading glasses, when used properly, allow the

---

[52] "The Myopia Myth" - 1974, by Donald Rehm

eyes to be relaxed while reading. Although there were also psychological factors involved, my own myopia was caused mainly by reading and writing, which similarly impacts the eyesight of countless millions of children around the world. But Myopia can be prevented and even reversed if caught in time.

My eyesight was 20/200 at one point, and now it is about 20/30 due to decades of good reading habits, meditation, ID-R, and the consistent use of reading glasses. Everyone would benefit by using reading glasses for ALL reading and close work, whether they "need" to use them or not. But this is CRITICAL for children when they begin reading, because their eyes are still developing until around adolescence, and will permanently adjust to the range of vision that they are most accustomed to. This is how we evolved. I hope that someday reading glasses will be provided for every student in all schools from first grade on. The solution is simple but unfortunately it is also easily ignored, and eye glasses are big business. For a more complete understanding of this topic I recommend Rehm's book and the website myopia.org.

Walking Pneumonia – or
Using Death as an Advisor

"Death is the only wise advisor that we have. Whenever you feel, as you always do, that everything is going wrong and you're about to be annihilated, turn to your death and ask if that is so. Your death will tell you that you're wrong; that nothing really matters outside its touch. Your death will tell you, 'I haven't touched you yet'."
– Carlos Castaneda, Journey to Ixtlan

One summer during the first few years of doing ID-R, when I went on my daily runs, I began feeling unusually tired. On hot days I would come home weak and very exhausted. This had never happened before so I treated it as a reaction, and discovered that it was. It led me to recall the time in the Summer of 1977 when I was twenty-nine and had walking pneumonia. I was managing a restaurant, working all the time, experiencing lots of stress, and getting little sleep.

I had just come home from work and was lying on the waterbed feeling complete exhaustion. My chest felt heavy, I had a bad headache, and I was burning up. Lynne took my temperature with a mercury thermometer. She looked at the reading and looked at me but didn't say anything. She shook the thermometer down and took my temperature again. I asked her what it was but she was silent. She said she wasn't reading it right or it wasn't working. She took my temperature a third time. Again she wouldn't tell me what it said. Finally she just showed it to me – 107 degrees! It took a moment for that to sink in. My first thought was that at 106 degrees you die!

I had a shock. My whole life passed before me and I realized I was wasting it. What was I doing managing a restaurant? I had other more important things to do! In that moment Death was my advisor. I decided to change my life. I jumped out of bed and told Lynne to get some ice. I ran in the bathroom and filled the tub with water. With some fortitude I slid into the cold water and we slowly added the ice. As my temperature dropped, I realized I wasn't just tired – I had walking pneumonia. I took lots of vitamin C and other nutrients, got a lot of rest, did meditation, and recovered quickly. But I quit my job the next week. It was quite a surprise to my employers, especially since they had just offered me the job of general manager of their entire chain of restaurants in the area, which I also declined. I decided instead to take time off work so I could concentrate on my true vocation. After working through this incident, my summer exhaustion after running completely disappeared. This reaction had been reactivated one day by the heat.

The Successfully Boring Voice

We are unaware of how our voice sounds to others until we hear it recorded and played back. To me, my voice always sounded weak and wimpy, and there was a particular quality to it I didn't like. One day I decided I needed to change my voice so I explored the idea that it was part of a stuck identity. It was.

When I was about six years old, our new babysitter was eating some candies. I went up to her and asked if I could have one. I was very enthusiastic and full of energy. She said "Not when you ask me like that!" She looked disgusted. She described my mannerisms, my voice, and my impatience, and told me how she felt put off by my whole approach. She said something more and made it clear that the answer was no. I walked away feeling there was something wrong with my voice. It was puzzling and I tried to figure it out. I realized I had too much energy and excitement for her. I went back to her and asked her again in a gentler way, but she didn't like that either. She told me I sounded like a cry baby or a little girl or something, and my attitude was still too perky for her. I had failed, and felt her criticism as a personal affront. That's when I had a shock. I felt there was something wrong with me. I realized that I needed to be emotionless and address her in the most uninteresting way I could. In that moment I knew what was required and created a very weak and boring voice. I made my request again in a tone of exaggerated disinterest. "That's much better," she said, and gave me a candy. Somehow that winning voice became habitual. Once resolved, that wimpish quality I despised was gone and I now had the ability to change my voice, but I still needed some help.

I found what I needed in the excellent book "Change Your Voice Change Your Life."[53] I practiced the voice training methods in the book and learned to use my natural voice. The result was amazing, but my new voice took me some getting used to. I first tried it out on my mother and some friends. I was afraid that they would wonder why I was talking so differently, and I was very hesitant at first. It was like I was changing my face or my identity because I was very identified with how my old voice sounded to me when I spoke, but to my surprise, no one even noticed. That could be partially due to the phenomenon of "change blindness" mentioned earlier. People whom I spoke with for the first time however, told me they liked my voice, which no one had ever said before. But if I had not resolved the "boring voice" identity, trying to improve my voice may not have worked at all.

Swimming Dysfunction

I was never a good swimmer and never really practiced until required to do so in high school. I went swimming with my friends as a kid but never liked it much. One day I was working on a feeling

---

[53] Change Your Voice Change Your Life" - 1984 by Dr. Morton Cooper

of being a failure when I discovered where my swimming difficulties started.

My father often bragged that he could swim like a fish. He tried to teach me to swim when I was a child, but he was not a good teacher. We were at a crowded public pool and I was maybe five or six. He was holding me by the waist so that I was horizontal in the water, and he told me how to move my arms and legs. But when I did what he said, I kept getting a face full of water and it was hard to breathe. I just didn't like the whole thing – especially him controlling me and his critical tone of voice when I didn't do it right. He was making me feel like a failure.

A shock occurred at the idea that I was going to have to endure this until I got it right. I found that thought unacceptable. I was done. In the power-zone I decided to fail, so that he would let me go. So I panicked and started thrashing around wildly until he pulled me upright. I told him I didn't want to swim anymore, at which point he publicly harangued me, telling me I was a quitter and saying, in an ugly voice, "You're no son of mine." I remember going back and sitting on my towel, feeling bad and humiliated. But this was largely a pretense, because secretly I knew I had won. I had accomplished my purpose which was to escape the intolerable situation. Just as a shock is a form of failure, our solutions, when they work, are a form of winning, even if they never serve us well again or are not seen as winners by others. We could say that we tend to unconsciously hold on to, and use, our winning solutions over and over, even though they are now problematic, but this actually happens automatically. After this session I felt like I would love to take lessons and improve my swimming abilities. I even bought a book on the subject but just never found the time to practice.

Summary

The kinds of unwanted conditions that can be caused by or influenced by past trauma is unlimited. So that's the first point – any condition or situation that is bothering you might be purely, or partially, a reaction that has little to do with your present reality. The goal is to resolve these states or manage them somehow. The approach used in these self-healing stories involves intentionally putting ourselves in the unwanted state in order to gain access to the unconscious aspects of it that keep it operating This enables us to permanently remove it. This is how ID-R works.

Next it is important to realize, as explained above, that when you are in an unwanted state, _your view of reality is determined by that state_, and it may be very difficult to see beyond that reality or to change your focus strongly enough to even modify that state. This is especially true if it is a physical state of dysfunction or pain. How to manage unwanted conditions, short of resolving them, is a very important subject and is covered in Chapter 18. Now let's go a bit deeper.

Chapter 9
Self-Healing Stories – Part 2
The Mind

"There is no normal life that is free of pain. It's the very wrestling with our problems that can be the impetus for our growth."
– Fred Rogers (Mr. Rogers)

No Charisma

I loved Miss Nathan. She was my fifth grade teacher until she was replaced by Mrs. Goodman. She left to get married to some bald headed guy. Naturally I didn't like the man, or the picture of him that she showed us – none of her students did – because we didn't want her to leave. Miss Nathan, through her enthusiasm and positive spirit, inspired me to work hard. I loved doing homework in her class, and when we were each assigned to do one report on a different American state, I did eleven ten-page reports. Miss Nathan thought highly of me for some reason and one day she asked me to stay for a few minutes after class during recess, and teach something to six other kids. Then she left the room.

Maybe I was supposed to inspire them by talking about how I did so many reports. I had written to the governor of each state I chose, and got back lots of information. It was fun! I stood behind the teacher's desk and began my momentary stint as Mr. Important. I felt elevated and rather puffed up. I was also overly serious. The other kids were immediately bored. I was talking *AT* them, not *TO* them. One by one they walked out before I was done. At one point I had a shock. I realized I had no control, no leverage, and no charisma, and my authority was slipping away! Maybe at the time I would have used the word "powerless." When we were down to two kids remaining, I said "That's all," and they left. I felt weak and inadequate. I walked out wondering how teachers maintained attention and control. What was their mysterious power and why didn't I have any? Hadn't I been put in charge? I was puzzled.

This, and several similar and relatively small traumatic experiences, were all hindrances later on, causing some degree of dysfunction when I had to address a group of people. On such occasions I would shift into whatever identity got triggered, and experience the resulting emotions and thoughts, like having no power or charisma.

The problem is that when we are looking from the viewpoint of a stuck identity it is very difficult to see past its perspective even when we know better – a point worth reiterating. Because it changes our view of the world and our reality, we then act as if that reality were true, which can be a severe limitation. However, we can never really see the degree to which we are inhibited by some of our reactions until they are gone and we can finally see the difference. It's like wearing colored glasses and then taking them off. And sometimes the difference is profound. My point is that if you have any reactionary states arising in any situation, the potential for improvement may be far beyond what you might think, because these states limit our ability to have any other perspective. This can be difficult to truly grasp until you've experienced it multiple times.

Public Speaking – or Humiliation 101

One day back in third grade it was my turn to give a short talk on some subject in front of the class. I had done "Show and Tell" before and thought this would be a piece of cake. All my friends called me a "brain" because they thought I was very smart even then, before I started reading dozens of books a week. So I was really full of myself before this talk. I thought I was going to "knock 'em dead" in the parlance of the time. I started out OK but something happened. I lost my train of thought and started to dissociate. Another personality was talking to me and I got confused. At some point I panicked and couldn't even speak. Finally the teacher said "Ok Dennis, that was fine, you can go back to your seat." I slunk off, eyes to the floor. Back at my desk I had another shock while considering my humiliation. I dropped the "I'm so smart" attitude and decided that I was no smarter than my "dumb" friends. I was just like them, and that was OK. I was in good company, and at least this attitude was better than being a failure.

In the second semester of fifth grade Mrs. Goodman asked me to participate in a class play. She had a high opinion of me and thought this would showcase my talent. I tried to say "No" but she wouldn't listen, so I gave up trying. But I was terrified of being in the play and could not bring myself to practice with the other students at the home of one of them, which was in walking distance from mine. So I never went, never learned the lines, and didn't even recall the name of the play. I worried about the play every day though, and had several shocks about it. But for some reason I was even afraid to tell the teacher that I couldn't do it. I thought that if I just didn't practice I could avoid the whole situation by default, and while I knew the teacher would be mad, I could live with that.

On the day of the play I sprang the news on Mrs. Goodman, and she was furious! I'd never seen her so mad! Still, I thought I was off the hook, but she came back to my desk and said that I would have to do the play anyway! Another shock! So I prepared myself for failure, and the play was a total fiasco! Mrs. Goodman's plan was to hide under a desk and whisper my lines to me. I tried to repeat her words but she was barely audible, and I screwed them up royally. Almost everything I said caused the whole class to burst into laughter. The play didn't last long.

If only the teacher had listened to me, had asked me about my reluctance, had considered my feelings, or understood that I had some serious issues, we could have avoided this. Afterward she told me she was very disappointed in me but didn't scold me further. I could sense that she realized I was just a kid, and that somehow this was not totally my fault. Most of my stage fright disappeared after resolving this experience. Years later however, I became curious about why I was dead set against doing the play. I realized there had to be more to this than just the embarrassment from the incident in third grade, and I was right – it was something else.

The X-Room – or A Snow Job

In third grade I was approached by a teacher with white hair about a special project. I'd seen her at school but I didn't know her. We'll call her Mrs. Snow. She led me into a room across the hall from my third grade classroom. This room, which I call the X-Room, was used mostly as an audio-visual and utility room for making copies and showing students educational films, and other things. I had never been in that room before, and its intoxicating aroma of mimeograph ink was a new experience. Mrs. Snow left and brought in a girl student, Monica, and had us sitting next to each other. She said this was an experimental class where we were going to be actors in a play. She made us feel important. She explained a few things about what we would be doing, and said the play was going to help teach other kids something about boys and girls, and babies. She told us when to come back the next day during recess, and we did.

Mrs. Snow gave us each a script and had us do some role playing. This whole thing may have gone on for maybe three or four days but it's very hazy. She didn't have us do anything sexual, but at some point, something I said made Monica get mad and she left the room, although I was only following instructions. However, this whole thing was starting to make me feel uncomfortable. Mrs. Snow ran after Monica and told me to stay there. When the teacher came back, she sat at a small desk facing me and spent quite some time writing something on a sheet of paper. She seemed worried and was talking to herself. I realized that she was afraid Monica would tell someone about our class. When she was done, Mrs. Snow handed me the paper and told me that she was going to bring Monica back in the room. I was supposed to read this paper to Monica, word for word. She was very adamant that I agree, although I had no idea what she had written. As she left she told me not to read the paper except to Monica.

Monica finally came in the room, alone, and said I was supposed to tell her something. We stood face to face and I read the paper to her. It was basically an excuse for what had happened, explaining that it was all part of an act that meant something other than what it seemed. As I read the paper I realized that this statement was putting all the blame for whatever caused Monica to be upset, on ME! So while I pretended to be reading the paper I changed it. I made up my own statement saying that my reading this statement was also part of the play and none of it was real. My revision was actually kind of brilliant. Monica left confused, but still mad.

I now realized that Mrs. Snow was up to no good and had betrayed me. I scrammed out of there and don't remember ever

seeing Mrs. Snow again, although I think I just avoided her. The
teacher I had in fourth grade also had white hair, which did cause
me to switch with my helper Denise. That teacher may have been
Mrs. Snow, but I really can't say for sure. However, I do remember
going into the X-Room again in fifth grade to watch a film with the
class. As I walked in the door I had a strange feeling, like there was
something mysterious about that room – something I couldn't
remember. So when Mrs. Goodman tried to get me to be in the
play ... well ... you get the picture. Things got triggered, and I'd had
my fill of plays.

My First Day of School

After I started reading "The Primal Scream" back in 1976 and
began trying to recall my early childhood, there were many
memories that arose spontaneously. Now, out of curiosity, I decided
to take a closer look at some of these. These first memories
appeared as isolated snapshots of a past scene, and while they all
seemed unimportant at first glance, they were all connected with
significant trauma. In one of these snapshots I was standing outside
my kindergarten classroom with my mother.

This was my very first day of school and there was a line of
children filing into the classroom and getting name tags, but my
mother and I were at the end of the line because I refused to go in.
This snapshot memory was a "stuck picture" trapped in the moment
of shock that occurred when my mother told me I had to go in and
I felt I was doomed. The idea of going to school had triggered an
earlier experience and I was terrified.

When that babysitter was molesting me when I was two years
old, she had told me that I was in school and she was my teacher,
and that what we were doing were called lessons. That morning
when I was told I was going to school, I threw a fit. When it was my
turn to go in the classroom I threw another tantrum, screaming and
pleading until my mother promised to stay there with me, outside
the door where I could see her.

As I sat there on the floor with all the other kids I kept looking
over to make sure mom was still there, and for a while she was. But
when I looked over and saw she was gone, I left my body for several
minutes. This was a spontaneous reaction. Eventually I felt safer but

was relieved when mom came back to pick me up. Later my father asked how I liked my first day of school. I told him there was a bubble in my head. I was trying to describe the OBE experience where I felt like a bubble above my physical head. He asked me what happened to it and I said "It popped"; we both laughed. We could learn a lot from children if we truly listened and tried to understand their experiences with an open mind.

In that earlier experience when I was two, after my parents realized I was being assaulted by the babysitter, we immediately went to her apartment and my father banged on the door. While he held me I pretended to be asleep. The sitter wasn't home. And yet my mother, having no one else to watch me, took me back to that sitter the very next day. She confronted this lady, who denied hurting me, but I threw a tantrum outside her door and would not go in for some time. My first day of school was a painful reenactment of that traumatic scene.

The Manly Face

About a year after starting my ID-R counseling practice, I was having coffee with Jeremy, a young pianist I met earlier that day at a local church. We were having a great conversation at a nearby café when suddenly I had the mistaken idea that he might be gay. Then I noticed that my face had changed. It was like I was wearing a mask and it was hard to change my expression. I was able to shake it off and we went to my office to do a session because he had an issue he wanted to clear up. Afterwards, I worked on this mask phenomenon and recalled the following.

In my third year of college, having had almost no social interactions with my classmates in college, high school, or any time after seventh grade, my social personality was very stunted. Although I knew a lot about many things, socially I was still about twelve years old and very naive in many ways. Some hometown friends would occasionally come up and visit me and we'd explore the town and have fun on weekends. I had a room with two beds in a coed facility and my friend Jeff came up and slept over one time.

We were going to get up early and explore the extensive hiking trails along the American River less than a half mile away. When we were getting ready to sleep, I suggested we push our beds together as if we were sleeping outside, but he said no. We had slept outside in sleeping bags right next to each other many times in the past and I was thinking this would be the same, and I was kind of enthusiastic about it. He said no again, and when I continued to promote the idea he finally shouted at me: "NO!" That's when I got it – and it was a bit of a shock. We went to sleep in silence.

When I awoke in the morning I remembered what had happened and didn't know how to face Jeff. That's when I had the shock that created the "manly face." Unsure of how to "be," I suppressed all thought of my faux pas the night before and became very manly! And so did Jeff! We talked about manly things like sports and motorcycles, and we spoke in manly voices – it was just like the "pillows" scene in the movie "Planes, Trains and Automobiles." It's hilarious now, looking back, although it was quite awkward at the time. The manly face was a mask to hide my embarrassment and humiliation, and to protect me from being misinterpreted. It confirmed that I was not gay and also hid my homophobia, a very prevalent condition back then, and one I have since resolved. Jeff must have had a similar reaction.

I have noticed and resolved many "stuck faces" over the years – faces that served as masks to hide something or to project something. You can also have stuck postures, voices, ways of walking or talking, and other stuck traits. Anything can be part of a reactive identity. Until you spend some time doing self-observation, noticing your reactions and your various mind-body states as they come and go, as I have done since I was a child, many of these experiences and topics like "stuck faces" may seem like things you have never experienced yourself, and hence may sound strange. But they are not. When you start becoming more mindfully aware of your own experiences, more of these phenomena will be recognized as something you have indeed experienced many times yourself.

The Black Leather Jacket Dysphoria

My brother Alan bought three black leather aviation jackets one Christmas in the late 1980's, as gifts for Blake and me, and for himself. The jackets were great but I never wore mine – it stayed in the closet for years. For some reason I just felt uncomfortable wearing it.

Twelve years later, I was investigating a pain in my right eye and recalled a confrontation with two seniors when I was a sophomore in high school. I had gotten a new black leather jacket for Christmas and was very proud of it. One day I was walking from my High School locker through the east hallway, when two older boys began harassing me. One of them said he really liked my jacket and asked me if he could try it on. I was feeling intimidated but, in the spirit of good will, I naively took the jacket off and gave it to him. He put it on and said he liked it and was going to keep it. When I asked for it back, he asked me how much I wanted it. He then said I had to fight him for it, and slapped me in the face. In my shock various thoughts came up, including the idea that I could easily kill him. I also had a thought that led me on a long twisted path in my mind to a passage in the Bible about turning the other cheek. I decided that I would do nothing, and a great sense of peace came over me.

The guy asked me if I was just going to let him hit me. He slapped me in the face several more times, but I felt my nonresistance was actually shaming him. Some students down the hall yelled at them to leave me alone, and the two bullies finally walked away laughing. The guy with my jacket threw it on the ground, and I walked over and picked it up. The other students came over to see if I was OK, which I was, and said these guys were just a couple of jerks who thought they could do anything because they were seniors. But I never wore that jacket to school again.

Once this incident was resolved, the former hesitation completely disappeared and I have happily worn my leather jacket ever since. This example illustrates how tuck identities can and do affect every aspect of our lives, and can be responsible for anything from major physical and emotional issues, to simple attitudes and preferences, and everything in between.

Arachnophobia

I had some fear and loathing of spiders, especially black widows, since I was a kid, and I used to have scary dreams of black widow spiders fairly often. I don't know if I would call it a spider phobia, but although I overcame this reaction for most spiders, I couldn't do it with black widows until I resolved two incidents.

At age nine I was examining the black widow webs in our garage. I was scared of the spiders but, being the scientist that I was, I also found them fascinating. Terrence was watching me as I investigated a big spider web and when I told him what I was doing he said I needed a closer look. He then grabbed me by the neck and shoved my face into the black widow's web. I struggled to break free and I did get away, but not before having a shock. In the shock I actually communicated psychically with the spider. I asked it not to bite me and promised to leave it alone. While this was going on, I sensed the spider's mind – it was very mechanical and robotic. I sensed no emotions and do not know if it was conscious, but it seemed to agree with my proposition. Anyway, I was not bitten, but got stuck with some strong feelings, especially the feeling of revulsion.

Most of the fear however, started earlier. When I was five my father and I were in the garage. He called me over and wanted to show me something. He was wearing black gloves and had something on his left hand. When I looked, I saw a big black widow spider crawling slowly on top of his glove. It was shiny and black and I thought it was beautiful, so I reached out to pick it up. In horror my dad yelled "No!" and jerked his hand away, causing the spider to land on the back of my shirt near my right shoulder. Then he yelled at me, with great fear in his voice, "Don't move! Turn around! Keep still!" Because of my father's tone and the fear in his voice, I became very frightened myself. He recovered the spider and killed it, and explained to me that they were very dangerous. This was the origin of my fear. After resolving this I had no more concerns, or scary dreams, about spiders.

The Wise Sitter – or How Would You Feel?

One day during the time period when I was working on the issues in this chapter, a relative was visiting with me, and before she left she said something that implied I had done something wrong. I gave her some excuse, defending myself verbally, but after she was gone I found myself continuing to talk to her in my head. I was making up excuse after excuse to justify my behavior. I quickly realized this was a reaction. I worked on it right then and soon found its source.

When I was six or seven I was home alone with a temporary babysitter named Sherry, while everyone else was gone. Larry, a friend of mine from down the street, kept calling me on the phone and I told him repeatedly that I didn't want to talk to him. Then he showed up at my door. I answered the door and yelled at him, I really insulted him and told him to go home. Sherry, who was reading in the front room and witnessed everything, told me that I was very rude and that if she were Larry, she would never talk to me again. I had a shock at the idea that I had done something wrong and might be in trouble. I shifted into making up excuses as to why my friend had deserved this, and why I did what I did. I made up excuse after excuse to justify my actions. This was the identity I was addressing, and which I needed to resolve in my session. Then I recalled the rest.

After listening to my excuses Sherry suggested I put myself in Larry's place and imagine how I would feel if I were him. So I did – but I was able to access his feelings psychically and really feel what he felt. And that was another shock! I realized that his feelings were as real as mine and that hurting him was like hurting myself! I decided that Sherry was right and that this insight was something I needed to help guide me in life. After thinking about this for a minute I went over to Sherry and told her that she was very smart. I then asked her if she could tell me some more smart things. She laughed and said she was flattered, but these were just things you learn while growing up.

We talked a while and Sherry explained a few other things about life which I thought were profound, and which made me think. I began to feel a huge thirst for knowledge. She then said that my parents should be teaching me these things, but I told her they didn't teach me anything. She said parents want to teach their children well, but sometimes they don't do as good a job as they are supposed to. Then I asked her if she could be my mom. She said I could only have one mother, and that I should ask *her* questions whenever I wanted to know something.

When my parents came home I heard Sherry talking with my mother, telling her I was a special kid and that I should be given every opportunity to learn. I never saw Sherry again but she did inspire me to ask questions.

The Undeserving

When I first started doing ID-R with others and wanted to promote my services, I decided to go to a particular event and pass out flyers. But I felt inhibited by a feeling that I would be bothering people. I cleared that up quickly but then another problem appeared. I felt that no one would believe me.

When I was around six years old I saw a strange cloud of gray light floating in the air in the middle of my bedroom one night. I crept out of my room and found my father in the living room drinking vodka. I told him there might be a ghost in my room and he just looked at me with disdain. He was drunk, and said it was nothing and I should go back to bed. In my shock of being so lightly brushed off, I felt unsafe and not believed. But I decided that to press the issue would be bad for me, so I crept back to my room and found that the phenomenon was gone. Working on this incident cleared that feeling up. but there was still something else in my way.

As I focused on this new obstacle I suddenly became aware of an awful feeling, a feeling that I didn't deserve to be part of the human race. It was like today I had been peeling off layers of negative self-image or self-esteem and had gotten to something very deep and heavy. It was something I had always remembered, but I only remembered part of it. When I was six years old I was playing with my youngest brother Blake who was two. I was trying to get a toy truck away from him and I got behind him and pulled his head back, thinking he would let go, but he didn't, so I kept pulling. I didn't realize I was choking him. Then his body went limp. I jumped up and yelled "Dad, there's something wrong with Blake!" He ran over, as my mother looked on, and said "Jesus Christ, what did you do?!" I told him, and he said Blake wasn't breathing. He was turning blue as I watched my dad holding him upside down by his ankles. That's the part that was always remembered. The aftermath was not.

Frightened, I ran and hid in the empty red vacuum cleaner chest in my parents' bedroom. After a few minutes my father found me, and when I stood up he asked me if I was happy now that my little brother was dead. He wasn't dead, he was fine, as I found out two minutes later when I saw him walking down the hallway.

But for those two minutes my father harangued me about killing my brother, until my mother walked in the bedroom and asked him what he had said to me. She scolded him and told me the truth. But it was too late. I had fallen to the floor and was pounding my fist and screaming "No, no, no!" I could see some of my helpers standing around looking sad. This was one of the most devastating moments of my life, and I had several more aftershocks related to this. I won't go into them all, but the end result was that I had to suppress all my feelings of grief, guilt, and horror, behind a fake identity that was founded on the idea that the whole choking episode never happened. This false identity was created when I first came out of my closet, after hiding there and contemplating things for several hours, amidst further shocks. I remember walking into the kitchen and seeing my mother cleaning the table. I didn't know how to *BE*, or how I could still fit into the family. But when she saw me, she treated me normally, as if nothing had happened. But something *HAD* happened! So I had another shock trying to reconcile this, and chose to play along, as if the recent events had never occurred. But the negative feelings and ideas of my self-worth were still there and affected me for much of my life after that, while this part of the incident was never consciously recalled. Deep down inside I felt like I had killed my brother, and those feelings were painfully difficult to relive. After this session I had no problem handing out my flyers. But the positive effects of resolving this traumatic incident were far reaching – indeed they were life changing.

Unfriended

Julian was my best friend at school in the sixth grade. Some of our adventures were quite mischievous and we were lucky we didn't get caught pulling some of our thoughtless pranks, like breaking windows, or turning off the lights at a local stadium one night in the middle of a packed music concert. But Julian laughed easily, told funny jokes, and was always cheerful and good company.

One day Julian and I were playing around with some exercise equipment I had. One contraption had two wooden bars connected by two long metal springs. You could stand on one bar and press the other bar over your head, pushing against the force of the springs. Julian was doing some repetitions of that when the thing broke, and the bar he was standing on sprung up and hit him in the left eye. My instant response was to laugh. It was like a scene from the Three Stooges, which was on TV every afternoon at the time.

Julian was stunned however. He said something like "It's not funny!" and left holding his hand over his eye without saying another word. I think my laughter was much worse for him than the injury. I initially thought he wasn't really hurt, but when I realized he was, I had a shock myself and felt a ton of guilt. I saw a drop of blood on the wooden floor and ran outside after him. I called his name as he rode away on his bicycle but he didn't reply.

We always had lunch together at school but the next time I saw Julian walking down the hall he was with some other guys and just sneered at me. I mentioned lunch, and he scornfully replied, "Who would want to have lunch with YOU?", and kept walking. I tried a few times to get back in his good graces with humor but he just told me to grow up and act my age. We had more classes together over the next six years but we never spoke more than a few words.

I saw Julian about twenty-five years later at a big local event, and we were happy to see each other. After initial greetings the very first thing he said to me was "Remember when we were at your house and that exercise thing broke and hit me in the eye?" That barrier between us was the first thing that had to be addressed. This was still years before ID-R, and I hadn't yet recalled all the details of the accident, but I was aware of the effects of trauma and the power of communication, awareness, feeling, and validation. I expressed how bad I had felt, and we talked about it a little bit. The hurt that Julian had felt, which caused him to unfriend me, as well as my shame and guilt, were still present after all that time, and that's how it is with all of our programming, if we don't take care of it. Some healing took place in that communication, and Julian and I have been back on good terms ever since. Clearing this up allowed me to be more open to having friends and less afraid of rejection.

Chapter 10
The Chronicles of Medic

*"I just had the experience of going to doctors and waiting to be
told what my cure was. And they would talk about pain
management, and I would think, well, you're not the doctor for me
because I'm not interested in managing my pain. I'm interested in
having my pain cured. And then I would go look for another
doctor, a cure doctor, and I never found the cure doctor."*
– Melanie Thernstrom (interview, 2010)

This chapter discusses some challenges I had with my own
physical issues. Although ID-R has been successfully used in
resolving a great many such issues in myself and others, including
chronic pain, numbness, and physical dysfunction, my efforts to
heal these things in myself eventually hit a big snag.

I've never had pain that took over my life or led me to the depths
of despair and depression. Nor have I had pain that tormented me
unbearably day and night and made it impossible to do anything
productive, but there are many who have, and do. But I have had
chronic pain that made for some miserable days, and weeks, and
months, including headaches that lasted hours or days, back pain
that made it difficult to walk or even get out of bed, painful leg and
foot neuropathy that made it difficult to sleep more than an hour at
a time without having to get up and walk around a bit, a month-
long bout of shingles that made it hard to focus in the day or sleep
at night, as well myriad episodes of acute recurring pain. I feel
deeply for those who suffer from pain more intense, chronic,
debilitating, and demoralizing than mine. Chronic pain, pain
which is more or less continuous for long periods of time, can be a
complicated condition with many different contributing factors,
and in spite of many great advancements in medicine, it is still
largely a mystery. There are many different kinds of chronic pain,
and often there is no cure. Although there are many helpful
treatments, finding a pain management program that is personally
sufficient can be difficult. One key factor that is often ignored
however, is the mind-body connection. But once this connection is

properly understood and utilized, cures can and do happen. I don't know a lot about chronic pain medically, but I do know a few things.

Medic, my internal helper, was the recipient of all my physical pain-trauma for forty-three years, and was the main part of my consciousness that handled it. And this wasn't a problem even after I integrated with her. I was able to resolve most pain and body issues that came up for me without even taking Medic into consideration. But when I decided I needed to experience Medic's pain, from her viewpoint, things changed. And that started with the Dead Octopus incident.

Dead Octopus

When I was eighteen a bunch of us teenagers, about a dozen or so, would get together to play tackle football on the weekends. Lenny was a tall lanky guy, much bigger than me, and when he had the football he ran like a prancing horse, kicking his knees up as high as his chin. The first time I saw him run with the ball I thought I wouldn't want to get in his way and get my head knocked off. But I did end up colliding with him one Saturday afternoon in the park.

It was a sunny summer day when I felt the impact of Lenny's right knee in the center of my right thigh – one of the biggest shocks of my life! I was rushing the quarterback when Lenny, who was blocking, crashed right into me. We were both running full steam. Our heads collided, impacting mine painfully on the right side, like getting hit with a bat. His shoulder hit my upper chest crushing my right hand against my shoulder, and this caused my right triceps to stretch and tear. The pain in my thigh was like a gunshot, and the force of the impact of Lenny's knee jolted my right hip, which has not been right ever since. When the shockwave from my thigh bone hit my spine, pain shot down both legs, up my back, and through my abdomen in many directions. I left my body immediately and stayed out for several seconds which was unusual for me in pain-trauma, and Medic was surprised to find me gone.

In the middle of her own shock and while experiencing sideways-time, Medic could see all the pain signals radiating through my body like frozen red and yellow lightening bolt spreading out from a central point, and she said to Buffer "Look at that! It looks like an octopus!" To which Buffer enthusiastically replied "Kill the octopus!" So as Medic was suppressing the pain, pushing it down and numbing it out, she chanted over and over the words "dead octopus," while picturing my body limp, numb, and lifeless.

When I came back in the body several seconds later, I was lying on the grass holding my leg and rocking back and forth. Blake called my name and when I looked up at him standing over me he said, "You were saying 'dead octopus'," but I was unaware of that. I struggled to stand up and found that both legs were completely numb. In fact the whole lower half of my body was numb and tingling, and my head felt like it was vibrating. I had another shock, picturing an ambulance and thinking I might have to go to the hospital. I even considered briefly that I might die. I walked around until some feeling came back in my legs, and then I sat under a tree with my dog, King, and rubbed my right leg for an hour or more. While I sat there, there was some kind of inner conversation going on, like someone was trying to help me or boost my spirits. Eventually I felt OK enough to walk home.

There was a huge bruise on my upper right thigh the next day, and that leg was not very functional for few weeks. Besides damaging my hip, I believe the head impact also cracked my skull and that this was a factor in my contracting bacterial meningitis many years later.

I remember sunbathing on the lawn in my early thirties, and noticing a numb spot on my right thigh. I took a pen and traced the borders. It was a roughly circular area the size of a baseball. At that moment I recalled the football injury. Later I worked on this incident with ID-R and regained some feeling there, but problems emerged later.

Reflexive Sympathetic Dystrophy

Several years after working on my football injury, a client named Julia came to me suffering from chronic pain. Julia had been diagnosed with RSD or "reflexive sympathetic dystrophy," also known as "complex regional pain syndrome"(CRPS). RSD often appears as pain and inflamation in some area of the body, usually after some kind of injury or physical damage. The symptoms can be complex and may seem way out of proportion to the apparent cause or trigger, like when I got tapped on the hand by a ruler (Chapter 2) and had pain there for many days. If I had also developed bruising and swelling, perhaps it could have been called RSD, although diagnosing RSD can be complicated. In Julia's case, the whole right side of her body was bruised, including her shoulder, arm, hip and right leg, as if she had been beaten. She didn't mention any swelling but she was in constant pain. She had tried many forms of pain treatment and had gotten little relief, but she didn't want to just rely on drugs. She could barely walk and her husband had helped her into my office.

RSD is not well understood. Studies have been done on the physiology involved, and there are useful correlations, theories, and treatments, but nothing conclusive about the cause as far as I know, except that it appears to be a neurological problem. My theory, based on the Identity Model, is that the symptoms of RSD are the effect of a trauma that has been reactivated, perhaps by a more recent trauma or trigger, the damage from which cannot account for the symptoms or their persistence. Why the symptoms are so pronounced and dominant, I can't say. The physical and psychological expression of every mindbody reaction we have, seem to be determined by many things. There may be other purely biological factors at play in RSD as well, making this a complex problem. I believe that if all related underlying trauma were resolved there could be significant improvement in cases of RSD and I am looking forward to seeing research done that would confirm this possibility. Spontaneous remission is also possible, and on rare occasions RSD can just suddenly disappear, which is something I would expect if it's mainly a psychosomatic condition.

So after some discussion I asked Julia a question that apparently no one had asked her before: was there a time when she first experienced this pain? Her reply was immediate: "When I fell off the mountain!" Her husband nodded – he had witnessed this. She described tripping and rolling down a mountainside. Her fall ended abruptly when she crashed into a huge boulder, injuring the whole right side of her body, breaking some bones, and resulting in bruising similar to what she had now. This had happened many years earlier and had healed. But something had reactivated this trauma, in my opinion, and she was suffering. However as we began the ID-R session the pain of the accident proved too much for her to process at this time, so we backed off. Since she was reluctant to consider reexperiencing the pain, at least for now, I got her into a more comfortable state and worked with her using hypnosis. I also gave her some instruction in self-hypnosis.

I have myself had several chronic conditions whose symptoms remained minor for long periods of time and then flared up with some intensity, after which they again receded to their previous rather innocuous states. The factors involved in the flare-ups included stress and continuous use of, or attention drawn to, the affected area (in my case usually by me working on the issue), and probably other things I'm unaware of. My nose injury described in Chapter 7B would sometimes get restimulated to the point where my nose would become painfully swollen and red on the side of the injury for a day or two, in the years before I finally resolved this issue.

Taming the Tiger

When working with Julia, I had told her that I had experienced a similar injury that had left me with numbness in my right thigh, and that I had cleared it up. But a short time after this I noticed I still had some numbness in that area. I decided that I had to resolve this issue completely before I could claim it was completely healed. When I proceeded to work on it however, addressing my old injury, I couldn't seem to make any headway. I decided, for the first time, to go into Medic's viewpoint and heal _her_ trauma. This made sense since it was Medic's traumatic memory that was actually suppressing my feeling in that numb area, and since our integration, I am Medic, so I didn't expect any problems. To reiterate how this works, I simply recall experiencing the trauma as Medic, and work through it from her viewpoint. If you had ten helpers who all experienced the same event, and you were all integrated, you would potentially have ten different perspectives of the same event. The football injury was experienced by me, Buffer, and Medic.

However, I was unable to get anywhere after a few sessions and decided to do it later. Soon however, I developed chronic pain in my right hip and lower back, obviously restimulated by my work on the "dead octopus" incident. This condition lasted about a year but I never tried to heal it. I had been jogging daily but now I could no longer run and was in constant pain. Finally, after being reminded by my brother Alan several times, I did address it, again working with Medic's trauma. The pain went away but other pains from the injury emerged of which I had been previously unaware. These included recurring pain on the right side of my head and jaw, my right shoulder, hand, and triceps, and pain in the numb area of my thigh, which was now both numb and painful at the same time. Although I was now able to run again, and the previous chronic pain in my lower back was gone, I now I had new chronic pains which I could not resolve. So I quit trying and did not address this injury again for several years, during which time the new pains were not very bothersome. In 2007 when I did work on this injury again in earnest, I noticed that other old injury somatics started to appear. I tried working on those as they came up, also from Medic's viewpoint, and they only got worse, but I kept at it.

Finally so many new conditions appeared that I felt I had lost control. I had aches and pains all over my body and some of my symptoms appeared to be very serious, including intense thirst and dehydration, a feeling that I was dying, strange waves of energy moving through my body, and my toes becoming painful and turning purple. So I took myself to an Urgent Care facility. After enduring hours of waiting and multiple tests that found nothing wrong, except that I was dehydrated, and after talking with a doctor who refused to see the whole picture, I was quite frustrated. I decided the next morning, after doing a blood sugar test which came out normal, that I would have to figure this thing out for myself.

I spent a few hours thinking about my situation and doing research until I felt I had a good explanation regarding the cause of my dehydration. It was a trauma I had experienced at about nine months of age, which suppressed my pituitary gland. I recalled that in the past whenever I had worked on this issue I would suddenly get very thirsty. I then decided to try and turn these reactions off by doing some deep relaxation meditation. I sat in silence for more than two hours, continually going deeper and deeper into physical relaxation, while visualizing all the reactions becoming dormant.

There was a point at which I felt a dramatic shift. The incessant thirst I had been experiencing, suddenly stopped, as if a switch had been thrown. My energy returned and every symptom I was feeling disappeared except for the purple toes. But my toes did stop hurting immediately and returned to normal in about a week. I thought my overall problem might have something to do with how Medic had processed pain, something I did not yet understand. So I decided to avoid working on any physical trauma for a while, until I could understand my situation better.

About a year later however, I again tried to work on the "dead octopus" incident and thought that if I just ignored anything else that came up I could keep all unrelated reactions at bay and be able to work on one issue at a time. But this strategy didn't work. Every time I went into Medic's viewpoint, painful symptoms from many other incidents started appearing. I stopped and restarted again a few more times, but finally I took a long break. I considered various solutions but realized that this was not a priority for me at this time, and it would have to wait. ID-R works like a miracle for many cases of physical pain or dysfunction, but mine was an unusual predicament, and I knew I could always work on this football injury again in the future. It's no surprise to me however that I developed severe arthritis in my right hip later on.

The Pain Chronicles

In her book "The Pain Chronicles" Melanie Thernstrom comments: "Understanding chronic pain as a disease of the central nervous system sheds light on the riddle of chronic pain, solving the question of why, for many pain syndromes, there is no clear cause, and why even in pain syndromes where there is a clear-cut cause of pain, the cause bears no clear relation to the severity of the pain."[54] What does that mean, "a disease of the central nervous system?" It simply means that the pain has a deeper cause than it would seem, and that we can't simply trace nerve pathways back to some physical or neurological source – it's something more complicated. It's a mind-body condition. Thernstrom's book is a chronicle of her odyssey in trying to heal her own agonizing chronic pain which

---

[54] "The Pain Chronicles" - 2014, Melanie Thernstrom [p 140]

emerged for no apparent reason, affecting her neck, right shoulder, arm, and hand, and plagued her for years from then on. She tried many different treatments, and chronicles the many different approaches she learned from doctors, medical researchers, and a wide range of health practitioners. In the end, she simply realized that chronic pain often goes deeper than simple physiology, and that there are many different treatments that do work for some people and many different ways to manage and reduce the perception of pain.

A major clue in solving the mystery of chronic pain is revealed however, when we discover that unexplained chronic pain is often actually the pain of past trauma that is continuously recycling through our system. Psychosomatic pain is the elusive "disease" of the central nervous system, and it can be healed if we address it correctly as a mindbody state that has its source in some past experience, and by bringing that experience fully into awareness. This includes seeing whatever aspect of the experience is keeping the pain trapped in the mind and body, as I have described throughout this book. I have seen both acute and chronic pain resolved completely in this manner. While there is much more for me to learn about all this, including finding a way out of my own particular dilemma, I believe this is the fundamental understanding that has been missing from mainstream medicine: the understanding of the deeper relationship between mind, body, and consciousness. This understanding ultimately suggests a new paradigm of existence.

Beyond

I had a sore appear on top of my right hand which formed a very small scab. But the scab never fell off and when I peeled it off it would bleed and form another scab. After the fourth time I did this, a red circle of inflamation appeared. I then had a flashback of being intentionally burned on that spot with a cigarette when I was a child, but I didn't try to resolve it. The inflamation soon disappeared and the scab healed, but then it came back a few years later following the same pattern. The red area again looked much like a cigarette burn. I have heard stories of cigarette burns and other marks from old trauma appearing on people's skin many times before, and have seen them in my own practice. I believe similar kinds of psychosomatic inflamation and degradation in tissue and function can and do occur inside the body's deeper tissues and organs as well, as a result of past trauma. Perhaps you have experienced something similar yourself.

As I alluded to earlier, the question of how a physical trauma from the past can manifest itself in the form of something physical like a bruise or a cigarette burn on the body in present time, duplicating a past injury, is one of the more difficult things to reconcile with the basic medical model. It's easier to say that past trauma has nothing to do with it, and look for some other way to explain these phenomena. But there is no need, because when the apparent source of the condition is resolved and its physiological expression disappears, the connection between the two is clear. Certainly we want a more precise understanding, and that is what the Identity Model seeks to represent. And if there are past or future studies that show a definite correlation between a past injury and its present time physical manifestation as a symptom, this would, of course, serve to validate this model even more.

The psychological and emotional repercussions of past experiences are more easily accepted than are any physical manifestations because we have all experienced emotional responses when thinking about the past or the future. And yet these emotional responses to memory or imagination also impact the body in a physical way, causing changes in heart rate, breathing, tears, sweating, adrenalin and other hormones, brain chemistry, behavior, and so forth. If you vividly imagine biting into a pickle right now, you will salivate. Think about something you are afraid of and your heart rate will increase. It's not a great leap from this universal observation, to think that a past experience, forced upon us by a traumatic memory, can bring up powerful feelings, fears, phobias, anger, and various psychological conditions. That would just be an amplification of what we all experience daily. However, the psychosomatic effects of past trauma, which come from the mind and affect the body, like acute headaches or chronic back pain, and many other conditions such as RSD/CRPS, are not generally recognized as trauma-related. By doctrine, such phenomena must have a physical origin, and currently there is no conclusive traditional model, no causative biological mechanism,

to account for the mind creating such effects, even though many
doctors accept that they do.

There are many practitioners, organizations, and facilities
around the world that are dedicated to investigating and treating
chronic and recurring pain of various kinds, from headaches and
migraines to RSD/CRPS, back pain and other conditions. But in
my opinion, any approach that does not consider the psychosomatic
factors and the effects of trauma would be ignoring at least 90% of
the problem. None of our problems exist in isolation. Our lives and
health are biopsychosocial in nature, a result of our physiology, our
environments, our psychological and emotional needs, and our
relationships. There are also however, many practitioners who DO
recognize the reality of mind, body, and consciousness as a unified
or interconnected system, and who utilize effective mind-body
techniques to resolve or manage pain issues. These practitioners
have witnessed, as I have, chronic pain being reduced, transformed,
and even cured, using these approaches. While there certainly can
be other explanations I'm unaware of, I would say that, in general,
these methods work because they have either: helped heal an
underlying physical issue, released and resolved an underlying
unconscious cause of the pain, removed or nullified a trigger, have
caused the unconscious source of the problem to become dormant,
or they have changed the way the person is processing the
experience of pain.

I haven't talked about pain medication since I am not a doctor
and rarely take any myself, but I do want to mention something.
Chronic pain that is mainly psychosomatic can often act as its own
trigger and keep itself going. In other words, the pain can cause a
situation, whether it is inflamation or triggering other pain in the
same area, so that it never lets up, like the Energizer Bunny, even
in sleep. But sometimes taking one effective dose of a pain
medication, if it takes all the pain away, can break the constant
restimulation cycle so that when the medication wears off the pain
doesn't come back until something triggers it again. I have seen this
happen many times. For example, with a headache that might last
many hours or even days, a couple aspirins might clear it up in an
hour, and it doesn't come back after the aspirin wears off. Any
method that takes the pain away for a while can do the same thing.

I have stopped several people's headaches in a few minutes using hypnosis.

To sum this all up, since chronic pain, and other chronic physical conditions as well, can be the result of many interacting biological, psychological, social, and environmental factors, a multifaceted approach addressing all these things, using all the tools we have, would be obviously the best way to go. A wonderful book that utilizes such an approach for pain is "The Pain Management Workbook" by Rachel Zoffness (2020).

My approach would be to try and resolve the issue first if possible and manage it in the meantime (see Chapter 18). ID-R seems to resolve these issues for most people most of the time if they are willing to do the work. As for me, I do have a few somatic issues that I would like to clear up, but they would require that I address some severe past physical traumas which are presently not causing me much concern. Whenever I do address them, it will be from my own original viewpoint, which has worked well in the past, leaving Medic out of the picture for now. I expect that eventually I will find the missing pieces of this puzzle. In the meantime, having resolved so much of my past trauma, even when I am in pain it's usually not a problem because that work has made me stronger in a lot of ways. I also have many tools for dealing with pain if I need to.

So at this point it appears that recalling my past experiences as Medic is risky business and something I'm avoiding at present. The Chronicles of Medic, a record of a lifetime of suppressed traumatic pain, will have to remain a closed book for a while.

In Part IV we will be looking at other ways of handling our unwanted conditions, including pain, apart from trying to resolve the underlying causes, which is not always the fastest or even the best way to go. First however, in Part III we'll take an excursion into the realm of real magic.

✳ ✳ ✳ ✳ ✳ ✳ ✳ ✳ ✳ ✳ ✳ ✳ ✳ ✳ ✳ ✳ ✳ ✳ ✳ ✳

The Safety Class

In fourth grade our class was bussed to another school to attend a lecture on something like health or safety. I actually don't recall anything about the lecture except that the teacher was male, because I became completely distracted. The room appeared to be a long rectangular music room with rows of benches descending from the door, like bleachers, along one of the long walls. There were musical instruments and other equipment stored at the far end. Our class, seated in the front, was sitting on the lower benches. Some of us sat crossed-legged on the floor and a class from this school was to be seated on benches above and behind us. We were seated first and the other kids filed in shortly afterward.

Suddenly I felt elated and instantly knew she was there – that girl! I turned around and spotted her as she sat down in the top row above me. I looked at her and grinned from ear to ear excitedly, as one might greet a long lost friend. The tall girl next to her saw what I was doing and nudged her, pointing me out. She spotted me and looked at me with a defiant glare. I couldn't say anything or keep staring at her as I didn't want to get reprimanded, but I did keep turning around and smiling at her as often as I could. Most of the time she looked away as if she were paying close attention to the lecturer, but from time to time she would glance at me and look away when I caught her.

Finally she stuck her tongue out at me. She seemed curious but not amused. I, on the other hand, was animated and joyous the whole time, and her presence seemed to fill me with new energy.

As we all stood up to leave, filing out in reverse order, I heard her taller friend who was ahead of her ask, "Do you know that boy?" "I think so," was her reply. This time I felt sure I would see her again.

* * * * * * * * * * * * * * * * * * * *

Part III

♻

Real Magic

* * * * * * * * * * * * * * * * * * * *

Chapter 11
Everyday Miracles

"Why, sometimes I've believed as many as six impossible things before breakfast." – Alice in Wonderland

This whole book is about magic – not witchcraft, wizardry, or prestidigitation, but real magic, the magic of life, of existence. Here magic refers to wondrous and beautiful things, to things that inspire awe, amazement, love, and delight. It also refers to the miraculous manifestation of an intention into being, to the power of creation. Magic is imagination becoming real.

The word "magic" has a complicated history and several definitions. It stems from the Proto-Indo-European language root "magh," which means "to be able." This word morphed its way through Persian, Greek, and Latin, to become the English word "magic." Magh also became the Sanskrit word "ma," which means "to create" and is the root of the word "Maya," which itself means magic. In ancient Vedic literature, Maya literally implies extraordinary power and wisdom. But Maya also refers to the illusion of life that hides from us the underlying reality of our true nature, the realization of which can set us free. This means that the very magic that makes our lives worth living and can fulfill our wildest dreams, can also be, at the same time, a trap.

We are exploring some deep questions in this book and I will address the ultimate nature of things in later chapters. But suppose it turns out that we live in a universe that is simply consciousness imagining everything into being, and that _we are_ that very same consciousness imagining at this moment that we are human beings, when in fact we are consciousness itself. We are, then, _everything we experience_, and ultimately the entire universe itself. In my lifelong examination of my own life I have come to believe that this is indeed the case. Our universe, in all its awesome wonder and complexity, is nothing other than self-aware Existence transforming itself, through the magic of imagination, through Maya, into the experiences that we call our world and our lives. We are living in a universe of infinite stories and infinite games, games even beyond human imagination and description, birthed into real experiences – games of magic in which any and all fantasies are manifested into being as our personal perception of reality. But it's a dream reality, real in appearance, but only so long as we are asleep and unaware of our true nature as consciousness itself, and therefore unaware that this dream world is only a projection of our minds. The only thing missing is our own personal realization of this truth, which we'll be exploring in Part IV. But in a universe where everything is a manifestation of imagination, anything is possible, and the things we consider paranormal, or impossible, become explainable.

The chapters in this section take us more deeply into the realm of the miraculous. Amazing experiences do occur in daily life, for all of us I'm sure, but they are most often suppressed and forgotten. During self-exploration however, memories of such things can and do arise, and they shed further light on who we are and how our minds work. Dealing with such memories is a normal part of ID-R and an essential part of this discussion. These chapters will also serve as preparation for my upcoming adventures with Patty.

In the course of doing my solo ID-R work I uncovered many experiences that were miraculous. The word "miracle" has many definitions and uses as well. Something thought of as an act of God or supernatural forces would be the most basic. Another common definition refers to something that defies scientific or logical explanation. Synchronicities, in the form of a meaningful and fortuitous coincidences that seems to beat incredible odds, are also often called miracles.

But both the words "miracle" and "magic" are just words used to describe something amazing or something we can't explain.[55] In the absolute sense, everything is a miracle since we really don't know where anything ultimately comes from. Indeed, the biggest miracle is probably that anything exists at all. The idea that at some time in

---

[55] Although I may use this word in other ways, in the context of this chapter "magic" primarily refers to any mysterious or extraordinary quality or power that is, or seems, miraculous. In this book the words "miracle" and "magic" refer to natural events or phenomena that simply defy common materialistic explanations, or to which I assign a non-physical cause.

the future we WILL know, or that we COULD know, how
everything came into being, in a scientific way, is pure
presumption. The fact is we DON'T know. For a truly complete
understanding of anything, we would have to know where the
whole universe came from and what it's actually made of. We don't.
We give names to things and describe them in terms of other things
but these are all relative and descriptive understandings. We may
feel comfortable with our knowledge of the world because we can
predict outcomes and we can see the "cause and effect" interactions
between people and things in our lives, but while this familiarity
helps us feel safe and helps us to survive and evolve, the ultimate
source of these things remains a mystery. So a miracle is nothing
more than something that defies expectation and explanation,
usually in some extraordinary way. We live in a universe which is
ultimately unexplained, and in which anything can happen – a
magical universe!

Approaching my own miraculous experiences in a scientific way
requires me to first accept them as data, and possibly real
phenomena – real in the sense that they are more than just my
personal psychic hallucinations. This means I must not dismiss
them out of hand simply because they freak me out, or because
I don't understand the mechanics of how the universe might allow
such things. Nor should I reject them because they violate my
current beliefs and assumptions, and especially not because they
violate the predominant consensus reality or popular opinion. My
stories are my personal experiences. If they are hallucinations or
delusions, or some other kind of misunderstanding, I have to find
this out for myself. If they are real, then the world is not what it
seems to be, at least in the minds of most of us. And guess what –
it's not.

I personally define a miracle as something whose origin and
governing principles lie outside the physical universe and its known
laws. Miracles are governed by spiritual laws. When I use the word
"spiritual" I'm simply referring to consciousness. In my view, the
world of time, space, matter, and energy is only a dream we are
having. Although ours is a real and lucid dreamworld to be sure, it
is governed by laws similar to those which govern dreams – the laws
of mind. In this view the physical universe and the principles that
control it are ultimately a complex set of rules which determine

what we will experience as conscious beings while appearing as mortal creatures within its domain. Our physical dreamworld is just one domain which lies inside the infinite vastness of consciousness itself.

I have experienced many amazing things. All of the MOST miraculous things I have experienced in my life were partially or completely forgotten until I recalled them in my ID-R sessions. Whether or not these experiences really happened (beyond my experience of them), why I believe they did happen, and whether this is important, will be discussed in Chapter 16. What is vitally important is that I was willing to look at the strange images that arose in my sessions and treat them as possible memories. This allowed the process to continue and resulted in many associated unwanted personal conditions being resolved.

There were many paranormal or magical experiences, however, that I never forgot. I have always remembered them precisely because their miraculous nature was <u>disputable</u>. Calling them miracles is actually just my opinion based on my understanding of the universe. I call these miracles "Wimpy ESP." What I like about them is that most of us can and do remember them. They are ordinary "everyday" miracles, but they are a peek through the keyhole in the door leading to our greater potential.

Wimpy ESP

Wimpy ESP is what I call the lightweight paranormal experiences most people seem to have, like reading minds, knowing the future, manifesting a parking space, remote viewing, knowing where things are etc. These kinds of miracles happen every day. The reason I call these things wimpy, even while they are manifestations of a higher reality, is that they can easily be called coincidental, random luck, or perhaps instances of finding meaning where there is none. No matter how fortuitous or unlikely an occurrence may be in these cases, the belief that there is some higher power or special ability involved that is beyond our understanding, usually has nothing substantial to support it, even though paranormal phenomena and abilities have long been scientifically proven to exist.

If my more extraordinary paranormal abilities in childhood were real, then those experiences would support the spiritual paradigm that I am partial to. But even though I intuitively have always felt that my experiences involved a higher reality, having been brainwashed in the "cult of materialism," also known as scientism, since I was a kid, I couldn't even accept my own truth with any certainty for much of my life.[56] But here are some of my close encounters of the wimpy kind.

The $32.50

One day I needed $30 to continue my nutritional experiments. I was using nutritional supplements to heal myself and my pets of various ailments. I was twenty-three, still living at home, had no job, no car, and was broke. And I was feeling desperate. I started pacing back and forth, which is how I like to brainstorm. For me, pacing induces a slight altered state by splitting my attention between walking and focusing on my question. I speculate this may actually be how EMDR works as well. While doing this, a light went on in my head, and suddenly I knew what to do! I would go FIND the money. I just knew that was the answer.

I went outside and felt compelled to start walking. I let some internal guidance system lead me down the street and around the corner. I crossed the street, a block away and went over the footbridge across the river that led to the nearby university. Once over the bridge I turned right and was amazed to find a $10 bill near some old train tracks. I scoured the area and found two more $10 bills in less than a minute. Then I walked around the nearby football field and found $2.50 in change on the grass beneath a tree. I knew I was done and came home. But it COULD have been a coincidence: a coincidence that I needed some money, brain-stormed about it, got an inspiration, followed that inspiration blindly with no information and no reasonable expectation of

---

[56] Scientism is another name for materialist reductionism, which is the idea that everything will eventually be explainable in terms of matter, energy, time, and space, or yet to be discovered physical laws. Mind and spirit are mere epiphenomena. This term emphasizes the religious tone of scientific dogma.

success, found exactly the amount I needed all in a few minutes, and did this once in my life, and never tried it again. But what are the odds?

The Black Bunny

One day in 1994 I was meditating and had a vision of a black rabbit staring at me. It was so crystal clear and significant that I would have remembered it even if nothing had come of it. Later that day I went for a walk by the river and saw a black bunny hopping around, which was obviously tame. Someone had released it, and the box was nearby. I knew I must have had the vision for a reason, so I decided to catch it. Being something of an animal whisperer I easily befriended the bunny, took it home, and gave it to my seven-year-old niece. She was happy to adopt it, especially since her own bunny, which I didn't even know she had, was lonely and needed a friend.

Danger Will Robinson

Once in the early 1980's I was walking to my car at 3:00 A.M. after work at a downtown tavern. As I approached my car, a dark image of something flashed across my field of vision from right to left. It was so vivid and sudden that I stopped short and took a step back. I decided this was a warning and I had better drive slowly. I even said this out loud to myself. Out of the parking lot I turned left onto 8th Street and then left again at the next corner where the traffic light was green. I was purposely going at a slower speed than normal. As I approached the next intersection at 7th Street I saw the traffic light was green so I didn't slow down. When I was about twenty feet from the intersection, a speeding car came out of nowhere running the red light and crossing my path from right to left. I knew immediately that this was the meaning of my vision. I can't know for certain that the car would have hit me if I had not had the vision that prompted me to drive more slowly, but the timing seemed just about right, and I was a bit intoxicated myself. This kind of thing has happened to me more than once. I have also heard several almost identical car stories from others.

Believing

I could easily think of a hundred personal experiences similar to those above, which would include reading minds, seeing the future, amazing luck, avoiding danger, willing things to happen, and many other such phenomena. None of these were ever forgotten, and their memories have occasionally crossed my mind. In the course of my work I have also discovered many other similar instances that I simply had not thought of since the time they occurred. I have also heard of many similar first hand experiences from people I know, and have been present during some of these. Now if the cause of these phenomena is indeed a relationship between mind and matter, between consciousness and the world, that science has yet to understand, then they are just as miraculous as levitating objects or making them disappear. But they are "wimpy" mainly because they lack the same powerful psychological impact on those who witness them, that those more phenomenal demonstrations do. These lesser miracles are too easily discounted or dismissed.

Few people would have any problem believing the above stories because they don't require any greater understanding of the universe. They could all be oddities of coincidence – entertaining but meaningless. The ability to move objects around by psychokinesis is a different matter, but because it has no conventional explanation, it cannot be real. But having no explanation does not alter the fact that something exists. I call this the "Closed Mind" fallacy – when some phenomenon is rejected simply because there is no conventional way to explain it. To claim such a thing must therefore be a lie, a delusion, or a false memory. That is, unless we don't really know as much about reality as we think we do. We don't. Miracles DO have a rational explanation, and within the spiritual domain in which they occur they are simply events like any other, and are not special. However, they are miracles to us because we don't see their cause, and we cannot fit them into our mechanical paradigm. This reminds me of the book "Flatland."[57] In that book, people living in a two-dimensional reality are visited by a three-dimensional being. The communication with this 3D being impacts their 2D reality in ways that seem miraculous

---

[57] "Flatland" - Edwin A. Abbott, 1884.

and cannot be understood using two-dimensional thinking. We cannot understand the miraculous with a mind that is programmed against it.

Pushing the Envelope

Here are some experiences that edge beyond the wimpy category. One night when Lynne and I worked together at the pizza parlor where we met, we were cutting pizzas on opposite sides of the cutting table. To show off, I cut my pizza at lightning speed. I heard Lynne say, in a sarcastic tone, "What are you doing, having a race with yourself?" A few moments later after handing our pizzas to the customers, I asked her what she meant. She asked me what I was talking about so I repeated what she had said. She just gave me a blank stare and finally said "I was _thinking_ that, but I didn't say it." I had expressed her thoughts word for word.

On another occasion we were in the library at a local Mormon church where Lynne's mother was doing genealogy research. I was perusing some book titles on a shelf when Lynne walked up to me and said she had to use the restroom. So I turned around and grabbed her hand and led her down a few hallways to the restrooms. I hadn't said a word. She gave me a strange look, and then went into the restroom. When she came out, she asked me how I knew she needed to go. I said "What do you mean? You came up and told me." Her reply was quite certain "No. I didn't. You just came up and grabbed my hand." Upon reflection, I realized that I had seen her approach me from the front while I was facing a shelf of books – some sort of dual consciousness was going on. Also, this was the first time I had ever been to that church and I was unfamiliar with the building. Yet I led her right to the restroom area, having never been there myself. I never forgot this, and it's not a simple coincidence.

I see evidence of psychic abilities in people all the time, although they do not. In early 1977 my brother Alan and I were managing a restaurant. One evening as I was getting off work and Alan was taking over, he burst into the office and said "I just had the weirdest experience. I was standing at the bar and I heard Lily say over the microphone, 'Alan you have a phone call', – it was plain as day! But I looked in the kitchen [where the microphone is for the loudspeaker] and Lily was over by the ovens! [nowhere near the microphone.]" As we talked the phone rang and Lily called out over the loudspeaker, "Alan, you have a phone call." Alan said to me "Hold on," and answered the office phone which was on the wall right next to him. He spoke for a moment, hung up, and continued his story, amazed at how vivid the experience was. Meanwhile, I just looked at him with a huge grin. Seeing my expression, he paused, and I said, "Do you realize what just happened?" "What?" "Lily just said those exact words over the microphone. You had a vision of the future!" He just said "Oh," his facial expression showing that he made the connection, and he left. If I had not pointed it out, I'm sure he would have missed it. I have often missed things like that myself, only to realize it later.

One Thanksgiving Day at a family gathering, I was talking to one of my nephews who was about eight or nine years old. I asked him who else was coming. He told me who they were and that they would be here in a minute because their car was just now coming through the subdivision gate. The gate was a quarter mile away and we were in the living room with no windows facing that direction. No one there had a cell phone back then and there had been no phone calls. I realized he must be seeing them psychically, so I asked "Do you see them?" He nodded and named the three people in the car, and mentioned that there should have been four. A minute later the doorbell rang and the three people he had named came in and explained why the fourth person wasn't there. I simply told my nephew "Very good!" Again, I could easily describe hundreds of similar stories. Why? Because I notice them and don't immediately dismiss them. When you have a miracle mindset, you're able to recognize possible miracles, and you will see them more often. And they're happening all the time.

Inner Guidance

One more experience that pushes the envelope comes to mind and is applicable here. I was three years old and was alone in the house with my father. He was very angry and upset about something. He was rummaging through drawers in his bedroom and I walked in and asked him what he was doing. He told me he was going away and tossed a revolver on the bed. I didn't know what a gun was but I knew that something was very wrong, and I felt a sense of urgency. I asked him where he was going. "You don't need to know where I'm going, I just won't be around anymore," he grumbled. So I told him I wanted to go with him and his reply was "You can't go with me; nobody can go where I'm goin'." There was a shock at the idea that something unknown and terrible was going to happen. I started to cry, pleading "Daddy don't make me cwy, don't make me cwy." These were the very words I heard back in 1977 during my mystical flashback episode, and the memory I'm describing arose during an ID-R session many years later, revealing their source.

My dad just yelled at me angrily, "Men don't cry! Grow up! Be a man! Be a man!" "But I'm just a little boy" I whimpered, and walked out of the room. I went into the living room and knelt down and cried into a chair. With my face in my hands, I wept with total abandon, as young children do. I had no idea what was happening or what to do. But suddenly I heard a noise in my head like radio static which kept getting louder until it got my full attention. Then it became a voice that had the feeling of a chorus of voices speaking in unison. The voice was urgent and told me exactly what to do. I ran out of the house and over to our next door neighbor's porch, and knocked on the door.

When the man came to the door all I could do was cry, "My daddy, my daddy" over and over, while pointing toward my house. The man walked me home and rang the doorbell. My dad came to the door and they talked. He told the man that I was just scared because I didn't know where he was, and that everything was fine. When the man was gone, my dad knelt down and thanked me and asked me some questions, but I didn't say anything. He later told my mother about this.

In 1976 when I was reading about Primal Therapy and began trying to remember my past, before the breakthrough discussed in Chapter 2, I was talking with my parents in the kitchen one day. I mentioned a couple of trivial memories I had recalled, and my dad then asked me if I could recall the time I helped him out. I started to dissociate. My mother commented "Oh, he wouldn't remember that." I didn't. In fact I blocked out this whole conversation as well, but it all came back to me when I discovered this childhood incident. Was the inner voice I heard as a child an angel – a spirit guide – Dennis–2 from the future – God – my own unconscious mind? I have no idea.

In the first year of doing ID-R for many hours every day, I was recalling some very amazing stuff, and gaining clarity on things I had already remembered. As I began recalling more miraculous things, they became easier to accept, and working through my traumatic encounters with Terrence, my petty tyrant, seemed to open my mind to recalling such things more easily, like the time I levitated to the ceiling. These memories encouraged me to accept the fact that anything is indeed possible.

Chapter 12
My Petty Tyrant

"Opportunities to find deeper powers within ourselves
come when life seems most challenging." – Joseph Campbell.

"The warrior who stumbles on a petty tyrant is a lucky one."
– Carlos Castaneda, "The Fire From Within"

"Compared to the source of everything [the Tyrant], the most
fearsome, tyrannical men are buffoons; consequently, they were
classified as petty tyrants." "A petty tyrant is a tormentor ... Someone
who either holds the power of life and death over warriors or simply
annoys them to distraction." When I read these words of Don Juan
in "The Fire From Within" by Carlos Castaneda in 1984, I saw the
petty tyrant as someone who forces you to exceed your limitations,
to go beyond what you thought was possible, and do more than you
believed you ever could. They can help temper the spirit, teach
forbearance, and assist one in losing self-importance. According to
Don Juan, a petty tyrant is an essential element on a warrior's path
to self-knowledge. I was thirty-seven at the time, but not until seven
years later did I begin to remember that, long ago, I had a petty
tyrant of my own.

Terrence was a relative who came to live with our family for a
year when I was nine and a half. He was seventeen at the time, a
senior in high school, and of course much bigger and stronger than
me. He also had a mean streak and seemed fond of tormenting me
whenever he had the opportunity. While my parents often
mistreated me, I never consciously considered them to be
adversaries. I depended on them and so our relationship was based
on that. While my feelings toward my parents varied from love to
hate and everything in between, depending on the situation, I dealt
with the challenges they presented by acquiescing to them in some
way. Terrence however was my nemesis. Regardless of how much
he tortured and terrorized me, I was always defiant and determined
to never give in. Being the oldest brother, I had previously bullied

my siblings around, but now my "top dog" status was effectively nullified. The very first day he moved in, Terrence had me on the floor on my stomach digging his knee into my back. When I called out to my father in the kitchen he just said, "You can take care of yourself," meaning that I should fight back and not be weak. This was the first instance with Terrence where I was pushed to draw upon unexpected resources.

I was in a lot of pain as Terrence, his left knee in the middle of my back, pulled painfully upward on my arms. I was at a loss as to what to do, feeling both helpless and angry. Then I heard a familiar sounding male voice somewhere around me that said "Turn your palms toward the floor, bend your elbows, and roll over to the right." I answered "What?" I don't recall if I verbalized it or just thought it. The voice replied, "Trust me," and the message was repeated. So I did as he instructed and rolled over, Terrence flew off, and I got up and walked away. I was fairly amazed. As I walked away I asked in my head "Who are you?" "Who do you think I am?" the voice answered, in a tone that implied I must be delirious. "It's me, Jeff." I thanked him and we talked for a few more seconds.

When Jeff and I met three years earlier in second grade he connected with me for some reason and kept talking to me although I rarely responded. But because he was loud, boisterous, and persistent, the opposite of me, we eventually became friends. However one day he wouldn't talk to me and I didn't understand why. I had asked him something but he remained silent. My intention was strong however, to understand what was going on. Then I heard him say, in my mind, that he didn't like that I was playing tetherball every day with Sonny, a Japanese boy. He wasn't looking at me and his jaw wasn't moving at the time, which I found curious, but the message was clear. So the next day I told Sonny I couldn't play with him any more, and then I told Jeff, verbally. He gave me a funny look, then resumed happily talking with me and our friendship continued. Upon reflection, after his help with Terrence, I felt we had a special connection. When Jeff moved away a few months later, I made sure we kept in touch, and we did so for many years.

In my many battles with Terrence my general resolve was to be strong and to not let him win. But he was clever. Sometimes he would pretend to be on my side only to gleefully betray me. And when he would physically torture me for long periods of time, although I never gave in, the suffering was agonizing. For example one time Jeff and I had made powerful slingshot rifles out of wood, rubber bands, and clothespins. Terrence wanted mine but I wrapped myself around it and he couldn't get it out of my grasp, even though he and his friend Arnold had me on the floor for what seemed like half an hour, pinching my skin, digging knuckles into my joints, and doing anything short of actual injury. However since I had Buffer and Medic to handle the major pain, my greatest challenge was to maintain the physical effort and resolve I needed to endure his attacks and hold on to my property, until he gave up or got bored.

Terrence was a troubled kid. His father had recently died and he and his siblings were split up. He had a lot of anger and insecurity and delighted in being a tyrant and in seeing what kinds of outrageous things he could get away with doing to my brothers and me. But because I didn't think he would actually injure or kill me, I did provoke him on many occasions. He was always checking his face for blemishes. Sometimes when walking by the bathroom and seeing him looking in the mirror, I would say "I see another pimple" and run off laughing. The following are some of our more amazing encounters.

The Compass

I was working on an issue and started repeating a word loop which made no immediate sense to me: "You can't find, my compass, you can't find my compass!" In fact it took several looping repetitions before I was sure of the words and the syntax. After a bit more work, I began to remember. The memory opened up with Terrence and me in the middle of a struggle. Almost every day he would bully me in some way and today we were in my bedroom where he had me on the floor and was pushing the point of a metal drawing compass closer and closer to my right knee. The point of the compass was like an ice pick. With both hands grasping his right wrist I fought with all my might to keep the compass at bay, but I was losing. When the point was about to go into my leg, I had a shock ... and the compass ... disappeared!

Terrence immediately jumped up in an attempt to find the compass, probably assuming I must have knocked it out of his hand. I remember being in a trance-like state and chanting over and over, "You can't find my compass!" There was some worry that the compass might not remain wherever it had vanished to. But the compass was gone, and was never seen again. He was still looking for it when I ran out of the room.

The Sonic Boom

Terrence and Arnold were chasing me when I ran in the house and hid in an empty vacuum cleaner chest in my parents' bedroom. We had been given both a red and a yellow chest years earlier when we bought the vacuum cleaner so we could decide which color we preferred, but the salesman never came back. The red chest was my favorite hiding place since I was five years old. It was padded and made a good seat also, and had a simple hinged lid with no latch. But Terrence knew about it. He came in the room and sat on top of the chest so I couldn't get out. He began teasing me by saying things like "I wonder where Dennis went? I guess I'll just sit here until I can figure it out." I pushed on the lid and when I realized I was trapped I started to panic and began screaming and thrashing around. Eventually I had a real shock at the idea that I might actually die. In the power-zone I found myself above the chest near the ceiling of the room. Everything appeared very dark for some reason. Then, from a higher level intention, I created a very loud explosive sound. BANG! The noise shook the walls. Terrence immediately jumped off the chest and I escaped. As I ran out the door I turned to see if they were coming after me, but they were frozen in wonder, so I stopped and watched them. Finally his friend Arnold said "It must have been a sonic boom!" "Yeah!" said Terrence. Now they had a way to make sense of it. I didn't know at the time what a sonic boom was, but I was happy they didn't know it was me.

The Hypnotized Robot Super-Soldier

Several years ago a red mark appeared on top of my right forearm near the wrist. It started growing fast and soon became an ugly looking cyst, although there was no pain. I speculated it might be anything from a spider bite to flesh-eating bacteria or cancer. I had decided a year earlier that whenever any physical symptom appeared I would work on it first with ID-R before seeing a doctor, no matter what it was, but because I was usually pressed for time and prone to worry about these things, I instead went to a clinic right away. The clinicians had no idea what this thing was, so after a few tests I went to a hospital and saw another doctor. She assured me it wasn't cancer but still had no other ideas. Joseph, a psychic friend of mine, suggested I put an herbal product on it, although I had mentioned nothing about it to him and all he saw was the bandage on my arm. The herb he mentioned was primarily used for burns. I had nothing to lose so I tried it, and also started doing ID-R. I immediately discovered the source of the cyst. It was a burn, but from long ago.

Terrence was with me and my little brother in the living room one evening when my parents weren't home. The four of us had formed a club called the Golden Eagles and Terrence was the leader. We would have imaginary adventures and tonight he was trying to hypnotize Blake and me. He told us we were robot soldiers and that he could hypnotize us so that we wouldn't feel any pain, and we would then be able to do anything. He did some passes with his hands and told us we were hypnotized. He had me hold my right arm out and began repeatedly chanting "You will feel no pain," while he heated the blade of his pocket knife with a cigarette lighter. After a few seconds he pressed the hot blade against my skin on the top of my right arm.

But in playing along with Terrence I had actually hypnotized myself, and I felt no pain. However, the blade wasn't hot enough to cause any damage. He looked baffled when I showed no reaction. So he told me I was a super-soldier and kept chanting, and heated the blade again, this time until it was red hot. Once again he pressed it against my skin for a couple seconds. In spite of the mild self-hypnosis, I had a momentary shock. The pain immediately disappeared, even while my skin sizzled and smoked, and again I didn't flinch. Terrence was amazed at the power of hypnosis and said to my brother "Now we'll try you." But Blake was having none of this and took off out the side door with Terrence chasing after him.

After being burned I ended up with a large red blister which turned into an ugly sore, but it never hurt and seemed to heal very quickly without leaving any scar. I believe something must have reactivated this incident decades later, causing it to reemerge in physical form on my arm. After working through this, the cyst, which had persisted for five weeks, immediately began clearing up and disappeared completely in about ten days. However it left a temporary and distinct rectangular scar, shaped just like the side of a pocket knife.

Clark Kent

I worked through many more traumatic encounters with Terrence, some of which will be mentioned elsewhere. But in the context of pushing me beyond my limitations, these last three incidents were the most amazing yet. They also solved a long-standing mystery of a recurring dream which I had many times for over thirty years. These dreams, which ceased once I understood them, probably began a few months after the events I'm about to share. In the dreams I could walk on air. By being very careful, I could step up in the air as if I were climbing an invisible staircase. Usually I was outside, but I never went higher than about eight feet. Sometimes I would have flying dreams, but very often I was unable to go very high, as if there were some kind of ceiling I couldn't get past. These sky-walking dreams were always intriguing and mysterious to me until I discovered their source.

Any issue we are trying to heal may require working through many incidents before it is resolved, since it could be made up of many parts or identities. The issue I was working on was a feeling that I had to stay hidden and out of the lime light, something I have felt all my life. So this feeling came up one particular day for some reason and led me to recall, at age ten, being on the back patio of our house facing Terrence, who was very excited. He was calling the kids who were in the back yard to come over and was telling them about something I did, but I couldn't recall what he was saying. Whatever it was, I was denying it and feeling afraid of being exposed somehow. After working with this for a while I heard his words: "Dennis can fly, everybody, c'mere, Dennis can fly!" And he looked at me as if he really believed it, saying "You should join a circus – you could make a million bucks!" But to me this was a frightening proposition and I wanted nothing to do with it. I kept denying that I did any flying, saying that it just looked that way because I had jumped really high. Everyone walked away, but Terrence followed me around for several minutes trying to convince me to join a circus or go on TV. I tried to convince him that he was imagining it all. But he wasn't. As I was working on this incident, which I labeled "Clark Kent" because I was trying to conceal my superpowers, I was having repeated flashbacks to what had actually happened a few minutes earlier.

Skywalker – or Door Number Three

I don't know what I had said or done to make Terrence so mad, but he was after me. He cornered me in the back bedroom but I managed to escape and was racing down the hallway. With Terrence in hot pursuit, I made it to the living room and had to make a split second decision. With the kitchen doorway blocked on my left I had two possible options. I could run straight for the front door, but it was closed and had a screen door also, and I would never be able to get them both open fast enough. To my right was the patio door but it was also closed and opened in the wrong direction to be viable. So I chose door number three – I decided to do the unexpected and ran diagonally between the doors toward the TV in the far corner of the room, hoping that this might confuse him or that some other option might show up. However, two steps into it I had a shock – I realized that although this was some creative "outside the box" thinking, it wouldn't work, and I was doomed! Suddenly, invisible stair steps appeared in front of me, which I quickly ran up using my hands and feet, yet feeling no weight or pressure on them at all, until I got to the ceiling. I turned around with my head and back against the ceiling, and looked down to see Terrence looking up at me. His mouth was wide open – he looked like he was seeing a ghost.

He turned and ran away, disappearing through the hallway door. I wasn't sure what to do at this point – my mind was blank. Then, not knowing how to get down, I had another shock and slowly I began to float down. I could see Terrence now, who was on his hands and knees peeking up from the hallway floor. I had raised my arms and it felt like some force or entity was lowering me to the ground. I recall now that in the power-zone there appeared to be two small transparent spirits helping me. They appeared as naked children like the spirit that helped me later with the train incident. As soon as my feet hit the rug I ran out the side door to the patio. That's when Terrence came running out, telling me it was OK and that he wasn't mad at me anymore.

Learning to Fly

After the Skywalker incident Terrence bugged me every day to teach him how to fly. During this time he wasn't mean to me which was a relief, but his persistence was wearing on me. I kept telling him that I had no idea how to fly, which was the truth, but he refused to let up. Finally one day I gave in. We were sitting on one of the twin beds in my brothers' room and I said "OK, here's what you have to do. First you have to be nice to me and my brothers for two weeks. You can't hurt us or take our stuff or anything like that, because it doesn't work unless you're a good person. Then I'll show you how to feel the air." This was a clever ruse but unfortunately I wasn't thinking very far ahead, and two weeks seemed like a long time for me at that age. So Terrence eagerly agreed and he became a very different person for two weeks. It was great – until the last day arrived. I had almost forgotten my promise by this time. But Terrence came up to me that day smiling, "Ok, I did the first part – I've been good for two weeks. So tomorrow you're going to show me how to fly after school, OK?" I agreed that he had been good and that I would teach him how to fly the next day.

What I remember most about the next day was that I was wearing an oversized dark-brown coat that was thick and warm and which I liked a lot. It was probably late spring but still a bit cold. I was walking out the front door thinking about my predicament. I pictured Terrence-the-terrorist flying around like a crazy smiling demon with great power, and I knew that I could not unleash such a thing on the world. Not that I had the faintest idea how to fly. It was just something that happened and not something I had any control over or that I thought I would ever do again. Still, I was afraid there might actually be something inside me that could impart this ability to him. I just didn't know. I lived in a magical universe where anything was possible, and that special power that allowed me to fly had to exist somewhere. I decided that I had to break my agreement, but I felt bad about it. Even though he was my enemy, I hated to hurt Terrence's feelings by denying him something he was so joyfully anticipating. I had experienced such disappointment myself in the past.

When Terrence came home all smiling and ready for flying lessons I told him I couldn't do it. I admitted that I had no idea how to fly. He didn't believe me and became furious. He said if I didn't teach him to fly tomorrow after school ... he would kill me.

Liftoff – or What Goes Up

The next day after school I reevaluated my decision and realized that it would be better to die than to risk giving Terrence any magical powers. I was wearing the same coat and remember walking around with my head down, resigning myself to my fate. Terrence and Arnold found me in the back yard. When Terrence demanded I show him how to fly and I said "I can't do it," he said "Well, then get ready to die." They each took me by an arm and a leg and began swinging me back and forth. I was facing the ground as they swung my body several times to gain momentum. I guess the idea was to throw me as high as they could, thinking I might save myself by flying. Of course, I'm sure Arnold didn't believe for one second that I could fly.

Finally Terrence began counting, and they released me on the count of three. I don't know how high I went – maybe seven feet – but I didn't fly. Instead I came right down on my head. There was a loud "crack" and I was out of my body. I could see them just standing there for a moment, and I heard something like "Oh shit!" Then they took off running, and I was alone. I was exterior and disoriented. I was aware of my body on the ground and tried to wake it up but it was unresponsive. I began floating around the backyard slowly spinning from right to left, in a confused daze of despair. It felt like I was dying.

Then there was a flurry of energy and I saw red and yellow lights around me. Someone else had arrived, also exterior, and very powerful. It was Patty, and she was very upset. She was upset with me for getting myself into this situation, and very angry with whoever did this to me. I don't know if I was actually dying but she healed my body. Then she took off after Terrence. I got up off the ground and dusted myself off but immediately switched with a helper and left my body again. I couldn't let Patty destroy Terrence. When I found them, Terrence was lying prone on someone's lawn near the sidewalk with Patty hovering over him. I had the feeling he had fainted from the stress of thinking he had killed me, but I wasn't sure Patty hadn't contributed to his collapse. I told her the story and convinced her to let him be, and she finally calmed down and left.

I was in the livingroom when Terrence walked in the house that evening, several hours later. As soon as he saw me his face lit up, and he ran over to me and grabbed my shoulders. "Dennis!" was all he said. It was identical to the Star Trek scene in the episode "Amock Time" when Spock discovered Kirk was still alive after he thought he had killed him in a ritual battle to the death. Terrence just looked at me in amazement for several seconds and then went off to the bedroom. I didn't understand why he was so happy to see me. I thought it was strange, but my memory of the day's events was pretty hazy by that time.

Retrospect

Terrence stopped terrorizing me after all this, which was near the end of his stay, but he couldn't hide his mean tendencies. I do remember a time when my brother and I were doing homework on the livingroom floor. Terrence walked by and made some badgering comment, perhaps threatening to step on my papers. He was all dressed up and leaving to participate in an event that had something to do with American Bandstand. Without looking at him I said "If you don't leave me alone I'll make you break out in pimples right now – and you KNOW I can do it." He didn't say another word.

After Terrence graduated, he immediately enlisted in the Navy. My father served in the Navy in WWII, and had convinced Terrence that it would be good for him. Terrence visited us briefly a year or so after enlisting, and he had grown at least six inches taller. That's the last time I ever saw him. I contacted Terrence almost 60 years later. We hadn't spoken in all that time. He had suffered several strokes and was in a rest home but very lucid. I mentioned that there were some amazing things that had happened back when he lived with us but I didn't give him any details that would help him remember anything. My plan was to give him some time to consider what I had to say and if he didn't remember anything I would reveal it all in our next talk.

So we had an interesting conversation, and he was quite open to the possibility of miraculous experiences, asking if what I did was like the main character in the movie "Carrie."[58] He didn't recall anything extraordinary during our talk, but he also didn't remember much at all about his stay. However, he did make an interesting comment at the end of our conversation. I explained that when we are faced with something that too greatly challenges our sense of reality, or is too unbelievable or frightening, we tend to block it from our memory. His immediate reply was "Or join the Navy."

---

[58] Carrie (1976) (2013)

Chapter 13
Tales of Power

"There are more things in heaven and earth, Horatio,
Than are dreamt of in your philosophy" – *Shakespeare*

My adventures with Terrence went way beyond wimpy ESP, which is why I had forgotten them shortly after they occurred. But even back when I was twenty-eight, after remembering scores of early OBEs, I began to occasionally recall some equally miraculous events from childhood, but since they were so extraordinary, I didn't know how to evaluate them. Every psychic thing I had recalled prior to this time was of the wimpy variety, except for some of the OBEs I had begun having where I was apparently perceiving the real world from an exterior viewpoint. Eventually I was able to take a better look at all these memories using ID-R, and many more amazing incidents came to light.

Taking my experiences as scientific data, I have tried to create a model that makes sense of them. The Identity Model, which I will describe later in Chapter 17, represents a universe in which all such experiences are possible. I have also allowed for the possibility that my more extraordinary recollections may not correspond to the reality of others, but I will explain later why I believe they are real, even if that is the case. My recalling of the childhood abilities I had forgotten, like seeing behind me and moving toys with my mind, gave me greater confidence in my more mundane psychic abilities as well. Still, cultural conditioning can be very difficult to overcome.

Toy Story – or Hiding the Truth
Ever since I was a kid I had dreams of toys moving by themselves. Usually they would follow me around but sometimes I would just watch them moving around on a wooden floor. One day I was working on an issue of feeling small in a group of people. This included feeling like an outcast in that something about me had to stay hidden, and this inhibited me from being more outgoing. As I

began examining this issue, I began recalling several of these dreams. As I was thinking about them, I had a flashback. Suddenly I saw my father's face; his jaw was dropped and he looked terrified.

I was around three years old and I was playing with some toys on the wooden floor in my bedroom. I had a little wooden train moving around by itself and some other things spinning in the air – they just seemed to do what I wanted them to and it made me laugh. My father walked in the room and I said "Daddy look!" ... silence. Then I heard him shout "Dennis, get away from there!" His tone was very serious and I looked around and saw his shocked face, which startled me. I'd never seen my dad scared before. "Son, come over here – by me – right now!" I ran over to him and looked toward where he was looking. I didn't see anything but by now I was frightened too. I could sense his feelings and there seemed to be some great danger around us.

My dad whisked me out of the room and into the kitchen where my mother was working. He told her "Don't go in the back bedroom, there's something in there." "What?" She asked. "I don't know." He paused ... "I think it's from outer space." This was 1950 and I'm sure he'd seen a few science fiction movies. "Ohhh" my mother groaned, as if to say "Give me a break." "I'm serious" he said, and left the kitchen.

I was standing there trying to figure out what was going on, and suddenly it was clear – it was ME! He was afraid of me! I had another shock at that, and thought that if they knew I was making the toys move they would throw me in the garbage – a threat they had used on occasion when I was not being cooperative. They were joking of course, but I didn't know that. I immediately made sure the toys weren't moving – I could see them from where I was – I could see through the walls. A few minutes later I walked in the bedroom and saw my dad with a screw driver taking apart the electrical outlet near the toys, as if that had something to do with it. I knew this was something I had to keep hidden or risk being literally cast out.

The Spelling Bee

This is another siddhi that I had for a short time. It could also be seen as a savant ability like some autistic people possess. In seventh grade I was selected to participate in a spelling competition and was allowed to leave my classroom and go to the school library. There were many other kids there and we were given a written multiple choice spelling test. I did well and was selected a day or so later for round two with fewer of us remaining. I liked spelling and had been praised for being a good speller early on. I don't know when this particular ability kicked in, but I don't recall it being there until we were given words verbally and had to spell them out loud. At the same time, I began feeling some pressure to not fail, although I haven't yet found a shock that might account for it. It worked like this: during the testing, whenever I was given a word, I could see it in my mind's eye, above my head in bright red letters on a very black background, and all I had to do was read what I saw – and I was never wrong, even if I had never encountered the word before. I was very much reminded of this when I saw the movie "Bee Season," by how the correct letters appeared in magical ways to Eliza, the protagonist, during the spelling bee.[59] After a while I lost any sense of pressure. The Spelling Bee was fun but I had no incentive or desire to win. I felt more like a messenger than a player.

I'm unsure how many days we were tested but I managed to make it to the grand finale of the Spelling Bee. There was a makeshift stage set up in the library, where we all stood in line and would file up to the front when it was our turn to be given a word. Every time I was given a word, I just read the letters that appeared in my mind. Simple. But I did feel a bit guarded because I had this secret. It felt a bit like I was cheating.

All was fine, and I was quite at ease up until the end when there were only three of us left, and it suddenly occurred to me that I might actually win! I started getting nervous. The idea of being in the spotlight as the winner was terrifying to me. This was probably triggering my Clark Kent identity. Up until then I had felt lost in the crowd, which was how I liked it, but the crowd was gone. When the tall skinny boy in front of me missed his word and left the stage it was down to me and a Chinese girl, and I was up next. I was about to win, and this could be my last chance to escape notoriety! I

---

[59] Bee Season" (2005)

had a shock and made a decision to lose. Now if I didn't want to win I could have just purposely misread the red letters, but the shock took over. In the power-zone I altered the spelling mechanism to spell the words incorrectly. When given my next word I could see that the red letters that appeared above me were gibberish, but I gladly read them anyway and was dismissed. I retired to my seat, much relieved, and happy to see the smiling girl get all the attention. The red letters never returned.

The Power Wall

After Terrence left and I got my own room back I awoke one night feeling a sense of power, like the whole room was charged with some kind of energy. My bed was up against the wall, which was to my right. I looked at the wall and it was dimly glowing with red light. I sat up on the side of the bed and noticed I could feel the energy in the air. The red glow in the wall disappeared but the energy was still there. The energy and I were connected. It was as if everything was magnetic and I could feel the force of everything around me. I was tuned in to it and I knew that I could use it. I went into my brothers' room where they were sleeping and I woke them both up. The night was still dark but the room was softly lit up by moonlight coming in through the south windows. I said "Watch this" and I levitated a tin cup a few inches off the night stand by moving my hands to guide the energy. Blake saw it and turned over and went back to sleep. Alan just said "You did it," quite matter-of-fact-ly and laid back down. I went back to my room. I had just felt like I needed to show them while the energy was still present. Later I found that with a little focus I could tune in to the energy-feeling at will.

Shades of Mimzy

In the movie "The Last Mimzy" two children develop psychic abilities after finding some high tech toys from the future.[60] There is a scene where the little girl shows her babysitter what she can do, and levitates several objects, called spinners, and has them all

---

[60] "The Last Mimzy" (2007)

moving around in the air. The sitter runs screaming out of the house. It reminded me of a similar childhood experience.

Not long after the Power Wall incident we got a new babysitter and housekeeper named Rosie, and she had been working for only a few days. One day when she was sitting on the couch in front of the coffee table smoking a cigarette, I asked her if she would like to see a magic trick. She said "OK" so I proceeded to levitate her pack of cigarettes off the table. Rosie immediately stiffened up and squeaked "You're the devil!" I saw that she was spooked so I let the cigarettes drop and tried to calm her, saying "No, it's just a trick." But she was too frightened, and wouldn't look at me. "Really. It's a magic trick. I got a magic set for Christmas" I pleaded. The latter was true. But Rosie was already reciting the Lord's Prayer and staring down at the floor. She did not budge from the couch and continued chanting all day until my mother got home from work. She told my mother that she had to quit, and gave her some excuse. I was watching the whole thing, and Rosie kept glancing over at me as she spoke, but said nothing of what had occurred. She never returned.

The Sorcerer's Apprentice – or My Wizard

I was working on a feeling of doubt I had about some of the miraculous things I was remembering, and I had a flashback of a dream I'd had sometime earlier. The dream was like a cartoon in which a sorcerer takes a boy into his secret laboratory as an apprentice, but something happens, and the boy runs away. It seemed like the sorcerer was really trying to steal the boy's soul or something. Then I began having flashbacks of fifth grade. This incident is cringeworthy, but it still makes me smile.

Sometime after the "Mimzy" fiasco, I was in the cafeteria at school during lunchtime watching Joe, the custodian, juggling some fruit for the kids, which he did from time to time. We would give him our apples and oranges and he would entertain us for a minute. But this time as I watched him from a distance, his whole body seemed to glow; especially his head and down his spine, and there were little pink lights, about the size of ping pong balls, dancing around him. I felt he must be magic and I got the idea that he could teach me something!

After school I went into the cafeteria where he was sweeping the floor. No one else was there. I hung around until he asked me if I was waiting for someone, and I asked him to teach me magic. He said he didn't know any magic and kept sweeping. I didn't leave, and I again asked about him teaching me, explaining that I knew some magic myself. He seemed annoyed and asked if I thought that juggling was magic. He said juggling was not magical and again denied that he knew anything about magic. He seemed nervous and told me I shouldn't be there.

Joe was probably in his forties, maybe younger, but I really can't say. I persisted, and finally I said, "I know you're magic because I can see lights around you." He stopped and turned around, and said, with some amazement, "You can see that?" I said yes and described the lights I saw, what colors they were (mostly pink and yellow) and where I saw them. He then said he could teach me magic but that it would change me, so I had to be sure that's what I wanted. I accepted that. He gave me an address, which was right down the street from the school, and said to be there at five.

I was very happy. There was no one else I could share my secrets with and here was a real wizard who was going to help me! When I showed up at his house he took me into a bedroom and said that this was the _magic_ room. There were a number of interesting things in the room, giving it the appearance of being somewhat magical, like a sorcerer's cave. I realize now that he probably set the room up that way for this occasion, and this was certainly the source of my dream. He left the room to get something and closed the door, but soon returned with a candle. He lit the candle and sat in a chair in front of me with the light off. He then told me a long boring story about some warrior on a journey looking for magic or something, but I was more interested in watching his aura glow and sparkle. I'd never seen that before. I was also perceiving a definite female presence around him, and a sadness about being trapped somehow and unable to exert any power, but I didn't understand these impressions.

After the story, he told me that men had a special magic, and he exposed himself. He had an erection and told me that it was magic. He asked if I could do that and I said yes, but that my magic was different and I wanted him to help me understand it. I was not surprised by what he did and never felt any fear or sensed any threat or danger about him. Actually I felt very special. No one had ever taught me _anything_ that I wanted to learn, and here was someone like ME, offering to teach me secret things – or so I thought.

So I ignored his vulgar impropriety, which was boring, and wanted to get to the REAL magic. I asked if I could show him what I could do and he said OK but didn't seem very excited. I figured I would show off and impress him. I needed an object. I looked at the items on his dresser and the first thing I considered was too small so I picked a larger one. It was a Magic 8-Ball – a four-inch black spherical toy that was popular in the 1950's for telling fortunes. I put it on the floor near his feet as he sat on the bed, and moved my hands on each side as if I were trying to raise a sunken softball from the bottom of a swimming pool.

The object rose about two feet when I heard a gasp and looked up. Joe had collapsed face down on the bed, moaning and gasping for air. The Magic 8-ball dropped loudly to the floor as I stood up. Joe's whole body was shaking like he was having some kind of seizure. I thought that he might be choking or having a heart attack. As I stood there a girl's voice in my head told me to get him some water, so I ran in the kitchen and came back with a glass of water. But another voice was now telling me to run. Joe was still shaking on the bed so I set the glass on the floor and hurried out of the house. I was actually worried that I had caused him to have a heart attack and that I might be put in jail.

As I quickly walked away from his house, Joe came to the door and said I didn't have to run. Then he saw a neighbor who was gardening next door. He yelled at me to say that he didn't touch me. Then he yelled "Please!" I didn't understand, but I yelled back "You didn't' touch me," and kept walking.

It was very disappointing that my wizard was just another pervert – a "dead" person, and not magical at all. And now I was back to being alone. I never saw Joe again at school. I may have suppressed my memory of seeing him there, but my feeling is that he quit.

The Magic Show

For some reason I was determined to levitate something without freaking anybody out, but I realized that I had to somehow disguise my ability as a trick. Since my brothers had seemed to be unaffected by my original presentation, I gathered three neighborhood boys and told them I was going to do a great magic trick. I got out my magic set and set up some small objects on the box. The box had the word "MAGIC" right on the front and had a picture of a smiling kid with a big black top-hat and a magic wand. With my friends gathered 'round, I started waving my magic wand over the objects on the box. I could feel the energy, but at the last second I had a shock. What if they DO freak out?! Then I wouldn't even have any friends. I balked, and intentionally failed to do any "magic." I told them I forgot how to do the trick, and my friends moaned as they got up and left. But at least they weren't afraid of me.

All of the incidents I'm relating here were, at the least, small traumas for me – every one involved a shock and the shock led to a stuck feeling or condition. It was in trying to resolve these conditions or discover the source of the feelings, that these stories unfolded. This is true for all the stories that follow as well.

Don't be Afraid

When I was thirty-four, I had a part time summer job working for a construction company that built residential houses. One morning we were building a house with prefabricated walls. Once a wall was lined up correctly on the ground, a bunch of us lifted the top end and raised it into position so it could be secured into place. While lifting one wall my left hand was too low and got crushed between the wall we were raising and the frame of the house. I yelled out and everyone stopped. I removed my hand and went out front and sat down.

Mitchell, the owner and foreman, immediately asked about my injury when it happened, and I said I couldn't tell how bad it was. I was still wearing my gloves and there was no blood but my left wrist felt seriously hurt. I couldn't move it and thought it might be broken. Mitchell said they would secure the wall and then see if I needed medical attention. So as the others finished with the wall I sat there holding my wrist. I seemed to drift into a quiet state. Then I heard a voice say "Don't be afraid." I felt the presence of "others" but thought it was my imagination. Then my whole left hand started getting very hot. Once again the voice said "Don't be afraid."

The heat increased until it seemed like my hand was on fire. The pain should have been unbearable but it wasn't. I felt something happening in my hand, like vibrations and things moving around and I had a shock at the idea that something miraculous might be occurring. When the heat faded away, I noticed the pain was gone and I was able to move my hand normally. I took off the glove and looked at my wrist, and it seemed normal. When Mitchell returned, I told him everything was fine. I figured I hadn't really hurt my hand much at all. But I seemed to be distracted for the rest of the day, as if I were trying to remember something, or connect with something that seemed important. The memory of what happened was fading though, and in the end I just let it go. I don't recall psychically asking for help at the time of the injury, and I have no idea who helped me or why.

Back to the Future

In the summer when I was thirteen my friend Jeff and I were having fun hiding from each other in a big field of huge rectangular hay bales. The bales were stacked high and the way they were set created a huge maze. While I was looking for Jeff, I tried to psychically see where he was. I knew I could do this sometimes. Instead, to my shock, I saw the future. I saw myself lying dead on my bedroom floor, in a puddle of blood. I saw Dennis–2 floating above me in the hay field and I heard him say "Sorry you had to see that." This made me somewhat reluctant to be psychic, as you can imagine, so I immediately suppressed the vision. Several months later however, that premonition came to pass.

In February during eighth grade I had an accident. Weeks earlier Jeff had shown me his latest invention: a small rocket made of tin foil that could fly a distance of up to ten feet. He had devised this by making a tin foil cylinder, using a pencil, and filling it with gun powder from the caps that were used in toy cap guns. We added phosphorus from the tips of wooden matches and more gun powder, adjusted the angle of our launch ramps and got them to go even farther. As usual, I took Jeff's idea and tried to expand on it. I decided to make a bigger rocket using an eight-inch metal pipe but I made the exhaust opening too small. My father saw it and decided it was too dangerous for us to mess with and told me he would set it off himself. I had attached a string fuse about six inches long. My father told my brothers and me to get far away and to hide behind something. He lit the fuse and knelt down about fifteen feet away holding the metal lid of our garbage can as a shield. The rocket exploded like dynamite and left the metal pipe almost flat. I was reprimanded, given a short lecture on how I could have been killed, and was warned to not try this again. Right.

Sometime later I was given an empty CO_2 canister from my friend Ross's pellet gun. I decided to make a bomb out of it using caps, matches, and gun powder from bullets I got for the bolt action 22 rifle I had received from the Sears catalog in December. Well ... when you're dealing with explosives you must be extremely careful. I wasn't. I was sitting in my bedroom at my desk packing the explosives into the metal tube when I did something stupidly careless, and the thing blew up in my face. I was rushed to the hospital with a piece of metal protruding from my left eyebrow. I spent a week or so in the hospital, and another three weeks at home recovering.

One of the recurring headaches I would get later on, occurred on the left side of my forehead, and I traced it back to this incident. I had worked on this incident before and realized that something amazing had happened, but the pain was not resolved. Now, working on this again, I got more of the details.

The explosion blew me backwards off the chair and I remember hearing a "pop" sound that seemed very far away. Then I found myself on the floor in a puddle of blood, just like in the premonition. But I didn't die. Something happened in the power-zone that altered the outcome of this injury. Each time I looked at the middle of the shock I had a flashback. I kept seeing myself stacking towels back in junior high school.

Three months or so before this accident, I was assigned to be a towel monitor in gym class. This meant that for a week, another boy and I had to spend gym class folding and stacking towels in the utility room next to the showers. We would then hand the towels out to the other boys when they were done showering. One day as we were stacking towels I started goofing off, acting silly and jumping around as if some wacky energy had just taken me over, and BOOM, I hit my head on a metal shelf. Hard! I was stunned and nauseous and went to the nurse's office. I was sent home for the day and I ended up with quite a bump. It was just above my left eye. As the weeks and months went by this area became noticeably thicker and felt hard, as if the bone had actually beefed up. You couldn't tell by looking at it but I could feel it with my hand, and was often curious about it.

Months later when the bomb exploded and I found myself on the floor, I was dazed but still conscious. An internal voice yelled at me to get up, and I ran to get help. My mother called an ambulance while I held my bleeding head over the kitchen sink. That's when my hand felt the piece of shrapnel protruding from my forehead. In the hospital the surgeon removed the thin metal fragment, which was roughly an inch square. Using pliers of some kind, it seemed like Dr. Rixford had to use all his strength to pry it from the bone. It actually took him two tries. I was under local anesthesia only, and remember the whole thing. He showed the fragment to me later and told my parents that if it had gone a fraction of an inch deeper I would have died.

The piece of metal that struck me hit the EXACT spot where my eyebrow had grown thicker. I had always thought that the bump being there was just a lucky coincidence. Now I believe that in the middle of the shock from the explosion that should have killed me, I changed the past. I caused my younger self to start jumping around for no reason and hit my forehead just right, to create the desired effect. In the material world time travel is impossible because it breaks the rules and presents a paradox. Something cannot happen that didn't happen. But Consciousness can do anything, and it can alter the entire timeline anyway it wants, like a writer going back and rewriting a chapter. I don't recall any timeline where the towel room accident DIDN'T happen, but it doesn't matter. In that timeline I would have died and would now be living another life with no memory of my previous existence anyway. We have unlimited power but we hide it from ourselves in order to play the game of life, as tragic as it often is.

Poltergeist – or Be Calm

In her later years, after my father died, my mother lived with me. One cold day in February 1993 my mother and I were in the dining room having our morning coffee. I was standing facing the table and she was sitting to my left. When I was in the real estate business, we sometimes referred to lawyers as "deal killers" because they would consider every negative contingency in any transaction. Mom was like a lawyer in that respect, because when I would describe to her some creative plan of mine, she would tell me all the reasons it wouldn't work. I often found this very helpful because I like to consider everything. But this morning when I expressed an imaginative idea, she made a comment that was invalidating and disheartening. I immediately got angry. I didn't express my anger outwardly, but instead imagined hurling my cup of coffee and smashing it against the wall across the table.

Instantly my mother grabbed her left side and said "Ooh." I looked at her and she said "Did you ever feel like something just bit you?" She'd been zapped. I had a strong feeling about her reaction and said, "Mom, I can't explain it, but I think that was me." I didn't know it then, but something within me had awakened.

That night sometime after 11:00 P.M., I was pacing up and down the dark sidewalk in front of my house, brainstorming. At some point my thoughts concerning a particular person triggered some anger. Then I heard some metallic rattling sounds coming from my car, which was behind me and to my left in the driveway. I stopped and listened. Nothing. I continued pacing and heard it again. I stopped, and this time the rattling continued. I walked over to the car and listened. There were a few metallic "clunks" coming from under the hood. I thought there might be some animal in there, maybe a cat, but I also had the idea that I was causing this. I was getting a bit frightened. I looked underneath the car, and as I did so the fan turned on briefly, by itself. Then all was quiet.

I stood there a minute and walked away. Immediately the fan came on again, this time for a bit longer. I walked back to the front of the car and the fan went on and off sporadically. I got the idea that I could WILL the fan to stay on longer, and when it came on again I tried to make it keep going ... and it did! Now I was feeling a rush of adrenalin – my whole body was tingling.

The fan continued to go off and on by itself. Then I heard the phone ring. My mother, was asleep so I ran in the house and answered it – no one was there. I hung up and as I walked back to the front door, I heard the car fan come on again. Then there was an explosion, like a firecracker, across the street in a neighbor's car port. I saw their porch light come on. The car fan was going on and off more frequently, and the phone rang again. I ran back in the house and answered it – no one there.

Now I felt like I was surrounded by dark forces – like the whole house was engulfed in a dark grey cloud. I felt surrounded and oppressed so I called my psychic friend Sandra. When she answered I was talking a mile a minute, telling her about the dark forces and everything that was happening.

Sandra interrupted me, not in her normal voice, but in the soft voice that was always right. "Be calm," she said. "What?" I asked. "That's what I'm getting, just 'Be calm'," she repeated.

But I ignored her. I was too energized. After I hung up, the car fan continued to go on and off. I called Sandra back once or twice more, and finally I went to bed. When I awoke in the morning I went outside to see if my car was still possessed. It was cold outside and I could see my breath in the air. I discovered later by reading the manual that the fan in my car was activated by a thermocouple that responded to heat. The fan was cold and should not have come on the night before and certainly not this morning. But when I got five feet from the car, the fan came on. This all felt personal somehow, and I headed back in the house to do a session so I could look into it.

I did my session in the back bedroom which I had converted into an office and study. My computer was on, which sported an old Intel 386 processor, and every time the car fan turned on it caused some static interference which I could hear over the speakers. The fan went on and off continuously up until a certain point in the session.

The essence of the identity state I was in, regarding what I was calling the "dark forces," was a concern about wanting to be a good person. It seemed that I was trying to control the dark forces somehow so they would not hurt anyone. And this is what I found.

When I was maybe seven or eight I had just gotten out of the shower. I put my underwear on and ran into the front room to get something. My father was there and said that my skin made him want to pinch it. He started pinching me all over on my arms and back, very rapidly, and it hurt. I tried to get away but he held me and kept pinching me. Suddenly he yelled and let go. He then fell on the floor and started rolling around yelling, and swatting at his body as if he were being attacked by a swarm of yellow jackets. Now something was pinching HIM. At the same time there were explosions in the air, like firecrackers, and a picture fell off the wall. Then other objects started moving or falling while the explosions and the yelling continued.

With all the noise and chaos going on around me, I felt the presence of a dark force, which I imagined as a dark grey cloud, that was causing all this mayhem. I knew this was connected to ME and that I had to stop it, although I didn't remember anything about the power-zone or about creating this force at this point. My concern caused me to have another shock and I immediately tried to be as calm as I could. I told the dark force to follow me and I slowly and calmly walked into my bedroom and closed the door. I lay down on my bed and continued to be calm with the intention of putting the dark force to sleep. The commotion in the living room stopped, and when all was quiet I put on my clothes and ventured out. My father walked past me as I entered the front room. "I don't know how you did that, and I don't want to know," he said dryly, without making eye contact.

In the first shock, which was the moment when my father's pinching frenzy became intolerable to me, I became exceedingly angry. The shock was knowing that I could not express this anger openly without his retaliation. From my rage I created a vengeful protective mechanism. My poltergeist wasn't an alter personality or a protecting spirit, but a piece of intelligent psychic machinery. It was me, operating on an unconscious level, but in this case the machinery was part of the shock and became an unconscious identity state of self-protection. I had created this mechanism to avoid responsibility for hurting my dad. I didn't want to be the bad guy, but I had to do something. In the power-zone when I started zapping my attacker, I created my actions as an automatic mechanism. I imagined this dark force to be something other than myself. After the shock however, I felt the need to stop it but I didn't know how – it was out of control by design. This created a second shock. In that shock I decided to calm it down, like I would do with an upset animal. The solution was to be calm myself, _just as Sandra had said._

As I worked on the first shock, I noticed that the static on the computer speakers had ceased. After this session the whole thing

made sense and I knew the poltergeist was gone. I went out to the
car and all was calm. The fan never again came on by itself and
there was no more mysterious rattling under the hood.
Nevertheless, I felt that I had missed an opportunity to display these
paranormal phenomena in a controlled study.

In truth however, the poltergeist was not something I could
actually control. It was a reaction, and often when you TRY to have
some kind of response or make something happen, what's known in
hypnosis as "the law of reversed effect" takes over, where you get the
opposite of what you intend. Viktor Frankl used this technique and
called it "paradoxical intention" – which just means my plan
wouldn't have worked.[61] These more recent events were always
remembered, but the origin of the poltergeist was forgotten shortly
after it occurred.

---

[61] "Man's Search For meaning"- Viktor Frankl, 1946

Chapter 14
Self-Healing Stories – Part 3
The Spirit

Suicide Interruptus – or
Riding the Mad Hornet

The hornet that stung me and began my bee phobia when I was fourteen, attacked me one sunny day while I was out hunting with my dog King. I was several miles from home walking down a dirt road along a tree-lined slough surrounded by plowed fields, with no buildings in sight, carrying my bolt-action 22. I was feeling depressed and overwhelmed by the circumstances of my life, and was contemplating suicide when I suddenly realized that I could use my gun! I had never thought of that before and began giving the idea some serious consideration. The hornet came out of nowhere, and for no reason began harassing me, buzzing all around my head sounding very angry, if that's a thing. At first it was just strange – nothing like that had ever happened to me, but I had no fear. I stopped and knelt down and was very calm. But the hornet kept buzzing my head, even while I remained motionless. Then I felt it land on my shoulder. That's when I panicked and ran off waving my arms. I was wearing a T-shirt and it stung me on the left upper arm as I ran down the levy embankment and off into a field. I ran about thirty yards and suddenly calmed down. It's unusual for hornets to lose their stingers, but I pulled a rather large one out of my arm. All thoughts of suicide had vanished. I wouldn't have killed myself anyway, but my thoughts about it were rudely interrupted. As it turns out, that was no ordinary hornet.

This incident was the shock that linked bees and wasps to my earlier fear of death when I was six, which I described in Chapter 5. That earlier incident also explains why I suddenly calmed down after a short run. Later, after integrating with Dennis–2, I had the thought that it was no coincidence that I was attacked by that hornet right as I was thinking of doing myself in. Although he knew me as well as I knew myself, Dennis–2 wasn't taking any chances. I discovered that he had actually commandeered the hornet, taking full control of it, and attacked me himself. It was a wonderful "pattern interrupt!"[62] Also looking through the hornet's compound eyes was fascinating – it was a real IMAX experience!

The Black Dot

When I was twenty-one, I started doing Zen meditation using a koan, which is a question you contemplate which may lead to a spiritual awakening.[63] My koan was "Who am I?" which I had immediately recognized as a profound question when I first encountered it. One day I decided to try and maintain my awareness of this question continuously throughout the day. Previously I had done a lot of meditation where I counted my breaths, from which I had developed a strong ability to focus. When I began this challenging endeavor, I was actually able to maintain meditative self-awareness for 24 hours a day, for about two and a half days. Eventually, the question "Who am I?" became a nonverbal awareness of looking into my own being, and this awareness was present even during sleep! I would get up from sleeping and notice that I had been aware the whole time, both of dreaming and of dreamless sleep. This "awareness" was aware of both the content of my dreams and of just being itself as "timeless being," whether I was dreaming or not. It felt powerful.

On the third day I was walking through the house when there was a sudden shock. All I remembered of this moment afterward was that everything went black and the blackness shrunk to a small black dot in front of me and vanished. But there was a lot of fear

---

[62] The term "pattern interrupt" refers to an NLP technique I learned from Tony Robbins where, to get someone to shift out of a negative state they are in, you do something unexpected or attention grabbing, repeatedly if necessary, to interrupt their current response pattern. This is discussed in depth in Chapter 18.

[63] A Zen koan is an unanswerable question posed to Zen students as a meditative puzzle meant to stimulate a spiritual awakening, a direct experience of the truth that is beyond thought or intellectual understanding.

there, and I didn't attempt to do any Zen meditation again for
twenty-two years.

After I had learned ID-R and knew how to successfully process
trauma and work with various altered states, I recalled the missing
pieces of this experience that I had blocked out. What actually
happened was that my awareness had suddenly expanded so that my
center of perception was above my head and I could see my body as
well as my house and the entire neighborhood for several blocks. I
also saw several people around me, as spirits, looking at me. Some
looked surprised, some looked afraid, and some looked happy, but I
had no idea who they were or what was happening. I was totally
spooked! In a state of panic I entered the power-zone and
immediately suppressed, and literally blacked out, the whole
experience. When I regained my previous perspective, I had
forgotten everything – except the black dot.

The expansion of my consciousness was a natural result of
maintaining self-awareness continuously for an extended time.
There is more I could say here but the bottom line is, I simply was
not prepared for this experience. Otherwise, this could have been a
profound breakthrough. I did other forms of meditation after that
experience, mostly for concentration and relaxation, but I did not
try Zen meditation or use my koan again until after this incident
was resolved. I believe the spirits I saw around me were just some of
my own helpers.

Pie in the Sky

When I was thirteen our family was in danger of losing our
home because we were behind on the mortgage. One afternoon I
was worrying about this and feeling sorry for my parents. Then I
remembered that I could levitate things and that Terrence had said
I could make a million bucks. Although I found the idea of being in
a circus scary, I considered that I might be able to help my parents
and save the house. I walked in the kitchen and saw a freshly baked
apple pie on the counter. No one else was home. I wanted to see if I
could still do it, so I tried to feel the energy, and it was there the
moment I thought about it. I moved my hands and the pie rose
about six inches off the counter.

As I calmly confirmed to myself that I still had this ability, the pie suddenly shot up to the right corner of the room in front of me and disappeared through the ceiling! In that same instant, from the spot where the pie vanished, came a resounding "NO!" I didn't hear the voice so much as felt the power of it and understood it. There was no emotion, no threat, no judgement of me in the voice, but it's intention was strong, unmistakable, and final – I would not be allowed to do anything of this nature, period! I wasn't alarmed because somehow I already knew I would be breaking some kind of rule. It seems I could get away with using my gifts to a small degree, but more public demonstrations were apparently forbidden.

No one questioned me about the pie, but later on, my mother spent a lot of time looking for her favorite pie pan. It was never found. We lost our house about a year later.

The Great Circus Disappointment – or Craving the Incredibles

I used to have an intense reaction of disappointment whenever something I had planned with someone else was delayed or cancelled. I worked on this issue many years ago after a girlfriend thoughtlessly decided to cancel our plans one day and didn't tell me, leaving me to wait for her for quite a while. This particular reaction originated however when I was about eleven, after I had acquired some tickets for a circus that was coming to town. The circus was arriving on a Saturday and my dad said he would take me, but when the day came he told me we weren't going. I was furious! I ripped up the tickets and went to my room, slammed the door, and fumed about it for a long time. I was very happy to clear up this reaction, but it turns out there was more to it.

Flash forward to 2018; there was a movie playing that I very much wanted to see. I wanted to ask a lady friend to see it with me but I didn't know her well so I hesitated. But for some reason seeing this movie with her seemed very important, and I couldn't stop thinking about it. This whole thing caused me far more concern than it warranted! I finally realized this was a reaction and did a session. This is another example of a reactive past experience intruding into present time to make something difficult when it should be easy. When you consider how much of our lives are hindered by these things it's quite amazing – life could be so much more peaceful and enjoyable! Here's what happened.

In that earlier incident, after my dad had promised to take me to the circus, and about a week before the event, I walked in the kitchen and mentioned to him how much I was looking forward to going. He said he was glad I reminded him because he had forgotten all about it. I had a shock when I realized this wasn't important to him at all, and there was a possibility we wouldn't go. I decided I had to keep reminding him and that I could lose this opportunity if I didn't keep it constantly on my mind. But every time I tried to get reassurance about it, he would give me the less than inspiring comment "We'll see." So now I was worried about missing the circus and constantly obsessing about it. This was the unwanted identity that had been bothering me in present time.

In this session I also realized why the circus was so important. Because Terrence, my petty tyrant, had said I should join a circus, when he discovered I could fly, I imagined circus people must know something about flying and other magical things. Since my "wizard," Joe the custodian, had turned out to be bogus, I imagined that this event might be my last opportunity to find magical people that I could actually learn from, so I had a lot of hope tied up in that idea. I still believed I lived in a world where magic was real. It *is* real of course, but not in the minds of most people, and eventually it became unreal to me as well. The movie I wanted to see with my friend, by the way, was one in which the main characters all had superpowers! This was a direct association to the circus incident. We did end up going to see the movie and it was great fun, but days earlier when I resolved this reaction, the importance and urgency of going vanished completely.

Unless we are completely "present," human interactions are most often just programs reacting to other programs. My father did take me to the circus once when I was three. During the show a monkey had been trained to run around the inner perimeter of the amphitheater along a metal railing just below the audience, and just inches from me. When I saw that very strange-looking creature rushing toward me and getting closer and closer, I didn't know what it was and became terrified. I started screaming and my dad had to take me home. So he could have had his own negative reaction to the idea of taking me to the circus, even though he probably didn't consciously remember anything of this past experience at the time.

Another Lesson

In eight grade I borrowed another boy's body for a few minutes so I could interact with Patty, as you will read in Chapter 23. When I got home, I bragged about it to my friend Ross. We were in my front yard with Timmy, a younger neighborhood boy. As I walked out of my front door I told Ross I could go into other people's bodies and make them do whatever I wanted. He laughed and thought it was ridiculous, so I asked him "Do you want to see?" I asked Timmy if I could borrow his body and he said OK, but I didn't consider the fact that he didn't understand what I was talking about. I told Ross "Watch," and as I stood there I left my body and went over to Timmy. I was able to push him out of his body but he became disoriented. I then danced around in his body for a few seconds saying some silly things that he would never say, and went back to my own body. Timmy fell to the ground in fetal position, covering his head.

Ross looked at me and asked "Did you do that?" He looked fascinated. I nodded "Mm Hmm." "Can you do it to me?" he asked. "I can try." I left my body and went behind Ross and looked in his head. I could see him in there, like a ghostly duplicate of himself, but something was wrong. He seemed to be stuck in there facing backwards somehow. In the state I was in I knew this was a problem – I could feel it. I went back and said to Ross: "It won't work with you – I think you could die." He looked over at Timmy, who was still on the ground, said he was going home, and left.

I went over to Timmy but he wouldn't move or say anything. Now I was worried. He hadn't known any better, and I now felt ashamed of my cavalier attitude. I had a shock thinking I may have seriously hurt him somehow. I went in the house and tried to figure out what to do, and I prayed to God that Timmy would be OK. I went back outside and told Timmy how sorry I was and that I would never do this again to anyone. I heard him say very clearly in my head, in a very adult voice, "Have you learned your lesson?" I said yes. He immediately got up and went home without speaking. The next time I saw him he seemed fine and acted as if nothing had happened. I didn't think what I did was wrong, but I really didn't expect anyone to get hurt.

The Dead World

"It is not now as it hath been of yore;—Turn wheresoe'er I may, By night or day. The things which I have seen I now can see no more."
– William Wordsworth

I had recently turned fourteen. After scaring people and possibly hurting them with my spiritual shenanigans, I began feeling that I had crossed a line, and that I had to do something about it. I decided that using my psychic abilities was a bad thing, and that was why no one else was doing what I could do. This was the first reactivation of the depressing past-life incident described in Chapter 4, and I was feeling like I didn't belong in the same world with everyone else. I started to understand how others felt when they saw something miraculous, and I became afraid of myself. It felt like the whole world was shifting.

One day something happened that led me to think more deeply about these things. After the Timmy-incident an adult neighbor saw me levitating something in my back yard and started yelling at me over the fence with some intensity. Her admonitions left me feeling troubled and confused. Some hours or perhaps days later I went into my bedroom and closed the door. I put a book on the floor and was going to attempt to levitate it. This felt like a big experiment. I was feeling that my power was wrong – not evil, just unacceptable or illegal – and I started to get scared. I felt bad enough about myself as it was, but this ability was something that separated me from everyone else – something I couldn't have if I wanted to be part of the human race. I wanted to believe I was like everyone else and that I didn't have any special abilities, meaning that I could not possibly levitate that book.

So I bent over and made the familiar movements with my hands, half-heartedly, pretending that I didn't really feel the energy fields around me. But when the book began to move I had a shock. This time it was terrifying! I stood up and whirled around. With my back to the book I stared out of my window and repeated to myself over and over "It's not happening, it's not happening!"

In that moment the Magical World died and I entered the Dead World. It was as if all the color drained out of existence, and everything faded to black-and-white. The world became empty of life, energy, and magic. It all became hollow, dead. I turned around and looked at the book lying on the floor. It was dead too. Even before I moved my hands to check, I knew I could no longer feel the energy. And I also knew that there never was any energy, and that nothing magical I had ever done before was real. What had previously been so innocent and natural was now impossible.

The Walking Dead

"But the white man, they believe everything is dead. Stone, earth, animals. And people. Even their own people." – Little Big Man, 1970

This new identity prevented me from accessing my previous abilities and affected the way I thought about such things. First, I could no longer remember that I had ever levitated anything, traveled out of my body, or had experienced anything magical. Many such things had been forgotten quickly anyway, but in my new persona as a "normal human being" I was now like everyone else – one of the walking dead. Like a drone in the Borg Collective, I had been assimilated.[64] But although my more powerful abilities had been stifled, I still had a sense of a spiritual connection to something beyond myself and felt that I had some special abilities even if I didn't remember them. Although I have now resolved this incident, I didn't regain any of my previous abilities because, as often happens, this shock awakened other powerful shocks which I have not yet looked into. But my fear of the miraculous appears to have greatly diminished.

---

[64] The "Borg Collective" refers to an alien civilization of cyborgs in the Star Trek universe. The Borg space ships invade planetary systems throughout the galaxy and assimilate other intelligent species into their collective by turning individuals into cyborg slaves and connecting them to their hive-mind. The Borg also integrate captured knowledge and technology into their own system to further their goal of achieving perfection.

Chapter 15
Spirit Releasement

*" Knowing or feeling that we are all connected to each other and
to the cosmos by more than our eyes and ears is not a new notion but
one as old as humanity. Traditional indigenous societies were fully
aware of nonmaterial connections and incorporated them into their
daily life. The modern world, however, continues to dismiss and even
deny these intangible links ... Consequently our mainstream culture is
spiritually impoverished, and the world we live in has become
disenchanted." – Ervin Laszlo, The Akashic Experience*

*"The reality, though, is that we are always in the company
of spirits and angels, in our inner depths."
– Emanuel Swedenborg, Secrets of Heaven 5036*

We are spiritual beings, beings of consciousness, by which I
mean we are not material beings, even though it may appear that
we are. We are intimately connected with everything and everyone
around us in ways we do not understand. Our true nature is
consciousness, and the realm of consciousness is unlimited. We
may think of space and time as unlimited, or of the universe as
infinite, but these are just concepts which allow us to imagine the
immensity of existence in perceptual ways. But without
consciousness, it's simply a truism that nothing in the universe
would ever appear to anyone, because there wouldn't BE any
conscious being to whom anything COULD appear.

Having an out-of-body experience is a universal phenomenon
and many people have recalled living past lives and alternate
simultaneous lives. Memories of these kinds of experiences and
many others require, if taken seriously, a different model of reality
than those which explain things in a purely materialist way. These
experiences imply that we do not require bodies and can exist
independent of them in some form – as spirits if you will. What
these experiences mean, and whether they are actually evidence of
anything beyond physical reality, will be considered later. What is

important here is that people *DO* have these experiences and it is useful to have workable alternative models of reality to explain them. By the way, such models have been around for many centuries.

Another thing that we experience is the psychic influence of others. How this is possible and why it happens can be debated but the fact is that conscious beings can, and do, affect each other. These effects can be through physical communication and interaction of course, but may also be transpersonal, that is, they operate through a modality that lies outside of the physical realm and within the greater realm of consciousness itself. For example, we may appear to be visited by people who are deceased. We may be visited by or influenced by people who are living but not in our physical presence at the time. In addition, we may also experience interactions with what we might call spirit guides, angels, saints, demons, the devil, troubled spirits, alien beings, gods or goddesses, our Higher Self, or God. Whether any of these concepts represent something real beyond their appearance, is unimportant for our immediate purposes. We simply take things as they are, or as they seem, and deal with them as necessary. Such visitations may be one time occurrences, or they may be prolonged relationships, and any of these can be beneficial, neutral, or detrimental to us in some way. In this chapter we will be exploring spirit communication and influence, spirit attachment, and spirit releasement. My personal stories in this chapter are provided to demonstrate some of the many ways our spiritual nature might be experienced in our everyday lives, when our hearts and minds are open enough to see it.

Sometimes when working with a client, we find that the source of some unwanted condition involves a conscious entity that is not a helper personality or any aspect of the person's mind or consciousness. Here we will simply call such an entity a "spirit." We say the spirit is attached if its connection to the person is ongoing, stuck, or intractable. In counseling we can usually make a connection and engage in communication with the spirit and come to a resolution so that the spirit leaves and the unwanted condition changes or disappears. Since spirits cannot generally be detected in any physical way, the question of whether there really was an external spirit present, after the point of healing, is a matter of opinion. But this is not as important as the healing that takes place, which is the primary goal. ID-R helps us locate the entity and resolve one's involvement with it, while Spirit Releasement Therapy, as I use it in my practice, is the process of resolving the connection or attachment on the part of the entity, who is the source of the condition. While either method alone might work, both processes are often necessary to completely resolve an attachment situation.

Spirit Releasement Therapy, or SRT, is a term coined by Dr. William Baldwin author of "Spirit Releasement Therapy: A Technique Manual" (1992). The best review of this book that I have read was written by American engineer and visionary Willis Harman, past president of the Institute of Noetic Sciences, IONS, of which I am a past member. IONS is a progressive collaborative group devoted to the exploration of consciousness and the human sciences. It was founded by astronaut Edgar Mitchell. Willis calls Baldwin's book "disturbing" but is willing to take it seriously, and in his review quotes psychologist William James: "In his 'Essays in Radical Empiricism', James defined this term: 'To be radical, an empiricism must neither admit into its construction any element that is NOT directly experienced, nor exclude from them any element that IS directly experienced.' (emphasis mine)"[65]

Harman's piece is a great basic summary of Baldwin's book, which is itself a major classic on the whole subject of spirit attachment and possession, and many other phenomena of consciousness.[66] Baldwin also studied the work of Edith Fiore, a licensed psychologist and earlier pioneer in this area. Another great book discussing these issues is "Multiple Man" by Adam Crabtree, and there are many others. Dealing with spiritual interference of various kinds can be essential in effectively removing an unwanted condition, and the possibility of such interference should not be

---

[65] Empiricism is a theory that states that knowledge comes only, or primarily, from sensory experience - from perception as opposed to thought. When studying consciousness, all experience, including extrasensory perception, is data.

[66] Noetic Sciences Review, NO.26 Summer 1993, Book Review, p.36

overlooked anymore than a doctor would overlook an infection in dealing with an injury. If the source of someone's problem IS a spiritual interaction, then of course the solution is to lessen or terminate that interaction. I mention the above resources because I must confine myself to providing only a brief glimpse into this subject based on my own experience.

There are a great many possibilities and variations in the types of possible spirit interactions, attachments, possessions, harassments, and assistance, and every case will be different. While I have found spirit attachments and influences in myself and others, they have so far, with a few exceptions, been relatively easy to handle, and the results have been excellent, but this may not always be the case. When comparing the effects of spirit attachments, past-life experiences, and the effects of present-life trauma, the overwhelming majority of problems, in my personal experience, stem from present-life experiences, and mostly from childhood. This observation may be due to my approach, which is this: I do not steer my clients in any particular direction. I always let them find their own answers.

Many problems have purely physical causes of course, like infections, toxins, injuries, genetic disorders, and so on. Still, it is very easy for a physical problem to trigger some past trauma, which will then become a complication, causing increased pain, problems with healing, emotional problems, or other symptoms – like my gall bladder pain mentioned earlier. Some people seem to be mostly troubled by past-life trauma while others seem to have nothing bothering them from past lives at all. Some may have many alter personalities and some have none, and some may have no spirit attachments and some may have many. Usually I find there is a combination of all of these things present, but everyone is different. Any spirit interaction, whether it's a simple communication or an actual attack, can be traumatic, leading to some unwanted condition later on. Spirit interactions can also be friendly, enjoyable, helpful, and not traumatic at all.

Many people seem to have spirits helping them and may refer to these spirits as guides, ancestors, relatives, friends, or angels. There is usually no reason to look further into these relationships if they are helpful and cause no problems, except maybe to understand them better. Often the extent of my assistance with helpful spirits, when they are present, is to help improve and clarify communications. I often suspect such spirits to be one's own alter personalities, or one's own unconscious mind or a "higher level" aspect of theirself (discussed later in this chapter), but very often they are not. The following stories are examples of spirit interactions that I have experienced or worked with.

Hannah's Fear – or Sad Lisa

In the 1990's a young lady named Hannah came to me to resolve a few issues. One was that she was unable to eat at restaurants without having a strong emotional and physical reaction. She would have these intense reactions before, during, and after being in a restaurant, and often have to leave abruptly. The start of this problem seemed to be a time when she was a child playing in her room alone. It turns out that the spirit of a young girl, who we'll call Lisa, began talking with her, and became attached. Sometimes I have the client try and integrate with the entity, if there is any possibility that it's an alter personality. When nothing happens in these cases we may proceed with SRT. This attachment with Lisa became a strong friendship – a stuck identity state in which Hannah felt happier and less alone. The restaurant anxieties were actually Lisa's reactions. Lisa had lot's of anxieties and there were some indications that Lisa had choked and died in a restaurant shortly before joining Hannah.

We used hypnosis to help Hannah relax and communicate more easily with Lisa. Lisa said that her need to stay with Hannah was "To have a life." In communication with Lisa we explained that it was time for her to have her OWN life, and to be healed of her anxieties. We explained to Lisa that it wasn't fair that Hannah had to experience her anxieties also. We reached an understanding, and after some work Lisa was able to communicate with helpful spirits that guided her toward a new life.

Hannah shed a few tears as she said goodbye to Lisa. I had Hannah fill the space within her that Lisa had occupied, with her own energy, and to seal any "openings" in her energy body. These are creative visualization techniques that provide a sense of security and protection, and possibly real protection on an unconscious level, whether or not they accurately depict what is actually happening with the physical body, or some kind of "energy body" on a spiritual level.

After the session just described, Hannah said that she was amazed, and wasn't sure she hadn't made Lisa up, but concluded she would not have done so. As always, I never suggested any of this but only asked questions in a neutral, non-leading way. Could my questions have been suggestions? My questions only hint at possibilities, and the instruction is for the client to only tell me what they see. I have no preference or expectations as to what people might find – I'm curious myself. If in the end they make something up that results in their problem resolving, the results are still valid. But I personally know, as do many others, that spirit interactions like these do occur, and my default position is to believe that Lisa was real. I have helped release many spirit attachments where the spirits seemed to be having no noticeable effect on the client, but releasing them always felt right to my client and to me. No one seems to want them to hang around. It's like finding a bug in your house, harmless or not!

Hannah's restaurant symptoms greatly diminished over the next two weeks. She told me that, because these symptoms had been so much a part of her, she expected them to still be there, and felt like she was trying to create them. After working on other issues I didn't hear from Hannah for years. This was typical in the past as I usually didn't follow up much with my clients. However she did call me one day a few years later about a project she was working on, and I asked her about the restaurant reactions. She said they went away completely and never returned.

An attached entity apparently has a safe haven within the host, where they have a place to rest and are not drawn into the continuous cycle of rebirth. However, they may not be completely conscious, and usually become dependent on maintaining their attachment. They may also be the source of unwanted thoughts, reactions, and compulsions as well.

David's Demons

In 1997 I had a dream that I was in my office working with a new client who was sitting on the couch in front of me, He appeared to be a young man with dark hair, and there was an older

man sitting in the chair to my right wearing a white shirt. The
young man suddenly stood up and started to walk out. I stood up to
face him as if to talk him out of leaving – something I wouldn't do –
and he tried to punch me in the face. It was a vivid dream and I
recorded it. I thought about it briefly, felt it might be precognitive,
and then dismissed it. The next week I got a call from a man who
wanted to bring in his grandson who had been diagnosed with
paranoid schizophrenia three years earlier. They came in a few days
later.

David was nineteen years old, had dark hair, and was seated on
the couch. His grandfather, Frank, was wearing a white shirt and sat
in the chair to my right. I didn't make the connection. Frank
thought David's problems might be the result of some Satanic cult
activity, and ritual abuse experiences from when he was about
thirteen and was staying in a group home. As I spoke with David it
was difficult to get very far because he was constantly turning his
head and talking to unseen "others" and slapping his body and
moving his hands like he was shooing away mosquitos. He said he
was being constantly harassed by various entities. I was trying to
develop some rapport so I could get his explanation of what he was
experiencing, and the history behind it.

Then suddenly I remembered the dream and knew what was
about to happen. I moved my chair a bit so I wouldn't be in his way
if David tried to leave, and less than a minute later he stood up
abruptly and walked out of the office just as he did in the dream.
He came back in and sat down a few minutes later, as I was talking
with Frank, and we agreed to end the session. I saw David a dozen
more times. Frank drove him to my office but David sometimes
came in by himself.

David told me he felt controlled by others but had no idea who
they were, and said he heard voices but said they didn't come from
within his mind, nor did they come from the external world. He
said it was more like they came from "other realms." What he was
primarily looking for in working with me was support. My biggest
difficulty with him was in maintaining fluid communication,
although a good portion of the time he was very lucid and we did
make some good headway.

It seemed like his problems originated when he started taking
drugs as a teenager and got involved with some abusive members of

one of the group homes he stayed in for a while. These people spoke of demons and Satan and tried to involve him in various cult activities. After our first session I joined various online schizophrenic chat groups to get an idea of how people with this diagnosis thought of their condition, I found that they almost unanimously believed they were being harassed by demons or mad spirits. David's doctor also called me a few weeks later and seemed to appreciate the work we were doing.

In the course of working with David we talked about spirit possession and harassment, multiple personalities, childhood trauma, and sexual abuse, and he told me he had all of these things going on. Before we could even begin to do ID-R or hypnosis we had to first focused on getting him into a state where he could stay in session and not be distracted by "the others" long enough to make some progress. We also had to understand his triggers and we agreed to only do what he could tolerate. So most of our time was spent helping him manage his condition so he could function well enough to work with his issues. David was rather soft-spoken but he had a helper personality named Joe who was angry and impatient. Most of our sessions were ended by Joe suddenly taking over and walking out, but David always stopped at the door and made another appointment.

Working with David was like helping a crippled person climb a mountain of rocks – it was slow and tedious. But by really connecting, listening, and accepting his reality, I was able to help him make sense of what was happening to him. I never felt he was lying or making things up and I was impressed with how he was able to sort things out on his own after getting some perspective. There were apparently dozens of entities harassing him but he was able to see that they mainly comprised two groups that were embroiled in some sort of conflict. He said the spirits around him would often want to speak through him and they would interfere with his thinking and his ability to find the right words. There were also some spirits who were kind and were trying to help him. David said he was able to see lights moving in and out of people, which seemed to be spirits and energies coming and going, and he could see the spiritual causes of physical phenomena. I believe these kinds of things are happening with all of us all the time, but David's being aware of them made it hard for him to pay attention to what people were saying and to the world in general. He was almost constantly in an altered state where he was only partially aware of physical reality. An apt metaphor might be to imagine having several vivid dreams going on at once while you are wide awake and having to sort out what was what. Things might get a bit strange. Was I just joining David in his delusion of spiritual influences when his condition was just a brain disease? No. My interpretation is plausible because I have experienced such influences myself and so have many others on many levels.

I believe that David's condition was the result of many factors including developmental trauma in early childhood, sexual abuse, spiritual assault, and drug abuse. Genetics, nutrition, and lifestyle could also have played significant roles. My guess is that all these things broke his brain to the degree that, in addition to the usual burden of devastating trauma, he was further made vulnerable to connection and attack by foreign spirits. He was no longer sovereign in his own body. The solution for his condition would probably require much attention to all these areas, with particular focus on physical health and nutrition, and perhaps medication, to heal his damaged brain and nervous system and seal the cracks, so to speak, so as to keep the intruders out.

Our sessions ended and David later spent some time in an institution after starting a camp fire in the living room of his apartment. He called me from the facility one day and thanked me. He said I had helped him more than anyone ever had. He had only come to me for support, which he got, but he was also able to confront his condition, see it in a new light, realize he wasn't helpless or alone, and begin to take some control.

A brief note on demons: There are all kinds of conscious beings in the universe, with varying degrees of ability depending on the games they are playing, and I consider them all as "people." A conscious being is just a separated viewpoint and it can adopt and identify with any form it wants, and all forms are temporary illusions. Although we can imagine them to be whatever we fancy, "demon" is just a word given to spirits with harmful intentions. I tend to agree with what Swedenborg wrote in "Heaven and Hell" when he said, regarding the creation of demons and angels as such: "No, all the people in heaven and all the people in Hell have come from humankind."

Night Attack – or
Eliminating the Competition

Occasionally as an adult I would be awakened at night by
strange heart vibrations, but I didn't explore them. Then, while
developing ID-R I had a dream of being attacked by an invisible
entity and I experienced these same sensations. In the dream I
engulfed the entity and carried it up through the ceiling and into
the sky. I worked on this dream the next morning. I found that one
night during High School I was awakened by the same heart
vibrations and left my body. There was a spirit attacking me while I
was sleeping and he was apparently trying to kill me by stopping my
heart. He didn't have the power to do this, but he had a lot of
emotional intensity, and I did feel something. I immediately
grabbed him and took him high up into the night sky. I recognized
him as a classmate of mine named Barry. Although we currently
had no classes together, I had known and liked Barry since
kindergarten and he always seemed happy and friendly. I scolded
Barry to never do this again. I also immediately knew why he had
attacked me. He was in love with Patty! But she wasn't interested in
him and I could feel his anguish. Apparently he had discovered her
connection with me and tried to take me out of the picture. As he
disappeared in the distance, I felt sad for him.

Sometime after this session I did the Flows process on a dream
for the first time. This process is covered in Chapter 20. There were
several unrelated elements in the dream, which centered around
what looked like a government building with pillars and steps. I was
able to find the meaning of each element and I was quite amazed at
how well this method worked. Then I remembered a tiny person
sitting quietly at the bottom of the steps. Doing "Flows" (see
Chapter 20) revealed that he was sad and remorseful. I soon
realized it was Barry, and I also received an apology. It was as if he
appeared in my dream to apologize. Perhaps I picked this up
psychically in the past, or maybe he even communicated this
telepathically to me at some point, and I incorporated that into this
dream.

This particular dream had come several years after Barry and I
had come face to face at a local event, decades after high school. I
had walked up to him and, without knowing why, I asked him if he

had seen Patty recently. This was strange because although I knew he knew *of* Patty, on a conscious level I had no idea if he knew her personally, and I had never before mentioned Patty to anyone except my friend Ross back in ninth grade. At this time I remembered nothing of the attack. Barry responded by shaking his head and looking away, but strangely said nothing, not even hello. Then something strange happened which seemed amusing at the time but also puzzled me. I spilled my drink on his shoe. I said "Oops, sorry," and walked away. Maybe unconsciously I still held a grudge at that time, but more likely this whole thing was a prank by Dennis–2. I have a feeling Barry apologized to me in spirit right then, or shortly thereafter.

The Seriously Irate Man

When I was eleven years old, I did something disgraceful – I engaged in some petty larceny that I was soon to regret. I found a letter addressed to a neighbor left in our mailbox by mistake. I opened it and found a check inside for the neighbor's grandson who was coming to visit. The five-dollar check was for the cost of his birthday party. Seeing an opportunity to profit from my creative talents, I easily changed the amount to fifteen dollars. I then put together a plan and practiced a script. I went to a local bakery and explained the check was a birthday gift. I bought a birthday cake for less than two dollars, and cashed the check myself, forging the name. My friend Jeff and I then went horseback riding, bought some snacks, and had a fun day. In my life at that time I had few examples of people being charitable or ethical. I didn't even consider the fact that my actions would be affecting other people or upsetting anyone. I mainly saw this as a problem to be solved, another interesting puzzle, and the risk made it somewhat exciting, although I had to suppress my feelings of guilt.

My elderly neighbor Elmer and another man, probably the boy's father, came to our door one day a week or two later and talked to my father about the missing check. He knew nothing of it and assured them his kids had nothing to do with it. A few days later I was playing alone in the backyard when suddenly I had trouble seeing. Everything became dim and fuzzy and there were explosions of light. Then I couldn't see at all. I realized something

was wrong and got scared. I lay on the ground and closed my eyes.
Now it felt as if my whole body was under some kind of electrical
attack. I heard an angry voice yelling at me and saying he knew it
was me and that he was going to kill me. I became worried that he
might succeed! At first the words were garbled, but as they became
more distinct there was a moment when I suddenly realized that
this was the birthday boy's father, a living person who was here in
spirit, and he was extremely angry about the check. I had a shock at
this realization and I felt a lot of guilt. I decided to remain silent,
but I also asked for help from Dennis–2.

The guy was trying to get me to admit what I had done because
he wasn't actually certain. Dennis–2, appearing as a spirit,
immediately told the guy that he was one of my guides, and I
definitely was not the one the man was looking for. He said that
there were several kids in the neighborhood who might have done
this, and who also fit the description given by the people at the
bakery of the boy who had cashed the check. Dennis–2 was very
convincing and soon the irate man left in disgust to do further
investigation. I was told to remain silent for a couple of minutes
until Dennis–2 was sure the guy was gone. During this ordeal I
realized that my actions had hurt people, and I knew that I would
never do this again. But I had to learn similar lessons when I failed
to foresee the hurtful effects of some of my later escapades.

When I finally got up, I realized that my nervous system had
been damaged. I was groggy and dizzy and my vision was impaired,
but Dennis–2 told me that these things would clear up. They did
clear up in a couple of days, but there was possibly some permanent
damage that affected me later in life.

Astral Allies – or Birds of a Feather

When I was around nine years old, I was awakened one night by
a presence and noticed that right above me were a bunch of boys
and girls, about seven or eight of them, mostly close to my age,
except one boy who seemed to be maybe ten years older. I only saw
their faces and they were all smiling and excited. They were talking
to me but I don't recall what they were saying. It felt like we were
all working together in some way, like part of a team. This seemed
like an introduction in which we had all heard of each other but

were meeting for the first time. When I first remembered this, decades later in 1992, I immediately felt that the older kid was Dr. Charles Tart, the consciousness researcher, although I had never met him. The feeling was very strong. I don't know who the other kids might have been but the feeling is that they all had life paths involved in advancing the understanding of consciousness and the mind. A few years ago I saw a date in a random article on the internet and knew immediately that this was Dr. Tart's date of birth. I located his biography online right away, and discovered that I was correct. I do not believe that I had ever seen his birth date before this, and his picture as a young man fit the vision I had as a child.

The Message

One day when I was nine or ten, I began hearing the voice of a deceased man who wanted me to do something for him. I tried to pretend I didn't hear him but he pestered me and repeatedly said that he knew I could hear him. Finally I addressed him, in thought, "OK, what do you want me to do?" He wanted me to write a note and give it to someone. I remember being in the front yard and walking in the house to find something to write on. I wrote the note in pencil on a small piece of paper, after which the man led me to the house where I was to take it. I went to the house, which was just a few houses down from mine and across the street, but I was reluctant to deliver the message. The man said all I had to do was to stick the note in the screen door. I was still hesitant so he said "Do you want me to do it?" I knew what he meant, and since I didn't want him taking over my body, I said that I would do it myself. I snuck up to the door and opened it slightly, closed it on the note, and ran away. The man had recently passed on, and the note was to his wife, but I don't recall what it said because it didn't have any emotional significance to me personally at the time.

The Great Escape

I had a client named Linda who claimed her ex-husband Jake, who was serving time in prison, was possessing her current boyfriend on various occasions, and threatening her. He would tell her his name and that prison could not keep him away from her. The boyfriend would later have no memory of this happening.

From the things she was telling me, I considered that Jake may have even possessed her on occasion as well. The reason I entertained these as possibilities was that I knew from my own experience that such things do happen. However, these experiences were very unsettling to Linda and she was questioning her own sanity. Since everyone this lady had talked to about this issue thought she was crazy, she found some relief in talking with me, and felt I gave her some helpful advice on dealing with the situation. I have heard many stories from people indicative of temporary possession, spirit attachments, psychic influence, and harassment that seem authentic, but with whom I did not work long enough to find the truth, and this was the case with Linda. But if you want to help someone you have to be willing to enter their reality. Then, if their interpretation of things is a delusion or a mistake, you will be able to help them see that for themselves.

At the Hour of Death – or I'm OK!

My mother, a long time smoker, died of lung cancer in 1994. I was her caretaker, and in the year or so before she died, many amazing spiritual events occurred, often startling both me and my ex-wife Lynne, who was helping out occasionally with housekeeping chores. Most notably my mother began to be aware of things beyond her physical perception. She knew psychically exactly when the hospice nurse was about to arrive, on occasion, and many other things. One night we were in the house alone and she was in bed. At this point she was unable to walk and used a wheelchair, which she needed help getting into. I was lying on a pillow, on the floor the front room with the hallway door closed, watching TV, drinking a coke, and eating ice cream.

I got up to go to the bathroom and as I walked down the hall past my mother's bedroom I saw her sitting up in bed. She began talking in a very animated manner, telling me that she had seen me in the front room watching TV and having a party, as if it were a big deal. She was wide awake and was in an unusually energized state. I went in and asked her what she saw. She described exactly what I had been doing, which I validated for her. Then I asked her when she had seen all this and she explained that she had just walked down the hall a minute ago. I paused a moment and said: "Mom, you know you can't walk down the hall. You just had an out-of-body experience!" She was quiet for a minute, thinking about that. We didn't discuss it further, as there was no need.

One day out of the blue my mother apologized to me. This was shortly before she passed on. She said she was sorry for everything that happened. I knew she meant all the trauma that I had experienced as a child that she was responsible for or could have done something about. It took me by surprise and I had mixed feelings. I felt in that moment that she didn't actually recall everything that had happened, and I felt some inner anger and frustration. But then something inside me relaxed and I knew this was coming from her heart. Another parting gift. My resistance disappeared and I thanked her and forgave her.

A few days before she died, I was working with my mother using hypnosis to help relieve her back pain as she was falling asleep. I did this every night for a while. On this particular night, a blue light appeared behind me and to my left. It was about the size of a cantaloupe and just hovered there. The most interesting thing about this experience was that I had no reaction to it. I didn't question it or even pay it any attention. It was there for several minutes and then vanished. I didn't even think about it until the next day, and it still seemed completely ordinary. But it wasn't, and now I was curious! When I did the Flows process on the blue light I got that it was a Being whom I was apparently familiar with on a higher level, and that it was emanating love, calming intent, and something else I cannot describe, but that was definitely some kind of support, all directed at my mother. Later I heard from a reputable source that angels or helpful spirits often appear as blue lights.

The day before my mother died a priest showed up at our house unexpectedly. He had not been called by anyone and we had not seen him for nine years, since he had officiated at my father's graveside memorial service. He said he just had a feeling he should stop by! My mother was a Catholic but had not been to church since I was a kid. She had mentioned a week earlier that some day she would like to receive Holy Communion.[67] This popped into my head and, as they were visiting, and I mentioned it. He then performed the ritual, which she took quite seriously. After the priest left, mom seemed very peaceful. She died the next day. This was not a random coincidence.

My mother died at home. That day she fell into a coma accompanied by the Cheyne-Stokes breathing pattern which I had seen before in a dying woman. I was unable to wake her and knew she didn't have long. I called my brothers and stayed by her side. After an hour or so she suddenly opened her eyes, looked at me and lifted her head slightly. She then said, in a weak voice, but with strong intention, "Tell everyone I'm OK!"

My first thought was that she was delusional, because I knew she wasn't OK – she was dying. She could see that I was confused and that I wasn't getting her message, so she cleared her throat and said again, very firmly this time, "_Tell everyone I'm ok!_"

Ahhh! Now I understood. She was already on the other side. I also had the distinct feeling that she was not alone. She immediately went back into the coma and passed away peacefully a few hours later while my brother Alan was with her. I delivered her message to several others but it didn't seem to impact them as it did me. I guess you had to be there. I'm grateful that I was.[68]

My mother had all her upper teeth extracted when she was around fifty-three years old and had to wear dentures. This whole episode was very traumatic for her and at the time she had little emotional support. I remember her crying for hours. I felt very sad for her. When she died, I found her dentures after the funeral. She had been buried without them. I felt bad about that too.

One night a few weeks after her passing, I had an OBE. In a dream I heard mom calling my name and I got out of bed and was

---

[67] Holy Communion is a sacrament in the Catholic church. When you receive Holy Communion, you're intimately united with Jesus Christ – he literally becomes part of you.

[68] For more stories of spiritual events around death and dying, read the phenomenal book "At The Hour Of Death" by Karlis Osis, 1997 or "Words At The Threshold" by Lisa Smartt, 2017

walking toward her bedroom when I suddenly became lucid. I
continued to her room and saw that she was propped up in bed on
her left arm. She was smiling at me and had all her upper teeth –
and they were glowing! I was instantly awake in bed, and knew that
she had just communicated with me, both to ease my own mind,
and to share her joy in being free from her body, and once again
whole, in spirit. She was telling me to not worry about the dentures
and that she was fine. I believe my mind created the dream images
I experienced during the OBE, from her actual communication,
which I don't remember. I believe many things that appear in our
dreams represent higher level experiences. Although we can often
remember our dreams, we are less often able to remember the
experiences that precipitated them, without some work.

Fred's Funeral

I liked Fred a lot. He was a cousin of mine on my mother's side
of the family, who lived in a neighboring city. Fred was much older
than I, a chain smoker with down to Earth wisdom and a keen sense
of humor that sometimes took me a few moments to grasp. When
he passed away, I attended his funeral. As I walked into the
sanctuary of the church where the service was being held, I saw
Fred's family members seated in the front pew and walked over to
greet them. But I stopped short.

There in front of me was Fred's open casket. The instant I saw
Fred, the entire atmosphere changed. There was such a strong
sense of presence that it felt like the whole space of the church was
charged with some kind of energy. This perception was so
pronounced, and so real and amazing, that I looked quickly around
to see how it was affecting everyone else – but no one seemed to
even notice. I was almost more fascinated by the fact that nobody
was aware of this energy, than with the energy itself! I'm calling this
feeling "energy" because that's how it felt, but I can't really describe
it except that I seemed to feel it with my entire body. It was
definitely not an emotional reaction to unexpectedly seeing Fred.
Perhaps the surprise of it created a momentary confusion that
expanded my awareness, similar to what happens in the power-
zone. Anyway, I decided to ignore the feeling, and after saying "Hi"
to everyone I took a seat several rows back.

During the service various people took the podium and said a few words honoring Fred. That's when I began hearing Fred talking to me. At first I thought it was something I was doing myself, for some unconscious reason, but I couldn't turn off the nonstop commentary. Finally I just said "Hi Fred, how are you doing?" His reply was something like "Feelin" pretty good." He seemed to be in a great mood and everything he said was amusing. When one of Fred's sons began talking and expressed how much Fred would have appreciated everyone being there, I heard Fred say in a humorous tone "I could have done without a few of them."

Now, I don't talk with dead people on a regular basis, and although we all have this potential, this was just something that happened. So I sat there, with Fred cracking jokes in my ear the whole time, and then toward the end he was gone. I don't know when I stopped feeling his presence, which I assume is what the energy was, but maybe I just got used to it until I didn't notice it anymore. I had lunch with Fred's wife, Sharon, a year later and told her the story. She was amused and said that it sure sounded like Fred. Sharon then shared her own beautiful story of when Fred had visited her after his passing.

King

One night in 1992 a friend of mine suggested that I try to communicate with Patty telepathically (see Chapter 22). After doing so, and while still in meditation, I sensed someone else present in the space around me. It seemed to be a little man in a small row boat that flew back and forth in the air above me. This man seemed to be mute and without thoughts. He also seemed to be guarding the space around me. I did the Flows process on him and soon realized that he was our dog King who had died eighteen years earlier. I had picked King from a large litter when I was eleven years old and he had been my best friend and a constant companion for my brothers and me for many years as we were growing up. King looked like a jet-black Labrador Retriever but was also half German Shepherd and was a bit slender like a Doberman. He was very friendly and highly intelligent. In those days before there were leash laws, he would follow me almost everywhere I went.

King was thirteen when he died, and I was twenty-four. He was shot in the side by a small caliber gun, probably while running around in the field next to our house. He made it home and died on our front lawn. That day I was sitting at the kitchen table reading the paper when I stood up suddenly and yelled "Where's King?" My parents were both in the room and said they hadn't seen him. I went to the sliding glass patio door and looked out at the field where King liked to sniff around. I called him from the door but he didn't come. I went back and sat down and a few minutes later my father left to go somewhere and came back in immediately to tell me I had better come outside. I found King dead on the grass with a bullet wound in his side, and called the Sheriff. I buried him myself in the field next to our fence.

Twenty-two years later I did a session on this incident, while tracking down the source of some anxiety, and got a closer look at my intuitive response to King's death. In the moment of his death I briefly left my body and went out to him on the front lawn. I saw him in the air above his body and he appeared as a pale yellow light, much smaller than his normal size. His appearance morphed in and out of the form of a dog. He seemed unconcerned that he had died – or oblivious to the fact. There was no communication in words but I could sense his intentions and emotions. He was his familiar happy self and glad to see me. In fact it is most likely that he came to me as I sat reading the paper that morning, prompting my response. In this session I realized that I had somehow kept him with me, but during that meditation back in 1992, when I first realized he was still around, I had assumed his presence was voluntary. Now I realized there was some kind of attachment involved. I had recorded many dreams over the years after his death where King was present, and I liked having him around, but I set him free a few years later when I released the Menagerie.

The Menagerie – Part 1

I have always had an affinity for animals. I felt a connection as a child early on, which led to the Menagerie. My first pet was a male collie puppy my parents brought home when I was around two and a half. I named him Cinder, because I was told Cinderella was a girl's name. Cinder and I didn't get along because he was always jumping on me and would knock over my blocks and chew on my toys. We had staring matches. When I complained and was asked if I wanted to keep Cinder I said no. My father got angry, put the dog outside, and shouted that I would never see him again. This was a shock to me, not because I would miss the puppy, since this did not occur to me, but because my father's anger was disturbing.

The next day Cinder ran in the house when my mother opened the back door that led to the kitchen, but he was quickly ushered out. I was in the kitchen at the time and literally did not see Cinder come in, even though I was looking right at him. That is the power of suggestion, especially when it occurs around a shock! My father's statement was like a posthypnotic command embedded in my unconscious mind. I remember being confused when I could not see Cinder while my mom was chasing him out of the house. Cinder was given away and I soon missed him. I realized we had something in common – an innocence and lack of pretense.

Later we had many assorted pets, and my affinity and connection to animals influenced the following incident. I didn't realize the consequences of this experience until years after recalling it. When I was around six years old, I found a cat in my back yard that was dying. As I walked up to it, I saw its spirit suddenly and unexpectedly fly out of its body, and I had a shock. I had never seen that happen before and I felt some responsibility. Perhaps it reminded me of losing Cinder, or I may have associated it with a similar incident involving Patty which I relate in Chapter 24. In the power-zone I reached out spiritually and grabbed the bodiless cat and kept it with me. I felt that if it left, it would be lost, and I wanted to keep it safe. What I failed to realize at the time I recalled this incident, was that the cat was still present, and I had not resolved the automatic reaction of keeping animal spirits with me if I was near them at the time of their death. This compulsion seemed to apply only to mammals.

Around 2001, which was eight years after I discovered the above incident, I felt a presence with me one day, and I asked who it was. The name that came up was "Blueberry." I then recalled a kitten we had once when I was a teenager. It had deep blue eyes and my mother called it Blueberry. I buried it after it had been backed over by a car. I was present when it died. Upon recalling this I realized that I had been compulsively sheltering the spirits of dead animals ever since that time when I was six.

I resolved the compulsive rescuing of animal spirits soon after that, and yet I didn't do anything about releasing those I was still harboring because I didn't take it very seriously. Also I felt that if these animals were still with me, they were safe and it wasn't causing me any problems. But I had no idea how many animal spirits I had been caring for. Quite a few it turned out. I later called them the Menagerie, and released them several years later when I saw them all in a vision. But knowing about the Menagerie helped me to understand the Bird People.

Uninvited Guests – or Intruder Alert

Many years before discovering the menagerie, and while I was attending a famous hypnotherapy school, I began to have a series of strange dreams which all appeared to be related. This was three years after I had begun doing ID-R. My mother had passed away months earlier and I was living alone at this time. These dreams occurred over a period of several months. At first there were two dreams involving people trying to break into my house. Then I had a few dreams in which I got up during the night and found a door or window open, so I closed it. I also dreamed that a fellow student, a lady who was in a class I was taking at the time and who was attracted to me, was paying me unwanted OBE visits at night. The general theme of these dreams was that some entity was trying to get inside and attach itself to me, so I did some protective meditations on that.[69] The following dream was more explicit.

In this dream I felt there was something wrong or out of place in my house and I walked in my kitchen and saw someone looking in the window, which faces the front yard. I yelled at them and went to the front door and found it open. Outside there were a dozen or more people, but they all had their backs toward me. I slammed the door several times but it wouldn't lock. Then I saw all the people

---

[69] Protective meditations include any visualizations, rituals, prayers, or auto-suggestions for the purposes of warding off any psychic attacks, attachments, or intrusions, and keeping oneself and ones space safe from such disturbances.

walking away from me. When I closed the door, I noticed it had writing on the back, as if made by a black marking pen. The sentences were written in angles to form the shape of a five-pointed star, but the writing was in symbols I didn't recognize. It looked like Chinese to me. Then I felt the people pushing on the door, and I knew they had no intention of leaving.

I grabbed the telephone and someone was already talking on it as I ran through the house – the phone had now become a radio and the announcer was talking about some opportunity. I saw that my extension phones were all off the hook, so I used the separate phone in my bedroom, got a dial tone, and called 911. But then the same announcer was on the phone talking about how I would not be able to reach the police. He was laughing now, and I knew he was one of the intruders. I ran to my office in the back of the house and grabbed my car phone but the intruders were already in the house. I ran back up the hall and struggled with them but everything went black and I could see nothing. Then I woke up.

Throughout this whole dream there was a sense of helplessness and frustration. Everything I tried worked against me, and I could make no headway. I was alone, and it felt like I was doomed. After waking, I speculated some group of entities was trying to connect with me against my will but had not yet succeeded.

A few days later I had a dream in which a child entity wanted me to help her. When I tried to counsel her, two other people showed up and said this was the wrong approach, and helped me realize that this entity wanted to attach itself to me. I sent her away with the help of other personalities and angels. I felt great sympathy, so I told her that she needed to have the right intention, in order for me to help her.

Mixed in with these intrusion dreams were dreams of large groups of animals. In one dream they were all floating and circling around a giant tree while I was trying to negotiate something with a lady seeking refuge for her daughter. The lady was Asian and had a very strong will, but I wasn't sure she wasn't evil. Later I had a dream in which a group of people had purposely burned themselves to death on a wooden platform. Finally I had the following dreams which prompted a session in which everything became clear.

Reinforcements - or
The Strange Turkey Invasion

After an hour of sleep I awoke and it seemed like I had been struggling for many hours with something. I recorded having a dream in which there were cats in my bed crawling over me and tormenting me or bothering me, and waking me up so that I couldn't get any good sleep. Although I was pushing them away, I was in a sort of stupor. It seems like they were supposed to be outside but they had gotten in. Then, in the same dream, it seemed like my top cover was sticking to me, so I got up and was struggling with it, trying to pull it off and get unentangled from it. It would wrap itself around my arms and legs like a snake, as I tried to walk down the hall. I threw it off of me and it jumped back on. After recording this dream I went back to sleep.

Later that same night I dreamed there was some kind of a commotion where I heard voices yelling or arguing. I wanted to get up and find out what was going on and see if I could help. As I walked down the hall there was an invisible force that was pushing on me and holding me back. I felt someone was in the house and I had to find out who it was. When I awoke, I thought I had been sleeping all night but only an hour had passed. It was like when you have a high fever and a minute seems like hours. Something had been interfering with my sleep and I felt like I'd been drugged. I recorded this as well.

When I dropped back into sleep a third time, I dreamed I came out of my room and I looked out toward the kitchen window because I heard some noise. There was a pecking sound which had been going on for a long time. I had been ignoring it but it finally got my attention enough to get up to check on it. When I first looked out the window, I saw some little birds pecking on the screen, but they were vague and gray. Then I noticed there were several huge tropical-looking birds out there perched on a tree limb, looking in at me. They had huge orange beaks and large eyes and were very colorful. They just stared at me silently. At some point I noticed some dogs and cats got in the house, and they weren't supposed to be inside.

Then, still dreaming, I imagined I woke up and believed the _previous_ scene had been a dream, and that now I was really awake, but actually I was now in something like a lucid dreaming state – it felt magical. While in _this_ state I walked into the kitchen from my bedroom because someone had come in, and found my brothers were both there. Alan was surveying everything and Blake was looking at all these small turkeys that were sitting on the floor. They had dog-like faces but otherwise looked like the turkeys you see in Thanksgiving decorations. There were a couple dozen of them. King was behind me and he sniffed a turkey and I explained to him that these turkeys were not to be harmed. With my brothers and King, I had my reinforcements.

The turkeys had come in through the kitchen window and the screen was knocked out. I told Blake that this was just like the dream I had right before they arrived, and that it must have been a premonition. I had a thought that we should _keep_ these birds, so we put them in the backyard. I considered the garage but thought they might be too messy in there. We started throwing them outside on the patio. It was the middle of the night but we had the patio light on. When I threw one bird out on the patio, it looked sad. It was hurt when it hit the ground and tried to crawl toward me. I felt sorry for it and suggested we try and be gentle as we moved them.

The Bird People

This last experience was more than a lucid dream, and it was in fact taking place in my own inner matrix - my own personal inner space. As I soon discovered, the birds were actually a group of people who had died in Vietnam during the war. They found that the only way they could attach to me was to disguise themselves as animals, since I had already created a sanctuary space for departed animal spirits. They thought they could merge with the Menagerie, and tried to do that for several weeks. They must have already been attached to me in some preliminary way. It seems that when they had tried to appear as cats and dogs, the other cats and dogs in the Menagerie didn't accept them. When they appeared as quiet and peaceful birds however, and agreed to my rules, I finally allowed them to stay.

I discovered all this when I did a session on this semi-lucid dream that morning. In the session I immediately connected with the group's leader, a Vietnamese lady who had been the matriarch of her village. About twenty-five years earlier her village had been burned and everyone had been killed. During the session she spoke through me and was extremely emotional, wailing about how "They burned our houses and killed our children," and I could see the tragedy through her eyes. When she died, she was quite lucid and very powerful. She gathered most of her traumatized people together as spirits and kept them with her. She then attached her group to an American soldier who was part of the attacking forces. Although this soldier was one of the perpetrators, he had strong spiritual abilities, and had many other attached spirits with him already.

Through a friend, I had made some kind of connection to this veteran soldier, although I never actually met him, and I had begun having dreams about him shortly before the Bird People showed up – dreams in which I was sharing some of his traumatic experiences. I believe he was seriously ill at the time of these dreams. This spirit group had been guided to relocate to me, and had believed it would be easier to do than it actually was. I feel that I had agreed to this on a higher level of awareness, but that the group had to accede to my requirements, and they were slow in doing so. In this session I did not release the Bird People, and for some reason, did not consider it. One of my hypnotherapy teachers hypnotized me in class and she spoke briefly with the leader of the group. The leader was still traumatized herself when talking about the massacre and this affected me so much that I had to stop the session. But I realized these people needed to stay with me awhile.

When I was working on the part of this chapter about the dream where something was written on my front door, I recalled that it looked Chinese, but I had forgotten about the lines forming a five-pointed star, until rereading the notes from my dream journal, twenty-three years later. It then occurred to me for the very first time to look at the Vietnamese flag. It's a five-pointed star!

There were a few more dreams which are worth relating because they revealed the disposition of the villagers and their ultimate departure. During one dream in which I was driving around in my car visiting people, something occurred to me, and I drove to a particular house and parked on the side of the road. I got out and went over to the garage, which was open. Inside were many cages on shelves lining the walls. The cages were everywhere, and inside the cages were giant owls. The owls were silent and beautiful, and each appeared to have its own cage. They seemed to accept their captivity, and I also sensed something magical about them, like they had some special power. They also emanated a sense of pride or self-respect. There were some baby owls there too, but they didn't look like owls yet. The whole place had a strange aura about it. It was an awesome sight.

There was a kid present who was taking care of the owls, and the feeling was that he had inherited a business. He seemed like a younger version of me. He had blond hair, was wearing a T-shirt, and was very focused on what he was doing. He had an attitude like he wanted me to butt out. I talked with him and asked him some questions about the owls. I mentioned how big they were and he said they were the biggest owls in the world. He said this was his business, that he'd been doing it for a long time, and that he was "real good" at it. I could see he was taking good care of the owls and I said "This takes a lot of work!" "Yeah" he said proudly. I noticed he had some high-tech cages, so I commented that those cages probably saved him a lot of time and effort. Again he said "Yeah" and added "but it's not all that much work." But I was thinking he had to feed them and clean the cages and so forth. However I also realized there was more going on here than I knew. In the dream I felt I was doing an inspection, and I decided everything was in order and that the owls were in good hands. I believe this dream represented a real and higher level inspection of the situation. By that I mean, this was a dream version of an experience I did not yet remember or of something I simply knew on a deeper level. The kid was a helper named Caretaker who took care of the animals. He was integrated after the Menagerie was released years later.

Then a few weeks passed, during which I had some dreams of talking to birds that morphed into people wearing gray shirts or robes. One night I was drifting off to sleep and thinking about the Bird People, when I saw some flashing lights behind my eyelids and felt some energy flows through my body. Then there was the feeling of someone giving me a hug and I heard a voice say "We'll be leaving soon." I asked the voice what they got from me and what I got from them, but I don't recall if I got an answer. My speculation is that they got some needed rest and orientation that allowed them to move on. For my part, I probably just wanted to help.

One day sometime later, weeks or months perhaps, I realized the villagers were gone – it was just a feeling. I didn't release them myself; they just left of their own accord. I had a dream shortly after that where I walked outside and saw a flock of birds land on a TV antenna a block away. There was a happy feeling there. I worked on this dream the next morning and discovered a message from the birds, which was simply "Thank you."

The Menagerie – Part 2

About ten years after the Bird People left I had a dream that became an out-of-body experience. As I began to become lucid, I found myself floating in my room and noticed that there were dozens of animals sleeping on my bed. In fact there were animals sleeping all over my room, which was dark and quiet, although it didn't actually look like my bedroom. There were lots of cats and dogs, smaller animals that may have been rats or guinea pigs, and there was even a sheep on my bed. Then I heard a low "Shhhhh" indicating I should be quiet and not wake the animals. I looked around and there was a giant cat to my right. The cat went through a door and motioned for me to follow. We went into a dark closet and I saw that it was really Patty in a cat costume. She told me she was here to help and it was time to let them go.

The next day I did a session and released the Menagerie. I felt that there were many spirits helping me with this. I also released my dog King. I rarely dream of him now.

The Stowaway

Maybe a year or so after releasing the Menagerie, I had an OBE one night, and as I was trying to move away from my bed I felt something restraining me. I flew around the room and felt something on my back. I struggled to throw it off and suddenly found myself back in bed, still in the OBE state, lying next to a young Asian lady. She smiled and said that I would not be able to get rid of her. She seemed very sure of herself and had no intention of leaving. I then woke up, and although it was the middle of the night I worked on this right then. The spirit lady was one of the Bird People, and she had not left with the others. The whole experience was very real and energetic. I worked on this for some time and she finally did move on. I did some exploration to make sure there were no others. In my case, none of the attached entities, whether people or animals, appeared to be connected with any unwanted conditions, except when the villagers were first pressing for asylum and interfered with my sleep. I believe the animals in the menagerie were dormant most of the time, except for King, and the Bird People had agreed to remain quiet and innocuous while they recuperated.

Stuck on You – or Who's Who?

I was reading a description of a man recalling the death of his wife in a past lifetime. He also recalled that they reunited later in another life. The description was very moving and after reading it I felt a huge wave of grief come over me and there were tears. This was very unusual so I worked on it immediately.

My vague impression is that this took place in Ireland during a plague. It seemed I was a man, Brian, who had lost his wife, and who then committed suicide. The first vision I had was of a small room, perhaps a one-room cabin, with a large window that made the whole room bright, and there was a man standing over a desk upon which were many bottles and other containers holding various herbs and potions. On the bed to the right was a lady lying face up under several covers. She was not moving. The man was me, and I was preparing some medicine to give to my wife when there was a loud banging at the door.

When I opened the door, I faced a large burly man, Connor, who said he was here for the body. Behind him were at least three other men, and a death wagon piled with dead bodies. I protested, saying my wife was not dead and they had to leave me alone. We argued intensely and Connor was yelling "There's nothing ya can do, ya have to let her go!" Finally Connor slapped me very hard. I dropped to my knees crying and screaming out the name "Mary Anne!" The men stood around me while Connor spoke to me rather gruffly. Then another man said "He'll be alright, just give him some time." They took Mary Anne's body and left. In my grief I decided I had nothing to live for and wanted to be with Mary Anne. I got my rifle and shot myself in the left temple, dying instantly.

As I recalled this experience, I felt a wave of pain shoot through my head from the left side. It was totally spontaneous and unexpected. The pain was real and visceral but very mild compared to traumatic pain I have recalled from my present life, and it felt completely released. What happened next was confusing. A few seconds earlier I had recalled Mary Anne pleading with Brian to not take his life. After the gunshot I heard her saying "Why did you do that?" I was looking at a golden ball of light in front of me, which I thought at first was Mary Ann, but I now realized that _I was the one asking the question_! Suddenly it was all clear. I was Mary Anne – and Brian was Patty. I went back to the beginning and looked at everything again, step by step.

When I first saw Brian, as I began the session, I was behind him as he prepared the medicine. I had not realized that I was recalling what I saw as Mary Anne, just before I attached myself to Brian. When I died and left my body, I went into his body and stayed with him until the end. I was afraid we would be separated, so I became totally joined with his body. I felt the fear of being separated from him, quite strongly in the session. Once I was attached to him I was aware of everything that Brian experienced, including his grief and his thoughts, and experienced it all as my own. I don't know who informed Connor of my passing, or how long it was after I died that the wagon came – it could have been days. But Brian was in complete denial. I thought, in the beginning, that Mary Anne was Patty because I definitely felt Patty's presence in this incident, not realizing that she was Brian in that life. This was a very surprising twist!

While I was attached to Brian (Patty) and shared all his experiences, I was very much identified with him, and felt like I _was_ him, yet there was a dim awareness that this was a self-created illusion – that I was identifying with him on purpose as a stronger way of holding on. So my own first-hand experience validates the literature on spirit attachments, which indicates that attached entities can experience everything we do, at least our physical perceptions, and that they may be drawn to connect themselves with people with whom they have a connection, or something in common like smoking, alcohol, and other addictions, or other interests.

Levels

The whole story of my connection with Patty Preston appears in Part V, but as I have mentioned, prior to 1991 I remembered almost none of my personal interactions with Patty. This is because, outside of our first few encounters before eighth grade, most of our contacts were traumatic for me in some way. In fact after college she rarely came to mind, and yet somehow she was always in the background. It seemed like sometimes I didn't remember her at all and at other times I was thinking about her just below the surface, as if there was some deep connection and we were part of some ongoing project. I would later discover that we had HUNDREDS of interactions that I had totally blocked from memory. These memories were not inaccessible, just well hidden.

While doing sessions regarding Patty, I recognized right away that I was operating on two different levels of being. I call my normal everyday waking state "Level–1." I am also in Level–1 when I am in the out-of-body state during sleep, when having a lucid dream, or during a personality switch. When I am in the higher state which I call "Level–2," I am usually out of my body but not always. These levels have little to do with "where" I am, like in or out of my body, but are levels of self-awareness where I have different degrees of access to spiritual perception and psychic ability. The quality and strength of these abilities can vary quite a bit, depending on the situation.

When I find myself in the Level–2 state, I have more clarity of myself as a spiritual being and more awareness of inner knowledge and purpose, which is not available at Level–1, and I also possess great psychic power. While operating at this level, I sense that THIS identity is my "real self," although not my highest or true self, and my Level–1 self seems more like a character I am playing. Another aspect of Level–2 is that when I am exterior at that level, I am not aware of any kind of body. Others who are in spirit may see me, but I have no idea what they see, although when I see someone who is also at Level–2, I usually see their human form wearing simple clothing, and their body has a soft glow. At this level I have all my normal perceptual faculties, but in spirit form, and yet for me there is no visible body unless I make an effort to see one. Also my ability to remember my Level–2 experiences is impaired when I return to Level–1. I also refer to my Level–1 self as my spirit-self.

Carlos Castaneda described a similar phenomenon in "The Eagles Gift" and "The Power of Silence." He called it the right and left side awareness, where the right-side awareness was the normal everyday state of consciousness and the left-side was a slightly higher state where he had great clarity of mind and felt as if he had previously been in a daze or half asleep. He began to access his memories of being in the left-side awareness as he progressed in his training. This sounds very much like Level–2. From doing this work I have been able to remember many events that occurred while in the Level–2 state. While I refer to these levels as levels of awareness or levels of consciousness, it would be more accurate to call them levels of mind, or levels of reality, in which our state of being encompasses a greater or lesser awareness of, and access to, our full potential. So Levels are STATES of being, like identities, but differ in their advantages and limitations, not unlike the different characters you might find in a video game.

In hypnosis there is a phenomenon called the "second-self." The second-self was discovered in the early days of the development of hypnosis. When a person is hypnotized, it is possible to contact an inner observer, who is not another personality but is apparently the person operating from a different state of awareness. The second-self knows much about the subject that the subject isn't consciously aware of, and speaks of the subject in the third person as if that person is a character they are continuously observing. This also sounds to me like Level–2. Now I don't know if anything Castaneda described regarding these levels came from his actual experience or just from his imagination, or if either of these descriptions are describing the same levels of awareness that I have experienced, but in all these cases, remembrance of the higher state is impaired from the viewpoint of the lower state. State-dependent memory is a well-documented phenomena. My "second-self," which is just me at Level–2, was the spirit who Hero was conversing with when he was giving a psychic reading to Faye, the lady at the tavern in the incident I described earlier. I suspect that Dennis–2 was constantly at Level–2 awareness, and it has been hard for me to recall most of his experiences even though I AM him.

Level–0 is the nighttime dream state, but not the state of deep sleep, which is actually not a state of mind at all, but more like a condition of no-mind. These level numbers are purely arbitrary. For me there seems to be another level just above Level–2 which may just be an expansion of that level so I'm calling it level 2.1. However I see Level–2.1 as a higher level because I cannot recall the experience of it at all. When in Level–2, if I do something miraculous, I sense that I did it but I cannot recall the experience of actually doing it. It's all blank – a missing aspect of awareness which I am calling Level–2.1. When I try to access my memory of Level–2.1 it feels like I'm going into a trance and I get a sense of what happened but no perceptual images. So I believe that Level–2.1 is a very powerful state which is far enough removed from Level–1 that I can't remember it at all. I consider Levels 2 and 2.1 as two aspects of the same level, since I can't recall most of my Level–2 experiences anyway. Also, my Level–1 self is not a creation of my Level–2 self, but a state I enter into from Level–2, just as a nighttime dream is a state I enter into from Level–1.

Level–3 is the Higher Self, the state from which all the other states are created. I speculate that the Higher Self is an enlightened godlike state that creates the world we see and the lower viewpoints from which we experience the world. It is a "self" only in the sense of having a mind separated from that of other Higher-Selves. In truth it knows it is not a self at all and the appearance of separateness is an illusion it entertains. It knows it is ONE with the reality from which all states emerge, which is consciousness itself. That the Higher Self is really enlightened is just my own speculation, but it does appear to have unlimited power. The Higher Self creates the lower level states but does not enter into them, identify with them, or lose itself in them, but experiences all of them while being free of them. While it may be that Level–2.1 and Level–3 are actually the same Level, for me there seems to be a difference. Level–2.1 contains a sense of me while Level–3 seems like another entity of which I am a small part. However I have had a couple of brief moments in which the Higher Self and I seemed to merge. These levels, and enlightenment, will be discussed more in Chapters 17 and 21.

So what level is the power-zone in? I believe the power-zone lies between levels and is not actually a state itself. By that I mean it is not a state we are IN but is more like what we ARE – pure consciousness. Very often people describe the power-zone as a state of peace or bliss – a state of no fear or concern. I have heard of people achieving a permanent spiritual awakening after having a sudden shock. The power-zone may simply be a moment of awareness of our true nature as consciousness in which we have access to our unlimited potential while still being identified with being a separate self. This awareness lies beyond time and space, and when we are in that momentary "time out" we are only limited by our thoughts and our immediate focus.

I recall that when I was about to get married, a picture of my fiancé and I appeared in the local paper. I hadn't authorized this and didn't know about it. When I saw the photo, I snapped into the Level–2 state and got angry – I didn't want Patty to see this article because I felt my marriage was a kind of betrayal. But for me at Level–1, Patty rarely came to mind, and the picture was no problem. It's clear that I can also have different identities within the Level–2 state. Sometimes I seem to be very focused and serious in that state, without much humor, whereas at other times I am much more carefree and happy. At Level–1, by contrast, although I'm not as carefree as when at Level–2, I'm usually very solution oriented, have a lot of humor, and often I don't take things very seriously, even important things, although I may seem to, because that's how we play the game.

My identities in these various states are all personas, driven by some underlying purpose. My purpose at Level–2 is to accomplish my mission in life and watch over Patty as well as to help others. My purpose at Level–1 has mainly been to transform myself so I can connect with Patty and accomplish my purpose, but I'm encumbered by all my programming. "Level–2 me" is more straightforward, but I'm rarely in that state.

As a final note I want to reiterate that when I speak of these levels of awareness I'm really describing levels of mind or levels of "awareness of," like levels of "reality" in a video game. Although these terms are useful, and I use them a lot, there are really no "levels" of awareness or consciousness, only levels of mind or domains within consciousness where we have different perspectives and different abilities. These levels sometimes seem like quantum states and other times appear to exist more as a continuum. It's confusing, even to me, how these levels of perception and ability work. Sometimes I have special knowledge and abilities at a certain level and other times I don't. The idea of the various levels of awareness that I am describing is just a way for me to categorize my experiences to better understand them. There may actually be many more levels, or perhaps in the future we will discover a completely different way to understand what is actually happening.

Summary

We live in a vast and amazing universe filled with unimaginable things. There are games within games and universes within universes happening all around us, and it's all consciousness. Nothing is actually material in the way we think it is, just as nothing is really material in a dream. The material world is an experience, just as a dream is an experience, and is in fact just a different kind of dream. The point I want to make here is that the realm we call the physical universe is just a subset of experiences that exists inside an even larger realm, the realm of mind, which itself exists within the ultimate realm of spirit, which is our own consciousness. And in the realm of spirit there are countless things happening that can influence us individually on a mental, physical, and spiritual level, while we are living our apparent physical existence. Since the spiritual influences come from beyond the physical realm, they cannot be directly affected by anything physical, but can be transformed through awareness, communication, and intention, which is spiritual power. ID-R and SRT help us to find and resolve any unwanted spiritual connections that are affecting us, and processes like these can give us more insight into what's going on at a level beyond our physical senses. Stories of the spirit realm can come from people we know or many other sources, like psychics, mediums, shamans, psychedelic visions, NDE's, dreams, hypnosis, and so on. While such accounts may sometimes seem bizarre, or give conflicting descriptions of spiritual reality, they are all filtered through our human minds and subject to individual interpretations. While I'm skeptical of many such stories I hear, I do believe that anything is possible, and that we can all have our own unique individual realities that may not correspond with those of others. We can use the stories of others as clues as to what might be, but it's up to each of us to find out how things are in our own reality, for ourselves

Ethics in the Spirit World

Many of the stories in this book are my experiences while operating in the spirit realm or while interacting with other spirits. As we follow our individual paths, we each have many connections with many others. One level of self-understanding is to discover our own past, what we have experienced, who we have been, and who we are connected to right now. This requires self-investigation. I expect that the ethics of our spiritual interactions is the same as for our physical encounters. Therefore I would suggest that the Golden Rule applies here, as always, and that love, empathy, compassion, humility, and respect be the ideal operating principles on every level. I admit that I may not always live up to these ideals myself, but the effort is ongoing. People who interfere with us spiritually in unethical ways will pay the consequences by experiencing the same. That's just cause and effect. However, while some may have other reasons or intentions, entities who attach themselves to us may be doing so out of desperation or fear, like a drowning person clinging to their rescuer. When it happens without our permission however, we might view spirit attachment as trespassing, like someone camping out in our back yard, or like a parasite, when their presence has negative effects.

While most of the spiritual influences depicted in books and movies are for nefarious or evil purposes, this may just be a distorted reflection of our own fears. Bad things do happen but we must not forget that we are powerful beings ourselves, and most of the problems we encounter in this regard are equally connected to our own actions and our own programming, as I have shown in the preceding stories. We can have as wide a range of interactions with spirits as we can with people in physical form.

Also, when operating in the spirit realm, on a higher level of awareness, we may find we have a different set of values, and that a different code of ethics applies there. For example, in a realm where no one really dies and death is seen to be only a transition, bodily life may not have the same value as it does for us when we believe we are mortal beings with only one life. The human body may be more clearly seen to be just a temporary vehicle, an avatar, for experiencing physical existence or communicating with others.

Many people have experienced channeling other entities, during which the other being takes over their body to some degree, in order to communicate with others. I prefer to call this kind of interaction "borrowing" or "sharing" rather than "possession," because it's temporary, occurs by mutual agreement, does no harm, and may even be beneficial. Many channelers, like Jane Roberts (Seth) or Esther Hicks (Abraham Hicks), have permitted this form of temporary "borrowing" by mutual agreement with the spirit. When the borrowing is hostile or by force however, even if temporary, this is hijacking, and obviously an ethical violation. I have experienced spirits asking for permission to speak or act through me (my body), and I have allowed it a few times and said "no" a few times. Of course these are things I would not presently even be aware of if I had not looked into them.

From a higher spiritual perspective it may be that our bodies are more like automobiles, which we might allow a friend to borrow, but which also might be abducted for a joyride by unwelcome intruders, under some conditions. All these kinds of things can happen, but how common they are, I don't know. I have also heard of people spontaneously finding themselves in someone else's body for a short time, maybe seconds or minutes, for no apparent reason, reminiscent of the TV series "Quantum Leap." Spiritual themes, like possession, body sharing, and especially body swapping where two people switch bodies, have been portrayed in many movies and TV episodes for decades. There is a wonderful movie from 2018 called "Every Day" in which a wandering teenage spirit finds theirself borrowing a different body, a body belonging to someone else the same age, every day. The other person never knows. There is also that memorable scene in the movie "Ghost" where Whoopi Goldberg's character Oda Mae allows ghostly Sam to use her body for a few minutes so he can touch his wife Molly one last time, and they dance together to the Righteous Brothers' "Unchained Melody." And in the movie "Wonder Woman 1984," the spirit of Diana's long deceased truelove returns to inhabit another man's body for a few days, when a magic stone grants her wish to have him back.

In light of all this, there are several stories I will tell, where both Patty and I borrowed another person's body in order for us to physically interact. In most of these experiences there was permission and mutual benefit. Other times the permission is unclear because I can't recall everything, but I assume it was there. While I'm simply reporting what happened, it's also important to understand that these things occurred while I was operating from a higher level, and not by any conscious intent from me – that is to say, not from my human level, or "Level–1 self." The things I do at Level–2 or beyond, are out of my human control, and the spiritual values and rules that govern these higher realms are not something I claim to understand.

And lastly I want to mention is that it is possible for any of us to telepathically communicate with each other intentionally, at least on a subliminal level, and we are actually communicating with others on a subliminal level all the time. Any time we are thinking about someone we know, we may also be connecting with them spiritually right then. That's why we might think about someone right before they call us on the phone. This might happen because they were thinking about us and we picked it up psychically, or we were thinking about them and they received a subliminal impression which inspired them to call. Also, if we think angry thoughts about someone we have interacted with, they may actually react to that, perhaps by thinking angry thoughts about us. If all of us were to subdue our angry and hateful thoughts about others while alone, who knows what might happen – we might change the world!

I believe we can all use this innate ability by intentionally communicating telepathically with people in order to promote a better relationship, to help them, or to reach an understanding if there has been some conflict. But just as in normal verbal communication, we must be willing to listen, and to communicate in a noncontentious way. This works best when we demonstrate compassion and empathy, and to do this we have to get our ego out of the way.

The way to communicate on this psychic level is to simply direct your thoughts to the person, say what you want to say, like a brief statement or question, and see if you get an immediate response. If you do, _it doesn't mean it's a real communication_, or that you should believe any impressions you get, but you treat it as if it is real, even if it's just a feeling. You then respond and continue to communicate until you feel satisfied, and say goodbye. If you get no response, that's fine too. It doesn't matter if you think it's all purely your imagination – just see what happens – you may be surprised. The applications of spiritual communications are unlimited. Just sending blessings or good intentions to people can produce amazing results. This can be misused as well, just as any communication can, and any misuse will naturally have negative karmic repercussions for the offender.

The spiritual things we do are simply expressions of our spiritual nature, in accordance with the games we are playing. On this level our actions can be angelic or demonic, just as they can on the human level. Our higher spiritual abilities are natural aspects of our being – they are "of consciousness" or "of God," if you will. Many of the more extraordinary spiritual things I relate in this book are just things that commonly happen outside of our ordinary perceptions and memory – and they probably happen to everyone.

Chapter 16
Memory and Reality

"History is an expansion of memory, and like memory it alone can explain the present and in this lies its most unmistakable value."
– Alfred Korzybski, Manhood of Humanity

"I believe in everything until it's disproved. So I believe in fairies, the myths, dragons. It all exists, even if it's in your mind. Who's to say that dreams and nightmares aren't as real as the here and now?"
– John Lennon

While I have been influenced by the experiences of many others, as well as the many philosophies and cosmologies that I have studied, the Identity Model, discussed in detail in the next chapter, is derived mainly from my own experience. And by "my experience" I'm of course referring to memory – and I've remembered a lot of strange and unbelievable things. Is any of it real? Did any of these things actually happen, or are they all some delusional product of my imagination? These are valid and necessary questions. And if my memories and my understanding of them _are_ correct, what does this say about reality? Well, it simply says that my current model of reality is theoretically valid, and if other similar models are valid, experiences such as mine should not be uncommon, and they are not! But maybe we're all crazy, so it's time to look into that.

Soon after I started this chapter, I realized that a deep and thorough discussion of memory and reality is well beyond the scope of this book. But there are a few very significant points I want to make, and I also want to explain why I believe that all the things I have remembered and presented in this book are true descriptions of my own experiences.

One real danger that comes into play with regard to memory occurs when we have previously decided how things are, how they were, or what is possible and what is not, and then judge our memories based on whether or not they conform to our preconceptions. If they don't, then to our mind they are not a true description of what happened, and must be rejected. Once we have adopted a world-view of how things are – one that creates a kind of coherence in our lives – this view becomes our internal map of reality. So when we reject our heretical memories, those which don't comply with that view, then, ipso facto, science is abandoned and truth is left in the dust, because we are choosing to believe what we want to believe rather than considering other possibilities. This alludes to that quote from Avatar (2009) "It is hard to fill a cup that is already full."

I once read a book on memory, the title of which I don't recall, where the author described an old memory of walking up a staircase. In the memory he was watching himself ascend the stairs from below. He used this memory to point out how faulty memory can be. Of course, in his view, this memory had to be purely imaginary, some kind of fabrication, since it could not be a real memory. How on Earth could he be watching himself from ten feet away? He didn't realize that he was making a completely unscientific assumption. He was trusting his unfounded concepts _about_ reality and memory instead of taking his experience as raw data that may have many explanations, including the possibility that this memory was an actual memory and not his imagination at all. People have dissociative experiences all the time. But because this author had no framework or model into which he could fit a different possibility, he simply dismissed it. It did not fit within his belief system. He then stated his faulty conclusion as if it were a fact, when it was merely a presumptive opinion. He could have been remembering a hallucination, or maybe that was not actually him walking up the staircase. He did not even discuss any other possibilities.

I was talking with a friend a while back who had taken a very injurious fall down some stairs two years earlier, and was still recovering. This was the first time he told me the whole story. And he told me that during his accident, he watched himself tumbling down the stairs from above. I have many memories of being exterior, and having worked with hundreds of others with similar experiences I know that these memories can be real memories, regardless of how you might wish to explain them.

Our hesitation in admitting that we have had an out-of-body experience, or any kind of spiritual experience, is partly a cultural thing. Our "science-based" culture tends to dismiss anything seemingly paranormal or miraculous, even though such experiences are commonplace. I won't go into the problems with popular scientific misconceptions and erroneous assumptions any further at this point, except to say that there is a tremendous bias against anything spiritual, or anything unexplainable by present scientific models, and this bias is the antithesis of science itself. Such bias can be overcome however, and to become better scientists we must look closely at our own psychology and be willing to confront the emotional leanings and unfounded assumptions that might lead us astray. This is especially important in the arena of consciousness research.

Most of the time, even for myself, the memories that emerge in ID-R are of completely believable ordinary situations. When memories arise that are easily believable, we have no problem with them, especially if they help with the healing process. Occasionally however, when working with others, some memories that come into view are hard for the client to confront or difficult to believe. Most often this is not because they conflict with my client's understanding of what is possible or impossible, but because what is remembered is too emotionally disturbing, or conflicts with their beliefs about themselves, their history, their parents, other people they have interacted with, or how the world should be. I have experienced these conflicts myself.

However, even ordinary shocks often contain elements of the extraordinary. This is because they constitute a momentary respite in a higher state of consciousness during which it is possible to perceive, know, and do things we ordinarily cannot. You may have by now recalled some extraordinary moments in your own life, even though you may still be doubtful as to their reality. Such things are often easy to discover, but they can be hard to believe and therefore are likely to be ignored, overlooked, or dismissed. Memories that a person is unable to confront, and is therefore strongly resisting, can certainly be very difficult to uncover. But once successfully confronted, painful or disturbing experiences become less so, and will become ordinary memories when the underlying trauma is resolved. But how do we reconcile those memories that do seem

implausible, impossible, miraculous, or just crazy, with our sense of
reality? In what context do they make sense and how do we know if
they are real or imaginary?

To tackle these questions we have to consider both memory and
reality. Although everything I have described about my own birth
memory is plausible, the question remains: is it really possible to
remember one's birth? And if it is, am I remembering it accurately?
If it's not possible, then where did this apparent memory come
from? And if I believe I have remembered a miracle, does that
mean miracles are possible, or have I made a mistake?

The Identity Model is a description of how consciousness
creates our experience and how we deal with trauma in the real
world – a world which is part of a reality in which _anything_ is
possible and _everything_ is a miracle. But when we are doing healing
work, whether or not something remembered actually took place at
all, either in the physical world or just in one's mind, is actually
irrelevant to the healing process. We don't need to verify anything.
If it works consistently, it's a valid method. Many techniques are
therapeutically valid, regardless that the explanations behind them
are unproven, incorrect, or unknown. However we do live in a
world that follows consistent rules, for the most part, and we need to
know how far we can trust our memory, especially when it serves up
things difficult to digest.

The memories that were hardest for me to accept were the ones
that required me to believe that my own parents, or another human
being, would do something so terrible and outrageous to another
person as what I was apparently remembering. Even when such a
memory seemed as real as any other, and "fit" into my life story as
well as any other, it has still been difficult. For example, one of the
most difficult memories for me was nothing miraculous but it was
so outrageous and raised so many questions that it challenged me
for a long time. This was mainly because of assumptions I was
making that I had to let go of. I've had clients who experienced
childhood mistreatment that was much more extensive and extreme
than mine, but my own recall of similar things has helped me to
better relate to their reality. The following memory arose
spontaneously.

Adrienne – or The Closet Mystery

I was lying on the floor relaxing in the summer of 1993 when I began to feel the sensation of movement. It felt like my whole body was swaying back and forth, as if I were sitting on a slow-moving swing. This was very visceral and pronounced, and I could turn it on and off. I decided to go with it, so I focused on it until it started to feel a bit like an OBE. Then my arms went numb, my hands tingled, my armpits hurt, and I knew I had something. So I got up, went to my desk, and did a formal session. Here is the story that unfolded.

I was maybe a year old and I could talk. I was lying on my back in a crib and making some noise when my mother came in. But it wasn't mom, it was Adrienne, my mother's mean helper. I looked at her and let her know I wanted my mommy. She said "How did you know I'm not your mother?" Her voice was stern. I got scared and became silent. Then she took something like rope or wire and wrapped it around me under my arms and hung me up in the closet like a coat, and closed the door. Because of the pain, I had already switched with Medic, who didn't scream or cry. We just hung there in the darkness, quietly swinging back and forth while our arms and hands went numb. Although it seemed much longer, it may have been less than a minute that we hung there in silence before my mother opened the closet door.

I heard her gasp at what she saw. She quickly took me down and was talking to herself, and me, frantically, trying to figure out what had just happened. She worried that a stranger might still be in the house so she went outside and stood on the front lawn holding me for several minutes. I don't recall her calling the police, but she did talk to someone, probably a neighbor. Then she called my father at work and he came home. I remember her telling him that someone must have come in the house when she wasn't looking, and tied me up in the closet. A very strange mystery.

Did this really happen? During the session I experienced the shock, felt the emotions and the pain, and this incident does explain all my symptoms, which went away as I worked on it. Although what I recalled is physically possible, I puzzled a long time over how she actually did it, thinking she must have used a wire clothes hanger. I've experienced some far worse things and yet, for some reason, it was easier for me to believe those, or miracles like levitating to the ceiling, than to believe this. But of course I don't have to believe any of it, and that's the beauty of ID-R. Even if my unconscious mind made all this up, which I'm sure it didn't, the images are quite clear, vivid, and convincing, and the narrative has left nothing out. When new bits of information surfaced later, they fit right in also, and this has almost always been the case with every newly recalled incident of mine throughout the years. Very rarely do I find anything that doesn't fit in easily and immediately.

Memory
"Scars have the strange power to remind us that our past is real."
– Cormac McCarthy, All the Pretty Horses

Understanding memory is exceedingly important and also very tricky. Memory, in its most general description, is the utilization of past conditions. For example, memory foam, when its form is altered by heat and pressure, will return to its previous shape when these forces are removed. It somehow uses its past condition to recreate that condition. How it actually does this is called memory.

With regard to our conscious experience, there are many kinds of memory: explicit – implicit – episodic – semantic – long term – short term – narrative – procedural – muscle memory – somatic memory – and others. Memory allows us to reproduce something from the past, whether it is a skilled set of movements, a body of useful information, or a conscious experience. The memory I want to discuss is explicit long term episodic memory. This, along with somatic memory, is what we utilize in ID-R and many other healing processes, as well as anytime we recall a past experience consciously. Explicit memory is whatever we can intentionally and consciously recollect, and "episodic" refers to specific episodes or incidents in our lives. Memory then, is our ability to bring past experiences back into our awareness, in some form.

Try to imagine what your life would be like without ANY memory, not even of the previous second. This may be an impossible task. I imagine it would just be the observation of the flow of immediate experience. In a sense it would be one-dimensional. Normally our mind lives in a kind of space that includes the immediate past and a vision of where we are headed, a kind of memory cache. Our attention is never solely on the tiny, imaginary pinpoint of "now," but hovers in between and includes what is, what was, and what might be. So with no past to reference, there would be no sense of the future and no sense of time at all! Even thoughts would seem to come from nowhere and would disappear into oblivion with no trace of having ever existed and no sense of their bearing on succeeding thoughts. You would have no sense of drawing upon past experience to make new decisions and no future upon which those decisions would have an impact, because even if you could imagine a future, the image of that future would also be immediately forgotten. So there would be no sense of a personal will. There would also be no sense of identity since there is no memory of who you were or what you did a second ago. Life, as an experience, would just be the totality of the present conscious moment, its content vanishing the instant it appears. Without memory there would be no experience of life as we understand it, because our understanding of life is based on memory, identity, and the flow of time.

Since suffering requires both identity and time, it too would be unknown. Unconscious memory could exist as autonomic impulses that assist survival, as in an amoeba, but without a conscious "narrative memory" that creates a sense of time and provides identity, context, and meaning to our lives, what would life be? To borrow a phrase from Mooji, our lives would be like "writing on water." The wondrous experience of life as we know it would not exist. There's more I could say along these lines, but from this perspective, as far as our human lives are concerned, memory is everything. And using connections between perception, memory, imagination, thought, and meaning, we construct our reality.

The images of our past experiences are connected by association. Think of grandma and you might immediately recall the smell of her chocolate chip cookies baking in the oven. Using these associations we create a conscious template, a temporal map, upon which we organize our experiences, and we call this template "chronological time." Our personal stories live on this template, and our lives seem to take place on it. So first let's consider this question: are _any_ memories of the past actually _real_?

Memory, as a process, is often defined as the encoding, storage, and retrieval of information. But this is not memory as we experience it; this is a theory of how our memory works. Memory itself, for our purposes, refers mainly to episodic memory – the conscious recall of past experience. And, leaving out any consideration of the cause, nature, or validity of memory, we will define it this way: *a memory is the mental reexperience of a past experience*, with some degree of fidelity, completeness, and vividness. Our memory theoretically enables us to recall any conscious experience we have had, and there are many theories as to how it works.

Although all memory takes place "now," a memory exists in contrast to an experience of the *immediate present*, which would include sense perceptions and mental experiences like thought and imagination that are occurring in consciousness for the first time. "Recall" is the bringing of an image of a *past* experience to *present* awareness. This past image can include anything we have previously experienced in any way, including all perceptions, thoughts, and emotions. For example when we remember the feeling of sadness we felt long ago at the loss of a pet, that sadness is an emotional image, just as the memory of what our pet looked like is a visual image.

However, although we may refer to certain impressions or images as "memories," that does not mean that they are accurate representations of the past or that they are real in any way beyond being immediate mental phenomena. *In order to be called memories they must be valid*. We'll explore that next.

False Memory
"Definitions create conditions." – Alfred Korzybski

"Nothing fools you better than the lie you tell yourself" – Teller

The generally accepted paradigm is that our memory is a recording of some kind, similar to a tape recording or a digital recording. The memory is neurologically encoded in the neurons of the brain in some way, perhaps holographically, and can be brought back to mind later for recall. The evidence for this includes the fact that vivid memories can be elicited through electrical or chemical stimulation of the brain, and problems with the brain can directly affect memory in very specific ways. Besides, it just makes sense that memory is stored in the brain and body if we are purely physical organisms and consciousness is just a byproduct of our physiology. And if memory is recorded in the brain in some physical form, it would naturally be subject to various problems and inaccuracies due to deterioration, alteration, or distortions in recording and playback, similar to what might occur with any other physical recording device. Indeed, our memory systems are famously imperfect, at least for most of us, and can fail us in many ways, and we do forget things, and may remember some things incorrectly. Traditionally these imperfections are thought to be due to possible faults in three main areas: the making of the memory, the storing the memory for subsequent retrieval, and accessing the memory later, although there are other factors involved as well. But if our experiences are not recorded properly, stored properly, or properly retrieved, then we may not remember things correctly, or at all. This has been borne out in experiments, and there are many ways that any of these three processes can be compromised.

So the presently accepted ideas about how our memories work do make sense, but they are still incomplete theories. Like the early models that portrayed the atom as a tiny solar system, they are good ideas derived from research and evidence, but will ultimately be discarded for better ones. The point is that we do not yet know what memories are, in the material sense, or how they are recorded, or if they are in fact recordings at all. It may seem silly to question some of these standard views, but most of our failures in science, and life, are failures of imagination. What if memories are neither recorded nor stored? What if they are something else? We should question everything, and we should consider as many alternative possibilities as we can. Scientists do this all the time, like when they dreamed up the "many worlds" idea of alternate timelines branching into parallel dimensions to explain how time travel might be possible without being a paradox. If these ideas have no other value, at least they make for some entertaining science fiction movies.

There is a lot of fascinating information and speculation available about human memory, especially concerning how fallible our memories can be, and I've seen much information over the years about false memories and how easy they are to produce. It's amazing how sure we can be that something we remember is real, when it is completely false or purely imaginary. The evidence is compelling! The only problem is, false memories do not exist. That's right – there is no such thing as a false memory – it's an oxymoron, like "original copy" or "jumbo shrimp." Let me explain.

A memory is an image in the mind. But what makes it a memory? Is it that we say it's a memory or that we believe it's a memory? Let's say someone vividly remembers being chased by a bear as a young child while the family was on vacation at a particular national park. And let's suppose that never actually happened, at least at that time, even though the person also remembers some details of the vacation correctly. Being chased by the bear could be called a false memory – a memory of something that didn't happen. But what is false about this memory? Is it the images or feelings that came up during recall? Those are just images and feelings. Nothing is false about them, because falseness is a judgement. The images and feelings are real, and they are just _there_. So is it the _belief_ that this event actually happened that's false? Well, if it didn't actually happen then yes, that belief is wrong. So it's actually the _BELIEF_ that's false, in the sense of being incorrect. But where did this vision of being chased by a bear come from? It could have been a vivid dream, a past life, a different incident where the person _was_ chased by a bear, or by a big dog named "Bear," at some other place, or perhaps it was imagined in the moment when it first came to light, and has been wrongly attributed ever since. But that doesn't matter – the source is irrelevant!

If we define a memory as anything that someone believes is a memory, then memory becomes nothing more than a belief in the accuracy of mental images. If the image that we believe is a true representation of the past is _not_ true, then we could call it a false memory, and many do. But it degrades the whole idea of memory to define it as a belief. It makes more sense to define a memory as the actual recall of a past experience, because that is what we expect memories to be, and this is the only reason those images that we call "memories" have special value. If we define a memory in this pragmatic way, as the _ACTUAL_ or _CORRECT_ recall of a past experience, then THERE ARE NO FALSE MEMORIES, only false beliefs regarding the past. So from here on in this book, a memory is, by definition, a recall, a reemergence into our awareness, of a past experience. By recall or reemergence, in this case, I mean a mental experience that accurately represents the past, without regard for the nature of that experience. The actual nature of the memory or how it is reproduced is irrelevant for now, whether it is a recording, a mental construction based on inner knowing, the actual past, or something yet to be discovered. So a memory is accurate by definition, and is a "memory" only to the degree that it *IS* accurate. A memory may be hazy or incomplete, and we may be confused about what it means, but to the extent that it is accessible, it is true. What we do with it is another matter.

And how do we know if a memory is true? We'll get to that later. However, if a *presumed* memory is inaccurate, to the degree that it is so, it is simply *not* a memory, or at least not the memory we might think it is. And consider this question: could you have an accurate memory and believe that it *didn't* really happen? Absolutely – it happens all the time – and we may declare such memories to be false even though they are not, like the example of the man walking up the stairs in the beginning of this chapter. But if we later found such a memory to be true, that is, a memory that we once believed was false, we wouldn't now say that the memory was previously false and has now <u>become</u> true, when it's obviously only our thinking that has changed. *The fallacy of the false memory concept is that we believe our memory is at fault, when it is actually our thinking.* To be sure, our memory <u>systems</u> can be faulty when they fail to bring up useful memories, or when they bring them up unclearly, but they don't bring up "false memories," they only bring up images which we must then evaluate or interpret. It is our evaluations and interpretations that are so often wrong.

To make this super clear, suppose we do get to the point with future biotechnology where we can erase or create memory impressions in a person's brain by some means, again assuming that memories are some kind of recording or physical condition. If we created a memory impression of something that never happened, and the person accessed that impression thinking it was a memory, isn't that a false memory? No. As I said, it's not a memory at all, it's just an image. Science fiction movies notwithstanding, it's just a trick. We may trust our memories and believe they are accurate, but mental images aren't memories unless they are true representations of past experience coming from your own memory system.

Similarly, if I showed you a photograph that was digitally altered to misrepresent reality, it's not a false image, it's just an image that shows something that isn't real – it's the idea that it's real, that is false. It's like fake news. A report is only news if it's an accurate report. *Fake news is NOT news at all,* no matter how good the made up eyewitness accounts or Photoshopped images are – it's just a lie – it didn't happen.[70] There are many areas in science and life where semantics is crucial, and this is one of them.

But why discard the term "false memory" altogether? Why not just redefine it more precisely as anything we think is a memory but isn't? Because again, that would just be a false belief. One problem is that the label "false memory" has been corrupted, misapplied, and misused, as has the word "hypnosis." However I think "hypnosis" can be reclaimed and redeemed whereas "false memory" cannot. But more importantly this concept corrupts the whole idea of what a memory is. Either we have memories or we don't. Images in our minds that are not reexperiences of past experiences, regardless of what they feel like or what we think about them, are simply not memories.

So there are no false memories, only false beliefs regarding memories and mental impressions. What have been called false memories are only false beliefs and interpretations regarding the images in our minds being true accounts of the past, when they are not. If I hypnotize someone and "implant" a memory by suggesting something and getting the person to imagine it very vividly, they may believe it is a real memory when they awaken – and it is. But it's a memory of what they imagined, not of something they experienced before the hypnosis, regardless of what I get them to believe. We can easily be tricked and we trick ourselves all the time. Sometimes we can feel very certain that something we

---

[70] This is a limited metaphor since news that is not intentionally misleading can be still be incomplete, inaccurate, or poorly reported, but we still would not call it fake. If a news reporter honestly reports something that turns out to be false, as often happens, that's just a mistake. "Fake news" is intentional.

"remember" is true even when there is solid evidence to the
contrary, because it feels true, it feels like a memory, and may make
perfect sense to us. Actual memories feel true because they _are_ true,
but that doesn't mean we understand them correctly. I use the term
"associative memory" (also called "reconstructed memory") to
describe the way we generally remember things, because most often
what we call memories are constructions, and they are usually
incomplete. Since our memory is rarely perfect, we usually have to
piece things together using association, to get a complete picture,
and this process has multiple issues affecting its reliability. I like to
call reconstructed memories "recollections" because they are RE-
collections of bits of memories.

Going further, what seems to be a simple memory, like an image
of a bird for example, is often a quite complex integration of
cognitive processes and different types of memory, including the
visual image, the context in which it is seen, any associated images
or knowledge connected with it, and various understandings of what
it all means. Any memory is actually a whole package of things,
similar to an identity state as defined in Chapter 5. When we are
very mistaken or completely wrong about what we think we
remember, the problem is that what we are _calling_ a memory is
usually a combination of memory, thought, and imagination. It may
be a memory of something we imagined, or bits and pieces of
memories of many past perceptions, feelings, knowledge, thoughts,
and imaginings, all pasted together to form a cohesive and
convincing picture. It seems real because it IS real, in many ways.
All the pieces can be real memories of real things, but when we are
mistaken, we are wrong because our construction or interpretation
is incorrect. In these cases we _are_ remembering, but if we are not
remembering where all the various images actually came from, and
are interpreting them incorrectly, our conclusions will be wrong,
and we will be deceived. We can say that we are remembering
incorrectly, in these circumstances, but we cannot say that our
faulty interpretation is a false memory. There is no such thing. But
there are _mistaken_ memories, just as there are mistaken ideas,
theories, or answers. A mistaken memory is a memory taken to be
something it is not, but it is not false any more than your perception
of a face that you see in a crowd is false because you mistake the

person to be a friend, and it turns out to be someone else. You saw what you saw, but your interpretation was false.

In the book "Mistakes Were Made (but not by me)" (2020) author Carol Tavris describes a vivid memory of her father reading a certain book to her as a child. She later discovered that this book was not published until after her father's death, rendering this "memory" false. In my view however, it would be more proper to say that her memory was only faulty in that she didn't remember ENOUGH so as to formulate her RE-collection more accurately. She believed the images in her mind showed the truth, when apparently they did not. I've experienced this many times myself, and I suspect most of us have.

We are learning more about memory all the time, and a better understanding of how our memory works will help us to better know what we can trust and what we can't.

True Memory

My definition declares all memories to be inherently true. But if there are no false memories, and our memories are fallible, the question then arises: _do actual memories, accurate reexperiences of the past, even exist?_ Maybe everything we think we remember is just some kind of useful approximation – except that usefulness depends on accuracy, and our memories are more than useful, they are essential. There are some deeper issues here, but what we are most often concerned about regarding our memories is how accurate they are, and this concern increases in proportion to the consequences of being wrong. Usually we just take our memory and its limitations for granted until there is some problem, discrepancy, or critical need for complete accuracy which forces us to double check or seek verification.

But accuracy is not always our primary concern in our use of memory. When I reminisce about a childhood Christmas morning when I felt happy and excited, I want to be able to experience that memory as vividly and as completely as I can – the wonderful fragrance of Douglas Fir, the magical colored lights, the emotions of wondrous anticipation, the mysterious packages, the cold chill in the wee hours of the morning, the taste of hot chocolate – purely for the enjoyment of it. Accuracy is of little importance here, although

I may feel it is entirely accurate. Other times there is a transformative function, as in ID-R or psychotherapy, and accuracy is again of less importance, taking a backseat to clarity, insight, and good results. Sometimes we use imagination to weed out any unpleasantness that might spoil our sacred remembrances, and we create our own happy "pseudo memories" to replace them. Maybe in my happy Christmas remembrance I left out some memories that might have spoiled the scene. But the bottom line question is, how can we know if anything we remember is really the way it was? By my definition, memory itself is _not_ malleable, as some suggest, and although we can interfere with memory in many ways, an altered memory is by definition, simply not a memory. But how we deal with what we remember does depend on many things.

Although we do remember things, and everything we remember is, by definition, a recall of past experience, and as such is a true representation of that experience, still, our memories are far from perfect. Most of us probably rely mainly on the associative memory process when recalling past experiences, which means that we directly recall bits and pieces of the past and construct a picture of what happened. We do this because we don't always get a vivid replay in our mind of the whole thing all at once, as if we were watching a 3D movie, although such experiences are possible. Still, this method of remembering works very well for us in everyday life. We can however, differ greatly in our individual abilities for recall. Some people can remember many things in great detail with remarkable accuracy and others couldn't tell you what they had for breakfast today. So this usual way of remembering can have many limitations, and for most of us the memories that we construct using associative memory are not crystal clear and complete. This means they are usually fragmented, and that can leave gaps to be filled in by guesswork and imagination, which we may do routinely as a matter of habit. This reminds me of how they replaced missing DNA fragments with approximations to breed dinosaurs in the movie "Jurassic Park."

What would an ideal memory be like? For me, it would, be 100% accurate as a representation of my actual experience, by definition, but I would also want it to be 100% as clear and vivid as when it was first experienced, 100% complete with no missing parts, and completely accessible instantly at any time. I would also want my memory completely under my control so that I am not bothered by old memories when I am not intentionally recalling them. I would call this ability to access past experience exactly as it was, "True Memory."

Is there any such thing as true memory? I believe so. One indication of this possibility is the fact there are perhaps a few dozen people in the world who can remember almost everything they have experienced in their lives with total accuracy. They have what is called Highly Superior Autobiographical Memory (HSAM). The TV series "Unforgettable" from 2011 was based on this. Although this kind of episodic memory is not what most of us experience and use in our daily lives, and it does have some limitations, I believe we all have the memory of everything we have ever experienced, including past lives and altered states, available in our unconscious minds. I have personally experienced the spontaneous recall of past episodes in my life and some past lives, and these memories were absolutely real and vivid. It was as if I were experiencing those scenes for the first time in the present moment, while at the same time, I knew they were memories. Every time we access _any_ memories, we are using our True Memory, although often with steep limitations. My present hypothesis is that the reason we don't have access to our complete memory in the ideal way I described above is due to our own internal programming. This programming inhibits our memory and blocks most of our more powerful abilities. I believe our characteristic amnesia regarding our past lives is one aspect of this programming and is a requirement for being born here in this world. I'll share my own experience with this in Part V.

True Memory then, would access a level of memory which brings forth a completely accurate and unblemished recreation of our past experience. How our memory actually works at the most fundamental level, is unknown. But whether the mind somehow re-creates our past from exact and true information, simply serves up recordings of our past, or somehow allows us to actually revisit our past, and regardless of HOW it does any of this, let's look at the result.[71]

The mental images called memory can be extremely vague in terms of vividness or so real they seem to be happening right now. They can also be very detailed and complete, or so fragmented as to convey very little useful information. Yet even without knowing what memories really are, or exactly how memory works, we use our memory effectively every day and treat memories as valid information about both the past and present state of our world. Also, when we consider whether any memory is clear, complete, vivid, and accurate, in comparison to real-time experiences, we need to know what these terms mean. A memory can be vague or clear, which means either you can tell what it is clearly or you only have a vague idea. It also can be partial or complete, in terms of the information we need. For example you may remember where you were eating dinner last Friday but you don't recall what you ate. And it can be as vivid and intense as the original experience, or hazy and dull. But most importantly, among the many elements we might consider about a memory, it can be accurate or inaccurate. What does this mean? We can know if a memory is clear, vivid, and complete, or vague, dull, and partial because these are subjective experiences – like rating pain on a scale of one to 10. But accuracy is another matter.

In daily life we depend on the accuracy of our memories to function and even to survive, and it is often important to recall things we've forgotten. I have successfully used hypnosis to help people find lost objects, sometimes many years after the fact, and long forgotten memories are recalled and validated by people all the time. Because the accuracy of what comes up using ID-R is usually unimportant to the goal of healing, it doesn't matter what happened twenty years ago or even that we are interpreting it all correctly. The results are what is most important. However, discovering such memories can give us an entirely new and life-altering view of ourselves and our lives, and the validity of that view

---

[71] If everything is consciousness and all events in time, space, and mind exist simultaneously, true memory might be an actual revisiting of past experience, or even future experience, in some form.

depends on whether these impressions truly represent reality.
Otherwise, one may be healed but also confused about what it all
means. For example my magical and spiritual views of life in which
miracles are real and virtually anything is possible are validated by
my memories of experiencing such things in the past. But if I
decide none of it really happened, then my views remain
unsubstantiated. I may still believe in these things, but surely
without the same conviction. So how can I know for sure?

Validation and Proof

At this point it is important to understand that there is no
objective way to determine the accuracy of a memory of an
experience on the _subjective_ level. For example, you may be having
a memory of something which is verified in every way by evidence,
but how can you know for sure that the images in your mind are
exactly the same as your original experience? You might know it in
your heart with metaphysical certainty, but other than that, there is
no other way to validate the actual experience, since it is yours
alone. Now if we _can_ know our memory is true in that way, with
that Godly certitude, we don't need any other validation, and that's
fine. But if we don't have that certainty, what can we do?

While we can't verify the accuracy of the memory of our
personal internal experiences in any external way, we _can_ verify the
accuracy of what our memory tells us about the world, and we do
that all the time, every day, like when we recall where things are
and how things work, and recognize the people and things around
us. We can verify all these memories with simple observation, or by
using records, witnesses, and physical evidence, to check the
details. This is of course what we normally do any time we want to
be sure of something, or we want to convince others.

On a personal level we verify the accuracy of our memories by
direct discovery or by finding evidence and indications. If I discuss
a past event with someone who shared it with me, and they describe
something I remember but have not yet talked about, that validates
for me that what I remember is real, if we use the word "real" in this
context to mean something that occurs within our collective
consensus reality. The term "consensus reality" denotes our shared

agreements about the world, which may be very broad or very narrow depending on our individual beliefs.

One day while waiting for a client who was late, I found myself getting irritated, which caused me to recall a dream from a few days earlier in which I was walking around a vacant lot looking at dismantled cars. When my client failed to show up, I felt angry, so I decided to work on that reaction. When I put myself in the "angry identity" viewpoint, my right foot started to hurt almost immediately.

The dream I had recalled turned out to be a memory of the following incident. My parents had left me and my brothers at a friend's house in the morning and said they would be right back, but they didn't come back all day. The friend was Derek, the auto mechanic, who remained busy in his garage the whole time and paid us no attention. We had to stay in the vacant lot in front of Derek's house for many hours with nothing to do. I got more and more upset about this as the day wore on and finally took out my anger by kicking one of the broken down cars. I almost broke my foot! After resolving this incident, my anger about waiting was gone and my foot stopped hurting.

Later that day I told my brother Alan about the dream. He said he remembered the incident, and before I could mention my foot he asked me if I remembered kicking the car. I consider that a strong validation that my memory was real. Remember, for now I am using the word "real" to describe anything that happens in the collective consensus reality of our shared experience of the world. The memory was of course a real experience for me, in and of itself, in my subjective personal reality. But does my brother's response prove that the event actually happened? No, not in any objective way, except perhaps between my brother and I. It only shows we have an agreement about the past. So what would prove it? That depends on you. For some, maybe this would be proof enough, and it did satisfy me.

Pragmatically I define "proof" as whatever convinces someone of something. We like to think that a proof is somehow set in stone as absolute reality, but in the relative world there is no such thing as absolute reality. You may have to think about this a bit, but any proof is only deemed a proof in someone's mind – there is no such thing as a proof outside of human thought. Things simply are what they are. This means that all "proof" is imaginary, regardless of how useful it may be. Also, there are degrees of convincedness. For example I might be convinced that I am right about something but would I bet $100 on it? A million dollars? My life? How convinced am I? So a proof is a subjective thing on several levels. A group of jurors in a court of law may reach a unanimous consensus about a verdict based on evidence, and we may abide by that verdict and call it proof of guilt or innocence, but it is still only an opinion. That opinion may be correct, or new facts may come to light that disprove it. We do the best we can, and we can indeed be right about things, but the question is always, how can we be sure?

We have all had the experience of being wrong about something we remembered, whether we were actually wrong or not. Sometimes we discover these errors by ourselves and realize our fallibility. But our memory is a tool, and like any tool, to be useful it must be used correctly. The way we use our memory is maybe 10% memory and 90% construction and evaluation. That's only a wild guess, but the point is, remembering isn't just memory, it's a process, and the process is fallible and the memories themselves can be inadequate for what we need at any given time. Also we often believe in something based _less_ on the evidence of our own experience, and more on past indoctrination, personal bias, and social influence, at the expense of truth. When we have all these factors and forces working against our own experience and memories, it is easy to doubt ourselves. This truth is often exploited by those who wish to suppress, gaslight, and control others.

I will explain why I believe my story and experiences are real, but in the end these are not provable in any absolute way. Nor is anything _you_ know. Also, no matter how forcefully stated or how true it may be, everything in this book is my belief or opinion. I'm not trying to convince anyone of anything. I only hope to stimulate your curiosity. You have to discover your own truth for yourself. Believe what makes sense and believe what works, but most importantly believe in yourself; it's all you've really got.

To sum things up, my current theory about human memory is that all experience exists simultaneously, and true memory happens when our attention is able to go to a past experience of ours in a way that allows it to enter our present awareness just as it was. But our ability to do this is limited due to the limitations of our minds in their current state of programming and our lower state of awareness. I'm also entertaining the idea that memory may be created in the moment of remembering. The source of the memory is the actual true information about the past. Let me explain. Our lives are stories. Suppose that when you read a novel, you picture the story in your mind, like a vivid daydream that includes all the details. You create all the characters and events based on the descriptions in the book, as if you were living it in your mind. Similarly. when we remember something, we are consulting the "book of consciousness" in which our own story is written, and we are reconstructing the memory from that true information, just as we do when imagining scenes while reading the novel. However, because we _are_ consciousness, we are imagining the memory into being from what we _know_. In this model the real memory exists only as information, not as recorded images. But that information is exact and perfect in every minute detail, even though it has no physical form and is not itself "stored" anywhere. Instead it is simply "known" at all times, consciously, by a higher level mind, and cannot be corrupted by any lower level process. But these are just theories.

Reality

"I believe there is no source of deception in the investigation of nature which can compare with a fixed belief that certain kinds of phenomenon are impossible." – William James

"Sit down before fact as a little child, be prepared to give up every preconceived notion, follow humbly wherever and to whatever abysses nature leads, or you shall learn nothing. I have only begun to learn content and peace of mind since I have resolved at all risks to do this."
– Thomas Henry Huxley

"Reality exists in the human mind, and nowhere else."
–George Orwell, 1984

Reality means _what is_, as opposed to what might be or what could be. In that sense our consciousness and conscious experiences are the only things we can know are real, because they *are.* This is my basic definition of reality, the "isness" of experience. But there is a second definition which is really a category of realities. Besides the reality of <u>what is</u>, there is also the imagined reality of <u>*what we believe*</u>, which is a "conceptual reality," and there can be many kinds of conceptual realities. The external world and what happens in it, apart from our actual experience of it, is really a lower level "conceptual reality" – a construct which we think of as existing outside of ourselves. This reality exists at the level of thought, which is the level where we communicate our agreements about what exists, what things are, and how things work. This is what we do when we play a game, like football, or when we form a government, where we all agree on what things mean, and the rules of engagement. Our most basic agreements about the world create the consensus reality we live in, and in our present world there are many things that almost all of us human inhabitants agree on.

Most of us with normal perception seem to perceive the same physical world, and we have developed sciences to understand how everything works in this world, as well as technologies to use this knowledge to our advantage. This paradigm is, for each of us, the most basic aspect of living as a human being on this planet, and is based on our physical perception of a world that appears external to us. We also adopt our own personal and tribal beliefs that may differ from the general consensus to varying degrees.

But sometimes things happen that seem to defy our ordinary experience and understanding of how things are. It's kind of like playing a game where someone seems to have incredible luck that we can't explain, and which should not be possible. We are dumbfounded until we discover that they have been cheating. For reasons I've discussed earlier, when things happen that don't follow the familiar rules, and don't comply with what we expect, like telepathy, psychokinesis, precognition, spiritual healing, or a thousand other things, the most common reaction is fear. Throughout history these fears, specifically fears toward those demonstrating or even discussing such phenomena, have led to persecutions, banishments, and executions in the name of science, religion, or law. Usually, instead of incorporating these experiences into our mainstream understanding of the world and enlarging our views of reality, we suppress and deny these experiences and their possible explanations. Even today those who pursue a greater understanding of such phenomena face tremendous challenges, are often ridiculed or even persecuted – they get "cancelled" and have their ideas relegated to the fringes of consideration.

But for many decades now, many serious researchers have studied these paradigm shifting phenomena, and have shown beyond any doubt that many paranormal abilities and phenomena are absolutely real. If you need to be convinced, the previously mentioned book "Irreducible Mind" covers the evidence in depth. I also suggest reading the works of Charles Tart and Dean Radin, two highly respected researchers in consciousness and parapsychology, and especially Tart's book "The Secret Science of the Soul" (formerly "The End of Materialism," the title I prefer) and Radin's books "The Conscious Universe," and "Real magic." Nevertheless, there are many who will never be convinced.

However, since proof of spiritual things is personal and subjective, as I said earlier, as is reality, there will never be any _physically causative_ explanation for those things whose cause is not physical. Since I experienced many miraculous things in my life that were immediately validated, I had never really felt any need for extra proof of their existence. But for me, starting back in the 1970s, the works of Tart were especially supportive and encouraging because they are based on real science, and I did feel that we needed mainstream scientific support if we were to create an acceptable model of the universe that explained these experiences, even while at the time, the only such phenomena I personally recalled were mostly of the wimpy kind described in Chapter 11. There may not be a great deal of agreement amongst different consciousness researchers about how it all works, in terms of an overall model, by which I mean how all these extraordinary phenomena and abilities integrate with the physical world, but I will give you my views in the next chapter where I posit that the physical world is simply one of many dreamworlds within consciousness.

When we recall something that defies explanation, or the reality of which lies outside our current belief system, it's normal to question our memory first, because it's easy to be mistaken. But remember, we don't really know the limits of possibility, and what we do know or believe is also based on memory. If we take what we recall simply as data, we have a better chance of finding out what is real than if we reject it because we think we already know.

The validation of things we remember regarding our material world experiences, by hard evidence and witnesses, can be an essential thing when needed for convincing others, but it's also wonderful for dispelling self-doubt. Even circumstantial evidence or clues can be uplifting in this regard. And if we want to make a case for what we recall, external evidence is of course the best way. When we are presented with evidence for things we didn't personally experience, we most easily believe in their plausibility if we have experienced the same or similar things ourselves in the past, or if they are things which we understand as part of our everyday reality. It is also important that the description of events makes logical sense. So if I had not mentioned any of those experiences in my life that conflict with the "ordinary" paradigm, which is the consensus reality of the material world in which nothing spiritual or paranormal exists, then my healing journey might be more believable to many people. But it would be 90% incomplete, dishonest, and far less helpful – and the world already has too many "black magicians."[72]

My Reality

I have many reasons to believe that all my experiences were real, and not just for me alone. But first let's be clear on one thing: _all_ experiences are real in the sense that we experience them. That is the one thing, besides consciousness itself, that we know for sure. We may not properly understand the true nature of those experiences or know where they come from, but we do experience them. Whatever else we think or believe about them is a matter of thought. When we remember things, we experience those images in our minds and conclude from intuition and present knowledge that they are memories. But if we need clarification or want further validation, we seek evidence. When our experiences coincide with those of others, we have the reality of our shared world, and in that reality there are two kinds of validation: the kind that supports our

---

[72] Those who propagate and enforce an unreal view of the world. See page 371.

own memory on a personal level, and the kind that convinces others, and these usually overlap.

Considering my memories of ordinary experiences, the main three questions would be, is it possible to remember such things as birth and other very early events at all, is it possible to remember such things accurately and in detail, and how can we know if any particular memory is real?

We can only study correlations regarding the memories of well-documented events, but this can provide evidence that it is indeed possible to remember things as far back as birth and prenatal experiences. For example if there were an audio recording of my birth we could see if I was recalling the words I heard with any accuracy. There are some studies that show we can have reliable memories before the age of three and a half, and very likely many more studies I am unaware of. People do actually remember prenatal, birth, and infancy experiences, and that's a fact. These memories are actually very common, but we just don't know how well they correspond to the real-world events they represent.

When early memories like this come up in ID-R, they are validated by the sensations and emotions that arise, by getting positive results, and by any new understanding they provide about the subject's life and experiences. Real world correspondence is usually unimportant except as a matter of curiosity. When doing early memory studies it would be important to test not only what people do ordinarily remember, but what we can _potentially_ remember using techniques like hypnosis, EMDR, ID-R, meditation, breath work, and psychotropic drugs. Our potential is much greater than most people realize.

When I recalled my birth, I was thirty years old and I had never remembered anything about it previously – but my body was remembering every time I got a headache. In considering my birth memories, as well as all of the more believable events in my life, I believe they are real because of the direct connection between the trauma and the pain or condition I was experiencing. In every case there was no internal doubt. That there was a positive healing result was an added confirmation for me. Also these memories were generally not strange or hard to believe, and I did not feel the need for any external verification. Furthermore, not only did these memories not conflict with anything else I remembered, nor did they pose any logical conundrums, for the most part, but they often explained, clarified, and filled in missing pieces of other memories and other aspects of my life. Therefore, there has been no reason to doubt them. That's not even mentioning the powerful subjective impact of reliving intense experiences, and the inner sense of reality they impart. Such an experience, by itself, is often enough to convince most people that a memory is real.

Even if those more believable memories of mine were complete or partial fabrications of my mind, working with them still served a very valuable healing function. If the story they tell about my life is unreal, then the time periods they represent are simply blank spots of total amnesia. If the memory of my birth was not real but just a fabrication, then all I have is a good story that might be some kind of approximation of the past. In that case why not accept it as being real anyway? In fact it is actually more difficult to explain this memory as unreal than to accept a simpler explanation that makes more sense – Occam's Razor. Finally, in my work with hundreds of clients in thousands of sessions, people have reported the same kinds of self-validating things as I experienced. At the very least there is definitely something real and powerful going on here in this work of self-exploration. And this is true with many other modalities including Primal Therapy, hypnotherapy, EMDR, Idenics, and every other form of trauma therapy or inner investigation.

My rediscovered memories that are questionable are of course those that defy a traditional materialist explanation, including everything paranormal, spiritual, or miraculous, as well as altered states of consciousness and multiple personalities. Let's call any such questionable memories "Q-memories." If you grant me that I experienced the things I say I did, as mental images that surfaced during my sessions, then it's really only my explanations of these possible memories that are questionable. Let's say for example that, during a session, I did experience what seemed like a memory of levitating to the ceiling when I was ten. My first question is, why did I experience that? My explanation is that this was a memory, I really did physically levitate, and such things are really possible. But if such a thing is not really possible, then there must be another explanation. Perhaps I imagined it and thought it was real, or I was remembering a dream or a hallucination – there are always many

possible alternate explanations for anything. So let me address all
Q–memories at once.

If any of my Q-memories of a physical nature are real, we simply
need a better model of the universe and the human mind to explain
it, since our present model is inadequate. There are in fact many
observed and accepted phenomena that the present physical model
cannot explain anyway, like the Big Bang, the speed of light, and
quantum entanglement. The Identity Model is my attempt to
correct this, although it is very basic. When considering things like
trauma, shocks, multiple personalities, altered states, OBEs, and
spiritual encounters, which are some of the more subjective things
that people experience, my explanations simply serve to fit them
into a useful construct, as any good model does. Whether or not my
explanations are useful for healing or inner exploration can be
EASILY TESTED, and the model can be adapted individually if
needed. I believe my Q-memories are real because they seem to be,
in every respect, just like my regular memories. The sensations,
emotions, thoughts, and shocks are all as they would be in any other
incident. There is nothing fundamentally different, except they defy
gravity, so to speak. They are not ordinary, but I believe them for _all
the same reasons_ I believe the memories that _are_ ordinary. Also, just
like those "ordinary" memories, working with them had a powerful
healing effect, and they all fit together seamlessly to tell a consistent
story with no continuity problems. And finally, they all have the
same strong subjective impact – they feel totally real. Additionally, I
should add that all these memories have been subjected to intense
inner exploration and consideration – I don't just believe any
images that appear in my mind to be memories of actual events ipso
facto – they have to satisfy all the conditions I have mentioned
above. Every story in this book fulfills those conditions.

A Separate Reality

*"Maybe each human being lives in a unique world, a private
world different from those inhabited and experienced by all other
humans ... If reality differs from person to person, can we speak of
reality singular, or shouldn't we really be talking about plural
realities?" – Philip K Dick*

There is no reason for me to try and prove anything in this book, because that is not what it's all about. I truly don't care if any of it is believed, although I would like my arguments and discussions to be considered in a rational and scientific way. What I do care about is the impact of my story and information on the lives of others, and I care about the usefulness of what I have shared and what I teach. Once you begin to discover your own inner reality, my story will become superfluous. And if you do recall anything as extraordinary as I have, we are not in the minority. I'm sure there are _billions_ of people on this planet who can consciously recall at least one real paranormal experience.

I have not put much effort into real world validation of my own experiences for myself, because it takes a lot of time and is no longer of any importance to me, although I won't deny it is nice when it happens. Still, I have done much soul searching regarding all this, and here is the million-dollar question: Could this whole story be an elaborate delusion constructed by my unconscious mind? And if so, why? And if I know it's all real, why even ask this question? For me this question is rhetorical, but I ask it first because we _must_ question everything, and second because questions like this will be asked anyway, and I want to address them in advance. Also, most people who do any kind of deep introspection either have recalled, or will recall, things that don't fit with the old paradigm, and they too will be asking questions like this. So this discussion is to provide further support for trusting ourselves.

But to answer the question of why my mind would fabricate elements of my life story that are not true, I would just have to make something up, but I can think of no reason I would do this that would make any sense whatsoever. Life is an adventure and the world has rules. If Patty and I had no spiritual connection, for example, then nothing that happened between us makes any sense at all, since she has been the driving force in my life. Yet everything in my story, from my perspective, fits together perfectly. Also, as I will suggest in the next chapter, our lives are being fabricated right now, imagined into existence by our Higher-Selves. Our lives don't have to follow any rules, but they do – that's part of the fun. Even if we don't understand much of it yet, there certainly is an order to our lives and there apparently _is_ a plan, and the more we know about ourselves, the greater the possibility becomes that we will understand that plan, even if it's just a game.

Experiences that are purely subjective can only be validated by oneself, and most of anyone's specific memories of material life, including yours, may not have a lot of evidence to back them up. But our stories serve as the background for everything we do. Much of my memory of my physical life, in addition to being believable and ordinary, is verifiable to myself, and others to some degree, but there is the possibility that specific elements of my story, both ordinary and extraordinary, do not correspond to real world events, or did not occur in the realities of the people involved. For instance, consider the incident where I was being chased by Terrence and levitated to the ceiling. I have no evidence that it happened in the real world. Although I did have the experience of it, no one remembers it except me. What if I had discussed it with Terence and he told me honestly that he never experienced any such thing, and what if that were true? If what I experienced never happened in his reality in this particular shared physical world, how do I explain that?

Although there is only one consciousness and we are ultimately all one, each of us is experiencing our own personal world. The Identity Model allows for any and all possibilities, and one possibility is that although our realities overlap, they may not always coincide. We may all have alternate lives going on simultaneously, and some of these may even be alternate versions of this life. This sounds very far-fetched I know, but nevertheless, my reality, as I experience it and remember it, is mine alone, just as yours is ultimately yours alone. If sometimes the evidence and the memories of others contradict what we remember, that can be quite disconcerting, but there is always an explanation.

One explanation is that our stories don't always have to mesh. I accept my story as my reality, even if some parts turn out to be separate from the physical reality of others. When we don't really know, it's easy to call such a discrepancy a delusion, a hallucination, a memory problem, or some other kind of mistake, and it may be. But it may also be that sometimes our separate realities play out differently because on some level we each prefer a different storyline. If this is true, it may cause confusion and other problems in our _shared_ storyline, but that doesn't change the fact that we had a real experience, albeit outside the current consensus world. In fact this happens every night when we dream. All that being said, while there are challenges to my memories, nothing has yet led me to believe that anything I experienced in the real world happened in an alternate reality. I only acknowledge the possibility. There are also people who have experienced unusual phenomena for which there is little or no physical evidence to support their claims – phenomena like alien abduction or satanic ritual abuse, among other things. Research indicates that such people often show the signs that something real and external happened to them – that it's not all in their heads – even though no physical evidence can be found. I can't explain these mysteries, but I can accept the possibility that these experiences are totally real. Perhaps they happened on a nonphysical level, in a past life, or they happened in an alternate reality – or maybe the evidence has simply been too well concealed – there are many possibilities.

As for me, there are no living witnesses who recall seeing me do anything miraculous, beyond wimpy ESP, as far as I know. My ex-girlfriend Natalie called me one morning in the '80s, and excitedly told me that I visited her the previous night while I was having an OBE. She was awakened and saw me hovering there in her room, smiling at her. This was totally real for her, but I didn't remember doing it. In the past when I read people's minds or communicated with others telepathically, I often got immediate validation, as I have described with Lynne. The most gratifying validations I get from others about the past, occur when we can share our memories of an experience we had together. I also feel validated when other people report experiences similar to mine that are either miraculous or otherwise subject to skepticism, and of which they have no doubt. While personal reality is subjective, objective reality is conceptual – it's a consensus of personal realities and requires agreement. There is no objective reality outside of our agreements about our own subjective realities.

The ideas in this chapter are primarily presented here to help you navigate your own reality. This whole book is about healing and self-discovery and finding a way to make sense of it all. For me, the Identity Model places my life and experiences in a feasible structure that, while it certainly doesn't explain everything, at least it makes sense to me and provides a solid theoretical foundation for a very workable program. We'll get deeper into this model in the next chapter.

* *

The Platoon Class

About half way through sixth grade our class started attending an hour-long science class held in the "science room," and taught by a teacher from another school. It was called a platoon class, and twice a week we would form a line and walk from our classroom down the hall and though the cafeteria to the new room. Mrs. Preston was in her thirties, had dark hair and blue eyes. She was a very good teacher and I liked her immediately. I would clown around with my friends in class, and when she caught me she was always firm but never mean. For some reason I felt like I knew her and my attention was drawn to her. It was curious; it was as if she had some secret wisdom or something, and if I paid attention I might see what it was.

One day Mrs. Preston mentioned that she had a daughter. Hearing this made me catch my breath. I was in a kind of stupor until class ended, and I was the last to leave. But ten feet out the door I stopped and seemed to have some intense conversation with myself. I then headed back into the room where she was on her knees putting away some books in a cabinet near the floor. I squatted down beside her and asked "So you have a daughter?" She said "I have two children. I have a son named Daniel and a daughter named Patricia." There seemed to be a hint of sadness in her voice – I don't know why, but I still remember the deliberate and restrained way she said their names, and I thought maybe one of her children might be ill or even dying.

Well, one day about a week or two later I walked into the classroom late, after the last recess period, and something was up! Something was new! Something inside me was literally jumping out of my skin! It was as if my vision suddenly left my body and was scanning the whole room. Physically, I stopped in my tracks next to the teacher's desk. I felt disoriented and elated at the same time. And then I saw her – that girl from before – the one I somehow knew!

In this classroom there were about thirty or more chair-desks in two sections, with about half on each side of the room and a large aisle down the middle. She was sitting in the middle on the side to my left. I deliberately walked past her and instead of sitting in my usual spot in the middle, I sat behind her in the section on the other side of the room. For some reason I was being careful. Mrs. Preston introduced her as her daughter Patty, who was from a different school and would be sitting in with our class for a few days.

I was distracted the whole hour, but when class was dismissed I got up intending to follow Patty but instead I turned around and walked to the rear of the room. I stood in front of the science display table which exhibited various unusual objects. I found myself staring down at the smooth bleached skull of a goat beneath the glass top of the long, waist-high display case, until Patty was gone. I don't remember what happened after that.

Patty attended the platoon class only a few more times, but each time I felt compelled to sit behind her so as not to be noticed. This was all very different from what happened in the "safety" class, and it was very mysterious. Also during the days Patty was there I seemed to lose track of time and sometimes left the class with a big headache.

In the session where I recalled this incident I was working on a dream I had that morning. In the dream, which was more like a vision, the elongated bleached skull of an animal appeared to hover in front of me as I was waking up. It was three-dimensional and amazingly vivid, which compelled me to investigate.

✳ ✳

Part IV

♻

Models of Transformation

✳ ✳

Chapter 17
The Identity Model of Consciousness

"New scientific ideas never spring from a communal body, however organized, but rather from the head of an individually inspired researcher who struggles with his problems in lonely thought and unites all his thought on one single point which is his whole world for the moment." – Max Planck

"And yet, in regard to the nature of things, this knowledge [physical science] is only an empty shell – a form of symbols. It is knowledge of structural form, and not knowledge of content. All through the physical world runs that unknown content, which must surely be the stuff of our consciousness."
– Sir Arthur Eddington – Space, Time, and Gravitation, 1920

Traditional science has gotten things backwards. Physicist Sean Carroll once said, in a statement opposing the idea of intelligent design, that the only assumption scientists make is that the world is not playing a trick on us. Well that's ridiculous! Firstly, even if he presumes to speak for all "scientists," this is <u>not</u> the only assumption scientists make. Scientists make many assumptions, most of which they are unaware, but which guide their thinking. Rupert Sheldrake covers a few of the more traditional and universal of these assumptions in his book The Science Delusion, but there are many more assumptions we make than he mentions.[73] Now there is nothing wrong with an assumption, as long as we are aware that it is only an assumption and may be entirely wrong. Secondly, I'm sure most scientists never even consider that they are being tricked by the world. That would imply deceptive intent by an intelligent

---

[73] "The Science Delusion" – 2012, by Rupert Sheldrake. This book was renamed "Science Set Free" in the U.S.

universe. They are however being deceived by their own minds. We all are.

When a magician creates an illusion, like materializing a rabbit out of an empty hat, it works because we are maneuvered into making some assumptions: we assume the hat was really empty or that the rabbit was not placed in the hat while we were being distracted, and we assume that we saw everything relevant that was going on. When we attempt to unlock the secrets of the universe by scientific investigation, it is easy for us to deceive ourselves by the assumptions we make, assumptions like objectivity, cause and effect, time and space, that consciousness has nothing to do with what we perceive, that we are not dreaming, and many others. One basic and rather arrogant yet perhaps necessary assumption is that our perceptions and our intelligence are sufficiently evolved to allow us to comprehend the universe, while in fact we have no idea if this is true. It is important that we find the humility to keep this in mind. There are also fundamental assumptions we all make as human beings, causing us to see the world in a certain way – but nothing is what it seems to be. This was revealed in the Upanishads more than four thousand years ago, that the world *IS* in fact, an illusion; it is not what it appears to be. If this is so, then reality, as we experience it, *IS* a trick, but one which we are playing on ourselves.

As I said earlier, the Identity Model of Consciousness is my attempt to make sense of the kinds of paranormal things most of us have experienced, from the viewpoint that these experiences provide real data about our conscious reality and the universe. This model is a radically empirical and pragmatic phenomenology. This mouthful of words just means that it's based on experience alone and attempts to understand the meanings and relationships of all the things we experience in a practical and useful way. It starts with the presumption that anything is theoretically possible until the basic fundamentals of existence are completely understood – that we can't really know anything for sure until we know everything. Like Eddington said in the quote above, we may know structure to some degree but we do not know content – what it all really is. But he also gave us the answer – consciousness. There are many models of existence and they all begin with assumptions, which are often in the form of unfounded or weakly founded, axioms – but even self-evident truths can be challenged. The Identity Model has a lot in common with other current models that hold consciousness to be fundamental or foundational in the universe, and is actually very simple. In fact I have already described it in bits and pieces throughout this book, so this chapter is basically a summary and discussion. We'll start with a deeper exploration of consciousness itself.

Virtual Reality

"The body itself is imagined in the Self, as is the whole universe."
– The Advadhuta Gita

A virtual reality is a simulation in which we experience something that isn't actually there in an objective way. A photograph is a simple example; you see a person but the person is not physically present. When watching a movie we hear and see the events on the screen and may even respond emotionally to the realism, but the people and events we perceive aren't really there, even in a 3D movie with surround sound with vibrating seats. Modern virtual reality gear can create extraordinary computer generated perceptions that seem very real. But a virtual reality experience is like a dream – a real experience but one that is not happening in our normally perceived physical environment. When we imagine something, like eating a delicious meal, or we reminisce about a conversation we had with a friend, we are creating our own virtual reality in our minds. But the line between what is real and what is virtual is purely conceptual. The Holodeck depicted on Star Trek TNG projected a simulated perceptual reality, with real physical objects one could interact with. The environments, people, and objects that were thus projected were simply not what they appeared to be, only sophisticated temporary forms. But since our "real" physical world also consists of sophisticated temporary forms, what's the difference? Perhaps our world is also not what it appears to be.

There are many ways to trick our minds into believing something is real. As conscious experience, all of our experience is real of course, regardless of what is causing it, but whether an experience is a virtual reality or an actual reality ultimately depends on the source of that experience. Is the source a movie projector, a VR headset, a computer, your imagination, a dream, a hypnotic suggestion, a hallucination, or the external world? Of course we may believe that our familiar external world is the only _true_ reality, but any "reality" is simply whatever you _believe_ is real in the moment. If there is a fundamental "rock bottom" reality, it would be a basic underlying foundational truth or system of principles, that is unchanging, regardless of anything else. Although that is also an assumption, most of us believe the physical world _is_ that reality. However, since we can only surmise the existence of a world outside of our experience, this is little more than a hypothesis, which I will explain shortly.

Presently the predominant mainstream materialist belief is that consciousness, including everything we experience, is the result of brain activity, or at least connected with it, and resides within our brains and nervous systems. This means we have no direct experience of anything we think of as being "out there" – that is, outside of our bodies or ourselves. Instead we are only interpreting nervous impulses from sense organs, out of which our brains create the entire universe of our experiences. In other words, _everything we experience is a virtual reality_, and our entire world and universe exists only in our heads. The wonderfully aromatic cup of hot coffee in your hands is an experience your mind has constructed from impulses relayed, supposedly, from the coffee cup's physical counterpart in an invisible, silent, yet "real" world – a world we can never see, hear, touch, or know directly.

Although we might understand and believe this scientific view, probably few of us ever contemplate what this really means or implies. It means we can never know that the world we experience is not some kind of dream – just like the world of the Matrix – a fabricated reality which is not a perception of any world "out there" that we think we are interacting with, but which is being generated from within. In the Matrix the impulses that created the sensations of being in a real world were generated by a computer, and piped into the brains of people who were plugged into it while they were asleep to the "real" outer world. But people were able to wake up from the Matrix to discover the truth.

When I was eighteen, I had this idea, which I probably got from watching Star Trek, long before the Matrix, that in the distant future we could build a computer that was indestructible and into which we could transfer our individual conscious minds so that we could all live forever in a utopian world – a virtual reality that was fully under our own control. This concept has been recently dramatized in the great futuristic TV series "Upload" from 2020. I envisioned that such a project would eventually include every conscious being in the universe. At that time I still thought that consciousness might be a product of a physical reality. My plan was based on many questionable assumptions, but the idea was that we could end all suffering and be eternally free. But if we are not experiencing a real physical world right now, as we believe we are, what are we experiencing? If we can't know if there really is an "external world," how can we truly know what we are, where we came from, or where we go after we die. Although we may adopt various religious, scientific, or philosophical theories to answer these questions, unless we have had some deep personal insight into ourselves, everything we believe about these things is purely conjecture. The profound implication of all this is that everything in the universe, as far as we can ever know, is only happening _inside_ us. There is nothing "out there." This is it! Which means we ARE experiencing the world directly – our experience IS the world. So what is experience? And what are we?

Consciousness and Space
"A map is not the territory it represents, but, if correct, it has a similar structure to the territory, which accounts for its usefulness."
– Alfred Korzybski, Science and Sanity

Like a map of the Earth showing the relative location of roads, rivers, and mountains, a "model" depicts an organization of things to describe the way in which they fit together, or interact and work together. Our model of chemistry depicts the structure and classification of atoms and molecules, describes chemical reactions and molecular bonds, and has practical applications. Models can also be improved upon or discarded in favor of better ones, which happens all the time, because models are just representations, and as statistician George Box said "All models are wrong but some are useful." The model presented here is a useful, but temporary construct to explain our experiences.

The Identity Model of Consciousness is not really a model of consciousness itself, but rather a model of how consciousness operates in creating the universe. In actuality consciousness itself cannot be modeled in the same way we could model, say, a new territory, an effective organization, a birthday party, or a molecule. Consciousness is similar to "space" in this regard. Even though space is an aspect of the material universe, and although every physical thing exists within it, we can't really model space itself. We know about space because of all the things it contains, like the Earth, stars, trees, cars, and people, and if there were no space, no "thing" could exist at all, at least not as we presently understand "things." So any model of the physical universe has to include space, and time as well, as necessary elements prior to anything else. And you are probably aware that even atoms are mostly space, being themselves an organization of subatomic particles in a sort of dance, with a nucleus in the center and electrons forming an outer shell with a comparatively vast space in between. An atom is 99.9999% empty space. And what are those subatomic particles made of? How much of each particle is empty space? When we get down to the smallest particles, we may find that they are just vibrations in space – like some kind of superstrings.[74] In the end, from a purely physical perspective, it may be that all of material existence consists of nothing more than modulations of space-time itself, much as waves in the ocean are just modulations of water!

And what *is* this thing we call space or space-time? Good question, since we might assume that even our hypothetical superstrings have to exist in some sort of etheric medium such as space. But the Michelson/Morley experiment seemed to rule out that space was any sort of "medium," so how could anything vibrate in it? But then space couldn't be purely "nothingness" could it? Who knows? There is the idea in theoretical physics that even space and time did not exist before the hypothetical Big Bang, that

---

[74] Superstrings are hypothetical particles that exists as vibrations in multiple dimensions of space-time. They are the foundation of every other particle in existence. Or something like that.

primordial nanosecond in which the entire space-time-energy-matter of the universe suddenly burst into existence. To even imagine this we would have to be able to imagine that "nothing" existed before that moment. But we can't actually conceive of "nothing" or nothingness. Sure we can imagine the absence of something, or an empty box, but not of the complete nonexistence of anything and everything – it can't be done. In fact the attempt to do so makes for a good Zen koan.[75] It's the same for "infinity" – we can understand what that word implies but we can't actually grasp it as an experience. Infinity is the imaginary end result of a process, like counting forever, just as nothingness is the imaginary end result of a process of removing everything, including space, time, and imagination. Space-time is the recognition of objective relationships like direction, distance, and motion between objects. Hence we describe space by the relationship of the objects and activities that occur within it, without knowing exactly what it is.

Similarly, although the Identity Model of Consciousness is not actually about describing consciousness, it is about describing the basic organization of what is _in_ consciousness, which happens to be _everything!_

The reality is that consciousness itself can only be described or defined by words that mean the same thing – words like "awareness" or "experience." So while its actual essence can be assigned words, consciousness itself cannot actually be described in relationship to anything else, as every other "thing" can. It can't be plugged into an equation – it doesn't fit those rules. Many have tried to explain consciousness but the reality is that consciousness cannot be explained directly. In fact it can't be "understood" at all – it's not a thinking problem. It's like the square root of a negative number in this regard. We can assume there is such a thing, give it a symbol, and call it an "imaginary" number but we can't really explain what it is beyond that. It's something that can't be, but is. It's a paradox. We can define consciousness as that which allows us to have experiences, or as "the knowing of experience," which is about the best we can do, but we've only sort of pointed to it; the real meaning must be intuited. And it is – we all know what

---

[75] The famous Zen koan "Mu" basically means "nothingness."

consciousness means, even though we can't explain it. Accordingly, any theory of consciousness is a theory of *US* – of "this" right here – this presence each of us calls "me."

So the Identity Model is about understanding that the universe is fundamentally nothing <u>*but*</u> consciousness, out of which has been created a system of relationships between conscious agents. Conscious agents are conscious entities. They are dynamic viewpoints in consciousness, like you and me, and include all the conscious experiences we have, like perceptions, thoughts, actions, and emotions. Even though consciousness itself can neither be defined, described, nor scientifically proven to exist, we still have to talk about it, and that can be a little bit tricky, but let's dive in.

What Is Consciousness?

So what is consciousness anyway? Well, as was once infamously expressed, "It depends upon what the meaning of the word 'is' … is." In this case it's true. "*IS*" is the present tense of the verb "to be" which means "existence." Yet consciousness does not exist because it is not a thing. We can't point to it and say "There it is." Consciousness is existence itself – it *IS* the *IS* It is the field in which all things appear to exist. And it so happens that Existence itself, the underlying substratum of everything, is self-aware. That is simply the nature of Existence. It didn't become that way, but rather it simply *IS* that way, always was, and there is no other way for it to be. Existence is consciousness.

Since consciousness is pure existence, the moment we try to explain it, we have left the realm of existence itself to talk about things that exist within that realm, like experiences or states of mind. The proof of consciousness is personal and subjective only, as is our own personal reality. Only consciousness is conscious, and there is, and can be, no objective proof of consciousness. So haven't I just explained or defined consciousness? No, not really. We can define the word anyway we like, but what it stands for cannot be described, and calling it "existence" or "being" simply points our attention away from everything else, although that may be a bit difficult to grasp. So existence is still an unknown, and as I said, consciousness cannot be understood by thinking, since it lies outside the realm of thought. We can only understand it mentally in terms of its creations. But we can understand it intuitively on its own terms when we transcend thought and the realm of creation, which is the realm of forms. We'll consider how to do that later.[76]

All that being said, consciousness is not a mystery unless we try to make it into a thing, a phenomenon which somehow evolved from that which was not conscious. Then it can _never_ be understood. We will explore this in more depth in Chapter 21, but understand that the activity of human beings trying to investigate consciousness is really consciousness pretending to investigate itself. "Being," the ultimate nature of the universe, already knows itself as Being, not through any process, but because that is what Being _IS_, whether we call it consciousness, being, existence, knowingness, awareness, nature, spirit, the Self, presence, the universe, infinite intelligence, or God. There is only one Being – one underlying self-knowing reality from which everything springs, and that Being is OUR Being, our everyday, ordinary consciousness, you and me – it is what _we_ fundamentally _are_. Although consciousness can't be proven to exist in any external way, it is the one thing we all know – that we are conscious. I Am! Consciousness proves itself to itself by being itself. Being _IS_ Knowing. It is the only absolute there is – absolute certainty of being – absolute self-luminous reality. If consciousness is "being" then it is a truism that it is UN-consciousness or NON-being that can't exist, except as an idea.

OK, I hope that wasn't too tedious, but now we have a place to start, although it may seem for now somewhat unsatisfying to our thinking minds. Somehow consciousness, the timeless essence of the universe, has brought into existence from itself, our individual minds and the world we know, including time and space, as our personal experience. But how? While materialists postulate that there were as yet unknown non-conscious mechanical forces present in the pre-Big-Bang reality, whatever that was, I have heard no explanations concerning this that make any sense. It's like an

---

[76] I like to capitalize Consciousness (or Existence, or Being) when I want to emphasize its role as the absolute foundation of the universe and the creator, the sustainer, and the intelligence behind everything in existence, and I use its lowercase form to represent awareness in general, and various levels or states of mind. But I'm not always consistent.

atheist version of "and then there was light." I don't have all the answers, but asking the question "How?" in this context, is based on an assumption that there is a time-dependent cause and effect process involved.

Consciousness however does not operate in any sort of mechanical way. In other words, there is no "how" – creation is an instantaneous act with no antecedents – it's a miracle. So while I can't explain "how" consciousness does what it does, any more than I can explain consciousness itself, I can give it a word: "magic." And magic is simply creative intention – imagination – something we all use every day. As the vampire Bill Compton says to Sookie in the TV series "True Blood": "You think that it's not magic that keeps you alive? Just 'cause you understand the mechanics of how something works, doesn't make it any less of a miracle – which is just another word for magic. We're all kept alive by magic, Sookie. My magic's just a little different from yours, that's all."

Everything is Consciousness
"Everything is part of what's creating every other moment – no mind could track all of those interrelationships happening simultaneously." – Adyashanti

Donald Hoffman, a cognitive scientist and author of "The Case Against Reality" suggests that the world we are experiencing is actually an interface between an unseen reality and our conscious minds.[77] Our perceptions are really only representations of the external world, like the icons on a computer screen that represent files and programs which we cannot perceive. We can however use these files and programs by interacting with the icons. He calls his

---

[77] "The Case Against Reality" - Donald Hoffman, 2019. Hoffman's further contention is that our particular representations of the world evolved in us through natural selection to optimize our survival and not to accurately reflect reality. This means that our neural interpretations appear as the images which will most likely insure our survival, and sometimes that means those images misrepresent the truth when that helps us stay alive. It can certainly be shown that our brains are creating illusions all the time in this regard.

model of reality the "Interface Theory of Perception" based on an
ontology called "Conscious Realism" in which consciousness is
fundamental, and the world we perceive consists entirely of
conscious agents. Since we already know we are experiencing a
virtual reality, this idea is most certainly true – that the images in
our minds are only representations of a hidden world that is very
different from what we see. This hidden world is like a movie
projector that is projecting all our experience on the screen of our
awareness. This means there is something _underlying_ our
experience that is determining exactly _what_ we experience. So the
question remains, what _is_ this hidden reality?

Hoffman suggests the idea that there may be no aspect of any
reality that is not a conscious experience by some conscious agent,
if I understand him correctly, and this is my contention as well.
Indeed, if everything is consciousness, then this proposition must be
true, which means that the universe, and everything in it, is simply
a network of conscious beings interacting with each other. The
Identity Model is primarily a description of this network and how it
might be set up.

Earlier in discussing levels of awareness I described a very basic
hierarchy of beings consisting of Higher-Selves, Lower-Selves, and
various levels of identity within the Lower-Selves. In my model, the
entire universe is being created and run by a set of rules held by
consciousness – ideas in the mind of God if you will. So the hidden
reality underlying all our experience is nothing other than these
very rules. These rules determine what each lower being in the
hierarchy will experience in any situation. This is just like a video
game where the programming determines that if you push a button,
something happens on the screen. Similarly, there is no "real tree"
behind our experience of the tree, but only the rules that cause us
to perceive the tree in some way if we encounter it. To say it
another way, these rules are simply the so-called natural laws that
run the universe. For example, the rules say if I turn around and
look behind me as I sit in my office, I will see a bookcase filled with
books. In our experiential domain as human beings on Earth, these
natural laws are none other than the principles of physics,
chemistry, biology, psychology, neurology, and metaphysics –
principles we discover and explore through observation using
science and logic. These laws are consciously held thoughts by

which consciousness conceives every detail of our lives, moment by moment, like the screenplay of a movie. Everything we experience happens according to that screenplay, and the reality that unfolds is the pure creation of imagination. Of course these rules are infinitely vast and complex and consistently implemented, and, as Cypher says in the movie, "there's way too much information to decode the Matrix." In other words our individual minds can never understand it all, and aren't meant to, although we can strive to understand more, as we are doing right now.

Not only is everything a creation of consciousness, but it's important to understand that everything we experience is also _made_ of consciousness. If you imagine holding an apple in your hand, what is the apple made of? Or an apple in a dream? They are purely imagination, mental images, modulations of consciousness. A dream apple has no seeds or cells or atoms, unless you imagine them. You might think of imaginary images or dream images as energy, but this would just be an idea. It's simpler than that. On the experiential level, the only level we can know them on, they are really just something we are aware of – forms within consciousness, like waves in an ocean, each wave different in its own way, but still just water. An imagined apple is consciousness in the form of an apple, and it's the same with a physical apple and everything else – every sight, sound, thought, or feeling. Nothing we experience or know can be anything other than consciousness. How all these forms can be so different and still just be forms of the same "substance" so to speak, is a good question. That's the magic of imagination!

Now if consciousness itself has the ability to _do_ anything at all, its abilities must be intrinsic to its nature. Just as the self-knowing nature of consciousness is its fundamental quality, so too must be its ability to imagine, to create. Since this seems to me to be the way it is, then consciousness, as the essence, power, and intelligence behind everything, is where the Identity Model starts. My contention is that consciousness is omniscient, omnipresent, eternal, immutable, and omnipotent, and that consciousness is the only thing there really is. If you try to find something that is not consciousness, all you will find is an idea that only exists within the consciousness of your own mind. I feel at least as justified in starting here as physicists may feel about assuming there are as yet undiscovered physical forces that brought the entire universe into being from a theoretical "unstable nothingness," as I heard one scientist call it. I think my nonsense is as at least as good as his.

Identification

"...the word consciousness to-day does no more than signalize the fact that experience is indefeasibly dualistic in structure. It means that not subject, not object, but object-plus-subject is the minimum that can actually be." – William James, "Does Consciousness Exist?"

Kidding aside, consciousness does appear to have all the qualities I just described, when considering it from a human perspective. In order to create conscious beings and the worlds they inhabit, consciousness appears to operate through *IDENTITY*. Everything that exists, only exists as conscious experience, and all experience requires an experiencer, a witness. The observer and the observed, self and other, form the essence of duality, and the impression that I am separate from everything I experience. Also, for an observer or "self" to exist there must be a sense of identification where the observer, at the very least, has a sense that it is separate from what it is observing or experiencing. Identification itself is difficult to explain, and it will be discussed more in the section on enlightenment, but for now we can just think of it as the sense of "I," as "I am"– one's personal sense of being.

When there is only empty consciousness present, without any forms, then we could say that the witness and the experience are one, although in actuality neither exists – there is nothing to witness. This is simply consciousness being (and knowing) itself, which is not something that can be imagined or described, even though it's happening in all of us right now. If there are forms (experiences) present but consciousness is seeing these forms as itself, without any differentiation, then the forms are moot, and nothing actually exists at all! I imagine these forms would be more like disembodied thoughts or possibilities. Consciousness therefore creates through the process of identification, which requires an imaginary separation of "self and other" because, as I said, and as James says in the quote above, nothing can exist without a witness.

However, this impression of there being a witness is an illusion. This supposedly separate entity "I" is imaginary and does not really exist at all, any more than water exists in a mirage. This does not mean that "you" don't exist, but it begs the question: what are you really?

As I hope will become clear in the discussion of enlightenment in Chapter 21, language is not adequate at this point to truly describe the shift from discussing the unitary field of pure consciousness, which has no inner distinctions, to the world of duality which we appear to inhabit, which is nothing _but_ distinctions and their relationships. I use phrases like "seems to be" and "appears to" a lot, as modifiers, because everything is an appearance, just as the images in a dream are appearances that "seem to be" what they represent. But we do not know that dreams are only appearances until we wake up from them and can evaluate them from a higher level of awareness and understanding. Anyway, my description of the basic structure of what appears to be going on may seem to imply that it takes place in time and in a particular sequence, but it's really about the totality of what is taking place in the present moment. Neither time nor cause and effect are involved in this creation, which is why we can't answer the question of "how" consciousness does what it does.

On the highest level then, consciousness creates imaginary separations within itself in the form of separate dynamic viewpoints – separate "Selves." These primary selves are what I call our Higher-Selves. Their separation is basically an intention that all experience within the minds of these Selves is private and is not shared with the other Selves. And this brings us to the definition of "mind." In this model, an individual mind is the totality of thoughts, forms, and abilities contained within one individuated Self. This setup is actually a game – it's just a story and purely make-believe.

Now these Higher-Selves are conscious agents, or entities, and have no inherent limitations. They in turn create their own imaginary worlds, and they populate and inhabit these worlds with viewpoints _they_ create and maintain within themselves which are therefore also conscious beings but _with_ limitations. These "sub-viewpoints" or Lower-Selves, are people like you and me as well as every other conscious being in our world, all of whom also appear to be separate from each other, and their limitations are intentional.

Remember, consciousness is just imagining all of this, and none of it is true except as a fantasy, even though the experiences created are absolutely "real" experiences and don't seem like fantasies at all. But our experiences are only modulations of consciousness, and the only thing that is real about them is our knowing of them, which is consciousness itself. This means that our experiences are only "real" as long as we don't see the deeper truth. From the lower viewpoints that we inhabit we can also create our own worlds and sub-beings, as we do in a limited way every night when we dream. Our dreams are conscious realities but usually with a very low sense of presence and very different rules.

Our Higher-Selves also communicate and share stories together in which their Lower-Selves can also interact. And these Lower-Selves also have different Levels of awareness, which I described in Chapter 15.[78] To recap, Level–2 is the level above normal waking-life consciousness, which is Level–1. Level–2.1 is a higher aspect of Level–2 that can't be remembered. Level 3 is the Higher Self, and Level–0 is the level of dreams. These level numbers are arbitrary, and the actual structure of things is likely much more complicated. The vastness of "all-that-is" is quite unfathomable. If we try to conceive of one mind doing all these things, creating zillions of other beings and operating each of them as they create sub-beings and zillions of other worlds as well as every atom, particle, and wave within them, it is of course literally unimaginable. But consciousness does this with no effort, no energy, and no difficulty whatsoever because it has no limitations or boundaries. You could call it an "all-powerful nothingness," but it is certainly not unstable.

Anyway, we have no problem thinking that a universe governed by physical laws can have those laws operating effortlessly and identically in every cubic nanometer of infinite space, because those principles, we assume, are somehow omnipresent and built into the entire space-time continuum of the universe. My main

---

[78] To reiterate, when I say levels of awareness I really mean levels of mind or levels of "awareness of," like levels in a video game. Although these terms are useful, and I use them a lot, there are really no "levels" of awareness or consciousness, only levels of mind which are domains within consciousness.

contention is that the universe is also self-aware and every principle in existence that governs everything we ever experience is a conscious act of creation. Furthermore, every particle in existence is really only a thought, a rule, information, in an underlying framework for the ongoing story of life – a framework which is only about determining what you and I and everyone else will experience in the next moment, as time unfolds. There are no actual particles anywhere, just as in the video game Super Mario Brothers, there is really no Mario, and no princess to rescue.

When we start with consciousness as the fundamental underlying reality of existence it solves a lot of problems, including the so called "hard problem of consciousness," the question of how consciousness could arise from unconscious matter and energy – this question simply disappears. Consciousness never arose from anything, nor is it a quality or property that anything has – it is existence itself and all things arise from IT.

What is perhaps the most difficult thing to comprehend in any universal model of consciousness is the idea that there is only one all-pervasive consciousness through which we all experience life as separate individuals. When I realized I had multiple personalities who were not me, and yet with whom I could merge, I found this totally baffling. I could not conceive of how there could exist another conscious "me" that I was unaware of. And yet there were many! This is also the case with all of us – our consciousness is not separate, only our minds. One metaphor I like to use is this. If you wiggle one of your big toes, you can feel it. Now if you wiggle a thumb you can feel that too. But does your toe feel your thumb? No – those two experiences are separate. You could say that one doesn't know the other. And yet these two experiences are ONE in YOU – you experience them both. Still, there is an apparent separation there. In the same sense we are all like the toes and fingers of a greater being, and we normally do not experience each other's feeling, thoughts, and perceptions although these are ALL experienced by the one consciousness at a level beyond mind. And this one consciousness is also OUR consciousness! It's only baffling while we remain confined to our limited viewpoints. But when we quiet our minds we can actually tap into that universal awareness and we actually CAN experience more than our limited perceptions normally allow. In fact we are picking up transpersonal impressions all the time without realizing it.

My model is most closely aligned with that of philosopher and computer engineer Bernardo Kastrup. In his book "Why Materialism Is Baloney" (2014) he suggests that the apparent separation between you and me and every other separate individual in the universe is similar to the dissociative separation between alter personalities in someone with multiple personalities. My own experience with multiple personalities is, in fact, how I came up with this idea myself. Kastrup calls the means of separation between individuals a "dissociative barrier," which is fine as a descriptive term. For me this description is metaphorical – there's no actual barrier as such. This dissociative separation is actually an illusion created by the Higher-Selves, just as the separation of Higher-Selves is an illusion created by Consciousness itself. The upshot of this is that we are all the multiple personalities of God, the one consciousness that creates and experiences everything we do, and which does this for all beings everywhere, and all at once. And this all seems to happen in a hierarchical way, similar to what I've described. Ultimately though, we truly are all one.

The Short Version

That was the long explanation of the underlying foundation of things. The short description is that consciousness creates separate dynamic viewpoints, Beings, our Higher-Selves, which create Lower-Selves like you and me through the illusion of separation and identification. The Higher-Selves then create countless worlds for us to inhabit, and unlimited games for us to play. Consciousness does all this using only imagination, creating forms within itself, from itself. You and I also have different levels of awareness and ability that we operate from, and all of this happens according to a plan following a set of principles and rules. In playing out the game of life together we are creating our own interactive and never-ending stories. I have no doubt however, that the actual organization of things is vastly more complex (or perhaps more simple) than I could ever imagine, involving multiple levels, hierarchies, variations, mazes within mazes, and other fantastical things. I realize that my model is of course incomplete and unsatisfactory on many levels, but it's a beginning. Still, as a preliminary gesture it does account for much if not all of human experience, including the spiritual and paranormal, as do other models that see consciousness as the fundamental underlying reality.

Now let's take a closer look at the ideas of self and mind. A so called "self" is most simply described as a "witness," a dynamic conscious viewpoint (person) that is aware of a world seemingly outside itself. The witness is therefore a particular viewpoint in "the All" (the totality of consciousness and its creations), and it is aware of whatever experiences are presented to it as well as whatever it creates for itself. This apparent duality of "self and other" exists in a kind of bubble of perception, or a separation of perception, at the very least. The bubble demarcates the boundary of an individual mind, which is that private subjective world in which the witness apparently resides. In other words we each live in our own private dreamworld, even as we seem to share that world with others through an interactive program, very much as was depicted in The Matrix, except that in our case the program is the will of Consciousness itself, which through our higher level selves, creates everything that happens. Our personal identification can then expand from the simple viewpoint of being a witness, to identification with a particular form such as a body, a personality, a story, a spirit, and countless other things within our world. Whatever we become strongly identified with then becomes an attachment that we take to be ourselves.

A basic overall identity can be simple or complex, and can also have many layers – we are a body, a human, male or female, straight or nonbinary, rich or poor, successful or struggling, happy or depressed. From there we might be a father, a mother, a manager, a queen, a president, a doctor, a soldier, a clown, a guru, or a deity, and those identities may be further modulated by attitudes like being important, loved, hated, needed, a hero, a victim, a villain, a winner, or a loser. Hence we can all have a huge supply of identities, both reactive and nonreactive, that can come into play at any time – whatever the game requires. But none of these things are who we really are. They are only roles, and even our roles can play different roles. Clarity is the first step in waking up out of all this identification and attachment into to a greater freedom, and that starts with recognizing that before any of this, we are the witness. We can start this process by simply asking ourselves "Who is experiencing all these identity states?" Then we can begin to move beyond even being the witness – beyond identification and separation altogether.

Models of the Universe

Since the universe is a creation of imagination and emerges from essentially nothing, that is, since it emerges from something that is not a thing but which is prior to "things," it has no inherent laws or structure other than those dreamed up by consciousness. There is no way that the universe _has_ to be, any more than a game has to be poker, basketball, or Minecraft – there is an infinity of possible games that can exist and an infinity of possible universes and structures that can exist as well. From a materialist viewpoint, according to physicists, even the theoretical Big Bang could have resulted in a universe with entirely different physical laws, including laws which do not even support life of any kind. And perhaps there are also many other universes created in other Big Bangs existing in their own alternate dimensions right now. So according to that theory too, there are many possible forms a universe can take. Different universes are really just different games, different Disneylands if you will, with many different rides and adventure theme parks. I've heard descriptions of many different kinds of universes that some people have claimed to have experienced, and they all have their own rules. But regardless of the nature of the various universes, be they heavenly, hellish, or something in between, they are all worlds of conscious experience – dreamscapes to play in.

So here we are, sharing this present world where at this time the predominant model of reality in the minds of humans is a material one, and that works just fine on the physical level. And this model will continue to evolve as we explore, experiment, and learn more about it. But when we try to incorporate our mental, spiritual, and paranormal experiences into this materialistic paradigm and they don't fit, we simply have to come up with something better to explain everything, rather than acknowledging only the facts that support our preconceptions. That's how science works. But there are many forces working against this particular change because, like I said, there is a conspiracy to hide the truth. That conspiracy however is unconscious and lies mainly within each of us individually.

In Castaneda's book "Tales of Power" Don Juan says to Carlos: "As one can see, the black magicians have already engaged all your allegiance." Carlos asks: "Who are the black magicians Don Juan?" "Our fellow men are the black magicians. And since you are with them, you too are a black magician. Think for a moment. Can you deviate from the path that they've lined up for you? No, Your thoughts and your actions are fixed forever in their terms. That is slavery."

With most of us conditioned and programmed since birth to see things in a certain way and to believe certain things, there is not only strong internal resistance to seeing things differently, but we ourselves become the enforcers of the consensus worldview that has captured us. While this indoctrination includes every aspect of life, varying with the social group we live in, when it comes to the materialist view of reality. _WE are the black magicians_. Even while there are countless variations of viewpoints within the basic materialist worldview, and a few ideologies that threaten to break out of it, most of us lie within its domain of influence and help sustain that influence. When faced with contrary information or anything that threatens the sanctity of our accepted paradigm, our reactions can run the gamut of emotions from curiosity and healthy skepticism, to suspicion, rejection, and cynicism, and all the way to pathological skepticism, fear, terror, anger, and violence. Even those who sincerely investigate this stuff suffer from this programming, including me. But all this can be overcome, even though much of this programming was put in place even before we were born.

The Earth Protocol

This is something I partially recall, and similar scenarios have been described by others, and that is that prior to being allowed to participate in this lifetime as a human being we had to agree to some rules, including that we forget our past lives and previous identities. I recall experiencing part of my indoctrination prior to this lifetime, and I have heard many similar descriptions of this process. In Michael Newton's 1994 book "Journey of Souls" for example, where hypnotherapy clients are regressed to looking at the "between-lives area" after recalling a past death, this forgetting is also described as an agreement. However the blocking of memory occurs on an unconscious level as a program, and such programs can be resolved.

One of the rules we agree to is what I call the "Earth Protocol." I considered calling it the "Prime Directive," because it does have some similarities to Star Trek's non-interference order which dictates that, as interstellar travelers, we are forbidden to reveal our advanced technology to less-evolved societies who aren't ready for it, lest they destroy themselves. The Earth Protocol addresses the fact that we are powerful beings who have agreed to operate at a reduced level as characters in a "lesser" game.[79] It simply demands that we play by the rules. This means that as human beings we can only use the natural abilities inherent in our biological forms, and a few of our lesser spiritual abilities, while we are here. We are not permitted to demonstrate our greater powers to others, at least not in any massive way, in the event that we are able to gain access to them. In other words, if I find I can levitate objects by my will alone, I can't join a circus and make a million bucks touring the world levitating pies. Those are the rules. But we all cheat a little, and sometimes a lot.

So the reason paranormal abilities and miracles aren't prime time news is ultimately because this is not allowed, and even if some of us somehow revive such abilities, we would immediately be reminded of our agreements to keep them private. I don't understand much about all these things or the subtleties of these particular rules, but I have received reminders of my agreement with these rules when I considered actions that would break them. I have also experienced "cease and desist" orders, and their enforcement when I broke the rules, many times, from the higher authorities who oversee these things. There does seem to be a relaxing of this protocol around spiritually awakened people, but I

---

[79] I call this a "lesser" game because even being a powerful "godlike being" is a game and not what we really are.

don't know why, or to what degree. It may also be that if enough people adopt a new paradigm and we develop a new general consensus, these rules can change.

But even if it were suddenly allowed at the current time, any public display of any real psychic ability that is not just a magic trick, would predominantly be met by others with fear, and, as depicted in scores of movies, government intervention. Even as it is, people reporting these kinds of experiences are often subject to intense ridicule and persecution, and are confronted with completely irrational arguments to debunk their claims, which is why so many times such things are never reported. If you yourself have recalled similar "unexplainable" things that you have done or experienced and which you've kept to yourself and dare not talk about, you know exactly what I mean.

Swedenborg and the Spiritual Universe

We explore our outer material world with the tools it provides, which includes our bodies, our senses, and the tools we create through technology, and we use our intellect to understand it all. To investigate the greater spiritual universe however, we have to go within ourselves where understanding involves more than intellect alone, and where the only tools we have are our own minds and inner resources. And that is exactly what Emanuel Swedenborg did back in the eighteenth century. After mastering most of the sciences of his day, for which he was quite renown, he began an inner exploration that is still one of the most profound spiritual journeys ever recorded. He visited heavens and hells and other worlds, spoke with God, Jesus, angels, demons, aliens, spirits, and deceased people, and described and elucidated many aspects of the spiritual universe. Being the son of a Christian minister, Swedenborg interpreted his experiences in biblical terms, and his visions revealed to him a new and profound understanding of the Bible as a great metaphor. He of course filtered his visions through his own cultural lens, and I suspect that if he had been a Hindu, a Hopi Indian, or a Zulu shaman, he would have been shown things in a different way, and would have had to integrate his discoveries with a different cultural worldview. So I believe what he described was itself a metaphor, and only one particular way of seeing our local universe, out of infinite possible variations. Nevertheless, his writings can be of great value to those who can relate to his Christian views, or who can see his work in a larger context, as I do.

To me, Swedenborg is describing a view of how the vast network of conscious beings and forces that we are a part of, functions. Although I have read little of his work, I do find Swedenborg's experiences and ideas useful and inspiring. And he does say that each of us comprises our own world, and our own Heaven and Hell, and describes it all as a manifestation of the One. Please understand that I'm not saying that anything Swedenborg or anyone else says is true, but just like everything I've mentioned in this book, it's all something to check out and see if it might apply to you and your life in some significant way.

Whenever we find something meaningful and useful, it becomes part of our own journey. Don't believe me or anyone else because you think they know something you don't. Instead explore, investigate, and make your own discoveries. Find out what's true for you. But don't get too attached to any beliefs – any belief is only a tool whose usefulness is often temporary.

Many people have described panoramic spiritual experiences, either in NDEs or great visions, which describe the structure and organization of the greater spiritual universe – visions like those of Chief Black Elk or the Myth of Er as recounted by Socrates. Many others claim to have spoken to God, saints, angels, spirit guides, aliens, and so forth. People like Betty Edie, Dannion Brinkley, Pam Reynolds, Eben Alexander, Anita Moorjani, Howard Storm, and many others, have described amazing near death experiences and written books about them. Profound experiences like these often transform the lives of those who have them, in a positive way. The question is, do they comprise a general description of our common spiritual domain, or are they just individual experiences with no particular relevance to anyone else? People who have such experiences are often adamant that their experiences are the way it is for everyone – that they have seen the truth and they are certain of it. Although in many cases these types of experiences are amazingly similar, other times they seem contradictory or incompatible. What do we make of that? The only area in which I find almost universal agreement is in descriptions of spiritual awakening or enlightenment, but this is an area where language is mostly inadequate.

As I suggested regarding Swedenborg, intense spiritual experiences usually can only be interpreted in terms of the person's present belief system and mental capacity, at least in the beginning. This is borne out in the book "At the Hour of Death" mentioned earlier, which is a fantastic record of a major long term study done on the spiritual and paranormal experiences of people, and those with them, around the time of their death. Many are visited by deceased relatives or friends, or by angels, saints, or other religious figures representative of their religious views. We create our own personal reality from a higher level, and its form can vary enormously from person to person, but we can always learn more about ourselves, who we are, who we've been, and discover more about the greater universe we live in, if we try.

Our Cortical Labyrinth – or
The Brain Game

"Neuroscientific explanations of human behaviour appeal to people because we're suckers for simplified, mechanistic brain-centred explanations – even if they're rubbish or don't make sense. Neurobabble makes nonsense brain 'science' more believable."
– Andrew Orlowski, 2015

"The brain enables the mind and thus the person. But neuroscience cannot yet, if ever, fully explain how this happens."
– Satel & Lilienfeld, Brainwashed, 2013

I haven't talked much about the brain, which is traditionally the supposed seat of the mind and consciousness. In many books and studies about the effects of trauma you will find numerous neurological explanations of how trauma affects our brains, bodies, and biochemistry. I also hear so much in psychology and self-help today that goes into great detail describing how what we do is managed and regulated by our brains, and how we might take control of our own neurology and chemistry, and manipulate hormones like oxytocin, cortisol, and dopamine, in order to change our behavior and emotional states. While such neurological explanations might help explain why we feel what we do and what drives us or inhibits us in many areas, how useful are they really, outside of medicine? They do describe how our bodies and minds work together and they can lead to new discoveries, but when we talk about the things we can do ourselves, or with support, to change our emotional states, resolve trauma, or have better relationships, understanding brain science is unnecessary. All the discussions about inner healing, in this book and many others, do not use or require any neurological explanations – this work is all experiential and requires only an experiential model. Most people have no idea how their cell phones work, on a technological level, but even children know how to use them and can do amazing things with them. Metaphorically our minds can be somewhat compared to the software on a computer. We can learn how to use the software programs on our computers with little or no understanding of how the computer hardware works, or even how the software programming code does what it does.

So regarding the brain, all the therapeutic remedies and exercises that actually work to help us heal our psychological dysfunctions and which do change our neurophysiology, work with or without all the neurobabble, and for reasons that, in many cases, can be understood without any reference to the brain at all. If we replace the word "brain" with the word "mind" in these kinds of discussions, and leave out all the talk about the amygdala, the hippocampus, the neocortex, and the pineal gland, nothing would be lost. In fact I think things would be easier to understand. All attempts to explain psychological problems or "mental illness" as purely metabolic issues are nonsense anyway. As I maintain throughout this book regarding our mindbody system, mind, body, and consciousness are one interactive ecosystem and ultimately part of a game created entirely by consciousness. A problem rooted in one of these areas will still affect all three.

Certainly all our brain functions are very important to study and understand for many reasons, and knowing how our bodies work is extremely useful to all of us. I'm not dismissing brain science at all. But when it comes to understanding and using the ideas I have discussed in this book, I have almost never heard any neurological explanations that made any difference – they always seem to me to be included just to add an air of scientific authenticity, but they feel

completely cluttersome and unnecessary. It is true that the mind
and brain have massive correlations. For everything we experience
and every action we take, there is undoubtedly something directly
related going on in the brain, whether that is the cause or the effect.
When you read a great book about the brain like Steven Pinker's
"How the Mind Works," you can see the enormity of what the brain
and body have to accomplish to allow us to do even the "simplest"
thing, like walking – it's not so simple. However, when we view a
human being as a complex machine run by an extraordinary bio-
computer, we get the feeling that everything can be explained by
materialism and cause and effect. And it can, _if that's what you
want._ But that doesn't mean it's so. No explanations are truth,
however useful they are, but all explanations _are_ thoughts in
someone's mind. And these thoughts are explanations because that
is the meaning they have been assigned, but there are always other
explanations – always. You might think that only one explanation
would be correct in understanding any given situation, but even if
that were true, people can and do accept explanations that have no
rational foundation at all. In the end, things are simply what they
are – explanations are secondary. Explanations are tools to help us
make sense of the world, but they change as we learn more.

Here's another viewpoint. Let's acknowledge the brain to be an
incredibly sophisticated biological computation system of which
the rest of the body and sense organs are peripherals. The brain is
like a car. You get in it and immediately your abilities are
predefined. There are things you can do and things you can't. The
car, just like any game, has rules – it gives you capabilities and
limitations. The car can roll but not jump, it can go forward and
backward, and turn, but it can't move sideways and it can't fly or
float like a boat. A car is an imposed limitation on you, as long as
you are strapped in. Although you can't swim or dance while in the
car, it does give you some abilities you would not otherwise have,
like high speed and long distance transportation, a radio, air
conditioning, and maybe a heater that warms your tush.

Our body is also a limitation we have to navigate. With its vast
interconnections among the seven basic physiological systems, it
constitutes a kind of labyrinth with the brain as the central control
center. It's our vehicle – like an Iron Man suit – part of a
sophisticated game we are playing called human life. Our human

experience is intimately tied to it as long as we are strapped in, and like a carnival ride, we are stuck in it until the ride is over. Look at any complex video game; it's the same thing on a much smaller scale. There are things you can do and specific ways to do them, as well as goals, obstacles, penalties, and rewards – just like life. Whether or not every iota of every experience we ever have is manufactured by our neuroplasm, it doesn't change what we are as conscious beings. And that very neuroplasm is being imagined into existence by Consciousness itself. It's all part of the show, what the Hindu's call Leela.

Therefore, if we are indeed spirits and if out-of-body experiences are what they seem to be and not ordinary dreams or imagination or just brain phenomena, then one question is, when we are exterior to the body how do we see or hear without eyes or ears? The problem with this question is that it proceeds from the false premise that we need something, a body or sense organs, in order to perceive the world, or to experience anything at all for that matter. In a dream you can have all kinds of perceptions with no sense organs at all. In actuality we are never "in" a body or "out" of a body – these are just experiences and interpretations. In the Identity Model, consciousness creates real experiences, sights, sounds, adventures, from whole cloth, just as our minds do in dreams, and requires nothing to do so – not atoms, molecules, energy, space, time, or brain cells.

But since human life is a lower level of a multi-tiered complex virtual reality, whether we need bodies or minds, eyes or ears, or anything else, depends on what game we are playing and what level of the game we are at. I have many times experienced being exterior and completely blind, or disabled in other ways, temporarily. So do we also have energy-level sense organs or spiritual sense organs, or a spiritual brain? Maybe, if that's how things are set up, although I have no experience of any of these things. But anything is possible, and finding out what is going on is what science is all about. Exploring consciousness however does take conventional science into new territory because it shows us that all reality is entirely subjective.

Many explanations of consciousness and paranormal phenomena fall into the category of what I call "spiritual materialism." Spiritual materialism includes all attempts to explain spiritual things in material-world terms by treating consciousness as if it were some form of energy or material that obeys certain metaphysical rules of cause and effect. Some theories try uniting the two paradigms, making this a universe of matter and consciousness somehow working in concert, which is a half-baked idea at best, since neither materialism nor consciousness is ever adequately defined. Attempts are often made to use quantum mechanics to show how the interplay of consciousness and matter determine reality. But there is no matter – matter is an experience, and experience is consciousness. There is nothing else. Panpsychism, the idea that everything in the universe is conscious, is also a mistake. To quote Rupert Spira "Only consciousness is conscious." I would also add that since consciousness is you, only YOU are conscious – but I'm talking about the real you, not the human you. In the end, matter and consciousness do not coexist, interplay, or co-create, and the universe does not contain or include consciousness – consciousness IS the universe. Even "consciousness" is just a word we use to represent that which knows experience. Self-aware Existence created all the relative dualities, like spirit versus matter, push versus pull, good versus evil, me versus not-me, and every other type of contrast and opposition, but they are all illusions, just as a movie in a theater is an illusion. Until we realize what's really going on – that it's all a projection of our minds – we will continue to be mesmerized by the world around us.

Another question that comes up in discussing the brain concerns whether or not we have free will. Discussions of free will rarely if ever adequately define the terms "free," "will," or the "we" who are supposed to have it. Our will, in the form of decisions, intentions, and efforts, is simply an experience, and seems "free" only because we have identified ourselves as its causative agent.

There is some evidence, although it is disputed, that the so-called "free" decisions we make actually happen in our brains milliseconds before we are even consciously aware of them! If that is true, it begs the question of who or what is choosing the course of our lives? Is it all just biology? However, these observations fail to consider the possibility that we might be UN-consciously aware (aware on a higher level) of our decisions before expressing them as behavior, because what consciousness is and who we are is never even considered. In any event, this whole brain game is part of a perfect illusion designed to make us believe we are something we are not. However, experiences that take place outside of the brain-body interface, like past life memories, NDEs, or paranormal phenomena, draw back the curtain and reveal the wonderful and mighty Wizard of Oz to be just another character in the story. The brain itself is an illusion – an icon in a magical game – a mental projection from a more fundamental and unseen reality. We'll revisit the brain again in Chapter 21.

According to many sages, including Robert Adams, our lives are preordained, as if we are watching a movie that we have no say in at present, because we wrote the screenplay in advance and we are just acting out a role. But we don't know that because we seem to be making free choices! On the other hand, since time is an illusion, then the writing of the script and acting it out may simply be one spontaneous happening! But until we know who and what we really are, the question of free will is moot. Still, we are told by those who see things more clearly, that there is indeed an element of free will here, and it appears the moment we step outside the identification with our character, and out of the story -- we have the freedom to not react, to not identify, and to wake up as pure awareness. So as a character in a story, we might possibly not have any so-called "free will," but it doesn't matter – we are not our characters. Furthermore, every decision is a spontaneous creation of consciousness -- which is our true Self. This means that ultimately there is ONLY free will! And, paradoxically, no one that has it.

Summary

The Identity Model says that everything is consciousness operating through a limitless network of individual viewpoints, using identification to create the illusion of an external existence in which there are innumerable worlds filled with other beings, and endless experiences. As real as it all is, we're living in a temporary dreamworld made of imagination. We ourselves are eternal consciousness, pure infinitely free spirit, impervious to harm, death, or suffering, except as an illusion, if we can only wake up. I find it easiest to describe all this in terms of games. A game is an adventure that follows a set of rules – and everything about the game is a rule. Just as in volleyball, where all aspects of the game are set forth in the rule book in exact detail – the court, the net, the ball, the players, and the rules of play – so it is in life. For each of us in our present situation, the rules of the world and our own psyche are something we have to discover for ourselves. Although everything around us is in constant motion and forever changing, there is an underlying order, as there must be in any game, if it's to be more than a chaotic psychedelic drug trip. For each of us on our individual journeys as spiritual beings, we live, die, learn, remember, forget, experience different levels of reality, and are reborn according to certain principles and patterns. These patterns may be called rules, laws, plans, karma, or stories. As humans we get programmed with patterns that become our stories, but which also cause suffering and limitation. We can be affected and influenced by any of the myriad forces around us, yet by recognizing that we are more than physical beings, and by looking more deeply into the experiences that change us and the influences that hinder us, we can not only heal ourselves of those limitations but we can also see more deeply into our spiritual nature and break free of the traps that cause our suffering. In the rest of Part IV we will look at how these ideas are incorporated into each of the three levels of healing and how we can use Identity Management, Identity Resolution, and Identity Transcendence to help us on our own journeys toward greater happiness and freedom.

Chapter 18

Identity Management

"A man likes to believe that he is the master of his soul. But as long as he is unable to control his moods and emotions, or to be conscious of the myriad secret ways in which unconscious factors insinuate themselves into his arrangements and decisions, he is certainly not his own master." – Carl Jung

"Whatever you are being, there is an intelligence and energy behind that which will draw to you those people, situations, and forces supporting that identity. Become a flower and you will attract butterflies and sunshine. Become lowly and you will attract vermin and darkness. If you don't like what you are being, change it. You do have a choice." – Pipananda

This book isn't a comprehensive self-improvement manual by any means, but I'm including this chapter because the Identity Model does provide a valuable new perspective in this area and helps explain why and how some methods work and others don't, and there are some important ideas I want to share.[80]

In Chapter 5 I described three basic levels of healing, and so far the focus here has been on the healing of unwanted mind-body conditions at their core, using Identity Resolution, because that is the main purpose of this book. Although ID-R eliminates unwanted states permanently, it is not always a quick fix and does take some time and effort, as well as money unless you learn to do it yourself or work with a partner. We often need something more immediate and convenient to use in our daily lives.

The second level of healing is management, and Identity Management (ID-M) includes all those things we can do to avoid or change negative states, short of resolving them, and to create and utilize positive states. Although ID-M is specifically about

---

[80] See the Bibliography for more recommended self-improvement resources.

managing our states, I like to include in this category all things that are considered self-improvement techniques not covered in the other two categories, like learning a skill for example, because they can all help us manage our lives and enjoy a better state of being. While there are many books and programs that can help us work on ourselves at a deeper level, the vast majority of self-improvement methods and healing modalities that are available in the world today are management techniques, which means they leave the root of the problem unchanged even if they successfully solve the problem on the surface. But that's OK. If you get headaches from using your cell phone for example, but you don't know the cause, it's fine to take an aspirin for the pain until you figure it out.

So the ID-M techniques available today include a wide variety of powerful tools to not only change your state but also to utilize your internal power and abilities more effectively and immediately. It's like learning martial arts for your mind! When you get yourself into a more empowered and positive mental and emotional state, it can change your physical state as well, in many ways. There are far too many useful methods to mention here, but whatever tools you use, the important thing is that you learn them well and use them consistently. No self-improvement method is any good if it's never used. I suggest trying out many techniques, and putting those that work the best for you into regular practice. Some you will want to include in your daily routines and rituals, and some are skills you can utilize whenever needed.

I will discuss here just a few of the most powerful methods you can use for yourself, and which I use every day, including self-observation, reframing, self-hypnosis, and meditation, with an emphasis on deep relaxation. I will suggest some other resources you can look into as well. The Identity Model simply presents these methods in a slightly different and more useful context.

You can create any identity state you want through learning, practice, and preparation, so that you generate that state automatically when needed, and really embody it. This identity becomes who you are in that setting, and even though you know it's only a useful persona, it can be very stable and powerful. But if you get triggered by something, that identity can be interfered with or get superceded by a reactive state like fear, anxiety, anger, or other dysfunction, so it's important to know how to deal with these things when they occur.

Self-Observation

"Self-observation brings man to the realization of the necessity of self-change. And in observing himself a man notices that self-observation itself brings about certain changes in his inner processes. He begins to understand that self-observation is an instrument of self-change, a means of awakening." – G. I. Gurdjieff

The first tool is one I call "Self-Observation," although it is actually more than that, and includes "not reacting." Gurdjieff taught Self-Observation as a spiritual practice, but for our purposes here it's more like advanced self-control. It's the most direct way to deal with unwanted identity shifts as they occur. There are two steps: noticing and not reacting.

Step one: Everything starts with *Self-Observation*: noticing our own behavior, thoughts, and feelings – even the most subtle – without judgement. We just want to observe. We can't deal with our reactions if we don't notice them. But this takes a greater level of "presence" than we might ordinarily have, and this may take some practice to develop. Another word for attentiveness to presence is "mindfulness," which is just being self-aware in the present moment. Try it now. Stop reading and let your body relax and let your mind be quiet for a moment, and really notice what's going on – what you feel in your body, the thoughts that come up in your mind, what you hear, see, and sense around you. There will be a lot going on that you were "tuning out" while reading. You will probably also notice some tension, which you can now let go of.

Take a step back from yourself for a moment and imagine these present experiences are happening to someone else and you are just watching. This will help create a sense of detachment as you observe these things – your breath, your heartbeat, your posture. Notice that <u>awareness</u> is present – be aware that you are aware. This is a good practice by itself, if only to help you become a more awake human being. This is also called "being in the now." I recommend reading some books on meditation and presence, like Eckhart Tolle's "The Power of Now," and just start becoming more present in your own life. This may seem boring at first, or even annoying, because we have become accustomed to being so focused on other things, and on being entertained, that we are oblivious to ourselves. But this is the first step toward connecting with inner peace and power!

One central goal regarding Self-Observation is to make it a habit, so that you can consistently notice when things change in your body and mind, and more specifically, when you _shift_ from one identity to another. When you notice a shift in state, it helps to remind yourself that you are not this new identity, simply the observer of it. This important aspect of Self-Observation is the beginning of dis-identification, which is remembering that we are NOT any of our identities, thoughts, or emotions, just as we are not the clothes we wear. Identification is much like being asleep. So as we begin to dis-identify with our various states by being more mindful of our own awareness, we may then start to identify with our true nature, which is not limited by its experiences. We'll explore this more in Chapter 21.

An exercise that will help you here is to plan in advance to spend a certain period of time observing yourself and especially noticing your identity shifts, which means noticing any changes in your physical and emotional states. For example you can plan to do this for the first ten minutes of a social gathering or some other event where you might have a variety of thoughts, feelings, and reactions. Be present (self-aware, in the moment, and slightly detached) and observe your own responses as you interact with others. Notice the changes in your facial expression, attitude, voice, posture, and other mannerisms. If you find any of this hard to do, the meditation discussed later in this chapter can help.

A quick note: Not everyone dissociates a lot, but it's good to understand what it is, and to try and notice it when it happens. Dissociation can take many forms, like spacing out, losing track of time, daydreaming, or forgetting things. Self-Observation will help you notice and acknowledge things like this. You may discover that sometimes you are not in control of what you are doing or saying, as if you have taken a back seat to some other force or presence within you. Just calmly observe this if it happens. Since dissociation may involve amnesia, you may simply notice that you don't remember something that just happened, or perhaps you find that you are not able to account for the last several seconds, minutes, hours, or days. I'm not kidding, this can happen. You may never experience this but if you do, and if you can discover what triggered this to happen, then you can practice handling that trigger, so that the next time it happens you can be more present and in control. Awareness is power. Reactions, including dissociation, can all be resolved once you become aware of them.

Not Reacting – or
The Pause that Refreshes

"When angry, count 10, before you speak; if very angry, 100."
– Thomas Jefferson

"The ability to observe without evaluating
is the highest form of intelligence." – J. Krishnamurti

Step two: The next step, and challenge, in doing Self-Observation, is *NOT REACTING* – to not do what the reaction wants you to do, whenever you get triggered. This is not easy and often requires more than just trying to exercise self-control. Instead you must "interrupt the pattern." "Pattern" is another word for a repeating reactive program, like getting nervous every time the phone rings. By just deciding not to react and halting your immediate impulses you have already interrupted the pattern momentarily, but the reactive state will still be there and you don't want any part of it affecting you. This may not happen completely until the reaction is resolved permanently, but there is a lot you can do in the meantime.

A "pattern interrupt" is anything that completely shifts your attention and captivates your mind enough to disconnect you from the state you were in. An interruption that comes from the outside, say from someone else, can shift you immediately out of one pattern and into another state completely, and we do this all the time with others by redirecting their attention or changing the subject. With a baby for instance, you might get them to shift from crying to laughing by doing something distracting and silly like jangling some keys in front of them, and laughing out loud. I once had the hiccups while talking with a friend on the phone. In the middle of our pleasant conversation she started yelling at me about the money I owed her. I was baffled! I didn't owe her any money! I asked her what the heck she was talking about! She asked me about my hiccups. *They were gone!* We both laughed. She had purposely interrupted my pattern. To do this for ourselves just takes awareness, intention, and a little practice, but the results can be amazing.

For example I once got angry when the bank returned a bad check someone had given me, and I noticed my reaction within a few seconds of opening the mail. That's Self-Observation. So while the initial automatic reaction of anger took over momentarily and clouded my self-awareness, I quickly recovered. To do this I first made my mind a blank and observed my breathing for several seconds. This interrupted my previous pattern and my anger subsided. I then reevaluated the situation. I saw that all the angry thoughts I had at first were not constructive. They were useless and caused me stress, and had their roots somewhere in the past. But now that I was more calm and composed, the answer as to what to do was simple and obvious. I made a decision about it and it was of no more concern. Counting to ten (or a hundred) really works!

Usually the first thoughts we have during a reactive shift are thoughts embedded in the identity and not thoughts we come up with voluntarily in the moment. They feel spontaneous and voluntary because we *did* come up with them voluntarily in the past, and that feeling is part of that identity. But the old thoughts and emotions are now just past programming. When you pause and take a mental step back, the reaction will pass, like a fever, if you do not succumb to it. This practice will gradually help you have much more control over your own feelings and behavior. Making important decisions when in a reactive state is usually a bad idea. It's better to get completely detached from the reaction, or even the situation, before even thinking about it.

Basically the easiest way to get completely out of one state is to *get into another state* – one that is very different or incompatible. To do that you have to change your immediate goal or intention. So you just start doing something else without hesitation and with total focus. Changing our physiology is one of the fastest ways to do this. You might just start laughing for instance, or smiling, or dancing. You can change your posture to one more congruent with the state you want to be in, which will actually bring forth that state! Your body chemistry will change, as well as your emotions and your thinking. We empower whatever we put our attention on. This is why counting works, watching your breath, noticing everything around you that is green, or just walking around the block. We give our mind something else to do. Be creative. There are many good books that go into way more detail for doing this. The real key here is that by changing your focus you have interrupted your previous thoughts and goals and made a conscious shift into a new identity state.

But be careful not to go back into the previous thought pattern. There is an innate urge to hold on to our reactions, and this is built into each reaction itself. This attachment is caused by our identification with these states. If I am angry, I will tend to want to remain angry because my anger is justified within the angry identity, due to whatever caused it in the past. But the past does not really exist and we are not our states. When we have a more calm perspective, we can make rational decisions and take more effective action.

By the way, many good methods that can help change our lives may be doing so mainly by this same process. They have us focus on doing some special technique, and this changes our focus and our goal, which is an identity shift, putting us in a different state. Then by continuing the process we reinforce the new identity until it is a familiar pattern that we can maintain even in the presence of former triggers. In addition, if we believe that the new technique will be effective, there is the added force of the mind-power effect. This will be reinforced if the method itself produces a very noticeable sensory impact – in other words, if it causes a physiological reaction we can feel. With these factors in play, the theory behind the method being used doesn't even have to be valid for this to work, but if it is valid then we have all of these things working together in our favor.

Once you get some insight into managing your own identities, you begin to realize what it really means to be controlled by reactive states. It may be shocking to realize that you have lived most of your life this way, once you begin to see that most of the reactive identities that have controlled you, besides being limiting and debilitating, are not actually even relevant to anything you want, or of any true value whatsoever! You may even begin to question who you really are. But that's a good thing!

An actual shock however, is a different kind of a reaction. If you are having a shock you will do whatever is necessary and this is not something you can plan in advance, although you may employ knowledge and skills you have previously acquired. After the shock however you may be in an unwanted state. Identity Management and Identity Transcendence techniques are the best resources to use at such times, so that you can get yourself into a better state and take care of your situation. You can always resolve the shock later.

You may have dozens of reactions every day, and the Self-Observation technique helps you to be aware of these reactions and not let them control you. You observe the reaction, interrupt the pattern, stop identifying with it, and take control by changing your focus to a completely different goal, which shifts you into a new and better state. In the beginning you may notice your reactions well after the fact, but gradually you will come to notice them immediately, and take charge more quickly. This practice could easily be a whole course in itself. These ideas are just some simple basics you can work with right now.

Here is a classic example of the power of redirected focus. As the story goes, on the last day of the American Civil War, General Grant was on the road with an excruciating migraine headache that had tortured him all night. Unexpectedly, an emissary from General Lee arrived with a note indicating that Lee wished to surrender! I'm sure Grant was overwhelmed. After all the blood, death, horror, and personal trials he had experienced, who knows what went through his mind in that moment, realizing the war was over! It may have even been a traumatic shock! But, by his own account, Grant's headache vanished instantly! What an epic and historic pattern interrupt! But Grant's "shift in state" was happenstance, and merely an example. There lies within all of us the power to intentionally change our state instantly and dramatically, and it starts with Self-Observation. Another powerful tool we can use to change our state of being is called "reframing."

Reframing

"Everything you have in life can be taken from you except one thing: your freedom to choose how you will respond to the situation. This is what determines the quality of the life we've lived. Not whether we've been rich or poor, famous or unknown, healthy or suffering. What determines our quality of life is how we relate to these realities, what kind of meaning we assign them, what kind of attitude we cling to about them, what state of mind we allow them to trigger."
– Dr. Victor Frankl, Holocaust survivor

"The greatest discovery of any generation is that a human can alter his life by altering his attitude." – William James

Is the glass of wine half empty or half full? Or is it just four ounces of wine? If it's raining outside is that a good thing or a bad thing? It depends doesn't it? Reality is not just the physical state of the external world but how we see it internally – what it means to us.

One of the greatest powers we all have is the ability to change our attitude, to find a different perspective so we see things in a different way. And how we see things can make the difference between success and failure, joy and suffering, the possible and the impossible, or life and death, because our perspective determines our response. We meet each situation with the identities and resources that are summoned up by it, whether they are reactive, previously learned, or spontaneously created in the moment. And because we have a say in what any experience means to us, we possess great power over our reality and our state of being, allowing us to make the best of any situation. The process of purposely changing what things mean and altering our attitude is called "reframing," and it is, in many ways, a superpower – real magic we can use every day.

Using reframing you can change the reality of any situation instantly. You may think that seeing things differently doesn't literally change reality but it does! As I said, reality is more than just the physical state of things. One afternoon when Lynne and I were first dating, my car broke down halfway home on our two-hour drive back from San Francisco. We had to park on the side of the road

and walk to a service station. Fortunately we were in the middle of a
town. But Lynne was grumbling – she was tired and very upset and
angry, and I could have been upset too, but in that moment I
noticed that I was actually feeling pretty good! So I changed the
meaning of our situation. I put my arm around her shoulders and
said "Look, there isn't any problem. It's a beautiful sunny day and
we're just going for a walk. Really! Just pretend for a minute. Isn't it
great?" She sensed my new attitude and played along. "There's a
hotel right over there and there's a restaurant" I said, pointing down
the road. "We can have a nice dinner and stay the night if we have
to – it'll be an adventure!" Instead of focusing on how our previous
plans were disrupted, we reframed this situation and acted as if we
had planned the whole thing. Both our attitudes quickly changed,
we had a great time, and my car was ready the next morning. The
situation went from being upsetting to being fun.

In seminars I have scribbled random odd shapes in different
colors on a white board and asked the audience what it was. It was a
mess that didn't look like anything. Then I placed a very ornate
picture frame around it. Suddenly it actually looked like some
avant-garde work of art. I had literally reframed it. The scribbling
went from being nothing to being something interesting and
possibly valuable. In war, the people who are seen as the enemy are
purposely reframed as being less than human, to make killing them
easier. In advertising, things being sold are associated with other
things that often have nothing to do with the products, but which
put them in a better light, or which help to create an artificial
meaning that is more attractive. Beer means fun, gum means love,
clothes mean status, and so forth.

There are different kinds of reframing because there are many
different types and levels of meaning, but overall, meaning is
information about relationships. It's an understanding of how things
interact and relate to each other, and without this understanding
nothing would be good or bad – actually nothing would mean
anything at all. And yet when we have learned that something has a
certain meaning, we generally accept that meaning as fact, until we
look more deeply into it, like Democrats good, Republicans bad, or
vice versa. In fact the way we see things is usually predetermined by
habit, previous learning, and programming, but we can change
that. Also, what something means depends on what aspect of it we

are focusing on. When we have a problem or find ourselves in a negative state and we want to get ourselves to focus on making a positive change, the challenge is in finding the meaning in our present situation that will best support us in doing so.

There are many ways to change what something means to you. You can change the context in which you see something, like I did when my car broke down, or you can change the value of something, you can change its purpose, or you can change what it is associated with. And when you find another meaning for it, you change what it *IS* – you change reality. There are many books and other resources for learning more about reframing – Tony Robbins book "Unlimited Power" is one – so I'm going to keep this short with a few principles and examples, but this is an essential tool to have in your toolbox and to use at every opportunity.

Reframing usually has two steps. First we choose what to focus on. There is something that poses a challenge, some disappointment or problem, some situation that is not optimal, or perhaps just a puzzle to solve. If I wanted apples and I got stuck with lemons, I can choose to focus on the problem or the solution. Focusing on the problem will bring out angry or anxious identities – in fact they might be triggered automatically. If we are mindful though, and using Self-Observation, we can squelch the reaction, quickly realize that we need to see things in a better light, and change our attitude. Then we look for the solution, which is step two.

Basically we are looking for a better meaning. The easiest way to find one is to ask a question, and the most general "skeleton key" question is "How can I see this in a better way?" Or, "how can I see this in a way that solves my problem?" You can, of course, be very specific in your phrasing about the problem, whether you want to feel better, be more hopeful, solve a conundrum, prevent a disaster, be inspired, deal with pain, or just survive.

Maybe I can't change the lemons into apples but I can see the situation as an opportunity to be creative and either get the apples I need or use the lemons. I can see it as a game or a puzzle, as well as a challenge to go beyond my previous plans. Maybe I made a mistake and I can see this as a learning opportunity. I can think about what lessons I have learned and consider how much that will benefit me in the future.

I can even view my disappointment as an <u>intervention from the</u> <u>universe</u> to keep me safe or lead me in a better direction, which is possible, even if I don't really know if this is true or not. For example maybe this was synchronicity because the apples I expected were contaminated and people would have gotten sick. The objective here is to get myself out of any impaired state and into the most resourceful state I can, by focusing on the meaning of this situation that most inspires me. It doesn't have to be true; it just has to be helpful. And what is the result? I solve the problem, I turn a disaster into a victory, I feel better, I get inspired and maybe even change my life in some way. Or maybe things turn out better than they would have, or my attitude inspires others and I have more confidence in myself – there can be countless positive outcomes and repercussions to changing the meaning of any experience. And if things don't turn out well I can reframe that outcome too. Things only mean what we think they mean.

So instead of thinking of something as a problem, what if your attitude was that this is exactly what you wanted to happen because it allows for the possibility of something better? Then you can look for what that is. Or you could ask: Why would God, my Higher Self, my Spirit Guides, or my partner or employer, put me in this situation? Be creative! When you look for answers, you will find them. Maybe the solution is to abandon what you had planned and do something completely different – to be spontaneous. If you go fishing and discover too late that you forgot your fishing pole, you can focus on the problem and be upset, or you can ask how this might be a great opportunity to do something else.

Here are a few more questions you can ask yourself that can change your perspective: What would make this OK? What good might come of this? What else could I be doing? What can I learn from this that might be important or helpful in the future? What is the hidden treasure in this situation for me or someone else? What do I now have that I didn't have before? How can I make this better than what it would have been? What is the best question I can ask myself right now? You can even ask everyone around you these same questions. So there are countless questions you can ask, and endless perspectives you can take, to change the meaning of any situation. Sometimes this might be very hard to do, but it is always within your power to try. Remember, what something seems to mean is <u>never</u> the only meaning it can have.

Sometimes when something unexpected happens, we just figure things out and make it work, or we just make a new plan and nothing needs to be reframed. Or it may be that our habitual way of framing things allows us to automatically see things in a positive way. Remember when you had a Lego set or Tinker Toys and you could construct anything you wanted from them? You just had to use your imagination. Remember the story of Apollo 13? As depicted in the movie of the same name, there is a scene where, in order to save the astronauts' lives during a crisis in which their ship's atmosphere was failing, the ground crew had to figure out a way to construct a $CO2$ filter from pieces of unrelated equipment that the space crew had onboard – "We have to make this [square filter] fit into the hole for this [round casing] using nothing but that [a pile of miscellaneous unrelated parts]." And they did![81] Reframing is about being creative, and changing reality is magic – it's a creative act! There may be many ways out of a jam, and reframing can help.

My personal attitude in life is that all is well and everything is unfolding as it should – something one of my favorite teachers, Robert Adams, said all the time. When that attitude is challenged and all seems definitely NOT well, my job is to see how it IS well, and to find the right context in which I can make the most of my situation. No matter what happens, I look for <u>the good in it that is present right now</u> that perhaps I just don't see, the <u>possible good</u> that can be created by utilizing what I have, and <u>the good that might come</u> from this situation later on. I try to stay focused in the present moment, to see things from the best perspective, and to be creative about the future. I see failure as a stepping stone, life as an adventure, beliefs as temporary tools, and love as the heart and purpose of everything. Unfortunately I don't always live up to my highest aspirations, but I keep trying. I take responsibility for every failure and try to learn something from it.

---

[81] "Apollo 13," 1995

More Reframes

Among countless possible reframes, here are two more to consider:

It Could Be Worse: No matter what unwanted thing happens, it could always be worse, possibly by orders of magnitude! Sometimes it helps to see things from a greater perspective by viewing your present situation in light of far worse situations that could have arisen but didn't. A terrible situation may then be seen to be less serious, or even nothing at all. If you are bothered by having a cold, be grateful you don't have cancer. Your carpet may be ruined by a toilet leak, but you can be grateful your house didn't burn down. This might seem silly until you try it, but it helps you appreciate what you have in the moment. Perspective is everything.

Goal Reframing: In the course of trying to accomplish something I have found it helpful on occasion to reframe my purpose, and the meaning of the outcome. Let's say I'm doing something to make money that is very successful but I feel unsatisfied. So I change my primary goal of increasing my wealth to having fun and being more creative instead, because those are my real values, and the money is secondary. In doing the same project with this change of focus, regardless of whether or not I make less money, or even more money, I will be accomplishing my primary goal of having fun and will no longer be unhappy.

Once I felt a strong connection to a lady and found I got very nervous around her. But she was not romantically interested in me. When I changed my goal to just being her friend, which actually felt more suitable, my nervousness disappeared. A different reality calls for a different response. We did become great friends and I soon realized that I had been misinterpreting my own feelings.

In the framework of a game, winning may be the goal. However sometimes what you _think_ you want is not what you _really_ want. In the movie "Rocky," Rocky is an out-of-shape, over-the-hill boxer who wins a chance to fight the world champion.[82] During his training he realizes that he can't beat the champ. He decides that

---

[82] "Rocky" 1976

all he really wants to do is to go the distance, something no one has ever done, so he can prove something to himself. And he does! What he might have previously seen as a loss, became a great win! Sometimes changing our goal to one that is more authentic, can line up forces within us that make us unstoppable. Why shoot for a goal that someone else has set for you?

In the TV series Star Trek TNG, the super-intelligent android, Data, is challenged to a mentally complex video game by an alien who is the preeminent champion.[83] Data loses the first match and is perplexed by this, so he asks for a rematch and they play again. This time he holds his own until his opponent finally quits in disgust. Data wins by default. He then reveals to his friends that he had changed his goal from winning to "not losing," and instead aimed for a tie! It's always good to know exactly _why_ you want something because this can sometimes reveal an easier, better, or more authentic objective, and provide greater inspiration and fulfillment. I've used this reframe many times in my life with much satisfaction.

Meditation
"Regular elicitation of the Relaxation Response can prevent, and compensate for, the damage incurred by frequent nervous reactions that pulse through our hearts and bodies."
– Herbert Benson, The Relaxation Response

Stress is our own agitated emotional and physical response to whatever we are experiencing. The body responds to physical stress by getting stronger, so the stress of exercise is good for us if not overdone. Good stress is simply a challenge that promotes strength and improvement. But we want to avoid stress that is harmful, and what is most commonly meant by the word "stress" in this regard, is the detrimental impact of the day to day mental and emotional challenges we face, which overall may be greater now than at any time in history due to the many unnatural and detrimental social, environmental, and economic conditions we face every day.

When we react to some triggering situation with an identity state created in trauma, our internal response lies in the realm of fight,

---

[83] "Star Trek TNG," season 2 episode 21,"Peak Performance"

flight, or freeze – our natural responses to danger. But these responses to non-traumatic situations are not natural, and lead to all the symptoms of stress. So if any experience affects us negatively in a way that goes beyond its immediate physical impact, that response is due to our own internal mindbody reactions. These reactions can raise our blood pressure, impair our digestion, and cause a whole host of hormonal and other chemical effects in the body. Such reactions can also include emotional and behavioral changes that affect every aspect of our lives. What we call stress is the impact of all these factors on our minds and bodies. I believe that a good case can be made for stress being the number one cause of premature death in the world today![84]

However this may be, our psychological programming is in operation all day every day, even in sleep. The traumatic experiences that have left their indelible imprints upon us, even when they are only active to the slightest degree, are affecting our mind and body continuously. The effects of all this depend on what programs are operating and their level of intensity. Mentally we may experience these reactions as changes in our mood and emotional states, and as any troublesome thoughts or images that enter our minds. Physically, this subliminal programming may result in tension, anxiety, pain, or any of countless other symptoms. Working in the background, these programs can interfere with any of our physical and mental functions. When we awaken in the morning, we are unaware that dozens of reactive programs are running, and more are being triggered to turn on throughout the day, as we shift in and out of the various identities that come into play. And yet we can become so accustomed to our dysfunctional programming that we don't even notice it.

---

[84] If we review the results of the ACE Study and if we consider that many traumatic reactions, which might be generally diagnosed as Developmental Trauma Disorder (DTD), are synonymous with stress, then for a large percentage of us, stress is involved in every health problem we have. So I think there is a good case to be made that, as a cause of premature death, stress surpasses all non-health related causes combined, including accidents, wars, and starvation, although stress has a large role in those deaths as well.

Anything we can do to turn these reactive programs off, prevent them from being triggered, or limit their effect or intensity, is useful. Among the most important things that can help with this, in general, include maintaining good health through proper nutrition and exercise, getting enough sleep, fresh air, and sunlight, drinking enough water, and having loving and supportive social relationships.

Activities like yoga, dancing, nature hikes, having more fun, love, laughter, or seeking peace of mind, meaning, fulfillment, and positivity in our lives, and anything else that contributes to happiness and better health, are all good. All these things work together to basically prevent reactions from being triggered, by reducing negative physical states of pain and discomfort, and by keeping us in our highest state of wellbeing. Maintaining good health includes limiting detrimental exposure to things like toxins in the air, water, food, and legal or illegal drugs, and also avoiding constant exposure to EMF and microwave radiation.[85] But the most powerful process we can use for this purpose is meditation, specifically that which promotes deep relaxation.

In his ground-breaking book "The Relaxation Response," mentioned earlier, and in his later book "Relaxation Revolution," Dr. Herbert Benson discusses his research in helping people reverse the detrimental effects of stress. He measured the effects of meditation on people's physical and mental wellbeing, and discovered that in meditation there comes a point where we experience significant positive benefits including changes in blood pressure, heart rate, nervous tension, anxiety, and many other measurable physiological and mental conditions. He called this phenomenon the "relaxation response" and has continued to study it, and the effects of various meditative practices, since his first book

---

[85] The harmful effects of EMF and microwave radiation on human physiology are considerable, and this has been scientifically proven beyond any doubt. But this is still a controversial issue because, like tobacco, wireless radiation is big business. It is also part of a global system that is not only designed to be addictive but, unfortunately, one upon which the majority of the world's population is now economically, socially, and emotionally dependent. You can find some resources on this in the Bibliography and at ehtrust.org.

was published in 1975. The relaxation response occurs after a certain period of time, around ten to twenty minutes, when doing any type of meditation that includes focusing your attention on one thing for an extended period of time so as to quiet the mind. In addition to the immediate benefits, the effects of regular meditation contribute to long term improvements as well.

Any form of meditation that follows Benson's guidelines will work and he mentions many different types in his books. My own recommendation with regard to the relaxation response is to keep the focus of attention on physical relaxation itself, either exclusively or in combination with another meditative practice. To do this I practice Yoga Nidra (yogic sleep) where one puts attention on various points around the body in a repeating cycle. My added suggestion is to RELAX each point as you notice it by releasing any tension, by visualizing relaxation, or by just "letting go." It's basically just a deeper form of progressive relaxation so I just call it "deep relaxation meditation" because the main focus is on relaxation to produce the relaxation response, and I abbreviate it as "Rx meditation" – an obvious reference to its healing benefits.

Once you are deeply relaxed, and find that state easy to maintain, you can simply continue this for the duration, or you may wish to focus on a mantra, repeating a certain word in your mind with each breath. Benson used the word "one" in his studies, or you can do the "I Am" meditation saying "I" mentally as you breathe in and "Am" as you breathe out. Or you can silently count your breaths by counting each exhalation, going up to ten, and starting over. You can also do Vipassana meditation by simply noticing the feeling of the breath as it enters and leaves the nose. Just do whatever practice you prefer, and maintain a passive attitude, letting everything be as it is. Maintaining a quiet, focused mind is difficult in the beginning, so every time you lose your focus just notice that, and come back to the meditation. This is a practice, not a test, and its purpose is to help you remain conscious of your own presence, so that your body can relax.

To begin, you basically want to have a quiet environment where you won't be interrupted, get in a comfortable position, close your eyes, and maintain a passive, non-reactive, and nonjudgmental attitude, especially toward yourself. Your breathing should be natural and uncontrolled, and I suggest you do at least 15 minutes a

day, preferably in the morning, but before eating, or wait at least
two hours after eating.

I do at least two one-hour meditations each day as part of my
spiritual practice, but I always devote at least 15 minutes of that
time to deep relaxation. I also take a few seconds to consciously
relax throughout the day, whenever I notice unwanted tension in
the body.

The effects of unconscious programing often appear in the body
as tension or pressure, which creates a feedback loop that keeps the
programs running. When we reduce the tension in our bodies,
which we can do even though it is unconsciously generated, we are
turning down the volume on the programs that are producing it.
We may even turn those programs off temporarily, although they
are still activated and can be retriggered. So deep relaxation
meditation is very powerful, but it is a management technique,
which means the programs that soften or turn off, are not resolved,
and the immediate effects may not be permanent. But you can
think of it like exercise or yoga, which you don't just do a few times
and stop – you make it part of your life. If you do deep relaxation
every day and remember to relax many times throughout the day for
a few seconds, so it becomes a habit, you should get all the long
term benefits of the relaxation response, including better health and
wellbeing. Of course the results will depend on your particular
situation.

The first benefit I got from using relaxation, early on, was
headache prevention and relief, including a lessening of pain and
duration, which I described earlier. This was immediate and
effective. I was also able to reduce my blood pressure significantly
on most occasions, but not all the time. After meditation I would
often feel full of energy and have a remarkable sense of wellbeing.
Many times during my first several years of doing meditation I
would find myself feeling happy for no reason, and upon reflection
I remembered I had meditated a short time earlier. My nightly deep
relaxation practice also led to me having the out-of-body
experiences I discussed in Chapter 3.

The most dramatic immediate physical effect I have had from
deep relaxation meditation is the amazing response I described
earlier in Chapter 10 (Taming the Tiger), when all the symptoms
that caused me to go to an urgent care facility suddenly vanished

after about two hours. The physical, mental, and spiritual benefits
of regular meditation are many, and you can find information on
this in many books, and on the web.

Unfortunately most people will stop meditating fairly quickly,
perhaps only trying it a few times. Until you try this yourself, and do
it long enough to repeatedly experience both the immediate
benefits and some long term benefits, it is easy to think that
meditation is doing nothing, and that you are wasting your time.
Modern civilization has conditioned us to seek continuous
entertainment and to keep ourselves busy. There are thousands of
influences vying for our attention all the time, both external and
internal, and we are constantly distracted and overstimulated. Many
people cannot set their cell phones down for even a few minutes.
To sit quietly doing nothing without feeling restless is not only
difficult for many people, but it may also invite all your "monsters
from the id" to surface in the form of feelings, thoughts, and
flashbacks. To stave this off, your mind may distract you with all
manner of thoughts and images. This persistent barrage of mental
activity is often called the "monkey mind." The best way to tame
the monkey mind is to make meditation a solid part of your life by
making it a part of your daily routine, preferably in the morning,
and by placing it in the middle of things that you *always* do. By
allotting a small amount of time for it, say 12 minutes, and sticking
to it, meditation will become a habit, and soon it will be an
indispensable part of your day. And daily meditation can even lead
to true spiritual insight and awakening. More on that in Chapter 21.

The Mind-Power Effect and Pointing the Bone

All of creation is imagination implemented by the power of
intention. We, as conscious beings, are always connected to that
unlimited power, but we are limited in its use partly because we
have agreed to a set of rules. Yet most of our limitations come from
our internal programming and conditioned beliefs. Still, we have
the potential, lying dormant within us, to work miracles. Sometimes
we rise above our limitations and go to a higher level, and amazing
things happen, but for most of us those times are rare. ID-R helps us
resolve the programming that hampers us, and most Identity
Management techniques can help us bypass or take control of it to

some extent, but it's also possible to just tap into our higher power intentionally. Hypnosis, self-hypnosis, the mind-power effect (formerly the placebo effect), and creative visualization are just a few names for using the power of intention to improve our lives. Simply holding a thought of what you want strongly in your mind for a period of time can bring about positive change. However, and I can say this from experience, even when we know we have that power most of us will seldom use it. So we need to develop the habit of using our intention on a regular basis, like doing a few minutes of Self-hypnosis or visualization every day, for example.

The power of our mind is well demonstrated by the "mind-power effect." This is still being called the placebo effect but that name has become antiquated. In medicine the word "placebo" refers to a substance or treatment that has no effect, in and of itself, but which is administered to a person as a psychological pacifier, or to promote healing through the power of the mind alone. This power is often attributed to the effects of strong belief or expectation, as well as a response to the authority of the source of the treatment. But to refer to the amazing power of the human mind, which we really don't understand at all, as a pacifier, is silly, don't you think?[86] And, as with all such things, there are those who acknowledge the Mind-Power Effect and those who believe it doesn't really exist. But in reality this effect is undeniable, and that it be taken into account has long been a requirement for any valid medical study. Besides my own experiences in life, and as a Hypnotherapist, I have heard hundreds of remarkable stories of the power of belief, faith, intention, and expectation, and many of these come from the medical profession where people were healed with inert medicine or sham medical procedures. What we believe and expect, and what authority figures tell us, can have powerful effects. And this can work for us or against us. When it works against us, it has been called the "nocebo effect." In Australia the Aborigines had a tradition of execution called "pointing the bone." If a shaman

---

[86] The"Mind-Power Effect" designation is catching on and has replaced the "Placebo Effect" in many places, including books like "Meditation as Medicine" by Dharma Singh Khalsa and Cameron Stauth, 2001, and "Mind Medicine" by Uri Geller, 1999.

with the proper authority pointed the bone at someone who had committed a serious crime, that person would inevitably die within a few days. Voodoo works in a similar way. We might say it was their own expectation that killed them. This almost happened to my mother.

When my mother was diagnosed with lung cancer, she was losing weight and had some back pain. She was seventy-three and had been a cigarette smoker for most of her life, and although the tumor was small, it had probably been growing for years. When the doctor gave her the diagnosis, she wanted to know how long she had to live. The doctor preferred not to give her the statistics but she insisted, so he said that people in her situation usually lived about a year. I was with her and watched her carefully. This news did not appear to affect her. The doctor explained that this estimate was just an educated guess, but my concern was that it might traumatize my mother, which could turn a guess into an internal pronouncement. I talked with her about the diagnosis and continued to quietly observe her mood for the rest of the day. She appeared to be fine.

The next morning however, was a different story. She could barely walk, and she shuffled around like a zombie. Whereas she used to take care of herself, cook meals, and do many of the household chores, today she couldn't even make coffee. She spoke in low whispering tones and needed me to do everything for her. She also mentioned something about only having six months to live, which is not what the doctor said. So that morning, once we were settled at the breakfast table, I asked her: "So Mom, did you have a shock?" We had a talk, and got to the bottom of her drastic transformation from a self-sufficient person to an invalid. We had done some ID-R sessions previously, so this didn't take long. She said "Well, I guess it finally hit me." She then described her shock while lying in bed, at the idea of her impending death, and her subsequent feelings, thoughts, and decisions. In less than ten minutes she was back to normal and remained so. She lived another two and a half years.

This story illustrates why anyone in authority, from parents, teachers, doctors, nurses, and counselors, to church officials, police, older siblings, or shamans, would do well to understand the power in their words, intonations, and body language, to do both great good and great harm.

If I were to suggest three golden rules to follow with regard to using the suggestive power of authority with others, the first would be DO NOT CAUSE TRAUMA. People get triggered all the time, which is not trauma, but do your best to not really overwhelm others, especially children or others who are in a sensitive state. That's always number one. But it's also important to be truthful and authentic in our communication, and the truth can sometimes be very traumatic, which can't be helped. Also people often traumatize themselves by their own thinking, which is out of our control. So we don't have to walk on eggshells regarding this, but we can do our best

The second principle would be DO NOT BE NEGATIVE – try to avoid imposing or suggesting any negative judgement or expectation on people who are in a very vulnerable place.

The third rule is BE POSITIVE – try and relate only the most positive or productive interpretations and expectations you can, whenever your words have great power in a sensitive situation. This could be another whole course in itself.

Self-hypnosis

Self-hypnosis is simply the process of creating positive intentions and images, called "suggestions," while you are in a quiet non-thinking state. You want to bypass your so called "critical thinking" which is actually mostly preconditioned thought and programming. If the intention is "To see myself as beautiful," because you don't, repeating an affirmation like "I am beautiful," may only stimulate your deep-rooted negative beliefs. To overcome this may require thousands of repetitions for it to make a dent on your self-perception, because it is constantly being countered by the opposite thought. This is the problem with so called "positive thinking" – it has to overcome any unconscious programming that is working against it. Hypnosis works because it installs the desired intentions and changes in the form of thoughts, images, and feelings, in the depths of your unconscious mind, bypassing or neutralizing the negative programming, so the process of change can begin immediately.

There are many good books on Self-hypnosis and visualization that go into more detail (See Bibliography) and I highly recommend you check them out or take a class. But for now the simplest way to begin is to do your daily meditation, and at the end when you are in a quiet state, simply state and envision your intended outcome clearly, several times. Think of it as planting a seed in your inner mind. Then let it go. Don't think about it. Your own inner power will take over. Keep your suggestions clear, simple, and few, and visualize the end result. It is often best to state the intention as a process that is happening, such as "I am getting better every day" or picturing a wart shrinking until it's gone. Generally the best results come from doing this daily for about twenty-one days but often the effects begin right away. Try this and see what happens! I once got rid of two warts at once after doing self-hypnosis for only four days. The warts began to shrink, and I knew I was done. They had been there for over a year but were completely gone in about ten days. Whatever changes you want in your life, doing regular self-hypnosis can help.

More Tools

Self-observation, reframing, meditation and self-hypnosis are just a few of the many Identity Management practices that can help us to be free of our automatic reactions and have more control over our lives. Whenever you find something that works well in this regard you can keep it in your purse or toolbelt to use as needed, or if it's something like exercise or meditation, you can make it a regular part of your life. Here is a short list of some other powerful ID-M practices I recommend exploring. I use them all with great benefit. See the Bibliography for more information.

– Creative Visualization can help you clarify and achieve your goals. Positive Self-Talk can help eliminate negative thought patterns and reinforce positive attributes.

– Asking a question of your unconscious mind, or of spirit, constantly, is something I do all the time. You keep asking one question, whenever you think of it, until you get an answer - and you will. Your question can be general or very specific like "How can I save more time?" or "What is my real mission in life?" When you get an answer it may not make much sense at first, or it may not seem feasible, but maybe you just need to reframe it or understand it better. You may get lots of answers. I just write them down and keep asking until I find one I can use.

– I use Routines and Rituals to weave things like exercise, self-hypnosis, and meditation into my daily schedule. Being consistent is important – the things we do consistently determine the outcome of our lives. An easy way to add something you want to do consistently to your life is to place it in the middle of things you already do. This method has been called "habit stacking" because you are linking your new behavior to a pattern that is already solidly in place. Until I have turned a new behavior into a habit, I use reminders like notes or alarms to keep me on track.

– "Focusing" is a great and simple technique I found in the book "The Power of Focusing" by Ann Weiser Cornell that helps us develop greater self-sensitivity and communication with our mind and body. And learning the Internal Family Systems approach to working with your own issues, can do incredible things. "The Internal Family Systems Workbook" by Richard Schwartz is a good source for this. Both of these methods can even resolve major issues.

– The assertiveness principles in Manuel Smith's book "When I Say No I Feel Guilty" are great tools to have and use for non-defensive communication and changing reactive patterns.

– Then there is the NLP modeling technology that Tony Robbins discusses in "Unlimited Power" and there are many other valuable ideas there, and even more in his book "Awaken the Giant Within" that you can learn and use to help create the life you want.

Whatever you want to change in your life, there are methods that can help you better manage things, and there are other methods you can use to resolve any deeper underlying issues. When an issue like anxiety or anger is resolved, managing it is of course no longer needed, but managing or resolving our limitations allows us to move forward. When we want to improve some aspects of life, like health, relationships, prosperity, wisdom, happiness, fulfillment, or spiritual growth, even when we have the motivation, knowledge, skills, and strategies to get there, we may still be limited by powerful unconscious forces which can stop us in our tracks. Many of the things blocking our way can be totally invisible until we take a closer look, which is what this whole book is about – waking up to ourselves. In the next chapter we will look into using some ID-R principles to bring some of those invisible forces out into the open.

Chapter 19
Identity Resolution

*"People will do anything, no matter how absurd, in order to avoid
facing their own souls. One does not become enlightened by
imagining figures of light, but by making the darkness conscious."*
– Carl Jung, Psychology and Alchemy

That's what Identity Resolution (ID-R) is all about – making the
darkness conscious. Resolution is the first level of healing where the
root cause of a problem is eliminated. ID-R is the process of
resolving the stuck identity states created during trauma, and
thereby healing the troubling or limiting conditions attached to
those states. Other effective means of handling trauma do the same
thing to some degree, but may describe it differently. The healing
that occurs is a natural consequence of self-awareness,
introspection, and gaining access to key aspects of our traumatic
memories – of bringing light to the darkness. In this chapter I will
describe ID-R in a bit more detail, with emphasis on what it takes to
do it for oneself, and then give you some simple instructions that
will help you gain a deeper understanding of the basic process, if
you are inclined to try it.

Summarizing my own experience, in using ID-R for myself I was
able to put an end to multiple headaches and other physical pains
and symptoms. I was able to resolve all kinds of fears, phobias, and
anxieties. I was able to change my attitudes regarding many
different things. I was able to put an end to dissociative reactions I
didn't even know I had and to integrate with many different helper
personalities that I had no idea even existed. I was able to recall
much of my childhood that had been selectively blocked, revealing
much trauma, and this gave me deep insights into many of the
mysteries in my life. Working with ID-R helped me to recall and
experience many things beyond what most of us ever remember
during the course of a lifetime. It not only gave me confidence that
almost any condition or problem resulting from the experience of

trauma can be resolved, but helped me understand people, the human mind, and consciousness in a whole new way. Also, recalling the paranormal and spiritual experiences that were present throughout my life gave me a much broader understanding of human existence. It helped me see our true potential and further validated the possibility of spiritual enlightenment. And ID-R enabled me to help others do the same, and to share all this with you. This approach has been healing, empowering, and enlightening.

That being said, ID-R is not a therapy. That's how I choose to see it. The idea that something is "a therapy" is a mental construct. As I pointed out in Chapter 18, how we frame something determines what it is for us. That's why I don't accept the concept of mental illness. I may use such terms, but mental illness is a medical concept that equates the mind with the body and sees a psychological problem as an illness. Although the body and mind do function as one system, they are not the same, just as the software running in a computer is not the same as the hardware. Here's a metaphor of how I see ID-R.

When we were in third grade, my friend Jeff and I rode our bicycles downtown to ride the escalators at JC Penney. It was the farthest we had ever traveled on bikes. We had some fun but eventually got kicked out of the store. Riding home however, we got lost. We differed strongly on how to find our way back, so we split up. Jeff followed his intuition and just went in the direction he felt was right. As for me, I didn't want to get more lost, so I rode back to Penney's and then backtracked my way home from memory, step by step, until I reached familiar territory. I knew my way would work, but Jeff was operating as a free spirit and wanted me to trust his judgement. He thought I was being a spoilsport and I felt he was being reckless and a stubborn idiot, while I was being smart and scientific. Jeff proudly beat me home.

The point of this story is that there was nothing wrong with us – no medical condition that needed fixing, We were just two lost kids who needed to find our way home, and we did, each in our own way. Considering our human condition, on the mental and spiritual side of things, home is just seeing things as they are, seeing through our illusions and misconceptions. When we see clearly what we need to see, everything falls into place naturally and our "problems" disappear. We only have these problems when we forget who we are and how we got into our present predicament. We can frame our psychospiritual difficulties in many ways, and they can be seen as illnesses requiring treatment, or as calls to remember and reclaim our own truth and power – a kind of shamanistic approach. I prefer the latter, and refer to myself as a spiritual counselor.

The Past is Present

ID-R has three basic uses. First it's a means to resolve any unwanted conditions or automatic reactions we may have. These reactions are stuck, or programmed, at an unconscious level as explained in chapters five and six. Secondly, ID-R can help you get things you want, like regaining or acquiring abilities you have lost or would like to have. Thirdly, it's like a master key for understanding yourself on a deeper level, by helping you recall your forgotten history, answer questions or explain any mysteries about your life, clarify memories, and it can even help you understand the meaning of your dreams. ID-R does all these things by addressing the internal blocks that hide the truth from us. These blocks are most often the result of trauma, at least on the human level.

Keep in mind however that, in my experience, few people actually want to explore their past or look deeper into their lives, and even fewer want to do this on their own, even if it might answer some important questions or help resolve some of their issues. There are many reasons for this, but basically the majority of us are so involved with the externals of life that we most often just want a quick fix for our issues and aren't looking for any deeper understanding. Also many people on a self-improvement path believe that the past is long gone and is best ignored. They feel it's better to live in the "now" and focus on creating a better future, and that rehashing the past is not only a waste of time but also the cause of many people's problems. Such people may be content with managing whatever issues arise without looking for root causes, until things get bad enough that they seek some form of intervention or therapy.

People on a spiritual path often have similar views and may also feel that the past doesn't matter because it isn't real, and that spiritual realization is the ultimate solution to everything. All these views have many valid points that I agree with, and yet all those who refrain from considering the past still fix things that get broken, correct problems that occur in their lives, and do things for learning and enjoyment. And when you realize that in our "not yet awakened" minds the past is actually _present right now_, with its effects being very real, you will see that dealing with the past to handle a present-time issue is no different from changing a light bulb or putting out a fire. In fact, those on a spiritual path will usually find that the first thing that gets in their way, as they become more open and receptive, are intense and difficult emotions, thoughts, and energies that arise spontaneously from their past experiences. Many spiritual traditions have ways to deal with these things, usually by accepting them and not resisting them. The feelings will eventually fade, even if very intense at first. If we try to avoid them or suppress them when they arise however, they can hinder, or even halt, further progress.

My feeling is that these various reasons for dismissing the past are just excuses that help us avoid facing it. Besides simply not understanding the role it plays in the here and now, I think that for most of us the avoidance of exploring the past, is primarily due to the pain and unwelcome feelings and realizations that are hiding there, and that's a valid concern. But whatever is hiding in the shadows in the back of our minds, it can all be brought into the light and resolved. And the past equally contains a great many unimaginable treasures. So I see no valid reason to avoid engaging the past, with the proper precautions, and most people with amnesia would probably want to get their memory back. Remember what Socrates said about an unexamined life? My own path includes both examining and resolving my past and working toward waking up to what I am, beyond those experiences. And while these two routes have different goals, they are completely compatible and complementary.

Solo

The solo ID-R process is basically very simple. First we bring the condition, limitation, or question to mind, sit with it, and notice all the feelings, thoughts, and sensations connected to it that are immediately present. Then we address a series of questions and

notice specific things regarding the condition. We are using our
natural abilities of attention, focus, memory, recognition,
imagination, feeling, and perception, among others. The questions
themselves, when addressed from the correct viewpoint, will trigger
the recognition of key hidden components of the primary source of
the condition. This happens automatically. As the inner source of
the condition reveals itself, many things can rise to the surface,
including intense emotions or sensations, painful memories, and
profound revelations. This can bring great relief from pain and
emotional distress, and will bring to light any unconscious
decisions, mechanisms, and other factors that are involved. When
all relevant aspects of the issue are seen, its resolution should be
spontaneous, and beliefs and attitudes will change accordingly. If
the issue is only to remember or clarify something, the ID-R process
makes it easier and can remove any memory blocks.

Becoming a Spiritual Warrior

Although the ID-R process is simple, that doesn't mean it's easy.
Not only do we have to become aware of things hidden in the
unconscious mind, which is difficult enough, but we are often
dealing with the most painful and frightening aspects of human
experience, and we can encounter massive resistence, especially
when doing this alone. Many people are afraid of going anywhere
near the traumas hiding inside them, and because of that they avoid
things like meditation or hypnosis, or anything else that might relax
their defenses. So the first thing to consider here is whether you
should do this type of work on your own at all. What happens in ID-
R sessions is that we are often recalling traumatic moments that
may contain very intense emotional and physical pain or other
intense mindbody feelings and reactions. We may also encounter
very disturbing memories that we may not want to experience
again, or recall things we may not want to believe or which
challenge our reality on many levels. The internal conflicts can be
profound. Many counselors feel there is also a possibility of being
retraumatized when working with trauma, even with help. Indeed,
doing inner work like ID-R on your own does require having the
mental fortitude necessary to face your pain and emotional distress

without being overcome by fear, while maintaining a degree of self-control.

The good news is that the more you do inner work like this, the stronger you become. Becoming a spiritual warrior is about developing strength of intention and a high capacity for facing the unknown and accepting whatever shows up. These qualities will increase over time. It also takes discipline and determination to keep going when it seems like you aren't getting anywhere. That's why it's best to start slowly by working with things you feel you can handle easily. And remember, whatever comes up has _already_ been experienced – it is already a part of you – and it's ALL you. So if you feel you have good ego strength and aren't subject to extended dissociative periods, intense PTSD manifestations, panic attacks, suicidal ideation, or psychotic episodes, and feel confident that you can handle whatever might arise, that's all good. The truth is, whatever you have experienced in the past, you have already survived and handled in your own way. Even so, remembering or reliving trauma can be challenging. That's why we have ways to stop reactions when they get too painful or out of control, and ways to get into a calm and non-reactive state whenever needed, and we will cover those shortly. But after reading all the instructions, if you don't feel comfortable doing this kind of work on your own, then don't. Either have someone assist you by reading the instructions to you, or have them just be there with you, or work with a counselor.

So the first principle here is to never take on more than you can handle. If what you're working on ever feels like too much, take a break. However, the feeling of it being too much may just be part of the issue, and if so, you will be working with that feeling during the session. Most of the time you will probably just breeze right through the issue you are working on, but sometimes we need to take a break and assimilate and adjust to things we remember, or feelings that arise. You can think of this as healing the trauma one small piece at a time, which makes it easier. Since we are dealing with traumatic shocks, and since every shock is "too much" in some way, the more you experience these "too much" moments, the easier they are to confront. But _do_ back off and take a break any time you need to gather your strength. It's like skin diving – occasionally you have to come up for air. Then go right back to it when you are ready.

Your New Superpowers

When I do ID-R for myself, it is always an adventure. I never know what I will discover, but whatever my goal for the session is, I do know that eventually I will find something of value, and occasionally something amazing and life changing. In fact for me the whole process is always amazing. It's like I'm sorting through a huge treasure chest of priceless artwork. Some sessions might be duds and others I may not complete right away, but most of the time the value is indeed beyond measure. Success in this work does require some patience, and it can often take some time before I feel I'm making any real progress on an issue, but it's more about being determined, focused, and in the zone. An average session takes about ninety minutes, but even if it takes hours of drudgery to finally get somewhere and the results are that I only clear up something minor, it's always worth it – it further validates the process and removes another internal block. I make it a point to finish every session but when I can't, I will usually start again as soon as possible.

Imagine digging for diamonds and knowing you will find some almost every time you dig! You might wonder how working through trauma can be fun, but it's like doing a physical workout to get stronger, even if it is painful. This reminds me of how Arnold Schwarzenegger, the world's most famous bodybuilder, described his difficult workouts as incredibly pleasurable, and yet he used to work out until he would actually vomit. Part of the pleasure that he connected to the "pain" was that he could see the results of his hard work almost daily, and he constantly visualized having the results he wanted. And of course he did reap great rewards for his efforts. And so will you. The more you experience the rewards of self-discovery and inner healing the more you will understand what I'm talking about, and your motivation to keep doing it will grow.

So where do we begin? Think of something you would like to change – some condition you want to get rid of, like anxiety, or some ability you would like to have, like more confidence. Or think of something about your life you would like to remember or understand better. Your goal can be huge or minor but it has to be something about you, not about someone else or something outside of you. A nagging partner or a rainy day may be unwanted conditions, but this is about changing yourself, not about changing other people or the weather. On the other hand some external conditions may actually change when *you* change. If you are jobless, after some effective work on yourself, a new job may seem to come out of nowhere. There can be many reasons for this. It also doesn't matter if you think that what you want is something that is impossible to achieve. It may very well <u>be</u> impossible, but you won't really know until you try, and even if you don't get what you want, you may still get something valuable from the session – maybe something even more valuable!

In an ID-R session we help you take a closer look at the problem. If it's some unwanted condition, we resolve it. If it's something you want, like more confidence, we work on whatever it is within you that stands in the way of that. The idea is that confidence, a forgotten memory, or whatever ability you wish to have, is already within you and has simply been blocked. This is an assumption, but one I believe in. After the session the problem may seem different, better, or even gone. If it's not gone then we work with any other parts of the issue that still need resolving. Some things may have several roots, or involve other issues that must be handled first.

When the effects of trauma are finally resolved, unconsciously imposed blocks and limitations fall away, and a new world opens up. A fun way to look at this is to recognize that every resolved issue gives you a new ability, and every new ability is like having a new Superpower. Whatever you could not do before, like being calm around bees, being able to smile, confidently giving a speech, or going to a social event without getting a headache, has become easy and natural. There's no limit to what you can change and what you can do. We are only stopped by our internal conditioning and limiting beliefs.

Take a sheet of paper and draw a vertical line down the middle. On the left side make a list of some of the problems or issues you would like to get rid of, whether mental or physical. You may not think of them all right now but take a few minutes and jot down whatever comes up. You can list all the biggest issues or limitations that are affecting you the most, and all your minor issues too – list *everything* you want to change, and don't be surprised if it's a large number. You also can include things you want to remember or abilities you would like to have. Then on the right side of the line, opposite each obstacle, describe the new superpower you will have when that issue is gone! You may also want to imagine how this new ability will change your life. This will add to your motivation! If you work on these issues successfully, those new superpowers will be yours! But more than all that, you will know yourself better and you will begin developing the realization of your greater untapped potential to be free and happy beyond measure.

Working on Yourself

Please note that the following information is for self-discovery purposes only and not to diagnose or treat any medical or psychiatric condition.

The brief process presented here is solely for the purpose of seeing how ID-R works and possibly discovering the source of an issue. There is much more to it, as you will have gathered from the previous chapters. Even so, the basics are here and you may get some benefit from doing this, like relief from something that is blocking or troubling you, for exactly the reasons given at the beginning of this chapter, and seeing what you need to see. Understand however, that since the whole panoply of ID-R methods will not be used, the objective is just to get some insight and see some things clearly. Among other things we will not be covering dissociation, helper personalities, spiritual influences, or looking more deeply into the power-zone. We will also not be covering the identity-bridge method for recalling the forgotten sources of our unwanted conditions.

Once you see and understand the general process of how we get stuck with all our programming, from your own observation, you can begin to have hope that real relief and change are possible, and other things discussed earlier may also make more sense. Often, just by being able to see where a reaction is actually coming from, our distress about it diminishes or may even disappear. Any other insights can be equally valuable.

Since not everyone will want to do this kind of work by themselves, and not everyone can, for various reasons, you can also do this with a partner. If you do it with a partner just have them be there with you for support. If you want them to read the questions to you, it's important the partner not do anything other than that, while you give the answers in your own time in your own way. They can acknowledge your answers with a neutral response like "OK," "got it," or "good." Unless they have some counseling experience they are there for support only, and conversation should be kept to a minimum. You can work out your own communication rules as you go. Your partner should also read this chapter.

Anyone can be helped with assistance by an experienced counselor, but a suitable partner may not be available. The question is whether we can do deep internal processing like this by ourselves. I believe those who develop a good understanding of what we are doing in using ID-R will also be able to use these instructions effectively on their own. This is why my training courses each require ten sessions with me. I don't think I'm that special however, and I believe many people can do what I did, but the only way to find out if you can do it yourself is to try. I think the main obstacle in doing solo work like this is that our own reactions, like fear and avoidance, get in the way, and we have a natural tendency to move away from pain. Also it takes some discipline, and it's very easy to get distracted. But even those limitations can be addressed and resolved like anything else.

A more complete presentation for solo ID-R with additional tools will require an entire volume of its own, which is in the works. Meanwhile the complete detailed instructions are currently only available in Part I of my ID-R Training Program.

But before we get into the simplified session instructions for gaining some insight it is important to have a way out of any uncomfortable feelings or thoughts that might arise.

Conscious Shifting

You may have heard the phrase "the way out is through." This is often true, but if we're not quite ready to go through something it's best to back off a bit and regroup. So if you ever start to feel overwhelmed by something, get confused, or feel like you're losing control, you need a way to change that on the spot. As I described in Chapter 18, the best way out of one state is to get into another one. To do that you first interrupt the pattern you are stuck in, and then focus on doing something else. A super-fast way to do that is to immediately change your breathing pattern. Clear your mind and inhale slowly through your nose for five seconds, hold your breath for five seconds, exhale slowly through your mouth for five seconds, and hold your breath for another five seconds. Do this several times. This is a form of "box breathing" and it will shift your state. The key is to totally focus on your breathing.

A common technique we use in hypnotherapy is to get into a peaceful state where we feel safe and strong, and link that to a code word or a physical anchor, like taking a deep breath and exhaling, or squeezing a shoulder, so that we can get into that state instantly whenever we want. You can do this by sitting quietly and remembering a time and place when you felt strong, safe, calm, and supported. Picture people around you who give you support or strength. You don't have to be in hypnosis. When those peaceful feelings are present, try and increase them – just really immerse yourself in them for a minute. Then you can choose a special code word to say silently to yourself, like the word "SAFE," "CALM," or "STRONG," with the intention that this word will shift you into this positive state whenever you use it. You can include a physical anchor to the code word as well, like a shoulder squeeze or tapping your hand on your chest.

Next, imagine being upset. Bring those feelings up and then take a deep breath, and go back to feeling better by doing exactly what you did before: get relaxed and calm again by remembering that same scene where you feel strong, safe, and calm. When those feelings are present, again try and increase them. Then repeat your code word and physical anchor with the intention that this will shift you into this positive state. Do this several times and practice this at least once before each session, as long as you feel it's needed.

In actuality, when consciously shifting out of a negative state in daily life by getting into a different state, the new identity state doesn't have to be calm and peaceful – it only has to be different and stable. Changing your physiology is the fastest way to do this, which is why breathing exercises work. You could also do jumping jacks, start laughing, play a game, or go for a walk. Do whatever works for you. Once your mind is engaged in the new activity and off the negative state for a short time, that state will fade, even if it includes physical symptoms or pain. If something comes up that doesn't temporarily go away, review what I did in Chapter 10, Taming the Tiger. So if something comes up in a session that you want to back off from, <u>shift out of it consciously</u> by using any of these methods, and go back to the session when and if you feel ready. You can also use any other method that works for you to get back into a better state.

Doing ID-R

If you are not ready to try this now, you can easily skip the rest of this chapter if you like, and come back to it later.

Do this in a quiet place where you won't be interrupted, as you would when doing meditation (see page 393). It's a good idea to take notes. These will be helpful while doing the process and afterward.

With ID-R you can target anything, including traumas, feelings, sensations, dreams, mental or physical conditions. What we want to do here is to work with something that is a problem or condition of some kind that is recurring. It could be a feeling, a reaction, or a recurring dream. In this lite version of ID-R we will first find a memory connected to the thing you want to address and then work through that incident for more clarity, to remove any blocks, and get some relief. If the condition is a recurring dream, we will use the strongest feeling in the dream as the target. If you want to look at a specific incident or trauma in your life that you are already aware of, you can skip Step 1 and go on to Step Two, if there is no resistance.

Handling Resistance

Before doing either of these steps, <u>ask yourself</u> if there is any part of you that does not want to deal with this, or is opposed to you knowing more about this condition or being free of it. If there is no sense of resistance, move on to Step One. If you do sense some internal resistance or are unsure, this must be handled first. Resistance can have many reasons and take many forms. Ask yourself the following questions:

✳ ✳

If I get rid of this condition will something bad happen?
If this condition is gone will I lose something? What's at stake?
Is there some value in things remaining the same?
– What do I gain?
Is there something I might discover that would be too upsetting?
If I resolve this issue will I be breaking a promise?
Is a part of me trying to protect me?
Does a part of me want to stop me or interfere for some reason?
Or just ask: "Why is there resistance?" and "How can we work together?"

Whatever answers you get, ask yourself if they are really true at this point in time. If you can see that any answer is not true, see if the resistance is gone. Whatever the answers are, you basically want to counsel yourself until you feel you can proceed without resistance. If you can't, choose another item to work on for now. When there is no resistance, proceed with Step 1.

Step One

Write down the feeling or reaction in question, like fear, guilt, jumbled thoughts, sweating, or whatever it is. Then hold it in your awareness – <u>really be in that state</u> – and ask yourself the following questions. Their purpose is to help you find a memory connected to this condition. Everything starts somewhere. Take your time. Ask each question a few times if needed. If nothing comes up, go to the next question. If you do get an answer, have a flashback, or remember something, write it down. As soon as you recall an incident <u>that feels right</u>, even if the memory is vague, that will be our target.

At this point skip any remaining questions and go to Step Two. If you get nothing from any of the questions, we will leave this subject and choose another condition to work on. You can always try again later. Remember to take notes and briefly write down your answers. We are looking for a specific incident or memory. You can also repeat this list a few times if necessary. <u>As soon as you find an incident to work on, skip the other questions and go to Step Two.</u>

If something better comes up, you can always work on that too. It's all up to you.

✳ ✳

Can you spot the first time you ever experienced this
feeling (or thought or sensation – whatever it is)?
If so, write it down and give it a label, eg: "Spanked on
birthday." If this incident feels right, go to step two.
Is this feeling connected to any particular person?
If so, is there a particular occasion where they are connected?
If this incident feels right, go to step two.

Is this feeling connected to any particular incident?
If you recall an incident that feels right, go to step two.

Is this feeling connected to any particular place?
If so, is there a particular occasion where they are connected?
If this incident feels right, go to step two.

Is this feeling connected to any particular object?
If so, is there a particular occasion where they are connected?
If this incident feels right, go to step two.

Step Two

Once you have a memory to work with, just relax and picture it in your mind. Become an observer of that memory as if you are there in the past, seeing what you saw, hearing what you heard etc. Since this incident had a negative effect on you, spot when that negative effect happened. Maybe someone yelled at you or you became aware of something disturbing. We'll call this the "shift." Something happened and your feelings and thoughts changed. Notice how you were before the shift – were you happy, sad, neutral, asleep? What were you doing or trying to do? This is your "before" identity. Note it. After the shift happened, notice how you felt and what you were trying to do, if anything. What was your goal? Note that. Give each identity a title to use later, like "happy me," "angry boy," or "terrified child." If none of this is clear yet, just continue.

If you noticed a shift, look more closely at it. Spot the exact moment things shifted. If it's too vague, that's OK. See if there is a moment of shock there, right at the beginning of that shift. This would be a disturbance that is overwhelming in some way. Review the "Shock" section on page 116 if you need to. The shock is really a transition. Spotting the shift is just seeing that there <u>WAS</u> a transition. The shock is the <u>CAUSE</u> of the shift, so you're just spotting the actual transition. That's all there is to it – something changed! As you continue this process, you may begin to have more clarity on what happened.

The next questions will help you with that. If you don't notice a shock or a shift, this can still be helpful. Ask each question repeatedly. For example, ask yourself: "In or around this shock (or shift, or incident) is there any emotion or feeling?" Then ask if there is any <u>other</u> emotion or feeling, since there may be several of each item. For example if there are decisions, try and get them all. When the answer is "no," move on. Here are the questions:

1. In or around this shock is there any: <u>Emotion or feeling</u>?
     If so, <u>feel that feeling, for that time</u>. It's especially important to feel your feelings and to feel them in the body or wherever they are. This includes negative and positive feelings. If a feeling is intense, just let yourself feel as much as you can. Back off if needed. There can be many emotions, so ask again and do the same. Take your time. Sometimes a checklist can help. Check for fear, anger, hate, betrayal, lost, disbelief, joy, love, peace, hurt, shock, hopeless, helpless, grief, sadness, guilt, shame, etc.

2.In or around this shock is there any: <u>Decision?</u> Repeat.

3. In or around this shock is there any: <u>Thought or question?</u> Repeat.

4. In or around this shock is there any: <u>Pain or Sensation?</u>
     If so, feel that pain or sensation? Repeat.

5. In or around this shock is there any: <u>Judgment?</u>
     (about anyone or anything, including self) Repeat.

6. In or around this shock is there any: <u>Effort or energy?</u>
   If so, feel the effort or energy. Repeat.

7. In or around this shock: <u>Does anything get suppressed?</u>
   (hidden, pushed away, prevented) Repeat<u>.</u>

8. In or around this shock: <u>Does anything get imagined?</u> Repeat.

9. In or around this shock:
   <u>Is there any time where you seemed to be out of your body?</u>
   If there was, just recall what that was like.

That's all for now. As you answer each these questions and feel the feelings, you may experience some relief or have some realizations or insights. If at the end of this you feel agitated, see if the agitation is part of that incident. If it is, then feel that feeling just as it was in the incident – feel it in your body or wherever it is. If it's not part of that incident, just relax and it will fade. You can investigate it later. There are many other questions that can be asked and more things we can do, but we will skip all that for now.

Now once again recall the identity you were in before the shift or at the beginning of the incident - like "happy me." Whatever that was, imagine being that character right now. Really be in that viewpoint and feel how you felt, then shift back to just being yourself in the here and now.

Now do the same with the identity after the shift, like "angry me." Be in that character's viewpoint just as you were in the past, and feel how that feels. Then shift back to just being you in the here and now. Recall any times you have shifted into that same identity or feeling state in the past in response to some situation or trigger. In your mind try and scan through all the times you ever had that particular reaction. Imagine all those memories and energies evaporating into space. When done, take a deep breath.

How do you feel? Were you able to remember more, feel the feelings, gain any insights? How does the condition you addressed seem to you now? Better? The same or different? Gone?

To sum this all up, my main purpose in describing this exercise is to help you see for yourself that our present conditions and reactions are directly connected to adverse experiences in the past, and that these traumatic moments are instigated by a shock, an overwhelming moment that causes a shift in our state of being. You can then directly see how these trauma-connected identity states become ingrained patterns that can affect us repeatedly throughout our lives. Even if there are parts of the memory that are still unclear or aspects of it that seem strange or confusing, or unfinished, the stuck or recurring aspect of it may be gone. You can always take a closer look later.

Chapter 20
Dream Magic

"The song 'Yesterday' that I wrote, I dreamed that song, And I woke up and there was this tune in my head. Well, now, that's magic." – Paul McCartney

"A dream which is not interpreted is like a letter which is not read." – The Talmud

In this chapter we will explore some simple but powerful techniques and tips for working with dreams, most of which I haven't seen anywhere else. Everything I have to say on this subject comes from the personal experiences of myself and my clients. Since this is not meant to be a complete exposition on dreams, lucid dreams, or OBEs, please check out the bibliography listing for this chapter if you want to learn more.

We all know what dreams are –the fanciful games of magic we play during sleep – but even when remembered, they often slip into oblivion if not written down or recorded immediately. Here's a definition from Wikipedia: "A dream is a succession of images, ideas, emotions, and sensations that usually occur involuntarily in the mind during certain stages of sleep. The content and purpose of dreams are not fully understood, though they have been a topic of scientific speculation, as well as a subject of philosophical and religious interest, throughout recorded history. Dream interpretation is the attempt at drawing meaning from dreams and searching for an underlying message."

In deep sleep we are not actively participating in anything – we are just pure consciousness, our true self. And because we are not distracted by anything, the totality of ourselves is available to us. This includes every experience we have ever had. What emerges from this totality in the form of a dream has some underlying force or intention behind it. The force may be pain, emotion, stress, desire, or frustration – something that is seeking release or acknowledgment. So a dream may also include an attempt to answer a question, or solve a puzzle we have been struggling with, or perhaps it's a wish fulfillment fantasy, or simply an expression of our inner creativity. Although it may contain frivolous and nonsensical material, a dream is most often a surface manifestation of something deeper, just out of sight and not readily apparent. Dreams can also be the vivid remembrances of out-of-body experiences or the shadows of spiritual adventures not yet recalled, including visits to other realms and higher states of being. Dreams can even be transpersonal messages, meant for us or someone else.

However, when a dream is recalled, its central meaning or purpose can be discovered using the appropriate methods. Dreams have been very important in my life and valuable in many ways. This chapter will provide a foundation for the many references I make to dreams in this book, and is dedicated to helping you better understand your own dreams, and get more out of them.

Freud called dreams the royal road to understanding the unconscious, yet many well-educated people still believe that dreams are the result of the random firing of neurons and don't mean anything. The doctor who saved my life many years ago when I had bacterial meningitis would personally come into work on his days off to give me an IV drip of antibiotics, after I had been kicked out of the hospital because I had no insurance. We met at his office daily for two weeks, and on the weekends when his staff was gone, we had some interesting discussions, especially about his years working with Mother Theresa in India. Although I tried to convince him otherwise, he still believed that dreams were just meaningless random brain activity. This silly notion became popular several decades ago. But if it were true, which it obviously is not, dreams would probably be more like white noise. It may be true that some dream content is triggered by random neural activity from which the mind then constructs the dream, but such activity is probably occurring all the time, even while awake.

"Meaning" implies a relationship or connection with something else. The meaning of a dream is simply whatever the dream is referring to, or what it represents in some way. There are many theories about dreams and many ways to interpret them. But what if you could just see where your dreams came from and know what they mean without having to interpret them at all? Well, you can!

Dreams come from within you and everything in every dream has some reason or cause for its being there. If this were not true, it would violate the principle of cause and effect. Even if dreams were triggered by random neural activity, the resulting imagery still comes from <u>your own mind</u>. The fact is that, besides being necessary for our physical and psychological wellbeing, dreams can be very useful. They can provide very powerful insights into ourselves and others, show us things we need to know, and be fountains of creativity and new ideas. While in the altered state of sleep, transpersonal perceptions and connections can also make their way into our dreams, giving us more to work with than we had before falling asleep. The meaning of dreams or dream elements can be trivial, or highly significant. Some dreams require no explanation at all, like solutions to problems or expressions of creativity. For example I have had several delightful new songs come to me in dreams.

I have been fascinated with dreams since I was a kid and often remembered them. I started recording my dreams when I was in High School and continue to this day. On looking back over the thousands of dreams in my journals, I have found a tremendous wealth of insight, understanding, and validation that has been invaluable in a great many ways. P.D. Ouspensky said that we are dreaming all the time, and this appears to be true. If you sit quietly and ignore your conscious thoughts, looking beneath the threshold of your perceptual awareness, you can see that just below the surface there is a lot going on, and not just dreams – our totality is with us all the time. During sleep our perceptions are blocked from awareness, and when we are in some other form of reverie such as meditation, or being in a sensory deprivation tank where our senses are similarly inhibited or ignored, dreams can become dominant in our awareness, and can appear quite vivid and intense. At such times, we might call them hallucinations, but they are more like lucid dreams.

In dream analysis, finding the meaning of a dream typically involves some sort of deciphering based on dream symbol interpretation, or various psychological models of dreaming. A good dream analyst or psychic may sometimes be able to help you connect with the true meaning of a dream, revealing wonderful insights, but in the end it is always you who makes the connection.

However, it is possible to discover what a dream means directly, without resorting to unproven or theoretical methods. Dream analysis then becomes mainly a method of examination and discovery and less reliant on speculation or interpretation.

Dreams are often much more than they appear to be if we take the time to look deeper. For myself, I find that many dreams are mainly memories of past experiences, sometimes entwined with more recent memories or extraneous images. Some dreams are premonitions, and some are symbolic of something I'm not quite aware of. Dreams can be a great many things and have a wide variety of meanings and purposes as we will see. And as Marc Ian Barasch amply demonstrates in his book "Healing Dreams,"[87] a dream can have vast and multiple connections to the past, present, and future, as well as to our own psychology and other people, all in fascinating and miraculous ways. And during lucid dreams, where we are fully conscious, we can also take willful action while in the dreamworld. In these states, which are a form of OBE, we have great power and the magical ability to alter the dream environment in many ways, and to even acquire useful information, and experience real healing that transforms our waking life.

The Flows Technique

To analyze my dreams I employ two main methods: ID-R and Flows. I use ID-R as a method of memory recovery if I suspect the dream is a memory or comes from one. I put myself in the viewpoint in the dream where I was experiencing something significant and ask a series of questions that can trigger recognition. Often the most significant part of the dream is an emotion or feeling. Since the feeling is often one I've had before, I try to recall the most recent time I had this feeling, as well as the very first time. This will often reveal the source and purpose of the dream. There is usually something traumatic involved in memory dreams, but not always.

While the intrinsic meaning of a feeling, like anger or sadness, is usually obvious, why it's specifically there in the dream may not be.

---

[87] "Healing Dreams, Exploring the Dreams That Can Transform Your Life" - Marc Ian Barasch, 2000

For example if I am angry at someone in a dream for stealing from me, it may make sense to be angry in the context of the dream. But why am I having that dream? I may find that someone did steal from me in the past or that I was angry for some *OTHER* reason. The anger is really already inside of me and is manifesting itself in the dream. Once I become aware of the source, I know that the dream is an expression of unresolved past anger. Finding the source of the emotional aspect of a dream usually reveals that the dream grew out of those feelings as they came to the surface. They may have come to the surface for many possible reasons, such as a recent experience that reminded me of the past in some way.

Earlier I referred to some dreams that led me to recall some traumatic incidents, like the "Sorcerer's Apprentice" dream and the "Toy Story," dream, and there are more in Part V. This has also been true for scores of other dreams. All these dreams had an emotional pressure behind them, as if the issues wanted my attention so they could be released. Addressing the dominant feelings can definitely help to resolve recurring dreams, which are recurring because they have something important to reveal, or some stress to release.

A simple process, and one I use most often, is called the "Flows" technique. Any dream is composed of elements, perhaps many, such as feelings, thoughts, objects, people, and situations. I picture a significant element in the dream out in front of me, usually with my eyes closed. I picture it as it was in the dream and I ask myself the following question: "Is there anything that flows or is flowing from that thing (person, object, space, energy, or whatever) to me?"

Then I just look at what I'm visualizing, and see what comes up. This requires some patience. If I get nothing right away, I wait a few seconds and ask the question again. It's a very good idea to take notes. I write down whatever comes to me. It can be anything, like a message, thought, feeling, energy, a gift, intention, or attitude. If I get something, I acknowledge this by silently (in thought) saying to the dream element "I got that." Let's say it's a person in the dream. I visualize or mock up the person in front of me and ask myself the question. If I get the feeling the person is sad, that's a flow. I say to the mockup of the person "I got that" regarding the sadness. This is meant to be a simple acknowledgment, not anything else, and not part of a conversation. Just think of it as the completion of a communication process.

Then I ask the question again. Maybe the person is waving goodbye or I suddenly see a butterfly. Again I respond with "I got that." I would continue like this until I get no more flows from the person or object. I often get enough understanding this way. Sometimes the image or element will change into something else as you work with it, perhaps becoming something it was representing symbolically, or even becoming the opposite of what it first seemed to be. If this happens, you just continue the process with this new image, even if the meaning has now become clear. Do this part first before doing the next step.

If you feel you didn't get enough understanding, you can use Flows again by asking relevant questions of the person or element, like: "Why are you here?" You can ask any questions that occur to you. Again, repeat the same question and respond to the answers, which are also flows, with "I got that." The purpose here is not to get real answers but just to see what comes up. The answers are not necessarily true, although they can be, but they may reveal something of value or have some real meaning for you. You may feel that you are, yourself, creating the flows and the answers you get. It doesn't matter whether this is true or an illusion. Everything is a projection of your mind anyway. However, you are becoming aware of things you were not aware of before, which is the whole point.

When you are done, the process can be completed by making several pictures or mockups of the element in front of you and doing something with them using your imagination. Do whatever you like. You can make them vanish, turn them into rainbows, absorb them, send them to Tahiti, or any of a million things. The idea is that they are your creations and under your control, so you do something with them in order to be done with them. Working with mockups in this way is a creative process that can be very insightful, and it can have a beneficial or healing effect as well. While often this may not seem to do anything, sometimes the effect can be startling!

Do these processes on any element in the dream that you want to understand better. Or do it on every aspect of the dream to see what turns up. That's all there is to it. However it is important to recall and record the dream immediately when you first remember it, bringing it as much into consciousness as you can so you can get the most details. Then work on the dream as soon as possible. The stronger your connection with that altered state in which the dream occurred, the more information you can get.

How do you know when this method is working? The impressions you get are instantly validated by you – it's simply a deeper means of perception. If I handed you a flower and asked you to smell it, you can tell me immediately if you can smell it. The fragrance is a flow from the flower to you, and is an aspect of the flower which you might not have noticed if I hadn't asked you to smell it. You now know more about the flower. With a dream item it's the same thing. There are subliminal aspects present waiting for recognition. The end result is that you feel satisfied that you understand the dream better. If you don't, then it didn't work for that dream, and you can try another method. But I find that it does work remarkably well most of the time. It supercedes the need for interpretation by helping you see the meaning directly, and is one of the most simple and powerful tools I know.

This process opens a portal to let the meaning into your conscious mind. It works because we are focusing on actually receiving subliminal information rather than just thinking about the dream. All the answers and meanings are already within you. It's kind of like when you are trying to remember something and you only have a little information about it. Basically you ask yourself the question, and then wait. Your unconscious mind does the rest. Say you forgot the name of a celebrity, so you try to remember. You just ask inside for the name, remain silently receptive, and eventually it arrives. Or you picture the person or recall something about them, and then you wait. You are holding a door open for the answer to come in, and it does. The Flows process is similar, and has other applications as well, both in ID-R and in life.

Nightly Treasures

Like a garage-sale Rembrandt, dreams are treasures, but only when you recognize them for what they are and don't ignore them. Dreams are keys to understanding, but I want to reiterate here that only you can know what your dreams mean. Even if someone were able to correctly interpret your dreams or psychically know what they mean, this would still be second hand knowledge for you. When you find out for yourself, you know for sure, and in the process you also open inner doorways that can bring real relief, and provide deeper insight and validation than any outside interpretation can ever give you.

But it does take some work. First you must remember your dreams, which is best done immediately when you awaken. I even record dreams that seem stupid or meaningless because later on they may prove valuable. For many years I had a notebook on my night stand, then a tape recorder. Now I use a dedicated digital voice recorder. If you use the voice recorder on your cell phone, I recommend turning off all EMF signals including phone, wifi, bluetooth, and GPS at night. This radiation is biologically harmful, contrary to what you may have heard, and can also interfere with sleep, and you don't want it close to your head for eight hours a day. You will also sleep better!

To help me remember my nighttime adventures, I also have a "reminder" list taped to a cardboard poster next to my bed. This printed list includes all the things I experience most often in dreams or OBEs, like flying, spirits, animals, Patty, other friends and people I know, places I've lived, cars, sex, food, becoming lucid, running, hiding, and more. Make your own list of things you commonly dream about or experience at night. Just going over your list for a minute upon awakening can help you recall many dreams you might never remember. Record them right away.

I don't work with every dream of course, only those that have some strong emotions, are in some way provocative, or intuitively feel important. Once you have a dream that you want to explore, you have to take the time to do the Flows process and memory work, or some other method like self-hypnosis or ID-R. I recommend taking these processes seriously and doing them in a formal and complete way, as opposed to being sloppy, just asking a few questions and giving up. The effort is well worth it, and you will be developing a good habit.

Working with dreams has also helped me recall the details of OBEs, lucid dreams, and forgotten real life experiences that were not traumatic. When I recall lucid dreams, OBEs, or other spiritual experiences that occur while asleep, I see them as real life events which I may not be recalling completely. I use ID-R or Flows to get further information and understanding. The sources of some of my past dreams were actually higher level OBEs that I did not recall, some of which occurred the same night as the dream. For example once I dreamed I was talking to Lynne when we were dating and was trying to get her to go somewhere with me, but she was refusing to budge from her chair and I was feeling frustrated. While working on the dream, I recalled that I had left my body and visited her on the same night as the dream. I was trying to get her to leave her body and go somewhere with me so I could show her something. I actually tried to pull her out of her body to wake her up in the OBE state, but she remained asleep. I would pull her half way out and she would snap back in, so I finally gave up. I hadn't recalled the OBE, but a distorted representation of it emerged as the dream of her sitting in a chair in a kind of stupor.

In addition to providing personal revelations, dreams have been the source of many creative ideas, works of art, scientific discoveries, and inspiration for myself, and many others throughout history. The inspiration for the discovery of the benzene ring by chemist August Kekul is a famous example, as is the melody for Paul McCartney's song "Yesterday" which came fully formed in a dream. McCartney ran to the piano and played the tune immediately when he woke up, so he would remember it.

Another noteworthy phenomenon is that when you do any kind of significant psychological or spiritual work and you make progress, especially some kind of breakthrough, your dreams may change. They may change in many ways including their general theme, mood, or content, and may also become more or less vivid, colorful, and intense. People have told me this and I have experienced it many times myself. I have not explored why this is so, but dreams do reflect our present inner and outer realities. Many years ago I was discussing dreams with a co-worker who said he never dreamed. This guy was charismatic but also had a troublesome antisocial streak. I could feel he was suppressing some deep anger. While we talked, I told him that we always dream but often don't remember. The next time I saw him he asked me what I had done to him! He was now remembering his dreams and they were very bizarre! It was funny to me but disturbing to him, so I explained how he might use his dreams and take more control of them. But this was shortly after

I started having OBEs, and I was still learning about dreams myself. I recommend the book "Conscious Dreaming" by Robert Moss as one great basic manual with many valuable tips and techniques for exploring dreams, and there are many others.[88]

The Varieties of Dream Experiences

So dreams can be any of the things already mentioned, including answers to some problem or situation you are dealing with, memories bubbling to the surface, premonitions, visions, or spiritual communications and guidance from others. The most valuable dreams for me were those that represented unresolved traumas, usually appearing as emotions, worries, desires, and frustrations. Dreams can also contain thoughts and images stimulated by the past day's events, a movie or TV show you saw, or a book you are reading. They can also be a jumbled mixture of any or all of the above. Sometimes elements appear in a dream simply because they are unacknowledged subliminal perceptions or subliminal messages from others, or from yourself. The variety of dream experiences is unlimited.

Every nightmare that I have worked on led me back to some traumatic experience. If a dream was a recurring one, whether pleasant or unpleasant, after processing it I never had it again. I had many dreams of being on the telephone and being unable to connect or get my message across. These stopped when I resolved an incident at age eleven where my mother told me to call the police on my father. As I was on the phone with the police, and while the two of them were arguing, my father kept yelling at me to hang up, which I finally did. There was a lot of confusion and conflict.

A dream can also be an imaginative representation of something that's actually happening while you are sleeping, such as music that's on the radio, a cat batting your eyelids, a sleep-learning tape that's playing, or anything else you might normally perceive, if you weren't asleep. Even a subliminal audio recording can influence your dreams. I remember a very colorful and vivid dream I had in

---

[88] "Conscious Dreaming, a Spiritual Path for Everyday Life" - 1996, by Robert Moss

the summer of 1966. There was an early morning space launch scheduled, and my family was watching it on TV while I was still in bed. There was a Gulf Oil Company commercial that came on during the broadcast which included a lively song about whaling ships. While this was playing, I had a dream in which I was watching a cartoon of a whaling ship bounding over huge ocean waves while the sailors were catching giant whales. The most vivid and beautiful part of the dream was the music I was hearing, which also inspired some amazing feelings. What I heard was an enhanced version of the song I was subliminally perceiving, The entire thing was quite magical. I then got up and watched the launch and saw the commercial when it came on again later. I realized immediately that the dream was imagined up from the commercial. I didn't record this dream at the time but I never forgot it. I recently found a video of that commercial on the internet.

Waiting for Natalie – A Healing Dream

This is a slightly edited transcript of an OBE I had when I was thirty-six. Although this is a lucid dream and an OBE, because I was occasionally fully conscious, the insights and healing nature of it would apply even if it were an ordinary dream:

"Power vibes, but not heavy and mostly at two spots on the back of my head. My response was to relax, not deeply, but more subtly. I rose up a few feet until I knew I was out. I went up to the ceiling and it was black and I was surrounded by darkness. I tried to go up through the ceiling, but the darkness wouldn't end. I said to myself "I'm out!" There was still a slight dreamlike quality and I was spinning. Then I saw images pop out of the darkness as if the darkness was a thick soup of images. Finally I burst into the sky and there were clouds and trees and it was a sunny day, but right before that I thought I might have shot into outer space. I flew for a while in the bright sky and then some force yanked me down and I dropped, whap, solidly to the ground feet first. I was 100 percent conscious, and totally in awe.

"I looked at the sky and it was now nighttime and the stars were so clear – my vision was beyond perfect, and I could see every star in the Pleiades! I was in the backyard of my childhood home. I looked behind me at the ant tree [this tree was always full of ants] and one of its limbs was glowing and making crackling sounds – the tree was humming with electricity. I raised my right arm to shoot a bolt of electricity at the tree. I felt I had to try this since it was a perfect opportunity. It took a while of visualizing, but I succeeded and the electricity shot out of my finger. I could feel the power through my arm and the whole sight was awesome! I split the tree in half. The sound was awesome too. Then I turned around and tried to fly, but I was stuck. Something was holding me down. Everything was extra real!

"The light was on in my brothers' room so I went to the window and saw them both sitting on their beds crying intensely, drenched in tears. I crawled in through the window and asked what was wrong. They said mom was dead. I asked why they thought that and Alan told me that dad had said he was going to bury mom today. Alan and Blake seemed to be about seven and five. I told them mom was fine and dad was just saying things because he was angry. However, I felt I was lying because I really didn't know what was going on. They stopped crying and became happy. I hugged them both and felt very close to them. Then I left.

"Again outside, I felt that now I could fly again, but the whole back yard was strung with strange wires that seemed to be in pairs. Finally I just flew right up through them and out into the night sky. Suddenly I was back in my room and I could see the walls. Without any break in consciousness I was back in my body, and I opened my eyes. The emotion and reality of the whole experience were on a higher level than ordinary daily reality. I feel like I'm more asleep now than I was then!"

So here is the context: At the time of this OBE, I was living across the street from my recent ex-girlfriend Natalie. I had been living with her in her apartment for a short time until she kicked me out a few weeks earlier. I was hoping we might get back together. Recently she had been going out at night and didn't come home until late. I would stay up worrying about her, and would watch her place from my window until I saw her lights come on and I could finally go to sleep. This ordeal was not fun. My worry was real but made no sense.

After a week or so of this I had the OBE. When I awoke, I realized that part of the experience was a real memory I had long forgotten! I had found my brothers very upset one day when I was nine. My father had been angry and had raged through the house saying things like "I'm gonna bury your mother!" Although I did reassure my brothers, I became worried myself since I was not certain everything was OK. So I sat outside on the front grass and waited the whole rest of the day for my mother to come home. I had my own shock when she was an hour late, and I became intensely worried. This was the source of my nightly anxiety. After this experience the worry was gone and I never waited for Natalie to come home again. In fact I felt so filled with energy after that experience that I called Natalie that same night and told her about it. Although this incident was no longer linked to Natalie, still, many years later, after I had developed ID-R, I had to work through this incident when it became the source of an ongoing state of worry linked with something completely unrelated.

What is most interesting to me is the unknown force that pulled me from the sky, held me on the ground, and prevented me from leaving until it had shown me what I needed to see – the scene with my brothers. Some unconscious intention had forced me to confront the source of my anxiety. Maybe it was my unconscious mind, or maybe Patty, Dennis–2, or my Higher Self. It doesn't matter. Two days later while in my hometown, out of curiosity I visited that childhood house. The tree in the backyard was still standing but the glowing branch in the dream had been cut off. The old clothesline was also there, but now had two extra sets of wires added to it.

Summary

Dreams are often worth remembering and working on. They are bringing things to the surface that can be valuable in many ways and even change your life. You can program yourself to remember your dreams using affirmations or self-hypnosis nightly, right before sleep, and by reviewing your dreams in the morning. Also you must record your experiences right away whenever you wake up, even in the middle of the night. Using a list of reminders to review in the morning can also help. Nightmares and recurring dreams and other nighttime problems can be permanently resolved when you find their source. You can ask your unconscious mind for dreams that give you answers or provide guidance. You can even overcome fears and other problems by confronting these things in your dreams and changing the outcome.

You can also train yourself to have incredible lucid dreams and OBEs which, besides being fun and exhilarating, have many uses, which includes being gateways to spiritual awakening. In recent years I began to occasionally have what I call "enlightenment dreams." In these dreams I'm doing spiritual inquiry or meditation during which I suddenly become lucid and have a brief glimpse of the true nature of reality. I'm having dreams like this now because I'm doing my spiritual practices, including self-inquiry and meditation, every day, and they have become a constant part of my awareness, even when I'm asleep. You can find more dream resources in the Bibliography.

Chapter 21
Identity Transcendence
& Enlightenment

"The trick, William Potter, is not minding that it hurts."
– T. E. Lawrence, Laurence of Arabia. 1962

"Do you want to know what my secret is? You see,
I don't mind what happens." – J. Krishnamurti, 1977

The third level of healing is transcendence. While
understanding the concept of Identity Transcendence can help us
in a healing sense, as well as in dealing with life in general, it goes
far beyond that into the realm of spiritual awakening.

The first quote above refers to T. E Lawrence slowly putting out
a match flame with his dry bare fingers, all the while smiling
peacefully. When William Potter tries it, he screams that it hurts.
"Of course it hurts" says Lawrence, and he tells Potter that the trick
is being OK with that. Transcendence is not about resolving a
problem, or even managing it, but about going beyond it. Nothing
gets fixed. It's about being OK regardless of the situation; It's about
being free. So it's not healing as we normally think of it, in the
sense of doing something internally or externally about the situation
itself, because the situation may remain unchanged. Instead,
transcendence is about "not minding" that it hurts – it's about being
OK with reality as it is, in which case no healing is necessary
because there is actually no problem. Identity Transcendence is
really about peace of mind and not suffering.

But this is a difficult thing to explain because it may seem to
conflict with our sense of reality. To be clear, when I use the word
"problem" here, it's not in the sense of a puzzle or a difficult
situation that has to be managed somehow, but only in the sense of
suffering. You see, if none of our problems included any kind of
suffering, and if they didn't bother us at all, they wouldn't really be

problems as we normally think of them, would they? And I'm using the word "suffering" in the sense of experiencing something inherently painful or upsetting. Of course there can be many degrees of suffering, from trivial to extreme, but it's all personal and subjective. In the "pebble in the shoe" analogy, when you have transcended the problem, the pebble still exists and it still may get under foot and cause pain or other limitations, but there is no problem in the sense of suffering, or as a disturbance of one's peace of mind. But how _does_ one "not mind" the pain?

Pain is usually equated with suffering, as are many emotions, and we may try to escape these things by fixing them if we can, or by avoiding or suppressing them. And problematic situations can automatically trigger painful emotions. So first let's look at _why_ things hurt, and where we can start in order to change that.

Suffering is a kind of interpretation. Everything we experience in life is actually an interpretation on many levels. On one level, perception is the processing of raw impressions into meaningful patterns – light becomes a beautiful sunset, sound becomes music or a dog's barking. These are interpretations. A dog's barking can also be interpreted as meaning an intruder is present, and a bird's song can signal sunrise. These are deeper levels of meaning. As we saw earlier, we have the power to change reality not only by taking action to change an external situation, when we can, but also by changing what things mean, which is our interpretation of what things are, and what our relationships _to_ them are. All these various interpretations create our reality. And we are all unique. What may cause one person to suffer may be pleasurable for someone else. But if something causes us to suffer, it is possible to transcend that suffering so that the experience is not a problem. This may sound like a kind of reframing, and it is similar in a way, but in this case we don't create a new way to interpret something. Instead we actually transcend the framework that is required for suffering to occur. It's actually a kind of "de-framing."

For example, in a dream suppose a lion is chasing you and you are running for your life. You may be terrified in the dream, but when you wake up the problem disappears. The framework in which the problem existed, the dream state itself, has been transcended. The problem is seen to be unreal, nonexistent, and is now of no concern and even laughable. But until you became aware of this greater truth, you suffered. If you had awakened to the fact that you were dreaming, while still in the dream, your fear could have vanished instantly, even if the lion was still attacking you. The framework that is necessary for us to suffer in waking life, although deeply ingrained, can also be transcended if we closely explore and examine what suffering really is. Then by practicing nonresistance and non-attachment we can begin to move beyond it.

Nonresistance

"I was gripped by an intense fear, and my body started to shake. I heard the words "resist nothing," as if spoken inside my chest. I could feel myself being sucked into a void. It felt as if the void was inside myself rather than outside. Suddenly, there was no more fear, and I let myself fall into that void." – Eckhart Tolle, The Power of Now, 1997

One aspect of suffering is resistance. Resistance can take many forms but if we can stop resisting a problem, our suffering may also stop. You know when you are resisting something – you are fighting it, being angry or frustrated with it, or trying not to feel it. To get to a state of nonresistance you first want to notice <u>how</u> you are resisting, and explore that, and then find a way within yourself to let it go. Here's an example.

One November many years ago I had an attack of shingles, which is caused by a reactivation of the dormant chickenpox virus. It attacks nerve trunks in the body, causing angry blisters on the skin and severe pain, as well as other problems. My outbreak was on the lower back and down my left leg. The pain was intense and constant, and lasted about a month. My only relief came during sleep, but the infection even made it difficult for me to fall asleep because no sleeping position was comfortable. I was treated for the virus and I was told there was only one pain medication that would work with this infection, but when I read the possible side effects there was no way I was going to take it. Instead I just accepted the pain, the constant itching, and other discomforts I won't describe. I accepted it all by not fighting it, and I didn't complain about it to myself either. This wasn't easy but I tried my best to not argue with the pain or resist it in any way.

I also found a positive use for the pain – I used it to remind myself to do self-inquiry, a spiritual practice I do as much as I can. I

questioned whether the pain was really causing suffering, what that
suffering actually was, and whether there was anyone actually
receiving the suffering, and I often found that I couldn't say that the
discomfort really bothered me. Sometimes I tried to pretend that I
was in agony, acting it out, and that always seemed silly, but it did
reinforce the feeling that my suffering was an illusion. I also saw
that struggling did no good anyway. I tried to see that the pain and I
were _one_, although that was more of a meditation.

Now, when I look back on the whole shingles affair, I can see
that my willingness to _accept reality as it is in the present moment,_
during that time, was a blessing. I remember one night in
particular. I was in pain and trying to go to sleep but there was no
position that was tolerable for even a few seconds. I finally stopped
resisting the discomfort and told myself that it was all OK, and I
went right to sleep. When I surrendered to reality, I was no longer
minding the pain.

This story illustrates one of the keys to practicing Identity
Transcendence as a method, and that is to not resist what you are
presently experiencing. Sure, if I had some medication at the time
that would have worked without side effects I would have tried it,
and there is nothing wrong with doing whatever you can to feel
better or to get cured. But suffering comes from resisting reality,
and reality is simply what is. As Adyashanti has said, if you fight with
reality you will never win. You can change reality, but whatever is,
IS. You don't have to like it, but if you simply see reality for what it
is, and don't fight it internally, then your suffering will decrease.
This takes practice. So anytime you are suffering, notice what you
are resisting and see if you can relax that resistance for a while.
Whatever the experience, whether it's anger, grief, fear, depression,
or intense pain, the key is not to try and suppress these things,
which is resistance, but to fully allow them to be present. Any
automatic resistance that seems beyond your control might then
also relax. This often allows amazing healing effects to take place.
Eckhart Tolle was angry and depressed when an internal voice told
him to resist nothing, and when he awoke the next morning not
only was all his suffering gone, but he had resolved the very root of
suffering itself, identification with the sufferer.

Non-attachment

*"All of our miseries are nothing but attachment. Our whole
ignorance and darkness is a strange combination of a thousand and
one attachments. And we are attached to things which will be taken
away by the time of death, or even perhaps before." – Osho*

Attachment implies we are stuck to something, holding on to
something, depending on something, or needing something, and if
that something is threatened or missing, we will suffer. Conversely,
if something we want or need is missing and we don't suffer, there
wasn't any real attachment to it – it's no problem and we move on.
So attachment implies we have a dependent relationship with
something or someone, upon which our sense of wellbeing or
happiness depends. And you can't be attached to something unless
you *are* something. An attachment is a relationship, and as such it
depends upon *identification*. So identification is the real problem.
We become *so* identified with something, whether it's our body, our
status, our affiliations, or even our beliefs, that we think we *are* that.
That is the ultimate attachment. When that identity is threatened or
lost it may feel like death. However, identification is never real. We
cannot *be* anything we experience because, as the one who
experiences that thing, it must necessarily lie outside of us. I'm
using the word "outside" in the sense of something being separate
from us. As I said before, we are not anything we experience,
including our many identities. But before we tackle identification
itself, let's explore what we can do about attachment.

Much of our suffering comes from our automatic negative
reactions to things, and these reactions have suffering already built
into them, so they are painful by nature. Our suffering in these
cases is mostly a reaction from the past, which means whatever we
are feeling or thinking, however painful, often has little or nothing
to do with what is happening right now. Seeing this clearly will help
us put things in a more realistic perspective. And by reframing any
situation that is distressing, the stress may disappear since it was a
reaction to the previous meaning we had given our experience, and
not inherent in the situation itself. There is nothing inherently good
or bad about a rainy day – we can see it as a disappointment or as a
blessing. Reframing is an Identity Management technique that
helps us to see that we *do* have a choice in our responses and how

they affect us, and this also helps us to dis-identify with unwanted states.

Until we give any situation a meaning, all situations are emotionally neutral. By neutrally observing an emotional reaction (even though the reaction itself isn't neutral) we become detached from it, which means we momentarily stop identifying with it, and with the identity state of suffering, however troubling it may have been. We then become the _witness_ of our experience, as if the experience belongs to someone else, or as if we are watching a movie. In Zen this is called "taking the backward step." In the words of psychologist and meditation teacher Tara Brach: "Whenever we step out of thought or emotional reactivity and remember the presence that's here, we're taking the backward step."[89] So when someone rejects me and I feel hurt, or criticizes me and I get angry, by "not reacting" I can reduce the "problem" immediately. So the practice of Self-Observation, which includes not reacting to things that get triggered, is also a method of non-attachment. It's the first step.

But what is it that makes a situation or an experience hurtful in the first place, such that we resist it and suffer, or have a shock? Often it is simply the meaning we give to the situation, a meaning that defines the situation as an unwanted condition or state of affairs, and connects us with internal fear or pain. This meaning has power because we believe it is true. Byron Katie suggests asking these four questions regarding any beliefs that are causing us to suffer: Is it true? Can I absolutely know that it's true? How do I react or feel when I believe that thought? And: Who would I be without that thought?[90] This may sound like a bit of cognitive therapy but it goes beyond logic by targeting our attachment to the belief. As we explore our beliefs more deeply we may begin to wonder, "_What if this thing I believe is NOT true? What if the opposite is true? Why do I care? What if it doesn't even really matter?_" These questions and others not only put us in a different identity state with a different goal, which is that of "questioning our beliefs," but they also help us

---

[89] Tara Brach's Blog: March 13, 2013 - The Backward Step (tarabrach.com)

[90] "Loving What Is: Four Questions That Can Change Your Life" - Byron Katie

recognize that our beliefs are just thoughts that may or may not be true, and may or may not even be relevant, and which certainly do not define who we are. We have the power to define our identity (which is only a transient character role anyway) by our own choice right now, based on our true values.

Let's say I lose my job because my company is downsizing. It's a job I have had for many years, and I get very depressed. I feel like a failure and everything seems hopeless. These feelings may arise out of the shock of being fired, or from an old forgotten trauma that has been reactivated by this turn of events. But my depression will most likely have some underlying thoughts and judgments which I can easily become aware of. These thoughts constitute a framework of beliefs that hold this depression in place. Now if I examine those beliefs I may discover that they are not really true, or that I simply can't really know if they are true or false. I may see that my painful emotions and negative thoughts are all based on these dubious or false beliefs. I may even see that if I did not entertain these beliefs there would be no real problem at all. Or I may see that without these thoughts I would not be able to complain or get angry or feel self-pity, and I would then feel helpless because those actions actually help me feel more powerful and in control, even while being expressions of pain. If I see that I have identified with these limiting beliefs, and feel I would be weaker without them, I can now question _that_ as well.

When I look into the underlying beliefs that support my depression and feelings of failure, and explore their origin, value, and validity, whatever I discover will help me to see things more clearly, without the filter of my previous misconceptions. Perhaps now I can just make some new decisions and move on. No bad feelings, no suffering, just another day of making choices, taking actions, and doing the best I can. Whether it is a romantic break-up, losing your job, getting a raise, or having a party, any situation only means what we say it means, and there is only suffering if we resist our experience and remain attached to meanings, situations, and desires that hurt us.

One of the maxims given by Don Miguel Ruiz in "The Four Agreements"[91] is to not take anything personally. We take things personally, especially when they are negative, when we feel some aspect of our identity has been assaulted. But when a dog barks at us do we take it personally? The dog is just doing what it naturally does and it means nothing in a personal way. We don't see those barks as insults or criticisms or invalidations, but with other people we do. And yet people are just behaving according to their nature also – their "barking" is mostly programming. Everyone has their own reality, which is supported by their experiences and beliefs, and it may be very different from yours. No one really knows you anyway, they only know their image of you, which is largely a fantasy. "Not taking things personally" is an easy way to think about practicing non-attachment when it comes to interacting with others. It simply means not reacting by being unattached to anyone's judgements, words, or behavior.

The bottom line is that even when you are already having a negative reaction, you can get immediate relief by becoming as unattached to that reaction as you can, by taking a step back, and by examining and questioning your underlying beliefs and feelings. You may find there is really no reason to suffer, and if some part of you believes that there is, or that you deserve to suffer, you may be able to see that this is also a reaction that has no basis in reality. If you can see that, perhaps you can let it go, or move on in spite of it and not be a victim of your own thoughts. This is the practice of non-attachment – to not react. When the situation no longer bothers you, whether you do something about it or not, you have transcended it.

Identity Transcendence, as a method, is a way to reduce suffering by recognizing the fact that we are not any of our identities, emotions, reactions, or thoughts. These basic methods of finding peace or happiness without fixing or healing anything can be incredibly helpful, but they are only stepping stones leading to a higher truth that brings complete liberation and true happiness. In fact whenever we practice nonresistance and non-attachment and live fully present in the moment, we are actually emulating that

---

[91] The Four Agreements" - Don Miguel Ruiz, 1997

higher truth. And when we have truly transcended identity itself and discovered that higher truth to be what we actually are, our own essential being, we have found enlightenment.

Enlightenment
"Enlightenment means waking up to what you truly are and then being that." – Adyashanti

"The world is an illusion, only Brahman is real, Brahman is the world." – Shankara

My journey in life began with trauma and I was guided to find a way to heal myself. But healing in this regard can be a never-ending process. Even when you are healed and thriving, new problems can arise and old problems can be reactivated. In fact it's inevitable. If we live countless lifetimes, suffering will never end. At some point we're going to want out of this cycle. For me, the whole point of self-discovery and healing is to help us realize that we are eternal spiritual beings and that we can awaken to our true nature and be forever free of all fear and suffering. Once we understand this we can focus on the ultimate life purpose of self-realization. But enlightenment isn't some state we can attain, it just a recognition of what we already are and the underlying truth that suffering is and always has been an illusion.

When I was about six years old, I was walking through the kitchen thinking about death. I don't recall exactly why I was thinking about death but it may have had something to do with my "Race with Death" experience a short time earlier. I was very curious about what would happen if I should die. As I contemplated what would it mean if I were to cease to exist, it made me wonder just what I _was_ anyway. I realized that if I died and my awareness somehow vanished, other people would still be conscious, so I tried to understand the difference between their consciousness and mine. But I wasn't just considering this, I was actually trying to see it. And in the instant I tried to see it, something happened, In that moment I saw – I knew – that everyone's consciousness was the same as mine, not just _like_ mine, but one and the _same_. Suddenly I realized that what I was, was consciousness! I could not have expressed my experience in these words at the time, but I realized in that moment that there was only one consciousness and that it was shared by everyone, and yet it was also, in a way, outside of everyone. I also realized that it could never die.

For a moment it was like I was merging into a rushing stream, like I was out of my body and experiencing other people's awareness. I actually saw these people and saw through their eyes. I didn't know them but they seemed to represent anyone and everyone. There was a moment in that realization that was so profound that it startled me. I felt like something overwhelming was about to happen, so I snapped out of it – but I never forgot it. This experience intrigued and baffled me any time I thought about it. I wondered at the time why nobody ever talked about this – about how we were all one. But I never mentioned it to anyone because I always got in trouble when I talked about experiences that other people never talked about, which included anything spiritual or paranormal. I had learned to keep such things to myself, as you may recall, and this seemed like another one of those things.

This early experience was a momentary glimpse of a higher truth, perhaps a tiny foretaste of enlightenment. Simply put, enlightenment is the realization that we are consciousness itself, spirit, pure awareness – nothing more, nothing less. But what this means, what it reveals about reality and ourselves, and the impact this realization has on our lives and experience, are what makes it significant for us as human beings. The key word is "realization." Enlightenment is not just some information or a deeper understanding of how things are, or something like a fleeting LSD trip, but a permanent change in the way a person experiences everything. It's an inner transformation and a radical shift in one's overall identity that puts an end to all fear, suffering, and want, for all time. It's the eternal salvation, the nirvana, the spiritual freedom, the ultimate joy and love, the "Kingdom of Heaven" that spiritual prophets and teachers have been talking about throughout history. As consciousness or spirit itself, we are totally free – nothing can touch us or affect us in any way. It is the realization of oneness with God, of oneness with "all-that-is," or as Jesus called it, "The All."[92]

---

[92] The Gospel of Thomas: (2) Jesus said, "Let him who seeks continue seeking until he finds. When he finds, he will become troubled. When he

The many miraculous and psychic experiences I had as a child and later, and even some of the remarkable altered states I experienced, were not insights into the truth of spiritual awakening – these things are all just mind games. What those experiences showed me however, is that we are powerful spiritual beings playing these amazing games in a universe of consciousness in which anything is possible. True awakening however reveals that this universe, in all its vast complexity and infinite beauty and diversity, is only a dream – an illusion that is real only as long as we remain asleep, so to speak. Enlightenment is called an "awakening" because it means waking up _out_ of the dream universe and _out_ of the identification with personhood. We wake up _to_ the truth that reveals us to be Consciousness itself, which, like a multidimensional movie screen, is the conscious space in which all experience is taking place. Eckhart Tolle's enlightenment sprang from the idea that he hated himself. As he considered this idea, he realized that for him to hate himself, there had to be two of him. But who hated who? And which one was really him? He observed later that this question was like a Zen koan.

End Game
"A strange game. The only winning move is not to play."
– Joshua, War games, 1983

I said earlier that when Consciousness created separate viewpoints as separate entities, this separation was an illusion, a pretense only, like playing multiple parts in a stage play, or like a child playing with dolls or toy soldiers – we play all the parts, and we know it is completely imaginary. But at some point in the hierarchy of Levels of Being, a kind of sleep is established where the pretense is mistaken for reality. We have forgotten the truth. This is the sleep of "duality," and this is what we must awaken from if we want to be free. Now, not being enlightened myself, I'm sure my words are not describing these things very accurately, perhaps no words can, but I like the analogy of describing the spiritual path as the highest and most magical game we can play, as human beings –

---

becomes troubled, he will be astonished, and he will rule over the All."

the game of escaping the ultimate trap of "self and other" and
waking up to freedom.

This reminds me of something my friends and I did a few times
as kids. We had a lot of old lumber in my back yard and we would
use it to make a wooden teepee with a thick central pole. The pole
supported boards leaning against it and completely surrounding it,
so it was quite dark inside. Then a bunch of us would get in this
cone shaped fortress and talk for a while. We made up a stories, like
maybe how we were war prisoners plotting to escape. Finally we
would kick down the central pole and the whole thing would
collapse on top of us. We spent the next ten minutes or so very
slowly crawling out from under the boards, being careful to not get
any splinters. We would scream and describe how we were fighting
off soldiers and monsters as we escaped our self-imposed trap. This
may sound like a silly game but that's what all games are – silly
diversions. People actually risk their lives or body parts doing things
like climbing Mt. Everest, race car driving, fighting wars, and many
other things. Our childhood teepee game contained the essence of
every game: create a situation, a goal, obstacles to that goal, and a
means to win. A game can be exceedingly complex or very simple.
The more challenging the game is, the greater the possibility of
losing – and the more you have to lose, the more exciting it is.

So there seem to be two basic perspectives of reality: duality and
nonduality. In the viewpoint of duality I am an individual. I have
identified with a body, a name, a personality, and a story. I exist as a
separate entity cast into a world of infinite things that are separate
from me. It is a world managed by rules, and I have relationships
within this world, both with the world itself and other individuals.
This world is a vast universe of many games, the most important of
which seems to be survival, in one form or another. If you don't
survive, as whatever kind of mortal creature you're pretending to be,
you can't play. But in the enlightened viewpoint of nonduality there
is only one reality and you are that. You are everything. You are not
an individual and there are no relationships, no universe, no time
or space, and no games. You are the All, and all is One. This is the
perspective of just being "awake."

But if enlightenment is the realization of our nonduality, of
unity, and the end of all games, why would anyone want it? We
want it because, as the Buddha said, life is suffering, and also

because this realization is the greatest joy, freedom, and fulfillment one could ever know – Nirvana, or the Kingdom of Heaven of which Jesus spoke. Or we may be intuitively drawn to this path just because it feels right.

In the universe of experience, time is infinite, and everything changes – nothing stays the same. The cycles of growth and decay, war and peace, life and death, joy and sorrow, happiness and horror, are never-ending. Living as a human being is a game, and has, as we know, considerable challenges and limitations. It may even seem objectionable to some to call life a game when we look at the massive suffering so many of us have to endure.[93] I have seen people get quite angry at the suggestion that suffering is an illusion or part of a game. Pain and trauma, disease and death, injustice and famine, "man's inhumanity to man" – how are these games? I understand this objection and I'm using the word game in a technical sense, as opposed to something we do for enjoyment, since enjoyment does not seem to apply with regard to the serious suffering side of life, at least from our limited human perspectives. Although as I pointed out, we do many things for "fun" that can include the risk of terrible suffering or death. On the other hand, life includes everything wonderful as well.

In my own case there has always been an inner level of my awareness that does not take life too seriously, even when terrible things are happening. On some level I know this is all a dream, a game, but one I have been committed to, until I began seeking a higher truth. Even in the future when we have enough understanding of the mind, body, and spirit, so that we can heal and prevent all physical, mental, psychological, and spiritual ailments, those understandings will only last for a limited time. Change is inevitable. And yet we are eternal. In reality it may be that we have all been gods and goddesses in the past, the creators of universes, and had incredible lives for millions of years, and that we have had

---

[93] When the Buddha said that life is suffering, the word he used was "dukkha" which has several meanings referring to unpleasant experience or suffering. Many contemporary Buddhists prefer to use the meaning of "unsatisfactory" or "unsatisfactoriness." Life has many pleasures but also contains horrible suffering as well. In that sense I would say that life is indeed unsatisfactory.

everything we ever wanted many times over, as free spirits roaming the cosmos. And yet here we are, operating as lower life forms on a wet planet in an insignificant star system. At some point on this roller coaster of existence we may just want the game to be over – we may just want to wake up and be free.

We do have many great methodologies that can help us be healthy, wealthy, and happy, but even if we succeed in those aspects of life, in the end we die. We start over and begin a new life somewhere else. A trillion years from now we may be at the top again and then later, back on the bottom. But when we see the truth of who we are, all that comes to an end. Nirvana literally means "to blow out" – to cease. Karma ends, delusion ends, needs end, and suffering ends. What we *ARE* does not end, but the games end, and we are free. This is the real "end game" – to finally get free and experience our true nature. I have had many tiny glimpses of this astonishing freedom, and I believe there are many authentic teachers, past and present, who embody this truth and who tell us about it from direct experience.

Still, the illusion of the universe and all its games seems to persist, in a way, even after enlightenment. The difference is that the universe is seen for what it is, which is only awareness, which is something that cannot be described – it is often referred to as being nothing at all, pure emptiness or silence. This means that nothing exists at all, even as an illusion. Of course this makes no sense whatsoever to our thinking minds. It's a paradox which the mind can never fully understand. Fortunately, it doesn't have to. The mind is itself an illusion, and enlightenment is the extinction of the mind. Once you see through the stage magician's trick, the magic is not just gone – you realize that it never was. Then, to paraphrase Mooji, once you are awake, then you can truly enjoy life. But how do we get there? How do we reach that eternal state of freedom, love, and joy?

A Path With Heart

"If you can see your path laid out in front of you step by step, you know it's not your path. Your own path you make with every step you take. That's why it's your path." – Joseph Campbell

Earlier I described the tremendous value of meditation, in various forms, as a mind-body technique for healing and general wellbeing. But these benefits are only byproducts – meditation for enlightenment has a much greater objective, which is spiritual awakening. By the way, although I have had some real insights that shed light on what enlightenment might be for me personally, much of what I say in this chapter comes from my study and understanding of many spiritual writings throughout history, and the words of those I consider to be enlightened teachers, both past and contemporary.

When I first became acquainted with the idea of enlightenment at the age of twenty, I immediately saw that the path to understanding life was an inner journey, not an outer one. I turned my scientific exploration inward, just as Emanuel Swedenborg did centuries ago. But there is nothing that he experienced, or that any spiritual teacher has realized, that is not available to all of us if we are willing to look within, and keep at it. The path to self-realization is fraught with many obstacles. Fear is the greatest obstacle, and fear comes in many forms and disguises. It's also easy to be misled by the traps in our own minds and the words and behavior of others. We must each find our own path. That's why I love this quote from "The Teaching's of Don Juan" by Carlos Castaneda:

"I warn you. Look at every path closely and deliberately. Try it as many times as you think necessary. Then ask yourself, and yourself alone, one question: 'Does this path have a heart?' If it does, the path is good; if it doesn't, it is of no use."

My original inspiration occurred in college when I first encountered the question "Who am I" in the first Zen book I read. That was where my spiritual path really started on a conscious level. After my "Black Dot" scare, discussed in Chapter 14, I was simply reluctant to do the specific practice that led to that experience. But after my OBEs and trauma discoveries made me less afraid of what I might find "inside" myself, and my subsequent resolution of the Black Dot incident, my fears dissolved. However it still took some time, and inspiration from friends, before I got firmly back on the enlightenment track, although on some level I never really left it.

There are many paths to enlightenment, including Zen Buddhism, Advaita Vedanta, Gnostic Christianity, Sufism, Jewish Kabbalah, the Yogic paths of Bhakti Yoga, Karma Yoga, Jnana Yoga, Raja Yoga, Atma Yoga, and many other spiritual practices and schools of meditation and chanting connected to many spiritual and religious teachings. Many wonderful books have been written on these subjects and some that I recommend are listed in the Bibliography. But it is important to find your own path, the one that resonates with you – your own "path with heart." Here I will briefly discuss my own practices.

I began doing Zen meditation by counting my breaths. I would set aside some time, maybe twenty minutes, and sit up straight in a chair with my feet on the floor while letting my body relax. The idea here is to keep your attention focused on a simple task in order to quiet the mind. You want to prevent yourself from being distracted by thoughts. This is not easy! The problem is that thinking reduces "presence" and puts us to sleep in that sense. I did improve my ability to concentrate by counting my breaths but the real goal is to be _present_. Although we are always conscious, when we are "present" we are more awake, alive, in the moment, and aware of our own existence. It's about being _aware that you are aware_, right now, in this moment. Take some time right now and try it – be aware that you are aware! That's presence! It's easy to do for a few seconds but then thoughts will come in and you will lose your presence, and you'll see what I mean – it's like going to sleep. Being present is a higher state of awareness. With practice it becomes easier to do for longer periods of time. Presence is our natural state and we would be present all the time but our self-awareness gets interrupted by our attachment to thoughts and other distractions.

Osho says that real meditation IS enlightenment. Since enlightenment cannot really be defined, the path is not about trying to achieve something, but simply about opening up to our own being. Adyashanti refers to "true meditation" as "resting AS awareness." This is Zazen, "just sitting" and allowing everything to be as it is, with no resistance. So when I meditate, I sit with the Silence, just being present, resting my attention on the source of everything: Awareness itself.

My current path is best described as the way of nonduality, also known as Advaita Vedanta. Nonduality is really the core of all these teachings. It refers to the essential oneness of all things and embraces many practices as well as all the ideas being discussed here. In addition to meditation I do self-inquiry which is a contemplation involving some form of the question "Who am I?" or

"What am I?" You ask the question but don't try and answer it. Instead just be quiet, or try and see who it is that is asking the question – who is thinking, feeling, breathing – who or what is it that is experiencing your life? You can see that awareness is present, but what is it that is aware? You may say "Me, I am aware," so you ask "Who am I?" This is my Zen koan. Right before my Black Dot experience I was "present" with this question more or less continuously for over two days. Since what we _are_ IS pure awareness, my attention was focused on awareness itself until I wasn't actually thinking of the question conceptually anymore because my looking WAS the question.

There are other contemplations which are also forms of self-inquiry, like trying to experience oneness, timelessness, the realization of "no-self," or the eternal silence. These are really all the same thing, but each different contemplation considers the truth from a slightly different angle. I refer to these different viewpoints as doorways, and there are many. I now usually sit on my couch for an hour twice a day doing meditation and self-inquiry. I also listen to material by teachers of nonduality most days while driving or doing chores. These teachers include Nisargadatta, Ramana Maharshi, Adyashanti, and many others, and old recordings by Robert Adams. Self-inquiry and mindfulness (being present) can be practiced any time, no matter what you are doing, and these have also become an integral part of my life.

Since 2006 I have had many insights that confirm for me that I am on the right path. Around this time I also began having lucid dreams related to truth-realization. As you recall, I have been having OBEs and lucid dreams my whole life. Some of my most profound glimpses of awakening have occurred in these states just prior to waking up from sleep, and they are not hallucinations. I call them "enlightenment dreams." Sometimes they are messages or lessons, and sometimes they are profound experiences verging on spiritual awakening. They often provide profound insights regarding my personal path or the truth itself. Usually they start out as ordinary dreams in which I am meditating or doing self-inquiry, but at some point I become lucid and find myself in a fully conscious out-of-body state during which the meditation takes me to a whole new level. The use of lucid dreams as a spiritual practice is described in "Tibetan Yoga and Secret Doctrines" by W. Y. Evans-

Wentz (1958), and in detail in the book "Dream Yoga" by Andrew Holecek (2016), which I highly recommend. Many of my spiritual insights are posted online in my Zen Blog.[94]

The following is an edited transcript of an enlightenment dream I had back in 2014:

Absolute Love

"One morning right before waking up I was doing meditation in the dream state and became lucid. So I was no longer dreaming that I was meditating but actually doing it, and I experienced a moment of oneness and entered a blissful state. I was immediately enveloped in a golden light, and while in that light I felt the deepest feeling of connection and safety I have ever experienced. I can't actually recall the feeling itself anymore, but I remember it being indescribable. I was in a place where I had everything I could ever want and I felt complete and safe and totally accepted beyond any doubt. I felt safe even in my vulnerability as a mortal being and with all my flaws, all of which seemed like a stick I was holding on to, which I could easily let drop away. These weren't thoughts but a knowing-feeling. And the presence that enveloped me was so strong and so perfect in its wholeness and its acceptance, and welcoming of me, that I could no longer distinguish myself from it. The only word I could find to express this experience later was 'love', and it was absolute and unconditional. But it was way beyond my previous experience or imaginings of love, so that at first I truly had no words for it.

"Everything around me and in me was love. It wasn't about being loved but about being HOME. Home might be a better word for this feeling. To be loved means you can also not be loved. Being home is assurance that there is ONLY love. I felt like a tiny child in all of this because the feeling was so vast. It was something I had never known before. This love was also 'forever' in the sense that it was not bound or limited by time. There was also the sense that 'home' is always here, standing right behind me. This was the first time, as far as I recall, that I had an experience of love. in any form, arise in meditation or inquiry, in my entire life." ... The next experience happened two years later.

The Magic Space

"I went to a weekly Vipassana group meditation, but this week instead of meditating we watched a movie, 'The Dhamma Brothers,' about an experimental meditation program in a prison. I'd seen it already and decided to meditate instead, so I paid no attention to the movie. While sitting there and keeping my mind quiet, there was a point where something startling happened. I shifted my body slightly in my chair and shifted my mental focus at the same time, and I instantly noticed that there was something in the background that *DIDN'T* shift, and my attention instantly went there. It was like if you were walking and your shoe fell off and you stepped back to get it. Suddenly the thing that didn't shift was no longer in the background but right up front, and I was aware that what had shifted was 'the whole universe!' The 'universe' included everything I thought of as me, and everything in existence, and everything that ever could exist, and it was all like a tiny speck, a drop of rain in an ocean of aware presence. I knew this speck included everything that could possibly exist because I saw the nature of 'things' in general, 'things' meaning anything I could be aware of. Curiously, neither the presence nor the universe it contained were 'me,' which was a bit confusing but not a problem. There just *WASN'T* any 'me,' unless I say that the whole thing was me, but the idea of a 'me' seemed unimportant since there obviously wasn't any need for such a thing.

"Two things stood out the most. The first was my sense of 'everything.' It was like the whole universe was swallowed up and included things I didn't realize were part of my universe because they were so familiar, and even subliminal, which is hard to explain. Foundational elements like my body, my sense of self, and the world, as well as space itself with all its stars and galaxies, were no longer foundational or even necessary. So that was surprising. The other thing I immediately saw was that nothing any teacher had ever said about enlightenment described 'this.' My response was like 'What!?!' It was totally wonderful and exciting, but just unexpected. It was as if I were seeing something no one else had ever seen before. But I wasn't actually seeing it – the seeing I'm talking about was more like an image created by my mind in response to a shift in understanding – I understood, for a moment, that the whole universe, including 'me,' was just a speck in a vast self-aware empty presence, which was like a sort of 'magic space' because it included a sense of aliveness, power, and infinite possibility. At the same time it rendered everything I thought of as real, inconsequential. There seemed to be no relationship between the presence and the universe, that is, the presence contained the universe but had no relationship with it, because the universe was simply not real." ... This experience lasted only a few seconds but its effect was indelible. I can still feel it lingering in the depths.

Transcending Identification

"You have made the mistake of identifying yourself with the body and mind. Therefore, the body and mind seems to control your life. But as soon as you switch identities, as soon as you begin to identify with consciousness, everything changes for you. You become happy, peaceful, joyous, blissful. It happens by itself. All you've got to do is to switch identities, and identify with reality." – Robert Adams

Enlightenment is something that happens automatically when one is ready, and is not something you can make happen – there are no steps to it – it's all about preparation. The more you learn about spiritual enlightenment, the more you see that it is not something you can know with your mind. You can understand the path, but not the experience. As Ramana Maharshi said, it's really about removing the ignorance that stands in the way of truth like clouds hiding the sun, because the truth is already here.[95] Spiritual practices only clear away unseen obstacles. They create an opportunity for the realization that will come "like a thief in the night."

A summary of the foundation of the Identity Model is applicable here, as it applies to enlightenment. Everything in all existence only exists as conscious experience and all experience requires an experiencer, a witness. Consciousness therefore creates through identification, which requires an imaginary separation of self and other, because nothing can exist without a witness. This is the essence of duality. The existence of a "self" is identification with a

---

[95] "Be As You Are" - The Teachings of Ramana Maharshi - 1985, David Godman

particular viewpoint, at the very least. But identification expands from there to include things like identification with a particular body, a personality, a story, and many other things, as previously described. This brings us to you and me.

My human identity state compels me to "believe" there is a "me," and that everything I experience lies outside of me. I recognize this belief as unfounded, but it exists as an inner unconscious conviction which I am investigating and hope to uproot. I further identify with my body and my life. But none of these things are really "me." Even the witness of my life is only an idea and not the real me. The real me, which is not a "me" or a self at all, is Consciousness. Although Consciousness cannot be described, it can be known, and is known, by Consciousness itself. But in order to have a life and all the adventures that come with it, which is the game the ancients called Leela, I must dwell in the illusion of duality, called Maya. Even what I say here is just illusion discussing illusion. Nothing actually exists and nothing is happening, from the "unidentified" perspective.

Identification is, therefore, the fundamental mistake that allows suffering to exist. Also every identity in our programming only has power because we identify with it, and that identification is built-in to every identity we have, whether it is stuck or not. Identification is the ultimate attachment – the attachment to "being something" or someone. The idea that I am a SEPARATE someone, or something, is called the ego. Ramana Maharshi called it the "I thought."

Teachers tell us we are already enlightened and just don't know it. Enlightenment is already what we are, and the truth is already the truth – nothing has to happen for awakening to be recognized, even though it seems otherwise. That we have to discover something we already know is a paradox, like when you are looking for your glasses only to find you are already wearing them. Your mistake was just a thought, and you simply failed to notice that your vision was already correct, so you continued to insist that it was not.

We are all destined to wake up anyway, but once we find ourselves on the spiritual path, it's good to know that the basic teachings of enlightenment are free and easy to find. So if the idea of spiritual awakening makes sense to you or if you are curious, check out the many books, videos, and teachings that are available by awakened people like Ramana Maharshi, Nisargadatta Maharaj, and Robert Adams and contemporaries like Adyashanti, Unmani, Mooji, Rupert Spira, Ellie Roozdar, Angelo Dilullo, and many others, who can elucidate this topic far better than I can. You can find the books I recommend for this chapter in the Bibliography. For starters I recommend "The Three Pillars of Zen" by Philip Kapleau, but there are many others. If you want a personal teacher you can find one, as I did, and I recommend you do. But what is mostly needed are a genuine curiosity, an internal commitment, and a sincere effort to awaken. But regardless of the path we choose for ourselves, methods like ID-R and EMDR, Idenics, hypnotherapy, mindbody therapies, Identity Management techniques, Identity Transcendence practices, and many others, can help us recover our health and power, and also help us to be happy and at peace regardless of life's disturbances.

* *

★ Seventh Grade

After Patty stopped coming to our science class in sixth grade, I saw her again later that semester during a school bazaar held annually in the cafeteria. I felt her presence and turned around, spotting her immediately. I watched her for a time, but something seemed to restrain me from talking to her. I was strangely cautious and subdued, and a bit spaced out. It was curious because I was not at all shy in sixth grade.

In seventh grade Patty and I went to the same school but we never saw each other. I have memories of hiding from someone or something for no apparent reason. I would just be standing in some spot for a few minutes unable to move. And then it would be over and I was allowed to resume walking. I never questioned this because it felt like I was in control and just following some kind of intuition. Way back then I had no idea that I had other personalities, and Dennis–2 was influencing me in ways I knew nothing about. He didn't want Patty and me to meet just yet, but eighth grade was a different story.

✳ ✳ ✳ ✳ ✳ ✳ ✳ ✳ ✳ ✳ ✳ ✳ ✳ ✳ ✳ ✳ ✳ ✳ ✳ ✳

Part V
♻
Patty Preston

✳ ✳ ✳ ✳ ✳ ✳ ✳ ✳ ✳ ✳ ✳ ✳ ✳ ✳ ✳ ✳ ✳ ✳ ✳ ✳

Chapter 22
First Contact

"Tis torture, and not mercy. Heaven is here where Juliet lives,
and every cat and dog and little mouse, every unworthy thing, live
here in heaven and may look on her, but Romeo may not."
– William Shakespeare

It was the first day of eighth grade and I was in my third period
"Home Room" class called "Basic," which was two hours of English
and history. I was sitting near the back of the room in the furthest
row from the door, which was to my left. The teacher was taking
roll call. I said "Here!" at the call of my name and just sat there in
my own little world. Unlike before, my intuition failed to alert me. I
seemed to be in a sort of trance or something. Then I heard her
name "Patty Preston?" "Here!" I was electrified. I could barely stay
in my seat, straining to see where she was sitting. She was on the
other side of the room by the windows. I was so preoccupied for the
next fifty minutes that I had no idea what the teacher said. I seemed
to be making some kind of connection to other realities, possibly
past lives – I even felt like a different person, wondering what I was
doing here in this body, in this room. I seemed to be scribbling
something on my desktop, drawing strange patterns or something. It
reminds me of the deleted scene in "E.T" where Elliot was drawing
electrical schematics on the classroom wall.[96] Finally the period was
over and it was break time. I shot out of my seat and headed for the
door. There were a lot of students in front of me but I saw her
walking out. I felt incredibly happy and free – it was like I was
surrounded by some amazing energy. My feeling of connection
with her was indescribable. I imagined going up to her, saying "Hi,"
engaging her in light hearted banter, being funny, making her
laugh, and everything would just be perfect. Birds would sing,
fragrant flowers would burst into bloom out of nowhere, and the
sun would shine brightly ever after. But sadly ...

---

[96] E.T. the Extra-Terrestrial, 1982

Half way to the door I froze – it was as if I'd been caught in the flash of a nuclear blast. All my dreams were destroyed in an instant and I knew that I could not talk to her – I could not approach Patty in any way. So I stopped, and proceeded to walk out slowly, making sure to avoid her.

In that fateful moment, which seemed to last a long time, some inner had ambushed my attention, and, in graphic technicolor 3D, had shown me why I must NOT make contact with Patty. It was like I was pulled into another reality where this entity showed me scenes from my past, my sexual trauma, things I felt ashamed of, and things I'd done that hurt others. I don't recall much of it but he pulled out all the stops and made it clear that if we should meet now she would find me repulsive and would never love me. The horror of that prospect, and the shame, guilt, pain, and fear, were too much for my thirteen-year-old brain. I was devastated. I caved in and decided that he was right, it was all true, and I realized that I must, at all cost, avoid Patty Preston.

But something else was also present. There was a sense that somehow, someday in the future, things would be different. It was a cloudy thought at the time but there was a very strong force behind it. Way in the back of my mind was the intention and determination that I would solve this dilemma – that I would find a way out. In that same moment of shock I vowed to find a way through this obstacle, no matter how long it took.

So whatever our lives might have been, this moment set them on a different course. I never questioned what this inner voice had said or why he had intervened as he had, in spite of the fact that I later saw him as an unpredictable nemesis over whom I had no control.

This event left me sad and depressed, and all that happy enthusiasm was now turned inward with nowhere to go – imprisoned. I felt immediately exhausted. So from then on I watched Patty quietly in class, paid close attention to her every word and every conversation about her. It was as if I might find some clue, or something I could use to get myself out of this predicament. There was something I was missing and it seemed just out of reach. This was the beginning of a very long quest! I needed to find out how I could redeem myself, not so much to become worthy of Patty, as I somehow knew we were already connected, but to clear myself of all the garbage that had been heaped upon me since birth, to purify myself – to be free to be myself.

So I would avoid her, hide in the shadows, never speak to her, figure this thing out, conquer my demons, and come back fresh, victorious, and revived, so we could finally connect. I could live with that; at least it was hope, and that was all I had. Our only class together that year was this two-hour period. So I would remain inconspicuous; I would slip in and out unnoticed; I would be a ghost. That was my plan. But Patty would have plans of her own, and I had no idea who I was dealing with.

All the incidents discussed in this chapter were recalled in sessions I did from 1991 to 1995. In the beginning, a good percentage of my session time was spent addressing headaches and other physical symptoms, but I worked on whatever issues presented themselves each day. Patty made her first appearance in my sessions about three months after I returned home from Colorado. All I remembered about Patty at that time, on a personal level, was that I met her in eighth grade and that there was some kind of connection there. I also recalled saying "Hi" to her once in college. I had forgotten that September day in 1961 when the teacher called her name, but it burst into my mind while working on a feeling of being unable to approach any woman I was interested in. I always had a problem approaching someone for a first date and although I wasn't interested in anyone at the time, this feeling came up so I explored it, and it led me to the incident I just described. After recalling and addressing what had happened regarding Patty on that first day at school, I was left with a strange feeling. I explored that feeling the next day.

A Past Life Together

It was a vague feeling and hard to describe, but I discovered that even the tiniest, most ill-defined impression can be enough of a thread to backtrace to its source. As I went into the viewpoint of this feeling, I recalled lying in a hospital. I was an adult male and I was seriously injured and couldn't speak. The room I was in appeared dimly lit and there were beds all around me and the nurses were wearing some kind of odd hats and speaking French. I was desperately trying to get someone's attention. I managed to convey to a nurse that I wanted to write a note and she got me a tiny piece of paper and a pencil. With great difficulty I eventually was able to scribble something down. I gave the nurse the note and a short time later I heard her talking with someone. She was being told that the person whose name I had written on the paper had died. I left my body right then and found myself at the sight of a crashed plane.

The person I was worried about was a young woman named Annette, who I will refer to as Ana. Ana was still alive but unconscious. My name was Philippe and I had been flying a small two-seated plane over a field somewhere in France when there was a malfunction and we went down. Gravely injured in the crash, I had managed to crawl to a road and some people took me to the hospital, but they were unaware of the plane and I had been unable to communicate. Upon seeing that Ana was still alive, I willed myself back to my body but it was lifeless and I could not revive it. I hastened back to the plane and found that Ana had also perished, in order to be with me. We stood there face to face, exterior, looking at each other, appearing as we had in life. Then she became extremely upset and emotional. It was difficult to communicate with her so I mostly just tried to calm her down. After a while I was able to connect and promised her that we would be together in the next life. I assured her that I would find her and that we would never lose touch. Suddenly her mind seemed to go blank, and, as if she were being called by some unseen celestial Siren, she flew away from me and disappeared. I sensed that she was following some strong single-minded purpose that I could not interrupt.

I took off after Ana and found myself captured by a strong compulsion of my own, which led me through various dreamlike stages where I was being interviewed, instructed, conditioned, and controlled by other beings and forces. I was in the "between-lives area" and I knew that I would be made to forget my past lifetime. But I did something within myself to make sure that I did not forget Ana. I wanted to be born near her and be able to recognize her under any conditions, so I could fulfill my promise. Somehow I managed to conceal my memory of her, as well as my ability to spot her, deep in my mind where they could not be noticed and interfered with.

The last part of this journey involved being in a dark, park-like area with many other people waiting to be reborn. We were all standing on glowing circles of light which came in many different colors. I was made to stand on a red circle but I needed to be on the blue one nearby. I quickly hopped over to the blue circle when no one was looking. An attendant came over and thought something was wrong, but after checking with a supervisor, allowed me to stay where I was. I believe I had some inside help with this deception from someone I knew there. Eventually I was pushed, by some force, through the blue circle which became a hole, and I shot down through a tunnel.

At this point I noticed there was someone with me – an unseen male presence. I thought it was a spirit guide for a time, but I now believe it was Dennis–2 from the future. Whoever it was, this guide led me to my parents. I found myself in an elevator with a man wearing a gray hat. I followed him and he eventually walked by a lady sitting at a desk and I was told these were my future parents. I quickly entered my mother's body as if I were pulled in by some gravitational force. My impression was that she was already two weeks pregnant, but that's just a feeling. Once inside I hovered in the soft pinkish light of the space I was to reside in and something immediately got my attention. There was a hollow circle with a black dot in the middle, right above me, which seemed to have an invisible glow about it. It resembled a frog's egg, and there was another similar one above it which looked smaller because it was farther away. I asked my guide what they were and he said "Those are your brothers." I speculate that these particular eggs were glowing because they were being reserved.

It took a few more sessions to get all the details of that past-life experience with Ana, who I now believed was Patty in this life. Although I am presenting many of the stories involving Patty in chronological order, I actually recalled all the events in this book in random order over many years. So at this point I didn't recall ever seeing her before eighth grade, and didn't have all the details of the plane crash memory, or our first day of class together. However I now thought that since I better understood our connection, there wasn't anything more to know about Patty Preston, and I stopped thinking about her. But four months later I addressed the following incident.

How to Be a Jerk without Really Trying

I was sitting at my desk as class was letting out when Patty came up and started talking to me. We had finished working together on a group project a few days earlier. Today she was telling me about some event that was coming up. I think it was a dance and there was something about a "hayride." Eventually she asked me if I wanted to go. I had been trying hard to avoid any contact with her and I wanted desperately to get out of this conversation but I didn't know what to do. There was a moment of shock and I saw myself being very rude to her, telling her quite bluntly that I didn't want to go to any dance. I wasn't sure exactly what I said but I knew I hurt her feelings. After working through this incident in December of that first year of doing ID-R, I felt strongly compelled to send Patty a letter. This was thirty years later and I had no idea if she was still alive, if she would remember me, or where in the world she might be living. But I found her address and wrote her a nice letter, apologizing for my behavior in eighth grade. I knew this was a pretty strange thing to do and I had no idea how she would feel about it, but it felt important.

I mailed the letter the next day and then went on my daily run along the river bank, which was two blocks from my house. While I was jogging, I experienced a weird phenomenon. It was like I had been a foot tall my whole life and suddenly I was now ten feet tall. Then I was small again and then big, and each time my viewpoint expanded to being tall, the world got brighter somehow. When this phenomenon stopped, I felt tall and expanded and had the strange thought that I could now be successful, as if I had just broken free of some restraint that had literally kept me small and limited in many ways. This was very bizarre and I couldn't wait to get home to work on this thing and find out what it was.

That evening in session I recalled a later incident on that same day that I had hurt Patty's feelings. I was walking home from school, thinking about Patty and feeling bad about what I had done. While still on the school grounds I had a shock at the thought that I had ruined my chances with Patty forever. Most of the traumatic shocks we have in life are in response to our own thoughts, and often these thoughts are not about anything we know for sure, and are just things we imagine. And any shock, regardless of the cause, is a traumatic moment that can have mild or devastating consequences.

In this shock I decided that I would somehow make this up to Patty in the future, and _until then_ I would never be a success. In my heart I promised Patty that I would not do all the things I had planned – college, biophysics, making important discoveries – instead I would be nothing, until I fixed this. And in a bubble above my head I saw myself sending Patty a letter in the future. At that moment I was actually looking at some dog poop on the ground and decided that I was as low as that, and my viewpoint actually became contracted. All the way home I felt small and low to the ground like an ant, and the world appeared dim and huge. I had another shock when I got home, and I lay on my bed depressed and teary eyed for a long time, while the sound of accordion music floated through my window from my Italian neighbor's house next door.

John Galusha, my Idenics teacher, once said to me, regarding the perpetuity of the decisions we make in traumatic moments, that shocks don't contain a clause that says "until Tuesday." But I discovered that in actuality they can – just like a post-hypnotic command, a shock can contain anything. Sending the letter did release some aspects of this incident, resulting in my experience while running, and I now understood why I felt the need to send it. In the few years prior to that time, I had been reading lots of success books, like Tony Robbins' "Unlimited Power" and others, but I never applied what I learned. As long as this promise to not be successful remained active and locked away deep inside, there would always be something holding me back. There were other things holding me back too, but at least this one was now gone. Patty's invitation to the dance at school had come shortly after our first meeting.

The Report – or "Hi, I'm Patty"

After that first day of class I avoided any eye contact with Patty and tried to remain as anonymous as possible. But I watched her and listened to her conversations, feeling that any information I could get might help me in some way. I remember watching her walk past me when she was passing out papers, and noticed her head had an odd concave shape and there was a thought in my mind "that will do," meaning that, although it was unimportant to me, this body that she was occupying in this life would be good for her. Our eyes did meet a couple of times accidentally, causing me a shock each time, but I managed to avoid any further contact.

A few weeks into the history class we were made to form groups to collaborate on a paper on some assigned topic. Each row of about six students formed one group, and Patty was in my row, sitting a few chairs behind me. I wanted to be sitting at the back of the room near the door for a quick exit, but when we picked our seats, the end seat was too close to Patty, so I sat at the front of the first row. I always remembered our first meeting. Patty came up to the front of my desk and introduced herself: "Hi, I'm Patty." She seemed to be taking charge of our group.

I had a shock and suppressed everything I was trying to hide from her, including every negative thought and memory I had about myself, as if she would be able to see them if I didn't. The collateral damage of this, which stayed with me for decades, was that my sexuality was also completely suppressed, because I had equated anything sexual with pain, guilt, and shame.

But I then shifted into a higher state of awareness, and although I was aware of my internal effort to suppress things, I had tremendous clarity. However, it is possible that I was being influenced by Dennis–2. As we talked, I was connecting with her, revealing who I was – as if to say "It's me, Philippe – remember? I'm here!" In this moment of connection it felt like I was trying to awaken something inside her – like I was nudging her to recognize me. She liked to touch people when she talked, and she lightly touched my left hand as she made a point. That's when I noticed her hand was shaking – in fact her whole body was slightly trembling – and I knew I had made the connection. Inside I was smiling. This of course was not what I wanted in my normal state, but apparently, from this higher point of view, (or perhaps from Dennis–2's point of view) her recognition was imperative.

When our group got together to start working on the paper, something to do with Africa, we had to decide who would present the paper to the class. I volunteered right away so I wouldn't have to work with the others. I had a fear of public speaking but I wasn't thinking ahead. I was compelled by the urgency of the moment to avoid any interaction with Patty now and in the future, and I also avoided eye contact with her during this meeting. About a week or so later they gave me the paper I was to read and I took it home and studied it. On the day I had to read it I was very nervous. I realized that this could have been a big mistake because if I did poorly I would be a failure in Patty's eyes. I had to do a good job to prevent her from having a bad impression of me. I was sitting at my desk minutes before it was my turn to speak, feeling my angst, and whispering over and over "I can't make a mistake! I can't make a mistake!" I was really just putting more pressure on myself. Then I heard a voice in my head suggesting very clearly "Say 'I WON'T' make a mistake'." A light bulb went off in my head as I realized this was much better, and started silently chanting this new mantra until I was called upon.

This teacher, Mrs. Mosely, liked to experiment and do things differently, and although most of her ideas were duds, many were simply unusual, like changing our seating assignments periodically. So for this report I didn't have to face the class to give my talk. Instead I stood at my desk facing the teacher, who was sitting at her desk in the front of the room.

I began reading the paper, but suddenly I couldn't see the paper at all. I could only see straight ahead. I was speaking directly to the teacher, and although I could see her, it was like I was looking through a fish bowl. Everything was a bit blurry and distorted. I kept trying to look down at the paper but I couldn't feel my hands or move my head. I worried that I would drop the paper on the floor. I heard myself speaking and noticed I was using some big words and saying things that weren't in the paper. Since there was nothing I could do, I just tried to stay calm and pay attention to the words that were coming out of my mouth. When I was done, the fish bowl disappeared and I seemed to be back to normal.

The open-mouthed look of incredulity on the teacher's face was priceless. She was quiet for a moment and then said "Well! ... I think Dennis deserves a big round of applause" and the sound of clapping hands filled the room. I returned to my seat and whispered a quiet "Thank you" to whoever that was. I didn't know about Dennis–2 or any of my helpers, but I knew some unknown force had just helped me out. At recess our whole group came up to my desk to compliment me. I remember Patty standing on the outside looking at me thoughtfully, but she said nothing. I don't know what she was thinking, but from then on it was cat and mouse.

Cat and Mouse

A year after first addressing it, I did more work on that incident where I had rejected Patty and hurt her feelings. Once I had begun discovering other personalities and integrating, I found one I called Meany, although he referred to himself as Harry. His job was to run interference for me by dissuading Patty from trying to befriend me or even talk to me. To this end he had to be blunt, forceful, unfriendly, and even downright mean. This was because Patty, it turned out, was a formidable adversary in this game of cat and mouse. She was like the Terminator, being virtually unstoppable. No matter what I said, she would not be put off. For every excuse I gave as to why I couldn't do something, she had endless solutions. I discovered that Meany was born during that conversation we had about the hayride dance, after my famous one-off report. I would tell her I didn't know how to dance and she would offer to teach me, or I would say I had no way to get there and she would say I could ride with her. Finally I reached the breaking point. I couldn't just say I didn't want to go anywhere with her, because that wasn't actually true, and I also didn't want to hurt her feelings. But I had to. Meany emerged from the resulting shock and said whatever he had to, to get her to stop, while I watched sadly from a few feet away. I of course realize that I am responsible for the actions of any of my helpers, having recruited them so to speak, but they were able to handle things I couldn't, and once they took over I usually had no way to stop them.

After that incident, Patty continued to try and connect with me. She would say hi to me if I looked at her and would try to engage me in conversation by asking me casual questions. I wasn't rude but I was becoming increasingly shy since many of these encounters were shocks in which I created quiet and reclusive identities. These identities would be triggered later in life in situations around women I was interested in.

One day she called me at home on the phone. I answered the phone, not expecting this tactic. I thought I was safe at home. I had not yet fully experienced the force of nature that was Patty Preston. I recall vividly how, as I spoke with her, her voice became hollow and thin and farther away, as if I were listening through a tin can. I heard myself actually having a conversation with her, which was confusing because I wanted to hang up. I still don't know how the conversation went, although it was Dennis–2 doing the talking. The call didn't last long and finally it was over. The next time the phone rang I had a shock at the idea it might be her, so I didn't answer it. After this, I had a startle response every time the phone rang. It's funny now, but this reaction lasted for years.

Forgetting Patty Preston

I never got a response from Patty to the letter I sent in December of 1991 but it didn't matter. I thought I was done with any obligation. I was doing several sessions every day and discovered ten more incidents with Patty over the next two weeks, then nothing for four months. Then she began appearing in my sessions with increasing regularity, and it began to bother me. What I was remembering revealed a strong attraction between us in school, and the more I remembered, the more I thought about her. Although I realized we were married in our last life, we didn't even know each other in this life, and I wanted to stop thinking about her. One evening near the end of June the next year, I went for a walk on the college campus we both attended for two years, which was near my house. I was remembering seeing her there, and had the idea that maybe I could force myself to forget her. Then a weird thing happened. I had a fleeting feeling that I could really lose my memory of her completely, and it scared me. I think this was an internal warning to not even consider it. I was dismayed.

That night I prayed to God for help. I wanted to resolve this Patty thing. The next day I got a phone call. Synchronicity! I had been advertising my ID-R services in local tabloids. A lady named Sandra called me and was interested in my work. She turned out to be a spiritual consultant and she asked me if I did trades. I explained my situation and my problem concerning Patty. I needed answers and this felt like providence, so I welcomed her services. The very first thing she said to me when I mentioned Patty was "She goes by Patricia." She then told me where she lived, that she had no children, and many other things that I later found to be 100 percent accurate. But the most important thing she convinced me of was that Patty and I had a profound connection that should be explored more deeply – that there was more I needed to know. She suggested that I try mentally communicating with Patty and that I look deeper into our past-life relationship.

So that night during meditation I tried to communicate with Patty psychically, which I had never tried before. I was surprised that I got some answers. They were mainly in the form of feelings. I immediately felt that she was angry with me, but the anger soon disappeared and I sensed a forceful encouragement from her to go deeper. I began the next morning.

When I looked again at our past life together as Ana and Philippe, I discovered that Ana had been pregnant when she died and this was part of the deep grief she was feeling. At the site of the plane crash I noticed the child spirit was watching us from a distance and he too appeared upset. The promise I made to Ana was not only that we would be together in our next life but that we would have children so that the child we lost might also return. My love and concern for Ana were very deep, and I knew this was what she wanted. When I connected with her and those feelings, I experienced a deeper sense of who Ana was to me – it went beyond our earthly personas and was as if we were a part of each other. There was a sense of love and beauty there that was totally unexpected. It engulfed me and I felt a new commitment to this wonderful Being who I now knew as Patty. This session started an avalanche. All but four of the next fifty sessions were on incidents connected to her. There were more than two hundred such incidents in the next three months, and many hundreds more over the next few years. Some of these interactions are described in the stories that follow, and there are still new memories emerging to this day.

Chapter 23
Adventures with Patty

"All is fair in love and war." – Francis Edward Smedley

Eighth grade was a brutal year for me in many ways. In addition to my traumatic interactions with Patty, I had an accident in November that left me with periodic nighttime seizures, and the bomb injury in the second semester which kept me out of school for over a month and left me feeling disfigured. However, the many magical things that happened in Home Room in eighth grade kept hope alive and inspired me to never give up. As with most of my experiences with Patty, I didn't remember any of these stories until they came to light in my sessions.

Zapped

In eighth grade in spite of my repeated rebuffs, Patty continued her ongoing campaign to try and get me to open up to her. Since being nice to me didn't seem to work, Patty started "poking"me. By that I mean, she would walk by my desk and knock my pencil on the floor, or accidentally bump into me. One dark windy day, as the rain poured outside, the teacher had her go up and down the rows passing out papers to everyone. She went down our row first and as she walked by me I felt an electrical shock in my left side and I knew intuitively that she had just "zapped" me. It was annoying, like someone had just poked me in the ribs with a mild cattle-prod. So as she walked up the next row I zapped her back. She stopped for a moment but didn't look at me. She had no other noticeable reaction, but she soon zapped me again and I reciprocated. This went on a few more times until she was done and sat down. I can't tell you how I was able to zap her except that it felt like an easy and natural ability at the time, so perhaps we were both operating at a slightly higher level to some degree, during this exchange.

The Body Repairman – or Another Man's Shoes

One day during the first semester, Mrs. Mosely chose Patty and a boy named Dewey to do something which I still don't understand. Remember, this teacher had some strange ideas, although she was probably just trying to be creative. Whatever they were doing, which I'm most likely describing incorrectly, probably took about fifteen minutes, but I'm guessing. After they started, the teacher left the room for some reason. There were two boxes. Box number one was on the teacher's desk, and box number two was on a smaller desk about ten feet to my right. Patty would take a card or paper from box one and carry it over to box two and do something with it, and Dewey would similarly take one from box two and carry it to box one, and they would walk past each other. Then they would go back and repeat the process, passing each other again. It seems they were writing something on a separate paper each time. I feel it had something to do with counting votes but I really have no idea. Anyway, everyone else was at their desk reading or doing homework. I pretended to take a nap and left my body. I seemed to dissociate a lot in that class and soon found that I could exit my body in a slightly higher state of awareness, at will.

Exterior, I went over to Dewey and communicated with him psychically. I perceived him as a ghostly version of himself inside his body. He turned his spirit head to face me as we talked. I asked him if I could borrow his body for a few minutes because Patty and I were friends. But he said "No," and I sensed he felt this would be violating some rule, and he was a stickler for rules. So I said OK and left. I came back a minute later and, keeping myself invisible, I made him very sleepy. When I saw that he was having trouble staying awake I reappeared, looking different, and wearing a white shirt that said "Body Repairman." I got his attention and, acting official, I told him that he had probably noticed he was having trouble staying awake. I explained that there was something wrong with his body and if I didn't fix it he would pass out. I told him he would have to leave his body for a few minutes so I could get in there, but the problem was simple and I would fix it right away. He was a bit annoyed by this interruption but agreed, so I said "Just stand right there in front of the teacher's desk and count to a thousand." This whole transaction only took a few seconds. He left and began counting while I took over his job of transferring cards.

As I walked past Patty, I looked at her and smiled. In this guise I had no fears or reservations and in fact I felt elated. It was similar to being Pete in fifth grade. I did the same thing every time we passed each other – I looked at her and smiled. Patty was quite puzzled at Dewey's mysterious behavior but then her expression changed and she stopped looking at me and seemed to be thinking. Then she gave me a knowing look and smiled as if she had caught me with my hand in the cookie jar.

After about three minutes Dewey reached one thousand and we traded places. I told him everything was now back to normal and went back to my desk. Patty and Dewey were done shortly and they took their seats. Before Patty took her seat though, she stopped briefly at my desk, knelt down, and whispered something to me. My head was still laying on my arms in nap position and my eyes were closed but she knew I was awake. "I know what you did" she said confidently, and walked away. The teacher still had not returned, so when the bell rang we all left.[97]

The Magic Rock

I had a dream very similar to the "goat skull" dream. It was a very lucid vision of a colorful rock. It was reddish overall and mottled with brown and black streaks. The rock was shaped like a roundish cube, with a few jagged edges giving it a crystal-like appearance, but I couldn't estimate its size. In the vision it seemed as big across as my hand, and it was just floating in front of me, slowly turning so I could see the whole thing. I soon discovered it was another memory from eighth grade.

It was getting close to Christmas and my fourteenth birthday was approaching. I was standing at home in the kitchen one night and I heard a voice that said, "Hold out your hand." It sounded more like a statement than a request. It was gentle, neutral in tone, and had no quality of gender. I stopped and kept listening. Then I heard it again, spoken exactly the same as the first time: "Hold out your hand" but added "and close your eyes." So I held out my right hand, palm up, and closed my eyes. And I saw something. It was a

---

[97] Beyond my tricking Dewey, this episode raises ethical questions which are discussed in Chapter 12.

vision of a colorful rock surrounded by darkness. It was slowly rotating. Suddenly I felt something cold in my hand and opened my eyes. There resting in my palm was the rock I had just seen, but smaller. It was about an inch across. There was a momentary shock at this alteration of reality. Again I heard the voice, sounding farther away now, say "It's a gift." I immediately closed my hand to hide the rock and looked around to be sure no one had seen what had just happened. I was alone, and I quickly ran to my bedroom and closed the door. I went to my desk and examined the rock. I didn't know where the rock came from but it felt magical and special. I hid it in a special place.

Reciprocations

A few days later around noon, on a weekend, I was in my bedroom when I heard a voice instructing me to get ready to go somewhere. He told me to put on a nice shirt and comb my hair, so I did. I know now that it was Dennis–2, but at the time I recognized this voice as my guide. The "guide" was a disguise Dennis–2 adopted when he needed me to trust him. I remember putting on a coat and being told to bring the magic rock. I was then instructed to stand in a certain spot in the middle of my room, to lean forward, and to not move no matter what happened. Suddenly I was in a different space. It was dark but I could make out vague objects around me. As my surroundings came more into focus I could see that I was in someone's dining room, facing the kitchen. There was a table on my left and a counter in front of me, and before that, a swinging door on the left that led to the living room. I was also now in a higher state of awareness and understood what was happening. This was Patty's house. I sensed there were some people in the living room making Christmas preparations. Patty walked in through the swinging door, and when she saw me she froze in her tracks. It took her a couple of seconds to recognize me. She then immediately considered her appearance and checked her hair with her hands.

I was smiling when she asked "What are YOU doing here?"

"I was invited" I said. We had a few words and I told her, "I can't stay – I just wanted to tell you I got your present." I was holding out my closed left hand. "What present?" she asked. "You have to come closer so I can show you" I replied.

She just stood there but I knew I could not move from my spot so I said "You have to come over here." She asked me some questions and moved closer, but was still too far away. "Closer" I said, and when she was near enough to see it clearly, I opened my hand and showed her the rock. "You sent this to me" I said, as she stared at the rock. "Do you remember?" She said something and looked up but I had vanished!

Patty was confused for a few seconds, wondering if this was real. But as she walked over to the kitchen counter she became elated. It was a miracle! She began pounding her fist on the counter and saying "I knew it, I knew it, I knew it!" She pondered this experience for hours. How I know what Patty was feeling and thinking however, requires a chapter of its own.

Patty was not to be outdone. I don't know when this happened, but it seems like a few weeks later. I was walking into my living room from the hallway when I saw a shimmering disturbance to my right, in front of the fireplace. It looked like heat waves that you might see above hot pavement in the summer, but was emanating various colors. As I watched it, the three-dimensional image of a girl appeared. I say "image" because I had the impression I was watching some kind of projection. The girl was standing in my livingroom surrounded by a translucent white light, and was holding something, but her image was distorted.

She looked at me and I said "Who are you?" I was scared but curious.

"Don't you recognize me?" she responded, audibly. "I'm not sure," I said, keeping my distance.

As the image corrected itself I could see it was Patty and she was holding a sheet of paper.

"How do I look now?"

"Better – you look normal" I replied. Because this experience lay outside our normal social context, I felt none of the angst I usually had around her.

"OK, here's what I want you to do" she said, sounding very sincere, as if this were some kind of solution to our unspoken dilemma. She began rapidly reading a list of about seven or eight things she wanted me to do, maybe more, but I knew I wouldn't do any of them, so I didn't try to remember what she was saying. I just watched, until her image faded out. She wasn't quite done reading when she realized her time was up, so, as she was losing contact, she tried to hand me the paper. I took a step forward to take it but she disappeared. She had let go of the paper but, as it floated downward, it too vanished in the same moment. I just stood there awhile, wondering if what I had just experienced was real. It now felt more like a dream. In my normal state of consciousness I didn't remember what I had experienced while in altered states, and at this point I no longer recalled anything about the magic rock, but I had a definite sense that there were things happening between Patty and me "behind the scenes." It's like I knew what was going on, and didn't know, at the same time.

Body Dysmorphic Disorder – or Being Quasimodo

The bomb accident impacted my life in many ways, and addressing the various issues it created, years later, not only revealed some important things to me about healing, but also provided some amazing insights into what is possible. At the time however, it was a new source of trials and tribulations, and wonders, with Patty.

During my stay in the hospital two kids from one of my classes came to visit me, and they gave me a get-well card signed by the teacher and the students. This was maybe on the third or fourth day after the accident. I didn't really know them and they didn't stay long. Maybe it was the way they were looking at me, or maybe it was just curiosity, but after they left I felt compelled to go look in the mirror. I remember the gown I was wearing and how dizzy I felt trying to walk over to the mirror which was on the wall near the door. I imagine I was also on a lot of pain medication.

But when I looked in the mirror I had the shock of my life. I was horrified! I looked worse than Frankenstein's monster. My face was horribly swollen and distorted, scarred, stitched up, and discolored in various shades of black, blue, purple, red, and yellow. In the shock, I felt my life was over – that all my hopes and dreams were shattered forever. I decided that I would live my life as a recluse and never let anyone see me. I was the Elephant Man, Deadpool, Quasimodo. Any chance I ever had with Patty was obliterated. I collapsed to the floor. My spirit was crushed.

An interesting aspect of that shock at the mirror is that while in the power-zone I was shown a book by an invisible presence that I believe was my Higher Self. Each page of this book was thick and hard and had a picture of someone that looked very strange and hideous to me. Some must have been alien beings. I looked at several pictures. Each picture was three-dimensional, appearing inside a box-like space within the page, and the images were moving, like short video clips. Nowadays we have digital photo frames that can do these things but this was in the 1960's and I had never seen or imagined anything like this before. The tone from my Higher Self, as he turned the pages, was one of humor. Perhaps he was trying to help me have a different attitude, but I was mostly just confused, and didn't understand the purpose of the book at all.

Devastated, I crawled back into the bed, hid under the covers, and tried not to let anyone see me again. That failed of course, and my family put me at ease by not acknowledging my hideousness in any way. But now I was terrified to see my own face.

When I returned home, I avoided looking in any mirrors or seeing my reflection anywhere. I imagined I was the distorted monster I had seen at the hospital – that image was stuck in my head. But it was a blurry image now because I had tried to block it out of my vision at the time, so I was seeing a suppressed version of it. What was still painfully present was the crushing hopelessness of my future.

One day during my first week at home I was sitting on the couch in the livingroom reading when I heard some girls' voices outside. I had an inner vision of Patty and her friend Rene outside the front door. When the doorbell rang, I yelled at my father not to answer it. He ignored me, and when he saw the two cute young girls standing there, he of course invited them in. I immediately ran to my bedroom and slammed the door. I refused to come out when my father called me. Patty chatted with my dad a bit and they left. They had brought me some cookies. But now I felt trapped in my own home.

One day, a week or two later, my friend Ross, who lived down the street, showed up unexpectedly when I was doing something on the patio. He came through the garage to the door that opened to the patio and suddenly we were face to face. I got angry and told him I wasn't ready to see anybody. He said he just wanted to see how I was doing since I hadn't called him. I actually hadn't called any of my friends since the accident. I had a short conversation with

him and he seemed to be undisturbed by my appearance. But I
went back in the house as soon as I could.

After confronting Ross and being told by my family that the
swelling and bruising were all gone, I got curious. When I felt my
face with my hands, it seemed OK except for the scars. So one day I
took a chance and glanced in the full length mirror on the back of
my parents bedroom door, for a split second. My face was its normal
color. I took longer and longer glances until I could see that I
wasn't hideous anymore. But I still felt hideous. I now had a mild
case of body dysmorphic disorder. But the fact was, I didn't really
care how I looked to my parents, my brothers, or really anyone
other than Patty. That remained true until years later when I started
dating and these awful feelings were summoned forth again.

The Inner-Light Support Group,
a.k.a. The Ugly Club

In the midst of my many new revealing sessions regarding Patty,
during the summer of that second year of using ID-R, I had a dream
in which a group of grotesquely deformed and mutilated people
were gathered around me. The leader, who was perhaps the hardest
for me to look at, put his hands on my shoulders and I was filled
with an amazing feeling of energy and started to fly above the
group. I began experiencing OBE feelings and woke up. This whole
experience felt very real, and in my next session I discovered that it
was.

While I was still in the hospital recovering from the bomb
explosion, and feeling terribly demoralized after seeing my
reflection, Patty visited me in spirit. She pulled me out of my body
while I was sleeping and took me on a journey. We flew through
the sky for some distance and then went down to Earth and entered
a building. Patty led me through a maze of rooms until we entered
a large area that was like our school gymnasium. We went to the
middle of the wooden floor and a large group of people started to
come in and gather around us. They were the same disfigured
people in my recent dream. Many had been burned, or maimed in
other ways, and the leader's body was completely charred. All this
was probably taking place in some astral realm.

As these unusual people gathered around me, Patty left and the
leader started talking to me. He explained that they had formed this

group of compassionate individuals in order to help people like me to recover from the emotional impact of the trauma of their disfigurement. He pointed out that there were many people in the world who had been mutilated far worse than me, and that they were still human beings and could still be happy and live fantastic lives. He said the body was just a shell and that true beauty came from within – we were all really made of pure spirit – pure light. As I became more present and aware, and started looking at the people around me, I realized that everyone there was actually happy and joyful, whereas I had first imagined that they were all as sad, pathetic, and as completely disheartened as I was.

Everything the leader said made sense, and I actually began to feel better. In the end I felt lighter, as if a weight had been lifted off me. The leader invited me to join the club and I said I would have to think about it. He then placed his gnarly, burnt hands on my shoulders and I felt a tingling throughout my spirit-body as if he was transferring energy to me. It felt totally physical. I began to rise in the air and saw the people waving goodbye. I awoke in the hospital bed briefly, imagined it was a dream, and went right back to sleep. I did not recall any of this when I awoke that morning, as far as I know, but I believe my visit with the Ugly Club may have helped me reframe my situation on an unconscious level.

Night Visit – or The Sparkling Chatterbox

I was sleeping one night at home during my month off from school, recuperating from my accident, when something awakened me. At first it sounded like white noise, like raindrops on a wet sidewalk, but as it grew louder it began to sound like a crowd of people talking. I couldn't discern where the sound was coming from so I opened my eyes and saw a white hazy cloud of light forming above my bed. The cloud became a rainbow of colors, with round twinkling spots of red, blue, and white, appearing and than fading out above me. It reminds me of the "Companion," a sparkling cloud of sentient energy, in the original Star Trek episode "Metamorphosis." As soon as I saw the emerging cloud of lights I was terrified. I closed my eyes and didn't move. I pretended to be asleep and tried to remain completely still. The sounds quickly congealed, becoming a single voice which I recognized as Patty's. She was happily chatting away nonstop telling me what was happening at school and in our classroom. Her voice was quite animated. This went on for several minutes while I remained as motionless as possible, not showing any signs of being awake, although I was inwardly quite tense. Even as her voice began to fade, she showed no signs of slowing down, as if she could talk all night. Finally there was silence, and with a sigh of relief I opened my eyes to the undisturbed darkness of the room.

I wasn't sure what had just happened, but it made me feel like I was a part of something vast and mysterious that I could not remember. It felt like I had amnesia. A "static OBE" state is what I call it when I feel like I'm just lying awake in bed but I'm actually having an out-of-body experience. Usually while in this state people experience sleep paralysis and will find they are unable to move if they try. This is usually explained by describing the physiological mechanism that blocks our muscle impulses and prevents us from acting out our dreams when we are asleep, which could be dangerous. I prefer to say that when we are exterior we are not really connected to the body but we still think we are. It is in this state that one may be able to leave the body if they relax all efforts to move physically, and instead try to move by intention alone. In a static OBE state one can have amazing experiences and mistake them for taking place in physical reality, when they are actually only happening in a non-physical realm, or in your mind. But in this particular case, although I can't say whether anyone else would have seen the lights or heard Patty's voice, I CAN say that during this experience I was in a normal waking state, could move my body, and was not having a dream or a static OBE.

Fight the Future

The whole idea of going back to school after the bomb accident was very troubling. Since I still felt as ugly as the image I saw in the mirror at the hospital, even though I could see I looked normal again, the idea of Patty seeing me was very upsetting. I stalled as long as I could but one day I was told I was going back to school on Monday, and I saw no way out of it. Still, on the morning I was to go to school I protested. I pleaded that I still wasn't ready, but to no avail. My mother had gone to work but my father waited so he could take me to school himself. They wanted to be sure that I went. As my father walked out to the car he asked me if I wanted to

stay home forever. He made it clear that the choice was mine. I
froze in the doorway. The shock came when I realized this was a
no-win scenario. My dad was right. If I stayed home there was no
hope for the future. If I went to school there would be hardship but
at least some possibility. I decided that I had to go to school because
everything I wanted in life depended on it.

At school I moved through the corridors like a spy, scanning all
horizons for any sign of Patty. Peeking around corners and hiding
behind bushes – well, maybe I didn't go quite that far. Due to
constant seating rotations in Home Room I was now seated at the
first desk by the door. Perfect. My plan was to be the last one to
enter, and the first to exit. I would slip in unnoticed and zip out at
each break. It was a hopeless fantasy. When I first walked by the
room at third period, there was a bunch of kids hanging out around
the doorway. I thought I might sneak in right then but I saw Patty
there and had a shock. I quickly walked on by, changing my gate
and posture to prevent being identified. I did this by switching with
one of my helpers.

I finally did make it to class, but of course the first thing the
teacher did was have everyone welcome me back. I felt
demoralized. I hung my head and tried to hide behind my hair.
When class was over Patty was on me before I could even blink,
wanting to know how I was feeling and hoping I was ok. All I could
do was hide my face and mumble. Fortunately things got better
from there, because hiding was futile. Patty was unremitting and
eventually I had to give up trying to be invisible.

One day toward the end of eighth grade my parents got a letter
that said I was to attend a school event – some kind of prom or
dance party. The letter said that this was a formal event and I had to
dress up and wear a suit. In my paranoia, I assumed that sending a
letter to my parents was some trick of Patty's to force me to attend a
school event. When I told my father I didn't want to go he got angry
and insisted that I was going and that he would buy me the clothes I
needed. I felt doomed. But I took the letter and hid it, and my
parents forgot all about it, and so did I.

Ninth Grade – or A Kiss is Just a Kiss

In the hundreds of encounters Patty and I had in Junior High,
High School, and College, the main theme was usually the same.

She made some attempt to communicate or interact with me, and I ran away. Sometimes she put her friends up to trying to convince me to attend things, like her fourteenth birthday party, which led to me having some intense arguments with them. Dennis–2, in the guise of my adversary, occasionally threw a wrench in the works by initiating interactions with Patty which I then had to extricate myself from. You might think I would have just given in to Patty at some point, but the drive to avoid her was a strong identity and an imperative force that overrode any other inclinations. Even so, there were occasions where I decided to stop running and actually tried talking with her. But Dennis–2 stopped me there too. It was all quite maddening.

The first day of ninth grade I discovered that Patty and I had one class together, our second period geometry class. She stopped by my seat before class and asked me how my summer vacation went. In my shock a new personality was created, and he told her he wasn't Dennis and that Dennis wasn't around. When she asked who he was, he said he was "Dennis' friend." I could hear the conversation and was distressed by the whole thing. Patty of course thought I was putting her on and played along for a bit. Some days or weeks later she made sure that I saw her kiss a boy outside in front of the classroom before class, just as I was walking up to the door. The kiss was obviously staged, and clearly a plan to make me jealous so that I might take some action. It did upset me of course, but there was nothing I could do. I made sure I looked sad during class and afterward she stopped by my desk and apologized, saying it was a mistake.

Later that year our geometry class won an award for selling the most magazine subscriptions in a school contest, and that morning we were ushered to another room for a party, with cake, ice cream, soda, and music from a radio. Patty was one of the students who took charge of the party. Since participation wasn't mandatory, I slipped out as soon as Patty wasn't looking. But I hadn't got ten feet outside before Patty came running out the door after me. She was holding something in her hand and had cake on her face. She tried to sell me on coming back in for cake and ice cream, telling me I didn't have to leave. In my bewilderment, Dennis–2 took over.

Dennis–2 walked straight up to Patty and kissed her on the lips. "What did you do that for?" she asked, looking awestruck and mystified – like she wasn't sure how to feel. "Because I wanted to" he replied, smiling confidently. "You can still come back in, there's lots of good stuff" she pleaded. "No thanks," he said as he walked away. I was not aware of the kiss, only of telling her "No." I remember deciding right then to never be happy again – I felt that everything I did with regard to Patty was hurting her. This doesn't mean I was never happy after that, only that I had another unhappy identity that could be triggered under similar conditions.

Agent 99

Every so often, because of Patty's persistence and her apparent acceptance of me as I was, I would get the idea that I could approach her and be normal. This always startled me because it conveyed a great sense of freedom which was normally deeply suppressed. If I could freely interact with Patty, I could do anything! When I had these thoughts it always felt like I was emerging from some deep depression, or a deep sleep. So one day after our second period class was over, I approached her to ask her about going to an upcoming school event. I felt confident and determined. More importantly I felt sane, like I knew what I wanted and it would all be OK. Patty was still in the classroom talking with someone, and as the conversation ended I walked up behind her and tapped her on the shoulder. Patty turned around but I barely got two words out before I found myself standing behind my body, watching.

Dennis–2 smiled and said "Never mind"and walked away. Patty followed and asked "Were you going to ask me to the dance Friday night? ... it's OK." But Dennis–2 kept walking and said "No, it was nothing."

As we left the classroom I started to panic, thinking I was possessed. Every time a switch happened, if I was somewhat conscious of it, it was very confusing. But as I considered my predicament I found I could talk with this entity that was interfering with me, and I told him he couldn't stop me. But he told me that he would hurt Patty if I tried this again. Somehow I knew he was bluffing and told him I didn't believe him. He then assured me that he could never hurt Patty but that there was someone else here who could. He then introduced me to a female personality who seemed like a secret agent. He assured me that she wouldn't have any problem pushing Patty around. I could see this new agent standing behind my adversary, and although she was silent, she looked strong and mean. I gave in. I later named her "Agent 99" after the lady spy in the TV series "Get Smart." I felt stifled in every direction, but I soon forgot this incident, as I did all my dissociative episodes. They disappeared as quickly as many dreams do when we first wake up and have a brief remembrance of them, before they fade into oblivion.

Every moment with Patty was another opportunity for me to embarrass myself, which I usually did. But Patty started doing more 'hit and runs' in High School, in which she would come up to me and tell me something or give me something and walk away before I could do anything stupid. For example in tenth grade on Valentines Day she handed me a heart-shaped locket with her picture in it. When I asked her what it was, she said it was a keepsake, opened it to reveal her picture, and walked away.

The Once and Future Date

This was one of the more embarrassing experiences I had with Patty. It happened in tenth grade sometime in the Spring. Dennis–2 had taken control and was talking with Patty in the main hall at school. He told her she was very beautiful. During the conversation she suggested we go on a date to see a movie. Dennis–2 agreed and the date was set for Saturday, which was several days away. Dennis–2 switched with me at the end of the conversation and I found myself looking into Patty's incredible blue eyes without a clue as to what had just transpired. I turned around quickly and walked away. I heard her say something as I was leaving and I asked inside what had just happened. I was told by an inner voice that we had made a date. I was skeptical and tried to forget about it.

However when Saturday rolled around I knew something was up. I knew this was supposed to be the day of our date but I was still doubtful that the date was real, although I kept looking out the window just in case. When I saw Patty's mother pull up with Patty in the car, I panicked. I ran in my bedroom and hid under the bed and lay there for half an hour in silence, not moving – hardly even breathing.

My father answered the door and invited Patty and her mother inside. He had no idea where I was, and talked with them for quite a while until it was apparent I was a no-show. After they left and I emerged from hiding, my father asked me where I had been and why I hadn't shown up for the date. I don't recall what I said, but whatever it was it provoked him to punch me right in the face, giving me a black eye.

That evening Patty's mother called and wanted to speak with me. She gave me a proper scolding, which I deserved, and told me that Patty was very upset. I heard Patty scream at her in the background "Don't tell him that!" I profusely apologized, since I didn't know what else to do, and the conversation ended. But things only got worse.

Hit Me – or The Earth and Moon Collide

As an adult I would occasionally have dreams of the moon crashing into the earth. These dreams took different forms and were always horrifying and tinged with a deep sense of depression. Working on one of these dreams revealed the following incident.

Back at school after the date fiasco in tenth grade, Patty confronted me in the main hallway and told me how despicable I was for standing her up. But it wasn't me she was talking to – it was Dennis–2. He totally agreed with her and said he was really sorry for what had happened and suggested that she should hit him as punishment. She asked "What?" and he said "Hit me on the shoulder like this, but hard, and gave her a soft punch in the shoulder. She said she didn't want to, but he said he deserved it and she should just do it. So she gave him a light tap on the shoulder. But he said "No, harder, like this," and hit her hard enough to hurt a little, but nothing like when my brothers and I would play this game. However, she clutched her shoulder, asked him why he did that, and turned around and left.

I switched back at that moment and saw her walking away. I asked inside what had happened and a voice said "You hit her." I instantly had a terrifying shock. I imagined my life was over. I had just hurt Patty and was obviously a danger to her. Although it was still morning, I left school and walked all the way home, about three miles. As I walked out of the crowded hallway I wished the world would end right then and imagined the moon crashing into the Earth and destroying everything. This image was very real, like a

3D movie, fueled by powerful emotions. This shock is what had produced those frightening dreams.

This incident had also triggered other past trauma. At home I lay in bed depressed all day. The next day I had a shock just considering how I could go back to school and face anyone ever again. I decided that I should never allow myself to be around Patty at all. Fortunately for me, in three years of High School, we never had a single class together.

My Confession

UN-fortunately for me, Patty had a mind of her own and her efforts never ceased. She was soon approaching me again doing hit and runs, and one day I decided I had to do something. I could feel my inner adversary trying to stop me, but somehow I had the strength to keep him in check, at least this once. So that day I went up to Patty in the hall when she was at her locker, and made my confession. I told her that I had no control over my actions and that the things I did and said were almost never what I wanted. I explained that the best thing for both of us was to just not talk to each other and stay as far apart as we could. She asked me if that was what I really wanted and I said no, but that it was the way it had to be. I left feeling strong but sad, and I knew I was doing the right thing. I wanted her to be safe. At the time I wasn't in a shy state at all but in a higher, more confident state. As I walked away she said to me, with the utmost sincerity and strength in her voice, "We'll figure something out!" I sensed a deep feeling of partnership in this moment, but I immediately let it go.

Strategies

Patty never did relent on trying to make a connection with me, and I continued to avoid her. To counter this, she devised various strategies to corral me. One day in eleventh grade I was walking down a hall at school and a girl from one of my classes started talking to me. It seemed innocent enough but shortly there were three other girls there. Then I saw Patty coming and knew it was a trap. As I headed into the boy's restroom that was close by, all four of the girls tried to block my way, and one of them grabbed my arm. Patty had put them up to this so she could talk to me, so I must

have been doing a good job of avoiding her. I broke away and hid in
the restroom until after the bell rang.

Another time in between classes, Patty introduced me to a blond
girl named Janet, and after saying a few words she left us alone. It
was awkward. I suppose Patty had the idea that if I would interact
with another girl I might eventually interact with her as well. But
Janet and I just stood there looking at each other. We exchanged a
few inane words and then she said something like "It was nice
meeting you" and I said "OK, see ya later," and that was it. Janet
seemed nice and she did try to talk with me a couple more times
but my responses were brief.

When we were seniors, Patty approached me to be her escort in
some school event. She walked beside me down the "Senior Walk,"
a shortcut across campus restricted to seniors, trying to convince me
to do this. Every time I said no, and gave some excuse, she
countered with a solution I couldn't refuse, but I had to. She would
buy me the clothes, provide transportation, show me the ropes.
Weary, I finally switched with Meany who criticized her loudly
until she gave up. Meany's words really upset me, but I had
relinquished control and had to take responsibility. However,
incidents like these just seemed to make Patty more aggressive.

Jock Strapped

Some months later I was walking down a wing of classrooms off
the main hall when, as chance would have it, a door opened and
Patty stepped out. When she saw me walking toward her, she held
the door open and stood blocking the rest of the walkway. By this
time she had become quite popular in school and had developed a
bit of an attitude. She looked confident and defiant as if to say
"What are you going to do now Dennis?" I could have walked
around her onto the lawn where several people were sitting and
talking, but instead I lifted up her elbow and walked under her arm,
without saying a word. She said "Ow" as I moved past her, and
although I knew I hadn't caused any pain, I felt terrible but kept
walking.

Then I heard someone asking Patty if I had hurt her, and Patty
saying "No, it's OK." The guy talking to her was someone she knew,
an athlete, probably a football player. He was several inches taller

than me, and eager to help a pretty damsel in distress. And he decided it wasn't OK.

As I walked down the outside walkway toward the main hall, I heard him yell at me. "Hey you, turn around! Hey!" When I turned to look at him, he was approaching me and said "I think you should apologize to the lady!" I felt an inner sigh as I knew this was going to be another dismal moment of ultimate humiliation. But suddenly I found myself walking down a different walkway halfway across the campus. Dennis–2 had come to my rescue, unbeknownst to me. I had forgotten everything that had just happened, and as always, when I lost time, I just took it in stride and didn't give it another thought. But let's go back to a few minutes earlier.

Dennis–2 turned halfway and glared back at the jock heading toward him. The idea was to not face him directly, or he might feel inclined to stand his ground, to save face. So, while mustering great energy, Dennis–2 gave the intense impression of someone who had no time for petty bullshit. The jock, who was still about fifteen feet away, repeated his request that I "apologize to the lady," as he moved closer. With his size, confidence, and righteous bearing, I'm sure he saw himself as a white knight.

But what emerged from Dennis–2 was unexpected. He displayed the most astonishing ferocity, momentarily restrained as if he could barely contain himself. This must have made him seem twice his size, and perhaps gave the impression of a volcano that was about to explode. Then, with a look of absolute confidence that could not be doubted, and the finality of death in his voice, he growled: "If you mess with me I will rip your fucking face off!" The energy must have been overwhelming. Startled, the guy actually took a step back. I wouldn't have been surprised if he had fallen over. He was speechless. Dennis–2 turned back and kept walking. He heard the guy say to Patty that I had apologized and her response was "It didn't sound like that to me." Dennis–2 smiled to himself, and walked a goodly distance before switching out.

The Prom

This was all memory work using ID-R; I could not find any shock, although there may have been one at the thought of missing the Prom, but a vision led to the following adventure. It was the night of the Senior Prom night, and of course I was not going. I

don't know why everyone in the house was gone but I was the only
one home. A strange drowsiness came over me as the sun was
setting, and I went and lay down on my bed, almost in slow motion.
At some point I found myself at the Prom, exterior, hovering around
the crowd of students and teachers. I surveyed the people. Patty was
talking with a blond guy and was standing on one side of the
crowded auditorium.

I finally found someone that suited my purposes and asked him,
spiritually, if I could use his body for a few minutes. He said sure,
but that I would have to wait a little while. He was a handsome jock
fellow from whom I thought Patty would accept a dance invitation.
However as time wore on and I repeatedly requested his help, he
kept putting me off. Finally he swore at me and said he never had
any intention of granting my request. His attitude was arrogant and
belittling. This made me very angry and I let him know it, but he
just laughed at me and there was nothing more I could do.

Dismayed I searched for another volunteer but it was getting
late. I had to find a young man with whom I could easily
communicate, which was actually a small percentage of those
present, for some reason. It also had to be someone who would be
willing to help. Finally I found a short guy who had come to the
Prom alone. He wasn't the most handsome guy and I wasn't sure
Patty would accept a dance from him, but at least he was willing.
We'll call him Bradley. When I told Bradley he would get to dance
with one of the prettiest and most popular girls there, he just
wanted to be sure he would remember it. I said he would, as long as
he kept quiet and let me do all the talking. I could tell he was
lonely and that this would be the highlight of his evening. Once I
was in his body Bradley left for a few minutes to check on someone,
and then returned. When I found Patty, her back was toward me
and she was talking with some people. When I asked if she would
like to dance she said OK but that she was busy right now.

I waited off to her right and stood there with my back to her so
that she would think I forgot. I didn't want her to take added
measures to avoid me. Finally she walked away and I felt she was
trying to stall, but I walked over and reminded her. I heard her date
tell her that she didn't have to dance with me. Then I heard him
say "Do you want me to tell him to take a hike?" But she said "No,

that's all right" and walked over to me and said "OK." By that time I think it was close to the last dance, but we danced to the next song.

I didn't know how to dance but I seemed to do OK. Perhaps my host was helping me out! As we were dancing, she didn't look at me and I could tell she was a bit uneasy, but I was looking at her and smiling. Her bored expression changed however when I said "I have a message from Dennis Alsop." She looked at me and asked "Do you know him?" "Um, Hmm" I nodded. She asked what the message was and I said: "He wanted to be here and dance with you but he couldn't, so he asked me to dance with you in his place." She began grilling me with all kinds of questions about Dennis, like how I knew him and for how long. I just made things up, but I did make sure I expressed Dennis' positive feelings for her. When the dance was over I walked away, and as I took leave of Bradley's body I asked him if he could remember everything. He said he could, and thanked me.

At school the next week Patty and a couple of her friends approached me as I ate lunch in my reclusive hideaway table outside, behind the cafeteria. I think she knew all my routines and hiding places. I tried to ignore her but she sat down in front of me and started talking. She asked me about the Prom and told me about how this guy had given her a message from me. I honestly didn't remember anything about the Prom and had no idea what she was talking about, since I had been in an altered state at the time. Even so, I did feel like I was hiding something, so I shifted into denial. I acted oblivious to the whole thing, only concerned with my lunch. She asked me if I knew Bradley and I said no. She said that was strange because he said he knew me and that we were friends. Nothing Patty said helped me remember anything, as far as I recall, and she gave up. Afterward, she and her friends stood behind me talking for a minute. Once again, she left confused.

School Daze

On the last day of High School I composed a note to give to Patty. I had the feeling I would never see her again if I didn't do something. I knew where her last period class was but found no sign of her as I watched the students streaming out of the school grounds, many for the last time. I did see her that night at the graduation ceremony however. Our eyes locked briefly, then she looked away. I thought about her all summer, but finally decided there was no hope and became apathetic

However, in the Fall, during the first few days at the local Junior College, I encountered Patty at the campus book store. We had a brief conversation during which I started to feel there was some possibility for real communication. However, as Patty and I were conversing, my nemesis started talking to me and warned me to break this off quickly or something awful would happen. I knew my optimism was too good to be true, and got out of there right away. After that Patty no longer approached me, although she did make sure she walked past me on several occasions, even when I thought I was in the clear, and I always found myself turning toward her and saying "Hi" in spite of my trying to look the other way.

I had several Level 2 out-of-body experiences over the next few years in which I was called to help Patty when she was in distress. And she visited me as well, but none of these experiences made their way into my everyday conscious awareness, and were only remembered many years later.

The Pizza Parlor Blackout – or Hello Stranger

As with all the other stories in this chapter, I didn't remember anything about this particular chain of events before doing ID-R. When I was twenty-four I got a job working in a local pizza parlor. I worked in the kitchen on weekend nights and worked at the soda and beer bar during the weekday lunch hours. I had not seen or heard from Patty in over four years. One day at home I answered the phone and a woman's voice asked to speak to Dennis Alsop. I said "That's me" and she told me her name was Patty Preston and that we knew each other in high school. I had a shock and quickly told her she had the wrong number. I explained that my name was Dennis Johnson and that I thought she had said Johnson. After a short dialog I hung up. The phone immediately rang again but I didn't answer it, and my phone paranoia returned. Although I was reading a lot of self-help books and trying different self-improvement methods, they didn't help much with my social anxieties, and of course all my previous programming with regard to Patty was still intact. However, I soon forgot about the call.

A few days later when I got home from work my father told me a
woman named Patty Preston had called and wanted to get in touch
with me. She said she was a teacher and that we went to school
together and she would like to talk. I told him I didn't know her and
had no idea why she would call me. He tried to convince me it
would be good to have a social life and he gave me her number, but
I threw it away. What I didn't know was that he had told her where I
worked.

One day, perhaps a week after Patty's call, I was working the day
bar by myself at the pizza parlor. The lunch crowd was gone and
the place was empty. At this point I had bussed all the tables and
had amassed a huge amount of glassware to wash. The sink area to
my left, and half the bar top, had scores of dirty beer mugs, coke
glasses, and pitchers waiting for me. I was putting some clean beer
mugs away when two ladies walked in.

I thought nothing of it as they ordered a small pizza at the
kitchen window. Suddenly however, the parlor was empty! I looked
in the kitchen to my right and there was only one cook when there
had been two a moment before. Then I looked to my left and was
startled to see that all the glassware had been washed and put away.
I couldn't believe it! I ran to the door behind the bar that led to the
scullery and opened it to look at the punch clock on the other side.
Forty two minutes had passed. I had no idea what had happened.
Normally when I lost time, I never remembered doing so. This time
it was different, possibly because it hadn't happened in years. I
remember thinking about this phenomenon as I made the thirty-
minute walk home from work that day, but it remained a mystery.
In processing all this eighteen years later however, I was able to
recall what had happened during the missing time.

When the two ladies who had ordered the pizza came up to the
bar to order drinks, I found myself face to face with Patty. She was
absolutely beautiful. When I looked in her eyes it was like tumbling
into empty space. But the only thing I could think of to do, in my
moment of shock, was to try and block my aura so that she couldn't
recognize me spiritually. I wanted to appear as someone she didn't
know. But Dennis–2 was way ahead of me. He used my shock to
instantly take over and he cordially served Patty and her mother
their sodas and went about washing all the glassware. When Patty's
mother went to the restroom, Patty came up to the bar and spoke

with Dennis–2 for a few minutes. I was exterior and heard everything, although I didn't remember it afterward, and I was very disturbed by their interaction, but there was nothing I could do.

Patty introduced herself and Dennis–2 said he did remember who she was, but acted like he didn't recall anything that had happened between her and me. He remembered only being in a class or two with her and mentioned some of her more recognizable school activities, which she downplayed as being overrated. During their conversation, Dennis–2 showed no interest in Patty and gave no impression that he would like to get together another time. Patty saw clearly that there was apparently nothing between her and this man to whom she had been mysteriously drawn. She courteously said "It was nice talking with you," he said the same, and she went back to her seat.

I further recalled that on my walk home I had thought about the mysterious lost time at work. I seemed to go into a trance in which I was fantasizing various things and having conversations with unseen people. I came to the conclusion that everything was OK and forgot about it. But later on at work, a coworker mentioned that Patty was working at a school where he was also working part-time as a substitute teacher. After that I often found myself constantly worrying that she might walk in one day, completely unaware that she already had.

After talking with Dennis–2, Patty was confused. She was trying to understand what she had been thinking, and how she could have been so mistaken. Something in her died that day, as she sat there lost in thought. Patty and her mother left, and this ended eleven years of Patty trying to connect with me, on the material plane anyway, after recognizing me in eighth grade.

These were some of the highlights of my early interactions with Patty Preston. It would be almost twenty years before we spoke again. But our continuous spiritual interactions never ceased, and served to drive the secret purpose of our lives to its eventual realization. Five years later I made my first breakthrough, and fifteen years after that, I discovered what our assignment was. We were covert operatives on a mission! But I discovered this only with Patty's help. She still had a few more tricks up her sleeve, and this story is about to take us even deeper down the rabbit hole!

Chapter 24
Lydia

"Curiouser and curiouser! Cried Alice"
– Lewis Carroll, Alice in Wonderland

Ordinarily, connecting telepathically with another person is not something most of us purposely try to do. Mental communication is a natural ability we all have, but I suspect most of us have many blocks against it. If we practice however, as I suggested earlier, we can improve this ability. Unless we become more mindful of our "intuition," our spiritual perceptions and communications will only be noticed randomly, and ignored as meaningless.

I had a low level telepathic connection with Patty and a few other people. But with Patty, it turns out, I needed something more. I was running a solo session in the summer of 1992 to find the source of some neck pain. I discovered an incident where Patty had a serious accident in which she hurt her neck. I had left my body to go and help her. I had already resolved this incident a few weeks earlier, as my own experience, but this time I seemed to be in Patty's viewpoint and I was experiencing *HER* neck pain. So I just went through the incident as if I were her. Memories and feelings came up, and the pain vanished. This was interesting. It didn't seem imaginary in any way, but I thought it was just some kind of empathy or psychic connection where I was simply aware of her experience.

The Atom

A couple of weeks later I did a session on a recurring vision I'd been having, which I called "The Atom." It had come to mind many times over several weeks. There was a circle with a black dot in the middle, like a hydrogen atom. At some point it reminded me of the two human egg cells I saw when, as a spirit, I connected with my mother and first entered my embryonic body. But this image seemed to be floating in a bright space. I soon discovered that this was an incident that happened right after Patty's conception and before my own birth, and that the atom was indeed a human cell. Patty and I were both present in spirit and I was feeling a lot of love and joy. This may have been our first encounter after our previous life together had ended.

In this incident I was about to do something that would help me protect Patty during her life. This was necessary due to some vulnerability she had which I have not yet identified. But she was worried that this might be dangerous for me. There was also the idea that what I was going to do would mark each of us in a way that other spirits might be able to see – like a kind of flag. In addition, this did pose some kind of risk to me, but I felt the risk was worth it. During the session I wasn't able to see exactly what I did, but it seemed to take a great deal of energy or effort. Somehow I created a link between Patty and me, so that I would always know when she was in trouble. Although we were psychically connected already somehow, that connection was not dependable in emergencies. This new link would allow me to instantly know if there was trouble. In creating this connection I felt considerable distress and I almost lost consciousness, but I did succeed. After this session I still had no idea how this link was supposed to work. One passing thought was that I had become two people, one of whom was always with Patty. But it was just an idea.

Two weeks later during a session, I recalled visiting Patty in spirit when we were around four or five. I was at her house and she was talking out loud to me as if I were physically there. She was unhappy that she had only gotten two pieces of bacon for breakfast but that next time she was promised three. When I looked at her, I saw another person in her head – a shorter girl with dark hair and bangs. Patty noticed that I saw her and said "Oh that's just Lydia, she never talks." When I looked in Lydia's eyes something weird happened and I had to look away. I felt dizzy. It reminded me of looking into parallel mirrors where the images go on forever.

At this point in the present session I realized that, in the Atom incident, I had created another personality to reside with Patty in her body, and that I had done this by my own effort while in a Level–2 state. Patty had named this helper Lydia. Whenever there was real trouble, I knew it immediately through Lydia and would come in spirit to help. On a conscious level though, I was completely unaware of Lydia and of this connection. After discovering Lydia, I had a vision. In the vision I watched Patty being born. I was there, and I was surprised that she had a full head of dark hair.

Lights Off

Two months later I was relaxing, trying to connect with something "in my space" to work with, when I started frantically repeating a word loop that sounded like "fa lahts off ah cah." The phrase clarified as I continued, and became "I can't find lights off!" repeated several times. The phrase made no sense to me, but I worked on the frantic feeling.

I found myself in Patty's viewpoint again, reliving a childhood trauma. She was possibly around four years old or so and her mother had brought home a kitten for her, which was jet black. Patty was very happy and excited. They were in the living room and her mother asked her what she wanted to name it. As Patty was thinking, her mother said "I bet if you turned the lights off you couldn't even see her." Patty immediately said "Lights Off, let's call her Lights Off."

That evening Patty was playing with the kitten in her bedroom. The kitten got under a loose cover on the bed and was striking at any movement Patty would make on the outside. Patty was on the wooden floor next to the bed. At some point, the cover fell off the bed with the kitten underneath. Patty started hitting the covers but couldn't determine where the kitten was and I believe Lights Off accidently got caught under Patty's knee. When she saw the kitten's spirit fly out of the room she started screaming "I can't find Lights Off!" over and over, until her mother ran in.

Her mother found the expired kitten under the cover. Patty didn't understand that the kitten had died and wouldn't let her mother take Lights Off out of the room. So her mother told her it needed to sleep now, and left it there in a little box with a sock over it and put Patty to bed. She later removed the kitten when she thought Patty was sleeping. But Patty didn't go to sleep right away, and was thinking about what had happened. When she realized that Lights Off had died, she blamed herself, and in her shock she made a decision. It was a solemn promise that from then on she would always be good to cats and love them, and never be mean to them.

In many visions I have had of Patty, she had cats around her, and some were black.

I realized that I was experiencing this incident as Lydia. I was actually in Lydia's viewpoint because, as an aspect of my own consciousness, her experience was available to me. Lydia's job was simply to experience everything Patty did, including her thoughts and emotions as well as her shocks, apparently. It must have been an extremely empathetic bond. But I wondered, having merged with her viewpoint, if Lydia and I were now integrated, as would normally be the case. If so, wouldn't my link with Patty now be gone? It appears the answer was no. Lydia was not an ordinary helper – I was supposed to access her experiences without integration occurring. Perhaps this is what made Lydia's creation so difficult, and dangerous. At some point Lydia and I did finally merge but I haven't been able to determine exactly when or why.

Lydia was not a two-way street however. When I had an upset or felt pain, Lydia was apparently not aware, or at least did not pass it on to Patty. However if I had a major trauma, Patty would usually show up, but most of the time there was some delay. On a few occasions however, she did seem to show up immediately, but she may have already been present. Other times she showed up several minutes late, and sometimes she never arrived at all. I'm sure however that there were many other factors at play that determined these things, including my simply not being aware of her presence.

Although I could now do sessions on Patty's shocks when they came up, I knew that I could not just "be Lydia"and know what Patty was doing in the present, or have ordinary access to her memories, so I never did try. It was more like Lydia and I were two different people with a one-way hot line for emergencies. This connection seemed to disappear later on, and I still don't understand the full dynamics of it all. Again, I can only report what happened. However, Lydia is the reason I know what Patty was feeling or thinking whenever there was a shock involved. In many of the incidents I recalled, where I came to Patty's aid in spirit, I also, at some point, recalled experiencing the incident as Patty did, through Lydia. However, any shocks Patty had while away from her body, I know nothing about. And occasionally Lydia had private shocks of her own.

The Lydia Diaries

The incidents that arose which I discovered to be Patty's shocks, as experienced by Lydia, appeared randomly. I would be working on some feeling or image thinking it was my own experience, only to find myself experiencing an incident in Patty's past instead. These sessions gave me more insight into her personality, and a better understanding of what she thought of me and my past behavior toward her. There were many, but I will describe just four of these experiences here. For the most part I'm describing these in the third person because otherwise it can get confusing, but I experienced these as Patty did, through Lydia.

The Great Makeup Caper

When Patty was in grammar school, she decided to bring some of her mother's makeup and other cosmetic articles to school to show her friends. She hid these things in her lunchbox and was heading out the door. The school was a short walk from her house. The shock occurred when her mother stopped her and made her open the lunchbox. She thought she was in big trouble. It wasn't a big deal however, and her mother did let her take a couple of things with her. This is an example of a shock where there was no real danger and I was not alerted.

Breathing Under Water

I had a dream of a small submarine and sensed an urgency to breathe accompanied by a feeling of panic and the idea that I was drowning. There was also the sense that this was a covert operation. It felt like a memory so I used ID-R. I worked through this incident and really thought it was something I had experienced as myself, but I did not recognize the location or the people and it did not seem like a past life.

I was swimming underwater in a small public pool by a park, and as I rose to the surface someone held my head down so I could not reach the air. I fought to reach the surface and at some point I panicked and thought I might drown. Then I heard a voice which gently told me "You don't need air ... be calm ... you'll be OK ... don't fight it." There was some spirit helping me and I felt some energy fill my body, or possibly it was air, and I no longer felt any need to breathe. In my imagination I pictured this spirit coming from a small submarine hiding at the bottom of the pool. Finally I got out of the pool and yelled at the girl who was responsible. I complained about this to some adults but to no avail – they didn't seem concerned that I had almost drowned. After resolving this incident I still felt there was something missing.

On thinking about this later I realized this could be Lydia's memory and I took another look. I was indeed wearing a girl's bathing suit. Which meant that the friendly spirit was probably me. After working on this a bit more I was able to recall helping Patty but it was not me this time, it was Dennis–2.

The Surprised Nurse

I don't know if Lydia slept when Patty did, or was continually vigilant. She was not aware of Patty's dreams and had none of her own, as far as I know. I however, have had dreams which turned out to be Lydia's memories, so you could say they are Lydia's dreams, or my dreams of being Lydia.

Once when Patty was in the hospital and completely unconscious, possibly under a general anesthetic, a male nurse did something unethical. Lydia immediately opened her eyes and said, quite matter-of-factly, "You shouldn't do that." The nurse, expecting it to be impossible for Patty to wake up, was quite shocked and hurriedly left the room. Lydia then quietly closed her eyes and resumed her station.

In the dozens of incidents I experienced as Lydia, I rarely had any way to determine what year it was, or Patty's age, except through deduction based on any clues I could find. Often there were no clues at all. This was especially true after our school years, because I had no context in which to place anything. I didn't know where in the world she was, knew none of her friends, and knew nothing about what she was doing. Since I knew nothing of her life outside my own encounters with her, and things I had heard, there was almost nothing to go on, especially since these experiences were very short snippets of memories. Without access to Lydia's complete memory I was working only with bits and pieces of recall.

In fact, sometimes I was not certain an experience WAS Patty's, unless I had also been present in spirit and experienced the incident as myself, being there to help her. Think about it – if someone knew exactly what you were doing and thinking right now, how much would they really know? Would they know who you are? Would they know where you are or anything else about you? If you were opening a letter addressed to you, maybe they could read your name, but my memories were not that detailed. Only during shocks were memories embedded in a way that were strong enough to understand clearly. Lydia knew she was not Patty but felt she was "one" with her. In a way, for Lydia it was like watching a movie and identifying with the main character, except that she could also feel everything.

The Miracle!

About two weeks after discovering the Magic Rock incidents, I was lying on my bed resting when I experienced a deep sense of alarm and said to myself "a miracle happened!" Then I dramatized it a bit repeating "It's a miracle, it's a miracle!" I began a session immediately and also had the thoughts "I knew it was true, I just knew it!"

These impressions were coming from Lydia's memories of the day I appeared in Patty's house to show her the magic rock. This time I will describe it as Patty experienced it, through Lydia's eyes.

"I left the others in living room wrapping presents to get something in the kitchen. When I walked through the door, I saw a boy standing there by the kitchen table. At first I was confused and it took me a couple seconds to realize it was Dennis from school. Then my first thought was about how I looked, especially my hair. Then I shifted into how I normally am around him. I said 'What are YOU doing here?' I was really startled to see him in my house! He said he was invited, and I immediately thought about who could have invited him, and how would anyone know about him anyway? So I asked him who had invited him and he said that I did.

"Now I thought he must have snuck in the back door, so I asked 'When?' But he just said he had a present for me so I asked where it was. He said I had to come and get it and held out his left hand. I went toward him but he said I had to be closer, and this all felt kind of mysterious so I just stood there. He said the present was to show me something. Now I thought that maybe he had a frog or a bug in his hand and I asked if it was alive. I was a little nervous because boys do things like that. He said 'No, but you have to come closer.'

"When I got closer, he told me he got my present. When I asked him 'What present?' he opened his hand and showed me the rock I had found a few days ago. I looked at it and he said 'You sent this to me and I got it – do you remember? I just wanted you to know.' I stared at the rock.

"*'YOU GOT IT?!'* The words just burst out of me with amazement when I realized what it was. But when I looked up ... he was gone!

"I looked out the window to see if he had run out the door. I had a shock because something was not right, but I decided I was safe and that it really was him. I also knew that this was *A MIRACLE*! I repeated to myself several times the words 'It's a miracle' and 'I knew it was true'. I pounded my fist on the counter top and repeated 'It's true, it's true, it's true, I know it's true' until I was satisfied that I would not forget what happened. Later I asked my mother if miracles were real and she said yes. I said, 'I think so too', but I didn't explain.

"The night when had I wished the pretty rock to be given to Dennis I was sitting on my bed with my eyes closed. As I held the rock, I had a strange experience, like some spirit was helping me, but I thought it was a dream. Then I couldn't find the rock so I pretended that the dream was real. But I was worried that it wasn't real and that the rock had just fallen under my bed, so I didn't look for it."

Plucking the Spider's Web

When Patty was possibly three years old, I was called to her by the feeling that something was wrong. I was exterior and found her on the couch in her living room unconscious. I could tell she was dying but I didn't know what was wrong. I went into the kitchen where her mother was at the stove cooking something. I urgently tried to communicate my concern until she stopped what she was doing and went to check on Patty. From her perspective she probably just "had a feeling." She found Patty unconscious, burning up with fever, and barely breathing. She began frantically shaking her and talking to her.

At that point I had a shock. Patty was dying and I didn't know what to do. In the shock my Higher Self took over and I seemed to be a tiny observer with no will of my own. My Higher Self was

communicating with one or two other beings. Perhaps they were
Higher Self beings also. They had noticed something unusual
about Patty and knew it was her connection to another being. Like
the spider expert who plucked the spider web in the 1990 movie
"Arachnophobia," to lure the deadly spider from its nest, they had
caused Patty's distress in order to draw me out and see who I was. It
felt like some understanding was reached between the higher
beings and I never sensed any kind of conflict. After my Higher Self
returned me to my previous state, Patty was immediately better, and
completely back to normal. Our cover was blown however, but I
had thought until recently that nothing ever came of it. Now it
occurs to me that it may have precipitated a later event which I call
the "Playground Incident," which was the experience that changed
both our lives.

The French Connection

I saw Lydia visually in many of my sessions. Lydia appeared to
me as Patty had looked in our last life. She looked exactly like Ana.
And Ana looked very much like the French singer Mireille
Mathieu. I had learned to play the guitar when I was sixteen and
was mainly into 60's rock, The Beatles, The Moody Blues, Joni
Mitchell, and all the music from the Laurel Canyon scene of the
late sixties. I had zero interest in French pop music. But when I first
saw Mireille Mathieu on the Tom Jones Show in 1969, I fell in love
with her immediately. Besides being an amazing singer, Mireille
sang in French, was short, and looked like Ana, including the bangs
– a perfect storm. I bought her records and even took a French
class. It was crazy, and I could not explain the infatuation. Her
music still connects me to some wonderful feelings I had at the
time, but this is an example of why it is so important to really know
where our feelings and inclinations come from. Unless we see these
things clearly, they can control us. This is the definition of
programming – being controlled by our own unconscious thoughts
and experiences.

While we're on the subject, when I was in my early thirties I
became infatuated with a coworker, a lady who had the same color
hair and eyes as Patty, was the same height, and about the age of
Patty when I had last seen her. And her name was "Patty!" Another
perfect storm! But since I barely even remembered Patty at that

point on a conscious level, I didn't connect this lady to her at all. Of course she was totally wrong for me in every way, but fortunately she wasn't attracted to me. Still, it was an awkward situation – just another example of the importance of self-understanding.

When our attraction to certain people is a reaction and not a real connection, or one not based on reality, then it cannot be authentic, and will most likely lead to disappointment. Many people are attracted to someone who is like one of their parents because they wanted something from that parent, like love, acknowledgment, or protection, which they never got. If the person they presently desire will never give them that either, that unavailability may be the very quality that hooks them, because it triggers the need, and the goal to fulfill that need. People who are compatible and readily available for such a person may appear uninteresting, or not be noticed at all. This is a common theme. But the "need" is itself is a program and a limitation – it is only past pain and not a real need. But when the old reaction is gone, a whole new world opens up. And this is true in any area of life.

Sometimes our programs are put in place intentionally however, for a good reason. For example we may not consciously know our life's purpose, and yet still be unconsciously guided to fulfill it. It really helps though, to find out what our purpose is. As the Oracle says to Neo in "The Matrix Reloaded," "You've already made the choice, now you have to understand it." And as another character says later "Our only hope, our only peace, is to understand it – to understand the 'why'." My unconscious connection with Patty continued to play out after our meeting in the pizza parlor, and eventually I did come to understand, and find peace in, the "why."

Chapter 25

Close Encounters
of Another Kind

*I shall always be near you in the garish day, and the darkest night
amidst your happiest scenes and gloomiest hours always, always, and,
if the soft breeze fans your cheek, it shall be my breath; or the cool air
cools your throbbing temples, it shall be my spirit passing by.*
– Major Sullivan Ballou, letter to his wife. 1861

I'm including this chapter because I believe the things I
describe here may be quite common and important to consider.
But since these spiritual encounters happen on different levels of
consciousness, and because they also challenge our beliefs, they are
rarely discussed or even remembered. My experiences also present
some ethical questions, which I addressed earlier at end of Chapter
15.

Since I didn't remember Patty's visit at the pizza parlor when I
was twenty-four, and had quickly forgotten her phone calls, she
rarely entered my conscious mind for over twenty years, until those
first ID-R sessions in 1991. But I did think about her on a
subliminal level. I believe that whenever I thought about her, I was
in a different state of awareness, and my thoughts of her were
quickly forgotten when I shifted out of it. In my personal notebooks
in which I recorded my brainstorming ideas on many subjects, I
never mentioned Patty, but I used a symbol to represent her. Not
really knowing her, I used that symbol to represent my highest
purpose, and the motivation to achieve something great, whatever
that turned out to be.

Visitations

What I began to discover in early 1992 was that my OBE
visitations with Patty had been fairly constant during childhood,
continued through college, and were ongoing after our
conversation at the pizza parlor as well. As it had been from the

beginning, some of our spiritual visits were trauma based, where one of us would show up to help the other during some emergency or tense situation. Our other visitations were spontaneous attempts to connect and communicate, out of love and partnership.

I had spiritual visitations from several other people in my life, (like the Astral Allies and others already mentioned) but these were mostly one or two visits to deliver a message of some kind. That's all I currently remember anyway. These other visits include spiritual communications from my mother, my friend Jeff, my brother Blake, and a few others.

The only other person I recall showing up in spirit more regularly, was my brother Alan, who would show up on occasion when I was having some difficulty. He would usually just ask me how I was doing and sometimes give me advice. He mostly just seemed to stand around, but he was actually doing something more. His presence always calmed me and I would regain my balance, so to speak. Once I was having a very bad day in college. I was in the physics lab and, due to the stress I was under, felt like I was going crazy. I switched with a helper who began cracking jokes with another student. In the meantime I was out-of-body and literally bouncing off the walls – slowly gliding back and forth, near the ceiling, from one side of the room to the other. Alan walked in the door, also in spirit, and asked me what was going on. He just stood there calmly looking around, hands in his pockets, not saying anything, until I calmed down and felt more stable, and then he left. Sometimes he would phone me out of the blue, just because he had a feeling he should check on me. He was often correct and I actually WAS having some difficulty, although I would usually just say everything was fine. Still, his call seemed to help me.

My Angel Friend

As a young child, Patty would visit me on occasion, in an exterior state, and we would have conversations. I didn't know her name; I just thought of her as my angel friend. I didn't connect her with the bus stop or the artifact encounters because I didn't recall them. One day when I was five, she asked me if she could borrow my body and play at my house sometimes. I thought about it and told her that since I belonged to my parents I would have to ask them for permission. She left, and later when my dad came home from work I asked him if it would be OK if my angel friend could go into my body for a little while when she came to visit me. He listened attentively and had me explain this carefully so that he could understand it. Then he said he would have to talk this over with my mother when she got home. He seemed understanding and sincere.

When my mom got home, my dad told her what I had said as soon as she walked in the door. He appeared excited and amused "You won't believe what Dennis asked me today – ya gotta hear this!" Then he turned to me and said "Tell your mother what you told me." I instantly realized I was being set up. His air and demeanor revealed that whatever I was going to say would be unbelievable, and that I would be the butt of a big joke. I saw clearly that he had never believed me, and realized that if I told my story I would just be ridiculed and invalidated. I couldn't have used those words at that age of course, but I felt it.

So I told him I didn't remember what I had said earlier. He tried to remind me and then tried to explain it to my mom. Of course it sounded ridiculous to my mother, and she scoffed at the whole idea I had even said such a thing. This made my dad angry, so I left the room. Perhaps a week or two later, while Patty was visiting me in spirit, I was following my dad around the house. The previous incident was far from my mind. I was seeing Patty as a white cloud of light above me. I happily chatted to my dad as we walked through the living room, "I have a friend who's an angel and she lives on a cloud." He angrily spun around and slapped me with the palm of his hand right on the forehead and said, "I don't want to hear any of that crap out of you ever again!" and left the room. In that shock I realized once again that I had to keep anything "special" like this to myself.

Bad Medicine

I visited Patty often as a child when she was sick. Once in the early '50's I went to her house where a doctor had arrived with his black bag and was going to give her a shot. But I sensed great danger and realized he was about to give her the wrong medicine, and that it could kill her. At the level I was at, I was connected to great power, and was able to change the medicine into water, so that the shot had no effect. I then helped Patty begin to recover. I discovered this incident after I had a dream of a short girl with a round face and dark bangs leading me to Patty and the dangerous situation. I didn't know who this dream girl was until I discovered Lydia a few months later.

Although I was often able to enter a Level–2 state when I was called to help Patty, I was usually unable to do this for myself. When my own life was seriously in danger, and I did not have access to that level, I was usually rescued by Patty or my Higher Self. Other times when my life was threatened there was no intervention at all, and I survived by more ordinary means. The miraculous gifts I had as a child came to me while I was in my normal Level–1 state, and I have no explanation for their appearance. From the time I was a child, there were many occasions when I would be around people who were sick or had some disability and I tried to heal them, often by touching them. Although I recalled nothing from my Level–2 experiences at those times, it just seemed natural for me to try, but there is no indication that my efforts at this level ever had any effect.

Closer Encounters

Our childhood visitations were mostly just about hanging out together for a few minutes and communicating. But Patty and I also had "communions" where one of us would visit the other by going into the other's body and we would merge together somehow. These communions, which were infrequent, were a merging of physical, emotional, and spiritual feelings, and are difficult to describe. There was a rush of energy and deep indescribable feelings of love, union, and bliss, where we also experienced what the other felt. These unions are another allusion to the Star Trek episode "Metamorphosis" where a human stranded on a distant planet shared a similar rapport with his alien companion.

I remember sitting at the dinner table when I was around twelve, and felt Patty enter my chest, like an invisible energy. There was no asking permission or anything, but it all felt natural. I could feel her need to be there and I didn't try to stop it. I just relaxed and went into a blissful state. I visited her occasionally in a similar fashion. These were not like possessions or "borrowings" where the other had control of the body, but just a shared experience of being together. These communions were intimately sensual but did not involve sexual feelings until later in adulthood, at which point they would sometimes trigger spontaneous orgasms, which, to our ordinary consciousness, seemed to come out of nowhere for no reason. I only remember these later experiences happening a few times.

The Queen of Hearts

The first communion I recall with Patty was when I was around seven and I had been told by my father to stay in the front room and not come out until I was willing to tell the truth. No TV and no toys. I had reported something, I don't know what, that should have been impossible for me to know. He demanded to know how I had acquired this information. When I explained how I knew, perhaps by being exterior, my dad thought I was lying. Even though I had lost my special vision when I was five, I still had special gifts that would come and go. I had visions, would see things while exterior, could read people's minds, and I would sometimes receive communications from other spirits. In this incident I had been sequestered for over an hour and was determined to stand my ground.

But Patty, in a high state of awareness, visited me in the form of an angel-like figure. The way she looked, with her colorful aura, reminded me of the Queen of Hearts in a deck of playing cards. She entered my body and lifted my spirit up to the ceiling and just held me, in our own protected space, like a bubble of silence. After being in a state of bliss for a while, all my concerns evaporated. She then told me to tell my parents whatever they wanted to hear and to keep my gifts a secret, and to never give them up. When I came back into my body I told my dad I was ready to tell the truth, and made up a lie that he could accept.

First Times

When I first had sex with a woman, I was twenty-four, and Patty was there in spirit. I wasn't thinking about her consciously but I felt very guilty, as if I were betraying someone. There was some kind of emotional shock at one point, and while working through that I remembered Patty hovering over my left shoulder and saying "That's OK, men need that." She seemed very Vulcan-like, and more concerned for me, because I was feeling guilty.[98] I don't recall if her subliminal words had any effect on me.

However, when I was there during *HER* first time, it set up a deep tension within me. I was about twenty-two, standing outside in my backyard in front of a blooming rose bush, when I had an ominous feeling and found myself exterior in a house in another city looking at clothes strewn about on the floor. Upstairs where she was in bed with the man, we communicated. She told me everything was OK, and said the tear in her eye was for me. On a higher level, her having sex with someone did not bother me, and it had nothing at all to do with our love and connection. But unconsciously on a more human level, it triggered a lot of emotions. At the time I worked on this I was doing many of my ID-R sessions in the dining room of a vacant house I owned. Right after I resolved this incident, I got out of my chair and stood in the kitchen for several minutes. I just stared at the chair. Everything was so still and quiet it was amazing. It was like I had been living with a constant screeching noise in my nervous system for twenty years, and it had suddenly stopped. I was totally calm.

LSD – or Who Spiked the Orange Juice?

I began this session with nothing specific in mind to work on, but I soon noticed a bright golden light in my space, when I closed my eyes. I followed it to a memory, and saw that the light was around Patty. It was her aura. She was attending a party, and I saw her sitting on the floor in a bright, mostly unfurnished, upstairs room with a lot of windows. It could have been a college classroom with the chairs missing or pushed up against the walls, or someone's very large apartment. There were maybe two dozen people at this gathering, standing or sitting around and talking. I was exterior and went there to protect her. This had to be around the year 1969.

Patty seemed to have come by herself, and a tall cheerful fellow had given her a glass of orange juice. She didn't know that it had been spiked with LSD. I was somehow alerted that something wasn't right and went there to investigate. The drug may have

---

[98] Referring to the unemotional and logical nature of Vulcans, in the TV series Star Trek.

already taken effect by the time I arrived. I was worried that Patty might have a bad reaction and I stayed with her for a long time. She was very spaced out, so I kept her focused on me while I presented her with positive images and feelings. I was also able to keep other people from interacting with her. I guided her while keeping her unaware that she had been drugged. Somehow I was able to eventually nullify the drug, or perhaps it wore off sufficiently, and Patty snapped out of her trance. When she got up and realized what had happened she confronted the gentleman with some angry words and left.

The sense that I get from what I can remember, is that many people had drunk the spiked orange juice, and most knew what was in it. The hosts saw this reckless deception as a kind of harmless experiment, disregarding the possibility of doing real harm.

Soul Mates

When Patty was in college, I visited her by temporarily borrowing the body of another student. I don't have all the details but I believe this lady was chosen by Dennis–2. I also don't know if I am Dennis–1 or Dennis–2 in this incident, since we are now one. Either way, it was me. The story unfolded from a vision. I was guided to a college campus and led to Jennifer, a student in her early twenties. Jennifer was about five foot two with long dark brown hair. She had more of an unassuming personality and was not as assertive or outgoing as Patty – more the opposite. Although Jennifer was a quiet person, she possessed a calming nature and an openness that drew people in. I spoke with her spiritually and it seems we already had an agreement. She would loan me her body six times and she would be co-conscious with me and provide the information I needed to navigate the school environment. Why she agreed to this and what I gave her in return I don't know.

When I first entered Jennifer's body I became very confused, because I forgot where I was, and WHO I was. Seeing that I was a woman, I wondered if I was reexperiencing a past life or had died, and started to panic. This confusion occurred possibly because I was used to being in a lower state of consciousness when in my body, and this "downgrade" in awareness would happen automatically when returning from a higher state. But I quickly recovered and realized what I was doing. Jennifer was exterior temporarily, so that I could get my bearings as myself, to avoid being even more confused. I then had several encounters with Patty, most of which are sketchy, except for the last one. I believe Jennifer and Patty had already been acquainted for a few weeks. I remember that I, as Jennifer, helped Patty move some boxes into her apartment using an elevator. I recall us talking a few times and having lunch together. Patty felt a strong connection with me, when I was present, but thought the connection was totally with Jennifer.

These visitations through Jennifer culminated with me watching Patty read a story book to a dozen or more grade school children. This was probably part of her curriculum. I was with her in a gym where there were bleachers. The bleachers seemed portable, like they could be rolled out or pushed back into a folded position. Patty was two rows above me to my left, reading to the kids who were seated below, looking up. When she was close to being done she asked me if I would like to read the rest. I said OK, came up to her level, and read to the end of the story. Patty then dismissed the kids and told me I did really well.

Then, while sitting there, we started talking about teaching, children, life, and other things. Soon we got into a fascinating philosophical discussion which included reincarnation and other spiritual things. We both got really into it. While we were talking, I began connecting with her very deeply and I could feel her connecting with me. The energy was amazing – we were both spellbound. Our faces were very close now. At an opportune moment I said, looking deeply into her eyes, "We could even be soul mates!" "Yes" she whispered, almost automatically. And then I kissed her.

It took a moment for her to snap out of the spell and realize what had just happened. She stiffened up and pulled away saying "I'm sorry, I'm not interested."

I quickly responded with "I'm so sorry. I don't know what came over me." But she had already stood up and gathered her notebooks and other things. I continued to apologize but she just said "That's OK, I'm just not interested." She said something else I don't recall, and walked away.

Patty saw Jennifer a few days later, walking through the campus, but Jennifer didn't seem to notice her or recognize her at all. They never spoke again. The connection she had felt with Jennifer was quite a mystery to Patty, and she felt a sense of loss. She never knew it was me.

Three's Company

One night back when I was thirty years old, six or more years after the last story and while Lynne and I were still living together, I was resting on the bed when she came in and sat on the edge of the bed near my feet. She faced me and asked "Why aren't we together?" I responded with "What are you talking about?" "We're supposed to be together" she asserted.

"We *ARE* together – I don't know what you're talking about" I said, as I watched her gazing right into my eyes. I was puzzled and starting to feel a bit alarmed, wondering if she was OK. She could see I was confused, and I was about to become more so. "I'm Patty Preston" she said.

My instant response was anger – I thought Lynne must have found Patty's name in my notebooks somewhere, although I was sure I had never written it down. My interest in Patty was always something I felt, on some deeper level, that I had to keep secret until things were different. There was a shock in which I felt something very important was being threatened here, just as I had when my friend Ross spoke with Patty in junior high school, against my wishes. I was considering what this meant and what I should do about it. I asked Lynne where she heard that name, and I tried to sit up, but suddenly I was unable to move. It was like some powerful magnetic force had immobilized every cell in my body – like being encased in cement. Now I was scared! Meanwhile Patty started reciting where she had lived and went to school, her parents' names and where they worked, and other things I knew, and many things I didn't know. I felt like I was losing all sense of reality.

But at some point I relaxed and went into a heightened state of awareness in which I realized this was indeed Patty. The binding force disappeared and we made love. However, after some time, Lynne began popping in and out. It was like alter personalities switching back and forth, and it was very obvious. When Lynne appeared she was highly energized and laughing, like she was at an amusement park, and then Patty was back and I could feel her strength, love, and calmness.

I remember at one point feeling quite empowered. I was in touch with that "communion" energy and I was telling Patty that I could give her an orgasm. I was quite sincere, but I didn't realize Lynne had returned. She mocked my sincerity, looked deeply into my eyes and said "Really? You can give me an orgasm?" and then began laughing hysterically, like it was the funniest thing she had ever heard – which made me laugh too. This whole situation had become comically unstable.

Finally Patty's presence just vanished and everything changed. Whereas before the atmosphere was supercharged, as if there were a live rock band playing continuously in the room, now everything was quiet and still. Lynne turned over and went right to sleep without saying a word. Except for my body still buzzing like I was totally wired on caffeine, it was as if this whole experience had never happened. The silence was startling.

The next morning I still had some memory of the night before. As we were sitting on the edge of the bed getting dressed for work, I asked Lynne if she remembered what happened last night, but she just said "What do you mean?" She already sounded irritated. Not knowing how to talk about this, I asked if she remembered acting like another woman. Lynne was prone to intense jealousy, although last night, while in a higher state, she expressed none at all. Her response was an angry "Why? Is this some woman you want to sleep with?" I just said "No. Never mind," and dropped the subject.

Patty visited me through Lynne briefly one other time that I recall, perhaps two weeks later. Not long after that I was standing in the living room looking at Lynne and felt the most incredible sense of connection and partnership. I loved Lynne but had never felt this feeling before. It overwhelmed me and I asked her to marry me. I didn't recall anything about Patty's visits at that point and didn't understand that I was associating my feelings for her with my future wife.

Lynne and I separated after a few months of marriage but remained good friends. I talked with Lynne about these visitations a year or so after I recalled them. Almost immediately she said that she must have given her permission. This story didn't seem to bother her in any way. Lynne also had other personalities and I had helped her do some integration. She had also had some OBEs and was aware of the reality of leaving the body. She was open to the possibility of Patty's visits, but did not remember the actual events. I wouldn't have remembered them either, without doing this work.

In some of my memories it's almost as if Patty and I would occasionally meet backstage during intermissions of a play we were performing in, completely aware that in life we were simply immersed the acting roles we had been assigned. But these high states of awareness are very vague. The way we go into different levels of awareness and compartmentalize memories is not something I understand very well. Before doing ID-R, I knew about Patty and some of my helpers some times and didn't most other times. Also sometimes I would have some Level–2 abilities while operating at Level–1. How all this is administered on a higher level, I have no idea. Again, all I can do is report what happened and propose a useful model to represent it.

Let Me Go

I was working with a feeling of grief which led me to an incident that occurred when I was thirty. It happened a few months after Lynne and I separated. I was sleeping and left my body. I felt I was being called away and arrived at what appeared to be a restaurant after closing time. It seemed like there were chairs set upside down on tables, but the environment was dark and vague. Patty was alone, standing against a table, and seemed to be waiting for someone. She was talking to me out loud, or perhaps in whispers. She was telling me that I had to let her go because we had not connected and she did not want to wait anymore. She was seeing a man she really liked, and needed to let me go. I listened to her with a heavy heart. In the end I knew that I had to let her go and conveyed that to her as a feeling. This communication was her effort to let go of something that seemed to be holding her back.

I remember waking up in the morning after this experience, and although I didn't remember it, I found myself in a somber mood all day, feeling as if there were something important I had forgotten. When I ran this session, which contained a lot of grief, I cried for almost an hour.

In this incident, although I knew Patty was talking to ME, I feel that, from her Level–1 viewpoint, she was talking to someone she felt a deep spiritual connection with, but whom she could not identify specifically as me or anyone else. She was talking to Pip, the name I use to represent my true "spirit-self"- which is me - my individualized viewpoint in consciousness, at Level–2. I derived this name from my past-life name, Philippe, and I have similarly given Patty the spirit name Ana. I believe we each recognize ourselves as spirits at Level–2. We are souls who travel from lifetime to lifetime, and we have been many different people, had many names, and played many different characters. Unfortunately, we identify with each of these characters and forget who we really are.

So Patty wasn't talking to "Dennis" specifically, but to the connection she felt in her heart. Although I go by the nickname Pip, I don't really feel like Pip, unless I am in Level–2 consciousness, because I am too identified with being Dennis. In truth, none of us are, as our most true identity, any character from this or any other life we have lived. Our experiences and personalities only constitute a story which defines the characters we are playing. Our souls, our individual spirit-selves, are also not who we really are. These too are illusions, according to my understanding, but their apparent existence gives rise to the universe, and life as we know it.

Beach Blanket Intervention

In a dream I saw a human form suspended in the air which led to this: Patty and a man I presume was her boyfriend at the time, were at the beach in the daytime. I had apparently tried to get this man to say something to her, by mentally communicating with him, but it had backfired. I don't know if they were previously arguing or if I caused it. I kept repeating something for him to say but it didn't work. Whatever I wanted him to say, he wasn't saying it. So as they were having this intense argument I was starting to get irritated because I was having no effect. I think the argument had something to do with a job or business she wanted to do or to continue, and possibly something about moving.

Finally it was too much for me and I decided, in frustration, to handle this myself. In the shift I suspended her boyfriend's spirit in a grey cocoon of energy about seven feet in the air. As he slept peacefully in the cocoon, I utilized his body. I looked at Patty and her face was very red. I immediately stopped the argument by saying that I changed my mind and that I agreed with her. Then I said I had something important to tell her. I believe we were sitting on a blanket and I asked her to sit closer.

She was still angry and baffled by my change of heart. I explained to her that I was not her boyfriend and that I couldn't tell her who I was except that I was a spirit guide. I said that when her boyfriend came back he wouldn't remember this conversation. I then said to her what I had wanted her boyfriend to say. I explained why she should not do what she wanted to do. I think it had something to do with danger. I may have also given her some other options. She listened, and asked some questions. She seemed to understand and agree that she had been too single minded. After I told her how to handle the man when he came back, I said "I'm going now," and I left. But I hung around in spirit for a bit,

When her partner returned he didn't say anything, so she asked him if he knew what he had just said. He said no. She told him that he had said he was a spirit guide and he laughed and denied it. She thought he was just being clever and creative, but she was still puzzled. She said that she would think about what he had suggested, and left. I think she made the right decision in the end. I recall following her in spirit as she walked toward a building up beyond the beach.

The actual placing of the boyfriend in the cocoon must have happened on a higher level of awareness because I cannot remember doing it, but it seems that there was a higher level agreement between us for this to happen. I believe that the boyfriend would not have agreed to let me have control of his body and that his Higher Self had allowed it to happen without his awareness. That's my best guess. Although there were other occasions where I was able to borrow another person's body, it was always with their permission, as far as I can remember, although as a child I was not always honest about my intentions.

Checking Out – or
The Story of a Man Named Jed

I was working part time at a downtown Bar and Grill, and it was lunch hour. I was in my early thirties and was one of four people in the small kitchen. The lunch rush was hectic as usual. I was doing something down by the end of the sink, away from the serving area, when everything went black and I felt like I was being sucked through a dark inky vortex. I found myself exterior in another city watching a woman being assaulted on a public sidewalk by two or three men (it's a little blurry). She was on her back on the sidewalk. I thought this must be Patty and tried to help her, but my body was ethereal in that I had no physical effect on the men. I tried pushing them away and hitting them but my hands went right through them, just like it was with Sam in the movie "Ghost" from 1990. No one else was around to help. I brought my face very close to the lady's to see if this was indeed Patty, but the only thing I was sure of was that she was very frightened. I was able to create, by intention, a force field around her body, just over her skin, to protect her, but it felt unstable.

I stood by a car parked on the street frantically wondering what to do, when I felt myself being pulled back into the blackness, and the scene started to fade away. Suddenly I was back in the kitchen. I was sure the lady must be Patty, and I had to get back to her! I turned around with my back to the stainless steel sink and slowly slid to the floor, until I was sitting on the thick perforated rubber mat. I didn't even know how I would get back there but I was still in an altered state and I could feel the internal effort that was maintaining the force field around Patty.

I spiritually said to Ron who was at the till dealing with customers, something like, "Hey Ron, I need your help." Ron was an ex-Vietnam vet in his thirties with a drill sergeant demeanor and a "battle weary" countenance that made him look a lot older than he was. Like a grey, ghostly head inside his physical head, I could see his spirit turn and look at me and ask, very straightforwardly, "What do you need?" I said "Keep everyone away from me." His reply was "You got it."

In my altered state of consciousness this all seemed quite normal! I was sitting on the floor leaning against the sink with my eyes closed but I still could see Leslie, all 300 pounds of her, rushing toward me saying "What's Wrong!?" Ron immediately turned to her and barked "Don't touch him!" She hesitated, but again moved toward me and again Ron barked his order: "Leave him alone, we'll work around him." Ron was definitely in command. Leslie backed off. The other cook, Mark, a laid back kind of guy, just took it all in stride and kept working. I was having a kind of dual awareness here because at the same time these things were happening, I felt myself pressing against a black inky wall behind me, worried that I couldn't get through, until it finally gave way.

Then suddenly I was back at the scene and it seemed like no time had passed. The force field was still holding as Patty struggled with the men holding her down. I frantically flew down the street to the main intersection seeking help but there were no pedestrians, just speeding cars. I imagined I was running, which slowed my flying down a bit and added to my frustration. I ran back to the scene and spotted a derelict across the street about fifty yards away under a freeway overpass. Jed, the derelict, was just standing there, watching. I ran over to him and pleaded with him spiritually to help, but he rigidly refused – he didn't want to get involved. I gave up, and the situation was getting desperate.

I ran back toward Patty and the attackers. Maybe about thirty seconds in real time had actually gone by at this point. In the middle of the street I called out to God for help. I was still basically at Level–1 awareness, unaware that there even was a Level–2. So I just surrendered.

Suddenly there was a presence all around me which swept me up until I felt like a tiny bubble inside it. I recognized this presence immediately as my creator. There was no question or doubt, just the undeniable certainty that I was a small part of this presence which was somehow me, a much bigger me, and yet somehow separate. There was no visible form but a definite sense of maleness and power from this presence, my Higher Self, which I sometimes call Big Guy. I felt muted and devoid of any will or control, but entirely safe. I also felt a bit befuddled. It was as if my ego were nothing more than a thought, tucked away for safe keeping.

Big Guy said to me "I'll show you how it's done!" He definitely had a sense of humor! Time, in the external world, had now stopped. We went over to Jed the derelict and Big Guy tried to convince him to go help, in a very positive way. But Jed was stubborn and saw nothing in it for himself except trouble. He had a snickering attitude. So Big Guy reiterated his request with more force: "Look, I was just being nice. You have two choices: either you can run over there and help that lady, and be a hero, or you can stay here and go deaf in your other ear (he was deaf in one ear) and I'll take your sight away too and you will be deaf and blind for the rest of your life." Jed sort of chuckled with the attitude of "right, like you can really do that." Meanwhile as I said, time had stopped, we were operating in sideways-time, and this was all spiritual communication.

But in the next instant Jed found himself totally blind – this lasted for a couple seconds in his experiential time - long enough for Jed to be jolted into the reality that this was no joke. In his shock he pictured his life as a deaf and blind man ... and then his sight returned. "Make your choice!" Big Guy said with finality. Time resumed. Jed immediately ran across the street waving his arms and yelling, and the men took off running. The day was saved. I am aware that after taking this action the hearing in Jed's deaf ear returned to normal and some other physical pain or difficulty of his also disappeared. Big Guy was aware of everything Jed experienced, and this enabled me to recall some of these things as well.

I opened my eyes in the noisy kitchen and stood up. "I'm back" I announced, and resumed work explaining that I had the flu and just needed a break. Later when Ron and I were alone in the Kitchen I thanked him for how he had handled the situation. He gave me an understanding look. "We all have our moments when we need to check out for a while," he replied. The event was still semi-lucid in my mind so I asked him "Do you want to know what it was?" "No, I don't need to know," he smiled, as if he already knew, and left for his break. My memory of this whole incident was suppressed from then on.

I called Ron 15 years after this incident, and he remembered that day in the kitchen as I have described it. I shared this story with him, but only a brief summary. He seemed to accept it without reservation.

I have lots of questions. Why do sometimes I have great power and other times not? If I could create a force field around Patty, why not just knock her attackers out? Well, in that moment it seems the force field was all I could manage at the level I was at. It seemed to take all my concentration. As for the ethics of what happened there with Jed, I can only report my experience. Assuming that directly stopping the thugs was a violation of some rule, I would have to say that my Higher Self did what I would have done myself if I had possessed the power. Would I have blinded Jed had he not complied? No. And why didn't my Higher Self just spook the

attackers some other way? I have no idea. I'm sure there were a
million ways to end the problem. At the time however, no other
solutions occurred to me, and I have no idea what my Higher Self
thinks, or if he even "thinks" at all, in the human sense.

The Christina Affair – or A Separate Reality

In 1985 when I was thirty-eight I briefly dated a girl named
Christina, who was recently divorced. We had met many years
earlier when we worked together. We stopped seeing each other
after a couple of months but kept in touch. Two years later, in the
spring, we went together to see a well-known local musician
perform with his band at a popular coffee shop. We took my car and
left hers at my house, and returned around midnight, after the
show. As we were saying goodnight, standing on the sidewalk by the
passenger door at the front of my car, she started beaming a huge
smile and stared at me. So I said "What?" and she said, very
dramatically, "Do you know what's happening!?" I didn't – I just
stared at her blankly, and she repeated, shaking me by the
shoulders, "Do you know what's happening!? It's me, Patty – Patty
Preston!" Suddenly the whole world seemed to fade out and we
were in a twelve foot dream-bubble – our own separate reality. My
car was within the bubble but everything outside of it seemed like
an impressionistic painting. Understand however, there wasn't any
physical bubble – it was just my own mental creation to help me
accept what was happening.

I immediately got very happy. It was like we were meeting in a
different dimension. We hugged each other and she told me she
didn't have much time. She said some things I don't recall, but I do
remember that she said she was getting married in two months but
that it was just a formality, as if it might bother me. But it was an
earthly marriage and had nothing to do with our bond. However, I
later realized that she really loved the man she was marrying and
that she had other reasons for saying these things. Then she said
"Let's have one last kiss," and she kissed me. I didn't care about
anything else – it was such an amazing delight just to be with her.
We were holding each other very closely.

"Uhh ... what are we doing?" Christina was back and found
herself unexpectedly close to me. She took a step back. "Hugging," I
said, in a light tone, smiling innocently. She relaxed and said "OK,"

but looked quite confused. The dream bubble was gone and my reality was back to being ... ordinary.

Christina said "That was weird," implying she needed more clarity. But I immediately changed the subject instead, commenting on how beautiful the night was, and pointing out the two brother stars in the eastern sky, Castor and Pollux, reciting their names. We talked for a minute more, and as she was leaving, walking around the front of my car toward hers, she stopped and asked "Do you think we could be soulmates?"

Me: "What do you mean?"

Her: "I don't know, I just had a strange feeling. Do you think we could be soulmates?"

Me: "Well, I believe in past lives so I think it's very possible" I said, nodding my head.

I was trying to conceal my memories of what had just happened, to prevent her from reading my mind. We said goodnight, and as she drove away, the memory of what had just happened quickly disappeared, as if it were a dream.

But I stayed outside for a while, pacing up and down the sidewalk. I went into a kind of intense daydream in which a lady was on trial for doing something wrong, and I was her lawyer. I continued this daydream until my arguments had secured the lady's freedom. I suspect that on some level I was questioning the ethics of what had just happened, although I believe a higher-level authority had given us license.

After remembering this incident, I had a dream of watering the garden in the front of my house. The dream turned out to be a memory of Dennis–2 regarding the same event.

When Patty had displaced her, Christina was suspended in a grey cocoon about seven feet off the ground. However, for some reason the cocoon was becoming unstable and about to unravel. To avoid any problems, Dennis–2 had pulled Christina, in spirit, out of the cocoon and, pretending to be me, kept her distracted. He showed Christina my nondescript front garden and proceeded to describe it to her as if it were the most fascinating work of art. This went on for the last minute or so of Patty's visit. Dennis–2 was quite

humorous and solidly held Christina's attention until Patty left and
Christina snapped back in the body.

About six years after these events, having now recalled them, I
called Christina and asked her if she remembered this incident.
She did, and it was still something of a mystery. I told her about
Patty and what had actually happened. She brought up her
"soulmates" comment herself, and said it made more sense now.
She then volunteered that she had sensed Patty's unintrusive
presence on two other occasions when we were seeing each other
back in 1985, and described them to me. I hadn't been aware of
Patty directly, but in each of those instances I did recall a particular
feeling – the same feeling of another presence that Christina had
just described to me. Patty had been watching us with some
disapproval or concern. Christina also recalled me showing her my
garden, with some amusement. I was surprised she remembered
that, but didn't tell her about Dennis–2.

Future Shock – or
A Cubic Centimeter of Chance

This next incident reminded me of a quote from "Journey to
Ixtlan" by Carlos Castaneda. Don Juan says: "All of us, whether or
not we are warriors, have a cubic centimeter of chance that pops
out in front of our eyes from time to time. The difference between
an average man and a warrior is that the warrior is aware of this, and
one of his tasks is to be alert, deliberately waiting, so that when his
cubic centimeter pops out he has the necessary speed, the prowess,
to pick it up."

In July of 1992 I recalled an incident from about three years
earlier, when I awoke in the middle of the night in a panic and said
to myself, "She's gonna die!" and passed out. I ran this incident and
discovered the following.

After I passed out I awoke to find myself hovering in the
morning air above a building in some distant city. I was watching
the entrance door. There was some invisible friendly presence with
me, Dennis–2 I imagine, who instructed me to keep watching and
seemed to disappear. But every time I had the urge to doze off and I
started to lose my attention he would "poke" me. I was feeling
peaceful and in a good mood. I watched for hours as cars and
people came and went. When I asked what this was about, my

guide just said to keep watching and it would become clear. I waited all day. Evening came and many cars pulled into the small parking lot and others parked on the street. There was some event going on. Then I recognized Patty getting out of a white car and my alertness tensed up – I felt I had to be ready for something. A few hours later the event was over and people began leaving the building. It was dark now and I hadn't yet sensed any problem.

As Patty walked out in the street to get in her car a big pickup was heading right for her. The driver, a guy wearing a purple shirt, was not paying attention, and it was clear that he was going to hit her. I had a shock and was immediately next to the driver in the truck. I grabbed the steering wheel and was able to turn it to the right. I was invisible to the driver who was resisting me but I was exerting considerable physical force. I also spiritually pushed on the front tires and fender all at once. I was able to get the truck to crash into the rear of Patty's car instead of hitting Patty. This was the only viable alternative I was capable of at that moment. Patty was unhurt. Her car was damaged though, and she was a bit shaken. After the police arrived and questioned the driver, they told Patty that he was drunk, and that he was claiming that the steering wheel had locked up and turned by itself. The police hauled the drunk guy off, and someone Patty knew gave her a ride home.

I didn't remember any of this the next morning when I woke up. That evening however, as I was leaving for an appointment, I stopped outside my bedroom, looked at my bed, and felt like there was something I had to do that very night – something urgent that I was forgetting. Then a thought came to me, a very strong thought, "I already took care of it." I felt satisfied, and left.

Can we go into the future and alter the course of events before they happen? Or go into the past to change what happens now? I believe that these things are possible because I experienced them, and because time and space are not mechanical entities – they are creations of consciousness and conform to whatever rules consciousness sets up for them. If something could happen in a dream, it can happen in "real" life, even if it normally doesn't.

However, our world is well organized and governed by rules. It's like a symphony of many interacting parts. When editing a movie for example, if you change something along the time-line, other things have to change to maintain the integrity and continuity of the screenplay. When time travel is involved, somehow things are made to conform so there is never a paradox or a problem. As I said before, this is not possible in a materialistic paradigm in which ANY time travel is a paradox. But the universe is not a physical reality – it is only a construct of consciousness – a dream.

On the other hand I don't know if any of these more incredible stories are true for anyone other than me – they are my own subjective experiences. But if any of my memories are confirmed to be true for anyone else, that can be useful. If not, it doesn't matter. Everyone is living their own experience and it is most important to believe in yourself. That being said, many of my rediscovered memories have been confirmed by others, although not anything overtly miraculous as yet, which is what I would expect, since memories of such things, as I have repeatedly pointed out, are commonly suppressed.

Chapter 26

A Greater Purpose

"Your mission, should you choose to accept it ..."
– Mission Impossible, 1966

After my first conversation with Sandra and my subsequent revelations about Patty it was even more obvious that there was a major connection between us. I had promised Patty in a previous lifetime that we would be together and I felt it was my fault that it didn't work out. There was still a mystery here I had to solve and I had a strong inner drive to keep going without really knowing why. This work I was doing was exciting and amazing and I knew it was my mission in life, but I realized that the things that were driving me, including my feelings for Patty, were unconscious. And I knew this was true for her as well, but there was a lot I still didn't understand. I thought about calling her but most of the things that stopped me before were still there. Every time I considered contacting her some new huge block would arise and I would have to work through it – and there seemed to be an unlimited supply of these things! Then there was a series of days in the summer of 1992 where every session was bursting with revelations. The stories that emerged from my sessions were like reading a novel backwards, and when I reached the first chapter, everything finally made sense. First there was more about our last lifetime together, followed by memories of a number of intense encounters in school and later, all of which indicated that Patty and I had some kind of secret agreement. And then the following adventures came to light.

Patty Dies – or
The Great Arcanoid Conspiracy

I don't know the month or year, possibly sometime around late 1986. It was in the morning and I was in my bedroom sitting on the bed. I had a strange feeling, as I usually did before leaving my body when Patty was in trouble, but suddenly Dennis–2 was present and he was able to distract me. He was very excited about this video

game he wanted to show me, which could be played while
operating at Level–2, which I was at that moment. Dennis–2 made
it seem extremely important and urgent that I play this game, as if I
would get something critically essential from it. He assured me that
there was plenty of time and this wouldn't take long.

The video game was constructed within my own inner matrix –
in my personal mental space – like I was playing it in a lucid dream
state. The game had some similarities to a video arcade game I had
been playing around that time called Arcanoid, but it was three-
dimensional, texturally beautiful and very complex, requiring
intense concentration and strategy. Once I got into it, it was
instantly addictive. I still remember it somewhat but it would be
difficult to describe how it worked. I found it totally captivating and
seductive because it was very entertaining and sophisticated and
required doing several things at once, which I could do at that level

While playing the game, I seemed to lose my external awareness
and all sense of time. At some point I felt a growing pressure and
finally snapped back to reality. I realized I was late. I abandoned the
game and found myself at the scene of a traffic accident. Patty was
lying on a stretcher in an ambulance. She was dying. In the state I
was in, I felt I could heal her, but although I tried to provide the
healing that she needed to live, for some reason it wasn't working
and she refused to re-enter her body. Facing me, she told me that I
had not accomplished a task that I had agreed to, and so there was
no more reason for her to live.

I had a shock, and in that shock I decided to accomplish the task
immediately. In the Level–2 state I was in I knew what I was
supposed to do, whereas in my ordinary Level–1 mind, I had no
idea. I was supposed to find a way to heal trauma and reverse
human programming so I could reclaim my freedom and memory
and help others do the same. I immediately left the scene of the
accident in order to do this, and when I returned less than minute
later I had set in motion everything I needed to accomplish my task.
To me, the few seconds I was gone in real time actually embodied
about two weeks of intense work in experiential time.

When I returned, I saw Patty and Dennis–2 standing in the
ambulance, smiling at me. Of course we all took up no space, being
in spirit, while the EMTs worked on Patty's body. In that moment I
knew that this had all been a trick. Patty had not been dying and

Dennis–2 had stalled me so that I would appear to arrive too late to save her. I also realized that all this had been necessary, and I was just happy that Patty would be OK. When I came out of my trance, I was sitting on my bed thinking that I had dozed off, since this sometimes happened during meditation.

But a lot had happened after my shock in the ambulance. I recall visiting many wise and knowledgeable people while in the power-zone and conversing with them in spirit. I also recall being physically present in many of these discussions. I can't tell if these were replays of past lives in which I had accessed some of this information previously, or if these meetings were taking place on some spiritual plane in the present. I recall talking with a shaman who lived in a cave and who knew about alter personalities and levels of consciousness, and a university professor who understood trauma. Most of my other travels and visitations are a blur. Then I spent many days in what seemed like a bright hotel room working out the details with charts and writing boards, determining how this knowledge could be best put to use.

Once I was satisfied that I had a method and model that would work, I needed to get the material into my everyday conscious mind. I went into my bedroom at home and hovered over my body which was still sitting frozen on the bed. In real time I suspect only a few minutes had passed. I tried to enter my body with all the information still in my awareness. The idea was that I would awaken from my "trance" with a head full of knowledge. But I couldn't do it. It was like trying to hit a baseball you just pitched to yourself. I tried several times but at one point I had a moment of anxiety when I thought I might lose all this information.

Next I tried to materialize a physical book in my room that contained everything. But I abandoned this idea too, when I realized it wouldn't be allowed by the higher spiritual authorities. Too much spiritual red tape (we'll get to that later). But I COULD communicate this to someone else and get THEM to write it down. I decided to find someone to share this with but it had to be the right person – someone I could communicate with who would understand these ideas and also be interested in making them public. I recall tuning into humanity like you might tune into a radio station on an old analog radio. It was like I was contacting thousands of minds all over the world. It was something like I

imagine Professor Xavier of the X-Men might experience. There
were many "voices" that I could indeed communicate with, but I
was looking for a certain feeling that I interpreted as "competent
interest."

Finally I found a guy in Florida. He was sitting in his back yard
in a lawn chair. I asked him if he could hear me and he said he
could. He was not afraid in the slightest and we talked very clearly
as if I were physically present. I told him what I wanted and he was
very open to it. We went inside and worked at his kitchen table for
hours. First I did some sessions with him and then instructed him
while he took notes. When I felt I had given him enough, he
assured me that he would get this published in some way. I
complimented him, encouraged him, and left.

Next I went three years into the future to see what he had done
with the information I gave him. He had worked with ID-R for
about a year and a half, although I don't know what he called it. But
then he just lost interest and seemed to be more involved with golf.
Disappointing. The next bright idea I had was to deliver ID-R to
many psychics and channelers all over the world simultaneously.
Certainly that would get enough attention to make it back to me,
which was the main goal, not only so I could resolve my own issues
and be able to communicate with Patty, but to somehow make sure
that the material was successfully introduced into the world in order
to do whatever it was supposed to do. My guess is that the Identity
Model and ID-R are supposed to have some significant impact on
the evolution of human understanding, creating a transformative
effect on humanity over time. That's my hope anyway, even if it just
plants a tiny seed. Also I'm sure there's more to this project than I
am aware of, and there is also the possibility it will fail.

I then entered a space from which I could make the necessary
psychic contacts, and as I was moving through this space I
encountered a Being who was hanging out right in my path. He
appeared like a head on the end of a very long tether, which
reminded me of a weather balloon. It could be that as I was
opening myself up to channelers, he was just the first one I became
aware of. At the time I thought it was just a lucky coincidence, but I
now think he was waiting for me. He was watching me go by and
said something like "Hi there – what's goin' on?" He was very
amiable and open.

So I stopped and conversed with him. I explained my predicament and he was very interested. This Being was actually a man living in the United States who did a similar type of counseling work already. He was exterior and we were communicating on a higher level. Although I would be unable to talk with him as I did with the man in Florida, he said that he believed he would be able to get the information into his conscious mind, something which I had been unable to do for myself. If he found these ideas useful he said he would incorporate them into his present practice. So I set up a workshop right there in what seemed like a bubble of dark empty space above the planet where it was quiet and peaceful. The man seemed to absorb everything, and when we were done I followed him down to Earth.

I found myself in a coffee shop watching an older man seated in a booth across from a woman. The woman got up to use the restroom and after a few moments the man pulled out a pen, turned over his paper place mat, and began writing furiously. His wife returned and said something but he raised his hand and kept writing. She knew he was having a brainstorm, and remained quiet. I watched until I was satisfied and left. I don't recall checking the future as I did with the previous man, but I may have.

During this session I didn't realize that the Being who appeared in my path was my Idenics teacher, John Galusha, until the very end when I recognized him as the man in the diner. His face and presence were unmistakable. I remembered John telling me about having a brainstorm in a restaurant, but I had pictured it differently, and seeing him in the diner was a surprise. This event happened at least four or five years before we physically met. In these sessions of mine, many mysteries were being resolved and pieces of the puzzle were rapidly falling into place.[99]

---

[99] I was hesitant to reveal this part of the story since it could be seen as me trying to take some degree of credit for something I had no part in. I might have left it out if it wasn't a critical and necessary element. But it's also true. This collaboration between John and I is what I remember and not something I made up. I like to think that the ideas I gave him were new revelations for him and critical for his development of Idenics, and I feel that this is so. After all, I had put a lot of work into it – my whole life actually. On the other hand, I don't have all the (continued on next psge)

The Playground Incident

Often during that especially revealing series of sessions in July of 1992, just as I was preparing to begin each morning, Dennis–2 would make a comment. Usually it was something like "You won't like this" or "Sorry about that," but always with a sense of humor. While I only knew the feeling or condition I wanted to address, he always seemed to know which incident was about to reveal itself. This morning the comment was an excited "This is *IT*!" I had discovered the previous incident the day before. I now understood that Patty and I were mutually involved in a project that eventually led to my finding Idenics and developing ID-R, but I didn't know why. Today's session explained many things!

I was six and a half years old. It was a summer morning and I was standing in the back yard facing the window of my parents' bedroom when I got a very strange feeling and passed out. I instantly found myself at the playground of an unfamiliar grammar school. Patty was lying on the ground unconscious and a teacher, Holly, was kneeling over her frantically trying to get her to wake up. Another teacher, whom we'll call Martha, stood watching nearby. No one else was there. I began screaming at Patty with great passion "You can't die, you can't die!" I was in a very intense state. Apparently Patty had slipped and fallen while playing on the jungle gym and may have broken her neck. Holly was extremely distressed and crying thinking that Patty was dead, but Martha said she thought Patty just had the wind knocked out of her and would be OK.

My screaming was interrupted by a calm and clear voice in the air above us. The communication wasn't actually sound or words, but a feeling that conveyed an understanding. The message basically said, "Everything will be all right, come here so we can talk." The voice was summoning Patty and me, and we both floated

---

details so I really don't know exactly what I gave him or how much he was actually able to transcribe. What I do know for sure is that John and I did have some spiritual communication and I was later guided to receive his training. This allowed me to move forward with my promised task. The extent of my contribution is uncertain and unimportant at this point. What is important is that in the end we both had what we needed. ID-R would not exist without John Galusha, Mike Goldstein, and Idenics.

upward in spirit, following the voice, and found ourselves in another place. It seemed like a dry desert area. We were on a flat patch of hard ground surrounded by huge boulders, some towering above us. It was a very bright day. Patty and I stood there, side by side, with her on my right, facing a man who looked to be in his late twenties. We'll call him Bob. He was about 5 foot eight and had blond hair and casual clothing, with a white T-shirt. But his appearance and clothing seemed to be in a constant state of flux so that I don't have a definite image of him. At one point he seemed to be wearing some kind of robe that looked like a karate gi, and then he was wearing blue jeans. Patty and I appeared as adults and were dressed in loose fitting and rather drab clothes. To some extent we all seemed to know and respect each other.

Bob then spoke to us. It was an impassioned proposition. I don't recall much of what he said, just a few bits and pieces. He said our civilization was in need of many changes, and he spoke of the suffering of humanity and there was something about helping the children of the world. After giving us his "Ted Talk," he asked if we would volunteer to help. What he proposed made sense to me at the level of awareness I was now at, but volunteering meant that Patty and I would probably never get together on the physical plane in this lifetime. There was a moment of silence as we considered all this. I looked down at the ground. I had made a promise to Patty, in her past life as Ana, that we would be together. I felt torn, but Patty turned to me and said, with no doubt or hesitation, "I want to do it." I can still see the compassion and sincerity in her face. So, released from my promise, I agreed.

The next step involved splitting my awareness into two separate viewpoints: Dennis–1 and Dennis–2. I have said that multiple personalities are not split off parts of a person and that nothing is fragmented, fractured, or split when they are created. This is true. Consciousness cannot be added to, subtracted from, created, destroyed, or divided up in any way, regardless of how it appears. While the creations of both Dennis–2 and Lydia were unusual in my experience of how alter personalities come into being, the end result was basically the same in each case: there now being two people where there was only one before. This time however, in the end we actually had two hosts.

After explaining what we were going to do, Bob stood on my left side and drew my attention by speaking to me while Patty did the same on my right side. At my present level of awareness I could do several things at once and I had the ability to split my attention in this way. They also seemed to be pulling me energetically in some fashion because I did experience some kind of external pressure. But as each of them engaged with me more deeply, it forced me to give all my attention completely to each of them from these two different viewpoints, until each side of me became unaware of what the other side was experiencing. Although I can describe this in words, it's impossible to imagine. This was all taking place however, within my own singular conscious domain – the domain of my Higher Self, if that makes any sense. Our Higher Self knows what all parts of us are doing, at all times.

Then while Bob instructed Dennis–2 on his role in our new life's purpose, Patty engaged me, Dennis–1, by holding my hands, gazing into my eyes, and singing to me. We were both in a very joyful and loving state of being, like two little kids. We then agreed that we would try our best to be together, which was part of the plan it turns out – the trying that is – and that we would make an effort to not forget each other no matter what happened. We also promised to never have children with anyone else, in honor of our love and our past-life commitment. She said that if she ever did forget me, I only had to say to her a special code word: "macaroni." She sang the first stanza of the song Yankee Doodle several times to help me remember. While I was doing the session on this incident, I kept hearing this song in the back of my mind, until I realized what it meant. I never tried saying the word "macaroni" to Patty after I discovered this, and I have no idea if it would have worked.

When the programming was done, Dennis–2 left. I had no clue what his unique instructions were. The instructions for Patty and I were simply to try and connect with each other. Our love would take care of the rest. However, there was now an unknown factor in the equation, in the form of Dennis–2, and we both knew the odds were against us ever having a relationship. But we also knew that Bob had chosen us for a reason, and that we had been given the opportunity to create something beneficial in the world that might help humanity in a deep and meaningful way.

When we were done, Patty and I returned to the playground. Since we had been operating in sideways-time during our meeting with Bob, only a few seconds had passed in real time. I was now at a level where I could heal Patty's injury and although Bob offered to heal her, I wanted to do it myself. Holly was still crying and shaking Patty hoping she would wake up, while Martha just stood there wringing her hands. In those days there were no cell phones and no 911. All in all, only two or three minutes had passed since the accident itself.

Suddenly Patty opened her eyes and got up as if nothing had happened, and walked away. Holly was stunned, and called to her: "Patty, are you all right?!" Patty had picked up a kickball. She turned to the teachers and said, quite matter-of-factly, "I saw Jesus and I got to talk to him." Then she carried the ball over to a grassy area and kicked it to the fence.

Holly, who had been sure that Patty had broken her neck and was dead, started crying uncontrollably and thanking God, rightfully believing she had just witnessed a miracle. Martha, now relieved, had stopped wringing her hands and probably thought she had been right all along. I was with Patty trying to talk with her, but Holly was being too noisy. I went over to Holly and whispered in her left ear "Be quiet." "Who said that?" she whispered. "It's me, Jesus" I pretended. "Let this be our secret." I felt this deception might be helpful. Holly stopped crying and quietly stood up, her faith renewed and probably feeling something indescribable, while I returned to be with Patty.

I don't know that Bob was really Jesus, but I like to think so. In truth I don't know if there even was a historical Jesus, although there is ample evidence and I personally believe there was. I also have some past-life memories that seem connected with him. Whoever Bob is, I did seem to know him at the time, and he held some position of higher spiritual authority regarding this world. Since then, on several occasions in my life, he has given me some helpful advice.

Dennis–2 seemed to disappear from my "space" after this session. I noticed an empty space above the front-left side of my head and presumed this was his normal location in my "energy field" so to speak. I thought that he was gone but this was not so. This session occurred three months before my integration with Bill.

I did not really understand much about multiple personalities or integration at the time and, being more concerned with issues surrounding Patty, I did nothing more about Dennis–2.

A month after my integration with Bill, Dennis–2 initiated our own integration one night while I was sleeping. I awoke around 3:00 A.M. with an excruciating headache and went into my study to work on it. However when I sat down in the chair, I went into a trance where Dennis–2 and I sat in chairs facing each other. We discussed many things and he said it was time to merge back together and that it would be difficult because he had created a wall of pain between us. He said there might be another shock created in the process. We did manage to merge but it was indeed traumatic. I went back to bed and didn't even remember that session until a few days later, during a _different_ session. During this _new_ session I recalled our meeting and integration and was able to resolve the shock and the pain that occurred at that time.[100]

Later on I worked on recalling my memories AS Dennis–2, but since Dennis–2 operated mostly in an exterior state and at a somewhat higher level of awareness, these memories have been difficult to retrieve. Dennis–2 and I, at the moment of our separation, were identical, like when John Crichton was "twinned" on the TV series Farscape, and, as with Crichton, from that moment on, our experiences and memories diverged.[101] Dennis–2 remained at the state we were in when we were working with Bob and Patty, and did not suffer any of the human trauma that I did after that day. It would have been great if I could have dropped all my Dennis–1 programming upon integrating with him, but my primary in-the-body persona is that of Dennis–1. So although I have access to some of his memories and untainted personality traits, because I AM Dennis–2, the changes have not been as dramatic as I would have liked. I have wondered if I would be better off if we hadn't integrated, by having him as a powerful helper, but I don't

---

[100] It is not normal for an ID-R session to be traumatic and this is the only time, with myself or anyone else, that this has ever happened. However this particular situation was designed to be difficult to resolve.

[101] "Eat Me" - Farscape, Season 3 Episode 6 - 2001

think so, and apparently it was important that we end our separation when we did.

When I woke up at home after the playground incident, I was lying on our big sofa with a big headache. My little brother had told our housekeeper that I was hurt and she found me unconscious and brought me inside. She had called my mother at work and was about to call a doctor, but then saw that I was awake. I had no recollection of the playground or anything that had happened. I took some aspirin and had a very long nap.

Dennis–2, Star Warrior

As Dennis–2, Bob gave me instructions on how to guide Dennis–1 so as to help him fulfill the mission we had volunteered for. The idea was to prevent Dennis–1 from connecting with Patty so that he would be forced to explore his own mind and find out what the problem was. The solution would be to find a way to resolve the unconscious programming that would be set up to prevent him from communicating with her. Eventually he would have to discover and integrate with me, his better ... I mean more privileged ... half. This was nothing like when Captain Kirk got split by the transporter into two polar opposite characters, one gentle and one aggressive, although Dennis–1 did often see me as "the enemy within."[102] Dennis–1 and I were identical at first. I simply got to operate from a higher level state. The idea was to help humanity take another leap forward in the understanding of consciousness and the mind. Although that description does sound a bit grandiose and pretentious, I just don't recall any details from my talk with Bob about what exactly our contribution would be, or how this project would help the evolution of human civilization. Since this depends on other people, maybe it won't. I only recall that, at the time, we understood it to be a worthy endeavor.

After I left Bob and the others, I went home. Floating outside the back door of our house which led to the kitchen, I looked up at the sky. In my exterior state I could see all the stars even though it was a bright summer morning. The sunny sky appeared dim and gray and the stars appeared exceptionally bright, alive, and magical.

---

[102] Star Trek TOS 1x04 - "The Enemy Within"

It was an amazing sight. Like Star Lord in "Guardians of the Galaxy," I needed a name.[103] I remember saying to myself "I'm Dennis Number Two, Star Warrior!" Remember, I was only six. I felt very strong and happy.

I then, as Dennis–2, went to my body which was lying on the couch. As I entered the body, I addressed Gordie and Medic and explained that we were on a new mission, and that I had to do something important and they were not to interfere. They agreed to leave me alone. Because of the nature of how I was created, if Dennis–1 and I were present in the body at the same time, we would naturally merge. There was nothing yet set up to prevent that. I had to create a wall between us.

Just a couple of weeks before we were born, our mother slipped and collided with the dining room table. She lay on the floor in pain for hours, unable to even get up to use the phone. The collision impacted our head just above the right eyebrow. The pain was excruciating.

In my heightened state I was able to magnify the intensity of this stored traumatic pain and connect it with being in the body so that I could not be in the body at the same time as Dennis–1 without terrible pain for both of us. Any time Dennis–1 and I were accidentally in the body at the same time, the pain would prevent us from integrating and force one or both of us to exteriorize. I had to traumatize myself to create this reaction.

After we integrated and became one, I worked on this pain, from the viewpoint of Dennis–2. This was a difficult incident to get through and took me several sessions. In the shock of applying the incredible pain to the body, as Dennis–2, I recall saying to myself many times, over and over, "It's for the good of the world."

The mystery of Dennis–2's mean and threatening behavior was now solved. The twist in the story, which became clear in working through these incidents, is that there was no real "adversary" who just wanted to interfere in my life. Everything Dennis–2 did as my antagonist was in alignment with the purpose of keeping Patty and me apart, while at the same time keeping her safe and letting her know that I still cared. If he had allowed Patty and me to connect, I

---

[103] "Guardians of the Galaxy" - 2014

would have never had the motivation to do what I did. And if Dennis–2 had not encouraged Patty to keep pursuing me, she may not have pushed me hard enough to keep me going. Still, this whole story seems ludicrous and full of holes, and the more I discover, the more questions I have.

Angels Weeping – or
The Girl Who Sees Everything

I was awakened by a dream during the night in January of 1993 after hearing a strong male voice. The words were very clear and close: "There is a girl who sees everything." The tone was one of discovery and amusement. I recorded the dream and uncovered this incident over the next few days. As usual, the incident was revealed in nonsequential pieces. At first I saw a young girl sitting on a wooden floor in her underwear. I only saw her from the back, and I heard the voice and phrase again. I was seeing this through the eyes of Lydia.

This event occurred sometime during eighth grade. Patty was upset and depressed and may have also just had a confrontation with her mother. She was crying and feeling deep sadness. Something wasn't working out. It had something to do with love, so I suspect it involved me, as well as whatever else was being triggered. So she reached out to God, and an angel appeared. By angel I mean a benevolent spirit who was there to help. The angel sat very close and began weeping in sadness with Patty. Three more angels soon arrived and also wept with her. After a while Bob appeared and greeted Patty, who was now in a heightened state of awareness. He then looked right at Lydia, saying "There is a girl who sees everything" and Lydia was suddenly standing behind Patty and was unable to move closer. She was locked out! This had never happened before and was quite a shock for Lydia. She experienced several strong emotions, including a great sense of loss. Lydia referred to Patty as "My One," and to lose that union would be devastating – it was her entire purpose for being. But Lydia was asked to remain silent and to let me, Dennis–1, know that everything was all right, since, because of Lydia's distress, I was now already alerted that there was a problem. She was also asked to leave the room so that she could not observe. At first Lydia complied, but not knowing where to go, she came to me.

I was alone in the kitchen that night, getting a glass of water. Suddenly I felt something was wrong and went into an altered state but did not leave my body. When Lydia showed up, I didn't know who she was at first. She was nearly hysterical. Breaking her customary silence, she explained everything that had just happened. I told her to follow me but to stay hidden.

Exterior, I went to Patty's bedroom and told Lydia to wait outside. I then made myself as invisible to spiritual detection as I could, blending into the wall. But I'm sure Bob knew I was there, despite my being in super-stealth mode. Bob was in front of Patty, dressed in a light-colored robe, and there were four other beings present, two on each side of a tall, bright window that appeared in the wall to Patty's left. These "angels" had no discernable gender, and wore thin blue and white pastel gossamer-like garments, with streaks of gold, that floated around them almost like translucent butterfly wings. Perhaps these garments were actually just their auras. Bob appeared to be showing Patty a vision of some kind, which she could see through the window of light, but I was unable to see it, and I felt a strong desire to respect their privacy. I realized that this vision was meant only for Patty, and that Lydia had been ejected so that I would have no access to it. Whatever this vision was, Patty was spellbound; it lifted her spirits and seemed to strengthen her in some very profound and lasting way.

When the vision was over, the window vanished, and Bob and the angels disappeared. Patty sat there a while, absorbed in thought. I summoned Lydia and we waited in silence. It was several minutes before Lydia was able to resume her familiar post. Whatever Patty experienced was for her alone. I still have no idea what it was.

Goddess

I was tracing back a feeling that felt like anxiety and discovered it was actually worry about Patty. She was very depressed and seemed to be having an intense inner conflict about having children. Patty was probably in her mid to late thirties at the time. Deep within her was a desire to have children but her unconscious promise to me would not allow it. On a conscious level perhaps she had made a resolute choice in the past against having children, or possibly motherhood had been prevented on a biological level, I don't know. On the outside she normally appeared happy and unconcerned with this situation. However today, on the inside, she was tortured and confused. I don't yet know what she was dealing with but I suspect that some recent traumatic event had brought on deep feelings of grief and had possibly triggered her past death as Ana, and the death of our unborn child.

When I arrived in spirit she was on the bed curled up in a ball, her head toward the foot of the bed and her face in the covers. Locked in this paralyzing internal dilemma of depression and grief, she was slowly sinking into oblivion. Her condition seemed to have come on in a short time. My feeling was that she had lost the will to live and saw no purpose in continuing on. I pictured her at the bottom of a deep dark well. I called down to her spirit but she would not respond. I tried to tell her it was OK to let go of her promise but she wouldn't even let herself hear me. All I could do was sit there and watch her spirit die. That she might physically die, I didn't know, but her despair was profound.

My concern over Patty's pain was also intense. I was drawn in to her depression and was very identified with this drama. All I could do was to stay there with her and share her pain, and die with her if it came to that. Even in the OBE state the idea of death, of ceasing to exist, seemed real to me at the time. I felt I had failed her, and in a gesture of support, I imagined being with her in death. As I did this, I experienced a shock at the thought of actually dying, and in that altered state I asked God to help Patty, and I just surrendered myself to whatever might happen.

Immediately time seemed to stop, and through what appeared as a window behind me, a golden ball of light entered the room, growing to a diameter of maybe five feet, and bathing us both in radiant energy. In the past when I called out to God from an altered state, Big Guy would sometimes arrive, appearing as an invisible but distinctly male presence, as I described earlier, to help me out. But this "God" was different. This was Patty's Higher Self – *HER* creator. Although she could have appeared as anything, her presence was definitely feminine. There was a gentleness about her. I suspect it was her voice that alerted me to Patty's presence at the bus stop, as I described in the prologue. In the center of the sphere of light was a transparent crystal with many facets. The crystal seemed to represent infinite power. I received a feeling of "Hello."

In the presence of this beautiful Being I felt approval, acceptance, and limitless unconditional love, which left me feeling like I was the tiniest drop in an ocean of bliss. I blended with this feeling. The Goddess seemed to hold my concern for Patty before her in the air, as if beholding a flower. A woman's voice echoed within me as a synesthesia of deep rich sound, swirling light, and supreme authority, saying "Only your love can heal this," and then the room disappeared and I was in the light. The love I experienced was wonderful and indescribable – it was unending and all pervading. Everything was golden light.

I briefly thought this might be the end of my earthly existence. But then Patty's limp and lifeless spirit was brought into the light with me and our consciousness seemed to merge. In the light we were safe and we shared each other's feelings. Then slowly, like a transfusion, life began to flow into Patty's heart. The light surrounding us became a transparent crystal sphere that took us on a magical journey. The Goddess left, and we began traveling through time and space at great speed.

We seemed to have physical bodies now, although they looked different, and I was holding Patty tightly. She had her head on my chest and was very weak. Visions of our past lives together, highlights of past moments of joy and companionship surrounded us on all sides as we visited one after another. An image of some mutual experience would expand from the swirling panorama and we would enter the scene, as if we were having a lucid dream together. There was a kind of dual consciousness where we were reliving our experiences but at the same time standing outside of them. It was like watching a movie together because we were able to comment on it at the same time. We felt bodiless during each of these episodes. From lifetimes as primitive life forms, to primitive humans, to advanced beings with incredible power, we recalled sharing joy, comedy, and adventure, and some loss, but above all, our deep bond of love and connection. There were countless relationships as friends, lovers, and family members of every kind. We had been everything to each other in many different forms, and we also had countless children together.

I pointed these things out to her in a gentle yet lively way, and as I got her to look, she began to remember. This tour was arranged for us and I had no control over it, but the memories were each awakened in my mind as the scenes unfolded. We continued to encounter moments of great beauty as we spun and glided through this vast inner universe. As her attention grew stronger Patty gradually became revitalized by the memories and the fun we were experiencing. Her energy came back and she began joining in more on this playful excursion, sharing her own memories and feelings about the things we were seeing. She began to smile and laugh, and we were both very happy!

Patty was now back to normal, at which point the sphere seemed to run out of energy and we were back in her room. I was sorry that it had to end. We had reexperienced so much that it seemed like we had been gone for days, but it was perhaps only a few seconds in normal time. The sphere disappeared and Patty awoke and arose from the bed, feeling better. She may have had a vague feeling that she had talked with God. Or perhaps she recalled having a strange dream. Or maybe she remembered nothing at all. But there was now a sense of peace and a definite feeling that her decision about children was the right one. Whatever had been bothering her had faded away.

Patricia – or Patty in Real Time

I wasn't considering whether any of my memories were real to anyone other than me, but there were so many memories that had been validated in many ways, I just assumed it was all true. The only person I really confided in was Sandra, and although she did believe me, she also realized my story was quite strange. I'm sure it was like nothing she had ever heard before. After a month of sessions which included the discovery of the Playground incident and our mutual mission, but before integrating with Dennis–2, I felt the need to contact Patty. I wasn't sure what to say to her, or how I would even approach the subject of our previous interactions, but I thought that it was time to have a real conversation. Unfortunately there still was a lot I didn't know, and if I had waited another year to communicate with her I might have been better prepared, but I really don't think it would have changed anything. So I found out where she was living and got her phone number. I hadn't spoken with her in twenty years. I made the call around noon.

When I addressed her as "Patty" the very first thing she said was
"I go by Patricia" – exactly as Sandra had told me during our first
conversation ("She goes by Patricia"). She had gotten my letter in
December and thought it was "heartfelt," but swore that she didn't
remember me at all. I wasn't prepared for that. In my naive
excitement, and because of the enormous effect all these sessions
were having on me, I expected something different. I hadn't even
considered the fact that I too had forgotten her for many years. It
was interesting that for the entire conversation, which only lasted a
few minutes, Patty appeared to be in a heightened state, and
seemed anxious to end the conversation. I asked her a question and
she said "I don't want to play this game." She said it twice.
Confused and not knowing what to say, I let her go. This was
embarrassing. I realized many things after that brief interaction,
including the fact that, although Dennis–2 was not preventing it, I
was still not ready to talk with her.

After the call ended, the first thing I asked myself was whether
that was really her. I was confused. But a voice in my head
(Dennis–2) said it was, and I could feel a deep inner confirmation
–I knew it was her. I also felt something relax inside. I determined
that whatever I knew about our mission at this point, it was
definitely not over. I had developed ID-R and had resolved some
things, but I was a long way from the finish line. I continued to
reach out to Patty a few more times by mail and by phone for about
nine months before I gave up.

First I sent Patty a letter trying to explain why I had called but it
was returned unopened. I called her a second time about six
months later in early February, and this time she was much calmer,
but made it clear that she didn't want to talk with me. I was still
unprepared. I had needed to make a convincing impression and
failed to do so. I thought that just being able to communicate
openly with Patty for the first time in my life would somehow
magically make everything right. But I didn't understand the true
nature of this project. I also didn't understand the power of all the
traumatic programming I had amassed in all those years of hiding
from Patty. But most importantly, I had never even considered her
own unconscious reactions.

Cataclysm

Immediately after the second phone call, I experienced tremendous anxiety. When I worked on this, it turned out to be Patty's anxiety that I was experiencing as Lydia. Patty was experiencing this when we talked on the phone the second time even though she had appeared much calmer. The feelings were coming from an incident many years earlier when Patty was in an embarrassing situation and determined to make sure that I never found out about it, although I myself see it as no big deal. But for her at the time, it was an emotional cataclysm in that it brought about a profound change in her. She decided to have a "new life," and created a new persona. In a way she became a different person, as I did in being Pete. But part of being "Patricia" was to have no connection to me, and because she had been thinking of me subliminally at that time long ago, talking to me now was a trigger for the same awful feelings she had back then. This earlier event was the final barrier which divorced me from her life. Understanding this incident gave me more insight into how big a wall she had built between us after giving up on me. Even though she didn't now remember me, all the trauma was still there. I realized that the tables had now turned. Now it was me chasing her instead of the other way around, and I didn't like making her uncomfortable. I remembered how abysmal it had been for me when I was the mouse.

Blasted – or Cocoon Me If You Can

On a higher level however, something else was going on. Two nights after my last conversation with Patty I experienced the most intense energy phenomena ever. I had been asleep less than two hours when I was hit by a blast of blue and white energy coming from the far left corner of the room that swept me up out of my body and suspended me in the air about six feet above my bed. The "energy" felt like electricity touching every cell of my body, and it came all at once in a big rush, but it was not unpleasant. Then there was a magnetic feeling as if my etheric body was really a ball of energy itself but was being held in its human shape by magnetic forces which simultaneously lifted me upward. When I neared the ceiling, I felt my spirit body being held in that position for a few seconds, vibrating. I had the impression that the energy I was feeling was thickening, like it was being wrapped around me in layers. Abruptly however, the forces dispersed and I snapped back into my physical body as if I were connected to it by rubber bands that had been stretched to their limit, and then released.

Within seconds another blast of energy hit me, and I experienced the same phenomena, and again I snapped back. During all of this I was trying to relax and allow the process to happen. I seemed to know what this was all about. Patty was trying to suspend me in a cocoon so she could borrow my body and leave me a written message, and I was trying to cooperate. These phenomena continued for hours but the effort was unsuccessful. For some reason I was not able to enter the exterior sleep state. The feeling I had was that something within me was too strong or too awake. Perhaps I was just unable to surrender to the process, as much as I tried, or maybe I tried too hard. Sometime earlier I had consciously considered doing the same thing to Patty to get a message to her, but I have no memory of ever trying to do so.

An Angel's Kiss in Spring – or The Hickey

A few days later I had another amazing experience. Around 3:00 A.M. on St. Valentine's day in 1993 I was awakened by a presence in my room. I was in a static OBE state and was seeing the room from the viewpoint of my physical eyes, although my eyes were closed. I could not move but only observe. A foot above my feet and to my right was a ball of white light, about the size of a softball, emanating a powerful presence. Although the orb was very bright it did not light up the room, which remained pitch black. Remember though, I was probably not viewing the physical room but its astral counterpart. I was in my ordinary Level–1 mind and said loudly "I love you Patty." The orb then moved quickly toward me and as it got to my left shoulder it emitted a high-pitched squeal that sounded like a tape recorder on fast forward. It reminds me of the Star Trek episode where alien intruders were moving so fast they were invisible to the eye, and sounded like mosquitos to the Enterprise crew.[104] Then the orb moved through my left shoulder and disappeared. I became physically awake instantly and recorded

---

[104] Star Trek TOS season 3 episode 11, "Wink of an Eye"

the experience on my recorder, emphasizing how real and intense it all was. My first words were "There was a light, and it was *absolutely* there!"

That morning when I got up and went to take a shower, I looked in the mirror. There, on my left shoulder, was a strawberry size red mark, roughly circular. She had given me a hickey! Of course I went through a checklist of other things it could be – a bug bite, a bruise, a rash, but it was none of these. I took a picture of it and it was the only picture on that roll of film that didn't turn out – it was all black. I told some people about this experience and showed them the hickey, but that was a mistake. I'm sure they thought I was having a crazy moment, as we all do once in a while.

Tagged – or Fairies and Unicorns

Later that night, while thinking about the previous night's visitation, I had the idea of returning the favor and visiting Patty, and leaving her with a similar mark. The instant I had this idea I felt a deep feeling inside which I can only describe as an internal "Yes!" like a decision had been made on some deep level. But I had no real conscious intention of actually attempting anything, mainly because I didn't have the ability. I had retained no conscious psychic abilities for more than thirty years, nothing I could do intentionally anyway at Level–1. This was simply an amusing thought.

When I awoke the next morning, I began recording my dreams. I had forgotten about the spiritual hickey idea until remembering the first dream where I was talking with Patty and there was something about tattoos! I immediately got excited at the possibility that I had actually done it. And apparently I had! From the dream that it spawned, I was able to recall an actual Level–2 OBE visitation in which I knelt by Patty's side as she slept. I spoke softly to her and touched her right shoulder with my finger, creating a red mark similar to the one she had given me.

The other dream I had that night was about a trial of some kind. A lady prosecuting attorney was trying to ridicule the idea of past lives. She was trying to discredit a younger lady, the defendant in the trial, and who had taken the stand. She asked her if she believed in other silly things, like fairies and unicorns. My mind created this dream from Patty's own thoughts that morning when she saw the mark on her own shoulder in the mirror. Patty had arisen before I was awake, and she had a shock about the possibility of this being a sign of something miraculous. She was not thinking about me in any way, but had a feeling that something very strange had happened. She was whispering to herself. In her mind she was imagining talking to an older woman, perhaps her mother, about these possibilities, and imagined persuasive arguments against a magical cause. In other words, she was convincing herself that this bruise must have some ordinary explanation.

After the hickey incidents I was pretty hyped up. The things I was experiencing were real and inspired me to keep trying to connect. But after everything I had experienced in that second week in February, I knew that there was too much working against us, and that I had to stop. Nothing I could ever say would overcome Patty's internal blocks, and it was actually still very important that we did not connect at this time since the mission was only half completed. After realizing all this I made a decision, and ceased trying to communicate with Patty on the physical level. I understood at this point that the only thing I could do was to finish my work. I had a lot to accomplish, and I was a long way from being the person I wanted to be.

Working It All Out

So Ana and Pip died in France and were born near each other in their next life as Patty and Dennis. They had a very strong connection as spiritual partners and were pursuing their intention of being together and having a family in this new life. But this goal was changed when, as children, they were approached by a powerful being who asked them to join an effort to help humanity. After agreeing to this project, they had to reprogram themselves to carry it out, because it conflicted with their original life purpose. They knew they would sacrifice sharing this life together but it was for a good cause, and they would always find each other again.

Now that I knew the whole story of my life, the basics anyway, it finally made sense. The idea was that my unconscious programming would force me to run from Patty, while my love for her would drive me to find a way to resolve all that programming and finally reach out to her. In the end, hopefully, our efforts would contribute some very valuable information to the world. Now I understood why I had been drawn to books as a child and why I wanted to know everything. I knew why I had been attracted to Patty from the time we met at the bus stop, and why I could never connect with her later on. Everything that had happened, everything I did and everything Patty did, all fit together perfectly like a massive jigsaw puzzle. But that doesn't mean I understood everything. As I said earlier, this story is bizarre, the plot is full of holes, and I still had a million questions. But at least I did realize that our lives had been dedicated to something beyond our initial plans – something much larger than us – a greater purpose.

But why all the drama and secrecy? Instead of us being secret agents, even to ourselves, why couldn't Bob just give us the information we needed, which he probably already knew anyway, and help me write a book and train others so that Patty and I could still be together? What kind of game was this? This whole scenario seemed silly to me. Instead of creating this complicated and painful challenge it could have been much easier. It relates to an age-old conundrum: why didn't God just create a perfect world? Why do pain and suffering exist? Why does everything have to be so complicated and messy? There are so many unknowns! One answer is, there is no God or higher intelligence, and the world is just the result of random mechanical processes. But that's not how it is. The answers lie in a higher truth, and nothing is as it seems.

The Game of Life

I have discovered, as have many others, that this world is governed by higher level intelligent beings, perhaps higher aspects of ourselves, who enforce the rules by which we live. These rules are like the rules of any game – there is the basic format of the game, including the space in which it is played, and the rules of play. In the game of poker, if you have a bad hand, why not just grab the deck and take any cards you want, since you have the physical power to do so? Because it's against the rules, you would be cheating, and the other players might shoot you, if you're in the Old West. Also, if that were allowed there would be no challenge. The game would be pointless and no fun at all. Even though as spiritual beings we ultimately have unlimited power and can do anything, in this game of life on Earth, the rules prohibit us from using that power, and so there are things we are not allowed to do. As I said, I have very little understanding of these rules, but I feel that if I did understand them better, this project of ours, Patty's and mine, would completely make sense, as much as any game does anyway.

So life does indeed appear to be a game. Perhaps we are here to learn, to grow, to work off bad karma, to love, to have adventures, and we are ultimately here by our own choice, even though, in spite of enjoying the most sublime wonders, we also experience unimaginable horrors. As I said in Chapter 1, through the limitless magic of creation there are infinite games that can be played and an eternity in which to play them. However, because of what my own spiritual insights have shown me, I believe life is actually an illusion – a dream that, from a higher perspective, ultimately has no reality, like a movie.

Many spiritual teachers have suggested that life is simply entertainment and that there is no ultimate purpose to it, because any purpose or meaning can only exist within the context of life itself, not outside it, which is the realm of the ultimate. I believe, as Stephen Hawking has said, "The meaning of life is what we choose it to be."[105] So we are the creators, players, and umpires of our own game, and WE determine its meaning and purpose. However, while operating at a lower level of awareness where we do not know who we really are, we remain at the mercy of the unconscious forces within us – we are pawns in our own game – and we suffer. This was discussed in detail in Chapter 21. But whether or not these ideas sound reasonable to you at this point, or have any validity, all I can do is report my own story and share what I've learned and what I think about it all.

For some time after I recalled the Playground Incident, and my initial hesitation in accepting Bob's challenge, I wondered about my choice. I have lived most of my life in poverty and have few things most people would see as the trappings of success, but this is not to say I'm not happy. Indeed I have experienced great happiness for no apparent reason almost daily for many years. Although I'm extremely rewarded by my work and helping others, by my relationships with friends and family, and by the many simple

---

[105] "Stephen Hawking's Grand Design," 2012, episode 2: "The Meaning of life"

pleasures of life, the truth is I don't actually need anything to be happy. Indeed I'm realizing more and more all the time that my very nature is happiness. But in human terms, if I had it to do over again would I make the same choice?

The Decision – or A Life With Less Meaning
"You didn't come here to make the choice. You've already made it. You're here to understand why you've made it."
– the Oracle, The Matrix

One day in hypnotherapy class in 1995 we did an exercise where we were invited to revisit some important decision we had made in the past that had changed our lives, and explore, via time progression, what might have happened if we had chosen differently. After choosing which decision to change, we all lay on the floor while the teacher hypnotized us and guided us through the process. I chose to work with the decision I made that day on the playground with Patty. Instead of going along with Patty and accepting Bob's invitation, I declined. I then followed the timeline forward from there.

In the vision that unfolded, Patty and I met in school, dated and got married. We had children and had our own careers. We were both very creative. I became an artist, a musician, and an inventor, and she worked as a designer and organizer, and was very good working with people. We were very happy for a time. But there was something missing in our lives and we eventually drifted apart emotionally. There seemed to be some internal sadness we both shared. My decision to play it safe and live a life that ultimately felt less meaningful had created a rift. While my intention was for us to share a wonderful life together and fulfill my promises, deep inside we were both lamenting the call of a higher purpose left unfulfilled. Although we did help others and do meaningful things, we were losing interest in our ordinary lives, and thought we were losing interest in each other. In the end our happiness had diminished and we didn't know why. This vision was my own unconscious construction of course, but it felt very plausible. I know we made the right choice, even though it was a huge sacrifice, and I wouldn't change it for anything.

Although I had given up trying to communicate with Patty in 1993, I still looked forward to some future time when we could sit down together, perhaps over coffee, and have our first real, worldly conversation.

Chapter 27
My Breakfast with Patty

"But of course there's a problem, because the closer you come, I think, to another human being...the more completely mysterious...and unreachable...that person becomes. I mean, you know, you have to reach out, you have to go back and forth with them...and you have to relate, and yet you're relating to a ghost or something."
– Andre, My Dinner with Andre

"A bond built amongst the stars can't be tampered by an earthly experience, trust the distance, twin flames always meet again."
– Nikki Rowe

"That's why love stories don't have endings!
They don't have endings because love doesn't end."
– Richard Bach, "The Bridge Across Forever: A True Love Story"

I thought that one day I would be done, that I would have accomplished whatever this mission is supposed to be, and that all the barriers and reactions in my mind regarding Patty would be gone, at which point it would be the most natural and easy thing in the world to have some real communication with her. However, even now I have not reached that internal highland. I can't really describe very well my state of mind with regard to Patty, after discovering everything I have discussed so far, so my behavior probably doesn't make much sense. I chose the first quote above because it represents my frustration with my own situation. The closer I seemed to get to a breakthrough with Patty, the stronger the wall between us seemed to become, like the Chinese finger trap – the harder you pull the tighter it gets. But this is how it was supposed to be, until it wasn't.

Regarding my own personal development, I had certainly resolved many issues and I had come a long way. Many of my major issues were gone and I was no longer dissociating, which resolved some embarrassing social issues, although I had never been aware

of these issues in the past. And after all my inner work I felt much
stronger physically and had much more confidence in some areas
than ever before. But Patty was still pretty much a kind of phobia.
Even during our telephone conversations something wasn't right. I
understand now that there was a "wall of agreement" between us to
not connect although we consciously knew nothing about it. This
prevented us from ever having a true "meeting of the minds" so to
speak. We both understood that until my part of this mission was
done, there could be no kind of reunion. At the time of those
conversations I still felt like I was a million miles away from where I
wanted to be mentally, psychologically, and emotionally. I had to
accept that we were following our chosen paths and that those paths
might not cross again for lifetimes, for all I knew. The only thing to
do was to stay positive and keep moving forward as best I could.

   And there was another problem because there were still issues
holding me back from doing my best. After my unsuccessful initial
attempts to communicate with Patty my passion for my work kind of
died. I stopped working on myself as fervently as before and found
myself wasting time and making bad decisions. After coming close
to death with meningitis I faced some big challenges, and my life
began to seem rather pointless. I felt that I had failed. On the other
hand, whenever I did dive into working with others or myself, and
whenever I started doing research or writing, I got very inspired for
a while. But there was something wrong, and it was eating away the
years. Still I had this idea that one day, even if by then we may have
grown old, this "wall of agreement" would be gone and we would
have a real conversation. So I did think about it from time to time.

   I imagined the two of us having breakfast at a local diner some
chirpy Summer morning, just two old friends who had been long
out of touch, spending an hour or two talking over coffee —
catching up. Although it would be nice to be able to establish that
my own experiences were true in Patty's world, as well as mine, if
indeed they are, this whole idea of getting together was less about
validating anything to myself, and more about opening that closed
door between us. It's like having a loved one with amnesia and
trying to get them to remember some little snippet of the past. So I
would probably not mention anything too personal or radical. I
would just want to be able to connect with her and have a normal
conversation. Although if I had my final conversation with Terrence

to do over again, I would do what I didn't do then – I would try and jog his memory by telling him what really happened, which I had totally planned to do later. Unfortunately he passed away before we could have that second talk.

So by far the most important motivation for me regarding Patty was about clearing up this internal obstacle within myself that had been preventing us from connecting all this time. I felt hamstrung and incapacitated. But that was all on me, and no conversation was going to fix that. Also, now that the tables had turned and she wanted no such interaction, I had to come to terms with letting her go, and turn my focus to finishing what we had started. Even in my dreams, Patty made it clear that we were not to physically communicate. I also noticed that I had to constantly push myself out of my comfort zone in order to do anything, but I felt confident that when I had truly fulfilled my part of the mission, I would know it.

The Year of Living Dangerously

I had begun writing this book in fits and starts around 2004 but never really worked on the issues that were slowing me down. Then early in January 2012 at the age of sixty-four, I had a panic attack that came out of the blue, triggered by something that turned out to be laughable. But suddenly I had many physical and emotional issues come into play all at once, including some of the earlier issues that had sent me to Urgent Care, as I described in Chapter 10. I saw various doctors, and for about a year, because of my symptoms and how I felt, I was sure I was going to die, although, other than mild hyponatremia, there were no medical indications of any serious problem. My biggest concern during this time was that I would not finish this project. But I realized that there are higher forces at play and that this character I'm portraying, this person I call "me," is actually a manifestation of my Higher Self, and that whatever I'm here to do will get done, because ultimately it's not really up to me. I've heard Robert Adams say this many times – "I am not the doer" – and it helped me to let go of my attachment to the future so I could surrender to the present moment. This brought me great relief.

There was a time in the late Spring when I submitted a prayer regarding my death, which I felt might be soon. I forget the words I used but I remember the response. I heard a male voice in my mind which said "You must walk your path to the end." I thought that meant I was going to be OK and would finish my project so I asked "So I get to walk to the end?" To which he replied "There are no assurances!" I then realized I could take nothing for granted. We all walk our paths to the end, in a sense – that's just a truism, but he was encouraging me to keep moving forward with my goals. Although this wasn't completely reassuring, it did remind me that I was not alone and never have been. "Who is this?" I asked. "You know who this is" was the response – and he was gone. I knew it was Bob.

A couple of years earlier I began having this recurring daydream, which seemed to appear for no reason. I thought I was just playing around with a possibility. I imagined that Patty was sick and in the hospital dying and I was visiting her, borrowing other people's bodies, with their permission, so that I could talk to her and comfort her. In this daydream, Patty and I had decided that she would depart this life before me, although I don't know why. I didn't like this daydream, and thought these ideas were just random musings playing out in my head, although I knew her becoming sick was always a possibility. But I had believed for a long time that if Patty should die, that I would also die shortly afterward, if not immediately.

For several weeks, beginning in July of 2012, I had a series of troubling dreams, many involving Patty. But right before that I had a very strange experience while I was sitting up in bed one night around 11:30. I was thinking about how we deal with the miraculous experiences we have in life. Sometimes we block anything paranormal out of our minds instantly, and never even remember those things because they caused a psychic shock. But more often, in that shock, we first try to make sense out of our experience by explaining it to ourselves in an ordinary materialistic way. I call it "miracle-cancelling" when we try and find an explanation that is NOT spiritual or non-physical, for something extraordinary. Sometimes we just can't. We may then just assume there IS such an explanation, but since we're tired of looking for it, we dismiss the experience, or put it with the X-Files on a shelf in the back of our minds.[106] But often we will keep thinking about it until we are satisfied that we have found an ordinary explanation that works for us, and then we will stop questioning it. Case closed. We may still wonder about it and have some doubts, but we feel safe because we have found an explanation we can accept. But remember, ANYTHING can be explained away if we try. And ANY strange experience could always be a coincidence or a hallucination or a mis-perception

So I was noticing that in my own case I was looking at the miracles I have put on that back shelf and ignored. It's as if they have no place in my life but are part of a separate reality. Something seemed very wrong about that, and there was a feeling that if I could somehow bring those experiences more into the reality of my daily life, I would be greatly empowered. As I reflected on these things I reached down with my left hand under the covers, for no apparent reason, and touched my left knee. I felt something hard there on top of my knee – it felt like a small rock but it was stuck to my knee and didn't move. Startled, I uttered "What the hell!" under my breath, and instantly threw the covers off. For a few seconds I stared at the kidney-bean sized bump under the skin of my left knee. Then I grabbed my leg several inches above the object in case it was some kind of blood clot. As I contemplated what to do while staring at this bump, which was as hard as a rock when I touched it ... it vanished. It didn't shrink back under the skin or get smaller or move anywhere – it just faded away before my eyes, like a disappearing ghost.

The first thing I did was to try and figure out what it could be. I examined the skin of my knee and there was nothing there. I called my brother Alan, who worked in the medical field, to see if he had any ideas. I hated to bother him so late at night, since he had helped me out a lot lately and I had been acting like a hypochondriac for months, but he had no ideas. I thought about this phenomenon for a while and decided to use the Flows technique on the strange bump. During this process I realized that

---

[106] "The X-Files" was a TV series from 1993. The title referred to secret files kept by the FBI on unsolved cases that involved paranormal or unexplained events.

this was not a hallucination or anything physiological, but a miraculous manifestation created by Patty to help me see exactly what I do with these kinds of experiences. This experience helped me to answer the question I had been pondering right before I reached down and felt the bump.

The appearance of the bump was not a shock, although I did shift into a state of alarm, but after it vanished I immediately questioned the reality of what I saw. Specifically, did I really see it fade away like a ghost or was I mistaken? So I sat there remembering exactly what I saw, as if maybe that memory would turn into something more understandable. But I saw what I saw. Then later I tried to think of many possible physical explanations including that maybe it was just something physiological that is rare and undocumented. Even after realizing it was a miracle – a metaphysical phenomenon – I still found myself looking for alternative explanations. I also noticed that the reality of the event was fading – that the power of the mystery and magical nature of it, was disappearing. I was placing this file on a shelf in the back room of my mind, in Warehouse 13, along with the Arc of the Covenant, and the Roswell Spacecraft. But now, by examining this process while it was occurring, I had more clarity. When an experience doesn't fit with our understanding of the world or with the social consensus of what is real, it is very hard to maintain a sense of its reality. The only real solution is to change our view of the world.

I have always remembered a significant number of the miracles I have experienced in my life, although most were of the wimpy variety, and part of what helped me do this was that I recorded them in my journals. So the key is to look for them, write them down when they occur, and make an effort to remember them often. This involves developing a "miracle mind-set" where you are looking for and expecting miracles every day. They can be tiny or huge, like knowing the phone is about to ring or surviving death against all odds. Noticing the phases you go through when you witness a possible miracle is also helpful – things like exploring alternate explanations, questioning whether you actually saw it, fear, feeling crazy, and acceptance of the possibility of the miraculous – which simply refers to forces beyond our present understanding.

My "miracle bump" experience inspired me to hold periodic group meetings where people could share their own miraculous experiences. I call these meetings the "Spirit Power Circle." This is a sacred ceremony following the Native American "way of council" where a dozen or more of us gather in a circle and, using a "talking stick" we take turns sharing our stories of miracles we have experienced.[107] Participants are encouraged to trust and share things they may feel reluctant to share and things they perhaps have never told anyone about. This is a powerful method that helps us make the miraculous more acceptable and accessible.

Apocalypse Now – or Dreams of the End

After the "miracle bump" phenomenon, I began having dreams in which various friends and relatives, who are presently alive, had died or were in the hospital, and I had a few dreams about a coming apocalypse. I also had several dreams where the theme was that time was running out or I was too late for something. Although I had not dreamed of her for months, Patty appeared in several of these dreams, as well as in a few other dreams that seemed unrelated to these subjects at the time. The dream that stands out most was the following, which I worried about quite a bit for a while:

"Patty was staying in some facility and something was wrong with her. It seemed like a hospital. There was a big group of people assigned to watch over her, and I was one of them. She was aware of my being assigned to her but she didn't know who I was, and I didn't tell her. She was kind of "out of it," not in a stupor but just tired and recovering from something, so I stayed close to her. Patty could move around but was depressed. She allowed me to help her, and there was something going on between us, but maybe it was just that she understood that I was like a nurse and would be there for her. There was a big lady who was in charge. She seemed to be in the middle of everything and I had to follow her rules. There was also the feeling that this lady was the one who had assigned me to Patty, or maybe she was just allowing me to be there.

"There were lots of other people in the area around Patty, who was sitting in a chair at first, and then later was sitting on the floor. I

---

[107] Adapted from the book "The Way of Council" by Zimmerman and Coyle, 2009

made sure she had some food. At one point I had to leave and it
seems like I was back home on my daily walk. I was thinking that
this was my chance, and that the universe had set this visitation up
so Patty and I could get to know each other. I felt I should do
everything I could to communicate with her and get to know her, so
as to create a physical world relationship. In the dream, I returned
from my walk to where Patty was, because I was afraid to leave her
for too long. I was wearing a white coat and I watched her to see
how she was doing. I saw her watching some live show in an area of
the hospital where a group of people was singing or something, and
she was moving and clapping her hands. I felt sad. I was thinking
about how I know her shape and that I would know her anywhere.
But I wasn't referring so much her face or the shape of her body,
but more to the shape of her energy field, for lack of better words.
As I stood behind her, I was looking at her hair, and it was slightly
gray in some places but very dark. I just wanted to be next to her,
although she didn't see me. Then she disappeared and I woke up."

At first when I was interacting with Patty in this dream, she
didn't seem to be in a good mood. It was as if I had asked her a
question like, was she hungry, and she acted like maybe she was
senile or had Alzheimer's or something, and was irritated with me.
However, there was also a sense that she was going to recover. It
seemed that many of the people around her knew her better than I
did, but they didn't seem to be interacting with her.

At some point in the dream I was thinking about a past
conversation I had with her in spirit, about under what conditions
would I risk my life or give my life for her, so that she would
understand my future actions. But in the present dream she didn't
seem to acknowledge me much. I believed afterward that this
dream, which was an ordinary dream and not an OBE, represented
a real-world experience that I don't recall, in which I was visiting
Patty in a hospital. In the dream it seemed like I was there
physically, borrowing someone's body, but maybe I was just there
spiritually and she didn't recognize me. I don't know if the other
people helping her were actually physical people or spirits.
Whether or not I actually did any such thing, and how I might have
accomplished it, I don't yet know. Joseph, a trusted psychic friend
of mine, later told me that the big lady running everything in the
dream was an angel.

In working with Flows on this dream, I got that Patty wanted to interact with me but she couldn't allow herself to. I also got some flows of loneliness and introversion where the external world was seeming less real and important to her. Also present were my own feelings of sadness and regret that I can't be with her. I recalled that I was thinking about what kind of fruit she would like. I felt that this situation was set up this way as an opportunity for us to communicate somehow, and that it would work out, but I don't know what that means. There is one point where she is sitting in a wheelchair and her head is bandaged. It seemed like she had some kind of stroke or brain problem. Patty was obviously in some reduced state of health, so perhaps this experience was really about saying goodbye.

For some reason I didn't explore this dream further, but I discussed it soon afterward with some friends in case anything came of it, although I eventually decided not to try and contact Patty in real life, in any way. I recalled the recurring daydream I had earlier about her being in the hospital, and realized it may have been something I knew was going to happen, on a deeper level. I also felt some internal compulsion to push this whole thing out of my mind, so after a few days I let it go, and forgot about it.

Phasing Out – or What Dreams May Come

That summer, in the middle of July, I ran across some new videos by Michael Raduga on the internet about developing OBE skills and I read his free OBE Manual.[108] While I disagree with much of his current understanding of what OBEs are, and his framing of the whole phenomenon, and I though reject his calling the OBE state "the phase," I found his techniques to be amazing and invaluable! The very first night after being exposed to his material I had a very strong OBE and was able to intentionally maintain it for several minutes. This was phenomenal! I had never been able to do that before. When I became slightly lucid while sleeping that night, I was able to recognize instantly that I was exterior. We actually wake up or come close to the waking state

---

[108] The Phase – Michael Raduga, 2011. See the current website at remspace.net

many times in every normal sleep period, so normally I would have thought I was just awake and let myself drift back into unconsciousness. This time however, once I became lucid, I rolled out of my body and flew across the room. I immediately started using the new techniques to maintain and deepen the OBE state, but because I had not expected this to happen so soon, I hadn't preplanned any tasks to accomplish, which is very important. But I did explore my surroundings and had some interesting experiences, including a premonition of something that happened the next day. I also had some communication with a friend I had not spoken with for several years, who described to me how her life was going. I called her six months later and she confirmed that the information in that communication was completely accurate. I awoke pretty excited and began training myself to use these new skills over the next several months.

When having an OBE it is good to be prepared with a list of several tasks to carry out so that you don't waste the experience, and so you don't flounder while trying to decide what to do, which can cause you to wake up in bed. And checking your task list in the morning is a great way to remember any OBEs you may have forgotten, because the memories can easily vanish from consciousness, just as they do with dreams or any experiences that occur in an altered state. I began having about two OBEs every week at this point, and usually my first task was to visit Patty. This was actually a goal I had in my OBE's for many years prior to this time, and I was usually unsuccessful because my OBEs were so brief. Even now I was having little success with this goal and I was also unable to speak with Bob. I think there was an internal block to these things but I never worked on it. My secondary goals, like flying, walking through walls, looking in a mirror, getting answers to questions, moving objects with my mind, and many others, were mostly successful. But regardless of the tasks, the experiences themselves were astonishing and magical. Imagine being in a totally real and magical world, fully conscious, where you can do almost anything!

Voice of the Wizard

In late October I had the following OBE adventure. It was the most amazing Level–1 OBE experience I had ever had! Remember, most OBEs we hear about, except for some NDEs, probably take place in Level–1 consciousness, which means we have everyday awareness while operating in another domain outside of our normal material world, although sometimes our experiences may be much more clear, real, and intense, than normal, surpassing anything we experience on the human level. This is hard to describe. A Level–2 OBE is something else, because you have more awareness of your nature as a spiritual being and greater access to true power, but these experiences are seldom remembered. That October night, my plan was to accomplish three tasks. The first task in this OBE was to find Patty and see if she was OK. Next I wanted to look in a mirror, and then I wanted to communicate with the Spirit of the Cannabis plant and ask a question. I accomplished all of those tasks, and experienced many other amazing things, in this extended OBE, but I will only relate part of it here.

After waking up in a dream I found myself hovering in the air above a street carnival and I quickly remembered my three tasks. However I got momentarily distracted by some extraordinary experiences. Most memorable was that as I rose higher in the air I saw a mountain looming in front of me in the distance. The mountain seemed ominous somehow and I felt like it was pulling me toward it. This was a compelling vision but I turned away from it and set out to find Patty. I later identified this mountain and Mt. Arunachala.[109]

Seconds later I found myself outside a house facing a teakwood door. I stood there for a moment, astonished by how conscious I was. I felt the door frame and it was so real I wondered for a moment if I might be dead. I heard a man cough in the house and I smelled cigarette smoke. I opened the door, ran inside, and glimpsed someone disappearing into a back bedroom. I called Patty's name and went in the room but nobody was there. There was a noisy television on so I turned it down. I thought about that later because normally things like light switches or machines don't work in these astral realms because they are just images, although I have willed them to work on occasion. Then I saw a mirror on the

---

[109] Mt. Arunachala was the home of Sri Ramana Maharshi, the great Indian sage, and is considered to be the mountain that dissolves the ego. It is said to be a form of Shiva (God), and represents ultimate wisdom.

wall so I ran over and looked at my reflection, and had a good laugh. I was in such a stable state of awareness that I didn't have to use any techniques to maintain my focus at this point. I decided I would find a phone and call Patty. I looked around and spotted a black cordless phone, picked it up, and dialed zero. I thought I would ask the operator to connect me with Patty.

As I put the receiver to my ear, I heard what sounded like a mischievous wizard who was speaking in the most affected and overly dramatic raspy voice. He was like a cartoon character. He said something like "How may I help you on your mystical quest?" I immediately asked, quite forcefully, "Where's Patty?" I wondered later why I asked where she was, since I thought I knew where she was, and felt I should have asked to speak with her or at least asked how she was doing. The wizard, as if sensing my impatience, kindly responded, sounding quite bemused and speaking as if he were telling a ghost story around a camp fire on a dark night:

"She is lost in the recesses of her own mind, locked into a mental loop, a puzzle which keeps her confused and wandering, circling. The two of you are locked into a shared fate, a dance of destiny that must work itself out until all is revealed. You will face great fear and you will have to break through unknown barriers alone, and together."

I was listening intently, trying to memorize everything the wizard was saying, since I knew I could forget it all when I returned to my body. In fact I actually DON'T recall everything that he said. I was also delightfully mesmerized by the wizard, the quality of the sound, and the reality of this whole experience. I marveled at it all as I listened. Then the wizard went off into a philosophical dissertation, as if he were talking to someone else, and I felt we were done, so I put down the phone and walked out the door.

I noticed there was something in my mouth that I was chewing, which was tasty and chewy like beef jerky or something, again totally real. I walked out into a garden, bent down, and smelled a fragrant flower that looked like alyssum – incredible! More magical things happened but I returned to my body intentionally after a young relative named Sarah arrived to see what I was doing. Sarah appeared as a golden ball of light, but I knew it was her, and I believe she was actually spiritually present since we had been talking earlier that night and she was sleeping in the apartment right below mine. At that point, the Spirit of the Cannabis plant told us we weren't safe being there. "Let's get out of here" I said as I grabbed Sarah and we spun upward in a whirlwind of golden light. Then she streaked off toward the horizon and I opened my eyes in bed. I spent the next hour recalling as much as I could and recording the whole experience.

I regret that I didn't look deeper into this experience right after it happened, but I believe I was not supposed to, and that the wizard was being cryptic for a reason. When I did work on this OBE, I got that the wizard was indeed keeping information from me that I wasn't yet ready to know. Of course any information we get in a dream or an OBE is not necessarily real or true in any way. Although such information could be true, it should never be assumed to be valid, but simply seen as something to explore. Exploring this information can lead to real memories and insights however, as well as other clues to consider. For example if I had explored the dream where Patty was in the hospital I would have discovered that she had indeed been in a hospital with a serious health condition at that time.

A Conversation with Patty – or Spirits Having Flown

In January I had another OBE experience with Patty. I became lucid in a dream and began deepening and stabilizing my state. Then I noticed I was in the kitchen of the childhood home I lived in throughout elementary school and junior high. I went over to the telephone and picked up the receiver, but heard nothing. I spoke into the phone anyway asking for Bob, and when there was no response I just started asking questions like how was I doing on my mission and asking for some guidance. I was careful at this point to maintain my awareness because when I lose my focus I tend to drop quickly back into the dream state, and it almost happened here. I realized I needed to dial something so I dialed zero for help and I heard a girl's voice.

I asked "Who is this?" She paused for a moment and I thought maybe it was Patty. As soon as I had that thought she answered in a perky tone "It's Patty!" as if someone had read my mind and was just pretending to be whoever I wanted them to be. But I did feel like Patty would hear me so I just started talking to her as if she were there, and I asked her if she remembered me. Finally she said she did remember that I had sent her some things in the mail and she had thrown it all away, or had put it somewhere. She said that she had then gone out and indulged in some things like a facial and a massage, which sounded like an effort to push me, and any feelings I had stirred up, out of her mind. She kept chatting away about her various indulgences in a carefree teenage voice. I asked her if she remembered our last life together when we were going to have children, but had died in a plane crash. Her voice started to get weak and sad, sounding like a frightened little girl.

So I asked her if she remembered when we met Jesus. She said no, so I proceeded to tell her the whole story. I described the playground incident, our conversation with Bob, and our promises to each other. I told her how much I admired her great compassion, and that it was such an amazing decision for her to choose to help others and sacrifice her own desires. I spoke fast and with great passion because I wanted to tell her everything. I could feel the emotional energy building up like a cyclone, creating an almost physical pressure. Indeed everything except the phone and my body became blurry as if the world was spinning around me. At some point, while I was explaining why everything happened the way it did, I noticed Patty hadn't spoken for a while and I felt a sudden shift in my awareness, the scene faded, and I opened my eyes.

I recorded the experience immediately, and realized I had made many mistakes. I felt I had wasted the opportunity by talking too much and made plans to do better next time. I realized the voice on the phone was not necessarily Patty but I do believe we were spiritually in contact there. And what happened next adds to that conviction,.and makes it clear to me why I took that opportunity to explain everything, pouring my heart out to her over the phone. A couple of hours after awakening that morning I found out through a friend on the internet, that Patty had died the previous August. She had been fighting brain cancer for over a year. She was sixty-four.

When I heard the news, it was like my heart dropped out. In spite of us not having any kind of normal relationship or even really knowing each other, just the fact that we were here on the same planet felt like we had a worldly connection. Although on a higher level of awareness I already knew she had died, when that knowledge reached me at Level–1 it was still very depressing. The world suddenly felt flat, meaningless – like a garden without flowers, or a concert without music. I realized then that her presence had been a continuous influence on me, infusing my every breath with meaning and purpose. The life I had been living was somehow dependent on her being here, and that was not really a good thing. In some ways I had been too close to her, not just in a protective way with Lydia, and her being my inspiration for our mission, but I had allowed myself to be less involved with other people, and to remain in a general state of reclusiveness and hiding. So I felt disgusted with myself because I had neglected to work through those issues, and I had not accomplished all that I thought I should have. I felt Bob had misjudged me, and that I was unworthy of this mission. I was lacking something essential, and I had failed.

I thought about Patty and found myself hoping that she had a fulfilling life with lots of love and joy, because I knew there were disappointments. I also knew that I had to continue to live and finish what I had promised, as best I could, even if it was too little too late. But again, I don't really understand it all, and I do believe that everything is unfolding as planned, according to a higher intelligence.

But at least it now made sense why I had panicked over nothing a year earlier, and why I had thought for the last year that I was going to die when there was nothing wrong. I was picking up on Patty's condition and her feelings, which triggered my own reactions. I also now felt somehow released from fear and curiously free, which also added to my feelings of guilt and disgust, but I realized that all this was part of something we had worked out together which I didn't yet understand consciously, and I knew I still had a lot of work to do. I also knew that my own negative feelings were just reactions that I could easily resolve when I put my mind to it.

The same day I received this sad news, I had lunch with some old classmates, one of whom had been close friends with Patty in High School. We spoke about Patty, and although I revealed little of my personal history with her, many things were validated during our conversation, regarding Patty and me. Later my brother Alan checked in on me to see if everything was all right, so I'm sure he psychically picked up on my distress. I acknowledged his intuition and told him what was going on.

Dreams of a Dying World

In the following weeks I began reviewing many of the dreams I had recorded over the last two years, to see if there were any more clues about what was going on with Patty during that time. There were quite a few. I had forgotten all these dreams about Patty but began to recall most of them as I listened to the recordings. Many of them contained little hints that she was having some serious problems. Also during this time, as I reviewed these dreams, I often heard the song from the "Wizard of OZ," "If I Only Had a Brain," in the back of my mind, as if Patty were singing it and laughing. The following dream occurred in the Summer of 2012, a day or two before her death, and my sense while reviewing it was that she was unconscious, possibly in a coma. This is mostly an unedited transcription. At the time I had no idea that this dream might have anything to do with Patty. I do a lot of work with computers so computer files serve as metaphors in many of my dreams. Memories and clarifications, which I added later, appear in italics.

"Mid August 2012: In the last dream there were two identical computer document files – one was in a folder and its duplicate was in a subdirectory under that one and I couldn't remember which one I had edited last. I thought about this a long time in the dream and decided I would continue to edit the one in the subdirectory and I would copy the one in the upper directory to another location as a backup because, if I had edited that one and the files were different, I would have whatever changes I made there *[in the new location]*. So I would keep both files and start editing the one I thought I had edited last and move that one to the upper directory and move the other one somewhere else, so I'm only editing one. But during this whole thing there's this feeling that the world is ending, a strong feeling that time is running out because there was an earlier dream with that same feeling.

"*[Could the identical file represent Lydia? Or did it mean that of the two of us, there would now be only one? Or maybe somehow these files represent memory tracks, namely Patty's and Lydia's. Or maybe it just represents that I had to make some decisions about dealing with the situation.]*

"In the earlier dream people were running around in this world – some world, like a particular world separate from mine somehow – slowly dying. It's like food was running out or something was running out – it could be time. In this world there is some internal space in my body or organ, some organ, that had been eaten away to make room for something more essential – I don't know what that was – but in this world where things were dying, I think things were eating each other. I remember there were smaller creatures like mice or cats or something that I was competing with and everything was slowly starving to death, and the end was coming soon. It seemed like there should be a sense of loss of whatever had been eaten away in my body but there wasn't, there was … it was just the way it was. I was surprised that I wasn't more emotionally affected by that, but it was some kind of survival thing where, because I had this space. I could like, store more energy there or something. And then I was thinking 'Hey, wait a minute now, as long as I get enough vitamins …' and I thought 'I AM taking vitamins! You know I could last a pretty long time and maybe most other creatures or people aren't taking these things that I'm taking so they won't last as long.' So it was like the theme was death and that you can't escape it or something like that, but there was some … something had happened to the whole world – the whole world was like, uh, on its way downhill.

"[This is obviously about Patty who was dying – I believe she died two days later but I don't know any details. I was unaware of her situation until several months after she crossed over. She died of brain cancer but I don't know any particulars of her treatments or anything. I later had a very strange dream about brain surgery, although I believe the type of cancer she had was inoperable. But cancer often causes cachexia where the body starves to death as it is competing with the cancer cells for nourishment.

"[This dream appears, for me, to indicate that her death was a sacrifice meant to help me let go of the hope of meeting with her, as well as to help me release fears that are holding me back from what I have to do, which is the 'something more essential.' In any event, it has had this effect. The organ could symbolically be my heart or it could be her body. The 'space' is the freedom from the burden of worrying about her, and all the other baggage I'm carrying around that is now rendered inconsequential. In the dream I recognized there

was going to be a great loss but I was not distraught over it, which
surprised me, but I believe this was all expected and part of a destiny
we had both already come to terms with on a higher level. Although
Patty was 'a world separate from mine,' in many ways, she was my
world – still is.]"

The Memorial

Later that Spring I traveled to another state to attend a memorial
for Patty. I didn't know anyone there but I was seated in this
magnificent and very ornate church with a large group of Patty's
friends and relatives, and participated in the proceedings. Several
significant things happened that day but one miracle stands out.

After a break at the end of the service I was sitting behind
everyone, by myself, just feeling the energy of the place, while
people visited with each other. Out of nowhere a lady came up and
sat in the seat right in front of me, facing me, and introduced
herself. She was very open and direct, and looked me right in the
eye. Her name was Theresa, and she had been Patty's personal
massage therapist and healer, as well as a psychic friend and
spiritual advisor, for the last twenty years. We talked about ourselves
for a few minutes to get better acquainted. She told me that Patty
had been doing all the right things to stay healthy, which included
a good diet, exercise, and meditation, so Theresa was quite
surprised by the cancer.

Then, after I revealed something of my spiritual connection with
Patty, and described some of my prophetic dreams regarding her
illness, Theresa realized Patty and I were true soulmates. She then
communicated to me what was basically a summary of Patty's final
weeks. She told me that Patty had completed everything she needed
to at the end, had achieved her main goals, tied up all loose ends,
and felt satisfied that she had lived a good life. Her body had been
cremated and her ashes scattered in a place she loved. Tears welled
up in my eyes as Theresa spoke. It was as if she was delivering a
personal message to me directly from Patty, and it touched my
heart. I expressed my deep appreciation, and before Theresa left I
asked her what had prompted her to come up and talk with me. Her
answer was that when she saw me she felt an overwhelming
intuitive compulsion to talk with me – like it was something she

had to do before she did anything else. I believe she was being guided.

Rain Check

Later I reviewed my dreams from July 2011, which I thought might have been around the time Patty first became aware of her condition. I just wanted to see if there were any clues to help me understand things better. I discovered several dreams, all occurring in a two-week period, which may have represented her condition and its cause. In one dream there were "bad" computer files on Patty's computer that had been massively replicated from a good file, but which served no real purpose. These files were related to some project or hobby of hers and they were supposed to be copies of a security key but they didn't work right because they contained false information. There was a feeling that if one of these files came into operation, something very bad would happen. My guess is that the bad files represented cancer cells. There were feelings of sadness and doom in this dream, and I was there trying to figure out a solution.

In another dream there were small rocks or brown blobs or splotches on Patty's floor, and some were radioactive. Someone was helping me as we tried to sort out the safe blobs from the bad ones. Perhaps these represented something toxic in her environment. In these dreams there was a feeling that something harmful was being set in motion, but whatever it was, it seemed inevitable, and I felt powerless to change it.

So I never did have my breakfast with Patty, sharing the aroma of fresh hot coffee and deep thoughts on a sunny day with the birds chirping outside. Although we may have had a dream conversation in the kitchen in the morning, it wasn't exactly what I had in mind. But at least I understood that we had decided long ago that our project had to come first. Perhaps on a human level I hadn't totally accepted that, which ironically was a requirement for the project – my not accepting it that is. But I really just wanted more closure, not so much for myself, but I felt something was left undone. It didn't seem right that Patty should leave this world without consciously knowing her own story, the story I tried desperately to relate to her disembodied voice on the astral telephone. I realize she already knew everything anyway, on a higher level, yet somehow that still isn't very satisfying. But it's that very dissatisfaction that tells me I'm not done, and which keeps me going.

I will end this story with a profound quote from Joseph Campbell's "The Power of Myth" because I have found it to be true in my life even before I reached my present advanced age, and I believe it applies to us all:

"In his splendid essay called 'On an Apparent Intention in the Fate of the Individual,' Schopenhauer points out that when you reach an advanced age and look back over your lifetime, it can seem to have had a consistent order and plan, as though composed by some novelist. Events that when they occurred had seemed accidental and of little moment turn out to have been indispensable factors in the composition of a consistent plot." "And Schopenhauer concludes that it is as though our lives were the features of the one great dream of a single dreamer in which all the dream characters dream, too; so that everything links to everything else, moved by the one will to life which is the universal will in nature."

Chapter 28
Games of Magic

"There are dimensions of your being and a potential for realization and consciousness that are not included in your concept of self. Your life is much deeper and broader than you conceive it to be here. What you are living is but a fractional inkling of what is really within you, what gives you life, breadth, and depth. – Joseph Campbell, "The Power of Myth"

"But when you find out the game that's being played is erroneous, a joke, it is only a game, you wake up and you stop playing. You become absolutely, totally free." – Robert Adams

At the end of your Hero's Journey you have brought something new into the world. It may be information, an invention, a recipe, an object, a game, a vision, a song or other work of art – it could be anything. But most importantly it's a story of transcendence. And the story is an inspiration, and an invitation for others to follow their own bliss, to accept the call to a greater purpose, to face their own fears, to make their own journey, and to share their own story – and we are all enriched by this. My deeper experiences have led me to not only understand but to actually see, that we live in a universe that is only consciousness – a spiritual universe – and that we are immortal beings of incredible power and unlimited potential, playing games of magic throughout eternity. I believe that we will each continue this great adventure until such time as we awaken to discover the truth: that our separateness from Consciousness as individuals is an illusion.

As living beings we are playing roles, identifying with our bodies and our characters, and living countless lifetimes in countless worlds. But what we really are, individually and universally, never dies. And after this life we're off to star in our next movie – we just move on to "another ball game," as a friend of mine said a few years ago right before he passed on. And in this life in which we appear mortal and limited and in which we seem to have forgotten who we truly are, we are still always connected to the infinite power within ourselves, and we have helpful and guiding spirits and friends all around us, in many different forms, even when we think we are alone. Our all-powerful Higher Self is actually just a higher level of our own awareness pretending, through us, to be human. No matter how bad things get, that power is always with us, and eventually we will realize that "*that power*" IS us. Prayer, or asking for help from God, Spirit, the Universe, or our spiritual allies, always helps, even when it doesn't appear to, or when the asking seems futile.

In the nineteen sixties one of my favorite TV shows was "The Outer Limits," and my favorite episode was a two-part story called "The Inheritors." In this story, four American soldiers fighting in Vietnam were wounded around the same time, each having been shot in the head. They all should have died but didn't, and were transported home in a coma. Not only did they all fully recover, but each man developed a genius IQ. Agent Ballard, the FBI detective investigating these men, also discovered that each man had developed a second brain wave pattern, and that this new pattern was identical in all four men. He traced the metal in the bullets these men had been struck with to a meteorite in Vietnam that had apparently contained the genetic material of an alien life form. Ballard was unable to detain these men, and after they recovered and left the hospital they all disappeared. But eventually Ballard did manage to track them down. He discovered that one of the men had become rich in the stock market and was sending money to the other three. He also found that each of these other three men had become experts in different scientific fields and that they each felt compelled to carry out a project without knowing why. Even though none of these men knew each other, they had become psychically connected, and eventually met at a warehouse that one of them had leased. They were working together to build a spaceship. While the government had unsuccessfully tried to stop them, they had also gathered together a select group of disabled children to go on a journey to a distant planet. These children were quickly healed when they entered the special atmosphere of the completed ship. They had accepted the invitation to inherit their own world and begin a new civilization far from Earth. The four soldiers accepted this too, once the plan revealed itself in each of their minds. Since the warehouse was protected by a force field, the FBI could not intervene. As the Outer Limits "control voice" narrates the concluding monolog, we see the spaceship leaving the Earth, heading for the stars.

What intrigued me most about this story was the idea of a group of people working together on a secret project which none of them really understood, but which served a higher purpose. In this story each soldier was an essential part of the plan. I didn't know at the time that this was exactly what Patty and I were doing, in concert with many others, but I believe that is what a great many of us are actually doing here on Earth right now. I feel very connected to all the people who are trying to help others by understanding and working with trauma, as well as to all those studying the mind and consciousness, or helping others to improve or wake up. And even if our current roles seem to be small, every role is essential, and one's role can also change over time. However I do think it's incredibly helpful for us to know what our human purpose is, in this life, and this is something that can often be discovered with ID-R.

Circles

Everything happens in circles, in spirals. A circle is the reflection of eternity. It has no beginning and it has no end" — Goethe

There is an enormously profitable multifaceted industry aimed at those of us seeking self-improvement and success in the many aspects of our lives, like health, fitness, finances, relationships, happiness, and so forth, and much of what is available is very valuable and essential. But many of our ideals in these areas are just images sold to us by others for personal gain, or they are part of a culture we never had any say in. Even many purveyors of happiness and enlightenment are selling "truth" in a way that cheapens or subverts its real meaning and true value.[110] And yet there is not actually a "right" way to live our lives or a "right" way to be, or even a best way, in general. Every "way" of living or being in this world simply has a different set of realities to contend with, and a different set of values and consequences. There can be a best way to get what we want, but it all depends on what we want, and *we tend to want to*

---

[110] For one of many possible examples, and an excellent expose, read Ronald Purser's 2019 book "McMindfulness."

live in ways that are compatible with our programming, even when
that programming is detrimental. We acquire our beliefs, our
associations, our wants, our ideals, our moral values, and our sense
of what is normal, from our families, our teachers, our education,
our friends, our society, our religion, our celebrities, advertising,
TV, magazines, comic books, social media, our traumatic life
experiences, past lives, and even cereal boxes. So what we want may
not even be our own choice.[111]

As I have already pointed out, everything around us in this world
is trying to influence us in some way, and this manipulation is very
effective. And I don't just mean people. Even an apple is putting
out a fragrance to get you to eat it and spread its seeds around, and a
virus might make you cough so it can propagate its genetic
material. In the midst of this saturated dust bowl of persuasive
agents and infectious memes that we live in, with everything
pulling us in one direction or another, our happiness depends on
finding our own "path with heart," not only in spirituality but in
every other area of life as well. In counseling others I have often
asked this question: If you won a billion dollars in the lottery and
money was no longer an issue, what would you do? With survival
issues off the table, what are you drawn to? What did you dream
about doing as a child? What passions have you given up on? What
makes you happy and what do you love? Sometimes they already
know and sometimes the answer has been buried so deep and for so
long that the person has no idea, or just thinking about it makes
them sad. Or they may reply with something frivolous that has no
real heart. But when we focus steadily and sincerely on that
question, an answer will eventually emerge. Deep down we already
know.

In 1991 if I had actually won the lottery instead of finding some
of the answers I was looking for, my life most certainly would have
been better in many ways, but only temporarily and not in any of
the ways that really matter. However I can only see that in
hindsight. Ultimately I do believe the only real wealth is spiritual

---

[111] I highly recommend Jonathan Haidt's 2013 brilliant book "the
Righteous Mind" for a deeper understanding of how our moral values
develop and why they can differ so much between different cultures and
groups.

freedom, and our greatest joys lie in love, connection and contribution. Still, when our efforts toward success and fulfillment are fruitful it's great, up to a point, to be able to get past internal road blocks, to get free of limitations, to become the person we want to be, to find love, health, happiness, fame and fortune, to win at the game of life, to create a legacy, and to see a bigger picture of who we are and what we can do. But then we die and do it all over again, and we still don't know who we REALLY are.

We will surely continue to evolve and advance, even to the point of godliness once again, only to eventually fall. It's an endless cycle – a series of circles spiraling upward and then dwindling back down again, over the course of innumerable lifetimes. At some point on this never-ending journey we will all be drawn to waking up from the dream of personal existence, to our true nature, life itself. It's inevitable. Of course if you believe this one life is all there is for you, then you will live by that dictum. But even then, given that we are governed so much by unconscious forces, how much of what you do or decide is under your own control? Isn't self-knowledge still preferable to sleepwalking through life, bound by beliefs that may not even be true? Expanding our awareness and self-understanding is always something we can choose.

My present life's journey awakened within me all the memories and amazing stories I have related to you, and led to all my questions, ideas, and speculations as well. And these experiences have not only altered my life in many helpful ways but they have also changed things within my being in a way that has brought me closer to the deeper realization I seek. I reverse-engineered these experiences into the Identity Model and incorporated what I learned into this book. From my own experience I can tell you that all our lives are far deeper and more complex than we know. We really are living in a dream world with access, ordinarily, to only the tiniest part of it. In addition to the vast network of connections we have to our own past experiences and the various levels of our own minds, we are all connected to each other in mysterious and complicated ways, and it's all a super-amazing game that never ends, as long as we're caught up in it.

Now with all the stories I've told, the miracles I've experienced, and the powerful changes I've been through, it's natural to wonder why I'm not rich or famous, why I have to hobble around with the effects of various maladies like millions of others, and why I have to grow old and eventually die like everyone else. Why am I not perfect? And if I had all these super abilities why can't I just heal myself and manifest everything I want? I have to laugh. The answer to these questions is simple. I'm playing the game of being human, just like everyone else, and acting out my appointed role. Also, none of those amazing and miraculous things were really under my control. Everything I experienced "just happened." Control is an illusion. But somehow I know inside that I wouldn't change a thing, and I can't explain that except to say it's all part of the game that has to play itself out. To quote Morpheus in "The Matrix Reloaded": "What happened, happened, and couldn't have happened any other way."

While our present life is a game, with its own particular rules, goals, obstacles, consequences, and rewards, it is in turn part of a much larger game. And in this continuous cycle of birth and death, we suffer, and often that suffering stays with us unconsciously, as has been demonstrated throughout this book. But healing is also possible, by resolving issues, managing them, or transcending them completely. There is a way out of every trap. And in this world, the ultimate path toward spiritual awakening is always available – we always have the option of choosing to free ourselves, and there are more tools and resources available to help us with this than ever before in human history. We can awaken because we are _already_ consciousness – the truth is _already_ here and we just have to tune into it. As Jesus said, the Kingdom of God is in the midst of us and within us, but we don't see it. The Buddha said that the truth we seek is our fundamental nature, just obscured by a deceptive mind. We _are_ the universe – we are, in our essence, Consciousness itself, and all of life is an expression of God, the heart of our being. We are already perfect and have everything we could ever want. We just have to see it.

Changing the World

"I'm a pessimist because of intelligence, but an optimist because of will." "Whatever the situation, I imagine the worst that could happen in order to summon up all my reserves and will power to overcome every obstacle." – Antonio Gramsci

Here in this final chapter I want to leave you with some suggestions about how you might best utilize the information in this book, and how I hope it might have impacted you. At the end of Gabor Maté's book The Myth of Normal, the author talks about charting a course to creating a saner society where every individual, every group, and every institution that runs or governs our various social systems, is more compassionate, understanding, communicative, and "trauma informed" – in other words, more essentially human. He also describes some of the many huge difficulties we face in dismantling the multi-tentacled behemoth of forces and institutions that shape and maintain the thinking and behavior patterns that are ever-increasingly dragging humanity down the tubes. That may sound pessimistic but unfortunately it's true in many ways. When we look at the big picture, the challenges seem almost insurmountable. Maté himself admits that he is in many ways more comfortable describing the problem, which he has done brilliantly, than offering solutions for creating a trauma informed society. But he does offer some great ideas about where to start. My take on all this is that whatever the plan, it begins with us and expands person by person. Each of us becomes a catalyst by helping others, recommending books and resources, promoting institutional changes, and conducting ourselves in ways that epitomize what we believe – we walk our talk. Mahatma Gandhi said it this way:

"We but mirror the world. All the tendencies present in the outer world are to be found in the world of our body. If we could change ourselves, the tendencies in the world would also change. As a man changes his own nature, so does the attitude of the world change towards him. This is the divine mystery supreme. A wonderful thing it is, and the source of our happiness. We need not wait to see what others do." This is often paraphrased as: "Be the change you want to see in the world."

There has always been suffering in the world – it's the nature of life. But given that our knowledge and technology have come so far in the last few hundred years, it's disheartening to see that we, as human beings, have not really evolved much overall in our humanity. For such an intelligent species it's appalling the amount of unnecessary and preventable suffering happening in the world on so many different levels, from disease, poverty, and starvation, to crime, injustice, wars, and cruelty – man's inhumanity to man. Aside from our natural survival instincts, and human tendencies, I see trauma, and the perpetuation of it in all its forms, as one of the major factors in all of this. It's even more appalling that the vast majority of us consider the very things that cause or contribute to these problems as being normal or even necessary, when so much that is happening in our homes, workplaces, societies, and nations is seriously abnormal and unnatural. And yet much of the information we need and the answers we seek are already available and growing constantly! What's missing is the communication, agreement, and cooperation toward a common goal of healing the system. Everyone has their own agenda and their own life issues to contend with, and governments and religions have not succeeded here either. It's up to us individually to do what we can, plant seeds in our own way, and set an example.

Moving Forward
"The greatest achievement of humanity is not its works of art, science, or technology, but the recognition of its own dysfunction, its own madness." – Eckhart Tolle, A New Earth (2005)

Eckhart Tolle suggests in his book "A New Earth" that we are all entering a new era of awakened consciousness that will change our civilization from within. I hope so. But he makes it clear that this will only happen by necessity because the alternative is annihilation – remember the Krell? I do believe every problem has its causes and its solutions, and that eventually everyone wakes up and becomes totally free. The question is "when?" Will it take a thousand years? A million more lifetimes? Why wait?

Because we are all unique as individuals, our paths are also unique. Now that I am more free to see my past and to understand my potential, my path is to continue to heal myself, help and teach others, and to wake up. Of course I have many other temporary or ongoing goals in the areas of health, finances, living conditions, relationships, and enjoying life, and I have many ideas and beliefs that support me in these things. But no one has to believe what I believe or choose my path or anyone else's – we all must do what feels right for ourselves and our own unique situations. So rather than taking anything I have said to be true, unless you have found it to be so in your own experience, take it all as inspiration and motivation to find and awaken your own inner knowing and power. It's up to you to utilize the great many helpful tools, resources, and people that are available all around you. Here are some suggestions.

First, see your own dysfunction, your own madness, and be honest – see the logs in your own eyes. That's number one. Seek to really know yourself! This requires self-observation, not occasionally but as a reflex, a part of life, like breathing. Clearly seeing the "*person you have been*" may be hard, even frightening, but it's the first step. And I will say it again, that character is not the real "you." It's mostly an expression of your internal programming. As you more deeply observe this character, whom you have taken to be yourself, new revelations will come to light. Whatever it is, it's all good because it leads to the freedom to live more from your true and authentic nature and to discover what that is. Once you can honestly see your dysfunction, and you're more cognizant of your unwanted conditions and where they will lead you if left unchecked, don't despair! Do something about it – heal those wounds, those monsters from the id. Read, listen, converse, meditate, work on yourself, get assistance and support through counseling etc. Do whatever you need to do to undo the damage wrought on you since birth by a misguided world. As I said, healing is a path, a mindset, a lifestyle of being mindful enough to know when you are being *reactive*, as opposed to being authentic and living from your heart, your essence. Then you can realign and transform those mental structures that are meant to serve you and not to imprison you, as you live your life. This includes being a trauma informed individual who sees and respects the effects of trauma in theirself and all others, and seeks to understand more. Weave the things you learn and the changes you make into the fabric of your life so they are part of your everyday reality. You will then naturally live life with more empathy, harmony, honesty, and authenticity toward your fellow beings. The golden rule then becomes more obvious and compelling. Treat everyone with kindness, compassion, and understanding, be grateful for all you have, seek inner peace always, and let your confidence and strength be expressed with humility. Then the cycle will be broken and you will not pass along the abuse, battery, and injustice done to you, and you will become a catalyst for a better world. You will also have ended the growth of new negative karma for yourself, the cause and effect consequences of harmful actions, and will have planted the seeds for a better future for everyone.

Find your life's purpose! It's there – you may have forgotten, but you are here for a reason. When you know what it is, it may or may not seem profound, but whatever it may be, you chose it or agreed to it and it's important to you and has many repercussions you can't see. Of course you can change your purpose or expand it but you will probably see that it is something you are already deeply committed to internally. Until you are sure, just do what you love and if you know what your purpose is, pull out all the stops. I know all these things are easier said than done – that's why I use ID-R.

Be observant of the miracles and synchronicities that are happening all the time – the real magic of life. Develop a miracle mindset so that you notice, and don't dismiss, the myriad opportunities that arise to see the bigger picture and experience the wonder, power, and inspiration of that mysterious infinite network of connections that we are all a part of. After all, it's all you, it's what you are! When you see anything that defies explanation, ASSUME it's a miracle or a message until you know otherwise, and notice how you feel about that. And share your experiences with those who will appreciate them. Trust your intuition. See what happens.

And consider the possibility of spiritual awakening, of finding out what you really are. It's really where everything I've suggested in this book ultimately leads. If you're curious about where you came from, why you're here, where you're going, and the truth of your real nature, then look into it, if it's not ALREADY part of your life. You CAN find out! It's the supreme "Temet Nosce," and NOTHING can surpass the joy, power, love, and freedom of discovering this truth for yourself. Awakening is about seeing the truth of your eternal being – a truth that is always available to you whenever you're ready to see it. This is the peace that passes all understanding and the truth that will set you free. But just following the principles of an awakening life, like the Buddha's Noble Eightfold Path, the teachings of Jesus, or any similar path, can also help you live more easily, freely, and peacefully, right now.

Ripples – or The Butterfly Effect

Now let's consider the bigger picture of our effect on family, friends, tribes, communities, institutions, societies, cultures, and countries. We humans are biopsychosocial beings and what affects one affects all – we all make ripples and ripples become waves, and waves become tidal forces. I was discussing the 1998 movie "Saving Private Ryan" with a friend many years ago, and the incredible scenes of the D-day invasion. While talking about the thousands of Allied soldiers who died, she described the impact of each death as a wave that moved out across the world, deeply affecting many others in many ways. I could see it in my mind: thousands of interconnecting waves branching out and touching thousands of families and millions of people – a massive global "butterfly effect" that would influence the entire future of the world.[112]

Any revolution of change starts individually – it starts with each of us. The positive changes in us move out into the world through our actions and our interactions with others, creating ripples that give rise to more ripples. We idolize famous people who had major positive impacts on the world, like Lincoln, Gandhi, or Einstein. But none of these people, whether world leaders, saints, inventors, innovators, artists, warriors, or revolutionaries, acted in a vacuum – they could not have done what they did without the support of like-minded people and a social environment that, to some degree, allowed them to do their thing. And that principle applies to those who spread hatred, death, and destruction as well – they also had their supporters. Everyone contributes in one way or another to the outcome, and the outcome is whatever we're experiencing right now, and tomorrow. So if you would like to see the tide of humanity change, be that change. That's it! Everyone in your sphere of influence will feel it. If you want to do more, do more. The greater

---

[112] The "butterfly effect" refers to the idea that a small change in one thing can result in massive effects in other things later in time – like an escalating domino effect. The name comes from the example of a butterfly flapping its wings in one place which eventually causes a tornado to form elsewhere, whereas without the butterfly that particular tornado would never have formed.

number of people you reach in a positive way, the bigger the waves you make and the greater the effect. The possibilities are unlimited.

Each new generation inherits a different world, so if you are a young person, realize that what this world becomes and what your children inherit depends on you. And if you are raising a young person, what they become also depends on you. And no matter how old you are, you can still create ripples that make all the difference. Just being our best and happiest selves is all it takes to be part of the massive butterfly effect of millions of ripples feeding the tide of a massive and positive shift in our collective evolution.

A Final Word
One of the deep secrets of life is that all that is really worth the doing is what we do for others. — Lewis Carroll

"World peace must develop from inner peace. Peace is not just mere absence of violence. Peace is, I think, the manifestation of human compassion"– Dalai Lama XIV

Practically everything in this book is controversial, but why? Many of the kinds of experiences I've described in these pages which seem extraordinary are actually very common, although certainly not shared openly. They trigger various alarming reactions, like fear, because they are not understood. Since the beginning, humanity has dealt with unacceptable truths by ignoring them, ridiculing them, threatening them, and suppressing them. But the most problematic things about these inconvenient extra-ordinary experiences that people have, which incidently are not going to go away, are the explanations which make them out to be something other than mistakes or hallucinations. Adopting the alternate viewpoints of curiosity, acceptance, and openness to possibility, has obviously been one of my basic themes.

The main reason I have included my more controversial experiences in this book is that accepting them as experiences, if nothing else, allows for greater healing and self-understanding when you recall such things yourself. Such things HAVE come up and WILL CONTINUE to do so in many people's sessions, and must be dealt with whether they are considered to be real or not. Not very many people I know accept the idea that all my experiences are real events in the real world, and that's fine. Nothing questionable has to be believed; it simply has to be accepted as experience when it arises within you. Judgements can be made about such things later.

One aspect of being human is that everyone has a mind-set they have bought into, a paradigm they are ensconced in, a family, tribe, religion, or club they belong to, at least in their mind, and everyone has an opinion. And some of these things have been more or less burned into each of our systems with a branding iron and cannot simply be washed away with a few soapy aphorisms. The beauty of self-discovery is that we don't need explanations or opinions when we can find out about ourselves on our own. And we can do this if we are sincere and honest about it and have the right tools to really get into it. And of course it always helps to have the support of others! Aside from the challenges and difficulties inherent in the process of inner exploration itself, other problems can arise if we try to foist our personal revelations on everyone else – a mistake I made in the beginning. And even our own discoveries will evolve into new understandings as we shed the skins of our outdated ways of seeing things, and keep moving forward. Humility is crucial. This means we must always question everything, especially when we think we have the whole picture.

ID-R is about more than healing unwanted conditions or having useful tools. It is, most importantly, a means to show you what you really are and where you've been, even if it just gives you the tiniest glimpse. And when we start becoming fully aware of our healing potential, our higher states, our internal helpers, miracles, past lives, and our spiritual connections, all kinds of fascinating things begin to happen, and things change. This book has explored a wide range of topics but in the end it's not really about my story or even about ID-R. Ultimately this is about YOU. What are YOU going to do after you close this book? What is YOUR life purpose? What is YOUR destiny? How are you going to use the knowledge and many tools available in this world to your best advantage? There is nothing more valuable and hopeful than discovering who we really are, and I was drawn in that direction from the start. My life began with trauma and was shaped by trauma, and understanding life and the healing of trauma has been my passion. There is nothing more important to me than what I have discovered about myself – and what I have learned is that we are all One Family and One Being, that love, compassion, communication, and cooperation can change the world, and that there is such a thing as eternal happiness and spiritual freedom.

But even to begin awakening to something different, to activating our greater potential, there usually has to be a catalyst of some kind, even when the motivation for change is already there. Sometimes the catalyst is a single word or a kind gesture, and sometimes it's a traumatic shock. But whatever the experience, the catalyst often starts as a compelling idea or feeling. Whether it comes from a vision or revelation, a person, a book, or an observation, or maybe from a voice in our head or some feeling inside, once the idea takes hold, the idea that we have greater potential than what we have been systematically led to believe since birth, and if it has enough explosive force, then our paths can diverge from those of mediocrity or stagnation and deterioration. Sometimes by just contemplating some of the things we've explored here, people have insights that bring about massive changes. I've had people call me up years after we had a single conversation, telling me that our talk changed their lives. In each case, at the time of these conversations, I had no idea that what I said might have any significant impact, because all I did was relate a tiny bit of the material in this book. But it was the right thing at the right time – ripples.

I was reminded of these previous encounters a few days before beginning this chapter when a lady named Colleen called me. We had a brief conversation seven years ago and she had just recently found my business card while rummaging through some things. She wanted to thank me for helping her back then. Colleen couldn't even tell me what I had said to her – all she recalled is that she went home feeling different, looked at her life, ended her alcohol addiction, as well as some other addictions, and put her life on a new track. She enrolled in some programs and is now helping others. Of course she did all this on her own, and she had that potential in her all along. I felt that potential when we met; I remember her cheerful enthusiasm and vibrant energy. And when the fuel is present, all we need is a spark to start a fire. Although she only came in to pick up a computer I had built for her, something I did for a while as a hobby, she was curious about my counseling, which led to a discussion. Whatever I said to her was apparently the spark she needed. And if that's all this book is for someone, that's a good start.

Patty and I could have lived different lives, but we chose to do something that we believed would help others and be worth the effort. We made promises designed to keep ourselves on track without our being consciously aware of it. A lot of good has already come from all that, and I trust that much more will follow. And now the unconscious decisions and motivations that have driven me since childhood have led me here, to this paragraph, and these final words.

My spiritual advisor has pointed out my tendency to be too self-critical, so I won't dwell on my many mistakes and failures along the way. Instead, here's what I feel really good about. I feel good that I finished this book, finished my ID-R training manuals and have started training people. I feel incredibly grateful that I survived everything I've been through, the worst of which I have not shared, and that I was able to recall everything that I have so far. I am proud of the fact that I kept my promises and that I did at least try to connect with Patty. I feel honored that I was entrusted with this project even if I still don't see the bigger picture.

But think about it – what would life be like if we lived in a rational and compassionate world that wasn't ruled by fear, greed, or ego – a world governed by love where we all helped each other survive and thrive – where people were not programmed and forced to believe any dogma or doctrine? Well, for that to happen we need a tipping point, a critical mass of people who are not governed by internal negative programming. I first encountered this promising idea decades ago: the idea that we could have a better world if we were all sane and not run by trauma infected minds. But there wasn't enough sanity and cohesion behind those promoting that idea at the time, to make it work. This kind of vision is not something that can be enforced in any way by any organization, religion, or government – it can only be supported. It starts with each of us individually, and advances as we assist, encourage, and support each other in making real changes and in developing a deeper understanding of life.

When we live by love instead of fear, compassion instead of hatred and greed, when we are guided by motives that serve humanity instead of exploiting each other for profit and power, then we can all be encouraged and empowered in that positive and peaceful revolution, and will have reached the tipping point for profound change. Given the current state of divisiveness in the world, like the hopeful lyrics to that John Lennon song, this may be hard to even imagine. But we must imagine it because that's where everything starts, with imagination — and imagination is magic!

Epilogue

I came down with something totally awful in early 2021. It reminded me of the flu at first in that I felt weak and had body aches and pains all over. A few previous conditions that I had been experiencing for over a year, like vertigo and eye pain, suddenly escalated. The muscle pain and fatigue were awful enough, but within days I couldn't sleep for more than an hour at a time due to foot and leg cramps. I suffered from this for two weeks and got little help from my doctors, as test after test showed everything to be normal. Because of the pandemic, I didn't feel I could get the attention I needed to help me figure this thing out.

I was fairly sure my symptoms were the aftereffects of an asymptomatic covid-19 infection – a syndrome called PASC. I had been exposed to the virus early-on and had many symptoms of long covid. The only useful help I got was from an online "long covid" support group. Most of the people in the group who were commenting were also finding few answers or solutions, although we did share some helpful advice. I was sent to the hospital emergency room once due to a lab error, and more tests there showed nothing. The ER doctor said there was not enough known about covid-19 and that he had no answers for me, and sent me home. My symptoms were quite debilitating and mimicked those of many other conditions including Guillain-Barré Syndrome, ME/CFS, Vitamin B6 overdose, CIDP, and small fiber neuropathy, but I had none of these.

At this time I was waiting for more tests. If I did indeed have long covid and/or some other autoimmune condition, I realized it might be a long battle to recover. Regardless of all that, I was concerned and took many steps to get well. One thing I added to my daily meditation was to reach out spiritually to my Higher Self and to all my allies — my friends, family, and connections in the spirit realm, whoever they might be. I wasn't being specific; I was just putting out an SOS. I also do this often in behalf of my friends.

After the first week I wasn't getting better and sleep was more and more disturbed and sporadic. One morning I had a very vivid dream as I was awakening from my last nebulous bit of sleep. In the dream there was a knock at my door and when I opened it there were two well-dressed ladies standing there, a tall woman in her twenties and a younger one next to her who seemed to be her daughter, although they weren't that far apart in age. They asked me if I was Dennis but it was obvious they already knew me. I asked who they were and what they wanted. The tall lady said they were relatives of mine and had come to move in and stay with me. There seemed to be a large group of other people behind them who were also "family," although they were vague silhouettes. I felt disoriented and said they could not all move in because I was sick, weak, disheveled, did not have the space, and this would overwhelm me. The ladies looked somewhat bewildered at my response. This dream now took on characteristics of an OBE because my vision became impaired, but as I suddenly became more conscious, I was able to make myself see clearly again.

That's when I saw there was a teenage girl with silver braces on her teeth, standing next to me on my right. She was very friendly and chatty and began telling me about these people and explaining that they had a new last name, which sounded foreign. The ladies and the others went out to the street and I closed the door. Then I saw a couch being pushed in through my patio door and I ran over and pushed it out. I went out on the patio and the teenager was there, and again she began happily chatting with me. I felt like I knew her and started to feel better about the other people. Then I woke up. This dream, or semi-OBE, was so real that I was compelled to work on it as soon as I could.

In working with this dream I noticed more details, like the fact that all three of the women had a slight oriental look to their eyes. I also soon realized the ladies' intention. These were the "Bird People" and they had heard my call and had come to help me! The tall lady was the powerful matriarch of the Vietnam village who had kept her group together after they were all killed. The shorter woman had been her daughter in that lifetime, and the chatty girl had been the stowaway who had left my space long after the others. Wherever they were now, whether in physical form somewhere or not, by their outfits and demeanor they seemed to be healed and strong, and doing quite well. In this session I telepathically welcomed their help and felt overwhelmed by their gratitude. I hadn't helped these people for any reason other than compassion, and this was quite a surprise.

That night, after their arrival, I slept better than I had in a long time, and I began to feel some very gradual improvement over the next few weeks, although my condition was still worrisome and debilitating four weeks after the mystery illness began. Three years later my debilitating condition has improved but has not gone. I have no idea how much help they might have been capable of or whether they are still with me in some way, but regardless of how things turn out for me health-wise, the appearance of the Bird People afforded me some wonderful emotional support. I felt this was a remarkable experience and worth sharing. If I had never explored my life as I have, I would have never known that I had helped them or that they had returned the favor – I would only remember having some strange dreams.

※ ※ ※ ※ ※ ※ ※ ※ ※ ※ ※ ※ ※ ※ ※ ※ ※ ※ ※

A few weeks after finishing the first draft of this book I had a dream about Patty in which she came by to visit me. She and I were alone in the livingroom of a house that I seemed to own. We talked for a while and everything was cordial, which was a new experience for me, even in a dream. It was like we were getting to know each other after a long time apart. I handed her a large basket containing a mother cat and several kittens, and then left the room to get something else. When I returned to the room, she was gone. I didn't try to talk with her for a few days, although I did have her phone number. It felt like I wanted to give her time to adjust to something. Finally I called her, and we talked briefly. She said the cats were wonderful. She told me that the mother cat became ferocious and quite frightening when looking at her own reflection in a mirror, but with Patty she had now become a friend.

In considering this dream I realized that the mother cat was a reflection of the role that Patty had to play with me in the end, in order to keep her distance. The dream revealed that she was now at peace with that. The feeling was that the past was over and we would be communicating more. And the kittens were symbolic of course, but really they were just love.

Acknowledgments

Writing this book was a labor of love, but that was only the first step. Then came the reviews and suggestions from friends, and doing daily revisions and uncounted hours of editing over several years. I didn't realize however, how difficult it would be for an unknown author to find an agent or a publisher. Deciding to self-publish meant that I would have to do everything myself. Without all the support and financial backing of a major publishing company, I decided I didn't need to write a bestseller – I just wanted to get my book out there. Build it and they will come. But I did have a lot of support, not just at the end but throughout this whole adventure. This book evolved not only from my own life experiences and those of my clients and friends, but with the help, support, and knowledge of many other people. Here I wish to acknowledge with sincere thanks, appreciation, and gratitude, some of those people most instrumental in the completion of this work.

No one was more important in my own evolution and the development of this book than the late Patty Preston, whose real name will have to remain anonymous for now. Her presence in my life is the heart of everything.

I want to express my deepest love and gratitude to my brothers Kerry Alan Alsop and Randy Blake Alsop for their lifelong support of me and my work and for helping me get through some tough times. Their acceptance, validation, and support never wavered when I started sharing with them some of the pretty outrageous things I was remembering. They have always been there for me.

My sincere thanks and appreciation to Mike Goldstein and the late John Galusha of Survival Services, for the training I received in learning Idenics, and for their understanding and hospitality. Idenics was instrumental to the development of ID-R, and in that, changed my life.

I also wish to acknowledge my hypnotherapy teachers, Randal Churchill and Marlene Mulder. They were my instructors at the Hypnotherapy Training Institute when I took their courses back in 1994 through 1998. Their friendship and trust, the deeper lessons they taught me, and their encouragement, has made them part of my "inner circle of support" visualization whenever I need to bolster my confidence.

I am deeply grateful for my friend Sabrina Mouzes, my personal muse, confidante, and partner in crime, who has supported me and inspired me more than I can say, since we met decades ago. Our spiritual connection even once saved my life. Her guidance has been especially helpful in the final stages of this work.

Much appreciation also goes to my friend Susan Pitkin, who listened with an open mind for countless hours to my stories as they were unfolding, almost from the beginning, when I had no one else I could share these things with. Similarly I am thankful for my late friend and biggest supporter Michael Eakin, who encouraged me for many years and shared many of his own extraordinary experiences with me.

Heartfelt thanks go out to my friend Dat On, a spiritual healer, teacher, and acupuncturist with whom I recognized a spiritual connection when we first met. He has mysteriously supported me for many years, reviewed my first draft of this book, and repeatedly encouraged me to self-publish.

And I greatly appreciate all the friends and relatives who read and reviewed the early manuscripts of this book and gave me invaluable feedback. Their positive and negative criticism, important suggestions, and help with editing, resulted in many revisions, and a far better end result. These contributors include: C.C. Fish, Dat On, Ed Pejack, Taj Bhadori, Gail Francisco, Tori Burdick, David Halterman, Toni Barnett, Kerry Alsop, Devin Alsop, Kaylee Jones, and Diana Wolfe.

And thank you to all those who contributed to my initial fundraiser to get this book published, and to those who offered additional support later including: Gail Francisco, Dat On, Taj Bahadori, Toni Barnett, Ed Pejack, Frank Vera, Devin & Lauren Alsop, Skylar Alsop, Kellye Alsop, Mary Steva, Tori Burdick, Craig & Gail Costa, Joy Hope, Sheila Ford, Maria Rosado, Melissa Elam, Patty McDonald, Eunice Green, Diane Adams, Bob Hong, Gay Lynn Saunders, Scott Hall, Wendy Schulenburg, Aaron Black, and all those who wished to remain anonymous.

And finally I thank "Bob," Patty, and the Universe for entrusting me with this project, and I hope I didn't screw it up too badly.

Bibliography

This section lists sources referred to in each chapter, followed by additional related resources that I have read, relevant to the material in that chapter. While I do not agree with everything in most of these books and I strongly disagree with some of the theories and explanations expressed in several of them, they all have something of great value to offer and they help us see the human condition from different angles.

First I want to mention the four most important books relevant to the ID-R process and working with trauma. These books are all brilliant, with the first of these being the most important with regard to trauma counseling, and that is "Eye Movement Desensitization and Reprocessing (EMDR) Therapy" <u>Third Edition</u> – 2018, by Francine Shapiro. Next are: "The Body Keeps the Score" – 2014 by Bessel van der Kolk, "The Myth of Normal" – 2022, by Gabor Maté, and "Internal Family Systems Therapy" <u>Second Edition</u> – 2019, by Richard C. Schwartz and Martha Sweezy.

* * * * * * * * * * * * * * * * * * * *

Preface and Introduction:

Exceptional Human Experiences: A Brief Overview - from the EHE website: EHE.org, 1999

The Body Keeps the Score – Bessel van der Kolk, 2014

The Myth of Normal – Gabor Maté, 2022

Chapter 1:

Real Magic – Dean Radin 2018

Chapter 2:

The Primal Scream – Arthur Janov, 1970

Birth without Violence – Frederick LeBoyer, 1975

Chapter 3:

The Sun and the Shadow – Kenneth Kelzer 1987

Journeys Out of the Body – Robert Monroe, 1971

Far Journeys – Robert Monroe, 1985

The Ultimate Journey – Robert Monroe, 1994

Autobiography of a Yogi – Paramahansa Yogananda, 1946

The Relaxation Response – Herbert Benson, 1975

Unlimited Power – Anthony Robbins 1986

The Teachings of Don Juan – Carlos Castaneda, 1968

A Separate Reality – Carlos Castaneda, 1971

Journey to Ixtlan – Carlos Castaneda, 1972

Tales of Power – Carlos Castaneda, 1974

The Phase – Michael Raduga, 2011

Chapter 4:

Idenics: An Alternative To Therapy – Mike Goldstein, 2007

Chapter 5:

EMDR – Francine Shapiro & Margot Silk Forrest, 1997

Getting Past Your Past – Francine Shapiro, 2013

The Myth of Normal – Gabor Maté, 2022

Irreducible Mind – Edward Kelly et al., 2007

Games People Play – Eric Bern, 1966

Brave New Medicine – Cynthia Li, MD., 2019

The UltraMind Solution – Mark Hyman MD., 2009

Chapter 6

Eye Movement Desensitization and Reprocessing (EMDR) Therapy, Third Edition – 2018, by Francine Shapiro

Proof of Heaven – Eben Alexander, 2012

The Assault On Truth – Jeffrey Masson, 1984

Multiple Personality Disorder – Dr. Colin Ross, 1989

Trauma and Recovery – Judith Herman, 1992

The Complete Letters of Sigmund Freud to Wilhelm Fliess1887-1904 – Jeffrey Masson, 1985

The Body Keeps the Score – Bessel van der Kolk, 2014

The Future of the Body – Michael Murphy, 1992

Emotional Healing at Warp Speed – David Grand, 2001

Brainspotting – David Grand, 2015

Chapter 6 (continued)

The Divided Mind – John E, Sarno, 2007

An Autobiography of Trauma – Peter Levine, 2024

Chapter 7A

Stranger in the Mirror – Marlene Steinberg, 2001

Diagnostic and Statistical Manual of Mental Disorders, 5th Edition – American Psychiatric Association, 2013

When Rabbit Howls – Truddi Chase, 1987

Chapter 7B

Sybil – Florence Schreiber, 1973

Zen Combat – Jay Gluck, 1961

Psycho-Cybernetics – Maxwell Maltz, 1971

The Minds of Billy Milligan – Daniel Keyes, 1981

Internal Family Systems Therapy" 1995, by Richard C. Schwartz with Martha Sweezy., 2020

Katherine, It's Time – Kit Castle, Stefan Bechtel, 1989

The Control of Candy Jones – Donald Bain, 1979

Videos:

Joan Baez: "I Am a Noise," 2023, An American documentary film

Multiple Personality Disorder: The Search for Deadly Memories, – HBO, 1993

Chapter 7C

The Seven Sins of Memory – Daniel Schacter, 2001

The Four Agreements – Don Miguel Ruiz, 1997

Chapter 8

Getting Past Your Past – Francine Shapiro, 2013

See Without Glasses – Ralph J. Macfadyen, 1963

Chapter 8 (continued)

The Myopia Myth – Donald Rehm, 1981

Change Your Voice Change Your Life – Dr. Morton Cooper, 1984

Chapter 10

The Pain Chronicles – Melanie Thernstrom, 2014

The Pain Management Workbook – Rachel Zoffness, 2020

Waking the Tiger – Peter Levine, 1997

Chapter 11

Flatland: A Romance of Many Dimensions – Edwin A. Abbott, 1884

Chapter 12

The Fire From Within – Carlos Castaneda, 1984

Chapter 13

"Man's Search For meaning" – Viktor Frankl. 1946

Chapter 15

The Akashic Experience – Ervin Laszlo, 2009

Spirit Releasement Therapy – Dr. William Baldwin, 1992

Secrets of Heaven – Emanuel Swedenborg, 1749-1756

The Presence of Other Worlds: The Findings of Emanuel Swedenborg – Wilson Van Dusen, 1974

Essays in Radical Empiricism – William James, 1912

The Unquiet Dead: A Psychologist Treats Spirit Possession Edith Fiore, 1987

Multiple Man – Adam Crabtree, 1985

At The Hour Of Death – Karlis Osis, 1997

Words At The Threshold – Lisa Smartt, 2017

Chapter 16

Mistakes Were Made (but not by me) – Caroll Tavris and Elliot Aronson, 2020

Irreducible Mind – Edward Kelly et al., 2007

Real Magic – Dean Radin 2018

The Conscious Universe: The Scientific Truth of Psychic Phenomena – Dean Radin, 1997

The Secret Science of the Soul (formerly "The End of Materialism") – Charles Tart, 2009

Chapter 17

Space, Time, and Gravitation – Sir Arthur Eddington, 1920

The Science Delusion (Science Set Free in the U.S.)
– Rupert Sheldrake, 2017

The Case Against Reality: How Evolution Hid the Truth from Our
Eyes – Donald Hoffman, 2020

Why Materialism Is Baloney – Bernardo Kastrup, 2014

Tales of Power – Carlos Castaneda, 1974

Journey of Souls – Michael Newton, 1994

How the Mind Works – Stephen Pinker, 1997

Chapter 18

The Power of Now – Eckhart Tolle, 1999

A New Earth: Awakening Your Life's Purpose – Eckhart Tolle, 2005

Unlimited Power – Anthony Robbins, 1986

Awaken the Giant Within – Anthony Robbins, 1992

The Relaxation Response – Herbert Benson, 1975

The Relaxation Revolution – Herbert Benson, 2011

Meditation as Medicine – Dharma Singh Khalsa and Cameron
Stauth, 2002

Mind Medicine – Uri Geller, 1999

Self Hypnotism: The Technique and Its Use in Daily Living
– Leslie M. LeCron, 1964

Chapter 18 (continued)

Self Hypnosis and Other Mind Expanding Techniques
– Charles Tebbetts, 1989

The Power of Focusing – Ann Weiser Cornell, 1996

When I say No I Feel Guilty – Manuel Smith, 1979

The Internal Family Systems Workbook – Richard Schwartz

How I Found Freedom in an Unfree World – Harry Browne, 1973

Creative Visualization:– Shakti Gawain, 1998

How to Change Your Mind – Michael Pollan, 2018

Psychedelic Healing – Steven Goldsmith, 2011

Chapter 19

The Manufacture of Madness – Thomas Szasz, 1970

The Myth of Mental Illness – Thomas Szasz, 1974

Chapter 20

Healing Dreams – Marc Ian Barasch, 2000

Conscious Dreaming – Robert Moss, 1996

Chapter 21

Be As You Are, The Teachings of Ramana Maharshi
– David Godman, 1985

The Three Pillars of Zen – Philip Kapleau, 1966, 1989

I am That - Nisargadatta Maharaj, 1973

Chapter 21 (continued)

Tibetan Yoga and Secret Doctrines" – W. Y. Evans-Wentz, 1935, 1958

Dream Yoga – Andrew Holecek, 2016

The Open Secret – Wei Wu Wei, 1965

Silence of the Heart – Robert Adams, <u>original 1997 Acropolis ed. only</u>

Chapter 27

The Phase – Michael Raduga, 2011

The Way of Council – Zimmerman and Coyle, 2009

Chapter 28

A New Earth – Eckhart Tolle, 2005

* * * * * * * * * * * * * * * * * * *

Author's Note: This book uses left-aligned text rather than traditional justified formatting to enhance your reading experience, maintaining natural word spacing and flow for easier comprehension of complex material. The Electra font used in the printed editions was chosen for its warmth and excellent readability.

www.ingramcontent.com/pod-product-compliance
Lightning Source LLC
Chambersburg PA
CBHW021208130626
46554CB00004B/1127